WEB PROGRAMMING DESKTOP REFERENCE 6-IN-1

Written by

Michael Afergan

Rick Darnell

Brian Farrar

Russ Jacobs

David Medinets

Robert Mullen

Mícheál Ó Foghlú

D1560963

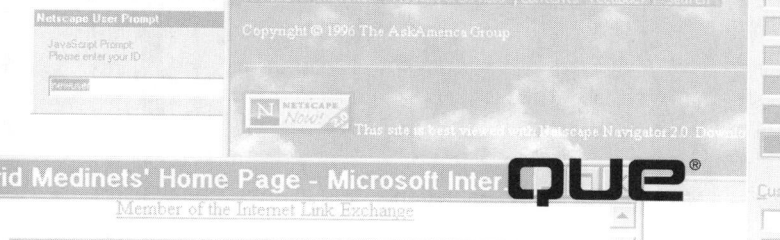

Web Programming Desktop Reference 6-in-1

Library of Congress Catalog No.: 96-71427

ISBN: 0-7897-1028-5

98 97   6 5 4 3 2

Interpretation of the printing code: the rightmost double-digit number is the year of the book's printing; the rightmost single-digit number, the number of the book's printing. For example, a printing code of 96-1 shows that the first printing of the book occurred in 1996.

Screen reproductions in this book were created using Collage Plus from Inner Media, Inc., Hollis, NH.

Composed in *Stone Serif* and *MCPdigital* by Que Corporation

Contents at a Glance

Contents

Credits

President
Roland Elgey

Publisher
Joseph B. Wikert

Publishing Manager
Fred Slone

Senior Title Manager
Bryan Gambrel

Editorial Services Director
Elizabeth Keaffaber

Managing Editor
Sandy Doell

Director of Marketing
Lynn E. Zingraf

Acquisitions Editor
Al Valvano

Production Editor
Maureen A. McDaniel

Assistant Product Marketing Manager
Christy M. Miller

Strategic Marketing Manager
Barry Pruett

Technical Editor
Sundar Rajan

Technical Support Specialist
Nadeem Muhammed

Software Relations Coordinator
Patricia J. Brooks

Acquisitions Coordinator
Carmen Krikorian

Editorial Assistant
Andrea Duvall

Book Designer
Ruth Harvey

Cover Designer
Dan Armstrong

Production Team
Stephen Adams
Debra Bolhuis
Marcia Brizendine
Kevin Cliburn
Linda S. Cox
Julie Geeting
Tammy Graham
Jason Hand
Daniel Harris
Dan Julian
Daryl Kessler
Tony McDonald
Casey Price
Erich Richter
Laura Robbins
Sossity Smith
Marvin Van Tiem

Indexer
Tom Dinse

About the Authors

Michael Afergan began working with Java early in the spring of 1995 through his research work at the MIT AI labs. Since then, he has carefully studied its growth, developing practical applets for large businesses as an independent consultant. Michael is a founding member of TeamJava, a network of Java professionals, and is also a weekly contributor to Digital *Espresso*, Java's online weekly digest. Michael was a contributing author for *Using Java* and has taught Java overseas.

Although only 18, Michael has been programming for ten years and even taught a class on computer science at MIT. Captain of his high-school wrestling team, Michael was accepted to every school to which he applied, including MIT, Princeton, UPenn, and Cornell. He is currently attending Harvard University, where he was accepted for early admission. You can reach him at **mikea@mit.edu**. His official Web page address is **http://www.ai.mit.edu/people/mikea/resume.html**.

Rick Darnell is a Midwest native currently living with his wife and two daughters in Missoula, MT. He began his career in print at a small weekly newspaper after graduating from Kansas State University with a degree in broadcasting. While spending time as a freelance journalist and writer, Rick has seen the full gamut of personal computers since starting out with a Radio Shack Model I in the late 1970s. When not in front of his computer, he serves as a volunteer firefighter and member of a regional hazardous materials response team.

Brian Farrar received his B.A. from Wabash College in 1985 in English and economics. He completed an MBA from Indiana University in 1987. He began his career at GTE and progressed through a series of positions until 1994, when he left to start an Internet and intranet consulting practice for Metamor Technologies. Through this consulting practice, Brian has helped some of the largest companies in the world decide on and deploy Internet technologies to solve business problems. His most recent Que title is *Special Edition Using ActiveX*.

Russell L. Jacobs is a programmer/analyst for The Prudential. He is also the president of SoftWare Alchemy. He has been programming on the PC for ten years using Pascal, BASIC, C, and C++ in the DOS, Windows, OS/2, and NT environments. Russ has contributed his expertise as technical editor for over ten Que books, including *Visual Basic 3 By Example, OS/S 2.1 Red Book for Developers*, and *Killer Borland C++*.

David Medinets has been programming since 1980, when he started with a Radio Shack Model I. He still fondly remembers the days when he could cross-wire the keyboard to create funny-looking characters on the display. Since those days he has spent time debugging Emacs on UNIX machines, working on VAXen, and messing about with DOS microcomputers. David lives in Flanders, NJ with his wife Kathy and his two computers. He works at Prudential Insurance in Roseland, NJ, producing reams of printed output. His prior work has included co-authoring *Special Edition Using Turbo C++ 4.5 for Windows* and creating CD-ROMs, Windows Help files, and electronic books. David can be reached at **medined@planet.net** with any comments.

Robert Mullen is a computer book author, HTML author, freelance writer, and editor-at-large living in northern California. Robert has authored or co-authored more than 16 computer books for personal computer users. Robert also publishes a computer industry watchdog publication called *CoolBlue! Magazine* at **http://www.askamerica.com** on the World Wide Web.

Mícheál Ó Foghlú is a lecturer in Applied Computing and Information Systems at Waterford Regional Technical College, Ireland (**http://www.rtc-waterford.ie**). Up until September 1996, he was working in the Computer Services department at University College, Galway, Ireland (**http://www.ucg.ie**). His interests include Natural Language Processing, WWW programming and development, Linux, computing using the Irish language, and Z39.50. When not slaving over a hot computer, he is sometimes seen nursing a quiet pint while listening to loud Irish music, and/or meandering through the hills in no particular direction. He can be contacted at the e-mail address **ofoghlu@indigo.ie**.

We'd Like to Hear from You!

As part of our continuing effort to produce books of the highest possible quality, Que would like to hear your comments. To stay competitive, we *really* want you, as a computer book reader and user, to let us know what you like or dislike most about this book or other Que products.

You can mail comments, ideas, or suggestions for improving future editions to the address below, or send us a fax at (317) 581-4663. Our staff and authors are available for questions and comments through our Internet site, at **http://www.mcp.com/que**, and Macmillan Computer Publishing also has a forum on CompuServe (type **GO QUEBOOKS** at any prompt).

In addition to exploring our forum, please feel free to contact me personally to discuss your opinions of this book: I'm **74671,3710** on CompuServe and **avalvano@que.mcp.com** on the Internet.

Thanks in advance—your comments will help us to continue publishing the best books available on new computer technologies in today's market.

Al Valvano
Acquisitions Editor
Que Corporation
201 W. 103rd Street
Indianapolis, Indiana 46290
USA

Introduction

Wouldn't it be nice if you could find one book that carried detailed reference material on six of the day's hottest Internet programming topics? You've found it. You're holding it.

The explosive growth of the Internet has created an abundant array of new programming languages and tools. These new languages and tools introduced new commands, new APIs, and new syntax structures to be learned. Until this book, no comprehensive language or command references have been available for these new Internet tools. *The Web Programming Desktop Reference 6-in-1* will become the first source programmers turn to for information and the one book they cannot do without.

This is *the* must-have Internet development tool. It combines six complete books in a single comprehensive reference:

- A *complete* HTML reference—in alphabetical order by command
- A *complete* Perl reference—organized by command in UNIX sort order
- A *complete* Java reference—organized by library, class, method, and field
- A *complete* JavaScript reference—in alphabetical order by command
- A *complete* VBScript reference—in alphabetical order by command
- A *complete* ActiveX reference—including coverage of the ActiveX Control Pad
- The book also contains more than 100 pages of navigation tables and indexes to guide you through the material.

Using This Book

The Web Programming Desktop Reference 6-in-1 is designed to provide quick and easy access to commands, standards, and programming tips.

This book is not a tutorial—you should already know the fundamentals of the various languages and standards. Instead, this book is a definitive reference work for the Web programmer.

If you are new to any of the languages in this reference book, Que has any number of books to help bring you up to speed:

- See Que's *HTML By Example* or *Special Edition Using HTML*, for two bestselling HTML tutorials.

- Get up to speed with the latest version of Perl in *Perl 5 By Example* from Que, or delve deep into Web programming with *Special Edition Using Perl for Web Programming* from Que.

- Learn Java programming quickly with *Special Edition Using Java* from Que.

- JavaScript programming is the focus of Que's *JavaScript By Example*.

- To learn VBScript programming, check out *Special Edition Using Visual Basic Script* from Que.

- And there's always *Special Edition Using ActiveX* if you need to master the intricacies of Microsoft's newest standard.

Each reference has been divided into its own section, and each section starts with a brief introduction. The introductions cover some basics about the language or standard, talk about key issues for that section, and set out the format and icons for the section. The introductions are followed by the detailed command references. There may also be additional material included in each section, such as special indexes, jump-tables, lists, or glossaries.

No matter what you are looking for, make sure to make use of the index in the back of the book. The index is arranged alphabetically, so you should be able to quickly locate your topic.

Conventions Used In This Book

Que has more than a decade of experience developing and publishing the most successful computer books available. With that experience, Que has learned what special features help readers the most. Look for these special features throughout the book to enhance your learning experience.

Several type and font conventions are used in this book to help make reading it easier:

- *Italic type* is used to emphasize the author's points or to introduce new terms.

- Screen messages, code listings, and command samples appear in `monospace typeface`.

- URLS, newsgroups, and anything you are asked to type appear in **boldface**.

Tip

Tips present short advice on a quick or often overlooked procedure. These include shortcuts that can save you time.

Note

Notes provide additional information that may help you avoid problems, or offer advice that relates to the topic.

Caution

Cautions warn you about potential problems that a procedure may cause, unexpected results, and mistakes to avoid.

Part I

HTML

Chapter 1

Understanding the HTML Reference Section

In this section, you'll find an entry for every accepted element or "tag"(and entries for tags that are anticipated to be accepted) in the various HTML standards/extensions in use. Turn to Part I of this book to find out more about categories, compliance, and so on.

The HTML elements in this section are in alphanumeric sort, as you would expect to find in an encyclopedia. If a tag manipulates the visual presentation of a browser, a figure is provided to help illustrate the effect caused by the use of that tag.

Every effort has been made to build the most comprehensive and up-to-date reference of the HyperText Markup Language in encyclopedic format. Note that there are several related conventions that are not part of the HTML standard but that can be called up or manipulated from an HTML document. Many of the most advanced math elements and server-side includes, for example, are not part of the HTML standards now in development. The scope of this book is constrained to HTML standards observed by browsers offered by Netscape, Microsoft, and Mosaic and the HTML 2/HTML 3.2 standards.

New tags will be added to this book as they are recognized, adopted, and implemented in products such as Netscape Navigator, Internet Explorer, and Mosaic or as they're included in subsequent HTML standards.

Every effort has been made to document every HTML tag you may run across. While individual attributes may not be represented by specific entries (as do all tags), a few tag/attribute combinations merit a specific entry and have been granted one.

Don't forget to check the Macmillan Computer Publishing Web site at **http://www.mcp.com/mcp/** for updates on subsequent releases of this book and other HTML references.

HTML Categories

Most HTML tags fall into families or functional categories. Tag categories are being developed by standards and proposal groups in the hopes of organizing individual tag development and standard enhancement efforts into clearly defined areas for the focus of more specific groups of practitioners.

The categories defined in this section of the book coincide with the HTML 2 and HTML 3.2 specification categories with some minor modifications. The HTML 2 and HTML 3.2 specifications are thoroughly supported by Netscape and Microsoft. In addition, both companies have introduced their own enhancements in the form of tags called *extensions*.

As the HTML standards mature, individual categories are expected to proliferate and become areas of specialty for many HTML authors.

The following sections detail those categories and their descriptions.

General
This category includes the basic page formatting tags required in every HTML document.

Forms
Forms tags are specific to authoring works that accept or act on input from the person viewing a page.

Tables
Table support is new to HTML 2 and is not fully supported on earlier versions of HTML and older browser software.

Frames
Frames are an extension of Netscape's interpretation of the HTML 3.2 standard. Currently, proper authoring of frames requires the HTML author to write three sets of documents, each set readable by three classes of browsers: those that employ proprietary extensions, browsers that are HTML 3.2 compliant, and, of course, legacy browsers that do not render frames at all.

Structural Definition
Structural definition takes advantage of the browser software's ability to format text without further input from the HTML document.

Miscellaneous
This category is host to tags that are not effectively included in other, more distinct categories.

Special Characters
Tags that are designed to work with characters that are not included in the lower ASCII character set are included in this category. The International Standards Organization (ISO) Latin characters are special characters.

Backgrounds and Colors

This category includes the tags that manipulate background imagery and colors used in HTML documents.

Lists

Lists provide the HTML author with the ability to organize content in hierarchies within a document.

Dividers

Dividers are objects that are employed by every browser to separate bodies of text or graphics in an HTML document.

Links and Graphics

This category includes all viewable images that must be rendered by a browser, not created by one. Links take that reader to another point in the same page or to another URL entirely.

Presentation Formatting

The presentation formatting category includes all font handling tags that manipulate which font is used, which point size is used, which color is used, and so on.

About HTML Extensions

Microsoft has presented another set of HTML tag categories that is closer to supporting Microsoft's goal for Internet Explorer's integration into every Microsoft application.

Many of the Netscape and Microsoft extensions are integrated into emerging HTML standards as they are revised. Correspondingly, some tags become obsolete because of disuse or poor performance.

At the time of this writing, Microsoft has done much to enhance the power of its HTML browser, Microsoft Internet Explorer. By introducing tags, such as <BGCOLOR>, which gives the Web author the ability to use shades of colors instead of just sixteen primary colors and <MARQUEE> that scrolls text across the browser's display, Web browsing has been made significantly more interesting.

The organization that actually sponsors HTML standards, W3C, did not include many tags that are proprietary extensions of HTML 2. If you want your Web pages to be rendered by the majority of browsers, consider avoiding the use of these extensions unless they are properly rendered by both of the latest versions of Netscape Navigator and Microsoft Internet Explorer.

About the HTML Reference Chapter

Chapter 3, "HTML Reference," is the part of this book that describes HTML tags and attributes. Some tags include a graphic or a table. Other tags do not. Some tags occupy more than a single page so that they are documented properly.

The following sections describe the kind of information you can expect to find on each page in the HTML Reference Section.

Command Header

This section displays the name of the HTML element described on that page or pages.

Compliance

This section deals with compliance issues and the relevance to the content of the reference section. Icons are used to indicate whether readers can expect a given element to work properly if they are staying within the scope of these levels of compliance:

 Netscape. This icon indicates that the latest versions of Netscape Navigator will render this element properly.

 Internet Explorer. This icon indicates that the latest versions of Internet Explorer will render this element properly.

 Mosaic/XMosaic. This icon indicates that the latest versions of Mosaic and XMosaic will render this element properly.

 HTML 2. This icon indicates compliance with this set of standards.

 HTML 3.2. This icon indicates compliance with this set of standards.

Syntax

This section provides an example of how the covered element appears in an HTML document. Includes beginning and ending tags if both are used.

Definition

This section defines the use for the element as originally intended. Any general discussion of the element appears in this section.

Example Syntax

This section provides an example of how the element is used in an actual line in an HTML document. Also, if a figure is displayed on the same page, every effort has been made to display the result of the example syntax in that figure.

In Actual Use

If a figure (screen shot and caption) imparts value in a visual way, it is included here. The "Example Syntax" section is used for this illustration.

If a figure is not useful, the "In Actual Use" section is not included.

Related Elements

If appropriate to the element being discussed, this section has a table that informs the reader of related HTML elements that can be used outside or inside the discussed element.

Some elements do not require a "Related Elements" section, in which case it will be omitted.

Chapter 2

HTML Quick Tables

Research has shown that people use reference materials in two basic ways. People who already have basic knowledge of concepts can recognize keywords in a book's index and find what they need. People who don't necessarily know what to look for in an index often rely on a table of contents to find information on a more topical footing.

To support these two different mindsets, we've produced two quick tables that speed you to several other tables that contain specific page numbers for the information you seek. These tables act as intelligent agents that lead you to the information you seek. Less guesswork, hassle, and time wasted!

How to Use Quick Tables

The "Building Pages Task-By-Task" table leads you to the most popular HTML tags used when authoring popular Web page elements.

The "Top Commands in Each Category" table directs you to other tables where the most popular tags and attributes are listed by the most popular categories.

Many people discover that hotlinking between tables (and the elements that they point to) can help find a tag or attribute in a minimum of time!

Building Pages Task-by-Task

To find out new ways to work with various HTML tags and their attributes, refer to the jump table on this page. Find a category of interest to you and then jump to a corresponding table that can help you complete your understanding of these basic concepts. Then use your new-found knowledge to build your Web pages.

Building Pages Task-by-Task	
To Find Out How To...	**Go to Page...**
Format Your Text	112-122, 42-43, 33-37
Lay Out Your Text	132-133
Display a Graphic Image	83-85, 94-95
Present a Background	30
Create a Hot Spot Image	97
Size Images for Best Performance	83-85, 94-95
Build a Marquee	98-99
Create an Image Map	97-98

Format Your Text

The tags listed on this page are among the most commonly used tags for formatting the appearance of text on a Web page. Managing the choice, color, and emphasis of fonts is a key factor in making your pages easier to read, and correspondingly, more memorable to the reader.

Tags	Go to Page...
<B>	24-26
<CODE>	43-44
<DFN>	49
<EM>	55
<FONT>	58
<I>	81-82
<KBD>	90-91
<STRONG>	124-125
<TITLE>	136

Lay Out Your Text

The HTML tags in this table represent the HTML tags most commonly used for organizing text on an HTML page. A good HTML author thinks about the way text is placed on her pages. Use these tags to layout your text so that readers can easily and quickly understand the meaning.

Tags	Go to Page...
<BODY>	34-35
 	37-38
<H1>	68-70
<H2>	70-71
<H3>	72
<H4>	73

Tags	Go to Page...
<H5>	74
<H6>	75
<HEAD>	76
<P>	110-111

Display a Graphic Image

The tags listed in this table are the most popular tags used for displaying graphical images on a Web page. With a little forethought, the HTML author can use the tags in this table to make the most of the display of images on their Web pages.

Tags	Go to Page...
<IMG>	83-85, 94-95
ALIGN	22
HSPACE	79
ISMAP	89
SIZE	60, 87, 120-121
SRC	66, 123
VSPACE	145

Present a Background

These tags play a role in displaying a background image. While they are few in number, the sensible use of background imagery and audio has a profound impact on any Web page.

Tags	Go to Page...
<BACKGROUND>	26
<BGCOLOR>	30
<BGPROPERTIES>	30
<BGSOUND>	31
<BODY>	34-35
DYNSRC	54
INFINITE	85
LOOP	95
SOUND	122

Create a Hot Spot Image

Hot spots link a user to another part of the current page, another site, another URL, and so on. The use of graphics as an anchor for a hotspot is one of the most creative elements evident in the most enticing Web pages.

Tags	Go to Page...
<A>	20
COORDS	47
HREF	78-79
<IMG>	83-85, 94-95
ISMAP	89
MAP	96-97
NAME	64, 98, 103, 119
SRC	66, 123
USEMAP	141

Size Images for Best Performance

Images don't have to be resized with image management software just to be used in a Web page. Today's preeminent browsers let you resize any image to your specifications.

Tags	Go to Page...
ALIGN	22
COORDS	47
HSPACE	79
<IMG>	83-85, 94-95
SRC	66, 123
VSPACE	145

Build a Marquee

Marquees are a recent addition to HTML publishing but they are catching on fast. Microsoft's Explorer browser paved the way for scrolling text in the form of a marquee. Expect to see more browsers begin to adapt this exciting medium for your messages.

Tags	Go to Page...
ALIGN	22
BGCOLOR	30
LOOP	95
MARQUEE	98-99

Create an Image Map

While creating an image map may seem a bit daunting at first, the use of image maps has overtaken the use of multiple, stand-alone images as hot spot vehicles to other points on the Information Highway.

I

HTML

Tags	Go to Page...
<A>	22
<ALINK>	96-97
<HREF>	78-79
METHODS	102
NAME	64, 98, 103, 119
URL	140
<VLINK>	144

Top Commands in Each Category

This table directs you to the most commonly used tags in the most popular tag categories. This table is especially useful to those who normally rely on the detailed index found at the rear of this and other reference books.

Top Commands in Each Category	
To Find The Top Commands For...	**Go to Page...**
Backgrounds and Colors	30-31
Links and Graphics	78-79
Lists	91-94
Forms	60-62
Tables	133, 137
Frames	62-63, 104-105
Netscape Extensions	157, 161
Internet Explorer Extensions	157, 159

Backgrounds and Colors

The backgrounds behind your scenes (and the colors you use to make them) can be a pleasant surprise and a refreshing inspiration to readers of overly "busy" Web pages. Use the tags in this table to change the colors of your backgrounds, text, tables, and so on.

Tags	Go to Page...
ALINK	96-97
BACKGROUND	30-31
BGCOLOR	30
<BODY>	34-35
COLOR	59
LINK	144
VLINK	144

Links and Graphics

Everyone agrees that the really cool aspect of the Web is its ability to take you off to a distant point of interest that you didn't know was there. Links and graphics tags, when used with text or imagery can send the readers of your Web page to places previously unknown...and beyond!

Tags	Go to Page...
<A>	20
ALIGN	22
<HREF>	78-79
<IMG>	83-85, 94-95
ISMAP	89
MAP	96-97
NAME	64, 98, 103, 119
SRC	66, 123
USEMAP	141

Lists

Organizing thoughts and short sentences into meaningful, easy-to-read lists can make your pages easier to comprehend and a lot more user friendly. The tags in this table are used to present text in different list formats.

Tags	Go to Page...
<DD>	48
<DIR>	50
<DL>	52
<DT>	53-54
<LI>	92-94
<MENU>	100
<OL>	107-108
<UL>	140
VALUE	142

Forms

Forms give the HTML author a way to collect meaningful information for processing or forwarding to another agent. The tags in this table are used to present the elements of a form on an HTML page.

Tags	Go To Page...
CHECKBOX	41
<FORM>	60-62
INPUT	86
METHOD	102
<SELECT>	117-118

Tables

Tables are a recent but welcome addition to HTML authoring. Tables help you organize text and graphics so that they relate to each other in rows and columns for easier reading.

Tags	Go to Page...
<CAPTION>	39
CELLPADDING	39
CELLSPACING	40
NOWRAP	130, 135
ROWSPAN	131, 135
<TABLE>	127-128
<TD>	129
<TH>	133
<TR>	137

Frames

Frames are another way that you can create a unique interface for your Web site. Frames are ideal for table of contents, fixed interface elements, and better forms and results.

Tags	Go to Page...
<FRAME>	62-63
<FRAMESET>	66
NAME	64, 98, 103, 119
ROWS	67
SRC	66, 123

Netscape Extensions

Netscape technology has played a major (if not a decisive role) in the proliferation of the Internet and the World Wide Web. Netscape browsers have been the harbingers of some of the most well received extensions to each successive, evolving HTML standard.

Tags	Go to Page...
ALINK	96-97
<BIG>	31-32
ISMAP	89
<MAP>	96-97
RECT	115
<SMALL>	121-122
<SUB>	125-126
<SUP>	126
USEMAP	141
VLINK	144

Internet Explorer Extensions

While Internet Explorer is a relative newcomer to the World Wide Web, Microsoft's Internet Explorer browser has introduced some of the most striking enhancements to the HTML standards in the form of the <MARQUEE> extensions and attributes, among others.

Tags	Go to Page...
BGCOLOR	30
LOOP	95
MARQUEE	98-99

Chapter 3

HTML Reference

In this section, you'll find an entry for every accepted (or anticipated to be accepted) element or "tag" in the various HTML standards/extensions in use. Turn to Part I of this book to find out more about categories, compliance, and so on.

The HTML elements in this section are in alphanumeric sort, as you would expect to find in an encyclopedia. If a tag manipulates the visual presentation of a browser, a figure is provided to help illustrate the effect caused by the use of that tag.

Every effort has been made to build the most comprehensive and up-to-date reference of the HyperText Markup Language in encyclopedic format. Note that there are several related conventions that are not part of the HTML standard but that can be called up or manipulated from an HTML document. Many of the most advanced math elements and server side includes, for example, are not part of the HTML standards now in development. The scope of this book is constrained to HTML standards observed by browsers offered by Netscape, Microsoft, and Mosaic and the HTML 2/HTML 3 standards.

New tags will be added to this book as they are recognized, adopted, and implemented in products such as Netscape Navigator, Internet Explorer, and Mosaic or as they're included in subsequent HTML standards.

!--

Compliance

Syntax

```
<!--......-->
```

Definition

The `<!-->` tag allows the author of an HTML document to place comments in the code that can only be seen while editing the document.

See also *COMMENT*.

Example Syntax

```
<!-- Document: INDEX.HTM 1.6 1996/03/25 17:33:48 -->
```

A

Compliance

Syntax

```
<A>...</A>
```

Definition

The `<A>` tag, which stands for "anchor," denotes the beginning and the end of a statement containing some form of a hypertext link. This tag allows the user to link to another location within the same HTML document, to another Web site, to an FTP server, and so on.

See *HREF* for more on creating hypertext links with the `<A>` tag.

Category

Links and Graphics

Example Syntax

```
<A HREF="http://www.askamerica.com">
```

Related Elements

Related Elements	This Element Can Be Used Inside `<A>`	`<A>` Can Be Used Inside This Element	Find It on Page Number
HREF	✔		78-79
METHODS	✔		102
NAME	✔		64, 98, 103, 119

Related Elements	This Element Can Be Used Inside <A>	<A> Can Be Used Inside This Element	Find It on Page Number
TITLE	✔		136

ADDRESS

Compliance

Syntax

```
<ADDRESS>...</ADDRESS>
```

Definition

The <ADDRESS> tag offers a way to format a small body of text into a format that resembles a conventional letter header. The <ADDRESS> tag provides mailing or contact information, often on a page that is intended to look like a conventional "analog" letter. The text inside the <ADDRESS> and </ADDRESS> tags is in italics.

Category

Structural Definition

Example Syntax

```
<ADDRESS>Robert Mullen<BR>

Box 32<BR>

Chicago Park, CA 95712-0032</ADDRESS>
```

Related Elements

Related Elements	This Element Can Be Used Inside <ADDRESS>	<ADDRESS> Can Be Used Inside This Element	Find It on Page Number
<A>	✔		20
<B>		✔	24-26
<BODY>		✔	34-35
<BODYQUOTE>		✔	33-34

(continues)

(continued)

Related Elements	This Element Can Be Used Inside <ADDRESS>	<ADDRESS> Can Be Used Inside This Element	Find It on Page Number
 	✔		37-38
<CITE>	✔		42-43
<CODE>	✔		43-44
<EM>	✔		55
<FORM>		✔	60-62
<I>	✔		81-82
<IMG>	✔		83-85, 94-95
<KBD>	✔		90-91
<P>	✔		110-111
<PRE>	✔		113-114
<SAMP>	✔		116-117
<STRONG>	✔		124-125
<TT>	✔		138-139
<VAR>	✔		142-143

ALIGN

Compliance

Syntax

```
ALIGN=[LEFT][RIGHT][CENTER][TOP][BOTTOM][MIDDLE][TEXTTOP][JUSTIFY]
```

Definition

ALIGN is an attribute meant to apply further presentation formatting to a body of text (using LEFT, RIGHT, JUSTIFY, CENTER, or TEXTTOP) or a graphic (using TOP, MIDDLE, or BOTTOM).

Category

ALIGN is used in every Category except Dividers and Backgrounds/Colors.

Example Syntax

```
<IMG SRC="MYFILE.GIF" ALIGN=TOP>
```

ALINK

Compliance

Syntax

```
ALINK="#RRGGBB">
```

Definition

The ALINK attribute defines the color of the "active link." Change the color mix used by ALINK by specifying color saturation in red (R), green (G), and blue (B). You can specify generic colors by specifying RED, GREEN, BLUE, and so on.

Category

Links and Graphics

Example Syntax

```
<BODY ALINK="#FFFFFF">
```

ALL

Compliance

Syntax

```
ALL
```

Definition

ALL is an variable used in the CLEAR attribute, which formats text to appear along the left, right, or below a line break.

Category

Dividers

Example Syntax

```
<BR CLEAR=ALL>
```

AU

Compliance

Syntax

`<AU>...</AU>`

Definition

The <AU> tag is used to identify the author(s) of an HTML document. This tag is most commonly used by groups of HTML authors working in a cooperative environment. The <AU> tag often appears in corporate and commercially-prepared Web pages. Client browsers do not display this text.

Category

Miscellaneous

Example Syntax

`<AU>Authors: Harold and Tim Robbins. Copyright 1996.</AU>`

B

Compliance

Syntax

`<B>...</B>`

Definition

This tag displays the text between the tags in bold when viewed with a browser.

Category

Structural Definition

Example Syntax

`<B>Take $90 worth of books for only $3.</B>`

In Actual Use

Fig. 3.1   This is an application of the <B> tag.

Related Elements

Related Elements	This Element Can Be Used Inside <B>	<B> Can Be Used Inside This Element	Find It on Page Number
<A>	✔	✔	20
<ADDRESS>		✔	21-22
<B>	✔	✔	24-26
 	✔		37-38
<CITE>	✔	✔	42-43
<CODE>	✔	✔	43-44
<DD>		✔	48
<DT>		✔	53-54
<EM>	✔	✔	55
<H1>		✔	68-70
<H2>		✔	70-71
<H3>		✔	72
<H4>		✔	73
<H5>		✔	74
<H6>		✔	75

(continues)

(continued)

Related Elements	This Element Can Be Used Inside <*B*>	<*B*> Can Be Used Inside This Element	Find It on Page Number
<I>	✔	✔	81-82
<IMG>	✔		83-85, 94-95
<KBD>	✔	✔	90-91
<LI>		✔	92-94
<P>		✔	110-111
<PRE>		✔	113-114
<SAMP>	✔	✔	116-117
<STRONG>	✔	✔	124-125
<TT>	✔	✔	138-139
<VAR>	✔	✔	142-143

BACKGROUND

Compliance

Syntax

```
BACKGROUND="myfile.jpg"
```

Definition

BACKGROUND is an attribute of the <BODY> tag. The BACKGROUND attribute allows the HTML author to specify a graphics file to be tiled behind all other text and graphics on a page.

Category

Backgrounds/Colors

Example Syntax

```
<BODY BACKGROUND="images/clouds.jpg">
```

In Actual Use

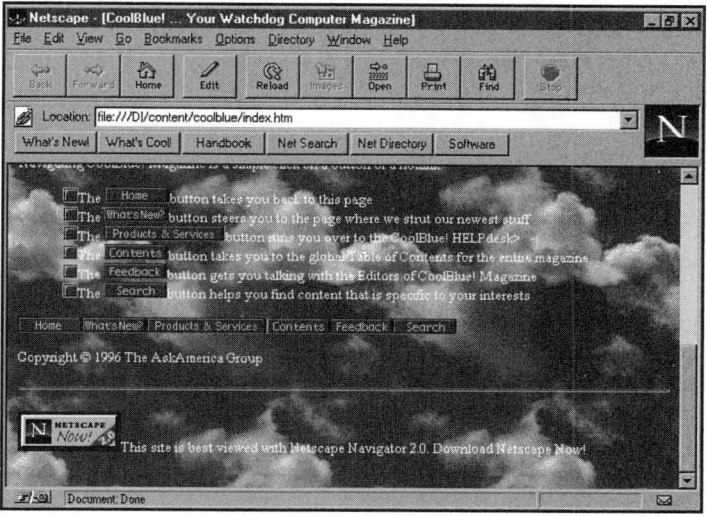

Fig. 3.2   This is an application of the BACKGROUND tag.

BANNER

Compliance

Syntax

```
<BANNER>...</BANNER>
```

Definition

The <BANNER> tag directs the HTML 3 compliant browser to render the <BANNER> graphic unmovable while the user scrolls the remainder of the content.

Category

Example Syntax

```
<BANNER>This is our Home Page!</BANNER>
```

BASEFONT SIZE

Compliance

Syntax

```
<BASEFONT SIZE=...>
```

Definition

The <BASEFONT SIZE> tag gives the author a way to establish or re-establish the default font size for all text that follows in the same document. All fonts are sized the same unless otherwise specified farther in the document. This tag is very useful to authors who are pasting large quantities of block text into HTML documents, that is, Internet publishers. The <BASEFONT SIZE> tag relegates the stated font size to an effective zero. Once the <BASEFONT SIZE> is established, authors use +1 or –1 to singly increment the size either larger or smaller from zero. The default <BASEFONT SIZE> is three unless otherwise specified using the <BASEFONT SIZE> tag.

Category

Structural Definition

Example Syntax

```
<BASEFONT SIZE=4>
```

BASE HREF

Compliance

Syntax

```
<BASE HREF=...>
```

Definition

The <BASE HREF> tag can be included in every page so that a reader can easily go to the home page if the reader has bypassed it to get to the current page.

Category

Links and Graphics

Example Syntax

```
<BASE HREF="http://www.askamerica.com/index.htm">
```

Related Elements

Related Elements	This Element Can Be Used Inside *<BASE HREF>*	*<BASE HREF>* Can Be Used Inside This Element	Find It on Page Number
<HEAD>		✔	76

BASE TARGET

Compliance

Syntax

```
<BASE TARGET="...">
```

Definition

Netscape supports the use of named windows. The TARGET tag gives the user the ability to name and open windows as long as the client browser is Netscape Navigator. Windows must be named in the HTML document's header in the same way variables are declared by programmers using traditional programming languages. The author may specify a default window to be opened in lieu of other named windows should that secondary window not be named and a TARGET window be called by a hyperlink.

Category

Links and Graphics

Example Syntax

```
<BASE TARGET="ABOUT_WINDOW">
```

BGCOLOR

Compliance

Syntax

```
BGCOLOR=# ...
```

Definition

The BGCOLOR tag establishes the background color of the page. You can either use text-based color names such as RED, GREEN, or BLUE, or you can specify colors as a hexadecimal number.

Category

Backgrounds/Colors

Example Syntax

```
<BODY BGCOLOR="RED">
```

or

```
*<BODY BGCOLOR=#ff0000>
```

BGPROPERTIES

Compliance

Syntax

```
BGPROPERTIES="..."
```

Definition

When the author places the BGPROPERTIES tag within the <BODY>...</BODY> tags, a non-scrolling image appears on a solid background color. This image creates an impression much like that of a watermark seen on traditional stationary.

Category

Miscellaneous

Example Syntax

```
<BODY BACKGROUND="OUR_COMPANY_LOGO.GIF" BGPROPERTIES=FIXED></BODY>
```

BGSOUND

Compliance

Syntax

```
<BGSOUND=...>
```

Definition

The <BGSOUND> tag provides the author with a way to play a background sound file (WAV, AU, or MID) to anyone viewing their HTML document, as long as that viewer has a PC with sound capability. The sound file plays when the document is opened by the viewer. The SRC attribute indicates the physical location of the file on the server. The LOOP attribute determines the number of times the audio file is played; for example, LOOP=4 plays the file four times. The LOOP=INFINITE attribute plays the file repeatedly.

See also *LOOP*.

> **Note**
>
> Mosaic will not play a MIDI file using the BGSOUND tag.

Category

Miscellaneous

Example Syntax

```
<BGSOUND SRC="MY_SOUND_FILE.WAV" LOOP=INFINITE>
```

BIG

Compliance

Syntax

```
<BIG>...</BIG>
```

Definition

The <BIG> tag allows the author to raise the font size of portions of text by one size increment, without further text formatting. For example, you may want to emphasize words in a sentence by making them one font size larger.

Category

Structural Definition

Example Syntax

```
<BIG>Search</BIG> Coolblue! Magazine for the content that interests you.
```

In Actual Use

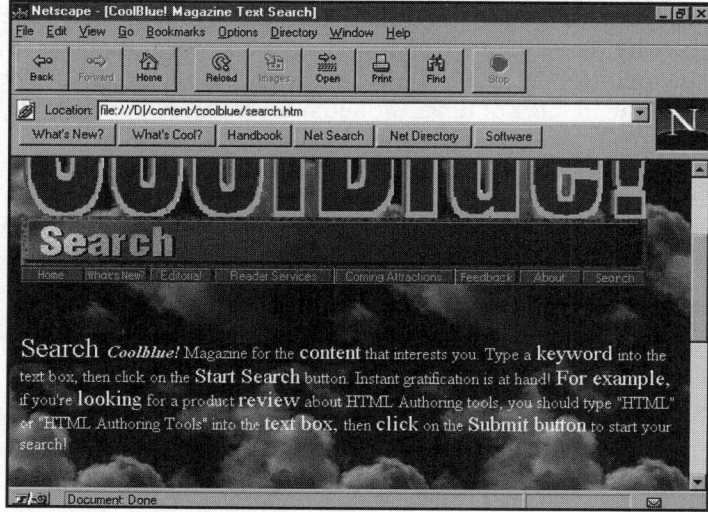

Fig. 3.3 This is an application of the `<BIG>` tag.

BLINK

Compliance

Syntax

```
<BLINK>...</BLINK>
```

Definition

Directs the browser to "blink" the specified text. Only Netscape supports this tag.

Category

Presentation Formatting

Example Syntax

```
<BLINK>Click on a button!</BLINK>
```

BLOCKQUOTE

Compliance

Syntax

```
<BLOCKQUOTE>...</BLOCKQUOTE>
```

Definition

The <BLOCKQUOTE> tag causes the client browser to indent the specified text on both sides. <BLOCKQUOTE> also includes a paragraph break before and after. Some browsers show an italic font when the <BLOCKQUOTE> tag is used.

Category

Structural Definition

Example Syntax

```
<BLOCKQUOTE>"in the future, everybody will be famous ..." Andy Warhol.
</BLOCKQUOTE>
```

In Actual Use

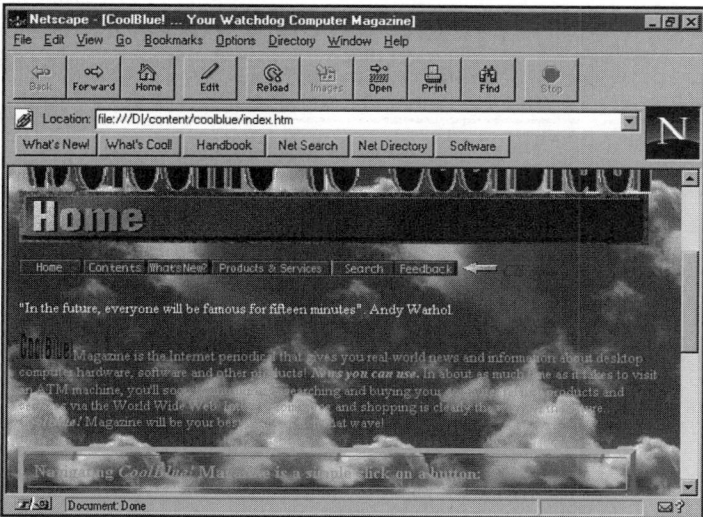

Fig. 3.4 This is an application of the <BLOCKQUOTE> tag.

Related Elements

Related Elements	This Element Can Be Used Inside <BLOCKQUOTE>	<BLOCKQUOTE> Can Be Used Inside This Element	Find It on Page Number
<ADDRESS>		✔	21-22
<BLOCKQUOTE>	✔	✔	33-34
<BODY>	✔		34-35
<DD>	✔		48
<DIR>		✔	50
<DL>		✔	52
<FORM>	✔	✔	60-62
<H1>		✔	68-70
<H2>		✔	70-71
<H3>		✔	72
<H4>		✔	73
<H5>		✔	74
<H6>		✔	75
<HR>		✔	77-78
<ISINDEX>		✔	87-88
<LI>		✔	92-94
<MENU>	✔		100
<OL>		✔	107-108
<P>		✔	110-111
<PRE>		✔	113-114
<UL>		✔	140

BODY

Compliance

Syntax

    <BODY>...</BODY>

Definition

All text, images, and formatting visible to the user must occur between the
<BODY>...</BODY> tags. Comment, <HEAD>, and other "for your eyes only" lines
should occur before the <BODY> tag to prevent these lines from being displayed by
the client browser.

Category
Structural Definition

Example Syntax
```
<BODY> Your entire HTML document goes here... </BODY>
```

Related Elements

Related Elements	This Element Can Be Used Inside <BODY>	*<BODY>* Can Be Used Inside This Element	Find It on Page Number
<ADDRESS>	✔		21-22
<BACKGROUND>	✔		26
<BGCOLOR>	✔		30
<BGMARGIN>	✔		26-30
<BLOCKQUOTE>	✔		33-34
<BODY>	✔		34-35
<DIR>	✔		50
<DL>	✔		52
<FORM>	✔		60-62
<H1>	✔		68-70
<H2>	✔		70-71
<H3>	✔		72
<H4>	✔		73
<H5>	✔		74
<H6>	✔		75
<HR>	✔		77-78
<HTML>		✔	80
<ISINDEX>	✔		87-88
<LINK>	✔		94-95
<MENU>	✔		100
<OL>	✔		107-108
<P>	✔		110-111
<PRE>	✔		113-114
<TEXT>	✔		132
<TOPMARGIN>	✔		136
<UL>	✔		140
<VLINK>	✔		144

BORDER

Compliance

Syntax

```
BORDER= ...
```

Definition

Draws a border around a table or an image. The author can specify the color or the width of the border in pixels.

Category

Presentation Formatting

Example Syntax

```
<P><A HREF="MY_URL"><img src="images/netscape.gif" alt="[Netscape Icon]"
border=5 </P>
```

BQ

Compliance

Syntax

```
<BQ>...</BQ>
```

Definition

The <BQ> tag is synonymous with the <BLOCKQUOTE> tag. The <BQ> tag directs the client browser to indent both before and after each line of text. <BQ> causes a paragraph break before and after. Some browsers display an italic font with <BQ>.

Category

Structural Definition

Example Syntax

```
<BQ>"in the future, everybody will be famous ...." Andy Warhol.</BQ>
```

Related Elements

Related Elements	This Element Can Be Used Inside <BQ>	<BQ> Can Be Used Inside This Element	Find It on Page Number
<ADDRESS>		✔	21-22
<BLOCKQUOTE>	✔	✔	33-34
<BODY>	✔		34-35
<DD>	✔		48
<DIR>		✔	50
<DL>		✔	52
<FORM>	✔	✔	60-62
<H1>		✔	68-70
<H2>		✔	70-71
<H3>		✔	72
<H4>		✔	73
<H5>		✔	74
<H6>		✔	75
<HR>		✔	77-78
<ISINDEX>		✔	87-88
<LI>		✔	92-94
<MENU>	✔		100
<OL>		✔	107-108
<P>		✔	110-111
<UL>		✔	140

BR

Compliance

Syntax

Definition

The <BR> tag directs the client browser to insert a line break in an HTML document. If the <BR> tag is used with the <IMG> tag, text following an image can be aligned with the left or right side of the image. The CLEAR attribute can used, in conjunction with an image, to center text directly below image. The <BR> tag (used alone) has the same effect as a carriage return on a typewriter. The <BR> tag can follow text on the same line, or it can be on a line of its own.

Category
Presentation Formatting

Example Syntax
```
My Name<BR>
My Street Address<BR>
My City, My State, My Zip<BR>
```

Related Elements

Related Elements	This Element Can Be Used Inside 	 Can Be Used Inside This Element	Find It on Page Number
<A>		✔	20
<ADDRESS>		✔	21-22
<B>		✔	24-26
 	✔		37-38
<CITE>		✔	42-43
<CLEAR>		✔	23
<CODE>		✔	43-44
<DD>		✔	48
<DT>		✔	53-54
<EM>		✔	55
<H1>		✔	68-70
<H2>		✔	70-71
<H3>		✔	72
<H4>		✔	73
<H5>		✔	74
<H6>		✔	75
<I>		✔	81-82
<KBD>		✔	90-91
<LI>		✔	92-94
<P>		✔	110-111
<PRE>		✔	113-114
<SAMP>		✔	116-117
<STRONG>		✔	124-125
<TT>		✔	138-139
<VAR>		✔	142-143

CAPTION

Compliance

Syntax

```
<CAPTION>...</CAPTION>
```

Definition

The <CAPTION> tag places a header or caption directly before the rows and columns of a table. <CAPTION> and its attributes must be included within the <TABLE> tags. A caption can be aligned to either the TOP, which is the default, or BOTTOM of the text line. The <CAPTION> tag centers enclosed text on the line.

Category

Tables

Example Syntax

```
<TABLE><CAPTION>Captions are centered by default</CAPTION></TABLE>
```

CELLPADDING

Compliance

Syntax

```
CELLPADDING=...
```

Definition

Specifies the thickness of a cell wall in a frame.

Category

Frames

Example Syntax

```
CELLPADDING=3
```

CELLSPACING

Compliance

Syntax
    CELLSPACING=...

Definition
CELLSPACING is an attribute used in creating tables. The CELLSPACING attribute directs the browser to display the specified number of blank spaces between the cell borders and the content of the cell.

Category
Frames

Example Syntax
    CELLSPACING=3

CENTER

Compliance

Syntax
    <CENTER>...</CENTER>

Definition
As a stand-alone HTML tag (not an attribute of another HTML tag) <CENTER> directs the client browser to center text or an image. Some HTML tags, such as the <BLOCKQUOTE> and <BQ> tags, also center by default. Since CENTER is also used as an attribute of many other HTML tags, check the context of CENTER in any HTML tag using the CENTER attribute for complete usage and definition in context.

Category
Structural Definition

Example Syntax
    <CENTER>Any text or image can be centered by the browser.</CENTER>

CHECKED

Compliance

Syntax

```
CHECKED
```

Definition

The CHECKED tag sets the default setting of a check box or radio button to "on" or "checked" by default.

Category

Forms

Example Syntax

```
<INPUT CHECKED>
```

CIRCLE

Compliance

Syntax

```
...=CIRCLE
```

Definition

CIRCLE one of three attributes of the AREA SHAPE tag/attribute combination. The CIRCLE attribute specifies that the shape of the clickable part of an image is in the shape of a circle.

Category

Links and Graphics

Example Syntax

```
<AREA SHAPE=CIRCLE/MAP>
```

CITE

Compliance

Syntax
```
<CITE>...</CITE>
```

Definition
Text within the <CITE> tag is italicized.

Category
Structural Definition

Example Syntax
```
<CITE>This text will be italicized.</CITE>
```

Related Elements

Related Elements	This Element Can Be Used Inside <CITE>	<CITE> Can Be Used Inside This Element	Find It on Page Number
<A>	✔	✔	20
<ADDRESS>		✔	21-22
<B>	✔	✔	24-26
 	✔		37-38
<CITE>	✔	✔	42-43
<CODE>	✔	✔	43-44
<DD>		✔	48
<DT>		✔	53-54
<EM>	✔	✔	55
<H1>		✔	68-70
<H2>		✔	70-71
<H3>		✔	72
<H4>		✔	73
<H5>		✔	74
<H6>		✔	75
<I>	✔	✔	81-82
<IMG>	✔		83-85, 94-95
<KBD>	✔	✔	90-91
<LI>		✔	92-94

Related Elements	This Element Can Be Used Inside <CITE>	<CITE> Can Be Used Inside This Element	Find It on Page Number
<P>		✔	110-111
<PRE>		✔	113-114
<STRONG>	✔	✔	124-125
<SAMP>	✔	✔	116-117
<TT>	✔	✔	138-139
<VAR>	✔	✔	142-143

CODE

Compliance

Syntax

```
<CODE>...</CODE>
```

Definition

Text within the <CODE> tag appears in a monospace font when viewed through a browser. The author may tailor the font in size, font name, or other font treatment.

Category

Structural Definition

Example Syntax

```
<CODE>This text is displayed using Courier New.</CODE>
```

Related Elements

Related Elements	This Element Can Be Used Inside <CODE>	<CODE> Can Be Used Inside This Element	Find It on Page Number
<A>	✔	✔	20
<ADDRESS>		✔	21-22
<IMG>	✔		83-85, 94-95
<B>	✔	✔	24-26

(continues)

(continued)

Related Elements	This Element Can Be Used Inside <CODE>	<CODE> Can Be Used Inside This Element	Find It on Page Number
 	✔		37-38
<CITE>	✔	✔	42-43
<CODE>	✔	✔	43-44
<DD>		✔	48
<DT>		✔	53-54
<EM>	✔	✔	55
<H1>		✔	68-70
<H2>		✔	70-71
<H3>		✔	72
<H4>		✔	73
<H5>		✔	74
<H6>		✔	75
<I>	✔	✔	81-82
<KBD>	✔	✔	90-91
<LI>		✔	92-94
<P>		✔	110-111
<PRE>		✔	113-114
<SAMP>	✔	✔	116-117
<STRONG>	✔	✔	124-125
<TT>	✔	✔	138-139
<VAR>	✔	✔	142-143

COMMENT

Compliance

Syntax

```
<COMMENT>...</COMMENT>
```

Definition

The <COMMENT> tag tells the client browser to ignore text between the tags. The <COMMENT> tags are used to embed text in an HTML document, yet make it visible to those who read the HTML source code for that document. <COMMENT> is popular with those who are sharing documents with multiple authors, allowing the tracing of individual edits (and dates of those edits) among multiple authors in a work group environment. Well commented source code is generally accepted as an instrument of professional programmers world-wide.

See *!--* for more on inserting comments into HTML documents.

Category

Miscellaneous

Example Syntax

```
<COMMENT>Last edited by Bob Mullen, 8/15/96.</COMMENT>
```

COMPACT

Compliance

Syntax

```
... COMPACT
```

Definition

Most often used with the <MENU> tag, the COMPACT attribute directs the client browser to minimize spaces between individual paragraphs of text in a menu list.

Category

Lists

Example Syntax

```
<MENU COMPACT>
```

CONTENT

Compliance

Syntax

```
<META...CONTENT="...">
```

Definition

CONTENT is an attribute of the <META> tag. The CONTENT attribute, when used in conjunction with the HTTP-EQUIV and REFRESH attributes, determines how often the specified image [URL] is to be refreshed on the browser screen, in seconds.

See also *META*.

Category

Links and Graphics

Example Syntax

    <META HTTP-EQUIV="REFRESH" CONTENT=2 URL=HTTP://www.bob.nuts.htm>

CONTROLS

Compliance

Syntax

    ... CONTROLS

Definition

CONTROLS is an attribute of the <IMG> tag. The CONTROLS attribute directs the browser to display a VCR-like panel of buttons below the display of an AVI file or video clip. This panel of buttons can be used to control the playing of the video clip.

Category

Miscellaneous

Example Syntax

    <IMG DYNSRC="MY_CLIP.AVI" CONTROLS>

COORDS

Compliance

Syntax

    COORDS=...

Definition
This attribute indicates the vector coordinates that are intended to be "clickable" in an image map. Image maps must be supported by the server for any client browsers to render them properly. Some ISPs do not support image maps because of legacy server software. In the following example, the user clicks within the coordinates of the image map to link the specified Web site.

Category
Links and Graphics

Example Syntax
```
<AREA SHAPE="RECT" COORDS="150, 25, 250, 125">
```

CREDIT

Compliance

Syntax
```
<CREDIT>...</CREDIT>
```

Definition
This tag is used to indicate credit for material included in a document. Credit is often given to sources and individuals who are being quoted directly.

Category
Miscellaneous

Example Syntax
```
<CREDIT>Photo used by permission of The Bettman Archives.</CREDIT>
```

DD

Compliance

Syntax
```
<DD>...</DD>
```

Definition

The <DD> tag is part of the formatting of a definition list. The <DD> tag directs the client browser to display an indented definition below the definition term. The <DD> and <DT> tags are useful, for example, in formatting multiple glossary or dictionary entries in an HTML document.

Category

Structural Definition

Example Syntax

```
<DD><IMG SRC="IMAGES/BULLET2.GIF" ALT="[BULLET]" THE
    BUTTON TAKES YOU BACK HOME TO THE FRONT COVER ... </DD>
```

Related Elements

Related Elements	This Element Can Be Used Inside <DD>	<DD> Can Be Used Inside This Element	Find It on Page Number
<A>	✔		20
<IMG>	✔		83-85, 94-95
<B>	✔		24-26
<BLOCKQUOTE>	✔		33-35
 	✔		37-38
<CITE>	✔		42-43
<CODE>	✔		43-44
<DD>	✔		48
<DIR>	✔		50
<DL>	✔	✔	52
<EM>	✔		55
<FORM>	✔		60-62
<I>	✔		81-82
<ISINDEX>	✔		87-88
<KBD>	✔		90-91
<MENU>	✔		100
<OL>	✔		107-108
<P>	✔		110-111
<PRE>	✔		113-114
<SAMP>	✔		116-117
<STRONG>	✔		124-125
<TT>	✔		138-139
<UL>	✔		140
<VAR>	✔		142-143

DEL

Compliance

Syntax
```
<DEL>...</DEL>
```

Definition
The <DEL> tag provides the author with a method of noting document content that has been deleted from the working body of the document as rendered by the client browser. This tag is most useful to groups of authors who edit shared HTML documents or to authors who are editing a document with a revised URL.

Category
Structural Definition

Example Syntax
```
<DEL>The upcoming celebration will be held in Nevada City!</DEL>
```

DFN

Compliance

Syntax
```
<DFN>...</DFN>
```

Definition
DFN stands for "defining instance." The <DFN> tag is used to delineate sub-definitions in a definition. A similar effect is found in a traditional dictionary where there are multiple definitions for the same term. The <DFN> tag provides the author with a method of organizing multiple, related instances into a compact area as a single definition. Line feeds can arrange each defining instance onto it's own line, you can see in the "Example Syntax" section.

Category
Structural Definition

Example Syntax
```
<DFN>This text will be displayed as a unique "definition".</DFN>
```

DIR

Compliance

Syntax
```
<DIR>...</DIR>
```

Definition
The <DIR> tag provides a way for the author to create a list that is compact and has narrow columns. A common use for the <DIR> tag is in alphanumeric indexes of content. The <DIR> tag constrains each item in the list to 20 characters.

Category
Structural Definition

Example Syntax
```
<DIR> <LI>NY Cities
<LI>Manhattan
<LI>Yonnkers
<LI>White Plains
<LI>Queens
<LI>Rochester</DIR>
```

Related Elements

Related Elements	This Element Can Be Used Inside <DIR>	<DIR> Can Be Used Inside This Element	Find It on Page Number
<BLOCKQUOTE>		✔	33-34
<BODY>		✔	34-35
<DD>		✔	48
<DIR COMPACT>	✔		50
<FORM>		✔	60-62
<LI>	✔	✔	92-94

DISC

Compliance

Syntax

    ... DISC

Definition

DISC is an attribute of the <LI> tag. If you want to bullet an entire unordered list with dots, use the DISC attribute after the <LI> tag. The client browser bullets each item in an unordered list with one of three bullets: DISC, CIRCLE, and SQUARE. DISC is the default bullet style. The author can specify any of the three attribute types on any item on a list by specifying different attributes on individual lines inside the <LI> tags.

Category

Lists

Example Syntax

    TYPE=DISC

DIV

Compliance

Syntax

    <DIV>...</DIV>

Definition

Divisions are another means for the author to present entire paragraphs of text. In Netscape Navigator, attributes of <DIV> are LEFT, RIGHT, and CENTER. With other client browsers, divisions are used to organize content into chapters and sections using the CLASS attribute.

Category

Structural

Example Syntax

    <DIV ALIGN=CENTER>This paragraph of text will be centered.</DIV>

DL

Compliance

Syntax

    <DL>...</DL>

Definition

The <DL> tag directs the client browser to display content as a list of terms and definitions, as in a glossary. The term is displayed flush left, with the term's definition slightly indented. Definition terms are displayed within one third of the total available display area. The COMPACT attribute directs the client browser to display a definition list in the smallest area possible.

Category

Lists

Example Syntax

    <DL>
    <DT>Fish<DD>A reptile that dwells in water.
    <DT>Bird<DD>A reptile that dwells out of water.
    </DL>

Related Elements

Related Elements	This Element Can Be Used Inside <DL>	<DL> Can Be Used Inside This Element	Find It on Page Number
<BLOCKQUOTE>		✔	33-34
<BODY>		✔	34-35
<DT>	✔		53-54
<DD>	✔	✔	48
<FORM>		✔	60-62
<LI>		✔	92-94

DOCTYPE

Compliance

Syntax

    <!DOCTYPE...>

Definition

The <DOCTYPE> tag is used to indicate to a server that the document is in HTML. The <DOCTYPE> tag is always placed before the <BODY> section of an HTML document.

Category

Structural Definition

Example Syntax
```
<!DOCTYPE HTML>
```

DT

Compliance

Syntax
```
<DT>...</DT>
```

Definition

DT stands for "definition term." Used in definition lists, <DT> presents text as the term before the definition, aligned to the left on the page. The definition follows the term.

See *DD*.

Category

Lists

Example Syntax
```
<DL>
<DT>Fish<DD>A reptile that dwells in water.
<DT>Bird<DD>A reptile that dwells out of water.
</DL>
```

Related Elements

Related Elements	This Element Can Be Used Inside <DT>	<DT> Can Be Used Inside This Element	Find It on Page Number
<A>	✔		20
<B>	✔		24-26
 	✔		37-38
<CITE>	✔		42-43
<CODE>	✔		43-44
<DL>		✔	52
<EM>	✔		55
<I>	✔		81-82
<IMG>	✔		83-85, 94-95
<KBD>	✔		90-91

(continues)

(continued)

Related Elements	This Element Can Be Used Inside <DT>	<DT> Can Be Used Inside This Element	Find It on Page Number
<SAMP>	✔		116-117
<STRONG>	✔		124-125
<TT>	✔		138-139
<VAR>	✔		142-143

DYNSRC

Compliance

Syntax
```
DYNSRC= ...
```

Definition
DYNSRC, which stands for "dynamic support," is an attribute of the <IMG> tag. The <DYNSRC> attribute specifies the location of a video or AVI clip (or VRML world) to be run in a window. Usually represented by a still image on a page, the client browser plays the file when the user moves the mouse pointer over the image or when the user clicks the representative image. AVI and VRML worlds can be played by default when a page is opened. The client browser must utilize inline video to display the DYNSRC attribute properly.

Category
Miscellaneous

Example Syntax
```
<IMG SRC="MY_FILE.GIF" DYNSRC="MY_MOVIE.AVI">
```

EM

Compliance

Syntax

`<EM>...</EM>`

Definition

The `<EM>` tag, which stands for "emphasis," directs the client browser to italicize the rendering of text. Some more obscure client browsers may render text inside `<EM>` tags in both italics and bold for added effect.

Category

Structural Definition

Example Syntax

`<EM>This text is displayed in italics!</EM>`

Related Elements

Related Elements	This Element Can Be Used Inside *<EM>*	*<EM>* Can Be Used Inside This Element	Find It on Page Number
`<A>`	✔	✔	20
`<ADDRESS>`		✔	21-22
`<B>`	✔	✔	24-26
` `	✔		37-38
`<CITE>`	✔	✔	42-43
`<CODE>`	✔	✔	43-44
`<DD>`		✔	48
`<DT>`		✔	53-54
`<EM>`	✔	✔	55
`<H1>`		✔	68-70
`<H2>`		✔	70-71
`<H3>`		✔	72
`<H4>`		✔	73
`<H5>`		✔	74
`<H6>`		✔	75
`<I>`	✔	✔	81-82
`<IMG>`	✔		83-85, 94-95
`<KBD>`	✔	✔	90-91
`<LI>`		✔	92-94
`<P>`		✔	110-111
`<PRE>`		✔	113-114
`<SAMP>`	✔	✔	116-117
`<STRONG>`	✔	✔	124-125
`<TT>`	✔	✔	138-139
`<VAR>`	✔	✔	142-143

EMBED

Compliance

Syntax
```
<EMBED ...>
```

Definition
The <EMBED> tag allows the author to display a file and allows that file to then be edited by the user. When the user clicks the file, the associated application on the user's machine is launched to edit the embedded file. An application must be associated with the embedded file type for the <EMBED> tag to properly perform. The WIDTH and HEIGHT attributes determine the dimensions (in pixels) of the displayed object. The original file located on the server is not edited.

Category
Links and Graphics

Example Syntax
```
<EMBED SRC="MY_IMAGES/MY_IMAGE.GIF" WIDTH=350 HEIGHT=150>
```

ENCTYPE

Compliance

Syntax
```
ENCTYPE ...
```

Definition
ENCTYPE is an attribute of the <FORM> tag. The ENCTYPE attribute uploads a file to the server based on input from the user. The user names the form to be uploaded in a text box in a form. When the user clicks the submit button, the file is sent to the specified URL (a location on the server).

Category
Links and Graphics

Example Syntax
```
<FORM ENCTYPE="FILENAME" ACTION="MY_URL" METHOD=POST>
```

FIGURE

Compliance

Syntax

```
<FIGURE>...</FIGURE>
```

Definition

The <FIGURE> tag tells the client browser to display the image file (an URL) named within the <FIGURE> tag.

Category

Links and Graphics

Example Syntax

```
<FIGURE SRC="/IMAGES/MY_IMAGE.GIF"></figure>
```

FILEOPEN

Compliance

Syntax

```
START=FILEOPEN
```

Definition

FILEOPEN is an attribute of the <IMG> tag. Used to play a video clip, the FILEOPEN attribute instructs the client browser to play the video clip immediately once the file is opened by the user.

See also *DYNSRC, MOUSEOVER,* and *LOOP.*

Category

Links and Graphics

Example Syntax

```
<IMG SRC="MY_IMAGE.GIF" DYNSRC="MY_BARBEQUE.AVI" START=FILEOPEN>
```

FONT

Compliance

Syntax

```
<FONT>...</FONT>
```

Definition

The <FONT> tag provides the author with a means of customizing how text appears with regards to font type, size, and color as well as other attributes. While most client browsers accept manipulation of text with most <FONT> attributes, some browsers accept more attributes than others. For example, Internet Explorer's FACE attribute of the <FONT> tag is not recognized by other client browsers.

Category

Presentation Formatting

Example Syntax

```
<FONT FACE="Arial,Lucida Sans,Times Roman" COLOR=RED FONT SIZE=-1>
```

Related Elements

Related Elements	This Element Can Be Used Inside *<FONT>*	*<FONT>* Can Be Used Inside This Element	Find It on Page Number
COLOR	✔		59
FACE		✔	59
SIZE	✔		60, 87, 120, 121

FONT COLOR

Compliance

Syntax

```
<FONT COLOR=...>
```

Definition

The COLOR attribute of the <FONT> tag determines the color applied to the text between the <FONT>...</FONT> tags. Color can be selected using two different criteria. The first is by naming the actual color (for example, RED, BLUE, and so on). The second is by specifying the shade using a hexidecimal reference that indicates the percentages of red, green, and blue. The "Example Syntax" section indicates the color of red in hexadecimal format. Some browsers do not recognize the use of hexadecimal when specifying colors.

Category

Presentation Formatting

Example Syntax

```
<FONT COLOR=#ff0000>This text is RED!</FONT>
```

FONT FACE

Compliance

Syntax

```
<FONT FACE=...>
```

Definition

The FACE attribute is an attribute of the <FONT> tag. The author can name the font used to display text. The author may specify up to three fonts, each to be used in the event that the preceding font is not available on the client browser's system. If the specified fonts are not found on the client browser's system, the browser uses its default font.

Category

Structural Definition

Example Syntax

```
<FONT FACE="CG OMEGA,Lucida Sans,Arial"></FONT>
```

FONT SIZE

Compliance

Syntax
```
<FONT SIZE=...>
```

Definition

The SIZE is an attribute of <FONT> tag. The author can change the relative size of a font by specifying how much larger or smaller the font should appear. The SIZE attribute increases or decreases the SIZE of the BASEFONT setting. To instruct the client browser to make the font size one size larger, the statement reads <FONT SIZE=+1>; in other words, the font size one size larger than the BASEFONT size whether that be default or author-defined. The default BASEFONT size is 3. The acceptable settings for the SIZE attribute are 1, 2, 3, 4, 5, 6, and 7 in both positive and negative.

Category

Structural Definition

Example Syntax
```
<FONT SIZE=+1></FONT>
```

FORM

Compliance

Syntax
```
<FORM>...</FORM>
```

Definition

The <FORM> tag provides a means of accepting input from the user. Information collected on a form can be displayed by the browser or sent to the server. Several attributes can be used with the <FORM> tag. Forms are normally a collection of inputs on a page. Users can click check boxes, radio buttons, and drop-down lists to make selections. Users can also enter text into text boxes. When the user clicks the submit button, the contents of the form are processed. The attributes of the <FORM> tag are too numerous to detail here. Use the jump table to find descriptions of relative tags and attributes on other pages of this book.

Category

Forms

Example Syntax
```
<P><FORM ACTION="FEEDBACK.HTM" METHOD="POST"><INPUT TYPE="HIDDEN" </P></FORM>
```

In Actual Use

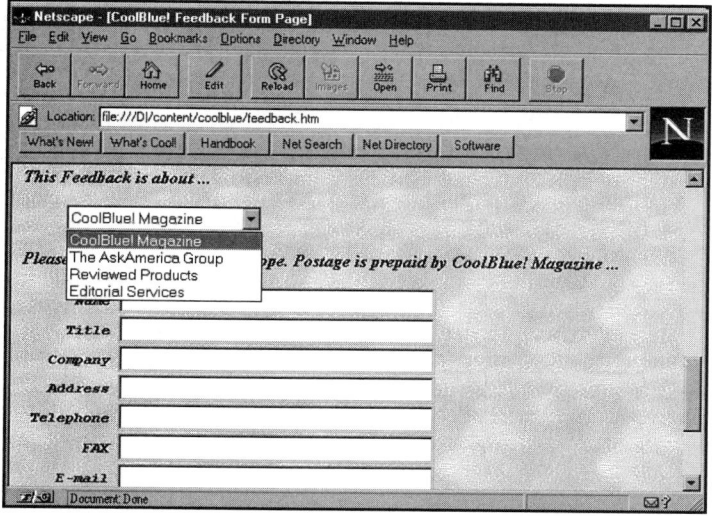

Fig. 3.5 This is an example of a form's drop-down list and text boxes.

Related Elements

Related Elements	This Element Can Be Used Inside <FORM>	<FORM> Can Be Used Inside This Element	Find It on Page Number
<ACTION>	✔		89
<ADDRESS>	✔		21-22
<ALIGN>	✔		22
<BLOCKQUOTE>	✔	✔	33-34
<CHECKED>	✔		41
<CONTROL>	✔		46
<DD>		✔	48
<DIR>	✔		50
<DL>	✔		52
<H2>	✔		70-71
<H3>	✔		72
<H4>	✔		73
<H5>	✔		74
<H6>	✔		75
<HR>	✔		77-78

(continues)

(continued)

Related Elements	This Element Can Be Used Inside <FORM>	<FORM> Can Be Used Inside This Element	Find It on Page Number
<INPUT>	✔		86
<ISINDEX>	✔		87-88
<LI>		✔	92-94
<MAXLENGTH>	✔		87, 99
<MENU>	✔		100
<METHOD>	✔		102
<NAME>	✔		64, 98, 103, 119
<OL>	✔		107-108
<P>	✔		110-111
<POST>	✔		113
<PRE>	✔		113-114
<SELECT>	✔		117-118
<SIZE>	✔		60, 87, 120, 121
<SRC>	✔		66, 123
<TEXTAREA>	✔		132-133
<UL>	✔		140
<VALUE>	✔		142

FRAME

Compliance

Syntax

    <FRAME...>

Definition

Netscape provides the Web author with the ability to create windows called *frames*. When used alone, the <FRAME> tag simply defines a single frame that's part of a group of frames called a *frameset*. The <FRAME> tag can utilize six attributes that determine the functionality and dimensions of the frame: FRAME NAME, FRAME MARGINWIDTH, FRAME MARGINHEIGHT, FRAME NORESIZE, FRAME SCROLLING, and FRAME SRC. These attributes are described in detail on other pages of this book.

Category
Frames

Example Syntax
See the six attributes for the <FRAME> tag for examples of usage.

FRAME MARGINHEIGHT

Compliance

Syntax
```
<FRAME MARGINHEIGHT= "...">
```

Definition
The MARGINHEIGHT attribute of the <FRAME> tag determines how much *vertical* space (in pixels) exists between the object located in a frame and the top or bottom inside edges of that frame. The client browser determines the appropriate MARGINHEIGHT if none is specified in the HTML document.

Category
Frames

Example Syntax
```
<FRAME MARGINHEIGHT=2>
```

FRAME MARGINWIDTH

Compliance

Syntax
```
<FRAME MARGINWIDTH="...">
```

Definition
The MARGINWIDTH attribute of the <FRAME> tag determines how much *horizontal* space (in pixels) exists between the object located in a frame and the left or right inside edges of that frame. The client browser determines the appropriate MARGINWIDTH if none is specified in the HTML document.

Category

Frames

Example Syntax

```
<FRAME MARGINWIDTH=2>
```

FRAME NAME

Compliance

Syntax

```
<FRAME NAME="...">
```

Definition

The NAME attribute gives the HTML author the ability to name to FRAME windows that hyperlinks in other HTML documents can target. The NAME attribute of the <FRAME> tag is optional and must use alphanumeric characters.

Category

Frames

Example Syntax

```
<FRAME NAME="MY_FRAME">
```

FRAME NORESIZE

Compliance

Syntax

```
<FRAME NORESIZE>
```

Definition

The NORESIZE attribute tells the client browser that the frame is not resizable by the user. Users typically resize frames by dragging a frame edge to a new position. The edge of an adjacent frame affected by the FRAME NORESIZE attribute is non-resizable. By default, Netscape allows all frames to be resized.

Category

Frames

Example Syntax

```
<FRAME NORESIZE>
```

FRAME SCROLLING

Compliance

Syntax

```
FRAME SCROLLING="..."
```

Definition

The HTML author can enable scroll bar capability to a frame. YES always displays scroll bars on that frame. The three possible settings are

```
FRAME SCROLLING=YES

FRAME SCROLLING=NO

FRAME SCROLLING=AUTO
```

The AUTO setting only displays a scroll bar when more content exists than can be seen in the frame. Netscape uses the AUTO setting by default.

Category

Frames

Example Syntax

```
FRAME SCROLLING=AUTO
```

FRAME SRC

Compliance

Syntax

```
<FRAME SRC="...">
```

Definition

The HTML author can tell the client browser to display the contents of an HTML document in a frame by using the FRAME SRC="..." attribute. Apply the standard rules for using any URL with the SRC attribute.

Category

Frames

Example Syntax

```
<FRAME SRC="HTTP://WWW.MY_HTML_DOCUMENT.HTM>
```

FRAMESET

Compliance

Syntax

```
<FRAMESET "...">
```

Definition

The FRAMESET tag defines the region of the screen in which the client browser constructs a frame. All FRAME dimensions and attributes are placed inside the FRAMESET tag. The FRAMESET tag must be used in lieu of the <BODY>...</BODY> tags or frames are not shown by the client browser. The FRAMESET tag and its attributes can be nested within other FRAMESET tags and attributes.

Category

Frames

Example Syntax

```
<HTML>
<HEAD>
</HEAD>
<FRAMESET>
</FRAMESET>
</HTML>
```

FRAMESET ROWS

Compliance

Syntax

```
<FRAMESET ROWS="...">
```

Definition

The ROWS attribute when used with the FRAMESET tag determines the width of each frame in pixels, percentage of available space, or at the browser's discretion. Variables (settings) for this attribute must be separated by commas. The "*" setting directs the browser to determine the optimum row size. The author may assign multiple settings that match the number of frames. The author can assign any combination of the three available setting types, separated by commas. By placing a number before the "*" setting (for example, "2*") in a compound setting statement, the author directs the client browser to double its assignment of space based on its assessment of the space available.

Category

Frames

Example Syntax

```
<FRAMESET ROWS=25>
<FRAMESET ROWS="50%">
<FRAMESET ROWS="*">
<FRAMESET ROWS="25,2*,50%">
```

FRAMESET COLS

Compliance

Syntax

```
<FRAMESET COLS="...">
```

Definition

The COLS attribute when used with the FRAMESET tag determines the height of each frame in pixels, percentage of available space, or at the browser's discretion. Variables (settings) for this attribute must be separated by commas. The "*" setting directs the browser to determine the optimum column size. The author may assign multiple settings that match the number of frames. The author can assign any combination of the three available setting types, separated by commas. By placing a number before the "*" setting (for example, "2*") in a compound setting statement, the author directs the client browser to double its assignment of space based on its assessment of the space available.

Category

Frames

Example Syntax

```
<FRAMESET COLS="25">
<FRAMESET COLS ="50%">
<FRAMESET COLS ="*">
<FRAMESET ROWS="25,2*,50%">
```

In Actual Use

Fig. 3.6 The Netscape Web pages exhibit an exciting use of frames.

H1

Compliance

Syntax

```
<H1>...</H1>
```

Definition

H1 stands for "heading 1," a first-level heading in a body of text. The client browser presents text inside the <H1> tag in a predetermined font presentation. There are six headings numbered one through six.

Category

Structural Definition

Example Syntax

```
<H1>How about a little <B><I>CoolBlue!</I></B> feedback? </H1>
```

In Actual Use

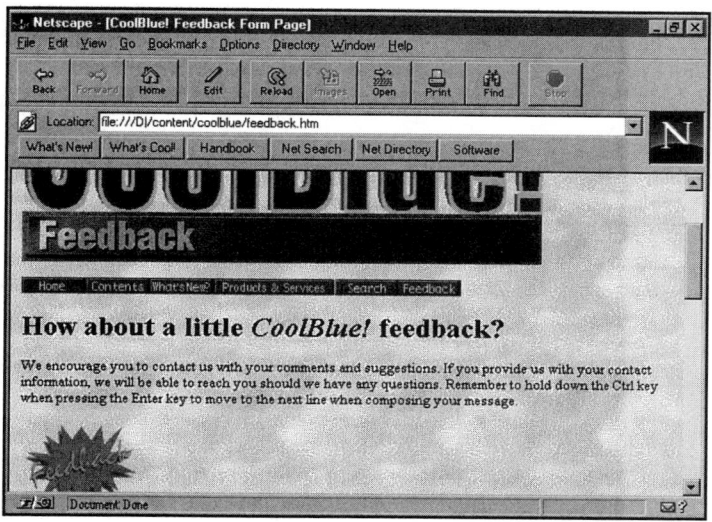

Fig. 3.7 This is the result of the example syntax.

Related Elements

Related Elements	This Element Can Be Used Inside <FRAME>	<FRAME> Can Be Used Inside This Element	Find It on Page Number
<A>	✔		20
ALIGN	✔		22
<B>	✔		24-26
<BLOCKQUOTE>		✔	33-34
<BODY>		✔	34-35
 	✔		37-38
<CITE>	✔		42-43
<CODE>	✔		43-44
<EM>	✔		55

(continues)

(continued)

Related Elements	This Element Can Be Used Inside <FRAME>	<FRAME> Can Be Used Inside This Element	Find It On Page Number
<FORM>		✔	60-62
<I>	✔		81-82
<IMG>	✔		83-85, 94-95
<KBD>	✔		90-91
<SAMP>	✔		116-117
<STRONG>	✔		124-125
<TT>	✔		138-139
<VAR>	✔		142-143

H2

Compliance

Syntax
```
<H2>...</H2>
```

Definition
H2 stands for "heading 2," a second-level heading in a body of text. The client browser presents text inside the <H2> tag in a predetermined font presentation.

Category
Structural Definition

Example Syntax
```
<H2><IMG SRC="BUTT07B.GIF" HEIGHT=80 WIDTH=112 ALIGN=LEFT> OK,
<B><I>CoolBlue!</I></B> ... What's New? </H2>
```

In Actual Use

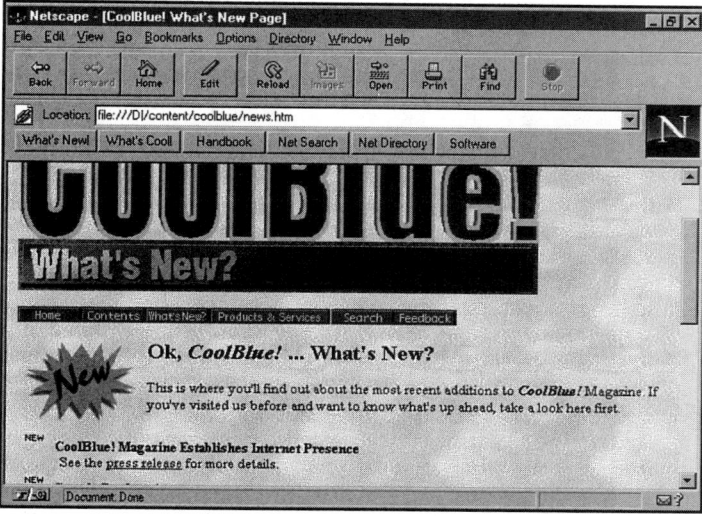

Fig. 3.8 This is the result of the example syntax.

Related Elements

Related Elements	This Element Can Be Used Inside <H2>	<H2> Can Be Used Inside This Element	Find It on Page Number
<A>	✔		20
ALIGN	✔		22
<B>	✔		24-26
<BLOCKQUOTE>		✔	33-34
<BODY>		✔	34-35
 	✔		37-38
<CITE>	✔		42-43
<CODE>	✔		43-44
<EM>	✔		55
<FORM>		✔	60-62
<I>	✔		81-82
<IMG>	✔		83-85, 94-95
<KBD>	✔		90-91
<SAMP>	✔		116-117
<STRONG>	✔		124-125
<TT>	✔		138-139
<VAR>	✔		142-143

H3

Compliance

Syntax

```
<H3>...</H3>
```

Definition

H3 stands for "heading 3," a third-level heading in a body of text. The client browser presents text inside the `<H3>` tag in a predetermined font presentation.

Category

Structural Definition

Example Syntax

```
<H2>Your heading text goes here...</H2>
```

Related Elements

Related Elements	This Element Can Be Used Inside *<H3>*	*<H3>* Can Be Used Inside This Element	Find It on Page Number
`<A>`	✔		20
`ALIGN`	✔		22
`<B>`	✔		24-26
`<BLOCKQUOTE>`		✔	33-34
`<BODY>`		✔	34-35
` `	✔		37-38
`<CITE>`	✔		42-43
`<CODE>`	✔		43-44
`<EM>`	✔		55
`<FORM>`		✔	60-62
`<I>`	✔		81-82
`<IMG>`	✔		83-85, 94-95
`<KBD>`	✔		90-91
`<SAMP>`	✔		116-117
`<STRONG>`	✔		124-125
`<TT>`	✔		138-139
`<VAR>`	✔		142-143

H4

Compliance

Syntax

```
<H4> .... </H4>
```

Definition

H4 stands for "heading 4," a fourth-level heading in a body of text. The client browser presents text inside the <H4> tag in a predetermined font presentation.

Category

Structural Definition

Example Syntax

```
<H4>Your heading text goes here...</H4>
```

Related Elements

Related Elements	This Element Can Be Used Inside <H4>	<H4> Can Be Used Inside This Element	Find It on Page Number
<A>	✔		20
ALIGN	✔		22
<B>	✔		24-26
<BLOCKQUOTE>		✔	33-34
<BODY>		✔	34-35
 	✔		37-38
<CITE>	✔		42-43
<CODE>	✔		43-44
<EM>	✔		55
<FORM>		✔	60-62
<I>	✔		81-82
<IMG>	✔		83-85, 94-95
<KBD>	✔		90-91
<SAMP>	✔		116-117
<STRONG>	✔		124-125
<TT>	✔		138-139
<VAR>	✔		142-143

H5

Compliance

Syntax

```
<H5>...</H5>
```

Definition

H5 stands for "heading 5," a fifth-level heading in a body of text. The client browser presents text inside the <H5> tag in a predetermined font presentation.

Category

Structural Definition

Example Syntax

```
<H5>Your heading text goes here...</H5>
```

Related Elements

Related Elements	This Element Can Be Used Inside <*H5*>	<*H5*> Can Be Used Inside This Element	Find It on Page Number
<A>	✔		20
ALIGN	✔		22
<B>	✔		24-26
<BLOCKQUOTE>		✔	33-34
<BODY>		✔	34-35
 	✔		37-38
<CITE>	✔		42-43
<CODE>	✔		43-44
<EM>	✔		55
<FORM>		✔	60-62
<I>	✔		81-82
<IMG>	✔		83-85, 94-95
<KBD>	✔		90-91
<SAMP>	✔		116-117
<STRONG>	✔		124-125
<TT>	✔		138-139
<VAR>	✔		142-143

H6

Compliance

Syntax
```
<H6>...</H6>
```

Definition
H6 stands for "heading 6," a sixth-level heading in a body of text. The client browser presents text inside the <H6> tag in a predetermined font presentation.

Category
Structural Definition

Example Syntax
```
<H6>Your heading text goes here...</H6>
```

Related Elements

Related Elements	This Element Can Be Used Inside <H6>	<H6> Can Be Used Inside This Element	Find It on Page Number
<A>	✔		20
ALIGN	✔		22
<B>	✔		24-26
<BLOCKQUOTE>		✔	33-34
<BODY>		✔	34-35
 	✔		37-38
<CITE>	✔		42-43
<CODE>	✔		43-44
<EM>	✔		55
<FORM>		✔	60-62
<I>	✔		81-82
<IMG>	✔		83-85, 94-95
<KBD>	✔		90-91
<SAMP>	✔		116-117
<STRONG>	✔		124-125
<TT>	✔		138-139
<VAR>	✔		142-143

HEAD

Compliance

Syntax

```
<HEAD>...</HEAD>
```

Definition

The <HEAD> tag begins (and ends) a part of an HTML document that refers to the document's usage context. The <TITLE> tag is normally enclosed in the <HEAD> tag, as is the <META> tag.

Category

Structural Definition

Example Syntax

```
<HEAD>
<TITLE>CoolBlue! ... Your Watchdog Computer Magazine</TITLE>
<META NAME="GENERATOR" content="Mozilla/2.01Gold (Win32)">
</HEAD>
```

Related Elements

Related Elements	This Element Can Be Used Inside <HEAD>	<HEAD> Can Be Used Inside This Element	Find It on Page Number
<BASE>	✔		28-29
<HTML>		✔	80
<ISINDEX>	✔		87-88
<META>	✔		101
<NEXTID>	✔		103-104
<TITLE>	✔		136

HR

Compliance

Syntax

<HR>

Definition

The <HR> tag draws a horizontal rule that is self-justifying and shaded for a 3-D look by default. The ALIGN attribute of <HR> can set the rule to justify to the LEFT, CENTER, or RIGHT. The NOSHADE attribute of <HR> removes the rule's default shade. The HEIGHT attribute of <HR> determines the height of the rule. The <HR> tag also accepts a WIDTH attribute that allows the HTML author to specify the width of a rule in either pixels or in the percentage of the available display space.

Category

Miscellaneous

Example Syntax

<HR>

In Actual Use

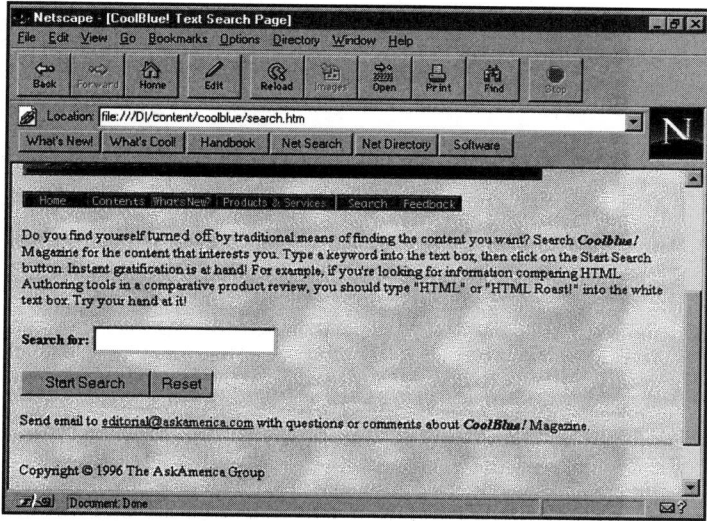

Fig. 3.9   This is an example of the <HR> tag.

Related Elements

Related Elements	This Element Can Be Used Inside <HR>	<HR> Can Be Used Inside This Element	Find It on Page Number
ALIGN		✔	22
<BLOCKQUOTE>	✔		33-34
<BODY>	✔		34-35

(continues)

(continued)

Related Elements	This Element Can Be Used Inside <HR>	<HR> Can Be Used Inside This Element	Find It on Page Number
<FORM>	✔		60-62
<NOSHADE>		✔	105
<PRE>		✔	113-114
<SIZE>		✔	60, 87, 120-121
<WIDTH>		✔	131, 135

HREF

Compliance

Syntax

```
<HREF...>
```

Definition

The <HREF> tag precedes a specified hypertext link.

The <HREF> tag can refer to

- Another URL on the WWW with the following syntax:

  ```
  <A HREF="HTTP:// ...">
  ```

- A WWW newsgroup with the following syntax:

  ```
  <A HREF=NEWS:NEWSGROUP>...</a> An FTP site with this syntax:
  <A HREF="FTP://...">
  ```

- A Gopher server with the following syntax:

  ```
  <A HREF="GOPHER://...>
  ```

- A mail program with the following syntax:

  ```
  <A HREF="MAILTO:ANY_MAIL_ADDRESS" TITLE="ANY_SUBJECT">
  ```

  > **Note**
  >
  > Some browsers ignore the TITLE attribute of HREF MAILTO.

- A NEWSRC file with the following syntax:

  ```
  <A HREF="NEWSRC:...">
  ```

- A non-default news server with the following syntax:

        <A HREF="NNTP://...">

- A telnet site with the following syntax:

        <A HREF="TELNET://...">

- A WAIS index server with the following syntax:

        <A HREF="WAIS://...">

Category

Links and Graphics

Example Syntax

See the earlier "Definition" section.

HSPACE

Compliance

Syntax

    HSPACE="..."

Definition

The HSPACE attribute is used by several tags. When used with the <IMG> tag, the HSPACE attribute sets the amount of blank space in pixels beside an image. Not all tags that use the HSPACE attribute are recognized by all browsers.

See also *IMG* and *MARQUEE*.

Category

Links and Graphics

Example Syntax

    <IMG SRC="HTTP://MY_IMAGE" HSPACE=3>

Related Elements

Related Elements	This Element Can Be Used Inside <HSPACE>	<HSPACE> Can Be Used Inside This Element	Find It on Page Number
<IMG>		✔	83-85, 94-95
<MARQUEE>	✔		98-99

HTML

Compliance

Syntax
```
<HTML>...</HTML>
```

Definition

The <HTML> tag indicates the absolute beginning and end of an HTML file. All other HTML tags must be used inside the <HTML> tag.

Category

Structural Definition

Example Syntax
```
<HTML>
<BODY>
<H1>This is an HTML document with only on line of text in it!</H1>
</BODY>
</HTML>
```

HTTP-EQUIV

Compliance

Syntax
```
<META HTTP-EQUIV="REFRESH" CONTENT=2>
```

Definition

HTTP-EQUIV is an attribute of the META tag. When used, this attribute directs the client browser to periodically refresh an HTML document.

See also *META*.

Category

Links and Graphics

Example Syntax

```
<META HTTP-EQUIV="REFRESH" CONTENT=5>
```

I

Compliance

Syntax

```
<I>...</I>
```

Definition

Text within the <I> tag appears in italics.

Category

Presentation Formatting

Example Syntax

```
<H3><I>Please address your return envelope. Postage is prepaid by CoolBlue!
Magazine ...</I></H3>
```

In Actual Use

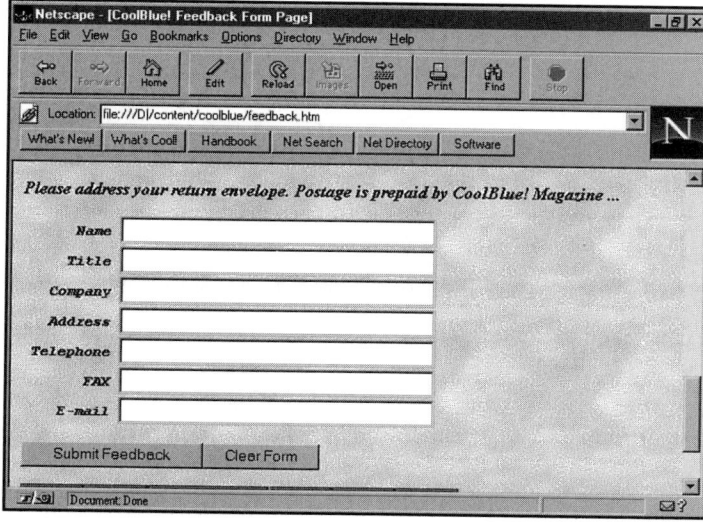

Fig. 3.10 This is the result of the example syntax.

Related Elements

Related Elements	This Element Can Be Used Inside <I>	<I> Can Be Used Inside This Element	Find It on Page Number
<A>	✔	✔	20
<ADDRESS>		✔	21-22
<B>	✔	✔	24-26
 	✔		37-38
<CITE>	✔	✔	42-43
<CODE>	✔	✔	43-44
<DD>		✔	48
<DT>		✔	53-54
<EM>	✔	✔	55
<H1>		✔	68-70
<H2>		✔	70-71
<H3>		✔	72
<H4>		✔	73
<H5>		✔	74
<H6>		✔	75
<I>	✔	✔	81-82
<IMG>	✔		83-85, 94-95
<KBD>	✔	✔	90-91
<LI>		✔	92-94
<P>		✔	110-111
<PRE>		✔	113-114
<SAMP>	✔	✔	116-117
<STRONG>	✔	✔	124-125
<TT>	✔	✔	138-139
<VAR>	✔	✔	142-143

ID

Compliance

Syntax

```
ID="..."
```

Definition

ID is an attribute for the <A> and <TABSTOP> tags. When used with the <A> tag, the ID attribute is used to specify an alias for a name such as a file or URL. When the ID attribute is used in the context of the <TABSTOP> tag, the ID setting sets that tabstop at the current geographical location in the HTML document.

Category

Structural Definition

Example Syntax

```
<A ID="MY_LABEL">
```

IMG

Compliance

Syntax

```
<IMG=...>
```

Definition

The <IMG> tag directs the browser to display a specified image. There are several attributes for the <IMG> tag. A graphics file need not be permanently resized to be displayed in varying contexts; however, the HTML author may direct the browser to resize with specified WIDTH and HEIGHT attributes. A clear BORDER, specified in pixels, can be applied to an image. An image can be aligned with the ALIGN=TOP, ALIGN=MIDDLE, ALIGN=BOTTOM, ALIGN=LEFT, and ALIGN=RIGHT attributes.

The ALT="..." attribute substitutes text specified by the HTML author in the event a specified image cannot be displayed. The CONTROLS attribute directs the client browser to display a VCR-like set of controls to be used in the play of AVI or other motion picture files. An HTML author can specify the location of the motion picture file to be played with the DYNSRC="..." attribute. Note that <IMG> is not rendered with character-based client browsers. Various attributes of the <IMG> tag are also not rendered with some client browsers. See the index of this book for other attributes used with the IMG tag.

Category

Links and Graphics

Example Syntax

```
<IMG SRC="IMAGES/HOMELOGO.GIF" BORDER=0 HEIGHT=153 WIDTH=575>
```

In Actual Use

Fig. 3.11   This is the result of the example syntax.

Related Elements

Related Elements	This Element Can Be Used Inside <IMG>	<IMG> Can Be Used Inside This Element	Find It on Page Number
<A>		✔	20
<ADDRESS>		✔	21-22
ALIGN	✔		22
<B>		✔	24-26
<CITE>		✔	42-43
<CODE>		✔	43-44
<DD>		✔	48
<DT>		✔	53-54
DYNSRC	✔		54
<EM>		✔	55
FILEOPEN	✔		57
<H1>		✔	68-70
<H2>		✔	70-71
<H3>		✔	72
<H4>		✔	73
<H5>		✔	74
<H6>		✔	75
HSPACE	✔		79

Related Elements	This Element Can Be Used Inside <IMG>	<IMG> Can Be Used Inside This Element	Find It on Page Number
<I>		✔	81-82
INFINITE	✔		85
ISMAP	✔		89
<KBD>		✔	90-91
<LI>		✔	92-94
LOOP	✔		95
MOUSOVER	✔		102
<P>		✔	110-111
<SAMP>		✔	116-117
SRC	✔		66, 123
<STRONG>		✔	124-125
<TT>		✔	138-139
<VAR>		✔	142-143
USEMAP	✔		141
VSPACE	✔		145
WIDTH	✔		131, 135

INFINITE

Compliance

Syntax
```
... =INFINITE
```

Definition
INFINITE is a setting of the LOOP attribute. The LOOP attribute of the <IMG> tag allows the HTML author to specify how long a moving picture is to be played. If LOOP=2 is used, the moving picture appears for two seconds. If you use LOOP=INFINITE, the moving image continuously replays.

Category
Links and Graphics

Example Syntax
```
<IMG SRC="MY_IMAGE.GIF" DYNSRC="MY_MOVIE.AVI" LOOP=INFINITE>
```

INPUT

Compliance

Syntax
```
<INPUT "...">
```

Definition
The `<INPUT>` tag directs the browser to send information to the server, usually the contents of a FORM.

Category
Forms

Example Syntax
```
<INPUT NAME="Control" TYPE=IMAGE SRC="MY_IMAGE.GIF">
```

Related Elements

Related Elements	This Element Can Be Used Inside `<INPUT>`	`<INPUT>` Can Be Used Inside This Element	Find It on Page Number
ALIGN	✔		22
CHECKED	✔		41
`<FORM>`		✔	60-62
MAXLENGTH	✔		87, 99
NAME	✔		64, 98, 103, 119
SIZE	✔		60, 87, 120, 121
SRC	✔		66, 123
VALUE	✔		142

INPUT SIZE

Compliance

Syntax
```
<INPUT SIZE="...">
```

Definition
The `SIZE` attribute of the `<INPUT>` tag gives the HTML author a way to specify the length in characters of a input field. The `MAXLENGTH` attribute of the `<INPUT>` tag determines how many characters can be input from that field.

Category
Forms

Example Syntax
```
<INPUT SIZE="35">
```

ISINDEX

Compliance

Syntax
```
<ISINDEX "..." >
```

Definition
This tag directs the client browser to display the following message, along with a text box: `You can search this index. Type the keyword(s) you want to search for:`. XMosaic and other browsers may display this information differently.

Text submited with this small form is posted back to the page's URL as a query or to a CGI script.

Category
Forms

Example Syntax
```
<ISINDEX>
```

Related Elements

Related Elements	This Element Can Be Used Inside *<ISINDEX>*	*<ISINDEX>* Can Be Used Inside This Element	Find It on Page Number
`<BLOCKQUOTE>`		✔	33-34
`<BODY>`		✔	34-35

(continues)

(continued)

Related Elements	This Element Can Be Used Inside *<ISINDEX>*	*<ISINDEX>* Can Be Used Inside This Element	Find It on Page Number
<DD>		✔	48
<FORM>		✔	60-62
<HEAD>		✔	76
<LI>		✔	92-94

ISINDEX PROMPT

Compliance

Syntax

```
<ISINDEX PROMPT= "...">
```

Definition

The PROMPT attribute of the <ISINDEX> tag gives the author a way to substitute a customized text message for the default text message.

See *ISINDEX* for the default text message.

Category

Forms

Example Syntax

```
<ISINDEX PROMPT="Why not use your own text prompt instead?">
```

ISINDEX action

Compliance

Syntax

```
<ISINDEX ACTION= "...">
```

Definition

The ACTION attribute of the <ISINDEX> tag sends submitted text to a specified gateway program.

Category

Forms

Example Syntax

```
<ISINDEX ACTION="SEARCH_ME">
```

ISMAP

Compliance

Syntax

```
ISMAP
```

Definition

The ISMAP directs the client browser to use a script that resides with the document on the server. When the user clicks an image, the ISMAP tag directs the browser to look for instructions in a specified map file (.MAP).

Category

Forms

Example Syntax

```
<A HREF="MY_MAP.MAP"> <IMG SRC="MY_IMAGE.GIF" ISMAP></A>
```

KBD

Compliance

Syntax

```
<KBD>...</KDB>
```

Definition

The <KBD> tag directs the browser to render specified text in a bold, fixed-width font. This tag is typically used to exemplify a keyboard entry made by the user.

Category

Structural Definition

Example Syntax

```
<KBD>Type your own message here!</KBD>
```

Related Elements

Related Elements	This Element Can Be Used Inside <KBD>	<KBD> Can Be Used Inside This Element	Find It on Page Number
<A>	✔	✔	20
<ADDRESS>		✔	21-22
<B>	✔	✔	24-26
 	✔		37-38
<CITE>	✔	✔	42-43
<CODE>	✔	✔	43-44
<DD>		✔	48
<DT>		✔	53-54
<EM>	✔	✔	55
<H1>		✔	68-70
<H2>		✔	70-71
<H3>		✔	72
<H4>		✔	73
<H5>		✔	74
<H6>		✔	75
<I>	✔	✔	81-82
<IMG>	✔		83-85, 94-95
<KBD>	✔	✔	90-91
<LI>		✔	92-94
<P>		✔	110-111
<PRE>		✔	113-114
<SAMP>	✔	✔	116-117

Related Elements	This Element Can Be Used Inside <KBD>	<KBD> Can Be Used Inside This Element	Find It on Page Number
<STRONG>	✔	✔	124-125
<TT>	✔	✔	138-139
<VAR>	✔	✔	142-143

LANG

Compliance

Syntax

    <LANG>...</LANG>

Definition

The <LANG> tag indicates that a language other than the base language of the document is in use.

Category

Structural Definition

Example Syntax

    <LANG> For our Japanese friends, here is the same joke in their native
    tongue... </LANG>

LH

Compliance

Syntax

    <LH>...</LH>

Definition

The <LH> tag renders enclosed text as a header for a list.

Category

Structural Definition

Example Syntax

```
<UL><LH>This sentence appears as a header before this bulleted list:</LH>
<LI>This is list item #1
<LI>This is list item #2
<LI>This is list item #3
</UL>
```

LI

Compliance

Syntax

```
<LI>
```

Definition

The <LI> tag is used to direct the browser to display the following text as a line item on a list. Lists can be ordered, unordered, or bulleted. Lists are bulleted by default. The TYPE= attribute of the <LI> tag changes the type of characters used to order a list: TYPE=A (use uppercase letters), TYPE=a (use lowercase letters), TYPE=I (use large Roman numerals), TYPE=i (use small roman numerals), and TYPE=1 (use Arabic numerals). The VALUE attribute of the <LI> tag directs the browser to begin ordering with the number specified. The <LI> tag needs no closing tag.

Category

Structural Definition

Example Syntax

```
<P>Here are the latest press releases. You may want to
<A HREF="search.htm">search</A>
for topics by keyword.</P>
<UL>
<LI>5/1/96 -- <B><A HREF="pr01.htm"><I>CoolBlue!
</I>Magazine Establishes Internet Presence</A></B> </LI>
</UL>
```

In Actual Use

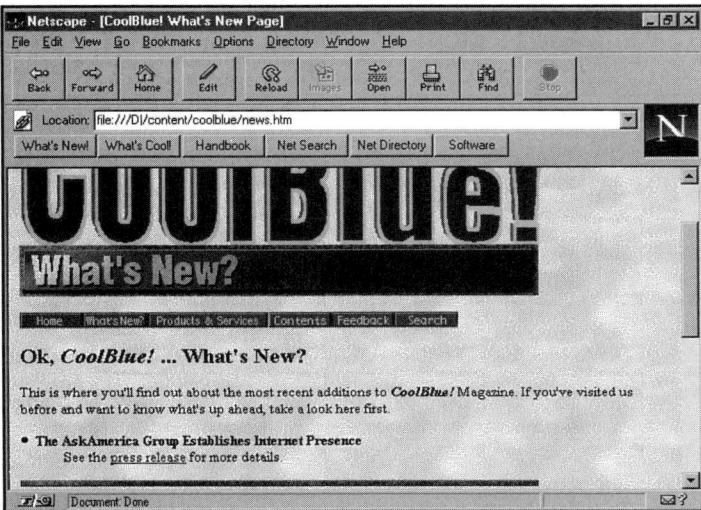

Fig. 3.12   This is the result of the example syntax.

Related Elements

Related Elements	This Element Can Be Used Inside <*LI*>	<*LI*> Can Be Used Inside This Element	Find It on Page Number
<A>	✔		20
<B>	✔		24-26
<BLOCKQUOTE>	✔		33-34
 	✔		37-38
<CITE>	✔		42-43
<CODE>	✔		43-44
<DIR>	✔	✔	50
<DL>	✔		52
<EM>	✔		55
<FORM>	✔		60-62
<I>	✔		81-82
<IMG>	✔		83-85, 94-95
<ISINDEX>	✔		87-88
<KBD>	✔		90-91
<MENU>	✔	✔	100
<OL>	✔	✔	107-108
<P>	✔		110-111

(continues)

(continued)

Related Elements	This Element Can Be Used Inside *<LI>*	*<LI>* Can Be Used Inside This Element	Find It on Page Number
<PRE>	✔		113-114
<SAMP>	✔		116-117
<STRONG>	✔		124-125
<TT>	✔		138-139
<UL>	✔	✔	140
<VAR>	✔		142-143

LINK

Compliance

Syntax

    <LINK...>

Definition

The <LINK> tag gives the HTML author the ability to specify a named file (URL) or text as a "hypertext link" to another document (or another point) in the same document. Other tags use an attribute called LINK. See the index at the back of this book to find other tags that use an attribute called LINK.

Category

Links and Graphics

Example Syntax

    <LINK HREF="/MY_FILES/MY_FILE.HTM>

Related Elements

Related Elements	This Element Can Be Used Inside *<LINK>*	*<LINK>* Can Be Used Inside This Element	Find It on Page Number
<HEAD>		✔	76
HREF	✔		78-79
METHODS	✔		102

Related Elements	This Element Can Be Used Inside *<LINK>*	*<LINK>* Can Be Used Inside This Element	Find It on Page Number
TITLE	✔		136

LISTING

Compliance

Syntax

```
<LISTING>...</LISTING>
```

Definition

The <LISTING> tag renders text in a fixed-width type.

Category

Structural Definition

Example Syntax

```
<LISTING>This text is displayed in fixed width.</LISTING>
```

LOOP

Compliance

Syntax

```
<...LOOP=...>
```

Definition

LOOP is an attribute of the BGSOUND tag. LOOP directs the browser to either play a sound as long as a page is active (for example, LOOP=INFINITE) or to play a sound for any specified number of seconds (for example, LOOP=3).

Category

Miscellaneous

Example Syntax

```
<BGSOUND SRC="MY_AUDIO_FILE.WAV" LOOP=INFINITE>
```

LOWSRC

Compliance

Syntax

```
<...LOWSRC="...">
```

Definition

LOWSRC is an attribute of the <IMG> tag. The LOWSRC attribute allows the HTML author to display a low resolution image intended merely to represent another higher-overhead, higher-resolution image.

Category

Links and Graphics

Example Syntax

```
<IMG SRC="MY_URL" LOWSRC="MY_IMAGE.GIF">
```

MAP

Compliance

Syntax

```
<MAP "..."></MAP>
```

Definition

The <MAP> tag specifies a collection of hot spots for a client-side image map.

See also *MAP NAME* and *MAP AREA*.

Category
Links and Graphics

Example Syntax
```
<MAP NAME="MY_MAP"></MAP>
```

MAP AREA

Compliance

Syntax
```
<MAP AREA="..."></MAP>
```

Definition:

AREA is an user-clickable region of a client side image map.

See also *MAP* and *MAP NAME*.

The MAP AREA SHAPE attribute renders the clickable shape as a rectangle (MAP AREA SHAPE=RECT), a polygon (MAP AREA SHAPE=POLY), or a circle (MAP AREA SHAPE=CIRCLE).

The MAP AREA SHAPE="..." attribute makes a round portion of an image clickable with the following example syntax:

```
MAP AREA SHAPE="0,25"
```

0 is the center of the circle, and 25 is the number of pixels on a radius.

The MAP AREA COORDS="..." attribute gives the HTML author the ability to specify the clickable rectangular or circular region of an image. If, for example, the top 50 percent of a rectangular image is desirable for use, the four vector points of a 100-point square image are specified with the following:

```
MAP AREA COORDS="0,0,100,50"
```

or

```
MAP AREA COORDS=LEFT
```

You can also use TOP RIGHT or BOTTOM.

COORDS must be specified in pixels. The NOHREF attribute of MAP AREA, when used with MAP AREA attribute, directs the browser to disallow clicking of the named area. Any area of the image that's not identified by an AREA tag is rendered as NOHREF as default. The HREF attribute, when used with MAP AREA, specifies a link to another URL.

Category

Links and Graphics

Example Syntax

```
<MAP AREA SHAPE=RECT>
```

MAP NAME

Compliance

Syntax

```
<MAP NAME="...">
```

Definition

NAME is an attribute of the <MAP> tag. This attribute allows the HTML author to label the <MAP> with a name made up of any characters.

See also *MAP* and *MAP AREA*.

Category

Links and Graphics

Example Syntax

```
<MAP NAME="MY_NAME">
```

MARQUEE

Compliance

Syntax

```
<MARQUEE>...</MARQUEE>
```

Definition

The <MARQUEE> tag gives the HTML author a way to create a scrolling text marquee. A marquee can be left or right-aligned on the page.

Attributes of the <MARQUEE> tag are:

- BGCOLOR="..."　Specify the background color of a marquee in hexidecimal format.

- DIRECTION="..."　Specify the direction of the scrolling action as either "LEFT" or "RIGHT".

- ALIGN="..."　Specify whether the marquee text is aligned to the TOP, MIDDLE, or BOTTOM of the marquee.

- BEHAVIOR="..."　Specify that the text slides onto the page and then stops with the SLIDE attribute, that the text bounces from side to side with the ALTERNATE attribute, or that the text repeatedly scrolls across the page.

- HEIGHT　Specify the height of the marquee in either pixels or a percentage of the page.

- WIDTH　Specify the width of the marquee in either pixels or a percentage of the page.

- LOOP　Specify the number of times a marquee scrolls in either the number of scrolls (LOOP=5) or indefinitely with the LOOP=INFINITE or LOOP= -1 settings.

- VSPACE and HSPACE　Specify the amount of clear space adjoining a marquee in pixels.

- SCROLLDELAY　Specify the time between scrolls in milliseconds.

- SCROLLAMOUNT　Specify the space between scrolled text in pixels.

Category
Miscellaneous

Example Syntax
```
<MARQUEE DIRECTION=LEFT>This text will scroll to the left.</MARQUEE>
```

MAXLENGTH

Compliance

Syntax
```
<INPUT MAXLENGTH="...">
```

Definition:
MAXLENGTH is an attribute of the <INPUT> tag. The MAXLENGTH attribute specifies how many characters are allowed to be entered into a text box by the user.

Category
Forms

Example Syntax
```
<INPUT MAXLENGTH="50">
```

MENU

Compliance

Syntax
```
<MENU>...</MENU>
```

Definition:
The <MENU> tag is used to direct the client browser to display following paragraphs of text as items on a list. The <LI> tag is used to specify the beginning of each paragraph on the menu list.

Category
Structural Definition

Example Syntax
```
<MENU>
<LI> This is item one.
<LI> This is item two.
<LI> This is item three.
</MENU>
```

Related Elements

Related Elements	This Element Can Be Used Inside <MENU>	<MENU> Can Be Used Inside This Element	Find It on Page Number
<BLOCKQUOTE>		✔	33-34
<BODY>		✔	34-35
<DD>		✔	48
<FORM>		✔	60-62
<LI>	✔	✔	92-94
<MENU>	✔		100

META

Compliance

Syntax

```
<META "...">
```

Definition

The <META> tag is used to indicate special instructions for the client browser or the server. The <META> tag must be placed as part of the <HEAD> in an HTML document.

The following are the attributes for the <META> tag:

- HTTP-EQUIV="REFRESH"   Directs the browser to repeatedly reload the document in the number of seconds specified in the CONTENT attribute.

- CONTENT="..."   Specifies the number of seconds that should elapse between successive document reloads.

- URL="..."   Specifies the full URL path name to be reloaded; if not specified, the current document is reloaded.

HTML authors can use the <META> tag and its attributes to produce slide shows using HTML documents.

Category

Structural Definition

Example Syntax

```
<META HTTP-EQUIV="REFRESH" CONTENT=5 URL=HTTP://WWW.FOO.COM/INDEX.HTM>
```

Related Elements

Related Elements	This Element Can Be Used Inside <META>	<META> Can Be Used Inside This Element	Find It on Page Number
HTTP-EQUIV	✔		80
NAME	✔		64, 98, 103, 199
CONTENT	✔		46
<HEAD>		✔	76

METHOD

Compliance

Syntax

```
<FORM  METHOD=...>
```

Definition

METHOD is an attribute of the <FORM> tag. The METHOD attribute directs the client browser in processing the information collected on a form. When the user clicks the Submit button, the proscribed METHOD is carried out. The content of a form can be posted as an URL on a server or mailed as an HTML file. The content itself can be formatted as "fields" using the following characters:

```
field1=field1 contents&field2=field2 contents&...&fieldn=fieldn contents&
```

& delimits fields, + inserts a space, and %0D%A inserts a line feed.

Category

Forms

Example Syntax

```
<P><FORM ACTION="_VTI_BIN/FEEDBACK.HTM" METHOD="POST"><INPUT NAME="VTI-GROUP">
</P>
```

MOUSEOVER

Compliance

Syntax

```
<...=MOUSEOVER>
```

Definition

MOUSEOVER is an attribute of the <IMG START> tag. The MOUSEOVER attribute directs the client browser to begin playing a movie file when the mouse pointer is moved over the icon representing the movie file.

Category

Miscellaneous

Example Syntax

```
<IMG SRC="MY_MOVIE_ICON.GIF" DYNSRC="MY_AVI_FILE.AVI" START=MOUSEOVER>
```

NAME

Compliance

Syntax

```
<A HREF NAME= "...">
```

Definition:

NAME is an attribute of the <HREF> tag. The NAME attribute directs the browser to link to the HTML file specified as part of the NAME attribute. The NAME attribute can also specify a link within the same document.

Category

Links and Graphics

Example Syntax

```
<P><A HREF NAME="INDEX.HTM"><IMG SRC="BHOME2.GIF"></A>
```

NEXTID

Compliance

Syntax

```
<NEXTID= "..."
```

Definition

The <NEXTID> tag is generated by some HTML editors. The <NEXTID> value is a variable that can be assigned by an editor to reference a document. The <NEXTID> value is a scheme used only by editor programs and is not generally used by "human" HTML authors.

Category

Links and Graphics

Example Syntax
```
<NEXTID N=Z147>
```

NOBR

Compliance

Syntax
```
<NOBR>...</NOBR>
```

Definition

The <NOBR> tag prevents the browser from inserting a line break even when word wrapping is appropriate. Some strings of text should not be broken under any circumstances. A good example of a string of text that should remain unbroken is a long URL.

Category

Structural Definition

Example Syntax
```
I don't want this URL broken by a browser:
<NOBR>http://www.askamerica.com</NOBR>
```

NOFRAMES

Compliance

Syntax
```
<NOFRAMES>...</NOFRAMES>
```

Definition

The <NOFRAMES> tag directs the browser to display specified text only in the event the browser is not capable of rendering frames.

Category:

Miscellaneous

Example Syntax

```
<NOFRAMES>This text will be displayed in lieu of framed content.</NOFRAMES>
```

NOHREF

Compliance

Syntax

```
<A HREF= "..." NOHREF>
```

Definition

HREF is an attribute that directs the browser to exclude the named range from being clickable. The HREF attribute is generally considered redundant since only named, clickable ranges can cause an action when clicked upon.

Category

Links and Graphics

Example Syntax

```
<AREA SHAPE="RECT" COORDS="0,0,100,50" NOHREF>
```

NOSHADE

Compliance

Syntax

```
<HR NOSHADE>
```

Definition

NOSHADE is an attribute of the <HR> tag. The <HR> tag directs the browser to draw a horizontal rule on a page. The <HR> tag draws a rule with a shaded or 3-D look by default. The NOSHADE attribute directs the browser to refrain from the shaded or 3-D look.

Category

Structural Definition

Example Syntax

```
<HR NOSHADE>
```

NOTE

Compliance

Syntax

```
<NOTE>...</NOTE>
```

Definition

The `<NOTE>` tag directs the browser to display text and graphics in one of three classes: NOTE, CAUTION, or WARNING. An image can be used in addition to text in a note. The `<NOTE>` tag will be part of most style sheets in the future.

Category

Miscellaneous

Example Syntax

```
<NOTE CLASS=CAUTION SRC="CAUTION.GIF">The IRS will fine you if you're a late
filer!</NOTE>
```

NOWRAP

Compliance

Synta-

```
<...NOWRAP...
```

Definitio

NOWRAP is an attribute used in formatting text in paragraphs and tables. The NOWRAP attribute directs the browser to refrain from word wrapping the specified text. This attribute is useful for displaying long URLs, math formulas, or programming code, wher the meaning of the text is adversely effected by word wrapping. Manual line breaks ma be inserted in text described in a NOWRAP statement.

Category

Structural Definition

Example Syntax

```
<P NOWRAP>This is the URL you need: HTTP:/WWW.ASKAMERICA.COM></P>
```

OFF

Compliance

Syntax

```
<...WRAP= "...">
```

Definition

WRAP is an attribute of the <TEXTAREA> tag. The WRAP attribute prevents the browser from wrapping text inside an input text box.

Category

Forms

Example Syntax

```
<TEXTAREA WRAP=OFF></TEXTAREA>
```

OL

Compliance

Syntax

```
<OL>...</OL>
```

Definition

OL stands for ordered list. The <OL> tag, by default, directs the browser to number the list items inside the <OL> tags.

Category

Lists

Example Syntax

```
<OL>
<LI>This is list item one.
<LI>This is list item two.
</OL>
```

In Actual Use

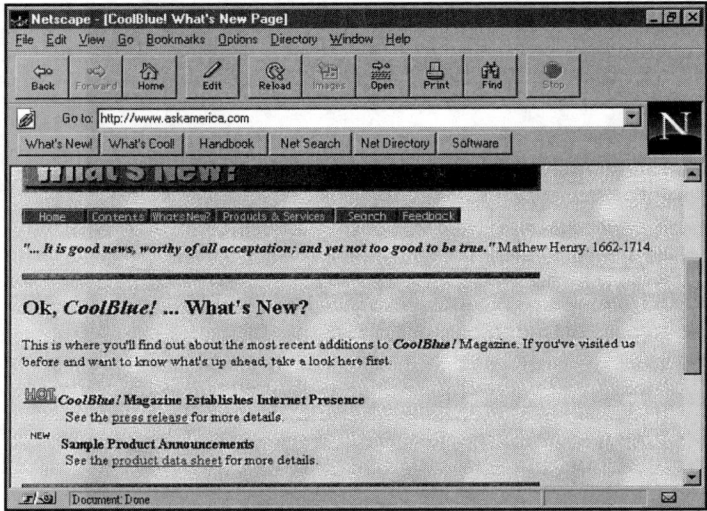

Fig. 3.13   Showing you the application of this example: "This is list item one, and so forth. "

Related Elements

Related Elements	This Element Can Be Used Inside <OL>	<OL> Can Be Used Inside This Element	Find It on Page Number
<BLOCKQUOTE>		✔	33-34
<BODY>		✔	34-35
<DD>		✔	48
<FORM>		✔	60-62
<LI>	✔	✔	92-94
COMPACT	✔		45

OPTION

Compliance

Syntax

```
<OPTION>...
```

Definition

The `<OPTION>` tag specifies that the following text is an item in a list box.

Category

Forms

Example Syntax

```
<P>
<SELECT NAME="Category">
<OPTION SELECTED>CoolBlue! Magazine
<Option> The AskAmerica Group
<Option> Product Reviews
<OPTION> Editorial Services </font></select>
</P>
```

In Actual Use

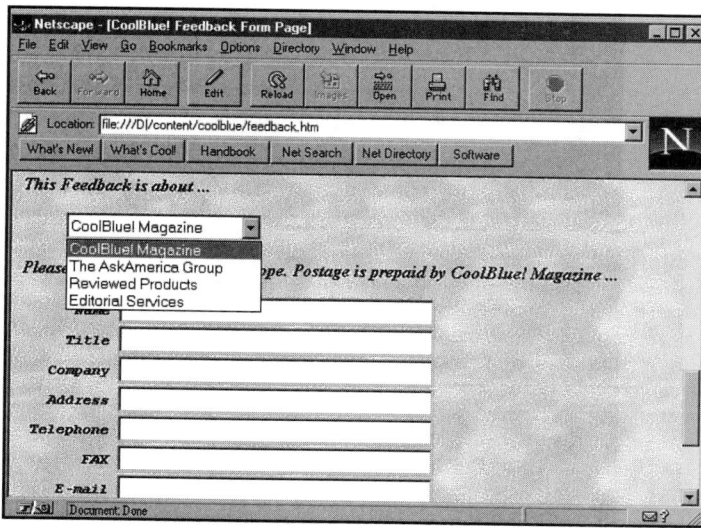

Fig. 3.14 There are four options on this list.

Related Elements

Related Elements	This Element Can Be Used Inside <OPTION>	<OPTION> Can Be Used Inside This Element	Find It on Page Number
<SELECT>		✔	117-118
VALUE		✔	142

P

Compliance

Syntax

    <P>...</P>

Definition

The <P>, or paragraph, tag denotes the beginning and ending of sentences to be displayed as a single paragraph. Some attributes of the <P> tag are not found in HTML standards prior to HTML 3.2.

Category

Structural Definition

Example Syntax

    <P>We encourage you to contact us with your comments
    and suggestions. If you provide us with your contact information, we will
    be able to reach you should we have any questions. Remember to hold down
    the Ctrl key before you press the Enter key to move to the next line in
    your message.</P>

Related Elements

Related Elements	This Element Can Be Used Inside <P>	<P> Can Be Used Inside This Element	Find It on Page Number
<A>	✔		20
<B>	✔		24-26
<BLOCKQUOTE>		✔	33-34
<BODY>		✔	34-35
 	✔		37-38

Related Elements	This Element Can Be Used Inside <P>	<P> Can Be Used Inside This Element	Find It on Page Number
<CITE>	✔		42-43
<CODE>	✔		43-44
<DD>		✔	48
<EM>	✔		55
<FORM>		✔	60-62
<I>	✔		81-82
<ADDRESS>		✔	21-22
<IMG>	✔		83-85, 94-95
<KBD>	✔		90-91
<LI>		✔	92-94
<SAMP>	✔		116-117
<STRONG>	✔		124-125
<TT>	✔		138-139
<VAR>	✔		142-143

PERSON

Compliance

Syntax

<PERSON>...</PERSON>

Definition

The <PERSON> tag denotes the name of an individual. Text specified with the <PERSON> tag is displayed exactly as it appears in HTML format. Use the <PERSON> tag to preserve capitalization formatting. If not enclosed inside paragraph tags (see *P*), a PERSON statement is not displayed by the browser.

Category

Structural Definition

Example Syntax

<PERSON>Robert deBeers MulHolland Ph.D.</PERSON>

PHYSICAL

Compliance

Syntax

```
<... WRAP=PHYSICAL>
```

Definition

PHYSICAL is an attribute of the <TEXTAREA WRAP> tag and attribute. The PHYSICAL attribute directs the browser to wrap text at the physical limits of the text box being displayed.

Category

Forms

Example Syntax

```
<TEXTAREA WRAP=PHYSICAL></TEXTAREA>
```

PLAINTEXT

Compliance

Syntax

```
<PLAINTEXT>...</PLAINTEXT>
```

Definition

Directs the browser to display specified text in fixed-width font, without formatting of any kind. The browser ignores any HTML commands between the <PLAINTEXT>...</PLAINTEXT> tags. The <PLAINTEXT> tag is slated for obsolescence in forthcoming HTML standards.

Category

Structural Definition

Example Syntax

```
<PLAINTEXT> This text will be displayed in a monospaced font!</PLAINTEXT>
```

POST

Compliance

Syntax

```
<...METHOD="POST">
```

Definition

When the user clicks the Submit button, the proscribed method (see *METHOD*) is carried out. The content of a form can be posted as an HTTP POST transaction to a named URL on a server.

Category

Forms

Example Syntax

```
<P><FORM ACTION="_VTI_BIN/SHTML.EXE/FEEDBACK.HTM" METHOD="POST"></P>
```

PRE

Compliance

Syntax

```
<PRE>...</PRE>
```

Definition

The <PRE> tag stands for "preformatted" text. The <PRE> tag is used to retains spaces and line feeds in bodies of text. This tag is useful in formatting an entire paragraph that the author would like the client browser to display verbatim.

Category

Structural Definition

Example Syntax

```
<PRE>This text will appear as you see it.
Complete with this line break.</PRE>
```

Related Elements

Related Elements	This Element Can Be Used Inside \<PRE\>	\<PRE\> Can Be Used Inside This Element	Find It on Page Number
\<A\>	✔		20
\<B\>	✔		24-26
\<BLOCKQUOTE\>		✔	33-34
\<BODY\>		✔	34-35
\<BR\>	✔		37-38
\<CITE\>	✔		42-43
\<CODE\>	✔		43-44
\<DD\>		✔	48
\<EM\>	✔		55
\<FORM\>		✔	60-62
\<HR\>	✔		77-78
\<I\>	✔		81-82
\<KBD\>	✔		90-91
\<LI\>		✔	92-94
\<SAMP\>	✔		116-117
\<STRONG\>	✔		124-125
\<TT\>	✔		138-139
\<VAR\>	✔		142-143
\<WIDTH\>	✔		131, 135

Q

Compliance

Syntax

```
<Q>...</Q>
```

Definition

The \<Q\> tag places quotes around the specified text.

Category

Structural Definition

Example Syntax

```
<Q>Use the Q tag to quote speech on a web page!</Q>
```

RECT

Compliance

Syntax

```
<...="RECT"...>
```

Definition

RECT is an attribute of the <AREA SHAPE> tag. The RECT attribute directs the client browser to accept clicks from a specified rectangular shape within a displayed image. The COORDS attribute is used to specify the actual coordinates of the clickable rectangle. The coordinates are separated by commas.

Category

Link and Graphics

Example Syntax

```
<AREA SHAPE="RECT" COORDS="100,50,50," HREF="HTTP://WWW.ASKAMERICA.COM>
```

S

Compliance

Syntax

```
<S>...</S>
```

Definition

The <S> tag directs the client browser to strike through any specified text.

See also *STRIKE*.

Category

Structural Definition

Example Syntax

```
<S>This text appears with a line though it!</S>
```

SAMP

Compliance

Syntax

```
<SAMP>...</SAMP>
```

Definition

The <SAMP> tag directs the browser to display specified text in a smaller font. If the <FONT FACE> tag is not used, the displayed font is fixed-width.

Category

Structural Definition

Example Syntax

```
<SAMP>A great way to display code in a body of text!</SAMP>
```

Related Elements

Related Elements	This Element Can Be Used Inside *<SAMP>*	*<SAMP>* Can Be Used Inside This Element	Find It on Page Number
<A>	✔	✔	20
<ADDRESS>		✔	21-22
<B>	✔	✔	24-26
 	✔		37-38
<CITE>	✔	✔	42-43
<CODE>	✔	✔	43-44
<DD>		✔	48
<DT>		✔	53-54
<EM>	✔	✔	55
<H1>		✔	68-70
<H2>		✔	70-71
<H3>		✔	72
<H4>		✔	73
<H5>		✔	74

Related Elements	This Element Can Be Used Inside *<SAMP>*	*<SAMP>* Can Be Used Inside This Element	Find It on Page Number
<H6>		✔	75
<I>	✔	✔	81-82
<IMG>	✔		83-85, 94-95
<KBD>	✔	✔	90-91
<LI>		✔	92-94
<P>		✔	110-111
<PRE>		✔	113-114
<SAMP>	✔	✔	116-117
<STRONG>	✔	✔	124-125
<TT>	✔	✔	138-139
<VAR>	✔	✔	142-143

SELECT

Compliance

Syntax

```
<SELECT...>
```

Definition

The <SELECT> tag directs the client browser to construct and display a drop-down list box with specified, using the OPTION VALUE= parameter, list box items.

Category

Forms

Example Syntax

```
<SELECT NAME="Countries">
<OPTION VALUE="1">USA
<OPTION VALUE="2">Canada
<OPTION VALUE="3">Mexico
</SELECT>
```

Related Elements

Related Elements	This Element Can Be Used Inside <SELECT>	<SELECT> Can Be Used Inside This Element	Find It on Page Number
<FORM>		✔	60-62
<OPTION>	✔		109-111
MULTIPLE	✔		119
NAME	✔		64, 98, 103, 119
SIZE	✔		60, 87, 120, 121

SELECT SINGLE

Compliance

Syntax

```
<SELECT...SINGLE>
```

Definition

SINGLE is an attribute of the <SELECT> tag. The SINGLE attribute directs the browser to only allow input of a single item on a drop-down list box.

See also *MULTIPLE*.

Category

Forms

Example Syntax

```
<SELECT NAME="Countries" SINGLE>
<OPTION VALUE="1">USA
<OPTION VALUE="2">Canada
<OPTION VALUE="3">Mexico
</SELECT>
```

SELECT MULTIPLE

Compliance

Syntax

```
<SELECT...MULTIPLE>
```

Definition

MULTIPLE is an attribute of the `<SELECT>` tag. The MULTIPLE attribute directs the client browser to allow the user to make multiple selections from a drop-down list box.

See also *SINGLE*.

Category

Forms

Example Syntax

```
<SELECT NAME="Countries" MULTIPLE>
<OPTION VALUE="1">USA
<OPTION VALUE="2">Canada
<OPTION VALUE="3">Mexico
</SELECT>
```

SELECT NAME

Compliance

Syntax

```
<SELECT NAME= "...">...</SELECT>
```

Definition

NAME is an attribute of the `<SELECT>` tag. The NAME attribute is the label used to name a drop-down list box.

Category

Forms

Example Syntax

```
<SELECT NAME="Countries">
<OPTION VALUE="1">USA
<OPTION VALUE="2">Canada
<OPTION VALUE="3">Mexico
</SELECT>
```

SELECT SIZE

Compliance

Syntax
```
<SELECT...SIZE="...">...</SELECT>
```

Definition

The SIZE attribute directs the client browser to build and make visible a drop-down list box using a specified number of list items. If the author requires a drop-down list with three options immediately visible, use "3" for the SELECT SIZE. To display just the first option on a list box with multiple options, specify a SELECT SIZE of "1".

Category

Forms

Example Syntax
```
<SELECT NAME="Countries" SIZE="1">
<OPTION VALUE="1">USA
<OPTION VALUE="2">Canada
<OPTION VALUE="3">Mexico
</SELECT>
```

SHAPE

Compliance

Syntax
```
<AREA SHAPE="RECT" ... >
```

Definition

SHAPE is an attribute of the <AREA> tag. The SHAPE attribute specifies the geometric shape of a clickable hyperlink of a displayed image. The author can choose from these six shapes: RECT, RECTANGLE, CIRC, CIRCLE, POLY, or POLYGON.

Category

Links and Graphics

Example Syntax

```
<AREA SHAPE="RECT" COORDS="50,50,150,150" HREF="HTTP://FISH.COM>
```

SIZE

Compliance

Syntax

```
<...SIZE= "...">
```

Definition

SIZE is an attribute of the <FONT> tag. The SIZE attribute directs the client browser to display specified text in one of seven possible sizes, from smallest to largest: -2, -1, -0, +1, +2, +3, and +4.

Category

Structural Definition

Example Syntax

```
<FONT SIZE=+4>This text is displayed in the largest font size.</FONT>
```

SMALL

Compliance

Syntax

```
<SMALL>...</SMALL>
```

Definition

The <SMALL> tag directs the client browser to display text in a font size smaller than the default text size. If a <BASEFONT> size is recognized by the browser, the <SMALL> font size will be one font size smaller.

See also *SIZE*.

Category

Structural Definition

Example Syntax

```
<SMALL>This text is smaller than the specified or defualt font size.</SMALL>
```

SOUND

Compliance

Syntax

```
<SOUND SRC="...">
```

Definition

The <SOUND> tag directs the browser to play a sound (*.WAV) file. HTML authors can further direct a client browser in the playing of sound files with the following attributes:

■ The LOOP="..." attribute directs the browser to repetitively play a specified sound file. Use LOOP=INFINITE to direct the browser to play the file over and over again.

■ The DELAY="..." attribute directs the browser to wait the specified number of seconds between the playing of a sound file. Use DELAY=3 to direct the browser to play the file between three-second intervals of silence.

Note that Mosaic is the only browser that utilizes the <SOUND> tag. Mosaic does recognize the <BGSOUND> tag, but even with this tag, Mosaic only plays .WAV files unless an external appliation is available.

Category

Miscellaneous

Example Syntax

```
<SOUND SRC="COOL_SOUND.WAV" LOOP=INFINITE DELAY=1>
```

SQUARE

Compliance

Syntax

```
<...=SQUARE>
```

I

HTML

Definition

SQUARE is an attribute of the <UL TYPE> tag. The SQUARE attribute directs the client browser to display square bullets on a bulleted list.

See also *UL, DISC,* and *CIRCLE.*

Category

Structural Definition

Example Syntax

```
<UL TYPE=SQUARE>
```

SRC

Compliance

Syntax

```
<...SRC="...">
```

Definition

SRC is an attribute of the <IMG> tag. The SRC attribute directs the browser to display an image if a file name or URL is specified.

See also *IMG.*

Category

Links and Graphics

Example Syntax

```
<IMG SRC="MY_LOGO.GIF">
```

STRIKE

Compliance

Syntax

```
<STRIKE>...</STRIKE>
```

Definition

The <STRIKE> tag directs the client browser to strikethrough the specified text. The <STRIKE> tag is supported by Netscape and Mosaic. The comparable <S> tag is supported by Netscape, Internet Explorer, Mosaic, and HTML 3.

See also *S*.

Category

Structural Definition

Example Syntax

```
<STRIKE>This text will have a line bisecting it!</STRIKE>
```

STRONG

Compliance

Syntax

```
<STRONG>...<STRONG>
```

Definition

The <STRONG> tag causes the browser to display specified text in bold type. Some legacy browsers display <STRONG> text in italics.

Category

Structural Definition

Example Syntax

```
<STRONG>Expect most browsers to display this text in BOLD type!</STRONG>
```

Related Elements

Related Elements	This Element Can Be Used Inside *<STRONG>*	*<STRONG>* Can Be Used Inside This Element	Find It on Page Number
<A>	✔	✔	20
<ADDRESS>		✔	21-22
<B>	✔	✔	24-26
 	✔		37-38
<CITE>	✔	✔	42-43

HTML

Related Elements	This Element Can Be Used Inside \<STRONG\>	\<STRONG\> Can Be Used Inside This Element	Find It on Page Number
\<CODE\>	✔	✔	43-44
\<DD\>		✔	48
\<DT\>		✔	53-54
\<EM\>	✔	✔	55
\<H1\>		✔	68-70
\<H2\>		✔	70-71
\<H3\>		✔	72
\<H4\>		✔	73
\<H5\>		✔	74
\<H6\>		✔	75
\<I\>	✔	✔	81-82
\<IMG\>	✔		83-85, 94-95
\<KBD\>	✔	✔	90-91
\<LI\>		✔	92-94
\<P\>		✔	110-111
\<PRE\>		✔	113-114
\<SAMP\>	✔	✔	116-117
\<STRONG\>	✔	✔	124-125
\<TT\>	✔	✔	138-139
\<VAR\>	✔	✔	142-143

SUB

Compliance

Syntax

```
<SUB>...</SUB>
```

Definition

The \<SUB\> tag directs the browser to display specified text in subscript form. The browser selects the next smaller font size for subscripting based on the font in use in the same paragraph—unless a font size is specified with the \<FONT\> or \<BASEFONT\> tags.

See *FONT, BASEFONT, SMALL,* and *BIG* for more on font sizing.

Category
Structural Definition

Example Syntax
```
<SUB>This text will be subscripted.</SUB>
```

SUP

Compliance

Syntax
```
<SUP>...</SUP>
```

Definition
The <SUP> tag directs the browser to display specified text in as superscript.

Category
Structural Defninition

Example Syntax
```
<SUP>This text will be superscripted.</SUP>
```

TAB

Compliance

Syntax
```
<TAB...>
```

Definition
The <TAB> tag directs the browser to set tabs at a specified location in text. The TAB ID="..." attribute names the text that is to serve as the next tab point. The TAB TO="..." attribute directs the browser to stop at the named tab. To align tabs, use the following settings with the ALIGN attribute: LEFT, RIGHT, and CENTER.

Category
Structural Definition

TABLE   **127**

I

HTML

Example Syntax

```
<TAB TO="MY_WORD">
```

TABLE

Compliance

Syntax

```
<TABLE>...</TABLE>
```

Definition

The <TABLE> tag denotes the beginning and the end of a table array. Note that some browsers do not recognize all of the following attributes of the <TABLE> tag:

- **ALIGN**   Sets table or text alignment using ALIGN=LEFT or ALIGN=RIGHT.

- **BGCOLOR**   Sets the background color of cells in a table.

- **BORDER**   Sets the width of the border in pixels.

- **BORDERCOLOR**   Sets the default color of a border.

- **BORDERDARK**   Sets the color of the dark side of a 3-D border.

- **BORDERLIGHT**   Sets the color of the light side of a 3-D border.

- **CAPTION**   Specifies the caption for a table.

- **CELLPADDING**   Sets the amount of clear space beside contents of a cell.

- **CELLSPACING**   Sets the amount of space between table cells.

- **WIDTH**   Specifies the width of the table in pixels or percentage.

Category

Tables

Example Syntax

```
<TABLE>
<TR>
<TH>This would be table heading text</TH>
<TD>This text would make up the first row.</TD>
<TD>This text would make up the second row.</TD>
<TD>This text would make up the third row.</TD>
</TR>
</TABLE>
```

Related Elements

Related Elements	This Element Can Be Used Inside <TABLE>	<TABLE> Can Be Used Inside This Element	Find It on Page Number
ALIGN	✔		22
BGCOLOR	✔		30
BODY		✔	34-35
BORDER	✔		36
CAPTION	✔		39
CELLPADDING	✔		39
CELLSPACING	✔		40
COLSPAN	✔		130, 134
NOWRAP	✔		106, 130, 135
<P>		✔	110-111
ROWSPAN	✔		131, 135
<TD>	✔		129
<TH>	✔		133
<TR>	✔		136
VALIGN	✔		141
WIDTH	✔		131, 135

TABLE ALIGN

Compliance

Syntax

```
<TABLE ALIGN="...">
```

Definition

ALIGN is an attribute of the <TABLE> tag, among others. The ALIGN attribute directs the client browser to display a table aligned to the LEFT, RIGHT, or CENTER of the browser's display area.

See also TD and TH.

Category
Frames

Example Syntax
```
<TABLE ALIGN=RIGHT>
```

TD

Compliance

Syntax
```
<TD>...</TD>
```

Definition
The `<TD>`, or table data, tag directs the browser to display a specified, single table cell.

Related Elements

Related Elements	This Element Can Be Used Inside `<TD>`	`<TD>` Can Be Used Inside This Element	Find It on Page Number
ALIGN	✔		22
BGCOLOR	✔		30
COLSPAN	✔		130, 134
NOWRAP	✔		106, 130, 135
ROWSPAN	✔		131, 135
TABLE	✔		127-128
VALIGN	✔		141

Category
Tables

Example Syntax
```
<TD>This text would make up the first row.</TD>
```

TD COLSPAN

Compliance

Syntax

```
<TD COLSPAN="...">
```

Definition

COLSPAN is an attribute of the <TD> or <TH> tag. The COLSPAN attribute indicates the number of cells adjacent and to the right that are to be combined into a single cell.

Category

Tables

Example Syntax

```
<TD COLSPAN=3>
```

TD NOWRAP

Compliance

Syntax

```
<TD NOWRAP>
```

Definition

NOWRAP is an attribute of the <TD> tag. The NOWRAP attribute directs the browser to prevent text wrapping within a cell.

Category

Tables

Example Syntax

```
<TD NOWRAP>
```

TD ROWSPAN

Compliance

Syntax

```
<TD ROWSPAN="...">
```

Definition

ROWSPAN is an attribute of the <TD> or <TH> tag. The ROWSPAN attribute indicates the number of cells adjacent and below that are to be combined into a single cell.

Category

Frames

Example Syntax

```
<TD ROWSPAN=2>
```

TD WIDTH

Compliance

Syntax

```
<TD WIDTH="...">
```

Definition

WIDTH is an attribute of the <TD> tag. The WIDTH attribute directs the client browser to display a table cell spanning a specified width of the table. WIDTH can be specified in pixels or in a percentage by adding the % sign after the specified digit(s).

Category

Frames

Example Syntax

```
<TD WIDTH=85%>
```

TEXT

Compliance

Syntax

```
<...TEXT="...">
```

Definition

TEXT is an attribute of the <BODY> tag. The TEXT attribute directs the browser to display text in the color specified in either the color name or in binary format.

Category

Presentation Formatting

Example Syntax

```
<BODY TEXT=RED>This text will be displayed in red!</BODY>
```

TEXTAREA

Compliance

Syntax

```
<TEXTAREA...>
```

Definition

The <TEXTAREA> tag directs the browser to create a space in a form that accepts input text from the user. The <TEXTAREA> tag has the following attributes:

- <TEXTAREA NAME="..."> Names the overall <TEXTAREA>.

- <TEXTAREA ROWS="..."> Specifies, in number of characters, the visible width of a <TEXTAREA>.

- <TEXTAREA COLS="..."> Specifies, in number of characters, the visible height of a <TEXTAREA>.

- <TEXTAREA WRAP=OFF> Directs the browser to turn word wrap off within the <TEXTAREA>.

- `<TEXTAREA WRAP=VIRTUAL>`   Forces the browser to accept text in long single lines but wrap the text in the visible part of the `<TEXTAREA>`.

- `<TEXTAREA WRAP=PHYSICAL>`   Directs the browser to send text with exactly as it is entered by the user.

Category

Forms

Example Syntax

```
<TEXTAREA NAME="MY_AREA" COLS=25 ROWS=5 WRAP=PHYSICAL>
```

TH

Compliance

Syntax

```
<TH...>
```

Definition

The `<TH>` tag directs the client browser to display text as a heading in the first row of a table.

Category

Tables

Example Syntax

```
<TH>This would be table heading text</TH>
```

TH ALIGN

Compliance

Syntax

```
<TH ALIGN="...">
```

Definition

ALIGN is an attribute of the <TH> tag. The ALIGN attribute determines how text is displayed in the table header. The possible attributes are LEFT, RIGHT, and CENTER.

Category

Tables

Example Syntax

```
<TH ALIGN=LEFT>This text will be aligned to the left in the first row of a
table!</TH>
```

TH COLSPAN

Compliance

Syntax

```
<TH COLSPAN="...">
```

Definition

COLSPAN, when used as an attribute of the <TH> tag, specifies how many cells in columns are spanned by the table header.

Category

Tables

Example Syntax

```
<TH COLSPAN=3>
```

TH NOWRAP

Compliance

Syntax

```
<TH NOWRAP>
```

Definition

When used in conjunction with the <TH> tag, NOWRAP directs the client browser to turn text wrap off in a table header.

Category

Tables

Example Syntax

```
<TH NOWRAP>This text will not be wrapped by the browser!</TH>
```

TH ROWSPAN

Compliance

Syntax

```
<TH ROWSPAN="...">
```

Definition

ROWSPAN, when used as an attribute of the <TH> tag, specifies how many cells in rows are spanned by the table header.

Category

Tables

Example Syntax

```
<TH ROWSPAN=3>
```

TH WIDTH

Compliance

Syntax

```
<TH WIDTH="...">
```

Definition

WIDTH, when used with the <TH> tag, specifies the width of a table header cell in either pixels or as a percentage of the entire table width.

Category
Tables

Example Syntax
```
<TH WIDTH=100%>
```

TITLE

Compliance

Syntax
```
<TITLE>...</TITLE>
```

Definition
The title of an HTML document. The <TITLE> text is displayed on the title bar of most client browsers.

Category
Structural Definition

Example Syntax
```
<TITLE>"Welcome To CoolBlue! Magazine"</TITLE>
```

TOPMARGIN

Compliance

Syntax
```
<...TOPMARGIN="...">
```

Definition
When used with the <BODY> tag, the TOPMARGIN attribute specifies how many pixels in height are rendered by a browser as margin space at the top of the page.

Category
Miscellaneous

Example Syntax

```
<BODY TOPMARGIN="10">The top margin of this HTML page is 10 pixels in
height!</BODY>
```

TR

Compliance

Syntax

```
<TR>...</TR>
```

Definition

The <TR> tag directs the browser to display the specified text inside a single table row.

Category

Tables

Example Syntax

```
<TR>This text will be in a cell all by itself!</TR>
```

TR ALIGN

Compliance

Syntax

```
<TR ALIGN="...">
```

Definition

When used in the context of the <TR> tag, ALIGN directs the client browser to display a table row LEFT, RIGHT, or CENTER.

Category

Tables

Example Syntax

```
<TR ALIGN=LEFT>The text in this table row will align to the left!</TR>
```

TT

Compliance

Syntax

```
<TT>...</TT>
```

Definition

The <TT>, or teletype, tag directs the browser to display the specified text in a monospaced font.

Category

Presentation Formatting

Example Syntax

```
<TT>This text will be displayed using Courier New by my MS Windows version of
➥Netscape Navigator!</TT>
```

Related Elements

Related Elements	This Element Can Be Used Inside <TT>	<TT> Can Be Used Inside This Element	Find It on Page Number
<A>	✔	✔	20
<ADDRESS>		✔	21-22
<B>	✔	✔	24-26
 	✔		37-38
<CITE>	✔	✔	42-43
<CODE>	✔	✔	43-44
<DD>		✔	48
<DT>		✔	53-54
<EM>	✔	✔	55
<H1>		✔	68-70
<H2>		✔	70-71
<H3>		✔	72
<H4>		✔	73
<H5>		✔	74
<H6>		✔	75
<I>	✔	✔	81-82
<IMG>	✔		83-85, 94-95
<KBD>	✔	✔	90-91

Related Elements	This Element Can Be Used Inside *<TT>*	*<TT>* Can Be Used Inside This Element	Find It on Page Number
<LI>		✔	92-94
<P>		✔	110-111
<PRE>		✔	113-114
<SAMP>	✔	✔	116-117
<STRONG>	✔	✔	124-125
<TT>	✔	✔	138-139
<VAR>	✔	✔	142-143

U

Compliance

Syntax

```
<U>...</U>
```

Definition

The <U>, or underline, tag directs the client browser to underline the specified text.

Category

Structural Definition

Example Syntax

```
<U>This text will be underlines!</U>
```

UL

Compliance

Syntax

```
<UL>...</UL>
```

Definition
The <UL> tag directs the browser to construct an unordered, bulleted list.

Category
Lists

Example Syntax
```
<UL>
<LI>This line of text is the first item in the list.
<LI>This line of text is the second item in the list.
</UL>
```

Related Elements

Related Elements	This Element Can Be Used Inside <UL>	<UL> Can Be Used Inside This Element	Find It on Page Number
<BLOCKQUOTE>		✔	33-34
<BODY>		✔	34-35
<COMPACT>	✔		45
<DD>		✔	48
<FORM>		✔	60-62
<LI>	✔	✔	92-94

URL

Compliance

Syntax
```
<...URL="...">
```

Definition
URL is an attribute of the <META> tag. The URL attribute specifies the full pathname of an URL to be loaded after the CONTENT specified time has elapsed.

See also *CONTENT* and *META*.

Category
Miscellaneous

Example Syntax
```
<META HTTP-EQUIV="REFRESH" CONTENT=5 URL=HTTP://WWW.ASKAMERICA.COM/COOLBLUE/
INDEX.HTM>
```

USEMAP

Compliance

Syntax
```
<... USEMAP="...">
```

Definition

USEMAP is an attribute of the <IMG> tag. The USEMAP attribute directs the browser to utilize the specified client side image map.

Category

Links and Graphics

Example Syntax
```
<IMG SRC="MY_URL" USEMAP="MY_IMAGE_MAP">
```

VALIGN

Compliance

Syntax
```
VALIGN="..."
```

Definition

VALIGN is an attribute of the <CAPTION> tag. VALIGN directs the browser to display a table caption at the TOP, MIDDLE, or BOTTOM of a table.

Category

Tables

Example Syntax
```
VALIGN="TOP"
```

VALUE

Compliance

Syntax

```
VALUE="..."
```

Definition

When used in the context of the <OL> or <LI> tags, the VALUE attribute directs the client browser to use the specified digit (number) as the first item number on the numbered list.

When used in the context of the <INPUT> tag, the VALUE attribute directs the client browser to use the specified text as default text for the control.

When used in the context of the <OPTION> tag, the VALUE attribute directs the client browser to use the specified text as the input of the control.

See also *OPTION*, *INPUT*, *OL*, and *LI*.

Category

Lists

Example Syntax

```
<INPUT VALUE="True">
```

VAR

Compliance

Syntax

```
<VAR>...</VAR>
```

Definition

The <VAR> tag directs the browser to display specified text in a smaller, fixed-width font.

Category
Structural Definition

Example Syntax
```
<VAR>This text will be somewhat smaller and fixed-width!</VAR>
```

Related Elements

Related Elements	This Element Can Be Used Inside <VAR>	<VAR> Can Be Used Inside This Element	Find It on Page Number
<A>	✔	✔	20
<ADDRESS>		✔	21-22
<B>	✔	✔	24-26
 	✔		37-38
<CITE>	✔	✔	42-43
<CODE>	✔	✔	43-44
<DD>		✔	48
<DT>		✔	53-54
<EM>	✔	✔	55
<H1>		✔	68-70
<H2>		✔	70-71
<H3>		✔	72
<H4>		✔	73
<H5>		✔	74
<H6>		✔	75
<I>	✔	✔	81-82
<IMG>	✔		83-85, 94-95
<KBD>	✔	✔	90-91
<LI>		✔	92-94
<P>		✔	110-111
<PRE>		✔	113-114
<SAMP>	✔	✔	116-117
<STRONG>	✔	✔	124-125
<TT>	✔	✔	138-139
<VAR>	✔	✔	142-143

VIRTUAL

Compliance

Syntax

```
WRAP="..."
```

Definition

VIRTUAL is an attribute of TEXTAREA WRAP. The VIRTUAL attribute directs the client browser to display text typed by the user, using word wrapping, but sends that text to the server, using single lines of text.

Category

Forms

Example Syntax

```
<TEXTAREA ROWS=5 COLS=30 WRAP=VIRTUAL>
```

VLINK

Compliance

Syntax

```
<BODY VLINK="...">
```

Definition

VLINK is an attribute of the <BODY> tag. The VLINK attribute directs the browser to display visited links with a specified color.

See also *BODY*.

Category

Links and Graphics

Example Syntax

```
<BODY VLINK=#00ff00>Visited shortcuts will be green!</BODY>
```

VSPACE

Compliance

Syntax

```
VSPACE="..."
```

Definition

VSPACE is an attribute of the <IMG> and <MARQUEE> tags. VSPACE directs the client browser to display the specified value in pixels as a clear area above and below an image or marquee text.

Category

Miscellaneous

Example Syntax

```
<IMG SRC="MY_URL" HSPACE=5 VSPACE=5>
```

WBR

Compliance

Syntax

```
<WBR>...</WBR>
```

Definition

The WBR, or word break, tag directs the browser to manually break a specified line of text even if that text has line breaking disabled.

Category

Structural Definition

Example Syntax

```
<WBR>This text will break regardless of previous tags applied.</WBR>
```

WRAP

Compliance

Syntax

```
WRAP="..."
```

Definition

WRAP is an attribute of the <TEXTAREA> tag. The WRAP attribute directs the browser to wrap text in the following three different ways:

- <TEXTAREA WRAP=OFF>   Directs the browser to send lines of text as they are typed. Word wrapping is not allowed. This is the default setting.

- <TEXTAREA WRAP=VIRTUAL>   The browser wraps text in a text box but inputs all text as one long line.

- <TEXTAREA WRAP=PHYSICAL>   The client browser word wraps text in the TEXTAREA and inputs wrapped lines individually at the line breaks.

See also *TEXTAREA*, *VIRTUAL*, and *PHYSICAL*.

Category

Forms

Example Syntax

```
<TEXTAREA WRAP=OFF>
```

Chapter 4

HTML Reference Tables

Characters from ISO 8859-1

Binary	Text	Description	Displays
		Non-breaking space	
&#177	&plusmn	Plus over minus sign	±
&#161	&iexcl	Inverted exclamation mark	¡
&#178	&sup2	Superscript two	2
&#162	&cent	Cent sign	¢
&#179	&sup3	Superscript three	3
&#163	&pound	Pound sign	£
&#180	&acute	Acute accent	´
&#164	&curren	General currency sign	¤
&#181	&micro	Micro sign	µ
&#165	&yen	Yen sign	¥
&#182	&para	Pilcrow (paragraph sign)	¶
&#166	&brvbar	Broken (vertical) bar	¦
&#183	&middot	Middle dot	·
&#167	&sect	Section sign	§
&#184	&cedil	Cedilla	¸
&#168	&uml	Umlaut/dieresis	¨
&#185	&sup1	Superscript one	1
&#169	&copy	Copyright sign	©
&#186	&ordm	Ordinal indicator, male	♂
&#170	&ordf	Ordinal indicator, fem	♀
&#187	&raquo	Angle quotation mark, right	»
&#171	&laquo	Angle quotation mark, left	«
&#188	&frac14	Fraction one-quarter	¼
&#172	&not	Not sign	Ø
&#189	&frac12	Fraction one-half	½

(continues)

(continued)

Binary	Text	Description	Displays
&#173;	&shy;	Soft hyphen	-
&#190;	&frac34;	Fraction three-quarters	¾
&#174;	&reg;	Registered sign	®
&#191;	&iquest;	Inverted question mark	¿
&#175;	&macr;	Macron	¯
&#215;	&times;	Multiply sign	×
&#176;	&deg;	Degree sign	°
&#247;	&div;	Division sign	÷

Color Tables

These two color tables will help you find a color name by referencing the Hex/RGB Value or find the Hex/RGB Value when you reference the color name.

Proposed Color Codes Sorted by Color Name		Proposed Color Codes Sorted by Value	
Find the Color Name Here	**Look Up the Value Here**	**Find the Value Here**	**Look Up the Color Name Here**
White	rgb=#FFFFFF	rgb=#000000	Black
Red	rgb=#FF0000	rgb=#00009C	New Midnight Blue
Green	rgb=#00FF00	rgb=#0000FF	Blue
Blue	rgb=#0000FF	rgb=#007FFF	Slate Blue
Magenta	rgb=#FF00FF	rgb=#00FF00	Green
Cyan	rgb=#00FFFF	rgb=#00FF7F	Spring Green
Yellow	rgb=#FFFF00	rgb=#00FFFF	Cyan
Black	rgb=#000000	rgb=#215E21	Hunter Green
Aquamarine	rgb=#70DB93	rgb=#23238E	Navy Blue
Baker's Chocolate	rgb=#5C3317	rgb=#236B8E	Steel Blue
Blue Violet	rgb=#9F5F9F	rgb=#238E23	Forest Green
Brass	rgb=#B5A642	rgb=#238E68	Sea Green
Bright Gold	rgb=#D9D919	rgb=#2F2F4F	Midnight Blue
Brown	rgb=#A62A2A	rgb=#2F4F2F	Dark Green
Bronze	rgb=#8C7853	rgb=#2F4F4F	Dark Slate Gray
Bronze II	rgb=#A67D3D	rgb=#3232CD	Medium Blue
Cadet Blue	rgb=#5F9F9F	rgb=#3299CC	Sky Blue
Cool Copper	rgb=#D98719	rgb=#32CD32	Lime Green
Copper	rgb=#B87333	rgb=#32CD99	Medium Aquamarine
Coral	rgb=#FF7F00	rgb=#38B0DE	Summer Sky
Corn Flower Blue	rgb=#42426F	rgb=#42426F	Corn Flower Blue

Proposed Color Codes Sorted by Color Name		**Proposed Color Codes Sorted by Value**	
Find the Color Name Here	**Look Up the Value Here**	**Find the Value Here**	**Look Up the Color Name Here**
Dark Brown	rgb=#5C4033	rgb=#426F42	Medium Sea Green
Dark Green	rgb=#2F4F2F	rgb=#4A766E	Dark Green Copper
Dark Green Copper	rgb=#4A766E	rgb=#4D4DFF	Neon Blue
Dark Olive Green	rgb=#4F4F2F	rgb=#4E2F2F	Indian Red
Dark Orchid	rgb=#9932CD	rgb=#4F2F4F	Violet
Dark Purple	rgb=#871F78	rgb=#4F4F2F	Dark Olive Green
Dark Slate Blue	rgb=#6B238E	rgb=#527F76	Green Copper
Dark Slate Gray	rgb=#2F4F4F	rgb=#545454	Dim Gray
Dark Tan	rgb=#97694F	rgb=#5959AB	Rich Blue
Dark Turquoise	rgb=#7093DB	rgb=#5C3317	Baker's Chocolate
Dark Wood	rgb=#855E42	rgb=#5C4033	Dark Brown
Dim Gray	rgb=#545454	rgb=#5C4033	Very Dark Brown
Dusty Rose	rgb=#856363	rgb=#5F9F9F	Cadet Blue
Feldspar	rgb=#D19275	rgb=#6B238E	Dark Slate Blue
Firebrick	rgb=#8E2323	rgb=#6B4226	Semi-Sweet Chocolate
Forest Green	rgb=#238E23	rgb=#6B8E23	Medium Forest Green
Gold	rgb=#CD7F32	rgb=#6F4242	Salmon
Goldenrod	rgb=#DBDB70	rgb=#7093DB	Dark Turquoise
Gray	rgb=#C0C0C0	rgb=#70DB93	Aquamarine
Green Copper	rgb=#527F76	rgb=#70DBDB	Medium Turquoise
Green Yellow	rgb=#93DB70	rgb=#7F00FF	Medium Slate Blue
Hunter Green	rgb=#215E21	rgb=#7FFF00	Medium Spring Green
Indian Red	rgb=#4E2F2F	rgb=#855E42	Dark Wood
Khaki	rgb=#9F9F5F	rgb=#856363	Dusty Rose
Light Blue	rgb=#C0D9D9	rgb=#871F78	Dark Purple
Light Gray	rgb=#A8A8A8	rgb=#8C1717	Scarlet
Light Steel Blue	rgb=#8F8FBD	rgb=#8C7853	Bronze
Light Wood	rgb=#E9C2A6	rgb=#8E2323	Firebrick
Lime Green	rgb=#32CD32	rgb=#8E236B	Maroon
Mandarin Orange	rgb=#E47833	rgb=#8E6B23	Sienna
Maroon	rgb=#8E236B	rgb=#8F8FBD	Light Steel Blue
Medium Aquamarine	rgb=#32CD99	rgb=#8FBC8F	Pale Green
Medium Blue	rgb=#3232CD	rgb=#9370DB	Medium Orchid
Medium Forest Green	rgb=#6B8E23	rgb=#93DB70	Green Yellow

(continues)

(continued)

Proposed Color Codes Sorted by Color Name		Proposed Color Codes Sorted by Value	
Find the Color Name Here	**Look Up the Value Here**	**Find the Value Here**	**Look Up the Color Name Here**
Medium Goldenrod	rgb=#EAEAAE	rgb=#97694F	Dark Tan
Medium Orchid	rgb=#9370DB	rgb=#9932CD	Dark Orchid
Medium Sea Green	rgb=#426F42	rgb=#99CC32	Yellow Green
Medium Slate Blue	rgb=#7F00FF	rgb=#9F5F9F	Blue Violet
Medium Spring Green	rgb=#7FFF00	rgb=#9F9F5F	Khaki
Medium Turquoise	rgb=#70DBDB	rgb=#A62A2A	Brown
Medium Violet Red	rgb=#DB7093	rgb=#A67D3D	Bronze II
Medium Wood	rgb=#A68064	rgb=#A68064	Medium Wood
Midnight Blue	rgb=#2F2F4F	rgb=#A8A8A8	Light Gray
Navy Blue	rgb=#23238E	rgb=#ADEAEA	Turquoise
Neon Blue	rgb=#4D4DFF	rgb=#B5A642	Brass
Neon Pink	rgb=#FF6EC7	rgb=#B87333	Copper
New Midnight Blue	rgb=#00009C	rgb=#BC8F8F	Pink
New Tan	rgb=#EBC79E	rgb=#C0C0C0	Gray
Old Gold	rgb=#CFB53B	rgb=#C0D9D9	Light Blue
Orange	rgb=#FF7F00	rgb=#CC3299	Violet Red
Orange Red	rgb=#FF2400	rgb=#CD7F32	Gold
Orchid	rgb=#DB70DB	rgb=#CDCDCD	Very Light Gray
Pale Green	rgb=#8FBC8F	rgb=#CFB53B	Old Gold
Pink	rgb=#BC8F8F	rgb=#D19275	Feldspar
Plum	rgb=#EAADEA	rgb=#D8BFD8	Thistle
Quartz	rgb=#D9D9F3	rgb=#D8D8BF	Wheat
Rich Blue	rgb=#5959AB	rgb=#D98719	Cool Copper
Salmon	rgb=#6F4242	rgb=#D9D919	Bright Gold
Scarlet	rgb=#8C1717	rgb=#D9D9F3	Quartz
Sea Green	rgb=#238E68	rgb=#DB7093	Medium Violet Red
Semi-Sweet Chocolate	rgb=#6B4226	rgb=#DB70DB	Orchid
Sienna	rgb=#8E6B23	rgb=#DB9370	Tan
Silver	rgb=#E6E8FA	rgb=#DBDB70	Goldenrod
Sky Blue	rgb=#3299CC	rgb=#E47833	Mandarin Orange
Slate Blue	rgb=#007FFF	rgb=#E6E8FA	Silver
Spicy Pink	rgb=#FF1CAE	rgb=#E9C2A6	Light Wood
Spring Green	rgb=#00FF7F	rgb=#EAADEA	Plum
Steel Blue	rgb=#236B8E	rgb=#EAEAAE	Medium Goldenrod

Proposed Color Codes Sorted by Color Name		Proposed Color Codes Sorted by Value	
Find the Color Name Here	Look Up the Value Here	Find the Value Here	Look Up the Color Name Here
Summer Sky	rgb=#38B0DE	rgb=#EBC79E	New Tan
Tan	rgb=#DB9370	rgb=#FF0000	Red
Thistle	rgb=#D8BFD8	rgb=#FF00FF	Magenta
Turquoise	rgb=#ADEAEA	rgb=#FF1CAE	Spicy Pink
Very Dark Brown	rgb=#5C4033	rgb=#FF2400	Orange Red
Very Light Gray	rgb=#CDCDCD	rgb=#FF6EC7	Neon Pink
Violet	rgb=#4F2F4F	rgb=#FF7F00	Coral
Violet Red	rgb=#CC3299	rgb=#FF7F00	Orange
Wheat	rgb=#D8D8BF	rgb=#FFFF00	Yellow
Yellow Green	rgb=#99CC32	rgb=#FFFFFF	White

Newsgroups for HTML Authors and Web Professionals

This table is a source of various newsgroups that focus on Internet related topics of interest to many HTML authors and Web Site Administrators. The column on the left of this table contains special-interest newsgroup addresses. The column to the right is a description of each newsgroup.

Browsers and Servers	Description
comp.infosystems.www.browsers.ms-windows	Web browsers for Windows 3.1 and Windows 95
comp.infosystems.www.servers.ms-windows	Web servers for Windows 95 and NT Web content development
comp.infosystems.www.authoring.cgi	Authoring CGI scripts
comp.infosystems.www.authoring.html	Authoring HTML
comp.infosystems.www.authoring.images	Using images
comp.infosystems.www.authoring.misc	Web authoring issues, Internet technologies, and Windows
alt.lang.basic	The BASIC programming language
alt.lang.vrml	VRML
alt.winsock	Windows Sockets, general languages, and tools
alt.winsock.programming	Windows Sockets programming

(continues)

(continued)

Browsers and Servers	Description
alt.winsock.voice	Voice-data
comp.lang.basic	More on the BASIC language
comp.lang.basic.misc	Yet more coverage of the BASIC language
comp.lang.basic.visual.3rdparty	Visual Basic 3-D add-ins
comp.lang.basic.visual.database	Database aspects of Visual Basic
comp.lang.c	The C programming language
comp.lang.c++	The C++ programming language
comp.os.ms-windows.apps.winsock.mail	Windows Sockets and e-mail
comp.os.ms-windows.apps.winsock.misc	Other Windows Sockets issues
comp.os.ms-windows.apps.winsock.news	Windows Sockets and news apps
comp.os.ms-windows.networking.misc	More networking
comp.os.ms-windows.networking.tcp-ip	TCP/IP
comp.os.ms-windows.networking.win95	Windows 95
comp.os.ms-windows.programmer.controls	Controls, objects, and VBXs
comp.os.ms-windows.programmer.tools.winsock	Windows Sockets programming
comp.os.ms-windows.programmer.tools.winsock	Windows Sockets programming tools
Tools and Technologies for the Enterprise	
comp.databases.ms-access	Microsoft Access
comp.databases.ms-sqlserver	Microsoft SQL Server
comp.os.ms-windows.nt.	Microsoft Windows
software.backoffice	NT/BackOffice
Data Security, Data Encryption	
comp.security.misc	Security issues
sci.crypt	Cryptography
technologiescomp.security.announce	Announcements in security technology

Chapter 5

Internet Glossary

The Internet can be rather confusing to new users. It has its own jargon, just as many professions or hobbies do. Learning the jargon can make the Internet less foreign to you. As the Internet has grown over the years, a whole vocabulary has developed to describe Internet features and related activities. As you read documents and participate in conversations on the Internet, you may come across terms that you are unfamiliar with. This section explains some of the most common terms you may encounter.

account   A user ID and disk area restricted for the use of a particular person, which is usually password protected.

ACM   Association for Computing Machinery, a professional society for people connected with the computer industry.

address   See *e-mail address* and *host address*.

Agent   The commercial version of the Free Agent newsreader.

alias   A short name used to represent a more complicated one. Often used for e-mail addresses or host domain names.

America Online   A commercial online service that gives its subscribers access to the Internet in addition to its other features.

analog   A form of electronic communication using a continuous electromagnetic wave, such as television or radio. Any continuous wave form, as opposed to digital on/off transmissions.

Archie   An application that enables you to easily search for information at anonymous FTP sites on the Internet.

archive   A repository of files available for access at an Internet site. Also, a collection of files—often a backup of a disk or files saved to tape to allow them to be transferred.

ARPA (Advanced Research Projects Agency)   A government agency that originally funded the research on the ARPANET, which became DARPA in the mid 1970s.

ARPANET   An experimental communications network funded by the government that eventually developed into the Internet.

article   Message submitted to a UseNet newsgroup. Unlike an e-mail message that goes to a specific person or group of persons, a newsgroup message goes to directories (on many machines) that can be read by any number of people.

ASCII   Data that is limited to letters, numbers, and punctuation.

ATM (Asynchronous Transfer Mode)   A developing technological advance in communications switching. This technology uses hardware switches to create a temporary direct path between two destinations so data can be exchanged at a higher rate.

attribute   A form of a command-line switch as applied to tags in the HTML language. HTML commands or tags can be more specific when attributes are used. Not all HTML tags utilize attributes.

AUP (Acceptable Use Policy)   The restrictions that a network segment places on the traffic it carries. (These policies used to be more prevalent when the government was running the Internet backbone.)

backbone   The major communications lines of a network.

bandwidth   The maximum volume of data that can be sent over a communications network.

bang   A slang term for an exclamation point.

bang address   A type of e-mail address that separates host names in the address with exclamation points. Used for e-mail sent to the UUCP network, where specifying the exact path of the e-mail (including all hosts that pass on the message) is necessary. The address is in the form of *machine!machine!userID*, where the number of machines listed depends on the connections needed to reach the machine where the account user ID is.

BBS (Bulletin Board System)   A system that allows you to connect to a computer to upload and download files and leave messages for other users.

binary   Data that may contain non-printable characters, including graphics files, programs, and sound files.

BinHex   A program that is used to encode binary files as ASCII so that they can be sent through e-mail.

bit   The basic unit of digital communications. There are eight bits in a byte.

BITNET (Because It's Time Network)   A non-TCP/IP network for small universities without Internet access.

bookmarks   Term used by some World Wide Web browsers for marking URLs you access frequently.

bot (IRC)   A program that watches an IRC channel and automatically responds when certain messages are entered.

bounce   An e-mail message you receive that tells you that an e-mail message you sent wasn't delivered. Usually contains an error code and the contents of the message that wasn't delivered.

bps (bits per second)   A units of measurement that expresses the speed at which data is transferred between computers.

bridge   A device that connects one physical section of a network to another.

browser   A utility that lets you look through collections of things. For example, a file browser lets you look through a file system. Applications that let you access the World Wide Web are called browsers.

BTW (By the Way)   An abbreviation often used in online conversations.

byte   A digital storage unit large enough to contain one ASCII character. Compare to *bit*.

CERN (The European Laboratory for Particle Physics)   Where the World Wide Web was first conceived of and implemented.

channel   An Internet Relay Chat term that refers to a group of people discussing a particular topic.

CIX (Commercial Internet Exchange)   A consortium of commercial providers of Internet service.

client   User of a service. Also often refers to a piece of software that gets information from a server.

CNRI (Corporation for National Research Initiatives)   An organization formed to foster research into a national data highway.

coaxial   A type of wiring where the signal wire is in the center of a shielded cable. Compare to *twisted pair*.

command line   Line on a terminal-based interface where you enter commands to the operating system. Some Internet accounts are command-line based.

compress   A program that compacts a file so it fits into a smaller space. This term can also refer to the technique of reducing the amount of space a file takes up.

CompuServe   A commercial online service that gives its subscribers access to the Internet in addition to its other features.

CPSR (Computer Professionals for Social Responsibility)   An organization that encourages socially responsible use of computers.

CREN (Corporation for Research and Educational Networking)   An organization formed by the joining of two different educational networks to enhance the capabilities of the two networks.

CWIS (Campus Wide Information Service)   A hypertext-based system that provides information about people and services on a campus.

cyberspace   A term used to refer to the entire collection of sites accessible electronically. If your computer is attached to the Internet or another large network, it exists in cyberspace.

daemon   A program that runs automatically on a computer to perform a service for the operating system.

DARPA (Defense Advanced Research Projects Agency)   Originally ARPA, the government agency that funded the research that developed ARPANET.

dedicated line   See *leased line*.

DES (Data Encryption Standard)   An algorithm developed by the U.S. government to provide security for data transmitted over a network.

dialup   A type of connection where you use a modem to connect to another computer or an Internet provider via phone lines.

digest   A form of a mailing list where a number of messages are concatenated, or linked, and sent out as a single message.

digital   A type of communications used by computers, consisting of individual on and off pulses.

DNS   See *Domain Name System (DNS)*.

DOD (Department of Defense)   A U.S. government agency that originally sponsored the ARPANET research.

domain   Highest subdivision of the Internet, for the most part by country (except in the U.S., where it's by type of organization, such as educational, commercial, and government). Usually the last part of a host name; for example, the domain part of ibm.com is .com, which represents the domain of commercial sites in the U.S.

Domain Name System (DNS)   The system that translates between Internet IP addresses and Internet host names.

dot address   See *host address*.

download   Move a file from a remote computer to your local computer.

ECPA (Electronic Communications Privacy Act)   A law that governs the use and restrictions of electronic communications.

EDUCOM A non-profit consortium of educational institutions that help introduce electronic information access and management into educational organizations.

EFF (Electronic Frontier Foundation) An organization concerned with the legal rights and responsibilities of computer usage.

e-mail An electronic message delivered from one computer user to another. Short for electronic mail.

e-mail address An address used to send e-mail to a user on the Internet, consisting of the user name and host name (and any other necessary information, such as a gateway machine). An Internet e-mail address is usually of the form *username@hostname*.

emoticon See *smiley face*.

encryption The process of scrambling a message so that it can be read only by someone who knows how to unscramble it.

ethernet A type of local area network hardware. Many TCP/IP networks are ethernet-based.

Eudora A popular e-mail application.

expire Remove an article from a UseNet newsgroup after a specified interval.

extension An enhancement or addition to an existing HTML standard. Extensions are usually referred to in the context of the HTML language. Netscape and Microsoft utilize extensions to the HTML standards that are proprietary to their own browser products. See also *browser*.

FAQ (Frequently Asked Question document) Pronounced *fak*, contains a list of commonly asked questions on a topic. Most UseNet newsgroups have a FAQ to introduce new readers to popular topics in the newsgroup.

feed Send UseNet newsgroups from your site to another site that wants to read them.

finger A program that provides information about users on an Internet host (possibly may include a user's personal information, such as project affiliation and schedule).

firewall A device placed on a network to prevent unauthorized traffic from entering the network.

flame Communicate in an abusive or absurd manner. Often occurs in newsgroup posts and e-mail messages.

forms Online data entry sheets supported by some World Wide Web browsers.

frame relay A type of digital data communications protocol.

Free Agent A popular shareware newsreader.

freeware Software that is made available by the author at no cost to anyone who wants it (although the author retains rights to the software).

FTP (File Transfer Protocol)   An Internet communications protocol that enables you to transfer files between hosts on the Internet.

FWIW (For What It's Worth)   An abbreviation often used in online conversations.

FYI (For Your Information)   An abbreviation used often in online conversations. An FYI is also a type of Internet reference document that contains answers to basic questions about the Internet.

gateway   A device that interfaces two networks that use different protocols.

gigabit   Very high-speed (1 billion bits per second) data communications.

gigabyte   A unit of data storage approximately equal to 1 billion bytes of data.

Gopher   An application that allows you to access publicly available information on Internet hosts that provide Gopher service.

Gopherbook   An application that uses an interface resembling a book to access Gopher servers.

GUI (Graphical User Interface)   A computer interface based on graphical symbols rather than text. Windowing environments and Macintosh environments are GUIs.

gzip   A file compression program originally designed to replace the UNIX `compress` utility.

hacking   Originally referred to playing around with computer systems; now often used to indicate destructive computer activity.

headers   Lines at the beginning of an e-mail message or newsgroup post that contain information about the message: its source, destination, subject, and route it took to get there, among other things.

Hgopher   A Windows Gopher interface.

home page   The primary document for a Web site. All other Web documents at that site are linked to the home page.

hop-check   A utility that allows you to find out how many routers are between your host and another Internet host. See also *traceroute*.

host address   A unique number assigned to identify a host on the Internet (also called IP address or dot address). This address is usually represented as four numbers between 1 and 254 and separated by periods; for example, 192.58.107.230.

host name   A unique name for a host that corresponds to the host address.

hosts   Individual computers connected to the Internet; see also *nodes*.

HotDog   A popular shareware HTML editor.

hotlist   A list of your favorite World Wide Web sites that can be accessed quickly by your WWW browser.

HTML (HyperText Mark-Up Language)   The formatting language that is used to create World Wide Web documents.

HTTP (HyperText Transport Protocol)   The communications protocol that enables WWW hypertext documents to be retrieved quickly.

hyperlinks   See *links*.

hypertext   An online document that has words or graphics containing links to other documents. Usually, selecting the link area on-screen (with a mouse or keyboard command) activates these links.

IAB (Internet Architecture Board)   A group of volunteers who work to maintain the Internet.

IEEE (Institute of Electrical and Electronics Engineers)   The professional society for electrical and computer engineers.

IETF (Internet Engineering Task Force)   A group of volunteers that helps develop Internet standards.

IMHO (In My Humble—or Honest—Opinion)   An abbreviation often used in online conversations.

Internet   The term used to describe all the worldwide interconnected TCP/IP networks.

Internet Assistant   A Microsoft application that enables you to develope HTML documents in Microsoft Word.

Internet Explorer   A Microsoft Windows 95 Web browser.

Internet Society   See *ISOC*.

InterNIC   The NSFNET manager sites on the Internet that provide information about the Internet.

IP (Internet Protocol)   The communications protocol used by computers connected to the Internet.

IP address   See *host address*.

IRC (Internet Relay Chat)   A live conference facility available on the Internet.

ISDN (Integrated Services Digital Network)   An emerging digital communications standard, allowing faster speeds than are possible using modems over analog phone lines.

ISO (International Standards Organization)   An organization that sets worldwide standards in many different areas. For example, the organization has been working on a network protocol to replace TCP/IP.

I

HTML

ISOC (Internet Society)   An educational organization dedicated to encouraging use of the Internet.

kill file   A file used by some newsreader software that allows you to automatically skip posts with certain attributes (specific subject, author, and so on).

knowbots (Knowledge robots)   Programs that automatically search through a network for specified information.

labels   The different components of an Internet host name.

LAN (Local Area Network)   A network of computers that is limited to a (usually) small physical area, like a building.

leased line   A dedicated phone line used for network communications.

links   The areas (words or graphics) in an HTML document that cause another document to be loaded when the user clicks them.

listproc   Software that automates the management of electronic mailing lists. See also *LISTSERV*, *majordomo*, and *SmartList*.

LISTSERV   Software that automates the management of electronic mailing lists. See also *listproc*, *majordomo*, and *SmartList*.

local   Pertaining to the computer you are now using.

local host   The computer you are currently using.

logon   Provides a user ID and password to allow you to use the resources of a computer.

lurking   Observing but not participating in an activity, usually a UseNet newsgroup.

Lycos   A popular Web search tool.

mailers   Applications that let you read and send e-mail messages.

mailing list   A service that forwards an e-mail message sent to it to everyone on a list, enabling a group of people to discuss a particular topic.

mail reflector   Software that automatically distributes all submitted messages to the members of a mailing list.

majordomo   Software that automates the management of electronic mailing lists. See also *listproc*, *LISTSERV*, and *SmartList*.

man command   A UNIX command that provides information about the UNIX command entered in the parameter command. (man is short for manual entry.)

MBONE (Multicast backbone)   An experimental network that enables live video to be sent over the Internet.

Merit (Michigan Educational Research Information Triad)   The organization that initially managed NSFNET.

MILNET DOD's (Department of Defense) network.

MIME (Multi-Purpose Internet Mail Extensions) An extension to Internet mail that allows for the inclusion of non-textual data such as video and audio in e-mail.

modem An electronic device that enables digital computer data to be transmitted via analog phone lines.

moderator A person who examines all submissions to a newsgroup or mailing list and allows only those that meet certain criteria to be posted. Usually, the moderator makes sure that the topic is pertinent to the group and that the submissions aren't flames.

Mosaic A graphical browser program used to navigate the World Wide Web.

MOTD (Message of the day) A message posted on some computer systems to let people know about problems or new developments.

MSN (Microsoft Network) A commercial online service run by Microsoft that allows access to the Internet in addition to its other features.

MUDs (Multiuser Dungeons) Interactive real-time, text-based games accessible to anyone on the Internet.

multimedia Presenting information using more than one type of media; for example, sound, text, and graphics.

NETCOM NetCruiser A complete Internet service package.

Netfind A service that enables you to look up an Internet user's address.

netiquette Network etiquette conventions used in written communications, usually referring to UseNet newsgroup postings but also applicable to e-mail.

NetManage The producer of Chameleon, a popular TCP/IP package that provides interfaces to a number of Internet services for Windows.

netnews A collective way of referring to the UseNet newsgroups.

Netscape A company that makes a popular commercial World Wide Web browser, Netscape Navigator.

network A number of computers physically connected to enable communication with one another.

NewsXpress A popular shareware newsreader.

newsgroups The electronic discussion groups of UseNet.

newsreaders Applications that let you read (and usually post) articles in UseNet newsgroups.

NFS (Network File System) A file system developed by Sun Microsystems that is now widely used on many different networks.

NIC (Network Information Center)   A service that provides administrative information about a network.

NII (National Information Infrastructure)   The government's vision of a high-speed network giving everyone in the country access to advanced computer capabilities.

NNTP (Network News Transport Protocol)   The communications protocol that is used to send UseNet news on the Internet.

nodes   Individual computers connected to a network. See also *hosts*.

NREN (National Research and Education Network)   A proposed nationwide high-speed data network to be used for educational and research purposes.

NSF (National Science Foundation)   Current supporter of the main Internet backbone in the U.S.

NSFNET   Network funded by the National Science Foundation, now the backbone of the Internet.

OC3 (Optical Carrier 3)   A protocol for communications over a high-speed optical network.

online   Existing in electronic form (for example, online documentation). Also, connected to a network.

OTOH (On The Other Hand)   An abbreviation often used in online conversations.

packet   The unit of data transmission on the Internet. A packet consists of the data being transferred with additional overhead information, such as the transmitting and receiving addresses.

packet switching   The communications technology that the Internet is based on, where data being sent between computers is transmitted in packets.

parallel   A means of communication in which digital data is sent multiple bits at a time, with each simultaneous bit being sent over a separate line.

PDIAL   A list of mailing lists maintained by Stephanie da Silva (**arielle@taronga.com**), periodically posted to the **news.answers**, **news.announce.newusers**, and **news.lists** UseNet newsgroups.

peer-to-peer   Internet services that can be offered and accessed by anyone, without requiring a special server.

PDN (Public Data Network)   A service such as Sprintnet that gives access to a nationwide data network through a local phone call.

PEM (Privacy Enhanced Mail)   A standard for automatically encrypting and decrypting mail messages to provide more secure message transmission.

PGP (Pretty Good Privacy)   An application that enables you to send and receive encrypted e-mail.

ping   A utility that sends out a packet to an Internet host and waits for a response (used to check if a host is up).

Pipeline   A complete Internet service package.

POP (Point of Presence)   Indicates availability of a local access number to a public data network.

port^1   A physical channel on a computer that allows you to communicate with other devices (printers, modems, disk drives, and so on).

port^2   An address to which incoming data packets are sent. Special ports can be assigned to send the data directly to a server (FTP, Gopher, WWW, telnet, and e-mail) or another specific program.

post   Send a message to a UseNet newsgroup.

postmaster   An address to which you can send questions about a site (asking if a user has an account there or if they sell a particular product, for example).

PPP (Point-To-Point Protocol)   A driver that allows you to use a network communications protocol over a phone line, used with TCP/IP to allow you to have a dial-in Internet host.

Prodigy   A commercial online service that gives its subscribers access to the Internet in addition to its other features.

protocol   The standard that defines how computers on a network communicate with one another.

provider   Someone who sells—or gives away, in some cases—access to the Internet.

public domain software   Software that is made available by the author to anyone who wants it. (In this case, the author gives up all rights to the software.)

RAS (Remote Access Service)   A service that enables other computers to remotely connect to a Microsoft Windows NT computer.

repeater   Device that allows you to extend the length of your network by amplifying and repeating the information it receives.

remote host   A host on the network other than the computer you currently are using.

rlogin   A UNIX command that enables you to logon to a remote computer.

RFC (Request For Comments)   A document submitted to the Internet governing board to propose Internet standards or to document information about the Internet.

router   Equipment that receives an Internet packet and sends it to the next machine in the destination path.

serial   A means of communication in which digital data is sent one bit at a time over a single physical line.

server   Provider of a service. Also often refers to a piece of hardware or software that provides access to information requested from it. See also *client*.

server side include (SSI)   An SSI is a command that directs the server to run a program, usually in the PERL programming language. SSIs are server-specific.

SGML (Standard General Mark-Up Language)   A powerful markup language that enables you to structure documents so that they can be displayed on any type of computer.

shareware   Software that is made available by the author to anyone who wants it, with a request to send the author a nominal fee if the software is used on a regular basis.

signature   A personal sign-off used in e-mail and newsgroup posts, often contained in a file and automatically appended to the mail or post. Often contains organization affiliation and pertinent personal information.

site   A group of computers under a single administrative control.

SLIP (Serial Line Internet Protocol)   A way of running TCP/IP via the phone lines to enable you to have a dial-in Internet host.

SmartList   Software that automates the management of electronic mailing lists. See also *listproc*, *LISTSERV*, and *majordomo*.

SMDS (Switched Multimegabit Data Service)   A type of high-speed digital communications protocol.

smiley face   An ASCII drawing such as :-) (look at it sideways), used to help indicate an emotion in a message. Also called emoticon.

SMTP (Simple Mail Transport Protocol)   The accepted communications protocol standard for exchange of e-mail between Internet hosts.

SNMP (Simple Network Management Protocol)   A communications protocol used to control and monitor devices on a network.

SONET (Synchronous Optical Network)   A high-speed fiber optic network.

store and forward   A type of system that collects information (like e-mail) for a user and then forwards the information when the user connects to the system.

subscribe   Become a member of a mailing list or newsgroup; also refers to obtaining Internet provider services.

surfing   Jumping from host to host on the Internet to get an idea of what can be found. Also used to refer to briefly examining a number of different UseNet newsgroups.

syntax   A statement that contains programming code.

T1   Communications lines operating at 1.544M/sec.

T3   Communications lines operating at 45M/sec.

tag   A slang reference for commands that are part of HTML. See also *HTML*.

tar (Tape Archive program)   A UNIX-based program that creates packages of directory structures.

TCP (Transmission Control Protocol)   The network protocol used by hosts on the Internet.

telnet   A program that enables remote logon to another computer.

terminal emulation   Running an application that lets you use your computer to interface with a command-line account on a remote computer, as if you were connected to the computer with a terminal.

thread   All messages in a newsgroup or mailing list pertaining to a particular topic.

toggle   Alternate between two possible values.

traceroute   A utility that allows you to find out how many routers are between your host and another Internet host. See also *hop-check*.

traffic   The information flowing through a network.

twisted pair   A type of cable where pairs of communications wires are twisted together to minimize interference. Compare to coaxial.

UNIX   An operating system used on many Internet hosts.

upload   Move a file from your local computer to a remote computer.

URL (Universal Resource Locator)   Used to specify the location and name of a World Wide Web document. Can also specify other Internet services available from WWW browsers. For example, **http://www.nsf.gov** or **gopher:// gopher2.tc.umn.edu**.

UseNet   A collection of computer discussion groups that are read all over the world.

user name   The ID used to log on to a computer.

UUCP (UNIX to UNIX Copy Protocol)   An early transfer protocol for UNIX machines that required having one machine call the other one on the phone.

UUDecode   A program that lets you construct binary data that was UUEncoded.

UUEncode   A program that lets you send binary data through e-mail.

Veronica   An Internet service that enables you to search the directories and files on Gopher servers for information of interest to you.

viewers   Applications that are used to display non-text files, such as graphics, sound, and animation.

virus   A computer program that covertly enters a system by means of a legitimate program, usually doing damage to the system; compare to worm.

VMS (Virtual Memory System)   An operating system used on hosts made by Digital Equipment Corporation.

VRML (Virtual Reality Modeling Language)   An experimental language that lets you display 3-D objects in Web documents.

WAIS (Wide Area Information Servers)   A system for searching and retrieving documents from participating sites.

WAN (Wide Area Network)   A network of computers that are geographically dispersed.

Web Chat   An application that enables you to carry on live conversations over the World Wide Web.

Web Crawler   A Web search tool.

WELL (Whole Earth 'Lectric Link)   One of the first Internet public access sites.

WHOIS   A service that lets you look up information about Internet hosts and users.

worm   A computer program that invades other computers over a network, usually non-destructive; compare to virus.

WWW (World Wide Web)   A hypertext-based system that allows browsing of available Internet resources. Also called the Web.

X-modem   A communication protocol that lets you transfer files over a serial line. See also *Y-modem* and *Z-modem*.

Y-modem   A communication protocol that lets you transfer files over a serial line. See also *X-modem* and *Z-modem*.

Yahoo   A Web site that contains lists of many topics to be found on the Web and includes a search tool to find sites you are interested in.

Z-modem   A communication protocol that lets you transfer files over a serial line. See also *X-modem* and *Y-modem*.

ZIP   Probably the singular most popular file compression and archive program for PCs.

Part II

Perl

Chapter 6

Understanding the Perl Reference Section

This section is a reference guide for the programming language called Perl. This book does not describe how to install Perl on your computer; if you do not already have Perl installed, it will not be very useful!

> **Note**
>
> If you want to install Perl and have access to the Internet visit the Central Perl Archive Network (CPAN). The master site is at **ftp://ftp.funet.fi/pub/languages/perl/ CPAN/**, and there are many mirror sites around the world. This is as much as can be found on Perl installation in this guide!

Perl has many uses, especially in UNIX system administrative tasks, which is where Perl was born and grew up. Perl stands for *Practical Extraction and Report Language*. Nowadays, Perl is seen by many as the ideal development language for Web server scripts.

This chapter describes the advantages of using Perl and outlines the structure of this section.

Why Use Perl?

People use Perl because it is quick, efficient, and easy to maintain when programming a wide range of tasks, in particular those involving the manipulation of text files. Also, there are many others using Perl who are prepared to share their code.

Rapid Development

Many programming projects are high level rather than low level. That means that they tend not to involve bit-level manipulations, direct operating system calls. Instead, they focus on reading from files, reformatting the output, and writing it to standard output—for example, a Web browser. With Perl, the programmer does not need to get involved in the details of how file handles and buffers are manipulated, how memory is allocated, and so on. You can tell it to slurp in the contents of a file and display it on the standard output device, but with all newlines replaced by tabs:

```
while ( <INFILE> )  {  s/\n/\t/;  print;  }
```

Let's not worry about the details of what's happening in that code example until Chapter 7, "Perl Overview." Just notice two things:

- It's very short.

- It's almost legible even without knowing any Perl, especially if you are familiar with C.

In a nutshell, that's the secret to rapid development: Write small amounts of powerful code without having to pause to consider awkward issues of syntax at every step.

Perl is pithy; a little Perl code goes a long way. In terms of programming languages, that usually means that the code will be difficult to read and painful to write. But although Larry Wall, the author of Perl, says that Perl is functional rather than elegant, most programmers quickly find that Perl code is very readable and that it is not difficult to become fluent at writing it. This is especially true of the high-level, macro operations typically required in Web development.

As it happens, Perl is quite capable of handling some pretty low-level operations, too. It can handle operating system signals and talk to network sockets, for example.

Compiler and Interpreter

A program by itself can't achieve anything. To carry out its work, it needs to be fed to either a compiler or an interpreter. Both have their advantages:

- A compiler takes a program listing and generates an executable file. This executable file can then be executed as many times as necessary, copied to other computers, and so on without the need for the program source code. This helps to keep program details confidential.

    Because the compiler only runs once, it can afford to take its time about generating the executable code. As a result, compilers tend to perform elaborate optimization on the program code with the result that the executable code runs very efficiently.

- An interpreter examines a program listing line by line and carries out the tasks required by the code then and there. There is no need for a separate compilation stage; once the program has been written, it can be executed without delay. This makes for a rapid development cycle.

There are advantages and disadvantages to both approaches. Compiled code takes longer to prepare, but then it runs fast and your source stays secret. Interpreted code gets up and running quickly but isn't as fast as interpreted code. You also need to distribute the program source code if you want to allow others to run your programs.

So which of these categories describes Perl?

Well, Perl is special in this regard; it is a compiler that thinks it's an interpreter. Perl compiles program code into executable code before running it, so there is an optimization stage and the executable code runs quickly. However, it doesn't write this code to a separate executable file. Instead, it stores it in memory and then executes it.

This means that Perl combines the rapid development cycle of an interpreted language with the efficient execution of compiled code. The corresponding disadvantages are also there, though: The need to compile the program each time it runs means a slower startup than a purely compiled language and requires developers to distribute source code to users.

In practice, these disadvantages are not too limiting. The compilation phase is extremely fast, so you're unlikely to notice much of a lag between invoking a Perl script and the start of execution.

In summary, Perl is compiled "behind the scenes" for rapid execution, but you can treat it as if it is interpreted. This makes it easy for you to tweak your HTML; just edit the code and let the users run it. But is that good programming practice? Hey, that's one for the philosophers.

Flexibility

Perl was not designed in the abstract. It was written to solve a particular problem and it evolved to serve an ever widening set of real-world problem categories.

It could have been expanded to handle these tasks by adding more and more keywords and operators, hence by making the language bigger. Instead, the core of the Perl language started out small and became more refined as time went on. In some ways, it actually contracted; the number of reserved words in Perl 5 is actually less than half the number in Perl 4, not more.

This reflects an awareness that Perl's power lies in its unique combination of efficiency and flexibility. Perl itself has grown slowly and thoughtfully, usually in ways that allow for enhancements and extensions to be added on rather than being hard-wired in. This approach has been critical in the development of Perl's extensibility over time, as the next section explains.

Extensibility

Much of the growth in Perl as a platform has come by way of the increasing use of libraries (Perl 4) and modules (Perl 5). These are mechanisms that enable developers to write self-contained portions of Perl code that can be slotted in to a Perl application.

These add-ons range from fairly high-level utilities such as a module that adds HTML tags to text, to low-level, down-and-dirty development tools such as code profilers and debuggers.

The ability to use extensions like these is a remarkable advance in the development of a fairly slick language and it has helped to fuel the growth in Perl use. It makes it easy for Perl developers to share their work with others; the arrival of objects in Perl 5 makes structured design methodologies possible for Perl applications. The language has come of age without losing any of its flexibility or raw power.

Web Server Scripts

Web servers generate huge amounts of HTML. The *M* stands for *Markup*, and you need lots of it to make your Web pages look more exciting than the average insurance contract. It's an awkward business though, with problems arising easily if tags are misplaced or misspelled. Perl is a good choice of language to look after the details for you while you get on with the big picture. This is especially true if you call on Perl 5's object-oriented capabilities.

Another facet of Perl that is of particular interest to many Web server managers is that Perl works very well with standard UNIX DBM files and support for proprietary databases is growing. This is a significant consideration if you plan to allow users to query database material over the Web.

Security

Security is a major issue when writing system administrative programs and on the Internet in general. Using Perl for scripting on your Web server, you can easily guard against users trying to sneak commands through for the server to execute on their behalf. There is also an excellent Perl 5 module called `pgpperl`, also known as Penguin, that allows your server to use public-key cryptography techniques to guard sensitive data from eavesdroppers.

Ubiquity

Lots of people on the Web already use Perl. Going with the flow isn't always the best approach, but Perl has grown with the Web. There is a lot of experience out there if you need advice. The Perl developers are keenly aware of Web issues as they add to Perl. And many Perl modules have been built with the Web specifically in mind.

Why Use Perl Summary

There are many reasons why you want to use Perl. It is small, efficient, flexible, and robust. Perl is particularly well suited for Web development work where text output is a major preoccupation. And if the reasons previously outlined aren't quite enough, consider this: Perl is completely free.

The Structure of This Section

This book falls clearly into two parts. Part 1 is a discursive overview of the Perl language, describing some things that are not easily summarized in tables. Part 2 is a set of reference chapters that describes the various aspects of Perl in detail:

- Chapter 7, "Perl Overview," describes all the features of Perl in a discursive manner. This chapter introduces the basic concepts of programming in Perl. Some things are not easily summarized in tabular form, even in a quick reference guide, which is why this chapter is included.

- Chapters 8 through 10 cover all Perl variables, operators, and functions in detail. Each of these chapters is arranged in a format that makes it easy to locate an item for reference. Icons mark each variable, operator, and function as being available in Perl 4, Perl 5, and NT Perl (the hip communications Win32 port).

- Chapter 11, "Perl Regular Expressions," and Chapter 12, "Perl Reference Tables," summarize regular expressions and list the standard Perl 5 modules.

II

Perl

## Chapter 7

Perl Overview

The *Perl Quick Reference* part is designed as a reference guide for the Perl language, rather than an introductory text. However, there are some aspects of the language that are better summarized in a short paragraph as opposed to a table in a reference section. Therefore, this part of the book puts the reference material in context giving an overview of the Perl language in general.

Running Perl

The simplest way to run a Perl program is to invoke the Perl interpreter with the name of the Perl program as an argument:

```
perl sample.pl
```

The name of the Perl file is `sample.pl`, and `perl` is the name of the Perl interpreter. This example assumes that Perl is in the execution path; if not, you will need to supply the full path to Perl too:

```
/usr/local/hin/perl sample.pl
```

This is the preferred way of invoking Perl because it eliminates the possibility that you might accidentally invoke a copy of Perl other than the one you intended. We will use the full path from now on to avoid any confusion.

This type of invocation is the same on all systems with a command-line interface. The following line will do the trick on Windows NT, for example:

```
c:\NTperl\perl sample.pl
```

Invoking Perl on UNIX

UNIX systems have another way to invoke an interpreter on a script file. Place a line like

```
#!/usr/local/bin/perl
```

at the start of the Perl file. This tells UNIX that the rest of this script file is to be interpreted by `/usr/local/bin/perl`. Then make the script itself executable:

```
chmod +x sample.pl
```

You can then "execute" the script file directly and let the script file tell the operating system what interpreter to use while running it.

Invoking Perl on Windows NT

Windows NT, on the other hand, is quite different. You can use File Manager (Explorer under Windows NT 4 or Windows 95) to create an association between the file extension .PL and the Perl executable. Whenever a file ending in .PL is invoked, Windows will know that Perl should be used to interpret it.

Command-Line Arguments

Perl takes a number of optional command-line arguments for various purposes. These are listed in Table 7.1. Most are rarely used but are given here for reference purposes.

Table 7.1 Perl 5 Command-Line Switches

Option	Arguments	Purpose	Notes
-0	Octal character code	Specify record separator	Default is newline (\n)
-a	none	Automatically split records	Used with -n or or -p
-c	none	Check syntax only	Do not execute
-d	none	Run script using Perl debugger	If Perl debugging option was included when Perl was installed
-D	flags	Specify debugging behavior	See table 2
-e	command	Pass a command to Perl from the command line	Useful for quick operations
-F	regular expression	Expression to split by if -a used	Default is white space
-i	extension	Replace original file with results	Useful for modifying contents of files
-I	directory	Specify location of include files	
-l	octal character code	Drop newlines when used with -n and -p and use designated character as line termination character	
-n	none	Process the script using each specified file as an argument	Used for performing the same set of actions on a set of files
-p	none	Same as -n but each line is printed	
-P	none	Run the script through the C preprocessor before Perl compiles it	

Option	Arguments	Purpose	Notes
-s	none	Enable passing of arbitrary switches to Perl	Use -s -what -ever to have the Perl variables $what and $ever defined within your script
-S	none	Tell Perl to look along the path for the script	
-T	none	Use taint checking; don't evaluate expressions supplied on the command line	
-u	none	Make Perl dumb core after compiling your script; intended to allow for generation of Perl executables	Very messy; wait for the Perl compiler
-U	none	Unsafe mode; overrides Perl's natural caution	Don't use this!
-v	none	Print Perl version number	
-w	none	Print warnings about script syntax	Extremely useful, especially during development

Tip

The -e option is handy for quick Perl operations from the command line. Want to change all instances of "oldstring" in Wiffle.bat to "newstrong"? Try

```
perl -i.old -p -e "s/ oldstring/ newstrong/g" wiffle.bat
```

This says: "Take each line of Wiffle.bat (-p); store the original in Wiffle.old (-i); substitute all instances of oldstring with newstrong (-e); write the result (-p) to the original file (-i)."

You can supply Perl command-line arguments on the interpreter invocation line in UNIX scripts. The following line is a good start to any Perl script:

```
#!/usr/local/bin/perl -w -t
```

Table 7.2 shows the debug flags, which can be specified with the -D command-line option. If you specify a number, you can simply add all the numbers of each flag together so that 6 is 4 and 2. If you use the letter as a flag then simply list all the options required. The following two calls are equivalent:

```
#perl -d -D6 test.pl
#perl -d -Dls test.pl
```

Table 7.2 Perl Debugging Flags

Flag Number	Flag Letter	Meaning of Flag
1	p	Tokenizing and parsing
2	s	Stack snapshots
4	l	Label stack processing
8	t	Trace execution
16	o	Operator node construction
32	c	String/numeric conversions
64	P	Print preprocessor command for -P
128	m	Memory allocation
256	f	Format processing
512	r	Regular expression parsing
1024	x	Syntax tree dump
2048	u	Tainting checks
4096	L	Memory leaks (not supported anymore)
8192	H	Hash dump; usurps `values()`
6384	X	Scratchpad allocation (Perl 5 only)
32768	D	Cleaning up (Perl 5 only)

A Perl Script

A Perl program consists of an ordinary text file containing a series of Perl commands. Commands are written in what looks like a bastardized amalgam of C, shell script, and English. In fact, that's pretty much what it is.

Perl code can be quite free-flowing. The broad syntactic rules governing where a statement starts and ends are

- Leading white space is ignored. You can start a Perl statement anywhere you want: at the beginning of the line, indented for clarity (recommended), or even right-justified (definitely frowned on) if you like.

- Commands are terminated with a semicolon.

- White space outside of string literals is irrelevant; one space is as good as a hundred. That means you can split statements over several lines for clarity.

- Anything after a pound sign (#) is ignored. Use this to pepper your code with useful comments.

Here's a Perl statement inspired by Kurt Vonnegut:

```
print "My name is Yon Yonson\n";
```

No prizes for guessing what happens when Perl runs this code; it prints

```
My name is Yon Yonson
```

If the \n doesn't look familiar, don't worry; it simply means that Perl should print a newline character after the text; in other words, Perl should go to the start of the next line.

Printing more text is a matter of either stringing together statements or giving multiple arguments to the print function:

```
print "My name is Yon Yonson,\n";
print "I live in Wisconsin,\n",
      "I work in a lumbermill there.\n";
```

That's right, print is a function. It may not look like it in any of the examples so far, where there are no parentheses to delimit the function arguments, but it is a function, and it takes arguments. You can use parentheses in Perl functions if you like; it sometimes helps to make an argument list clearer. More accurately, in this example the function takes a single argument consisting of an arbitrarily long list. We'll have much more to say about lists and arrays later, in the "Data Types" section. There will be a few more examples of the more common functions in the remainder of this chapter, but refer to the "Functions" chapter for a complete run-down on all of Perl's built-in functions.

So what does a complete Perl program look like? Here's a trivial UNIX example, complete with the invocation line at the top and a few comments:

```
#!/usr/local/bin/perl -w              # Show warnings

print "My name is Yon Yonson,\n";     # Let's introduce ourselves
print "I live in Wisconsin,\n",
      "I work in a lumbermill there.\n";   # Remember the line breaks
```

That's not at all typical of a Perl program though; it's just a linear sequence of commands with no structural complexity. The "Flow Control" section later in this overview introduces some of the constructs that make Perl what it is. For now, we'll stick to simple examples like the preceding for the sake of clarity.

Data Types

Perl has a small number of data types. If you're used to working with C, where even characters can be either signed or unsigned, this makes a pleasant change. In essence, there are only two data types: *scalars* and *arrays*. There is also a very special kind of array called an *associative array* that merits a section all to itself.

Scalars

All numbers and strings are scalars. Scalar variable names start with a dollar sign.

Note
All Perl variable names, including scalars, are case sensitive. $Name and $name, for example, are two completely different quantities.

Perl converts automatically between numbers and strings as required, so that

```
$a = 2;
$b = 6;
$c = $a . $b;   # The "." operator concatenates two strings
$d = $c / 2;
print $d;
```

yields the result

```
13
```

This example involves converting two integers into strings, concatenating the strings into a new string variable, converting this new string to an integer, dividing it by two, converting the result to a string, and printing it. All of these conversions are handled implicitly, leaving the programmer free to concentrate on what needs to be done rather than the low-level details of how it is to be done.

This might be a problem if Perl were regularly used for tasks where, for example, explicit memory offsets were used and data types were critical. But for the type of task where Perl is normally used, these automatic conversions are smooth, intuitive, and useful.

We can use this to develop the earlier example script using some string variables:

```
#!/usr/local/bin/perl -w                     # Show warnings

$who = 'Yon Yonson';
$where = 'Wisconsin';
$what = 'in a lumbermill';

print "My name is $who,\n";                   # Let's introduce ourselves
print "I live in $where,\n",
      "I work $what there.\n";                       # Remember the line breaks

print "\nSigned: \t$who,\n\t\t$where.\n";
```

which yields

```
My name is Yon Yonson,
I work in Wisconsin,
I work in a lumbermill there.

Signed:    Yon Yonson,
      Winsconsin.
```

Arrays

A collection of scalars is an array. An array variable name starts with an @ sign, while an explicit array of scalars is written as a comma-separated list within parentheses:

```
@trees = ("Larch", "Hazel", "Oak");
```

Array subscripts are denoted using square brackets: $trees[0] is the first element of the @trees array. Notice that it's @trees but $trees[0]; individual array elements are scalars, so they start with a $.

Mixing scalar types in an array is not a problem. For example,

```
@items = (15, 45.67, "case");
print "Take $items[0] $items[2]s at \$$items[1] each.\n";
```

results in

```
Take 15 cases at $45.67 each.
```

All arrays in Perl are dynamic. You never have to worry about memory allocation and management because Perl does all that stuff for you. Combine that with the fact that arrays can contain arrays as sub-arrays, and you're free to say things like the following:

```
@A = (1, 2, 3);
@B = (4, 5, 6);
@C = (7, 8, 9);
@D = (@A, @B, @C);
```

which results in the array @D containing numbers 1 through 9. The power of constructs such as

```
@Annual = (@Spring, @Summer, @Fall, @Winter);
```

takes some getting used to.

Note

An aspect of Perl that often confuses newcomers (and occasionally the old hands too) is the context-sensitive nature of evaluations. Perl keeps track of the context in which an expression is being evaluated and can return a different value in an array context than in a scalar context. In the following example:

```
@A = (1, 2, 3, 4);
@B = @A;
$C = @A;
```

the array @B contains 1 through 4 while $C contains "4", the number of values in the array. This context-sensitivity becomes more of an issue when you use functions and operators that can take either a single argument or multiple arguments. The results can be quite different depending on what is passed to them.

Many of Perl's built-in functions take arrays as arguments. One example is sort, which takes an array as argument and returns the same array sorted alphabetically:

```
print sort ( 'Beta', 'Gamma', 'Alpha' );
```

prints AlphaBetaGamma.

We can make this neater using another built-in function, join. This function takes two arguments: A string to connect with and an array of strings to connect. It returns a single string consisting of all elements in the array joined with the connecting string:

```
print join ( ' : ', 'Name', 'Address', 'Phone' );
```

returns the string Name : Address : Phone.

Because `sort` returns an array, we can feed its output straight into `join`:

```
print join( ', ', sort ( 'Beta', 'Gamma', 'Alpha' ) );
```

prints `Alpha, Beta, Gamma`.

Note that we haven't separated the initial scalar argument of join from the array that follows it: The first argument is the string to join things with; the rest of the arguments are treated as a single argument, the array to be joined. This is true even if we use parentheses to separate groups of arguments:

```
print join( ': ', ('A', 'B', 'C'), ('D', 'E'), ('F', 'G', 'H', 'I'));
```

returns `A: B: C: D: E: F: G: H: I`. That's because of the way Perl treats arrays; adding an array to an array gives us one larger array, not two arrays. In this case, all three arrays get bundled into one.

Tip

For even more powerful string manipulation capabilities, refer to the `splice` function in Chapter 10, "Perl Functions."

Associative Arrays

There is a certain elegance to associative arrays that makes experienced Perl programmers a little snobbish about their language of choice. Rightly so! Associative arrays give Perl a degree of database functionality at a very low yet useful level. Many tasks that would otherwise involve complex programming can be reduced to a handful of Perl statements using associative arrays.

Arrays of the type we've already seen are *lists of values indexed by subscripts*. In other words, to get an individual element of an array, you supply a subscript as a reference:

```
@fruit = ("Apple", "Orange", "Banana");

print $fruit[2];
```

This example yields `Banana` because subscripts start at `0` and so 2 is the subscript for the third element of the `@fruit` array. A reference to `$fruit[7]` here returns the null value, as no array element with that subscript has been defined.

Now, here's the point of all this: Associative arrays are lists of values indexed by strings. Conceptually, that's all there is to them. Their implementation is more complex, obviously, as all of the strings need to be stored in addition to the values to which they refer.

When you want to refer to an element of an associative array, you supply a string (also called the *key*) instead of an integer (also called the subscript). Perl returns the corresponding value. Consider the following example:

```
%fruit = ("Green", "Apple", "Orange", "Orange", "Yellow", "Banana");

print $fruit{"Yellow"};
```

This prints Banana as before. The first line defines the associative array in much the same way as we have already defined ordinary arrays; the difference is that instead of listing values, we list *key/value pairs*. The first value is Apple and its key is Green; the second value is Orange, which happens to have the same string for both value and key; and the final value is Banana and its key is Yellow.

On a superficial level, this can be used to provide mnemonics for array references, allowing us to refer to $Total{'June'} instead of $Total[5]. But that's not even beginning to use the power of associative arrays. Think of the keys of an associative arrays as you might think of a key linking tables in a relational database, and you're closer to the idea:

```
%Folk =    ( 'YY', 'Yon Yonson',
             'TC', 'Terra Cotta',
             'RE', 'Ron Everly' );

%State = ( 'YY', 'Wisconsin',
           'TC', 'Minnesota',
           'RE', 'Bliss' );

%Job = ( 'YY', 'work in a lumbermill',
         'TC', 'teach nuclear physics',
         'RE', 'watch football');

foreach $person ( 'TS', 'YY', 'RE' ) {
        print "My name is $Folk{$person},\n",
              "I live in $State{$person},\n",
              "I $Job{$person} there.\n\n";
        }
```

The foreach construct is explained later in the "Flow Control" section; for now, you just need to know that it makes Perl execute the three print statements for each of the people in the list after the foreach keyword.

The keys and values of an associative array may be treated as separate (ordinary) arrays as well, by using the keys and values keywords respectively:

```
print keys %Folk;
print values %State;
```

prints the string YYRETCWisconsinBlissMinnesota. String handling will be discussed later in this chapter.

Note

There is a special associative array, %ENV, that stores the contents of all environment variables, indexed by variable name. So $ENV{'PATH'} returns the current search path, for example. Here's a way to print the current value of all environment variables, sorted by variable name for good measure:

```
foreach $var (sort keys %ENV ) {
    print "$var: \"$ENV{$var}\".\n";
    }
```

(continues)

(continued)

The foreach clause sets $var to each of the environment variable names in turn (in alphabetical order), and the print statement prints each name and value. As the symbol " is used to specify the beginning and end of the string being printed, when we actually want to print a " we have to tell Perl to ignore the special meaning of the character. This is done by prefixing it with a backslash character (this is sometimes called *quoting* a character).

File Handles

We'll finish our look at Perl data types with a look at file handles. Really this is not a data type but a special kind of literal string. A file handle behaves in many ways like a variable, however, so this is a good time to cover them. Besides, you won't get very far in Perl without them...

A file handle can be regarded as a pointer to a file from which Perl is to read, or to which it will write. C programmers will be familiar with the concept. The basic idea is that you associate a handle with a file or device, and then refer to the handle in the code whenever you need to perform a read or write operation.

File handles are generally written in all uppercase. Perl has some useful predefined file handles, which are listed in Table 7.3.

Table 7.3   Perl's Predefined File Handles

File Handle	Points To
STDIN	Standard input, normally the keyboard
STDOUT	Standard output, normally the console
STDERR	Device where error messages should be written, normally the console

The print statement can take a file handle as its first argument:

```
print STDERR "Oops, something broke.\n";
```

Note that there is no comma after the file handle, which helps Perl to figure out that the STDERR is not something to be printed. If you're uneasy with this implicit list syntax, you can put parentheses around all of the print arguments:

```
print (STDERR "Oops, something broke.\n");
```

Note that there is still no comma after the file handle.

Tip

Use the standard file handles explicitly, especially in complex programs. It is sometimes convenient to redefine the standard input or output device for a while; make sure that you don't accidentally wind up writing to a file what should have gone to the screen.

The open function may be used to associate a new file handle with a file:

```
open (INDATA, "/etc/stuff/Friday.dat");
open (LOGFILE, ">/etc/logs/reclaim.log");
print LOGFILE "Log of reclaim procedure\n";
```

By default, open opens files for reading only. If you want to override this default behavior, add one of the special direction symbols from Table 7.4 to the file name. That's what the > at the start of the file name in the second output statement is for; it tells Perl that we intend to write to the named file.

Table 7.4 Perl File Access Symbols

Symbol	Meaning
<	Opens the file for reading. This is the default action.
>	Opens the file for writing.
>>	Opens the file for appending.
+<	Opens the file for both reading and writing.
+>	Opens the file for both reading and writing.
¦ (before file name)	Treats file as command into which Perl is to pipe text.
¦ (after file name)	Treats file as command from which input is to be piped to Perl.

To take a more complex example, the following is one way to feed output to the mypr printer on a UNIX system:

```
open (MYLPR, "¦lpr -Pmypr");
print MYLPR "A line of output\n";
close MYLPR;
```

There is a special Perl operator for reading from files. It consists of two angle brackets around the file handle of the file from which we want to read, and it returns the next line or lines of input from the file or device, depending on whether the operator is used in a scalar or an array context. When no more input remains, the operator returns False.

For example, a construct like the following

```
while (<STDIN>) {
        print;
        }
```

simply echoes each line of input back to the console until the Ctrl and D keys are pressed. That's because the print function takes the current default argument here, the most recent line of input. Refer to Chapter 8, "Perl Special Variables," for an explanation.

If the user types

```
A
Bb
Ccc
^D
```

then the screen will look like

```
A
A
Bb
Bb
Ccc
Ccc
^D
```

Note that in this case, `<STDIN>` is in a scalar context and so one line of standard input is returned at a time. Compare that with the following example:

```
print <STDIN>;
```

In this case, because `print` expects an array of arguments (it can be a single element array, but it's an array as far as `print` is concerned), the `<>` operator obligingly returns all the contents of `STDIN` as an array and `print` then prints it. This means that nothing is written to the console until the user presses the Ctrl and D keys:

```
A
Bb
Ccc
^Z
A
Bb
Ccc
```

This script prints out the contents of the file .Signature, double-spaced:

```
open (SIGFILE, ".signature");
while ( <SIGFILE> )  {
      print; print "\n";
      }
```

The first `print` has no arguments, so it takes the current default argument and prints it. The second has an argument, so it prints that instead. Perl's habit of using default arguments extends to the `<>` operator: if used with no file handle, it is assumed that `<ARGV>` is intended. This expands to each line in turn of each file listed on the command line.

If no files are listed on the command line, it is instead assumed that `STDIN` is intended. So for example,

```
while (<>) {
print "more.... ";
}
```

keeps printing `more....` as long as something other than Ctrl+D appears on standard input.

> **Note**
>
> Perl 5 allows array elements to be references to any data type. This makes it possible to build arbitrary data structures of the kind used in C and other high-level languages, but with all the power of Perl; you can, for example, have an array of associative arrays.

Flow Control

The examples we've seen so far have been quite simple, with little or no logical structure beyond a linear sequence of steps. We managed to sneak in the occasional `while` and `foreach`. Perl has all of the flow control mechanisms you'd expect to find in a high-level language, and this section takes you through the basics of each.

Logical Operators

Let's start with two operators that are used like glue holding Perl programs together: the `||` (or) and `&&` (and) operators. They take two operands and return either True or False depending on the operands:

```
$Weekend = $Saturday || $Sunday;
```

If either `$Saturday` or `$Sunday` is true, then `$Weekend` is true.

```
$Solvent = ($income > 3) && ($debts < 10);
```

`$Solvent` is true only if `$income` is greater than 3 and `$debts` is less than 10.

Now consider the logic of evaluating one of these expressions. It isn't always necessary to evaluate both operands of either a `&&` or a `||` operator. In the first example, if `$Saturday` is true, then we know `$Weekend` is true, regardless of whether `$Sunday` is also true.

This means that having evaluated the lefthand side of an `||` expression as true, the righthand side will not be evaluated. Combine this with Perl's easy way with data types, and you can say things like the following:

```
$value > 10 || print "Oops, low value $value ...\n";
```

If `$value` is greater than 10, the righthand side of the expression is never evaluated, so nothing is printed. If `$value` is not greater than 10, Perl needs to evaluate the righthand side to decide whether the expression as a whole is True or False. That means it evaluates the `print` statement, printing the message like

```
Oops, low value 6...
```

Okay, it's a trick, but it's a very useful one.

Something analogous applies to the `&&` operator. In this case, if the lefthand side of an expression is False, then the expression as a whole is false and so Perl will not evaluate the righthand side. This can be used to produce the same kind of effect as our `||` trick but with the opposite sense:

```
$value > 10 && print "OK, value is high enough...\n";
```

As with most Perl constructs, the real power of these tricks comes when you apply a little creative thinking. Remember that the left- and righthand sides of these expressions can be any Perl expression; think of them as conjunctions in a sentence rather than as logical operators and you'll get a better feel for how to use them. Expressions such as

```
$length <= 80 ¦¦ die "Line too long.\n";
$errorlevel > 3 && warn "Hmmm, strange error level ($errorlevel)...\n";
open ( LOGFILE, ">install.log") ¦¦ &bust("Log file");
```

give a little of the flavor of creative Perl.

The &bust in that last line is a subroutine call, by the way. Refer to the "Subroutines" section later in this chapter for more information.

Conditional Expressions

The basic kind of flow control is a simple branch: A statement is either executed or not depending on whether a logical expression is True or False. This can be done by following the statement with a modifier and a logical expression:

```
open ( INFILE, "./missing.txt") if $missing;
```

The execution of the statement is contingent upon both the evaluation of the expression and the sense of the operator.

The expression evaluates as either True or False and can contain any of the relational operators listed in Table 7.5, although it doesn't have to. Examples of valid expressions are

```
$full
$a == $b
<STDIN>
```

Table 7.5 Perl's Relational Operators

Operator	Numeric Context	String Context
Equality	==	eq
Inequality	!=	ne
Inequality with signed result	<=>	cmp
Greater than	>	gt
Greater than or equal to	>=	ge
Less than	<	lt
Less than or equal to	<=	le

Note

What exactly does "less than" mean when we're comparing strings? It means "lexically less than." If $left comes before $right when the two are sorted alphabetically, $left is less than $right.

There are four modifiers, each of which behaves the way you might expect from the corresponding English word:

- `if`—The statement executes if the logical expression is True and does not execute otherwise. Examples:

```
$max = 100 if $min < 100;
print "Empty!\n" if !$full;
```

- `unless`—The statement does not execute if the logical expression is True and executes otherwise. Examples:

```
open (ERRLOG, "test.log") unless $NoLog;
print "Success" unless $error>2;
```

- `while`—The statement executes repeatedly until the logical expression is False. Examples:

```
$total -= $decrement while $total > $decrement;
$n=1000;   "print $n\n" while $n— > 0;
```

- `until`—The statement executes repeatedly until the logical expression is True. Examples:

```
$total += $value[$count++] until $total > $limit;
print RESULTS "Next value: $value[$n++]" until $value[$n] = -1;
```

Note that the logical expression is evaluated once only in the case of `if` and `unless` but multiple times in the case of `while` and `until`. In other words, the first two are simple conditionals, while the last two are loop constructs.

Compound Statements

The syntax changes when we want to make the execution of multiple statements contingent on the evaluation of a logical expression. The modifier comes at the start of a line, followed by the logical expression in parentheses, followed by the conditional statements contained in braces. Note that the parentheses around the logical expression are required, unlike with the single statement branching described in the previous section. For example,

```
if ( ( $total += $value ) > $limit )  {
   print LOGFILE "Maximum limit $limit exceeded.",
   " Offending value was $value.\n";
close (LOGFILE);
   die "Too many! Check the log file for details.\n";
   }
```

This is somewhat similar to C's `if` syntax, except that the braces around the conditional statement block are required rather than optional.

The `if` statement is capable of a little more complexity, with `else` and `elsif` operators:

```
if ( !open( LOGFILE, "install.log") )   {
   close ( INFILE );
   die "Unable to open log file!\n";
   }
```

```
elseif ( !open( CFGFILE, ">system.cfg") )  {
    print LOGFILE "Error during install:",
    " Unable to open config file for writing.\n";
close ( LOGFILE );
    die "Unable to open config file for writing!\n";
    }
else  {
    print CFGFILE "Your settings go here!\n";
    }
```

Loops

The loop modifiers (while, until, for, and foreach) are used with compound statements in much the same way:

```
until ( $total >= 50 )  {
    print "Enter a value: ";
    $value = scalar (<STDIN>);
    $total += $value;
    print "Current total is $total\n";
    }
print "Enough!\n";
```

The while and until statements were described in the earlier "Conditional Expressions" section. The for statement resembles the one in C: It is followed by an initial value, a termination condition, and an iteration expression, all enclosed in parentheses and separated by semicolons:

```
for ( $count = 0; $count < 100; $count++ )  {
    print "Something";
    }
```

The foreach operator is special. It iterates over the contents of an array and executes the statements in a statement block for each element of the array. A simple example is the following:

```
@numbers = ("one", "two", "three", "four");
foreach $num ( @numbers )   {
    print "Number $num...\n";
    }
```

The variable $num first takes on the value one, then two, and so on. That example looks fairly trivial, but the real power of this operator lies in the fact that it can operate on any array:

```
foreach $arg ( @ARGV )    {
    print "Argument: \"$arg\".\n";
    }

foreach $namekey ( sort keys %surnames )  {
    print REPORT "Surname: $value{$namekey}.\n",
                 "Address: $address{$namekey}.\n";
    }
```

Labels

Labels may be used with the `next`, `last`, and `redo` statements to provide more control over program flow through loops. A label consists of any word, usually in uppercase, followed by a colon. The label appears just before the loop operator (`while`, `for`, or `foreach`) and can be used as an anchor for jumping to from within the block:

```
RECORD:  while ( <INFILE> )  {
    $even = !$even;
    next RECORD if $even;
    print;
    }
```

That code snippet prints all the odd-numbered records in `INFILE`.

The three label control statements are

- `next`—Jumps to the next iteration of the loop marked by the label or to the inner-most enclosing loop if no label is specified.

- `last`—Immediately breaks out of the loop marked by the label or out of the inner-most enclosing loop if no label is specified.

- `redo`—Jumps back to the loop marked by the specified label or to the innermost enclosing loop if no label is specified. This causes the loop to execute again with the same iterator value.

Subroutines

The basic subunit of code in Perl is a subroutine. This is similar to a function in C and a procedure or a function in Pascal. A subroutine may be called with various parameters and returns a value. Effectively, the subroutine groups together a sequence of statements so that they can be re-used.

The Simplest Form of Subroutine. Subroutines can be declared anywhere in a program. If more than one subroutine with the same name is declared each new version replaces the older ones, so that only the last one is effective. It is possible to declare subroutines within an `eval()` expression, these will not actually be declared until the runtime execution reaches the `eval()` statement.

Subroutines are declared using the following syntax:

```
sub subroutine-name {
            statements
}
```

The simplest form of subroutine is one that does not return any value and does not access any external values. The subroutine is called by prefixing the name with the &

character. (There are other ways of calling subroutines, which are explained in more
detail later.) An example of a program using the simplest form of subroutine illustrates
this:

```
#!/usr/bin/perl -w
# Example of subroutine which does not use
# external values and does not return a value
&egsub1; # Call the subroutine once
&egsub1; # Call the subroutine a second time
sub egsub1 {
    print "This subroutine simply prints this line.\n";
}
```

Tip

While it is possible to refer from a subroutine to any global variable directly, it is normally considered bad programming practice. Reference to global variables from subroutines makes it more difficult to re-use the subroutine code. It is best to make any such references to external values explicit by passing explicit parameters to the subroutine as described in the following section. Similarly it is best to avoid programming subroutines that directly change the values of global variables because doing so can lead to unpredictable side-effects if the subroutine is re-used in a different program. Use explicit return values or explicit parameters passed by reference as described in following section.

Returning Values from Subroutines. Subroutines can also return values, thus acting as functions. The return value is the value of the last statement executed. This can be a scalar or an array value.

Caution

Take care not to add seemingly innocuous statements near the end of a subroutine. A print statement returns 1, for example, so a subroutine that prints just before it returns will always return 1.

It is possible to test whether the calling context requires an array or a scalar value using the wantarray construct, thus returning different values depending on the required context. For example,

```
wantarray ? (a, b, c) : 0;
```

as the last line of a subroutine returns the array (a, b, c) in an array context, and the scalar value 0 in a scalar context.

```
#!/usr/bin/perl -w
# Example of subrotine which does not use
# external values but does return a value
# Call the subroutine once, returning a scalar value
$scalar-return = &egsub2;
print "Scalar return value: $scalar-return.\n";
# Call the subroutine a second time, returning an array value
@array-return = &egsub2;
```

```
print "Array return value:", @array-return, ".\n";
sub egsub2 {
    print "This subroutine prints this line and returns a value.\n";
    wantarray ? (a, b, c) : 0;
}
```

It is possible to return from a subroutine before the last statement by using the `return()` function. The argument to the `return()` function is the returned value in this case. This is illustrated in the following example, which is not a very efficient way to do the test but illustrates the point:

```
#!/usr/bin/perl -w
# Example of subrotine which does not use
# external values but does return a value using "return"
$returnval = &egsub3; # Call the subroutine once
print "The current time is $returnval.\n";
sub egsub3 {
    print "This subroutine prints this line and returns a value.\n";
    local($sec, $min, $hour, @rest) =
        gmtime(time);
    ($min == 0) && ($hour == 12) && (return "noon");
    if ($hour > 12)
        return "after noon";
    else
        return "before noon";
}
```

Note that it is usual to make any variables used within a subroutine `local()` to the enclosing block. This means that they will not interfere with any variables that have the same name in the calling program. In Perl 5, these may be made lexically local rather than dynamically local, using `my()` instead of `local()` (this is discussed in more detail later).

When returning multiple arrays, the result is flattened into one list so that, effectively, only one array is returned. So in the following example all the return values are in @return-a1 and the send array @return-a2 is empty.

```
#!/usr/bin/perl -w
# Example of subrotine which does not use
# external values returning an array
 (@return-a1, @return-a2) = &egsub4; # Call the subroutine once
print "Return array a1",@return-a1,
    " Return array a2 ",@return-a2, ".\n";
sub egsub4 {
    print "This subroutine returns a1 and a2.\n";
    local(@a1) = (a, b, c);
    local(@a2) = (d, e, f);
    return(@a1,@a2);
}
```

In Perl 4, this problem can be avoided by passing the arrays by reference using a `typeglob` (see the following section). In Perl 5, you can do this and also manipulate any variable by reference directly (see the following section).

Passing Values to Subroutines. The next important aspect of subroutines, is that the call can pass values to the subroutine. The call simply lists the variables to be passed, and these are passed in the list @_ to the subroutine. These are known as the parameters or the arguments. It is customary to assign each value a name at the start of the subroutine so that it is clear what is going on. Manipulation of these copies of the arguments is equivalent to passing arguments by value (that is, their values may be altered but this does not alter the value of the variable in the calling program).

```
#!/usr/bin/perl -w
# Example of subrotine is passed external values by value
$returnval = &egsub5(45,3); # Call the subroutine once
print "The (45+1) * (3+1) is $returnval.\n";
$x = 45;
$y = 3;
$returnval = &egsub5($x,$y);
print "The ($x+1) * ($y+1) is $returnval.\n";
print "Note that \$x still is $x, and \$y still is $y.\n";
sub egsub5 { # Access $x and $y by value
    local($x, $y) = @_;
    return ($x++ * $y++);
}
```

To pass scalar values by reference, rather than by value, the elements in @_ can be accessed directly. This will change their values in the calling program. In such a case, the argument must be a variable rather than a literal value, as literal values cannot be altered.

```
#!/usr/bin/perl -w
# Example of subrotine is passed external values by reference
$x = 45;
$y = 3;
print "The ($x+1) * ($y+1) ";
$returnval = &egsub6($x,$y);
print "is $returnval.\n";
print "Note that \$x now is $x, and \$y now is $y.\n";
sub egsub6 { # Access $x and $y by reference
    return ($_[0]++ * $_[0]++);
}
```

Array values can be passed by reference in the same way. However several restrictions apply. First, as with returned array values, the @_ list is one single flat array, so passing multiple arrays this way is tricky. Also, although individual elements may be altered in the subroutine using this method, the size of the array cannot be altered within the subroutine (so push() and pop() cannot be used).

Therefore, another method has been provided to facilitate the passing of arrays by reference. This method is known as *typeglobbing* and works with Perl 4 or Perl 5. The principle is that the subroutine declares that one or more of its parameters are typeglobbed, which means that all the references to that identifier in the scope of the subroutine are taken to refer to the equivalent identifier in the namespace of the calling program. The syntax for this declaration is to prefix the identifier with an asterisk, rather than an @ sign, this `*array1` typeglobs `@array1`. In fact, typeglobbing links all forms of the identifier so the `*array1` typeglobs `@array1`, `%array1`, and `$array1` (any reference to any of these in the local subroutine actually refers to the equivalent variable in the calling program's namespace). It only makes sense to use this construct within a `local()` list, effectively creating a local alias for a set of global variables. So the previous example becomes the following:

```
#!/usr/bin/perl -w
# Example of subrotine using arrays passed by reference (type globbing)
&egsub7(@a1,@a2); # Call the subroutine once
print "Modified array a1",@a1," Modified array a2 ",@a2, ".\n";
sub egsub7 {
    local(*a1,*a2) = @_;
    print "This subroutine modifies a1 and a2.\n";
    @a1 = (a, b, c);
    @a2 = (d, e, f);
}
```

In Perl 4, this is the only way to use references to variables, rather than variables themselves. In Perl 5, there is also a generalized method for dealing with references. Although this method looks more awkward in its syntax, because of the abundance of underscores, it is actually more precise in its meaning. Typeglobbing automatically aliases the scalar, the array, and the hashed array form of an identifier, even if only the array name is required. With Perl 5 references this distinction can be made explicit; only the array form of the identifier is referenced.

```
#!/usr/bin/perl -w
# Example of subroutine using arrays passed
# by reference (Perl 5 references)
&egsub7(\@a1,\@a2); # Call the subroutine once
print "Modified array a1",@a1," Modified array a2 ",@a2, ".\n";
sub egsub7 {
    local($a1ref,$a2ref) = @_;
    print "This subroutine modifies a1 and a2.\n";
    @$a1ref = (a, b, c);
    @$a2ref = (d, e, f);
}
```

Subroutine Recursion. One the most powerful features of subroutines is their ability to call themselves. There are many problems that can be solved by repeated application of the same procedure. However, care must be taken to set up a termination condition where the recursion stops and the execution can unravel itself. Typical examples of this approach are found when processing lists: Process the head item and then process the tail; if the tail is empty do not recurse. Another neat example is the calculation of a factorial value:

```
#!/usr/bin/perl -w
#
# Example factorial using recursion

for ($x=1; $x<100; $x++) {
```

```
        print "Factorial $x is ",&factorial($x), "\n";
}

sub factorial {
        local($x) = @_;
        if ($x == 1) {
                return 1;
        }
        else {
                return ($x*($x-1) + &factorial($x-1));
        }
}
```

Issues of Scope with *my()* and *local().* Issues of scope are very important with relation to subroutines. In particular all variables inside subroutines should be made lexical local variables (using `my()`) or dynamic local variables (using `local()`). In Perl 4, the only choice is `local()` because `my()` was only introduced in Perl 5.

Variables declared using the `my()` construct are considered to be lexical local variables. They are not entered in the symbol table for the current package. Therefore, they are totally hidden from all contexts other than the local block within which they are declared. Even subroutines called from the current block cannot access lexical local variables in that block. Lexical local variables must begin with an alphanumeric character or an underscore.

Variables declared using the `local()` construct are considered to be dynamic local variables. The value is local to the current block and any calls from that block. It is possible to localize special variables as dynamic local variables, but these cannot be made into lexical local variables. These two differences from lexical local variables show the two cases in Perl 5 where it is still advisable to use `local()` rather than `my()`:

■ Use `local()` if you want the value of the local variables to be visible to subroutines.

■ Use `local()` if you are localizing special variables.

Pattern Matching

We'll finish this overview of Perl with a look at Perl's pattern matching capabilities. The ability to match and replace patterns is vital to any scripting language that claims to be capable of useful text manipulation. By this stage, you probably won't be surprised to read that Perl matches pattern better than any other general purpose language. Perl 4's pattern matching was excellent, but Perl 5 has introduced some significant improvements, including the capability to match even more arbitrary strings than before.

The basic pattern matching operations we'll be looking at are

■ Matching—Where we want to know of a particular string matches a pattern.

■ Substitution—Where we want to replace portions of a string based on a pattern.

The patterns referred to here are more properly known as *regular expressions*, and we'll start by looking at them.

Regular Expressions

A regular expression is a set of rules describing a generalized string. If the characters that make up a particular string conform to the rules of a particular regular expression, then the regular expression is said to match that string.

A few concrete examples usually helps after an overblown definition like that. The regular expression b. will match the strings `bovine`, `above`, `Bobby`, and `Bob Jones` but not the strings `Bell`, `b`, or `Bob`. That's because the expression insists that the letter b must be in the string and it must be followed immediately by another character.

The regular expression b+, on the other hand, requires the lowercase letter b at least once. This matches `b` and `Bob` in addition to the example matches for b.. The regular expression b* requires zero or more bs, so it will match any string. That is fairly useless, but it makes more sense as part of a larger regular expression; for example, Bob*y matches `Boy`, `Boby`, and `Bobby` but not `Boboby`.

Assertions. There are a number of so-called *assertions* that are used to anchor parts of the patter to word or string boundaries. The ^ assertion matches the start of a string, so the regular expression ^fool matches `fool` and `foolhardy` but not `tomfoolery` or `April fool`. The assertions are listed in Table 7.6.

Table 7.6	Perl's Regular Expression Assertions			
Assertion	**Matches**	**Example**	**Matches**	**Doesn't Match**
^	Start of string	`^fool`	`foolish`	`tomfoolery`
$	End of string	`fool$`	`April fool`	`foolish`
\b	Word boundary	`be\bside`	`be side`	`beside`
\B	Non-word boundary	`be\Bside`	`beside`	`be side`

Atoms. The . we saw in b. is an example of a regular expression *atom*. Atoms are, as the name suggests, the fundamental building blocks of a regular expression. A full list appears in Table 7.7.

Table 7.7	Perl's Regular Expression Atoms			
Atom	**Matches**	**Example**	**Matches**	**Doesn't Match**
.	Any character except newline	`b.b`	`bob`	`bb`
List of characters in square brackets	Any one of those characters	`^[Bb]`	`Bob, bob`	`Rbob`
Regular expression in parentheses	Anything that regular expression matches	`^a(b.b)c$`	`abobc`	`abbc`

Quantifiers. A *quantifier* is a modifier for an atom. It can be used to specify that a particular atom must appear at least once, for example, as in b+. The atom quantifiers are listed in Table 7.8.

Table 7.8   Perl's Regular Expression Atom Quantifiers

Quantifier	Matches	Example	Matches	Doesn't Match
*	Zero or more instances of the atom	ab*c	ac, abc	abb
+	One or more instances of the atom	ab*c	abc	ac
?	Zero or one instances of the atom	ab?c	ac, abc	abbc
{n}	n instances of the atom	ab{2}c	abbc	abbbc
{n,}	At least n instances of the atom	ab{2,}c	abbc, abbbc	abc
{nm}	At least n, at most m instances of the atom	ab{2,3}c	abbc	abbbbc

Special Characters. There are a number of special characters denoted by the backslash; \n being especially familiar to C programmers perhaps. Table 7.9 lists the special characters.

Table 7.9   Perl Regular Expression's Special Characters

Symbol	Matches	Example	Matches	Doesn't Match
\d	Any digit	b\dd	b4d	bad
\D	Non-digit	b\Dd	bdd	b4d
\n	Newline			
\r	Carriage return			
\t	Tab			
\f	Formfeed			
\s	Whitespace character			
\S	Non-whitespace character			
\w	Alphanumeric character	a\wb	a2b	a^b
\W	Non-alphanumeric character	a\Wb	aa^b	aabb

Backslashed Tokens. It is essential that regular expressions are able to use all characters so that all possible strings that occur in the real word can be matched. With so many characters having special meanings, a mechanism is therefore required that allows us to represent any arbitrary character in a regular expression.

This is done using a backslash followed by a numeric quantity. This quantity can take on any of the following formats:

- **Single or double digit**—Matched quantities after a match. These are called *backreferences* and will be explained in the later "Matching" section.

- **Two or three digit octal number**—The character with that number as character code, unless it's possible to interpret it as a backreference.

- **x followed by two hexadecimal digits**—The character with that number as its character code. For example, \x3e is >.

- **c followed by a single character**—This is the control character. For example, \cG matches Ctrl+G.

- **Any other character**—This is the character itself. For example, \& matches the & character.

Matching

Let's start putting all of that together with some real pattern matching. The match operator normally consists of two forward slashes with a regular expression in between, and it normally operates on the contents of the $_ variable. So if $_ is serendipity, then /^ser/, /end/ and /^s.*y$/ are all True.

Matching on $_. The $_ operator is special; it is described in full in Chapter 8, "Perl Special Variables." In many ways, it is the default container for data being read in by Perl; the <> operator, for example, gets the next line from STDIN and stores it in $_. So the following code snippet lets you type lines of text and tells you when your line matches one of the regular expressions:

```
$prompt = "Enter some text or press Ctrl-Z to stop: ";
print $prompt;
while (<>)  {
   /^[aA]/ && print "Starts with a or A.  ";
   /[0-9]$/ && print "Ends with a digit.  ";
   /perl/ && print "You said it!  ";
   print $prompt;
   }
```

Bound Matches. Matching doesn't always have to operate on $_, although this default behavior is quite convenient. There is a special operator, =~, that evaluates to either True or False depending on whether its first operand matches on its second operand. For example, $filename =~ /dat$/ is true if $filename matches on /dat$/. This can be used in conditionals in the usual way:

```
$filename =~ /dat$/ && die "Can't use .dat files.\n";
```

There is a corresponding operator with the opposite sense, !~. This is True if the first operator does not match on the second:

```
$ENV{'PATH'} !~ /perl/ && warn "Not sure if perl is in your path...";
```

Alternate Delimiters. The match operator can use other characters instead of //; a useful point if you're trying to match a complex expression involving forward slashes. A more general form of the match operator than // is m//. If you use the leading m here, then any character may be used to delimit the regular expression. For example,

```
$installpath =~ m!^/usr/local!
    || warn "The path you have chosen is odd.\n";
```

Match Options. A number of optional switches may be applied to the match operator (either the // or m// forms) to alter its behavior. These options are listed in Table 7.10.

Table 7.10   Perl Match Operator's Optional Switches

Switch	Meaning
g	Perform global matching
i	Case-insensitive matching
o	Evaluate the regular expression once only

The g switch continues matching even after the first match has been found. This is useful when using backreferences to examine the matched portions of a string, as described in the later "Backreferences" section.

The o switch is used inside loops where a lot of pattern matching is taking place. It tells Perl that the regular expression (the match operator's operand) is to be evaluated once only. This can improve efficiency in cases where the regular expression is fixed for all iterations of the loop that contains it.

Backreferences. As we mentioned earlier in the "Backslashed Tokens" section, pattern matching produces quantities known as backreferences. These are the parts of your string where the match succeeded. You need to tell Perl to store them by surrounding the relevant parts of your regular expression with parentheses, and they may be referred to after the match as \1, \2, and so on. In this example, we check if the user has typed three consecutive four letter words:

```
while (<>)  {
    /\b(\S{4})\s(\S{4})\s(\S{4})\b/
        && print "Gosh, you said $1 $2 $3!\n";
}
```

The first four-letter word lies between a word boundary (\b) and some white space (\s) and consists of four non-whitespace characters (\S). If matched, the matching substring is stored in the special variable \1 and the search continues. Once the search is complete, the backreferences may be referred to as $1, $2, and so on.

What if you don't know in advance how many matches to expect? Perform the match in an array context, and Perl returns the matches in an array. Consider this example:

```
@hits = ("Yon Yonson, Wisconsin" =~ /(\won)/g);
print "Matched on ", join(', ', @hits), ".\n";
```

Let's start at the righthand side and work back. The regular expression (\won) means that we match any alphanumeric character followed by on and store all three characters. The g option after the // operator means that we want to do this for the entire string, even after we've found a match. The =~ operator means that we carry out this operation on a given string, Yon Yonson, Wisconsin; and finally, the whole thing is evaluated in an array context, so Perl returns the array of matches and we store it in the @hits array. The output from this example is

```
Matched on yon, Yon, son, con.
```

Substitution

Once you get the hang of pattern matching, substitutions are quite straightforward and very powerful. The substitution operator is s/// that resembles the match operator but has three rather than two slashes. As with the match operator, any other character may be substituted for forward slashes, and the optional i, g, and o switches may be used.

The pattern to be replaced goes between the first and second delimiters, and the replacement pattern goes between the second and third. To take a simple example,

```
$house = "henhouse";
$house =~ s/hen/dog/;
```

change $house from henhouse to doghouse. Note that it isn't possible to use the =~ operation with a literal string in the way we did when matching; that's because you can't modify a literal constant. Instead, store the string in a variable and modify that.

II

Perl

Chapter 8

Perl Special Variables

This section looks in detail at the special variables used in Perl. Understanding these variables is crucial to programming effectively in Perl. Some of the variables are essential for nearly all Perl programs, while others are merely useful shortcuts that can avoid the need to run external programs that extract information from the system.

Each variable may have three possible names:

- Long name (or English name)
- Intermediate name
- Short name

Most existing Perl programs use only the short name form. This is unfortunate, as the short name is usually a cryptic symbol. The use of these symbols in Perl programs may be daunting at first, especially in complex expressions comprising multiple variables. However, with the aid of this chapter, it soon becomes easy to identify their meaning and thus understand the programs.

The long name was introduced in Perl 5. This chapter lists all the special variables of this *English* name, in alphabetical order. In Perl 4, you must use the short name. In Perl 5, you can use any of the name forms, but if you want to use the long English name, you must include the following command:

```
Use English;
```

This command enables the long names in the Perl 5 program.

Sometimes (in particular where the same variable also exists in awk, the UNIX report processor) an intermediate name is also allowed. Again this requires the use of the English module and so is not available in Perl 4. This means that those who are used to the awk conventions can use them if they wish.

This chapter categorizes special variables in several ways to make it easier for you to use the list as a reference source. The most important of these categories is Scope, which can have the following values:

- **Always global**   These variables are global and have an unambiguous context (they need not be made local in a subroutine).

- **Localize**   These variables are global but may need to be made local in subroutines if the value is being changed (especially to prevent unplanned subroutine side effects).

- **Local**   These variables are always local and do not need to be made local explicitly.

The other important special-variable category used in this chapter is File Handle Call. Special variables that implicitly refer to the current active file handle can be explicitly bound to any existing file handle. This facility must be activated by the following call:

```
use FileHandle;
```

This enables calls of the forms

```
FILEHANDLE->method(EXPR)
method FILEHANDLE EXPR
```

The relevant *method* name usually is the full long name of the special variable. The optional EXPR is an expression for changing the current value of the file handle, as well as referring to another file handle for the purposes of the special-variable reference. This syntax may seem confusing at first, but when used consistently, it can make Perl programs with formatting much more readable.

Both the long English names and the use of file handles in references to formats are new features in Perl 5. If you are using Perl 4, you must use the short names and allow format operations to take place in relation to the current active file handle, which you can change by using the `select()` function.

$<l<digit>>

Compliance

Syntax

```
Short Name:        $1, $2, ... $<N>
Scope:             local (read-only)
```

Definition

These variables are used to refer back to pattern matches. In any pattern to be matched, sets of parentheses are used to mark subpatterns. These subpatterns are numbered from left to right. After a match has been made, each subpattern match is referenced by these variables, up to and including the number of subpatterns that are actually specified. $1 is the first subpattern, $2 is the second, and so on, up to and including $<N>, the Nth subpattern specified.

All subpatterns after the last one ($<N+1>, for example), are equal to undef.

Example

```
$_ = "AlphaBetaGamma";
/^(Alpha)(.*)(Gamma)$/;
print "$1 then $2 then $3\n";
```

Tip

If you have alternative patterns and do not know which one may have matched, try using $LAST_PAREN_MATCH instead.

$[

Compliance

Syntax

Short Name:	$[
Scope:	localize

Definition

This variable, which is usually set to a value of 0, represents the index of the first element in any array. Programmers who are used to using 1 as the index of the first element of an array could change the value of this variable to suit their preference.

Example

```
$[ = 1;
$_ = "AlphaBetaGamma";
$tmp = index($_,"Beta");
print "Beta located at: $tmp\n";
$[ = 0;
$_ = "AlphaBetaGamma";
$tmp = index($_,"Beta");
print "Beta located at: $tmp\n";
```

II

Perl

$ACCUMULATOR

Compliance

Syntax

```
Short Name:          $^A
Scope:               always global
```

Definition

This variable allows direct access to the line of output built up with the Perl formatting commands. Normally, this access is not necessary, but it is possible.

Example

```
$tmp = formline<<'FINISH', Alpha, Beta, Gamma;
@<<<<<<<<<  @!||||||||||||  @<<<<<<<<
FINISH
print "Accumulator now contains:\n $^A\n";
$^A = "";
```

$ARG

Compliance

Syntax

```
Short Name:          $_
Scope:               localize
```

Definition

This variable is the default pattern space. When reading a file, $ARG usually takes on the value of each line in turn. You can assign a value to $ARG directly. Many functions and operators take this variable as the default upon which to operate, so you can make the code more concise by using $ARG.

Example

```
$_ = "\$_ is the default for many operations including print().\n";
print;
```

$ARGV

Compliance

Syntax

```
Short Name:        $ARGV
Scope:             always global
```

Definition

When processing an input file, this variable provides access to the name of this file.

Example

```
print("Assuming this script has been called with an argument as a i/p file:_
while (<>){
    print "$ARGV\n";
    };
```

$BASETIME

Compliance

Syntax

```
Short Name:        $^T
Scope:             localize
```

Definition

This variable is the time when the Perl program was started, as measured in basic time units (seconds since the start of 1970).

Example

```
$nicetime = localtime($^T);
print "This program started at $^T (i.e. $nicetime).\n";
```

$CHILD_ERROR

Compliance

Syntax

```
Short Name:        $?
Scope:             localize
```

Definition

If a Perl script spawns child processes, you can examine their error codes by using this variable.

Example

```
'ls -lgd /vir';
print "Child Process error was: $?\n";
```

 ◄◄ See the $OS_ERROR variable for system error messages, p. 220

$DEBUGGING

Compliance

Syntax

```
Short Name:        $^D
Scope:             localize
```

Definition

Perl can be run in debugging mode. This variable allows the value of this flag to be accessed and altered.

> **Note**
>
> Debugging is only allowed if the version of Perl you are using was compiled with DEBUGGING specifically set.

Example

```
print "The debug flags are: $^D\n";
```

$EFFECTIVE_GROUP_ID

Compliance

Syntax

```
Short Name:          $)
Intermediate Name:   $EGID
Scope:               localize
```

Definition

In systems that support users and groups, as well as setting new users and groups within a process, Perl can access both the original and the effective user and group information. The effective group variable provides access to a list of numbers that represent the *effective group identifiers* (*GIDs*).

Example

```
print("Effective Group ID is a list of GIDs: $)\n");
```

$EFFECTIVE_USER_ID

Compliance

Syntax

```
Short Name:          $>
Intermediate Name:   $EUID
Scope:               localize
```

Definition

In systems that support users and groups, as well as setting new users and groups within a process, Perl can access both the original and the effective user and group information. The effective user variable provides access to a single number that represents the *effective user identifier* (*UID*).

Example

```
print("Effective User ID is one UID: $>\n");
```

II

Perl

$EVAL_ERROR

Compliance

Syntax

```
Short Name:      $@
Scope:           localize
```

Definition

Perl allows explicit calls to the eval() function to evaluate Perl syntax with a Perl script. This variable allows access to the returned error after such an operation. The error is a string that contains the relevant error message.

Example

```
print "Passing eval a malformed Perl expression:\n";
eval 'print "Hello';
print "Error: $@\n";
```

$EXECUTABLE_NAME

Compliance

Syntax

```
Short Name:      $^X
Scope:           localize
```

Definition

This variable provides access to the name of the Perl executable used by the script.

Example

```
print "Executable name of Perl is: $^X\n";
```

$FORMAT_FORMFEED

Compliance

Syntax

```
Short Name:          $^L
Scope:               always global
File Handle Call:    format_formfeed FILEHANDLE EXPR
```

Definition

When you use the Perl formatting commands, you can specify formats to manipulate centering and other formatting of the text. One additional option is to specify the exact code to be inserted between pages of output in the file. The default value is a form-feed character (\f), but this can be changed.

Example

```
if ($^L = '\f')
{
    print "The formfeed character is the default break between pages.\n";
}
```

$FORMAT_LINES_LEFT

Compliance

Syntax

```
Short Name:          $-
Scope:               always global
File Handle Call:    format_lines_left FILEHANDLE EXPR
```

Definition

When you use the Perl formatting commands, this counter, which exists for each file handle with an associated format, is decremented every time a line is output until it reaches zero, when a new page is generated. You can manually set this variable to zero to force a page break in the output.

Example

```
format EG_FORMAT =
@<<<<<<<<<<  @!!!!!!!!!!!!!! @>>>>>>>>> ^!!!!!!!!!!!
$one,       $two,           $three     $fitme
.
open(EG_FORMAT,">-");
select(EG_FORMAT);
$one = 'Left';
$two = 'Center';
$three = 'Right';
$fitme= "";
write;
$one = $-;
$two = $-;
$three = $-;
write;
$one = $-;
$two = $-;
$three = $-;
write;
select(STDOUT);
```

$FORMAT_LINES_PER_PAGE

Compliance

Syntax

```
Short Name:         $=
Scope:              always global
File Handle Call:   format_lines_per_page FILEHANDLE EXPR
```

Definition

Each format file handle has an associated number of lines per page, which you can access and change by using this variable.

Example

```
select (EG_FORMAT);
$one = 'Left';
$two = 'Center';
$three = 'Right';
$fitme= "";
write;
$one = $=;
$two = $=;
$three = $=;
write;
select(STDOUT);
```

$FORMAT_LINE_BREAK_CHARACTERS

Compliance

Syntax

```
Short Name:          $:
Scope:               localize
File Handle Call:    format_line_break_characters FILEHANDLE EXPR
```

Definition

When you are outputting a value to a formatted area by using the following format code

```
^!!!!!!!!!!!!!!!
```

(or the other multiple-line formats), the line-break character determines how strings are split into lines to fit into the formatted space. By default, the legal break characters are space, hyphen, and new line.

Example

```
select(EG_FORMAT);
$: = ' \n-';
$one = 1;
$two = 2;
$three = 3;
$fitme= "One-One-One-One-One-One";
write;
write;
write;
select(STDOUT);
```

$FORMAT_NAME

Compliance

Syntax

```
Short Name:          $~
Scope:               always global
File Handle Call:    format_name FILEHANDLE EXPR
```

Definition

Each format has a name, which may also be the name of the file handle. You can access the name directly through this variable.

Example
```
select(EG_FORMAT);
$one = $~;
$two = $~;
$three = $~;
write;
select(STDOUT);
```

$FORMAT_PAGE_NUMBER

Compliance

Syntax

Short Name:	$%
Scope:	always global
File Handle Call:	format_page_number FILEHANDLE EXPR

Definition

Because each format can produce multiple pages of output, this counter simply counts them.

Example
```
select(EG_FORMAT);
$one = $%;
$two = $%;
$three = $%;
write;
select(STDOUT);
```

$FORMAT_TOP_NAME

Compliance

Syntax

Short Name:	$^
Scope:	always global
File Handle Call:	format_top_name FILEHANDLE EXPR

Definition

Each format can have an associated format that is reproduced each time a new page is generated. (No equivalent automatic page footer exists.) By default, these are given the same name as the base format with a TOP suffix, although any name can be set.

Example

```
format EG_TOP =
            [Sample Page Header]
To the left  In the center To the right
-----------------------------------
.
open(EG_FORMAT,">-");
select(EG_FORMAT);
$- = 0;
$^ = EG_TOP;
$one = '111';
$two = '222';
$three = '333';
$fitme= "";
write;
write;
write;
select(STDOUT);
```

$INPLACE_EDIT

Compliance

Syntax

```
Short Name:        $^I
Scope:             localize
```

Definition

Perl is often used to edit files, and sometimes, the input file is also the output file (the result replaces the original). In this case, you can specify (with command-line options) the suffix to be used for the temporary file created while the edits are in progress. You can set or simply access this value from within the script itself by using this variable.

Example

```
$^I=bak;
print "Tmp file extension when editing in place... $^I\n";
```

$INPUT_LINE_NUMBER

Compliance

Syntax

```
Short Name:            $.
Intermediate Name:     $NR
Scope:                 localize (read-only)
File Handle Call:      input_line_number FILEHANDLE EXPR
```

Definition

This variable counts the number of lines of input from a file and is reset when the file is closed. The variable counts lines cumulatively across all input files read with the <> construct because these are not closed explicitly.

Example

```
print "The last file read had $. lines\n";
```

$INPUT_RECORD_SEPARATOR

Compliance

Syntax

```
Short Name:            $/
Intermediate Name:     $RS
Scope:                 localize
File Handle Call:      input_record_separator FILEHANDLE EXPR
```

Definition

By default, an input file is split into records, each of which comprises one line. The input-record separator is a newline character. This variable can be set to have no value (in which case entire input files are read in at the same time) or to have other values, as required.

Example

```
undef $/;
 open(INFILE,"infile.tst");
 $buffer = <INFILE>;
 print "$buffer\n";
```

$LAST_PAREN_MATCH

Compliance

Syntax

```
Short Name:        $+
Scope:             local
```

Definition

This variable returns the value of the last pattern marked with parentheses. In most contexts, you could simply use $1, $2, and so on rather than $+. When the pattern has a series of sets of parentheses as alternatives to be matched, using $+ is useful.

Example

```
$_ = "AlphaBetaDeltaGamma";
/Alpha(.*)Delta(.*)/;
print "The last match was $+\n";
```

$LIST_SEPARATOR

Compliance

Syntax

```
Short Name:        $"
Scope:             localize
```

Definition

When arrays are converted to strings, the elements are separated by spaces by default, which, for example, is what happens when arrays are printed. This variable allows you to specify any string as the list separator, which may be useful for output formatting or for other reasons.

Example

```
$" = ' ! ';
@thisarray = (Alpha, Beta, Gamma);
print "@thisarray.\n";
$" = ' ';
```

$MATCH

Compliance

Syntax

```
Short Name:        $&
Scope:             local (read-only)
```

Definition

This variable references the entire pattern that matched the most recent pattern matching operation.

Example

```
$_ = "AlphaBetaGamma";
/B[aet]*/;
print "Matched: $&\n";
```

$MULTILINE_MATCHING

Compliance

Syntax

```
Short Name:        $*
Scope:             localize
```

Definition

By default, Perl optimizes pattern matching on the assumption that each pattern does not contain embedded new lines; that is, it is optimized for single-line matching. If you are using a pattern that has embedded new lines, you should set this variable to a value of 1 so that this optimization is disabled and the correct result is obtained.

Example

```
print("\nTest 26 Perl Version ($])\n");
$_ = "Alpha\nBeta\nGamma\n";
$* = 0; # Assume string comprises a single line
/^.*$/;
print "a) Assuming single line: $& ";
print "(which is wrong - the assumption was wrong).\n";
$* = 1; # Do not assume string comprises a single line
```

```
/^.*$/;
print "a) Not assuming single line: $& (which is correct).\n";
$* = 0;
```

$OFMT

Compliance

Syntax

```
Short Name:        $#
Scope:             localize
```

Definition

This variable mimics the UNIX awk utility variable of the same name, which permits numeric formatting. The default value is

```
%.2g
```

See the UNIX awk documentation for information about the possible values.

Example

```
$# = "%.6g";
print 5467.4567, "\n";
$# = "%.8g";
print 5467.4567, "\n";
```

> **Tip**
>
> Use of the $OFMT variable is discouraged. You can format values by using the print() function.

$OS_ERROR

Compliance

Syntax

```
Short Name:          $!
Intermediate Name:   $ERRNO
Scope:               localize
```

Definition

If an operating-system-error condition exists, this variable is set to the error number and, if it is evaluated in a string context, to the equivalent error message. You can manually set the error number and then access the relevant error message in a string context.

Example

```
ls -lgd /vir';
print "OS Error was $!\n";
```

 ◄◄ See the $CHILD_ERROR variable for subprocess errors, which are not necessarily system errors, p. 208

$OUTPUT_AUTOFLUSH

Compliance

 4 **5** **NT**

Syntax

```
Short Name:         $¦
Scope:              always global
File Handle Call:   autoflush FILEHANDLE EXPR
```

Definition

If this Boolean variable, which is associated with a file handle, has a nonzero value, that file is autoflushed (the output is written after each print or write operation) rather than buffered.

Tip

When the output file is a pipe, it is best to set autoflush on so that other programs can access the pipe immediately after each write or print operation.

Example

```
select(STDERR);
$¦ = 1;
select(STDOUT);
print "Autoflush setting for STDOUT is $¦\n";
```

$OUTPUT_FIELD_SEPARATOR

Compliance

Syntax

```
Short Name:          $,
Intermediate Name:   $OFS
Scope:               localize
File Handle Call:    output_field_separator FILEHANDLE EXPR
```

Definition

This variable can alter the behavior of the print() function. The default behavior of print(), when it is given a comma-separated list of arguments, is to print each argument with no output separator. You can use this variable to specify any string as a separator.

Example

```
$, = "=";
print STDOUT a, b, c, "\n";
$, = "";
```

$OUTPUT_RECORD_SEPARATOR

Compliance

Syntax

```
Short Name:          $\
Intermediate Name:   $ORS
Scope:               localize
File Handle Call:    output_record_separator FILEHANDLE EXPR
```

Definition

This variable can alter the behavior of the print() function. The default behavior of print(), when it is given a comma-separated list of arguments, is to print each argument. If a new line is required at the end, you must add it explicitly. You can use this record-separator variable to specify any string as the end-of-record string, and you most commonly set it to the newline character to avert the need for explicit new lines.

Example

```
$\ = "\n";
print "No need for an explicit new line now.";
$\ = "";
```

Perl

$PERLDB

Compliance

Syntax

```
Short Name:         $^P
Scope:              localize
```

Definition

This flag represents the debug level of the Perl script. Normally, $PERLDB is used internally by the debugger to disable debugging of the debugger script itself.

Example

```
print "Value of internal Boolean debug flag: $^P\n";
```

$PERL_VERSION

Compliance

Syntax

```
Short Name:         $]
Scope:              localize
```

Definition

This variable represents the version string that identifies the Perl version that is being run. You can assign a value to the variable, if necessary. In a numeric context, the variable evaluates to a number made up of the version plus the (patch level/1000).

Example

```
$ver = $]+0;
print "So every test has tested the version $] (numeric $ver).\n";
```

$POSTMATCH

Compliance

Syntax

```
Short Name:          $'
Scope:               local (read-only)
```

Definition

When a string is matched by pattern, the pattern is actually split into three parts: the part of the string before the match, the part of the string that matched, and the part of the string after the match. Any of these parts could be empty, of course. This variable refers to the part of the string after the match.

Example

```
$_ = "AlphaBetaGamma";
/Beta/;
print "Postmatch = $'\n";
```

$PREMATCH

Compliance

Syntax

```
Short Name:          $'
Scope:               local (read-only)
```

Definition

When a string is matched by pattern, the pattern is actually split into three parts: the part of the string before the match, the part of the string that matched, and the part of the string after the match. Any of these parts could be empty, of course. This variable refers to the part of the string before the match.

Example

```
$_ = "AlphaBetaGamma";
/Beta/;
print "Prematch = $`\n";
```

$PROCESS_ID

Compliance

Syntax

```
Short Name:         $$
Intermediate Name:  $PID
Scope:              localize
```

Definition

In systems that support multiple processes, Perl can identify the process number of the Perl script current process (i.e. the process that is executing the Perl script itself) via this variable.

Example

```
print "The process ID (PID) is: $$\n";
```

$PROGRAM_NAME

Compliance

Syntax

```
Short Name:     $0
Scope:          localize
```

Definition

This variable contains the name of the Perl script that is being executed. You can alter this variable if you want the script to identify itself to the operating system as having a particular name.

Example

```
print "The program name is: $0\n";
```

$REAL_GROUP_ID

Compliance

Syntax

```
Short Name:          $(
Intermediate Name:   $GID
Scope:               localize
```

Definition

In systems that support users and groups, as well as setting new users and groups within a process, Perl can access both the original and the effective user and group information. The real group variable provides access to a list of numbers that represent the real group identifiers (GIDs). Effective GIDs may be set using flags in the script or explicit calls to functions. This will not alter the real GIDs.

Example

```
print("The Real Group ID is a list of GIDs: $(\n");
```

$REAL_USER_ID

Compliance

Syntax

```
Short Name:          $<
Intermediate Name:   $UID
Scope:               localize
```

Definition

In systems that support users and groups, as well as setting new users and groups within a process, Perl can access both the original and the effective user and group information. The real user variable provides access to a list of numbers that represent the real user identifier (UID). An effective UID may be set by flags on the script or explicit calls to functions. This does not alter the real UID.

Example

```
print("The Real User ID is a list of UID: $<\n");
```

II

Perl

$SUBSCRIPT_SEPARATOR

Compliance

Syntax

```
Short Name:              $;
Intermediate Name:       $SUBSEP
Scope:                   localize
```

Definition

This variable is used in emulating multidimensional arrays. The value must be one that is not used by any element in the array. The default value is \034.

Perl 5 directly supports multidimensional arrays directly, so the use of $SUBSCRIPT_SEPARATOR ($;) is not necessary.

$SYSTEM_FD_MAX

Compliance

Syntax

```
Short Name:              $^F
Scope:                   localize
```

Definition

By default, Perl treats three files as system files: 0, 1, and 2 normally, STDIN, STDOUT, and STDERR. The value of $^F is 2 by default. System files are treated specially; in particular, the file descriptors are passed to exec() processes.

Thus, file descriptors that number greater than $^F are automatically closed to child processes.

Example

```
print "The default maximum file descriptors is $^F\n";
```

$WARNING

Compliance

Syntax

```
Short Name:        $^W
Scope:             localize
```

Definition

This variable is a Boolean warning flag that you normally set to true by using the command-line -w switch, although you can set it within the script, if necessary. When this variable is on, the Perl program reports more verbose warnings.

Example

```
print "Boolean warning flag is set to: $^W\n";
```

%ENV{<variable_name>,<variable_value>}

Compliance

Syntax

```
Short Name:        %ENV{<variable_name>,<variable_value>}
Scope:             always global
```

Definition

This variable is an associative array that links the names of the environment variables to their values. This variable makes it easy to look up a value with the appropriate name.

Example

```
$tmp = $ENV{SHELL};
 print "The current SHELL is set to $tmp\n";
```

%INC{<filename>,<file-load-status>}

Compliance

Syntax

```
Short Name:          %INC{<file-name>,<file-load-status>}
Scope:               always global
```

Definition

This variable is an associate array that links the names of the required files to a status (whether they were successfully loaded). Normally, the Perl script itself uses this array to determine whether files have already been loaded so as to minimize the number of file loads that are carried out.

Example

```perl
require 'another.pl';
 $tmp = $INC{'another.pl'};
 print "The required file did exist: $tmp\n";
```

%SIG{<signal-name>,<signal-value>}

Compliance

Syntax

```
Short Name:          %SIG{<signal-name>,<signal-value>}
Scope:               always global
```

Definition

This variable is an associative array that links the standard signals to values. These values dictate the way that the script processes those signals. You can assign signal-handling subroutines to certain signals or set the script to ignore certain signals.

Example

```perl
$SIG{'HUP'} = 'IGNORE';
print "This process now ignores hangup signals.\n";
```

@ARGV[<N>]

Compliance

Syntax

```
Short Name:      @ARGV[<N>]
Scope:           always global
```

Definition

This variable is an array of the arguments passed to the script. Unlike the situation in the C language, the first element of this array is the first argument (not the program name). As the arguments are processed, the value of this variable can alter. As with all arrays you can specify each element with <N> referring to the element number.

Example

```
$Example46String = "There were $#ARGV arguments, first argument was
@ARGV[0]\n";
print $Example46String;
```

@INC[<N>]

Compliance

Syntax

```
Short Name:      @INC[<N>]
Scope:           always global
```

Definition

This variable is an array of the directories to search for included files. These directories are normally specified either at the command line when launching the Perl program or in an environment variable. As with all arrays you can specify each element with <N> referring to the element number.

Example

```
print "The possible include script directories are: @INC\n";
```

Perl

Chapter 9

Perl Operators

Perl has a range of operators, many of which are similar to the operators used in C. Also, many Perl functions can be used either as a unary operator or as a function. The difference in the syntax is that the function call has parentheses enclosing the parameters. The difference in semantics is that the function form has a higher precedence. All such operators are listed as functions rather than as operators in this book.

This chapter categorizes each operator in several ways:

- **Name**—Unlike the special variables, no standard long form exists for the name of each operator. You must use the symbolic name.

- **Precedence**—Each operator is categorized with a precedence number, the lowest number being the highest precedence. Higher-precedence operations are evaluated before lower-precedence operations.

- **Associativity**—Each operator may be left, right, or nonassociative. This determines the order in which operands are evaluated.

- **Type of Operands**—This category indicates whether the operator operates on numeric or string arguments, lists, or files.

- **Number of Operands**—Each operator can operate on one (unary), two (binary), or three (ternary) operands. (Some operators operate on a list of operands — the list being of arbitrary length. These are more commonly thought of as functions.)

- **Context**—Each operator can expect an array or a scalar context. Some operators have separate behaviors for each context.

The following lists the precedence of the operators:

1. TERMS, LIST operators (leftward)

2. ->

3. ++ --

4. `**`

5. `!` `~` `-` (Unary) `+` (Unary)

6. `=~` `!~`

7. `*` `/` `%` `x`

8. `+` (binary) `-` (binary)

9. `<<` `>>`

10. `NAMED` unary operators

11. `<` `>` `<=` `>=` `lt` `gt` `le` `ge`

12. `==` `!=` `<=>` `eq` `ne` `cmp`

13. `&`

14. `¦` `^`

15. `&&`

16. `¦¦`

17. `..`

18. `?:`

19. `=` `+=` `-=` `*=` `/=` `%=` `¦=` `&=` `^=` `<<=` `>>=` `**=` `¦¦=` `&&=` `.=` `¦=` `x=`

20. `,` `=>`

21. `LIST` operators (rightward)

22. `not`

23. `and`

24. `or` `xor`

This chapter contains detailed descriptions of these operators.

You may easily confuse some variables with some operators, so check Chapter 8, "Perl Special Variables," if the symbol is not described here.

Be aware that all Perl 5 (and many Perl 4) functions can behave as operators and as functions. The difference is in the syntax; functions have parentheses—as in `example()`. Operators which have a name rather than a symbol have been treated as functions and so are covered in Chapter 10, "Perl Functions," (this includes the file-test operators `-f etc.` and the pattern matching operators `m// etc.`).

!

Compliance

Syntax

```
Name:                  Logical negation
Precedence:            5
Associativity:         Right
Type of Operands:      Numeric, string
Number of Operands:    One (unary)
Context:               Scalar
```

Definition

The return value of this operation is 1 (true) if the operand has a false value that is defined as 0 in a numeric operand, a null string, or an undefined value. Otherwise, the return value is `''` (false), that is, a null string that evaluates to 0 in a numeric context.

Example

```
$one = !1;
$two = !22;
$three = !0;
$four = !'hello';
$five = !'';
print "1=$one, 2=$two, 3=$three, 4=$four, 5=$five, \n";
```

!=

Compliance

Syntax

```
Name:                  Relational not equal to
Precedence:            12
Associativity:         Nonassociative
Type of Operands:      String
Number of Operands:    Two (binary)
Context:               Scalar
```

Definition

The return value of this operation is 1 (true) if the string operands are not equal. The return value is `''` (false) if the string operands are equal. Every character in the strings is compared based on the character codes.

Example

```
$tmp = "aaa ";
$ans = "aaa" != $tmp;
if ($ans)
     { print "true\n"; }
else
     { print "false\n"; }
```

!~

Compliance

Syntax

```
Name:                  Bind pattern (with negation of return value)
Precedence:            6
Associativity:         Left
Type of Operands:      String
Number of Operands:    Two (binary)
Context:               Scalar
See also:              =~
```

Definition

This operator binds a pattern-matching operation to a string variable other than $. If the pattern match is successful, the return value is ' ' (false); if the pattern match is not successful, the return value is 1 (true).

Example

```
$tmp = "superduper";
if ($tmp !~ s/duper/dooper/)
     {print "Did not do a substitute, tmp still is: $tmp\n";}
else
     {print "Did a substitute, tmp now is: $tmp\n";}
```

%

Compliance

Syntax

```
Name:                  Modulus
Precedence:            7
```

Associativity:	Left
Type of Operands:	Numeric
Number of Operands:	Two (binary)
Context:	Scalar

Definition

The operands are converted to integers, if necessary. The left side is divided by the right side, and the integer remainder is returned.

Example

```
$ans = 48 % 5;
print "48 mod 4 is: $ans\n";
```

%=

Compliance

Syntax

Name:	Modulus assignment
Precedence:	18
Associativity:	Right
Type of Operands:	Numeric
Number of Operands:	Two (binary)
Context:	Scalar

Definition

This operation, like all the extra assignment operations, is a way to make the evaluation of the arguments more efficient.

Example

```
$ans = 48;
$ans %= 5;
print "48 mod 4 is: $ans\n";
```

&

Compliance

Syntax

Name:	Bitwise and
Precedence:	13

Associativity:	Left
Type of Operands:	Numeric (integer)
Number of Operands:	Two (binary)
Context:	Scalar

Definition

This operator performs a *bitwise and* on the binary representation of the two numeric operands; for example, each bit of the two operands are compared with a logical and operation and the resulting bits form the result.

Example

```
$ans = 456 & 111;
print "Bitwise and 456 & 111 is: $ans\n";
```

&&

Compliance

Syntax

Name:	Symbolic logical and
Precedence:	15
Associativity:	Left
Type of Operands:	Numeric, string
Number of Operands:	Two (binary)
Context:	Scalar

Definition

As in all logical operations, a null string and zero are false. This operator returns 1 (true) if both of the operands are true or null (false) if either operand is false or both operands are false.

Example

```
$ans = 1 && print("This will print.\n") && 0 && print("This won't print!\n");
if ($ans)
    {print("So it's all true!\n");}
else
    {print("So it's not all true. (expected)\n");}
```

&&=

Compliance

Syntax

Name:	Assignment logical and
Precedence:	19
Associativity:	Right
Type of Operands:	Numeric, string
Number of Operands:	Two (binary)
Context:	Scalar

Definition

This operator is a combination of the logical and assignment operators. This operator is more efficient when a new value is being reassigned to the same variable because the reference needs to be computed only one time.

Example

```
$ans = 1;
$ans &&= "eggs" eq "eggs";
if ($ans)
     {print("It's as true as eggs is eggs. (expected)\n");}
else
     {print("Not true, I'm afraid.");}
```

&=

Compliance

Syntax

Name:	Assignment bitwise and
Precedence:	19
Associativity:	Right
Type of Operands:	Numeric (integer)
Number of Operands:	Two (binary)
Context:	Scalar

Definition

This operator is a combination of the bitwise and assignment operators. This operator is more efficient when a new value is being reassigned to the same variable because the reference needs to be computed only one time.

Example

```
$ans = 456;
$ans &= 111;
print("Bitwise and 456 & 111 is $ans\n");
```

*

Compliance

Syntax

Name:	Multiplication
Precedence:	7
Associativity:	Left
Type of Operands:	Numeric
Number of Operands:	Two (binary)
Context:	Scalar

Definition

This operator returns the numeric result of multiplying the two numeric operands.

Example

```
$ans = 7 * 10;
print("$ans (expected 70)\n");
```

**

Compliance

Syntax

Name:	Exponentiation
Precedence:	4
Associativity:	Right
Type of Operands:	Numeric
Number of Operands:	Two (binary)
Context:	Scalar

Definition

The operation x**y returns the value of x raised to the power of y.

Example

```
$ans = 2 ** 3;
print ("$ans (expected 8)\n");
```

**=

Compliance

Syntax

Name:	Assignment exponentiation
Precedence:	19
Associativity:	Right
Type of Operands:	Numeric
Number of Operands:	Two (binary)
Context:	Scalar

Definition

This operator is a combination of the exponentiation and assignment operators. This operator is more efficient when a new value is being reassigned to the same variable because the reference needs to be computed only one time.

Example

```
$ans = 2;
$ans **= 3;
print ("$ans (expected 8)\n");
```

*=

Compliance

Syntax

Name:	Assignment multiplication
Precedence:	19
Associativity:	Right
Type of Operands:	Numeric
Number of Operands:	Two (binary)
Context:	Scalar

Definition

This operator is a combination of the multiplication and assignment operators. This operator is more efficient when a new value is being reassigned to the same variable because the reference needs to be computed only one time.

II

Perl

Example
```
$ans = 7;
$ans *= 10;
print ("$ans (expected 70)\n");
```

+ (Unary)

Compliance

Syntax

```
Name:                Unary plus
Precedence:          5
Associativity:       Right
Type of Operands:    Numeric, string
Number of Operands:  One (unary)
Context:             Scalar
```

Definition

This operator does not actually have any operation on a numeric or a string operand. In certain circumstances, the operator can disambiguate an expression. When a parenthesis follows a function name, it is taken to indicate a complete list of the arguments to the function, unless the parenthesis is preceded by + to make the parenthesized expression just one of the list arguments for that function.

Example
```
@ans = sort +(5 + 5) * 10, -4;
print("@ans (expected 100, -4)\n");
```

+ (Binary)

Compliance

Syntax

```
Name:                Addition
Precedence:          8
Associativity:       Left
Type of Operands:    Numeric
Number of Operands:  Two (binary)
Context:             Scalar
```

Definition

This operator returns the sum of the two operands.

Example

```
$ans = 15 + 5;
print("$ans (expected 20)\n");
```

++

Compliance

Syntax

```
Name:                Autoincrement
Precedence:          3
Associativity:       Nonassociative
Type of Operands:    Numeric, string
Number of Operands:  One (unary)
Context:             Scalar
```

Definition

In a numeric context, the autoincrement adds 1 to the operand. If the syntax is prefix, the value before the increment is returned. If the syntax is postfix, the value after the increment is returned.

With a string operand (that has never been used in a numeric context), the autoincrement has a "magic" behavior. If the string is an alphanumeric expression, such as /^[a-zA-Z]*[0-9]*$/, the increment is carried out on the string, including a carry (i.e. the string "19" becomes "20" automatically just as if it were an integer).

Example

```
$ans = 45;
print $ans,   " (expected 45) ";
print $ans++, " (expected 45) ";
print ++$ans, " (expected 47)\n";
```

+=

Compliance

Syntax

Name:	Assignment addition
Precedence:	19
Associativity:	Right
Type of Operands:	Numeric
Number of Operands:	Two (binary)
Context:	Scalar

Definition

This operator is a combination of the summation and assignment operators. This operator is more efficient when a new value is being reassigned to the same variable because the reference needs to be computed only one time.

Example

```
$ans = 15;
$ans += 5;
print("$ans (expected 20)\n");
```

Compliance

Syntax

Name:	Comma
Precedence:	20
Associativity:	Left
Type of Operands:	Numeric, string
Number of Operands:	Two (binary)
Context:	Scalar, list

Definition

In a scalar context, the comma operator evaluates the operand to the left, discards the result, evaluates the operand to the right, and returns that value as the result.

In an array context, the comma operator separates items in the list. The operator behaves as though it returns both operands as part of the list.

Example

```
$ans = ('one', 'two', 'three');
print("$ans (expected three)\n");
```

- (Unary)

Compliance

Syntax

```
Name:                  Negation
Precedence:            5
Associativity:         Right
Type of Operands:      Numeric, string, identifier
Number of Operands:    One (unary)
Context:               Scalar
```

Definition

This operator returns the negated value of a numeric operand. If the operand is a string that begins with a plus or minus sign, the operator returns a string that has the opposite sign. If the argument is an identifier, the operator returns a string that comprises the identifier prefixed with a minus sign.

Example

```
$ans = 45;
$ans = -$ans;
print("$ans (expected -45)\n");
```

- (Binary)

Compliance

Syntax

```
Name:                  Subtraction
Precedence:            8
Associativity:         Left
Type of Operands:      Numeric
Number of Operands:    Two (binary)
Context:               Scalar
```

Definition

This operator returns the first operand minus the second operand.

Example

```
$ans = 50 - 10;
print("$ans (expected 40)\n");
```

II

Perl

--

Compliance

Syntax

```
Name:                 Autodecrement
Precedence:           3
Associativity:        Nonassociative
Type of Operands:     Numeric
Number of Operands:   One (unary)
Context:              Scalar
```

Definition

This operator decrements its operand. It also returns a value, but you have the choice to return the existing value (before any decrement takes place) or to return the new value (after the decrement takes place) by using the prefix notation or the postfix notation. So if $x is 56, --$x returns 56 and $x-- returns 55, though in both cases the new value of $x is 55. This subtle difference is often important when one wants to both decrement a value and perform a test (for example with conditions in a loop).

Unlike the autoincrement operator, ++, this operator does not operate on strings.

Example

```
$ans = 45;
print $ans,   " (expected 45) ";
print $ans--, " (expected 45) ";
print --$ans, " (expected 43)\n";
```

-=

Compliance

Syntax

```
Name:                 Assignment subtraction
Precedence:           19
Associativity:        Right
Type of Operands:     Numeric
Number of Operands:   Two (binary)
Context:              Scalar
```

Definition

This operator is a combination of the subtraction and assignment operators. This operator is more efficient when a new value is being reassigned to the same variable because the reference needs to be computed only one time.

Example

```
$ans = 50;
$ans -= 10;
print("$ans (expected 40)\n");
```

->

Compliance

Syntax

```
Name:                 Dereference
Precedence:           2
Associativity:        Left
Type of Operands:     Special
Number of Operands:   Two (binary)
Context:              Scalar, array
```

Definition

This operator is new to Perl 5. The capability to create and manipulate complex data types with references provides flexibility in Perl 5 that was not present in Perl 4. This operator is just one of the aspects of this functionality.

The operands for this operator can be:

- A right side comprising array brackets or braces ([ ] or { }), and a left side comprising a reference to an array (or hash).

- A right side comprising a method name (or a variable with a method name), and a left side of either an object or a class name.

The operator allows you to access the elements in the data structure referenced by the left side (an array name, a hash name, an object, or a class name). Because there is no automatic dereferencing, you must use this syntax to dereference such a reference.

Example

```
@ans = (100, 200, 300);
$ansref = \@ans;
$ansref->[2] = 400;
print $ans[2], " (expected 400)\n";
```

Perl

•

Compliance

Syntax

```
Name:                   String concatenation
Precedence:             8
Associativity:          Left
Type of Operands:       String
Number of Operands:     Two (binary)
Context:                Scalar
```

Definition

This operator joins the two string operands, returning a longer string.

Example

```
$ans = "jordy" . " jordy";
print $ans, " (expected jordy jordy)\n";
```

..

Compliance

Syntax

```
Name:                   Range operator
Precedence:             17
Associativity:          Nonassociative
Type of Operands:       Numeric, string
Number of Operands:     Two (binary)
Context:                Scalar, list
```

Definition

In a list context, the range operator returns an array of values, starting from the left operand up to the right operand in steps of one. In this context, the range operator can use "magic" increments to increment strings, as with the autoincrement operator (++).

In a scalar context, the range operator returns a Boolean value. In effect, the return value remains false as long as the left operand is false. When the left operand becomes true, it becomes true until the right operand is true, after which it becomes false again.

The range operator can be used in a scalar context to set conditions for certain ranges of line numbers of an input file. This works because the default behavior when either operand is numeric is to compare that operand with the current line number (the $INPUT_LINE_NUMBER or $. special variable). Thus, it is easy using this construct to treat certain lines in an input file differently (in the following example the first five lines of the input file are surpressed from being output).

Example
```
@ans = 1..5;
print("@ans (expected 12345)\n");
open(INFILE,"<infile.tst");
while(<INFILE>) {
    print unless (1..5);
}
```

.=

Compliance

Syntax

Name:	Assignment concatenation
Precedence:	19
Associativity:	Right
Type of Operands:	String
Number of Operands:	Two (binary)
Context:	Scalar

Definition

This operator is a combination of the concatenation and assignment operators. This operator is more efficient when a new value is being reassigned to the same variable because the reference needs to be computed only one time.

Example
```
$ans = "jordy";
$ans .= " jordy";
print $ans, " (expected jordy jordy)\n";
```

/

Compliance

Syntax

```
Name:                  Division
Precedence:            7
Associativity:         Left
Type of Operands:      Numeric
Number of Operands:    Two (binary)
Context:               Scalar
```

Definition

This operator returns the product of the operands.

Example

```
$ans = 10/2;
print("$ans (expected 5)\n");
```

/=

Compliance

Syntax

```
Name:                  Assignment division
Precedence:            19
Associativity:         Right
Type of Operands:      Numeric
Number of Operands:    Two (binary)
Context:               Scalar
```

Definition

This operator is a combination of the division and assignment operators. This operator is more efficient when a new value is being reassigned to the same variable because the reference needs to be computed only one time.

Example

```
$ans = 10;
$ans /= 2;
print("$ans (expected 5)\n");
```

<

Compliance

Syntax

Name:	Numeric less then
Precedence:	11
Associativity:	Nonassociative
Type of Operands:	Numeric
Number of Operands:	Two (binary)
Context:	Scalar

Definition

This operator returns 1 if the left operand is numerically less than the right operand; otherwise, it returns null.

Example

```
$ans = 45 < 36;
if ($ans)
     { print("True.\n");}
else
     { print("False. (expected)\n");}
```

<<

Compliance

Syntax

Name:	Bitwise shift left
Precedence:	9
Associativity:	Left
Type of Operands:	Numeric (integer)
Number of Operands:	Two (binary)
Context:	Scalar

Definition

This operator shifts the operand left one bit in binary representation and returns the result. This is usually only used when processing some form binary data. For example it may be that a number is a representation of a series of flags (on/off Boolean values). One can use an integer of value 0 to 16 to represent five flags as the binary representation of all possible states ranges from 00000 to 11111 (this is 0 to F in hexadecimal). When processing data in this form it is often useful to use the binary shift operators to access individual bits. If you find the number modulus 2 this is the value of the least significant bit (1 or 0). If you shift the number to the right by one you effectively remove the least significant bit. If you shift by one to the left you effectively add a new least significant bit with a value of zero (doubling the actual value of the variable). See also ">>" for an example using such flags.

> **Caution**
>
> Bit shift operators depend on the implemention of storage on the machine being used and so may not be portable.

Example

```
$ans = 1024<<1;
print("$ans (Bitwise left shift of 1024 by 1 place)\n");
```

<=

Compliance

Syntax

Name:	Numeric less than or equal to
Precedence:	11
Associativity:	Nonassociative
Type of Operands:	Numeric
Number of Operands:	Two (binary)
Context:	Scalar

Definition

This operator returns 1 (true) if the left operand is numerically less than or equal to the right operand.

Example

```
$ans = 345 <= 345;
print("Comparing 345 <= 345 yields $ans. (expected 1 for true).\n");
```

<<=

Compliance

Syntax

Name:	Assignment bitwise shift left
Precedence:	19
Associativity:	Right
Type of Operands:	Numeric (integer)

```
Number of Operands:     Two (binary)
Context:                Scalar
```

Definition

This operator is a combination of the bitwise shift left and assignment operators. This operator is more efficient when a new value is being reassigned to the same variable because the reference needs to be computed only one time.

Example

```
$ans = 1024;
$ans <<= 1;
print("$ans (Bitwise left shift of 1024 by 1 place)\n");
```

<=>

Compliance

Syntax

```
Name:                   Numeric comparison
Precedence:             12
Associativity:          Nonassociative
Type of Operands:       Numeric
Number of Operands:     Two (binary)
Context:                Scalar
```

Definition

This operator returns 0 if the two numeric operands are equal. The operator returns -1 if the left operand is less than the right operand and +1 if the left operand is greater than the right operand.

Example

```
$ans = 345 <=> 347;
print("Comparing 345 with 437 yields $ans. (expected -1 for less than).\n");
```

=

Compliance

Syntax

```
Name:                 Assignment
Precedence:           19
Associativity:        Right
Type of Operands:     Numeric, string
Number of Operands:   Two (binary)
Context:              Scalar, list
```

Definition

In a scalar context, the assignment operator assigns the right operand's value to the variable specified by the left operand. The assignment operator returns the value of the variable.

In an array context, the assignment can assign multiple values to an array as the left operand if the right side results in a list.

Example

```
$ans = 43;
print("Assignment to \$ans: $ans (expected 43)\n");
```

==

Compliance

Syntax

```
Name:                 Numeric equality
Precedence:           12
Associativity:        Nonassociative
Type of Operands:     Numeric
Number of Operands:   Two (binary)
Context:              Scalar
```

Definition

This operator returns 1 (true) if the left and right numeric operands are numerically equal; otherwise, it returns null (false).

Example

```
$ans = 345 == 347;
print("Comparing 345 with 347 yields +$ans+. (expected null not equal).\n");
```

=>

Compliance

Syntax

```
Name:                 Comma
Precedence:           20
Associativity:        Left
Type of Operands:     Numeric, string
Number of Operands:   Two (binary)
Context:              Scalar, list
```

Definition

This operator is an alternative to the comma operator.

Example

```
$ans = (1 => 2 => 3);
print("$ans (expected 3)\n");
```

=~

Compliance

Syntax

```
Name:                 Pattern binding
Precedence:           6
Associativity:        Left
Type of Operands:     Special
Number of Operands:   Two (binary)
Context:              Scalar
```

Definition

The default string matched by pattern-match operations is $_. Any other string can be bound to a pattern-matching operation using the pattern-binding operator. The left operand is a string to be searched. The right operand is a pattern-match operation (search, substitution, and translation). The return value is true or false, depending on the success of the operation.

Example

```
$tmp = "superduper";
if ($tmp =~ s/duper/dooper/)
      {print "Did do a substitute, tmp now is: $tmp\n";}
else
      {print "Did not a substitute, tmp still is: $tmp\n";}
```

>

Compliance

Syntax

Name:	Numeric greater than
Precedence:	11
Associativity:	Nonassociative
Type of Operands:	Numeric
Number of Operands:	Two (binary)
Context:	Scalar

Definition

This operator returns 1 (true) if the left numeric operand is greater than the right numeric operand; otherwise, it returns null (false).

Example

```
$ans = 45 > 36;
if ($ans)
      { print("True.\n");}
else
      { print("False. (expected)\n");}
```

>>

Compliance

Syntax

Name:	Bitwise shift right
Precedence:	9
Associativity:	Left
Type of Operands:	Numeric (integer)
Number of Operands:	Two (binary)
Context:	Scalar

Definition

This operator shifts the operand right one bit in binary representation and returns the result. This is usually only used when processing some form binary data. For example, it may be that a number is a representation of a series of flags (on/off Boolean values). One can use an integer of value 0 to 16 to represent five flags as the binary representation of all possible states ranges from 00000 to 11111 (this is 0 to F in hexedecimal). When processing data in this form, it is often useful to use the binary shift operators to access individual bits. If you find the number modulus 2 this is the value of the least significant bit (1 or 0). If you shift the number to the right by one you effectively remove the least significant bit. If you shift by one to the left you effectively add a new least significant bit with a value of zero (doubling the actual value of the variable).

Caution

Bit shift operators depend on the implemention of storage on the machine being used and so may not be portable.

Example

```
$flags = 10; # i.e. Binary 01010 list of flags
for ($i=0;$i<=4;$i++) {
        # shift to make bit we want least significant (rightmost)
        # then find this modulus 2 to test this bit
        # (NB bit shift operations may not be portable)
        ($flags>>$i)%2 ? print "$i on\n" : print "$i off\n";
```

>=

Compliance

Syntax

Name:	Numeric greater than or equal to
Precedence:	11
Associativity:	Nonassociative
Type of Operands:	Numeric
Number of Operands:	Two (binary)
Context:	Scalar

Definition

This operator returns 1 (true) if the left numeric operand is greater than or equal to the right numeric operand; otherwise, it returns null (false).

Example

```
$ans = 345 >= 345;
print("Comparing 345 >= 345 yields $ans. (expected 1 for true).\n");
```

>>=

Compliance

Syntax

```
Name:                Assignment bitwise shift right
Precedence:          19
Associativity:       Left
Type of Operands:    Numeric (integer)
Number of Operands:  Two (binary)
Context:             Scalar
```

Definition

This operator is a combination of the bitwise shift right and assignment operators. This operator is more efficient when a new value is being reassigned to the same variable because the reference needs to be computed only one time.

Example

```
$ans = 1024;
$ans >>= 1;
print("$ans (Bitwise right shift of 1024 by 1 place)\n");
```

?:

Compliance

Syntax

```
Name:                Conditional operator
Precedence:          18
Associativity:       Right
Type of Operands:    Numeric, string
Number of Operands:  Three (ternary)
Context:             Scalar, list
```

Definition

This operator is like a symbolic if...then...else clause. If the leftmost operand is true, the center operand is returned; otherwise, the rightmost operand is returned. Either of the operands can return scalar or list values, and these values will be returned if the context allows.

Example

```
$ans = (45 == 45) ? "Equal (expected).\n" : "Not equal.\n";
print $ans;
```

List Operators (Leftward)

Compliance

Syntax

```
Name:                   All named list operators
Precedence:             1
Associativity:          Left
Type of Operands:       Special
Number of Operands:     List
Context:                List
```

Definition

Several functions require a list as a parameter. The list may be written with or without the function parentheses. These list functions are in fact operators that behave like functions when their arguments are in parentheses. If they are written with parentheses, everything within the parentheses is taken as the list argument to the function, and they behave as a TERM.

When the function call is written without parentheses, the precedence is slightly more complex. The list operator has a different precedence, depending on whether the comparison is to the left of the list operator (leftward) or to the right of the list operator (rightward). The list operator has higher or equal precedence compared with all operators to its left. Thus, in the following example, join is evaluated before print because print is to the left of join.

Example

```
print 'Ones ', 'Twos ', join 'hoho ', 'Threes ', 'Fours ', "\n";
```

List Operators (Rightward)

Compliance

Syntax

```
Name:                 All named list operators
Precedence:           21
Associativity:        Nonassociative
Type of Operands:     Special
Number of Operands:   List
Context:              List
```

Definition

Several functions require a list as a parameter. The list can be written with or without the function parentheses. These functions are in fact operators that behave like functions when their arguments are in parentheses. If they are written with parentheses, everything within the parentheses is taken as the list argument to the function, and they behave as a TERM.

When the function is written without parentheses, the precedence is slightly more complex. The list operator has a different precedence, depending on whether the comparison is to the left of the list operator (leftward) or to the right of the list operator (rightward). The list operator has lower or equal precedence compared with all operators to its right. Thus, in the following example, print is evaluated after join because join is to the right of print.

Example

```
print 'Ones ', 'Twos ', join 'hoho ', 'Threes ', 'Fours ', "\n";
```

Named Unary Operators

Compliance

Syntax

```
Name:                 All named unary operators
Precedence:           10
Associativity:        Nonassociative
Type of Operands:     Special
Number of Operands:   One (unary)
Context:              Scalar
```

Definition

In a similar way to list operators, named unary operators can behave as a TERM by being expressed with a function syntax, with the argument placed in parentheses.

When the function is written without parentheses, the precedence of these operators is lower than arithmetic types of operators but greater than the symbolic string and numeric comparisons. Thus, in the following example, the first int takes the result of the arithmetic division 7/2 as its argument, so 3 is printed. The second int is a term bound to 7, which returns 7 and then is divided by 2 to yield 3.5.

Example

```
print 'Ones ', 'Twos ', int 7/2, (int 7)/2, ' Fours', "\n";
```

TERMs

Compliance

Syntax

```
Name:                  TERMs
Precedence:            1
Associativity:         Left
Type of Operands:      Special
Number of Operands:    N/A
Context:               N/A
```

Definition

A TERM can be any variable, any expression enclosed in parentheses, any function with its arguments in parentheses, and also a quoted expression (using the so-called "quote" and "quotelike" operators). TERMs have the highest possible precedence; in other words, they are replaced by their return value when the entire expression is being evaluated before any other operator of lower precedence is evaluated. TERMs appear in this chapter on operators to show where they fall in the order of precedence.

Example

```
print 'One ', (1, 2, 3), "(expect One 3)\n";
```

\

Compliance

Syntax

```
Name:                  Reference
Precedence:            5
Associativity:         Right
Type of Operands:      One (unary)
```

```
Number of Operands:     Special
Context:                Scalar
```

Definition

This operator permits the creation of references and the use of complex data types. One example is the capability to create another reference to an existing array variable.

```
@ans = (100, 200, 300);
$ansref = \@ans;
$ansref->[2] = 400;
print $ans[2], " (expected 400)\n";
```

^

Compliance

Syntax

```
Name:                   Bitwise exclusive or
Precedence:             14
Associativity:          Left
Type of Operands:       Two (binary)
Number of Operands:     Numeric (integer)
Context:                Scalar
```

Definition

This operator returns the result of a bitwise exclusive or on the two operands.

Example

```
$ans = 456 ^ 111;
print "Bitwise xor 456 & 111 is: $ans\n";
```

^=

Compliance

Syntax

```
Name:                   Assignment bitwise exclusive or
Precedence:             19
Associativity:          Right
Type of Operands:       Numeric (integer)
```

```
Number of Operands:    Two (binary)
Context:               Scalar
```

Definition

This operator is a combination of the bitwise exclusive or and assignment operators. This operator is more efficient when a new value is being reassigned to the same variable because the reference needs to be computed only one time.

Example

```
$ans = 456;
$ans ^= 111;
print "Bitwise xor 456 & 111 is: $ans\n";
```

and

Compliance

Syntax

```
Name:                  And
Precedence:            23
Associativity:         Left
Type of Operands:      Numeric, string
Number of Operands:    Two (binary)
Context:               Scalar
```

Definition

This operator is the lower-precedence version of symbolic and `&&`.

Example

```
$ans = (1 and 3 || 0);
if ($ans)
    { print "true (expected)\n"; }
else
    { print "false\n"; }
```

cmp

Compliance

Syntax

Name:	String comparison
Precedence:	12
Associativity:	Nonassociative
Type of Operands:	String
Number of Operands:	Two (binary)
Context:	Scalar

Definition

This operator compares two string operands and returns -1 if the first is less than the second, 0 if the operands are equal, and 1 if the first operand is greater than the second.

Example

```
$ans = "abc" cmp "aba";
print("Comparing (cmp) abc with aba yields $ans (expected +1 aba > abc).\n");
```

eq

Compliance

Syntax

Name:	String equality
Precedence:	12
Associativity:	Nonassociative
Type of Operands:	String
Number of Operands:	Two (binary)
Context:	Scalar

Definition

This operator tests whether two strings are equal, returning 1 (true) if they are and null (false) if they are not.

Example

```
$ans = "abc" eq "abc";
print("Comparing (eq) abc with abc yields $ans (expected 1 true).\n");
```

ge

Compliance

Syntax

```
Name:                 String greater than or equal to
Precedence:           11
Associativity:        Nonassociative
Type of Operands:     String
Number of Operands:   Two (binary)
Context:              Scalar
```

Definition

This operator compares two strings and returns 1 (true) if the first string is greater than or equal to the second; otherwise, it returns null (false).

Example

```
$ans = "abc" ge "abc";
print("Comparing (ge) abc with abc yields $ans (expected 1 true).\n");
```

gt

Compliance

Syntax

```
Name:                 String greater than
Precedence:           11
Associativity:        Nonassociative
Type of Operands:     String
Number of Operands:   Two (binary)
Context:              Scalar
```

Definition

This operator compares two strings and returns 1 (true) if the first is greater than the second; otherwise, it returns null (false).

Example

```
$ans = "abc" gt "aba";
print("Comparing (gt) abc with aba yields $ans (expected 1 true).\n");
```

le

Compliance

II

Perl

Syntax

```
Name:                 String less than or equal to
Precedence:           11
Associativity:        Nonassociative
Type of Operands:     String
Number of Operands:   Two (binary)
Context:              Scalar
```

Definition

This operator compares two strings and returns 1 (true) if the first is less than or equal to the second; otherwise, it returns null (false).

Example

```
$ans = "abc" le "aba";
print("Comparing (le) abc with aba yields +$ans+ (expected null false).\n");
```

lt

Compliance

Syntax

```
Name:                 String less than
Precedence:           11
Associativity:        Nonassociative
Type of Operands:     String
Number of Operands:   Two (binary)
Context:              Scalar
```

Definition

This operator compares two strings and returns 1 (true) if the first is less than the second; otherwise, it returns null (false).

Example

```
$ans = "abc" lt "aba";
print("Comparing (lt) abc with aba yields +$ans+ (expected null false).\n");
```

ne

Compliance

Syntax

Name:	String not equal to
Precedence:	12
Associativity:	Nonassociative
Type of Operands:	String
Number of Operands:	Two (binary)
Context:	Scalar

Definition

This operator compares two strings and returns 1 (true) if they are not equal; otherwise, it returns null (false).

Example

```
$ans = "abc" ne "aba";
print("Comparing (ne) abc with aba yields $ans (expected 1 true).\n");
```

not

Compliance

Syntax

Name:	Not
Precedence:	22
Associativity:	Right
Type of Operands:	Numeric, string
Number of Operands:	One (unary)
Context:	Scalar

Definition

This operator is the lower-precedence version of symbolic not !.

Example

```
$ans = not 1;
print("Not 1 is +$ans+ (expected null)\n");
```

or

Compliance

Perl

Syntax

```
Name:                    Or
Precedence:              24
Associativity:           Left
Type of Operands:        Numeric, string
Number of Operands:      Two (binary)
Context:                 Scalar
```

Definition

This operator is the lower-precedence version of symbolic or ¦¦.

Example

```
open TSTFILE, "<nofile.txt" or print "The file doesn't exist\n";
```

X

Compliance

Syntax

```
Name:                    Repetition
Precedence:              6
Associativity:           Left
Type of Operands:        String and numeric (integer)
Number of Operands:      Two (binary)
Context:                 Scalar
```

Definition

The first operand must be a string, and the second operand must be an integer. The operator returns a string comprising the string operand repeated the specified number of times.

Example

```
print "Hello " x 5, "\n";
```

X=

Compliance

Syntax

```
Name:                 Assignment repetition
Precedence:           19
Associativity:        Right
Type of Operands:     String and numeric (integer)
Number of Operands:   Two (binary)
Context:              Scalar
```

Definition

This operator is a combination of the repetition and assignment operators. This operator is more efficient when a new value is being reassigned to the same variable because the reference needs to be computed only one time.

Example

```
$ans = 'Hello ';
$ans x= 5;
print("$ans\n");
```

xor

Compliance

Syntax

```
Name:                 Exclusive or
Precedence:           24
Associativity:        Left
Type of Operands:     Numeric, string
Number of Operands:   Two (binary)
Context:              Scalar
```

Definition

This operator returns 1 (true) or null (false) as an exclusive or of the two operands: the result is true if either but not both of the operands is true.

Example

```
for (0..1) {
    $a = $_;
    for (0..1) {
        $b = $_;
        print $a, ,' ', $b, ' ', ($a xor $b) ? 1 : 0, "\n";
        }
    }
```

Compliance

Syntax

```
Name:                Bitwise or
Precedence:          14
Associativity:       Left
Type of Operands:    Numeric (integer)
Number of Operands:  Two (binary)
Context:             Scalar
```

Definition

This operator returns an integer that is the result of a bitwise or between the two integer operands.

Example

```
$ans = 2 ¦ 1024;
print("2 OR 1204 is $ans\n");
```

Compliance

Syntax

```
Name:                Symbolic or
Precedence:          11
Associativity:       Left
Type of Operands:    Numeric, string
Number of Operands:  Two (binary)
Context:             Scalar
```

Definition

This operator returns 1 (true) if either of the two operands is true and null (false) otherwise.

Example

```
$ans = '' ¦¦ 'okay';
print("null ¦¦ okay is $ans (expected okay true)\n");
```

|¦=

Compliance

Syntax

```
Name:                 Assignment bitwise or
Precedence:           19
Associativity:        Right
Type of Operands:     Numeric (integer)
Number of Operands:   Two (binary)
Context:              Scalar
```

Definition

This operator is a combination of the bitwise or and assignment operators. This operator is more efficient when a new value is being reassigned to the same variable because the reference needs to be computed only one time.

Example

```
$ans = 2;
$ans |= 1024;
print("2 OR 1204 is $ans\n");
```

||=

Compliance

Syntax

```
Name:                 Assignment symbolic or
Precedence:           19
Associativity:        Right
Type of Operands:     Numeric, string
Number of Operands:   Two (binary)
Context:              Scalar
```

Definition

This operator is a combination of the symbolic or and assignment operators. This operator is more efficient when a new value is being reassigned to the same variable because the reference needs to be computed only one time.

Example
```
$ans = '';
$ans ||= 'okay';
print("null || okay is $ans (expected okay true)\n");
```

~

Compliance

Syntax
```
Name:                  Bitwise not
Precedence:            5
Associativity:         Right
Type of Operands:      Numeric (integer)
Number of Operands:    One (unary)
Context:               Scalar
```

Definition
This operator returns the bitwise negation of an integer operand. The result of this operation is sometimes known as the *one's complement*.

Example
```
$ans = ~1000000000;
print("Bitwise negation of 1000000000 is $ans\n");
```

Chapter 10

Perl Functions

Perl has a large number of functions that come as standard with most implementations, and an even wider range of additional modules, each with its own additional functions. This chapter lists all the standard functions alphabetically for reference.

Each function is assigned a category. There are two main categories: list operators, which can take more than one argument, and named unary operators, which can take only one argument. A secondary category is noted in parentheses so you can see, at a glance, the type of operation the function performs. This is a very rough categorization, as many functions might overlap in any category scheme.

For each function, the form of the arguments is listed. If there are multiple forms of calling the function, there will be multiple lines describing each form. The meanings of the arguments are described in the text.

The type of value returned by the function is listed. This is usually specified in more detail in the function description.

Two categories of functions, those dealing with sockets and those dealing with System V inter-process communications, are not dealt with in great detail. Both of these categories of function are direct counterparts of UNIX system functions.

-A

Compliance

Syntax

```
Category   named unary operator (file test)
Arguments  handle
Arguments  filename
Arguments  none
Return Value  integer (age of file in days since last
                       access relative to $BASETIME)
```

Definition

The file test operator takes one file handle or filename as an argument. It returns age of file in days since last access relative to $BASETIME. All file test operators can take a special argument underscore, which means that the test is carried out on the same file handle as the last file test, stat(), or lstat() call. If no argument is supplied, $_ is used.

Example

```
print "-A ", -A "/etc/fstab", "\n";
```

-B

Compliance

Syntax

```
Category   named unary operator (file test)
Arguments  handle
Arguments  filename
Arguments  none
Return Value  1 (true) '' (false)
```

Definition

The file test operator takes one file handle or filename as an argument. It returns 1 (true) if the file is binary. It returns '' (false) if the file is not binary. The first characters of the file are checked to see if the high bit is set and if a suitable number do have the high bit set, the file is assumed to be binary. If the file is empty, it is returned as binary. Because this test involves reading the file itself, it is best to test to learn if the file exists as a plain file (-f), first. All file test operators can take a special argument underscore, which means that the test is carried out on the same file handle as the last file test, stat(), or lstat() call. If no argument is supplied, $_ is used.

Example

```
(-B "/etc/fstab") ? print("-B fstab is binary\n") :
        print("-B fstab is not binary\n");
```

-b

Compliance

Syntax

```
Category  named unary operator (file test)
Arguments  handle
Arguments  filename
Arguments  none
Return Value  1 (true) '' (false)
```

Definition

The `file test` operator takes one file `handle` or `filename` as an argument. It returns `1` (true) if the file is a block special file (that is, a UNIX `/dev` device file). It returns `''` (false) if the file is not a block special file. All `file test` operators can take a special argument underscore, which means that the test is carried out on the same file `handle` as the last `file test`, `stat()`, or `lstat()` call. If no argument is supplied, `$_` is used.

Example

```
(-b "/dev/hda1") ? print("-b hda1 is block\n") :
    print("-b hda1 is not block\n");
```

-C

Compliance

Syntax

```
Category  named unary operator (file test)
Arguments  handle
Arguments  filename
Arguments  none
Return Value  integer (age of file in days since last
              inode change relative to $BASETIME)
```

Definition

The `file test` operator takes one file `handle` or `filename` as an argument. It returns `age of file in days since last inode change relative to $BASETIME`. All `file test` operators can take a special argument underscore, which means that the test is carried out on the same file `handle` as the last , `stat()`, or `lstat()` call. If no argument is supplied, `$_` is used.

Example
```
print "-C ", -C "/etc/fstab", "\n";
```

-C

Compliance

Syntax
```
Category  named unary operator (file test)
Arguments  handle
Arguments  filename
Arguments  none
Return Value  1 (true) '' (false)
```

Definition

The file test operator takes one file handle or filename as an argument. It returns 1 (true) if the file is a character special file. It returns '' (false) if the file is not a character special file. All file test operators can take a special argument underscore, which means that the test is carried out on the same file handle as the last file test, stat(), or lstat() call. If no argument is supplied, $_ is used.

Example
```
(-c "/dev/tty0") ? print("-c tty0 is char\n") :
    print("-c tty0 is not char\n");
```

-d

Compliance

Syntax
```
Category  named unary operator (file test)
Arguments  handle
Arguments  filename
Arguments  none
Return Value  1 (true) '' (false)
```

Definition

The file test operator takes one file handle or filename as an argument. It returns 1 (true) if the file is a directory. It returns '' (false) if the file is not a directory. All file test operators can take a special argument underscore, which means that the test is carried out on the same file `handle` as the last `file test`, `stat()`, or `lstat()` call. If no argument is supplied, `$_` is used.

Example

```
(-d "/") ? print("-d / is dir\n") : print("-d / is not dir\n");
```

-e

Compliance

Syntax

```
Category   named unary operator (file test)
Arguments  handle
Arguments  filename
Arguments  none
Arguments  none
Return Value  1 (true) '' (false)
```

Definition

The `file test` operator takes one file `handle` or `filename` as an argument. It returns 1 (true) if file exists. It returns `''` (false) if the file does not exist. All `file test` operators can take a special argument underscore, which means that the test is carried out on the same file `handle` as the last `file test`, `stat()`, or `lstat()` call. If no argument is supplied, `$_` is used.

Example

```
(-e "/") ? print("-e / exists\n") : print("-e / exists\n");
```

-f

Compliance

Syntax

```
Category   named unary operator (file test)
Arguments  handle
Arguments  filename
Arguments  none
Return Value  1 (true) '' (false)
```

Definition

The `file test` operator takes one file `handle` or `filename` as an argument. It returns 1 (true) if the file is a plain file. It returns `''` (false) if the file is not a plain file. A plain file is any file that is not a special block device (-b), a special character device (-c), a directory (-d), a symbolic link (-l), a pipe (-p), a named socket (-S), or a direct link to an I/O terminal (-t). All `file test` operators can take a special argument underscore, which means that the test is carried out on the same file `handle` as the last `file test`, stat(), or lstat() call. If no argument is supplied, $_ is used.

Example

```
(-f "/") ? print("-f / is plain\n") : print("-f / is not plain\n");
```

-g

Compliance

Syntax

```
Category      named unary operator (file test)
Arguments     handle
Arguments     filename
Arguments     none
Return Value  1 (true) '' (false)
```

Definition

The `file test` operator takes one file `handle` or `filename` as an argument. It returns 1 (true) if the file has the `setgid` bit set. It returns `''` (false) if the file does not have the `setgid` bit set. In UNIX, `setgid` allows an executable to run as if it were being run by the group, which owns the executable itself while executing (for example, if a binary is owned by the group `wwwstat`, and the binary has the `getgid` bit set, then that binary has access to all files that the `wwwstat` group can access while the binary is running, even when the binary is run by someone who is not actually a member of the `wwwstat` group). All `file test` operators can take a special argument underscore, which means that the test is carried out on the same file `handle` as the last `file test`, stat(), or lstat() call. If no argument is supplied, $_ is used.

Example

```
(-g "/vmlinuz") ? print("-g /vmlinuz has setgid\n") :
    print("-g /vmlinuz has not setgid\n");
```

-k

Compliance

Syntax

```
Category   named unary operator (file test)
Arguments  handle
Arguments  filename
Arguments  none
Return Value  1 (true) '' (false)
```

Definition

The `file test` operator takes one file `handle` or `filename` as an argument. It returns `1` (true) if the sticky bit is set. It returns `''` (false) if the sticky bit is not set. In UNIX, the sticky bit can mark an executable file to be held in memory when exited (for example, if the binary `ls` is marked as sticky, when the first person runs it, it is loaded from disk to memory and executed, but when the execution finishes, the binary stays in memory so that when the next person runs `ls`, it does not need to be loaded into memory again because it is already there). This is normally set for frequently used commands to optimize execution speed. All `file test` operators can take a special argument underscore, which means that the test is carried out on the same file `handle` as the last `file test`, `stat()`, or `lstat()` call. If no argument is supplied, `$_` is used.

Example

```
(-k "/vmlinuz") ? print("-k /vmlinuz is sticky\n") :
    print("-k /vmlinuz is not sticky\n");
```

-l

Compliance

Syntax

```
Category   named unary operator (file test)
Arguments  handle
Arguments  filename
Arguments  none
Return Value  1 (true) '' (false)
```

Definition

The `file test` operator takes one file `handle` or `filename` as an argument. It returns 1 (true) if the file is a symbolic link. It returns `' '` (false) if the file is not a symbolic link. All `file test` operators can take a special argument underscore, which means that the test is carried out on the same file `handle` as the last `file test`, `stat()`, or `lstat()` call. If no argument is supplied, $_ is used.

Example

```
(-l "/vmlinuz") ? print("-l /vmlinuz is symlink\n") :
   print("-l /vmlinuz is not symlink\n");
```

-M

Compliance

Syntax

```
Category  named unary operator (file test)
Arguments  handle
Arguments  filename
Arguments  none
Return Value  integer (age of file in days relative to $BASETIME)
```

Definition

The `file test` operator takes one file `handle` or `filename` as an argument. It returns the age of the file in days relative to $BASETIME. All `file test` operators can take a special argument underscore, which means that the test is carried out on the same file `handle` as the last `file test`, `stat()`, or `lstat()` call. If no argument is supplied, $_ is used.

Example

```
print "-M ", -M "/etc/fstab", "\n";
```

-O

Compliance

Syntax

```
Category  named unary operator (file test)
Arguments  handle
Arguments  filename
Arguments  none
Return Value  1 (true) '' (false)
```

Definition

The `file test` operator takes one file `handle` or `filename` as an argument. It returns `1` (true) if the file is owned by the real UID/GID and it returns `''` (false) otherwise. For the superuser, it always returns true. All `file test` operators can take a special argument underscore, which means that the test is carried out on the same file `handle` as the last `file test`, `stat()`, or `lstat()` call. If no argument is supplied, `$_` is used.

Example

```
(-o "/vmlinuz") ? print("-o /vmlinuz is owned by real uid/gid\n") :
    print("-o /vmlinuz is not owned by real uid/gid\n");
```

-O

Compliance

Syntax

```
Category  named unary operator (file test)
Arguments  handle
Arguments  filename
Arguments  none
Return Value  1 (true) '' (false)
```

Definition

The `file test` operator takes one file `handle` or `filename` as an argument. This function returns `1` (true) if the file is owned by the effective UID/GID and it returns `''` (false) otherwise. For the superuser, it always returns true. All `file test` operators can take a special argument underscore, which means that the test is carried out on the same file `handle` as the last `file test`, `stat()`, or `lstat()` call. If no argument is supplied, `$_` is used.

Example

```
(-O "/vmlinuz") ? print("-O /vmlinuz is owned by effective uid/gid\n") :
    print("-o /vmlinuz is not owned by effective uid/gid\n");
```

-p

Compliance

Syntax

Category named unary operator (file test)
Arguments handle
Arguments filename
Arguments none
Return Value 1 (true) '' (false)

Definition

The `file test` operator takes one file `handle` or `filename` as an argument. It returns `1` (true) if the file is a named pipe. It returns `''` (false) if the file is not a named pipe. All `file test` operators can take a special argument underscore, which means that the test is carried out on the same file `handle` as the last `file test`, `stat()`, or `lstat()` call. If no argument is supplied, `$_` is used.

Example

```
(-p "/vmlinuz") ? print("-p /vmlinuz is named pipe\n") :
    print("-p /vmlinuz is not named pipe\n");
```

-R

Compliance

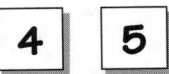

Syntax

Category named unary operator (file test)
Arguments handle
Arguments filename
Arguments none
Return Value 1 (true) '' (false)

Definition

The `file test` operator takes one file `handle` or `filename` as an argument. It returns `1` (true) if the file is readable by the effective UID/GID and it returns `''` (false) otherwise. For the superuser, it always returns true. All `file test` operators can take a special argument underscore, which means that the test is carried out on the same file `handle` as the last `file test`, `stat()`, or `lstat()` call. If no argument is supplied, `$_` is used.

Example

```
(-R "/vmlinuz") ? print("-R /vmlinuz is readable by effective uid/gid\n") :
    print("-R /vmlinuz is not readable by effective uid/gid\n");
```

-r

Compliance

Syntax

```
Category  named unary operator (file test)
Arguments  handle
Arguments  filename
Arguments  none
Return Value  1 (true) '' (false)
```

Definition

The `file test` operator takes one file `handle` or `filename` as an argument. It returns `1`
(true) if the file is readable by the real UID/GID and it returns `''` (false) otherwise. For the
superuser, it always returns true. All `file test` operators can take a special argument
underscore, which means that the test is carried out on the same file `handle` as the last
`file test`, `stat()`, or `lstat()` call. If no argument is supplied, `$_` is used.

Example

```
(-r "/vmlinuz") ? print("-r /vmlinuz is readable by real uid/gid\n") :
    print("-r /vmlinuz is not readable by real uid/gid\n");
```

-S

Compliance

Syntax

```
Category  named unary operator (file test)
Arguments  handle
Arguments  filename
Arguments  none
Return Value  1 (true) '' (false)
```

Definition

The `file test` operator takes one file `handle` or `filename` as an argument. It returns `1` (true) if the file is a symbolic link. It returns `' '` (false) if the file is not a symbolic link. All `file test` operators can take a special argument underscore, which means that the test is carried out on the same file `handle` as the last `file test`, `stat()`, or `lstat()` call. If no argument is supplied, `$_` is used.

Example

```
(-S "/vmlinuz") ? print("-S /vmlinuz is socket\n") :
    print("-S /vmlinuz is not socket\n");
```

-S

Compliance

Syntax

```
Category      named unary operator (file test)
Arguments     handle
Arguments     filename
Arguments     none
Return Value  integer (size) '' (false)
```

Definition

The `file test` operator takes one file `handle` or `filename` as an argument. It returns `size` in bytes as an integer if the file has a non-zero size. It returns `' '` (false) if the file has zero size. All `file test` operators can take a special argument underscore, which means that the test is carried out on the same file `handle` as the last `file test`, `stat()`, or `lstat()` call. If no argument is supplied, `$_` is used.

Example

```
(-s "/vmlinuz") ? print("-s /vmlinuz has non-zero size\n") :
    print("-s /vmlinuz does not have non-zero size\n");
```

-T

Compliance

Syntax

```
Category  named unary operator (file test)
Arguments  handle
Arguments  filename
Arguments  none
Return Value  1 (true) '' (false)
```

Definition

The `file test` operator takes one file `handle` or `filename` as an argument. It returns 1 (true) if the file is a text file. It returns `''` (false) if the file is not a text file. The first characters of the file are checked to see if the high bit is set, and if a suitable number are not set, the file is assumed to be text. If the file is empty, true is returned. Because this test involves reading the file itself, it is best to test to learn if the file exists as a plain file (`-f`) first. All `file test` operators can take a special argument underscore, which means that the test is carried out on the same file `handle` as the last `file test`, `stat()`, or `lstat()` call. If no argument is supplied, `$_` is used.

Example

```
(-T "/vmlinuz") ? print("-T /vmlinuz is text file\n") :
    print("-T /vmlinuz is not text file\n");
```

-t

Compliance

Syntax

```
Category  named unary operator (file test)
Arguments  handle
Arguments  filename
Arguments  none
Return Value  1 (true) '' (false)
```

Definition

The `file test` operator takes one file `handle` or `filename` as an argument. It returns 1 (true) if the file is a terminal tty device. It returns `''` (false) if the file is not. All `file test` operators can take a special argument underscore, which means that the test is carried out on the same file `handle` as the last `file test`, `stat()`, or `lstat()` call. If no argument is supplied, `STDIN` is used.

Example

```
(-t "/vmlinuz") ? print("-t /vmlinuz is tty\n") :
    print("-t /vmlinuz is not tty\n");
```

-u

Compliance

Syntax

```
Category  named unary operator (file test)
Arguments  handle
Arguments  filename
Arguments  none
Return Value  1 (true) '' (false)
```

Definition

The `file test` operator takes one file `handle` or `filename` as an argument. It returns `1` (true) if the file has the setuid bit set. It returns `''` (false) if the files does not have the setuid bit set. In UNIX, setuid allows an executable to take on the uid of the user ownership of the executable itself while executing. All `file test` operators can take a special argument underscore, which means that the test is carried out on the same file `handle` as the last `file test`, `stat()`, or `lstat()` call. If no argument is supplied, `$_` is used.

Example

```
(-u "/vmlinuz") ? print("-u /vmlinuz has suid set\n") :
   print("-u /vmlinuz does not have suid set\n");
```

-W

Compliance

Syntax

```
Category  named unary operator (file test)
Arguments  handle
Arguments  filename
Arguments  none
Return Value  1 (true) '' (false)
```

Definition

The `file test` operator takes one file `handle` or `filename` as an argument. It returns `1` (true) if the file is writable by the real uid/gid. It returns `''` (false) otherwise. For the superuser, it always returns true. All `file test` operators can take a special argument underscore, which means that the test is carried out on the same file `handle` as the last `file test`, `stat()`, or `lstat()` call. If no argument is supplied, `$_` is used.

Example
```
(-W "/vmlinuz") ? print("-W /vmlinuz is writable by real uid/gid\n") :
    print("-W /vmlinuz is not writable by real UID/GID\n");
```

-W

Compliance

Syntax
```
Category  named unary operator (file test)
Arguments  handle
Arguments  filename
Arguments  none
Return Value  1 (true) '' (false)
```

Definition

The file test operator takes one file handle or filename as an argument. It returns 1 (true) if the file is writable by the effective uid/gid. It returns '' (false) otherwise. For the superuser, it always returns true. All file test operators can take a special argument underscore, which means that the test is carried out on the same file handle as the last file test, stat(), or lstat() call. If no argument is supplied, $_ is used.

Example
```
(-w "/vmlinuz") ? print("-w /vmlinuz is writable by effective uid/gid\n") :
    print("-l /vmlinuz is not writable by effective uid/gid\n");
```

-X

Compliance

Syntax
```
Category  named unary operator (file test)
Arguments  handle
Arguments  filename
Arguments  none
Return Value  1 (true) '' (false)
```

Definition

The `file test` operator takes one file `handle` or `filename` as an argument. It returns 1 (true) if the file is executable by the real uid/gid. It returns `''` (false) otherwise. For the superuser, it always returns true. All `file test` operators can take a special argument underscore, which means that the test is carried out on the same file `handle` as the last `file test`, `stat()`, or `lstat()` call. If no argument is supplied, `$_` is used.

Example

```
(-X _) ? print("-X /bin/ls is executable by real uid/gid\n") :
    print("-X /bin/ls is not executable by real uid/gid\n");
```

-X

Compliance

Syntax

```
Category      named unary operator (file test)
Arguments     handle
Arguments     filename
Arguments     none
Return Value  1 (true) '' (false)
```

Definition

The `file test` operator takes one file `handle` or `filename` as an argument. It returns 1 (true) if the file is executable by the effective uid/gid. It returns `''` (false) otherwise. For the superuser, it always returns true. All `file test` operators can take a special argument underscore, which means that the test is carried out on the same file `handle` as the last `file test`, `stat()`, or `lstat()` call. If no argument is supplied, `$_` is used.

Example

```
(-x "/bin/ls") ? print("-x /bin/ls is executable by effective uid/gid\n") :
    print("-x /bin/ls is not executable by effective uid/gid\n");
```

-Z

Compliance

Syntax

```
Category  named unary operator (file test)
Arguments handle
Arguments filename
Arguments none
Return Value 1 (true) '' (false)
```

Definition

The `file test` operator takes one file `handle` or `filename` as an argument. It returns `1` (true) if the file has zero size. It returns `''` (false) otherwise. All `file test` operators can take a special argument underscore, which means that the test is carried out on the same file `handle` as the last `file test`, `stat()` or `lstat()` call. If no argument is supplied, `$_` is used.

Example

```
(-z "/vmlinuz") ? print("-z /vmlinuz has zero size\n") :
    print("-z /vmlinuz does not have zero size\n");
```

abs

Compliance

Syntax

```
Category  named unary operator (numeric)
Arguments numeric value
Return Value numeric
```

Definition

This function returns the absolute value of its argument (it ignores any sign).

Example

```
print("abs(-10) = ",abs(-10),"\n");
```

accept

Compliance

Syntax

```
Category  list operator (socket)
Arguments newsocket, genericsocket
Return Value integer (address of socket), '' (false)
```

Definition

This function performs low-level UNIX socket call `accept()`.

alarm

Compliance

Syntax

```
Category  named unary operator (process)
Arguments integer (seconds)
Return Value integer (seconds to previous alarm)
```

Definition

This function sets up a UNIX SIGALRM signal to be generated in the number of seconds specified. It is possible for Perl to trap such signals by calling specific signal-handling subroutines, such as `trap()`. Subsequent calls reset the `alarm()` time, retaining the number of seconds that were needed before the previous SIGALRM would have been generated. A call with zero seconds as an argument cancels the current `alarm()`.

Example

```
print("alarm(10) ",alarm(10),
" (to illustrate it needs to trapped c.f. trap)\n");
```

atan2

Compliance

Syntax

```
Category  list operator (numeric)
Arguments numeric, numeric
Return Value numeric
```

Definition

The atan2 function returns the arctangent of the arguments.

Example

```
print("atan2(60,2) = ",atan2(60,2),"\n");
```

bind

Compliance

Syntax

```
Category  list operator (socket)
Arguments  sockethandle, numeric (network address)
Return Value  1 (true) '' (false)
```

Definition

This function binds a network address to the socket handle; see the UNIX bind() call.

binmode

Compliance

Syntax

```
Category  named unary operator (i/o)
Arguments  handle
Return Value  1 (success) or undefined (error)
```

Definition

On systems that distinguish between text and binary files, this function forces binary mode treatment of the given file handle. In systems that do make the distinction, text files have the end-of-line characters (Carriage Return, Linefeed) automatically translated to the UNIX end-of-line character (Linefeed) when reading from the file (and vice versa when writing to the file); binary mode files do not have this automatic transformation.

Example

```
open(FIL,"file.dat");
binmode(FIL);
```

bless

Compliance

Syntax

```
Category  list operator (class)
Arguments  variable
Arguments  variable, classname
Return Value  reference
```

Definition

This function assigns a class to the referenced object. This class is either explicitly stated in the call, or the name of the current package is used if a second argument is not used in the call. The reference is returned.

> **Tip**
>
> Explictly state the class (use the two argument version of the call) if the code can be inherited by other classes, because the class in the single argument call would not return the required value.

Example

```
$tmp = {};
bless $tmp, ATMPCLASS;
print "bless() \$tmp is now in class ",ref($tmp),"\n";
```

caller

Compliance

Syntax

```
Category  named unary operator (scope)
Arguments  expression
Arguments  none
Return Value  1 (true) '' (false)
Return Value  (package, filename, line)
```

Definition

This function is used to test the current scope of a subroutine call. If evaluated in a scalar context, it returns 1 or '' depending on whether the current code has been called as a subroutine (this includes code that is included using a `require()` or an `eval()` call). In an array context, it supplies details of the calling context in a list comprising the `package` name, `filename`, and `line` of the call.

Example
```
sub testcaller {
    ($package, $file, $line) = caller;
}
&testcaller;
print "caller() Package=$package File=$file Line=$line \n";
```

chdir

Compliance

Syntax
```
Category    named unary operator (files)
Arguments   expression
Arguments   none
Return Value 1 (true) '' (false)
```

Definition
This function changes the current directory to the directory specified. If no argument is given, this call changes the current directory to be the home directory of the current user. It returns 1 upon success and `''` otherwise.

Example
```
chdir("/") ? print("It worked.\n") : print("It didn't work.\n");
```

chmod

Compliance

Syntax
```
Category    list operator (files)
Arguments   list
Return Value numeric
```

Definition

The first element in the list is the UNIX octal number representing the file permission. This function applies the mode specified by the octal number to all the files in the list that follows. It returns the number of files successfully modified.

Example

```
print "chmod() changed ",
chmod(0744,"/tmp/test1.txt","/tmp/test2.txt")," files.\n";
```

chomp

Compliance

Syntax

```
Category  list operator (string)
Arguments  list
Arguments  variable
Arguments  none
Return Value  numeric
```

Definition

This is an alternative to the chop() function. It removes characters at the end of strings corresponding to the $INPUT_LINE_SEPARATOR ($/). It returns the number of characters removed. It can be given a list of strings upon which to perform this operation. When given no arguments, the operation is performed on $_.

Example

```
$tmp="Aaagh!\n";
$ret = chomp $tmp;
print("chomp() ", $tmp, " returned ", $ret, "\n");
```

chop

Compliance

Syntax

```
Category  list operator (string)
Arguments list
Arguments variable
Arguments none
Return Value character
```

Definition

This function removes the last character of a string and returns that character. If given a list of arguments, the operation is performed on each one and the last character chopped is returned.

Example

```
$tmp = "1234";
$ret = chop $tmp;
print("chop() ", $tmp, " returned ", $ret, "\n");
```

Tip

Use chomp() (with $/ set to "\n") rather than chop() if you are unsure that the string has a trailing newline because chop() will remove the last character regardless, but chomp() only removes it if it is a newline.

chown

Compliance

Syntax

```
Category  list operator (files)
Arguments list
Return Value numeric
```

Definition

This function changes the ownership of the specified files. The first two elements of the list define the user ID and the group ID to set this ownership; the subsequent items in the list are the file names that are changed. The return value is the number of files successfully changed.

Example

```
print("chown() ");
chown(1,1,"/tmp/test1.txt") ? print("Worked\n") : print("Didn't work\n");
```

chr

Compliance

Syntax

```
Category  named unary operator (string)
Arguments  numeric
Return Value  character
```

Definition

This function returns the character indicated by the numeric argument.

Example

```
$E = chr(69);
print("chr() $E \n");
```

chroot

Compliance

Syntax

```
Category  named unary operator (files)
Arguments  directoryname
Arguments  none
Return Value  1 (true) '' (false)
```

Definition

This function is equivalent to the UNIX chroot() function. Given a directory name, this directory is treated as the root directory by all subseqent file system references, thus effectively hiding the rest of the file system outside the specified directory. This restriction applies to all subprocesses of the current process as well.

Tip

Normal UNIX security limits this function to the superuser, and it is normally used to make processes safer by only allowing them access to the subdirectory tree relevant to their purpose.

Example

```
print("chroot() ");
chroot("/") ? print("Worked.\n") : print("Didn't work.\n");
```

close

Compliance

Syntax

```
Category  named unary operator (files)
Arguments  handle
Return Value  1 (true) '' (false)
```

Definition

This function closes the file opened with the file `handle`. This operation flushes all buffered output. If the file `handle` refers to a pipe, the Perl program waits until the process being piped has finished.

Example

```
open(INF,"/tmp/test1.txt");
$ret = close(INF);
print("close() Returned ",$ret," on success\n");
```

closedir

Compliance

Syntax

```
Category  named unary operator (file)
Arguments  handle
Return Value  1 (true) '' (false)
```

Definition

This function closes the directory opened by `opendir()` by specifying the relevant directory `handle`.

Example

```
opendir(IND,"/tmp");
$ret = closedir(IND);
print("closedir() Returned ",$ret," on success\n");
```

connect

Compliance

Syntax

```
Category  list operator (socket)
Arguments  socket, name
Return Value  1 (true) '' (false)
```

Definition

This function is equivalent to the UNIX function call, which initiates a connection with a process, assuming that the process that is connected is waiting to accept.

continue

Compliance

Syntax

```
Category  flow control
Arguments  block
Return Value  n/a
```

Definition

A `continue` block is a syntax structure that allows a condition to be attached to another block (normally a `while` block). Any statements in the `continue` block are evaluated before the attached block is repeated.

Example

```
$i=0;
print "continue() ";
while ($i<10) {
      if ($i % 2)
          { print "${i}o "; next; }
      else
          {print "${i}e ";}
} continue {$i++}
print "\n";
```

cos

Compliance

Syntax

```
Category  named unary operator (numeric)
Arguments  expression
Return Value  numeric
```

Definition

This function returns the cosine value of the numeric expression supplied as an argument.

Example

```
print "cos() ",cos(60),"\n";
```

crypt

Compliance

Syntax

```
Category  list operator
Arguments  string, string
Return Value  string
```

Definition

This function is equivalent to the crypt() UNIX call (where available). It encrypts a string (the first argument) using a key (usually the first two letters of the first string itself) and returns the encrypted string.

Example

```
print "crypt() Password PA: ",crypt("Password","PA"),"\n";
```

dbmclose

Compliance

Syntax

```
Category  named unary operator (i/o)
Arguments  arrayname
Return Value  1 (true) '' (false)
```

Definition

This function undoes the linking of an associative array to a dbm file (see dbmopen()).

> **Note**
>
> This is depreciated in Perl 5; use untie() instead.

dbmopen

Compliance

Syntax

```
Category  list operator (i/o)
Arguments  arrayname, dbname, mode
Return Value  fatal error if dbm not supported (Perl 4)
```

Definition

This function links the associative array referred to by arrayname, to the dbm database (or equivalent) referred to by dbname (this name should not include the suffix). If the database does not exist, a new one with the specified mode will be opened (the mode being an octal chmod() style file protection).

> **Note**
>
> This is depreciated in Perl 5; use tie() instead.

defined

Compliance

Syntax

```
Category  named unary operator (misc)
Arguments  expression
Return Value  1 (true) '' (false)
```

Definition

This function returns a Boolean value depending on whether the argument is defined or not. There is a subtle distinction between an undefined and a defined null value. Some functions return undefined null to indicate errors, while others return a defined null to indicate a particular result (use a comparison with the null string to test for this, rather than using `defined()`).

Example

```
@iexist = (1,2,3);
print("defined() The array \@iexist ");
defined @iexist ? print("exists.\n") : print("does not exist.\n");
```

delete

Compliance

Syntax

```
Category  named unary operator (hash)
Arguments  expression
Return Value  value
```

Definition

Use this function to delete an element from a hash array, given the key for the element to delete, returning the value of the deleted element.

Example

```
%Hash = (1, One, 2, Two, 3, Three);
print("delete() Deleted ",delete($Hash{1}),"\n");
```

II

Perl

die

Compliance

Syntax

```
Category  list operator (i/o)
Arguments list
Return Value errorlevel
```

Definition

This function terminates execution of the Perl script when called printing the value of the list argument to STDERR (as if called with print(STDERR, list)). The exit value is the current value of $OS_ERROR ($!), which may have been set by a previous function. If this has a value of zero it returns $CHILD_ERROR ($?). If this is zero, it exits with errorlevel 255. If the error message string specified by the list does not end in a newline, the text ends "at $PROGRAM_NAME at line *line*, where *line* is the line number of the Perl script.

Example

```
die("die() Now we can give an example of die()...exiting");
```

do

Compliance

Syntax

```
Category  (flow)
Arguments block
Arguments subroutine(list)
Arguments expression
Return Value special
```

Definition

This is a syntax structure that allows repeated execution of a block of statements. The value returned is the result of the last statement in the block. Normally, an exit condition is supplied after the block. The second form where the argument is subroutine() is a depreciated form. The third form executes the contents of the file name specified by the expression (but it is better to use use() or require() instead, because this has better error checking).

Example

```
$i=1;
print("do ");
$return = do {
  print $i, " ";
  $i++;
} until $i==3;
print("Returned $return\n");
```

dump

Compliance

Syntax

Category named unary operator (misc)
Arguments label
Return Value N/A

Definition

This function causes the program to create a binary image core dump. This then allows the dumped image to be reloaded using the undump() function (if supported) which can effectively allow the use of precompiled Perl images. When reloaded, the program begins execution from the label specified. It is possible to set up a program that initializes data structures to dump() after the initialization so that execution is faster when reloading the dumped image.

each

Compliance

Syntax

Category named unary operator (hash)
Arguments variable
Return Value key, value

Definition

This function allows iteration over the elements in an associative array. Each time it is evaluated, it returns another list of two elements (a key, value pair from the associative array). When all the elements have been returned, it returns a null list.

Example

```
%NumberWord = (1, One, 2, Two, 3, Three);
print("each() ");
while (($number,$wordform)=each(%NumberWord)) {
  print("$number:(5Ôrdform ");
}
print("\n");
```

endgrent

Compliance

Syntax

```
Category  (system files)
Arguments  none
Return Value  1 (true)  '' (false)
```

Definition

This function closes the /etc/group file used by getgrent() and other group-related functions. It is equivalent to the UNIX system call.

Example

```
($name,$pw,$gid,@members)=getgrent();
$returned = endgrent();
print("endgrent() Closes /etc/group [$name,$gid]",
  " file returning $returned.\n");
```

endhostent

Compliance

Syntax

```
Category  (system files)
Arguments  none
Return Value  1 (true)  '' (false)
```

Definition

This function closes the TCP socket used by name server queries `gethostbyname()` and host-related functions. It is equivalent to the UNIX system call.

Example

```
$host = gethostbyname("lynch");
$returned = endhostent();
print("endhostent() Closes /etc/hosts [$host]",
    " returning $returned.\n");
```

endnetent

Compliance

Syntax

```
Category  (system files)
Arguments  none
Return Value  1 (true)  '' (false)
```

Definition

This function closes the `/etc/networks` file used by `getnetent()` and network-related functions. This function is equivalent to the UNIX system call.

Example

```
($name,$alias,$net,$net) = getnetent();
$returned = endnetent();
print("endnetent() Closes /etc/networks [$name]",
    " returning $returned.\n");
```

endprotoent

Compliance

Syntax

```
Category  (system files)
Arguments  none
Return Value  1 (true) '' (false)
```

Definition

This function closes the /etc/protocols file used by getprotoent() and protocol-related functions. It is equivalent to the UNIX system call.

Example

```
($name, $alias, $protocol) = getprotoent();
$returned = endprotoent();
print("endprotoent() Closes /etc/protocols ",
    "[$name,$alias,$protocol] file returning $returned.\n");
```

endpwent

Compliance

Syntax

```
Category  (system files)
Arguments  none
Return Value  1 (true) '' (false)
```

Definition

This function closes the /etc/passwd file used by getpwent() and password-related functions. It is equivalent to the UNIX system call.

Example

```
($name,$pass,$uid,$gid,$quota,$name,$gcos,$logindir,$shell) = getpwent();
$returned = endpwent();
print("endpwent() Closes /etc/passwd [$logindir,$shell] ",
    "file returning $returned.\n");
```

endservent

Compliance

Syntax

```
Category  (system files)
Arguments  none
Return Value  1 (true) '' (false)
```

Definition

This function closes the /etc/servers file used by getservent() and related functions. It is equivalent to the UNIX system call.

Example

```
($name,$aliases,$port,$protocol) = getservent();
$returned = endservent();
print("endservent() Closes /etc/servers [$name]",
    " file returning $returned.\n");
```

eof

Compliance

Syntax

```
Category  named unary operator (i/o)
Arguments  handle
Arguments  ()
Arguments  none
Return Value  1 (true) '' (false)
```

Definition

This function tests if the file pointer to file specified by the file handle is at the end of the file. This is done by reading the next character and then undoing this operation (so is only suitable on files where this can be done safely). If no argument is supplied, the file tested is the last file that was read. If the empty list is supplied, then this tests if all the last files supplied an argument to the Perl script are eof() (that is, it can be used as a termination condition in a while loop).

Example

```
open INF, "/tmp/test1.txt";
if (eof INF)
  {print "eof() TRUE\n";}
else
  {print "eof() FALSE\n";}
close INF;
```

eval

Compliance

Syntax

```
Category  named unary operator (flow)
Arguments  expression
Arguments  block
Arguments  none
Return Value  special
```

Definition

This function treats the expression like a Perl program and executes it returning the `return value` of the last statement executed. As the context of this execution is the same as that of the script itself, variable definitions and subroutine definitions persist. Syntax errors and runtime errors (including `die()`) are trapped and an undefined result is returned. If such an error does occur, `$EVAL_ERROR` (`$@`) is set. If no errors are found, `$@` is equal to a defined null string. If no expression is supplied, `$_` is the default argument. If the block syntax is used, the expressions in the block are evaluated only once within the script, which may be more efficient for certain situations.

Tip

eval() traps possible error conditions that would otherwise crash a program. Therefore, it can be used to test if certain features are available that would cause runtime errors if used when not available.

Example

```
$ans = 3;
eval "$ans = ;";
if ($@ eq "")
  {print "eval() returned success.\n";}
else
  {print "eval() error: $@";}
```

exec

Compliance

Syntax

```
Category list operator (process)
Arguments list
Return Value N/A
```

Definition

This function passes control from the script to an external system command. There is no retain from this call so there is no return value. Note that system() calls external commands and does return to the next line in the calling Perl program.

This is equivalent to the UNIX system call execvp().

Example

```
exec("cat /etc/motd");
```

exists

Compliance

Syntax

```
Category named unary operator (hash)
Arguments expression
Return Value 1 (true) '' (false)
```

Definition

This function tests if a given key value exists in an associative array, returning a Boolean value.

Example

```
%test = ( One, 1, Two, 2);
if (exists $test{One})
  {print "exists() returned success.\n";}
else
  {print "exists() returned an error.\n";}
```

exit

Compliance

Syntax

```
Category  named unary operator (flow)
Arguments  expression
Arguments  none
Return Value  value
```

Definition

This function evaluates the expression given as an argument and exits the program with that error. The default value for the error is 0 if no argument is supplied. Note that die() allows an error message.

Example

```
exit(16);
```

exp

Compliance

Syntax

```
Category  named unary operator (numeric)
Arguments  expression
Arguments  none
Return Value  numeric
```

Definition

This function returns the natural log base (e) to the power of expression (or of $_ if none specified).

Example

```
print "exp() e**1 is ",exp(1),"\n";
```

fcntl

Compliance

Syntax

```
Category  list operator (i/o)
Arguments  handle, function, packed_parameters
```

Definition
This function is equivalent to the UNIX `fnctl()` call. In Perl 5, use the `fntcl` module. In Perl 4, there should be some mechanism for linking the Perl functions to the system functions. This is usually executed when Perl is installed.

fileno

Compliance

Syntax
    Category named unary operator (i/o)
    Arguments handle
    Return Value descriptor

Definition
This function returns the file descriptor given a file `handle`.

Example
    `print("fileno() ",fileno(INF),"\n");`

flock

Compliance

Syntax
    Category list operator (i/o)
    Arguments handle, operation
    Return Value 1 (true) '' (false)

Definition
This calls the UNIX `flock()` function to access file locks. The `handle` is a Perl file `handle`. The operation is any valid `flock()` operation: place exclusive lock, place shared lock, unlock. These operations are represented by numeric values.

II

Perl

fork

Compliance

Syntax

```
Category   (process)
Arguments  none
Return Value  pid
```

Definition

The `fork` function calls the UNIX `fork()` function or equivalent to fork a subprocess at this point. Returns the process ID (pid) of the child process to the calling process; returns 0 to the child process itself. The calling program should `wait()` on any child process it `forks` to avoid creating zombie processes.

Example

```
$pid = fork;
# Chlid only prints this
if ($pid != 0) {
  print("fork() Forking a process duplicates o/p: $pid \n");
}
waitpid($pid,0);
# Child exits here
if ($$ != $origpid) { die; }
```

format

Compliance

Syntax

```
Category:    list operator (i/o)
Arguments:   format
```

Definition

This function declares an output `format` specification. These formats are used in conjunction with the `write()` function to control the output of variables and text to conform to a standard layout structure. Normally, the specification includes some variables, specifying how many characters to output and whether to justify these left, right, or centered. When `write()` is called, the actual values of the variables are used. This is useful for printing simple text reports and tables. The `format` specification itself is terminated by a period on a line by itself. The specification itself is in pairs of lines, the first describing the layout, and the second describing the variables to use in this layout.

Example

```
format STDOUT =
format() @>>>>>>> @>>>>>>> @>>>>>>>
        $t1,     $t2,      $t3
.
$t1 = One;
$t2 = Two;
$t3 = 3;
write;
```

formline

Compliance

Syntax

```
Category:      list operator (i/o)
Arguments:     picture, list
```

Definition

This function is not usually called explictly (it is an implicit part of the `format` mechanism). It allows direct manipulation of the `format` process by adding values to the `format` accumulator ($^A).

Example

```
$tmp = formline <<'FINISH', Alpha, Beta, Gamma;
formline() @>>>>>> @>>>>>> @>>>>>>
FINISH
print $^A;
```

getc

Compliance

Syntax

```
Category named unary operator (i/o)
Arguments handle
Arguments none
Return Value character
```

Definition

This function returns the next character in specified file `handle`. The file defaults to STDIN if none is specified. If there are no more characters, null is returned.

Example

```
open INF, "/etc/motd";
print "getc() ",getc(INF),"\n";
close INF;
```

getgrent

Compliance

Syntax

```
Category list operator (system files)
Arguments none
Return Value name
```

Definition

This returns the next group name (or undefined) in the /etc/group system file. In a list context, it returns extra information taken from this file (or null list). This function is equivalent to the UNIX system call getgrent().

Example

```
($name,$pw,$gid,@members)=getgrent();
print("getgrent() Examines /etc/group [$name,$gid] file.\n");
```

getgrgid

Compliance

Syntax

```
Category  named unary operator (system files)
Arguments  gid
Return Value  name
```

Definition

This function returns the next group name (or undefined) in the /etc/group system file with the supplied group ID (gid). In a list context, it returns extra information taken from this file (or null list). Equivalent to the UNIX system call getgrgid().

Example

```
($grname,$grpw,$gid,@members) = getgrgid(0);
print("getgrgid() Returns group name given GID [$grname]\n");
```

getgrname

Compliance

Syntax

```
Category  named unary operator (system files)
Arguments  name
Return Value  gid
```

Definition

This function returns the next group ID, gid, (or undefined) in the /etc/group system file with the supplied group name. In a list context, it returns extra information taken from this file (or null list). It is equivalent to the UNIX system call getgrname().

Example

```
($grname,$grpw,$gid,@members) = getgrnam("root");
print("getgrnam() Returns group GID given name [$gid]\n");
```

gethostbyaddr

Compliance

Syntax

```
Category  named unary operator (system files)
Arguments  address
Return Value  name
```

Definition

It returns the host name, (or undefined) in the /etc/hosts system file (or via a Domain
Name Server lookup) with the supplied host address. In a list context, the function returns extra information taken from this file (or null list). It is equivalent to the UNIX
system call gethostbyaddr().

Example (Perl 5 only)

```
use Socket;
@a=(140,203,7,103);
$addr=pack('C4',@a);
($name,$alias,$adrtype,$length,@address)=gethostbyaddr($addr,AF_INET);
print("gethostbyaddr() [$alias].\n");
```

gethostbyname

Compliance

Syntax

```
Category  named unary operator (system files)
Arguments  name
Return Value  address
```

Definition

This function returns the host address, (or undefined) in the /etc/hosts system file (or
via a Domain Name Server lookup) with the supplied host name. In a list context, it returns extra information taken from this file (or null list). This function is equivalent to
the UNIX system call gethostbyname().

Example

```
($name,$alias,$adrtype,$length,@address)=gethostbyname("lynch");
print("gethostbyname() [$alias].\n");
```

gethostent

Compliance

Syntax

        Category (system files)
        Arguments none
        Return Value name

Definition

gethostent returns the next host name, (or undefined) in the /etc/hosts system file (or via a Domain Name Server lookup). In a list context, it returns extra information taken from this file (or null list). This function is equivalent to the UNIX system call gethostent().

Example

        ($name,$alias,$adrtype,$length,@address)=gethostbyname("lynch");
        print("gethostent() [$alias].\n");

getlogin

Compliance

Syntax

        Category (system files)
        Arguments none
        Return Value name

Definition

This function returns the current login name from the /etc/utmp system file. It is better than the getpwuid() function for more information on the login because the information stored in /etc/utmp is limited.

Example

        print ("getlogin() ",getlogin(),"\n");

getnetbyaddr

Compliance

Syntax

        Category (system files)
        Arguments address
        Return Value name

Definition

getnetbyaddr returns the network name from the /etc/networks system file, given a network address. In a list context, it returns extra information from this file. This function is equivalent to UNIX's getnetbyaddr() call.

Example

```
($name,$alias,$addrtype,$net) = getnetent();
($name,$alias,$addrtype,$net) = getnetbyaddr($net,$addrtype);
print("getnetbyaddr() Reads /etc/networks [$name]\n");
```

getnetbyname

Compliance

Syntax

Category named unary operator (system files)
Arguments name
Return Value address

Definition

Returns the network address from the /etc/networks system file, given a network name. In a list context, it returns extra information from this file. Equivalent to the UNIX getnetbyname() call.

Example

```
($name,$alias,$addrtype,$net) = getnetbyname("localnet");
print("getnetbyname() Reads /etc/networks [$name]\n");
```

getnetent

Compliance

Syntax

Category (system files)
Arguments none
Return Value name

Definition

This function returns the next network name from the /etc/networks system file. In a list context, it returns extra information from this file. getnetent is equivalent to the UNIX getnetent() call.

Example

```
($name,$alias,$addrtype,$net) = getnetent();
print("getnetent() Reads /etc/networks [$name,$addrtype]\n");
```

getpeername

Compliance

Syntax

    Category named unary operator (socket)
    Arguments socket
    Return Value name

Definition

getpeername is equivalent to the UNIX system getpeername() system call.

getpgrp

Compliance

Syntax

    Category named unary operator (process)
    Arguments pid
    Return Value gid

Definition

This function returns the group ID (gid) of the process with the process ID (pid).

Example

```
print("getpgrp() ",getpgrp(0),"\n");
```

getppid

Compliance

Syntax

```
Category  (process)
Arguments none
Return Value pid
```

Definition

getppid returns the process ID (pid) of the parent process of the current process.

Example

```
print("getppid() ",getppid(),"\n");
```

getpriority

Compliance

Syntax

```
Category  list operator (process)
Arguments type, id
Return Value priority
```

Definition

This function calls the UNIX getpriority() function. The type is one of PRIO_PROCESS, PRIO_PGGRP, and PRIO_USER. The id is the relevent ID for this (pid for PRIO_PROCESS, pid for PRIO_PGGRP, uid for PRIO_USER). If zero is used as the id, the current process, process group, or user is used.

Example

```
print("getpriority() ",getpriority(0,0),"\n");
```

getprotobyname

Compliance

Syntax

```
Category  named unary operator (system files)
Arguments  name
Return Value  protocol
```

Definition

This function returns the protocol number from the /etc/protocols system file, given the protocol name. In a list context, it returns extra information from this file. getprotobyname is equivalent to the UNIX getprotobyname() call.

Example

```
($name, $alias, $protocol) = getprotobyname("IP");
print("getprotobyname() /etc/protocols [$name,$alias,$protocol].\n");
```

getprotobynumber

Compliance

Syntax

```
Category  named unary operator (system files)
Arguments  protocol
Return Value  name
```

Definition

This function returns the protocol name from the /etc/protocols system file, given the protocol number. In a list context, it returns extra information from this file. getprotobynumber is equivalent to the UNIX getprotobynumber() call.

Example

```
($name, $alias, $protocol) = getprotobynumber(0);
print("getprotobynumber() /etc/protocols [$name,$alias,$protocol].\n");
```

Perl

getprotoent

Compliance

Syntax

```
Category  (system files)
Arguments  none
Return Value  name
```

Definition

This returns the next protocol name from the /etc/protocols system file. In a list context, it returns extra information from this file. This function is equivalent to UNIX's getprotoent() call.

Example

```
($name, $alias, $protocol) = getprotoent();
print("getprotoent() Closes /etc/protocols [$name,$alias,$protocol].\n");
```

getpwent

Compliance

Syntax

```
Category  (system files)
Arguments  none
Return Value  name
```

Definition

getpwent returns the user name from the next entry in the /etc/passwd system file. In a list context, it returns extra information from this file. This function is equivalent to the UNIX getpwent() call.

Example

```
($name,$pass,$uid,$gid,$quota,$name,$gcos,$logindir,$shell) = getpwent();
print("getpwent() /etc/passwd [$logindir,$shell].\n");
```

getpwnam

Compliance

Syntax

```
Category   named unary operator (system files)
Arguments  name
Return Value  uid
```

Definition

This function returns the user ID (uid) from the /etc/passwd system file, given the user name. In a list context, it returns extra information from this file. It is equivalent to the UNIX getpwnam() call.

Example

```
($name,$pass,$uid,$gid,$quota,$name,$gcos,$logindir,$shell)
   = getpwnam("root");
print("getpwnam() /etc/passwd [$logindir,$shell].\n");
```

getpwuid

Compliance

Syntax

```
Category   named unary operator (system files)
Arguments  uid
Return Value  name
```

Definition

getpwuid returns the user name from the /etc/passwd system file, given the user ID (uid). In a list context, getpwuid returns extra information from this file. This function is equivalent to the UNIX getpwnam() call.

Example

```
($name,$pass,$uid,$gid,$quota,$name,$gcos,$logindir,$shell)
   = getpwuid(0);
print("getpwuid() /etc/passwd [$logindir,$shell].\n");
```

getservbyname

Compliance

Syntax

```
Category  list operator (system files)
Arguments  name, protocol
Return Value  port
```

Definition

getservbyname returns the port number of the service from the /etc/services system file, given the service name and the protocol name. In a list context, it returns extra information from this file. This function is equivalent to UNIX's getservbyname() call.

Example

```
($name,$aliases,$port,$protocol) = getservbyname("tcpmux","tcp");
print("getservbyname() /etc/servers [$name].\n");
```

getservbyport

Compliance

Syntax

```
Category  list operator (system files)
Arguments  port, protocol
Return Value  name
```

Definition

getservbyport returns the service name of the service from the /etc/services system file, given the port number and the protocol name. In a list context, it returns extra information from this file. It is equivalent to the UNIX getservbyport() call.

Example

```
($name,$aliases,$port,$protocol) = getservbyport(512,"tcp");
print("getservbyport() Problem with this! [$name]\n");
```

getservent

Compliance

Syntax

```
Category  (system files)
Arguments  none
Return Value  name
```

Definition

This function returns the next service name of the service from the `/etc/services` system file. In a list context, it returns extra information from this file. It is equivalent to the UNIX `getservent()` call.

Example

```
($name,$aliases,$port,$protocol) = getservent();
print("getservent() /etc/servers [$name].\n");
```

getsockname

Compliance

Syntax

```
Category  named unary operator (socket)
Arguments  socket
Return Value  address
```

Definition

This function is equivalent to the UNIX `getsockname()` system call and returns the address of the socket.

getsockopt

Compliance

Syntax

```
Category  list operator (socket)
Arguments  socket, level, optionname
Return Value  option
```

Definition

This function is equivalent to the UNIX `getsockopt()` system call and returns the socket option requested. However, if an error has happened, the function's return is undefined.

glob

Compliance

Syntax

```
Category  named unary operator (files)
Arguments  expression
Return Value  list
```

Definition

This function returns the `list` of files resulting from expanding the expression with any wildcards. This is equivalent to `<*.*>`.

Example

```
@files = glob("/tmp/*.txt");
print "glob() ",$files[1],"\n";
```

gmtime

Compliance

Syntax

```
Category  named unary operator (time)
Arguments  expression
Arguments  none
Return Value  list
```

Definition

Given a time as an argument (measured in seconds since 1 Jan 1970), `gmtime` returns a `list` of nine elements with that time broken down into seconds, minutes, hours, day of month, month, year, day of week, day of year, daylight saving enabled (daylight saving enabled is either 1 for on or 0 for off). If no argument is used, the current time is reported. If the system supports POSIX time zones, the time returned is localized for the Greenwich Mean Time.

In a scalar context, the `ctime()` style output (a string describing the time in readable form) is returned.

Example

```
($sec,$min,$hour,$mday,$mon,$year,$wday,$ydat,$isdst) = gmtime();
print "gmtime() 19$year-$mon-$mday\n";
```

goto

Compliance

Syntax

```
Category  (flow)
Arguments  label
Arguments  expression
Arguments  &name
Return Value  N/A
```

Definition

The first form transfers control flow in the program to the specified `label`. The second allows the evaluation of an `expression` to supply the label name to transfer control to. The third form is a way of passing control from one subroutine to another subroutine so that, to the original caller, it appears that the second subroutine was called directly.

Example

```
print "goto ";
$count = 1;
TESTGOTO: {
    print $count, " ";
    $label = "TESTGOTO";
    if ($count < 2) {
    $count++;
    goto $label;
    }
    else {
    goto FINISH;}
}
FINISH: print "\n";
```

grep

Compliance

Syntax

```
Category  list operator (lists)
Arguments  expression, list
Arguments  block, list
Return Value  list
```

Definition

This function evaluates the `expression` or `block` for each of the elements in the supplied list, returning a list of the elements that were evaluated as TRUE. The most common use for this is with a pattern match operation as the expression, and a list of strings to be processed.

Example

```
@a = ("One","Two","Three","Four","Five");
print("grep(), ",grep(/^T.*/,@a), "\n");
```

hex

Compliance

Syntax

```
Category  named unary operator (numeric)
Arguments  expression
Return Value  numeric
```

Definition

This function evaluates the `expression` as a hexadecimal string and returns the decimal equivalent.

Example

```
print("hex() ",hex("ff"), "\n");
```

import

Compliance

Syntax

```
Category  list operator (scope)
Arguments  list
Return Value  1 (true) '' (false)
```

Definition

In the Perl 5 module system, each module has a local import() method. This is called when use() includes modules.

index

Compliance

Syntax

```
Category  list operator (string)
Arguments  string substring
Arguments  string substring position
Return Value  position
```

Definition

index returns the position in the supplied string where the substring first occurs. If a position is supplied as an argument, the search begins at this element (thus repeated calls can find all occurrences if the found position is passed back as the argument to the subsequent calls). If the substring is not found, the return value is -1. All array element numbers are based on $[, which is normally set to zero. If this value is altered, it will change the way index() works. This is because index will start its search from $[if no position argument is supplied, and it will return $[-1 when there is no match found.

Example

```
$ans1 = index("abcdefghijiklmdef:-)","def");
$ans2 = index("abcdefghijiklmdef","def",$ans1+3);
print("index() def is at $ans1 and next at $ans2\n");
```

int

Compliance

Syntax

```
Category  named unary operator (numeric)
Arguments expression
Arguments none
Return Value integer
```

Definition

This function returns the integer part of the expression. It uses $_ as the argument if none is specified.

Example

```
print("int() ",int(345.678), "\n");
```

ioctl

Compliance

Syntax

```
Category  list operator (files)
Arguments handle, function, parameter
Return Value numeric
```

Definition

This function calls the UNIX `ioctl()` function with the specified packed parameter. It returns undefined if the operating system returns -1. It returns the string 0 but true if the operating system returns 0. Otherwise, it returns the value returned by the operating system.

join

Compliance

Syntax

```
Category  list operator (lists)
Arguments  expression, list
Return Value  string
```

Definition

This function returns the string comprising each element in the list joined with the string expression.

Example

```
@listone = (0, 1, 2, 3);
print("join() ",join("-",@listone),"\n");
```

keys

Compliance

Syntax

```
Category  named unary operator (hash)
Arguments  array
Return Value  list
```

Definition

This function returns a list comprising each key in the associative array passed as a parameter. In a scalar context, the number of keys is returned. The returned list is ordered by the internal storage requirements, so it is often useful to sort this array before processing.

Example

```
%assocone = (
   One, 1,
   Two, 2,
   Three, 3,
   Four, 4
   );
print("keys() ",join("-",keys(%assocone)),"\n");
```

kill

Compliance

Syntax

```
Category  list operator (process)
Arguments  signal, list
Return Value  1 (true) '' (false)
```

Definition

This function kills the processes with the `pids` in the supplied list by sending the signal level specified. If the signal level is negative, the process groups are killed.

last

Compliance

Syntax

```
Category  (flow)
Arguments  label
Arguments  none
Return Value  N/A
```

Definition

This causes control to exit the loop specified by `label` (or the innermost loop if none is specified).

Example

```
i=1;
print("last() ");
loop: while (I<10) {
   last loop if i=3;
   print(i);
}
print("\n");
```

lc

Compliance

Syntax

Category named unary operator (string)
Arguments expression
Return Value string

Definition

This function returns the lowercase version of any supplied expression.

Example

```
print"lc() ",lc("ABCDef"), "\n";
```

lcfirst

Compliance

Syntax

Category named unary operator (string)
Arguments expression
Return Value string

Definition

This function returns the string with the first character of the expression lowercased.

Example

```
print"lcfirst() ",lcfisrt("ABCDef"), "\n";
```

length

Compliance

Syntax

```
Category  named unary operator (string)
Arguments  expression
Arguments  none
Return Value  numeric
```

Definition

length returns the length of the string specified by expression. If no expression is supplied, $_ is evaluated.

Example

```
print("length() ",length("01234"),"\n");
```

link

Compliance

Syntax

```
Category  list operator (files)
Arguments  filename, linkname
Return Value  numeric
```

Definition

This function creates a new link named after the second argument linking to the filename specified in the first argument; returns 1 or 0 for success or failure.

Example

```
$result = link("/usr/local",:"/tmp/link");
print("link() $result\n");
```

listen

Compliance

Syntax

```
Category  list operator (socket)
Arguments  socket, queuesize
Return Value  1 (true) '' (false)
```

Definition

This is equivalent to the UNIX `listen()` system call. If you are using `accepts` on a socket, `listen` tells the system that it is available.

local

Compliance

Syntax

```
Category   named unary operator (scope)
Arguments  expression
Return Value  N/A
```

Definition

Modifies all the variables listed to be local to the current block. If there is more than one element, the list must be enclosed in parentheses. Any errors would be syntax errors. Although `local()` does prevent pollution of the global namespace with variables in subroutines, `my()` is safer than `local()` because it also creates new copies of the variables for each recursive call of a subroutine.

localtime

Compliance

Syntax

```
Category   named unary operator (time)
Arguments  expression
Arguments  none
Return Value  list
```

Definition

Given a time as an argument (measured in seconds since 1 Jan 1970), this function returns a list of nine elements with that time broken down into seconds, minutes, hours, day of month, month, year, day of week, day of year, daylight saving enabled (daylight saving enabled is either 1 for on or 0 for off). If no argument is used, the current time is reported. If the system supports POSIX time zones, the time returned is localized for the current time zone.

In a scalar context, the `ctime()` style output is returned (a string describing the time in readable form).

Example
```
($sec,$min,$hour,$mday,$mon,$year,$wday,$ydat,$isdst) = localtime();
print "localtime() 19$year-$mon-$mday\n";
```

log

Compliance

Syntax
```
Category  named unary operator (numeric)
Arguments  expression
Arguments  none
Return Value  numeric
```

Definition

This returns the logarithm (using the natural logarithm base e) of the `expression` (or of `$_` if none specified).

Example
```
print("log() ",log(2.5),"\n");
```

lstat

Compliance

Syntax
```
Category  named unary operator (files)
Arguments  handle
Arguments  expression
Return Value  list
```

Definition

The `lstat` function returns the file statistics of the file pointed to by the file `handle` (or a file `handle` produced by evaluating the expression). This is equivalent to `stat()`, but if the file is a symbolic link, the statistics are generated for the symbolic link itself rather than

map **335**

the file being linked to. Note that, like the `file test` operators, `lstat()` can take a special argument underscore, which means that the test is carried out on the same file `handle` as the last `file test`, `stat()`, or `lstat()` call.

Example

```
($device,$inode,$mode,$nlink,$uid,$gid,$rdev,$size,
$atime,$mtime,$ctime,$blksize,$blocks) = lstat("/tmp/link");
print("lstat() $device, $inode, $ctime \n");
```

m//

Compliance

Syntax

```
Category  named unary operator (pattern)
Arguments  m/<pattern>/<optionlist>
Arguments  /<pattern>/<optionlist>
Return Value  1 (true) '' (false)
```

Definition

This function searches the default string for the pattern using regular expression pattern matching. It returns 1 if a match is found. Otherwise, `''` is returned. The default string can be assigned to the match using either the `=~` or `!~` operators; otherwise, it is `$_`.

Example

```
$_ = "Happy MaN";
print "m// ",/n$/i,"\n";
```

map

Compliance

Syntax

```
Category  list operator (list)
Arguments  block list
Arguments  expression, list
Return Value  list
```

Definition

This function evaluates the specified expression (or block) for each individual member of the specified list. This is done by assigning $_ to each member of the list and evaluating the expression (or block). The value returned is the list of all these results (not necessarily one Perl element of the list).

Example

```
@result = map($_+1,(0,1,2));
print("map() ",@result,."\n");
```

mkdir

Compliance

Syntax

```
Category  list operator (files)
Arguments  filename, mode
Return Value  1 or 0
```

Definition

The mkdir function creates a directory with a name specified by the filename, with the mode specified by the octal mode. If it fails, $OS_ERROR ($!) is set to operating system error.

Example

```
print("mkdir() ",mkdir("/tmp/testdir",0777), "\n");
```

msgctl

Compliance

Syntax

```
Category  list operator (System V)
Arguments  id, cmd, arg
Return Value  special
```

Definition

This function is equivalent to the UNIX system call msgctl(), if supported, and provides a variety of message control operations as specified by CMD.

msgget

Compliance

Syntax

```
Category  list operator (System V)
Arguments  key, flags
Return Value  special
```

Definition

This function is equivalent to the UNIX system call `msgget()`, if supported, and returns the message queue identifier associated with key.

msgrcv

Compliance

Syntax

```
Category  list operator (System V)
Arguments  id, var.size, type, flags
Return Value  special
```

Definition

This is equivalent to the UNIX system call `msgrcv()`, if supported. This function reads a message from the queue associated with the message queue identifier, specified by `msqid`, and places it in the structure pointed to by `msgp`.

msgsnd

Compliance

II

Perl

Syntax

    Category list operator (System V)
    Arguments id, msg, flags
    Return Value special

Definition

The `msgsnd` function is equivalent to the UNIX system call `msgsnd()`, if supported, and sends a message to the queue associated with the message queue identifier.

my

Compliance

Syntax

    Category named unary operator (scope)
    Arguments expression
    Return Value N/A

Definition

This function declares each of the variables listed to be `local()` to the `block`. If more than one variable is specified, parentheses are required. The `my()` specification is stronger than the `local()` specification because it not only stops pollution of the global namespace but also creates a stack frame for subroutine calls so that recursive calls will behave as one would expect with local variables.

next

Compliance

Syntax

    Category named unary operator (flow)
    Arguments label
    Arguments none
    Return Value N/A

Definition
This operator allows branching within a loop so that the execution skips onto the next instance of the loop.

Example
```
print("next ");
@array = ("a","b","c");
loop: foreach $elem (@array) {
   next if $elem =~ /^a/;
   print $elem;
}
print "\n";
```

no

Compliance

Syntax
```
Category  list operator (module)
Arguments  module, list
Return Value  N/A
```

Definition
Using this function, particularly useful when using pragmas, is the reverse of `use()`.

Example
```
use integer;
# code using integer arithmetic here
no integer;
# back to floating point arithmetic
```

oct

Compliance

Syntax

```
Category  named unary operator (numeric)
Arguments  expression
Return Value  numeric
```

Definition

This function evaluates the expression as an octal string and returns the decimal value.

Example

```
print("oct() ",oct("88"), "\n");
```

open

Compliance

Syntax

```
Category:    list operator (files)
Arguments:   handle, filename
Arguments:   handle
Return Value TRUE (non zero) or FALSE (undefined)
```

Definition

This function opens a file using the specified file `handle`. The file `handle` may be an expression; the resulting value is used as the `handle`. If no `filename` is specified, a variable with the same name as the file `handle` is used (this should be a scalar variable with a string value referring to the `filename`).

The `filename` string may be prefixed with the following values to indicate the mode:

- `<`   Read, this is the default.

- `>`   Write.

- `+>`   Read/write—starting with new file.

- `+<`   Read/write using existing file.

- `>>`   Append.

- `<command> ¦`   Input pipe; the file name is actually a subshell command from which the file handle is piped.

- `¦ <command>`   Output pipe; the file name is actually a subshell command to which the output of the file handle is piped.

The special file name · can refer to either STDIN (·) when reading, or STDOUT (>·) when writing.

Example

```
open(FIL,"/tmp/notexist") ||
    print("open() failed as file did not exist.\n");
```

opendir

Compliance

Syntax

```
Category  list operator (files)
Arguments  handle, dirname
Return Value  1 (true) '' (false)
```

Definition

Opens a directory `handle` for the directory name specified. If the `dirname` is an expression, this can be evaluated to return a name.

Example

```
opendir (DIR, "/tmp/notexist") ||
    print("opendir() diled as directory dod not exist.\n");
```

ord

Compliance

Syntax

```
Category  named unary operator (string)
Arguments  expression
Arguments  none
Return Value  numeric
```

Definition

This function returns the numeric ASCII code of the first character in the expression (or $_ if none specified).

Example

```
print("ord() ",ord("A"), "\n");
```

pack

Compliance

Syntax

```
Category  list operator (records)
Arguments template, list
Return Value string
```

Definition

This function returns a packed version of the data in the list using the template to determine how it is coded. The template comprises a sequence of characters, each specifying the data type of the matching data item in the list.

Character	Description
@	Null fill to absolute position
A	ASCII string with spaces to pad
a	ASCII string with nulls to pad
b	Bit string (ascending bit order)
B	Bit string (descending bit order)
c	Signed char value
C	Unsigned char value
d	Double-precision float in the native format
f	Single-precision float in the native format
h	Hex string (low nybble first)
H	Hex string (high nybble first)
i	Signed integer value
I	Unsigned integer value
l	Signed long integer value
L	Unsigned long integer value
n	Short integer "network" order
N	Long integer "network" order
p	Pointer to a null-terminated string
P	Pointer to a structure (fixed-length string)
s	Signed short integer value

s	Unsigned short integer value
u	UUencoded string
v	Short integer "VAX" (little-endian) order
V	Long integer "VAX" (little-endian) order
x	Null byte
X	Back up a byte

A concise form of template can be used by appending a number after any letter to repeat that format specifier. For aA, the number uses one value and pads the rest. For bB, the number indicates the number of bits. For hH, the number indicates the number of nybbles. For P, the number indicates the size of the pointer structure. Using an asterisk in place of a number means to repeat the format specifier as necessary to use up all list values. Note that some packed structures may not be portable across machines (in particular, network and floating point formats). It should be possible to unpack the data using the same format specification with an unpack() call.

Example

```
Use Socketl
@a=(140,203,7,103);
$addr=pack('C4',@a);
($name,$alias,$adrtype,$length,@address)=gethostbyaddr($addr,AF_INET);
print("pack() ",@a, "packed as: $addr".\n");
```

package

Compliance

Syntax

```
Category  named unary operator (class)
Arguments name
Return Value N/A
```

Definition

Calling this function declares that all unqualified dynamic variables in the current block are in the scope of the specified package name. This is normally done in the header of a file to be included as a package or a module in other programs that require() or use(). Note that this does apply to variables declared as local() but not to variables declared as my().

pipe

Compliance

Syntax

```
Category  list operator (process)
Arguments  readhandle, writehandle
Return Value  1 (true) '' (false)
```

Definition

Links named pipes, like the UNIX function pipe().

pop

Compliance

Syntax

```
Category  name unary operator (array)
Arguments  variable
Return Value  value
```

Definition

This function removes the top item from the array specified and returns that element.

Example

```
@a = (1,2,3,4);
print("pop() ",pop(@a), "leaves ",@a,"\n");
```

pos

Compliance

Syntax

```
Category  named unary operator (pattern)
Arguments  variable
Return Value  numeric
```

Definition

Returns the offset that the last pattern match (m//g) reached when searching the scalar variable specified as an argument. It can be assigned to alter the behavior of the next match.

Example

```
$name = "alpha1 alpha2 alpha3 alpha4";
$name =~ m/alpha/g;
print("pos() ", pos($name), "\n");
```

print

Compliance

Syntax

```
Category  list operator (i/o)
Arguments  handle, list
Arguments  list
Arguments  none
Return Value  1 (true) '' (false)
```

Definition

Prints the list to the file represented by the file handle. If no file handle is specified, the default file handle is STDOUT. This default file handle may be altered using the select() operator. If no list argument is specified, $_ is printed.

Example

```
$return = print "print() ";
print "returns $return on success.\n");
```

printf

Compliance

Syntax

```
Category  list operator (i/o)
Arguments filehandle list
Arguments list
Return Value 1 (true) '' (false)
```

Definition

This function uses the C `printf` format specifiers to control the printed output. It is equivalent to

```
print filehandle, sprintf(list);
```

As with `print()` the default file handle is STDOUT.

Example

```
printf("printf() An integer printed with leading zeroes %05d.\n",9);
```

push

Compliance

Syntax

```
Category  list operator (array)
Arguments array, list
Return Value numeric
```

Definition

This appends the elements in the specified `list` on the end of the specified `array` and returns the new number of elements in the list.

Example

```
@a = (1);
$num = push(@a,2,3,4,5);
print("push() Added ",$num-1," elements to array: ",@a,"\n");
```

q/STRING/

Compliance

Syntax
```
Category  (string)
Arguments  q/string/
Return Value  value
```

Definition

This is a standard quote used to suppress special interpretation of characters, giving a literal string. You can use single quotes `'string'` or the letter q with delimiters. Any delimiter will do as long as it is not used in the string. The backslash character can be used to escape any reference to the delimiting character itself in the string.

Example
```
print(q!q// The only special character is the delimiter itself \!!, "\n");
```

qq/STRING/

Compliance

Syntax
```
Category  (string)
Arguments  qq/string/
Return Value  value
```

Definition

This is a double quote, used to allow interpolation of special characters within the string as required. You can use double quotes `"string"` or the double qq with delimiters. The backslash character can be used to disable the special meaning of interpolated characters, including the delimiter itself.

Example
```
$newline = "\n";
print(qq!qq// double quoted with interpolation! $newline!);
```

quotemeta

Compliance

Syntax

```
Category  named unary operator Î0attern)
Arguments  expression
Return Value  string
```

Definition

quotemeta returns the value of the expression with all the metacharacters backslashed.

Example

```
print(quotemeta("quotameta() I can use any metcharacter $ \ "),"\n");
```

qw/STRING/

Compliance

Syntax

```
Category  (list)
Arguments  qw/string/
Return Value  list
```

Definition

This function returns a list of words in string. Spaces are used as delimiters in the string to produce this list.

Example

```
print("qw// ",qw("1 2 3 4 5"),"\n");
```

qx/STRING/

Compliance

Syntax

```
Category  (process)
Arguments  qx/string/
Return Value  special
```

Definition

This is a back quote, used to allow interpolation of special characters within the string as required and then execute the resulting command as a system command. You can use back quotes 'string' or the letters qx with delimiters. The backslash character can be used to disable the special meaning of interpolated characters, including the delimiter itself. The return value is the return value of the system() call.

Example

```
print("qx// ",qx!du -s /tmp!);
```

rand

Compliance

Syntax

```
Category  named unary operator (numeric)
Arguments expression
Arguments none
Return Value numeric
```

Definition

This function returns a real number between 0 and the number evaluated as expression (the upper limit is 1 if no expression is specified). The upper limit must be positive. As the function calls a pseudorandom generator, it should be possible to generate the same sequence of numbers repeatedly unless the initial seed value is altered with srand().

Example

```
print("rand(), ",rand,"\n");
```

read

Compliance

Syntax

```
Category  list operator (i/o)
Arguments handle, variable, length, offset
Arguments handle, variable, length
Return Value 1 (true) '' (false)
```

Definition

Reads length bytes from file `handle` into variable (starting at offset if specified). It returns the number of bytes actually read.

Example

```
open(INF,"/etc/services") ¦¦ die "Error reading file, stopped";
read(INF,$result,10);
print("read() $result \n");
close(INF)
```

readdir

Compliance

Syntax

```
Category  list operator (i/o)
Arguments dirhandle
Return Value lname
```

Definition

In a list context, this function returns a list of the files in the directory specified by the directory `handle`. In a scalar context, it returns the next file name in the directory.

Example

```
opendir(DIR,"/tmp");
@file = readdir(DIR);
print("readdir() ",@files, "\n");
```

readlink

Compliance

Syntax

```
Category  named unary operator (files)
Arguments expression
Arguments none
Return Value value
```

Definition

This function returns the value of the symbolic link specified by `expression` (or `$_` if none specified). If symbolic links are not implemented, it gives a fatal error. If symbolic links are supported, but there is some system error, the error is returned in `$OS_ERROR` (`$!`).

recv

Compliance

Syntax

```
Category  list operator (socket)
Arguments socket, variale, length, flags
Return Value address
```

Definition

The `recv` function is equivalent to UNIX system call `recv()` and receives a message on a socket.

redo

Compliance

Syntax

```
Category  (flow)
Arguments label
Arguments none
Return Value N/A
```

Definition

This function passes control directly to the `label` without executing any continue block. If no `label` is specified, the innermost loop is used.

ref

Compliance

Syntax

```
Category  named unary operator (class)
Arguments  expression
Return Value  package
```

Definition

This function returns the package of a bless()ed variable, TRUE if the variable is a reference, or FALSE. The return value for TRUE is actually the type of the variable (for example, ARRAY, HASH, REF, SCALAR).

Example

```
$tmp = {};
bless $tmp, ATMPCLASS;
print "ref() \$tmp is now in class ",ref($tmp),"\n";
```

rename

Compliance

Syntax

```
Category  list operator (files)
Arguments  oldname, newname
Return Value  1 (true) 0 (fail)
```

Definition

This function renames files on the same file system from oldname to newname.

Example

```
$returned = rename("/tmp/test","/tmp/test2");
print("rename() returned $returned \n");
```

require

Compliance

Syntax

```
Category  named unary operator (module)
Arguments  expression
Arguments  none
Return Value  1 (true) '' (false)
```

Definition

If the expression is a scalar, the library specified by the `filename` is included (if it has not already been).

In Perl 5, if the expression is numeric, this requires that the version of Perl being used (in `$PERL_VERSION` or `$[`) is greater than or equal to the version specified.

Note that Perl 5 also has the `use( )` mechanism for including modules; `use( )` is more robust than required.

Example

```
require "cgilib.pl";
```

reset

Compliance

Syntax

```
Category  named unary operator (misc)
Arguments  expression
Arguments  none
Return Value  1
```

Definition

This function provides a way of resetting variables in the current package (especially pattern match variables). The expression is interpreted as a list of single characters. All variables starting with those characters are reset. The letters are case-sensitive (as Perl variables are). Hyphens may be used to specify ranges of variables to reset. If called without any argument, `reset` simply resets all search matches.

> **Caution**
>
> Use of this operator can reset system variables you may not want to alter. For example, be very careful with the following:
>
> ```
> reset A-Z;
> ```

return

Compliance

Syntax

```
Category  list operator (flow)
Arguments list
Return Value list
```

Definition

This function returns from a subroutine (or an `eval()`) with the value specified.

Example

```
sub test {
   return 1;
}
$test = &test;
print("return() Returned $test \n");
```

reverse

Compliance

Syntax

```
Category  list operator (list)
Arguments list
Return Value list
```

Definition

The reverse function returns the list given as an argument in reverse order. In a scalar context, it reverses the letters of its first argument.

Example
```
@a = (1,2,3);
print("reverse() ",reverse(@a),"\n");
```

rewinddir

Compliance

Syntax
```
Category  named unary operator (i/o)
Arguments  dirhandle
Return Value  1 (true) '' (false)
```

Definition
When reading a directory using readdir(), it is possible to reset the directory to the first file name.

Example
```
opendir(DIR,"/tmp");
print("rewinddir() (a): "
file: while ($file=readdir(DIR) {
   print $file, " ";
}
rewinddir();
print(" (b): "
file: while ($file=readdir(DIR) {
   print $file, " ";
}
print("\n");
closedir(DIR);
```

rindex

Compliance

Syntax
```
Category  list operator (string)
Arguments  string, substring, position
Arguments  string, substring
Return Value  position
```

Definition

This function is very similar to index() except that, instead of scanning for the substring from the first character in the string, it scans backwards from the last character. So, it returns the starting position of the last occurrence of substring in string (scanning backwards from the specified position or from the end if no position is specified).

Example

```
$ans1 = rindex("abcdefghijiklmdef:-)","def");
$ans2 = rindex("abcdefghijiklmdef","def",$ans1+3);
print("rindex() def is at $ans1 and next at $ans2\n");
```

rmdir

Compliance

Syntax

Category named unary operator (files)
Arguments filename
Return Value 1 or 0

Definition

This function deletes the directory specified (or $_) if it is empty and sets $OS_ERROR ($!) to the error value if there is a system error.

s///

Compliance

Syntax

Category (pattern)
Arguments s/pattern/replacement/options
Return Value numeric

Definition

This function searches the default string for pattern (a regular expression) and replaces this with the replacement string (the actual replacement behavior depends on the options). It returns the number of replacements made. The default string is set using either of the pattern binding operators (=~ or ¬~) or $_ is used if none have been bound. The valid options are

Option	Description
e	Evaluate the right side as an expression
g	Global (replace all occurrences)
i	Case-insensitive pattern matching
m	Ignore \n in string (multiple lines)
o	Optimize (compile pattern once)
s	Treat string as single line
x	Extended regular expressions

Example

```
$oldstr = "abcdefABCDEFabcdefABCDEF";
$newstr= $oldstr;
$str =~ s/abc/zzz/ig;
print("s/// $oldstr became $newstr \n");
```

scalar

Compliance

Syntax

```
Category   named unary operator (misc)
Arguments  expression
Return Value  value
```

Definition

This operator forces the argument to be interpreted in a scalar context, rather than as a list, so that it can override the default context if necessary.

seek

Compliance

Syntax

```
Category list operator (i/o)
Arguments handle, position, start
Return Value 1 (true) '' (false)
```

Definition

This function sets the file pointer to a specified offset position in a file. The offset is relative to the start that can have three values: 0 (start of file), 1 (current position), 2 (end of file). This allows the use of random access files, and the implentation of fast read algorithms (for example, binary search techniques) on file handles, especially with fixed-length data where the offsets are easier to calculate.

seekdir

Compliance

Syntax

```
Category list operator (i/o)
Arguments dirhandle. position
Return Value 1 (true) '' (false)
```

Definition

This function allows the position in a directory to be reset to a position saved with telldir(). This is useful when processing directories with readdir().

select

Compliance

Syntax

```
Category named unary operator (i/o)
Arguments handle
Arguments rbits, wbits, ebits, timeout
Return Value handle
```

Definition

This operator selects the default file handle used for I/O operations such as print() and write(). By default, STDOUT is selected, but this function can select any other file handle to be the default instead. The return value is the currently selected file `handle` (before any change) so it is useful to assign this to a variable in order to be able to restore the original `handle` as the default at a later stage.

The second form calls the UNIX system `select()` function.

Example

```
open(OUT,"/tmp/t.out");
$return = select(OUT);
print("This goues in /tmp/t.out.\n");
select($return);
print("select() restored to STDOUT.\n");
```

semctl

Compliance

Syntax

```
Category  list operator (System V)
Arguments  id, semnum, command, arg
Return Value  value
```

Definition

This function is equivalent to the UNIX `semctl()` function. This is a semaphore control operation with several variables.

semget

Compliance

Syntax

```
Category  list operator (System V)
Arguments  key, nsems, flags
Return Value  value
```

Definition

This function is equivalent to the UNIX `semget()` function and returns the semaphore ID.

semop

Compliance

Syntax

```
Category  list operator (System V)
Arguments key, opstring
Return Value 1 (true) '' (false)
```

Definition

The semop function is equivalent to the UNIX semop() function call and performs semaphore signalling and waiting functions.

send

Compliance

Syntax

```
Category  list operator (socket)
Arguments socket, message, flags, to
Arguments socket, message, flags
Return Value numeric
```

Definition

This function is equivalent to the UNIX system send() function and sends a message socket.

setgrent

Compliance

Syntax

```
Category  (system files)
Arguments  none
Return Value  n/a
```

Definition

This function rewinds the `/etc/group` file to the start of the file for subsequent accesses using `getgrent()`.

Example

```
print("setgrent() ",setgrent(), "\n");
```

sethostent

Compliance

Syntax

```
Category  named unary operator (system files)
Arguments  flag
Return Value  N/A
```

Definition

If called with an argument of 1, this function tells the system to keep a TCP socket open for name server queries such as `gethostbyname()`. If this is not, then the name server queries use UDP datagrams.

Example

```
print("sethostent() ",sethostent(1), "\n");
```

setnetent

Compliance

Syntax

```
Category  named unary operator (system files)
Arguments  flag
Return Value  N/A
```

Definition

This function rewinds the /etc/networks file used by getnetent() and other network-related functions. If the flag has a value of 1, then the file is kept open between calls to getnetbyname() and getnetbyaddr().

```
print("setnetent() ",setnetent(1), "\n");
```

setpgrp

Compliance

Syntax

```
Category  list operator (process)
Arguments  pid, pgrp
Return Value  1 (true) '' (false)
```

Definition

This function sets the current process group for the specified process (pid); if this is zero, the current process is set.

setpriority

Compliance

Syntax

```
Category  list operator (proxess)
Arguments  type, id, priority
Return Value  1 (true) '' (false)
```

Definition

This function calls the UNIX setpriority() function. The type is one of PRIO_PROCESS, PRIO_PGGRP, or PRIO_USER. The id is the relevent ID for this (pid, a pid for a group of processes, or uid). If 0 is used as the id, the current process, process group, or user is used. The priority is a number representing the level of priority (normally in the range 120 to 20) where the lower the priority, the more favorable the scheduling of the process by the operating system.

Example
```
print("setpriority() ",setpriority(0,0,-20),"\n");
```

setprotoent

Compliance

Syntax
```
Category  named unary operator (system files)
Arguments  flag
Return Value  1 (true) '' (false)
```

Definition
This function rewinds the /etc/protocols file used by getprotoent() and other protocol-related functions. If the flag has a value of 1, then the file is kept open between calls to getprotobyname() and getnetbynumber().

Example
```
print("setprotoent() ",setprotoent(1), "\n");
```

setpwent

Compliance

Syntax
```
Category  (system files)
Arguments  none
Return Value  1 (true) '' (false)
```

Definition
This function rewinds the /etc/passwd file used by getpwent() and other password-related functions.

Example
```
print("setpwent() ",setpwent(), "\n");
```

Perl

setservent

Compliance

Syntax

```
Category  named unary operator (system files)
Arguments flag
Return Value 1 (true) '' (false)
```

Definition

This function rewinds the /etc/services file used by getservent() and other service-related functions. If the flag has a value of 1, then the file is kept open between calls to getservbyname() and getnetbyport().

Example

```
print("setservent() ",setservent(1), "\n");
```

setsockopt

Compliance

Syntax

```
Category  list operator (socket)
Arguments socket, level, optname, optval
Return Value 1 (true) '' (false)
```

Definition

This function is equivalent to UNIX system call setsockopt() and sets the socket options.

shift

Compliance

Syntax
```
Category  named unary operator (array)
Arguments  array
Arguments  none
Return Value  value
```

Definition

This function takes the leftmost element from the array specified and returns that, reducing the array by one element. When no array is specified, the array of arguments passed to the Perl script, $ARGV, is used if the context is not in a subroutine; otherwise, the array of arguments passed to the subroutine, @_, is used.

The return value is undefined if the array is empty.

Example
```
print("shift() ");
while ($arg = shift) {
   print($arg,' ');
}
print("\n");
```

shmctl

Compliance

Syntax
```
Category  list operator (System V)
Arguments  id, cmd, arg
Return Value  value
```

Definition

This function is equivalent to the UNIX shmctl() function, and performs shared memory control operations.

shmget

Compliance

Syntax

```
Category  list operator (System V)
Arguments  key.size, flags
Return Value  value
```

Definition

This function is equivalent to the UNIX `shmget()` function and returns shared memory segment ID.

shmread

Compliance

Syntax

```
Category  list operator (System V)
Arguments  id, var. pos, size
Return Value  value
```

Definition

This function is equivalent to the UNIX `shmread()` function and reads from the shared memory segment ID.

shmwrite

Compliance

Syntax

```
Category  list operator (System V)
Arguments  id, string, pos, size
Return Value  value
```

Definition

This function is equivalent to the UNIX `shmwrite()` function and writes to the shared memory segment ID.

shutdown

Compliance

Syntax

```
Category  list operator (socket)
Arguments  socket, how
Return Value  1 (true) '' (false)
```

Definition

This function is equivalent to the UNIX `shutdown()` function and shuts down a socket.

sin

Compliance

Syntax

```
Category  named unary operator (numeric)
Arguments  expression
Arguments  none
Return Value  numeric
```

Definition

This function returns the sine of the expression in radians. If there is no explicit argument, `$_` is used.

Example

```
print("sin() ",sin(4), "\n");
```

sleep

Compliance

Syntax

    Category named unary operator (process)
    Arguments expression
    Arguments none
    Return Value numeric

Definition

This function causes the current process to `sleep` for the number of seconds specified in `expression` (if none is specified, it sleeps forever, but may be woken up by a signal if this has been programmed).

Example

    `print("sleep() ",sleep(5),"\n");`

---

socket

Compliance

Syntax

    Category list operator (socket)
    Arguments socket, domain, type, protocol
    Return Value value

Definition

This function is equivalent to the UNIX socket() system call and opens a specified type of socket and attaches it to a file handle.

---

socketpair

Compliance

Syntax

    Category list operator (socket)
    Arguments socket1, socket2, domain, type, protocol
    Return Value value

Definition

This function is equivalent to the UNIX `socketpair()` system call and creates a pair of sockets, which are unnamed, in the specified `domain`.

sort

Compliance

Syntax

```
Category  list operator (list)
Arguments  subname list
Arguments  block list
Arguments  list
Return Value  list
```

Definition

This function sorts the list specified and returns the sorted list. The sort method can be specified with the optional subroutine or block argument. A subroutine may be specified that takes two arguments (passed as global package variables, `$a` `$b`) and returns TRUE if the first is less than or equal to the second by any criteria used. Similarly, a block can be specified (effectively an anonymous subroutine) to perform this function. The default sort order is based on the standard string comparison order.

Example

```
@a = ("z","w","r","i","b","a");
print("sort() ",sort(@a),"\n");
```

splice

Compliance

Syntax

```
Category  list operator (array)
Arguments  array, offset, length, list
Arguments  array, offset, length
Arguments  array, offset
Return Value  list
```

Definition

This function removes the elements specified by `offset` and `length` from the array and replaces them with the elements in the list supplied as the last argument. A list of those elements removed is returned. If no `length` is specified, all the items from `offset` to the end of the array are removed.

Example

```
@a = ("a","e","i","o","u");
print("splice() ",splice(@a,0,3,"A","E","I"),"\n");
```

split

Compliance

Syntax

```
Category    list operator (pattern)
Arguments   /pattern/,expression,limit
Arguments   /pattern/,expression
Arguments   /pattern/
Arguments   none
Return Value list
```

Definition

This function manipulates a string, splitting the string denoted by the expression (or the $_ if none is specified) into an array of strings based on some separator string specified by the pattern (if the pattern has no specified whitespace as the default). An optional limit restricts the number of elements returned. A negative limit has no effect.

If not in a list context, the number of elements found is returned. In an scalar context, it returns the number of elements and puts the resulting array into the @_ array (the use of the @_ as the result is depreciated).

Example

```
print("spilt() ",split(/:/,"1:2:3:4:5"),"\n");
```

sprintf

Compliance

Syntax
```
Category  list operator (string)
Arguments  format, list
Return Value  string
```

Definition

This is equivalent to the C `sprintf()` call. The format is a string with special metacharacters to specify how many values/variables follow and how to represent each of these in the resulting string. This enables the explicit formatting of floating point and integer numbers (also enabling binary, hexadecimal, and octal formats).

Example
```
print("strintf() ",sprintf("%0d \n",9),"\n");
```

sqrt

Compliance

Syntax
```
Category  named unary operator (numeric)
Arguments  expression
Return Value  numeric
```

Definition

This function returns the result of evaluating the expression and finding its square root.

Example
```
print("sqrt() ",sqrt(4),"\n");
```

srand

Compliance

Perl

Syntax

```
Category  named unary operator (numeric)
Arguments  expression
Arguments  none
Return Value  1 (true) '' (false)
```

Definition

This function sets the seed used by the pseudorandom number generation algorithm when generating `rand()` numbers. In order to randomize the possible sequences, the seed should be set to a different value each time the script is called. The default behavior, when no expression is supplied, is to use the result of a call to `time()`. This is not a secure method of randomizing for scripts that need to be secure because it is possible to predict in what sequence the script will return.

Note that, when using a set of pseudorandom data generated using `rand()`, it is possible to generate exactly the same data repeatedly (without having to save the entire sequence) simply by stetting and saving the seed. Restoring the seed and calling `rand()` will then produce the same sequence again.

Example

```
srand(26);
print("rand() ",rand(),", ");
srand(26);
print(rand()," (should produce the same \"random\" number twice) \n");
```

stat

Compliance

Syntax

```
Category  list operator (files)
Arguments  handle
Arguments  expression
Arguments  none
Return Value  list
```

Definition

This function returns the file statistics of the file pointed to by the file `handle` (or a file `handle` produced by evaluating the expression). Note that, like the file test operators, `stat()` can take a special argument underscore; this means that the test is carried out on the same file `handle` as the last file test, `stat()`, or `lstat()` call.

Example

```
($device,$inode,$mode,$nlink,$uid,$gid,$rdev,$size,$atime,
   $mtime,$ctime,$blksize,$blocks) = stat("/etc/passwd");
print("stat() $device, $inode, $ctime \n");
```

study

Compliance

Syntax

```
Category  named unary operator (pattern)
Arguments  scalar
Arguments  none
Return Value  1 (true) '' (false)
```

Definition

When many pattern match operations are being performed on the same string, the efficiency of these patterns can be improved with the study() function. If no string is specified, the $_ is studied by default. The call sets up internal lookup tables based on the string studied so that pattern matching operations can use this information to processs the pattern match more quickly. Only one string at a time can be studied (subsequent calls effectively "unstudy" any previous study() removing the lookup tables). The function study() is often used in a loop processing lines of a text file where each line is studied before being processed with various pattern matches.

sub

Compliance

Syntax

```
Category  (flow)
Arguments  name block
Arguments  name
Arguments  name
Return Value  value
```

Definition

This is the syntax for a subroutine declaration. The full form defines a subroutine with the name and associates this with the statements in block. When evoked, it will return the result of the last statement executed in the block (often a return() statement). If no name is supplied, it is an anonymous subroutine (certain functions such as sort() allow anonymous subroutines as arguments). With only a name as an argument, the statement is a forward reference to a subroutine that is fully declared later in the script.

substr

Compliance

Syntax
```
Category list operator (string)
Arguments expression, offset, length
Arguments expression, offset
Return Value string
```

Definition
This function returns a substring of a string specified by expression. The substring starts at the specified offset and has the specified length. If the offset is negative, it starts from the righthand side of the string instead of the lefthand side. If the length is negative, it means to trim the string by that number of characters.

Example
```
print("substr() ",substring("okay",0,2),"\n");
```

symlink

Compliance

Syntax
```
Category list operator ((files)
Arguments oldfile, newfile
Return Value 1 or 0
```

Definition
This function creates a symbolic link from the existing file specified by oldfile to the specified newfile and returns 1 on success and 0 on failure. If symbolic links are not supported by the operating system, this will return a fatal error.

Example
```
print("symlink() ",symlink("/usr/local","/tmp/symlinktousrlocal"),"\n");
```

syscall

Compliance

Syntax

```
Category  list operator (i/o)
Arguments list
Return Value varies
```

Definition

This mechanism allows Perl to call corresponding UNIX C system calls directly. It relies on the existence of the set of Perl header files Syscall.ph which declares all of these calls. The script h2ph that is normally executed when Perl is installed, sets up the Syscall.ph files. Each call has the same name as the equivalent UNIX system call with the SYS_ prefix. Because these calls actually pass control to the relevant C system function, care must be taken with passing parameters.

The first element in the list used as an argument to syscall() itself is the name corresponding to the UNIX system call (that is, with the SYS_ prefix). The next elements in the list are interpreted as parameters to this call. Numeric values are passed as the C type int. String values are passed as pointers to arrays. The length of these strings must be able to cope with any value assigned to that parameter in the call.

Example

```
require "syscall.ph";
print("syscall() ",syscall(&SYS_getpid)," equivalent to $PID\n");
```

sysopen

Compliance

Syntax

```
Category  list operator (i/o)
Arguments handle, name, mode, permissions
Arguments handle, name, mode
Return Value 1 (true) '' (false)
```

Definition

This function calls the UNIX C open() function directly from the Perl script, which opens a file for reading or writing.

sysread

Compliance

Syntax

```
Category  list operator (i/o)
Arguments handle, scalar, length, offset
Arguments handle, scalar, length
Return Value 1 (true) '' (false)
```

Definition

This function calls the UNIX C read() function directly from the Perl script, which reads a line from the standard input source.

system

Compliance

Syntax

```
Category  list operator (process)
Arguments list
Return Value status
```

Definition

This call executes the specified list as an operating system call. The process to execute this command is forked and the script waits for the child process to return. The return value is the exit status of the child process.

> **Note**
>
> To capture the output from a system call, use the qx// (back quote mechanism) rather than system().

Example

```
print("system() ",system("ls -F /var > /tmp/t.tmp"),"\n");
```

syswrite

Compliance

Syntax

```
Category  list operator (i/o)
Arguments handle, scalar, length, offset
Arguments handle, scalar, length
Return Value 1 (true) '' (false)
```

Definition

This function calls the UNIX C `write()` function directly from the Perl script, which is an interactive write to another user process.

tell

Compliance

Syntax

```
Category  named unary operator (i/o)
Arguments expression
Arguments none
Return Value position
```

Definition

This function returns the current position in the file specified by the expression (which should evaluate to a file `handle`). If no `handle` is specified, the last file accessed is used. This value can be used by `seek()` to return to this position if appropriate.

Example

```
print("tell() ",tell(STDOUT),"\n");
```

telldir

Compliance

Syntax

```
Category  named unary operator (i/o)
Arguments dirhandle
Return Value position
```

Definition

This function returns the current position in the directory `handle` specified. This value can be used by `seekdir()` to return to this position if appropriate.

Example

```
opendir(DIR,"/tmp");
readdir(DIR);
print("telldir() ",telldir(DIR),"\n");
```

tie

Compliance

Syntax

```
Category  list operator (class)
Arguments variable, classname, list
Return Value object
```

Definition

This function binds a variable to a package class. It creates an instance of this class by running the `new()` method associated with that class. Any parameters for the `new()` method may be specified in the list.

The behavior depends on the way the package class is written, and on the type of variable. Most common are package classes written to support associative arrays. In particular, package classes exist to bind associative arrays to various databases.

The `tie()` mechanism hides all the complexities of implemention behind a simple interface so that, for example, the records in a database can be accessed by looking at the associative array bound to the database through an appropriate package class.

The example here uses the Configure.pm module. This module gives access to information about the machine on which Perl was installed. It is possible to bind an associative array to this class and examine this to find out the value of any of the configuration parameters.

Example
```
use Configure;
$return = tie %c, Configure;
print("tie() returned \"$return\" and ",
    "a sample value is $c{installbin}\n");
```

tied

Compliance

Syntax
```
Category  named unary operator
Arguments  variable
Return Value  object
```

Definition

This function was first implemented in Perl 5.002 and returns a reference to the object that the variable is an instance of. This is the0 same as is returned by the original call to tie() when it is bound.

time

Compliance

Syntax
```
Category  (time)
Arguments  none
Return Value  time
```

Definition

This function returns the time, in seconds, since 1 January 1970. The format can be converted into more useful parts using gmtime() or localtime().

times

Compliance

Syntax

```
Category (process)
Arguments none
Return Value list
```

Definition

This function returns a list of four elements representing the time, in seconds, used. The four elements represent the system time and the user time used by the current process and child processes.

Example

```
($usertime,$systemtime,$childsystem,$childuser) = times();
print("times() $usertime $systemtime $childsystem $childuser\n");
```

tr///

Compliance

Syntax

```
Category (string)
Arguments tr/searchlist/replacelist/<options>
Return Value numeric
```

Definition

This function translates all occurrences of items in the search list with the equivalent items in the replacement list. The string searched is the default search string bound by =~ or !=, or if no string is bound to the pattern match, the $_ string is used. The return value is the number of characters translated or deleted.

The valid options are described in the following table.

Option	Description
c	Complement (non-matching characters in search list are used)
d	Delete (delete any characters not in search list as well as translating)

Option	Description
s	Squash (if the translation results in a sequence of repeated characters from the replace list, then reduce this to one occurrence of the character)

The `searchlist` and the `replacelist` may contain the character to indicate a range of characters.

Example

```
tr/AEIOU/aeiou/      # Make all vowels lowercase
tr/[A-M]/[a-m]/      # Make first half of alphabet lowercase
tr/aeiou/ /c         # Replace all non-vowels with space
tr/aeiou/AEIOU/d     # Make all vowels uppercase and remove
                     # all other characters
tr/aeiou/-/s         # Replace all vowels with -,
                     # but only one - for adjacent vowels
```

truncate

Compliance

Syntax

```
Category     list operator (i/o)
Arguments    handle, length
Arguments    expression, length
Return Value 1 (true) '' (false)
```

Definition

This function truncates the file referenced by the file `handle` to `length`. An expression can be used that evaluates to the file `handle` if the operating system does not implement this feature.

uc

Compliance

Syntax

```
Category     named unary operator (string)
Arguments    expression
Return Value string
```

Definition

This function returns an uppercase version of the specified `expression`.

Example
```
print("uc() ",uc("This is All Caps"), "\n");
```

ucfirst

Compliance

Syntax
```
Category  named unary operator (string)
Arguments expression
Return Value  string
```

Definition

This function returns a `string` with the first character of the `expression` in uppercase.

Example
```
print("ucfirst() ",ucfirst("this is Capitalized"), "\n");
```

umask

Compliance

Syntax
```
Category  named unary operator (files)
Arguments newumask
Arguments none
Return Value  oldumask
```

Definition

This function sets the file mask using the specified `newumask`. It returns the `oldumask` so that it can be stored and restored later if required. If called without any arguments, it returns the current umask. This is the mechanism UNIX uses to modify the permissions of any files created.

Example
```
print("umask() The current umask is: ",umask,"\n");
```

undef

Compliance

Syntax
```
Category    named unary operator (misc)
Arguments   expression
Arguments   none
Return Value  value
```

Definition

This function undefines the value of the expression. The expression may be a scalar value, an array, or a subroutine (specified with a & prefix). When called without an expression, this function returns an undefined value.

unlink

Compliance

Syntax
```
Category    list operator (files)
Arguments   list
Return Value  numeric
```

Definition

This function deletes the files in the `list` and returns the number of files deleted.

Example
```
system("touch /tmp/t.tst");
print("unlink() ",unlink("/tmp/t.tst"),"\n");
```

unpack

Compliance

Syntax
```
Category  list operator (data)
Arguments template, expression
Return Value list
```

Definition

This function unpacks data that is packed with `pack()`. It uses the same template mechanism to specify the format of the data in the packed string. In a scalar context, the first value in the list is returned.

unshift

Compliance

Syntax
```
Category  named unary operator (class)
Arguments variable
Return Value 1 (true) '' (false)
```

Definition

This function undoes the binding between a variable and a `package` class that was created using `tie()`.

use

Compliance

Syntax

```
Category  list operator (module)
Arguments  module, list
Return Value  N/A
```

Definition

This function imports the specified module into the current block. The `import()` method defined for the package class represented by the module is evaluated. The specified list is passed as optional arguments to this `import()` method. If you do not specify a list argument, then the default methods for that module will be those imported. You can specify the empty `list()` in order to avoid adding any items to the local namespace.

Example

```
use English;
```

Note that this is the mechanism for implementing compiler directives known as pragmas. You can, for example, force all arithmetic to be integer-based by

```
use integer;
```

And then this can be turned off again with

```
no integer;
```

utime

Compliance

Syntax

```
Category  list operator (files)
Arguments  list
Return Value  numeric
```

Definition

This function sets the access and modification time of all the files in the `list` to the time specified in the first two items in the list. The time must be in the numeric format (that is, seconds since 1 January 1970) as returned by the `time()` function.

Example

```
$time = now;
print("utime() ",utime($time,$time,"/tmp/t.tst"),"\n");
```

values

Compliance

Syntax

```
Category  named unary operator (hash)
Arguments  variable
Return Value  list
```

Definition

This function returns the array comprising all the values in the associate array specified. In a scalar context, it returns the number of values in the array.

Example

```
%a = (1, "one", 2, "two", 3, "three");
print("vaules() ",values(%a),"\n");
```

vec

Compliance

Syntax

```
Category  list operator (fixed)
Arguments  expression, offset, bits
Return Value  value
```

Definition

This function uses the string specified by expression as a vector of unsigned integers. The return value is the value of the bitfield specified by offset. The specified bits is the number of bits that are reserved for each entry in the bit vector. This must be a power of 2 from 1 to 32. Note that the offset is the marker for the end of the vector, and it counts back the number of bits specified to find the start.

Vectors can be manipulated with the logical bitwise operators ¦, &, and ^.

Example

```
$vec = '';
vec($vec,3,4) = 1;       # bits 0 to 3
vec($vec,7,4) = 10;      # bits 4 to 7
vec($vec,11,4) = 3;      # bits 8 to 11
```

```
vec($vec,15,4) = 15;        # bits 12 to 15
# As there are 4 bits per number this can be decoded by
# unpack() as a hex number
print("vec() Has a created a string of nybbles, in hex: ",
   unpack("h*",$vec),"\n");
```

wait

Compliance

Syntax

```
Category  (process)
Arguments  none
Return Value  pid
```

Definition

This function waits for a child process to exit. It returns the process ID (pid) of the terminated process and -1 if there are no child processes.

waitpid

Compliance

Syntax

```
Category  list operator (process)
Arguments  pid, flags
Return Value  pid
```

Definition

This function waits for a specified child process to exit and returns pid of the terminated process and -1 if there is no child process matching the pid specified. The flags can be set to various values that are equivalent to the waitpid() UNIX system call (if the operating system supports this); a flags value of 0 should work on all operating systems' supporting processes.

wantarray

Compliance

Syntax

```
Category (flow)
Arguments none
Return Value 1 (true) '' (false)
```

Definition

This function returns 1 if the current context is an array context; otherwise, it returns ''. This construct is most often used to return two alternatives from a subroutine, depending on the calling context.

Example

```
return wantarray ? (8, 4, 33) : 3;
```

warn

Compliance

Syntax

```
Category list operator (i/o)
Arguments list
Return Value 1 (true) '' (false)
```

Definition

This function prints the supplied list to STDERR, like die(). If there is no newline in the list, warn() appends the text at line <line number>\n to the message. However, the script will continue after a warn().

write

Compliance

Syntax

```
Category  list operator (i/o)
Arguments expression
Arguments handle
Arguments none
```

Definition

This function writes a formatted record to the file `handle` (or the file `handle` that the expression evaluates to). If no file `handle` is specified, the default is STDOUT; this can be altered by using `select()` if necessary.

A format for use by that file `handle` must have been declared using the `format()` function. This defaults to the name of the file `handle` being used, but other format names can be associated with the current `write()` operation using the $FORMAT_NAME ($~) special variable.

y///

Compliance

Syntax

```
Category  (string)
Arguments y/searchlist/replacelist/<options>
Return Value numeric
```

Definition

The y/// operator is a synonym for the translation operator tr///.

Perl

Chapter 11

Perl Regular Expressions

A regular expression is a way of specifying a pattern so that some strings match the pattern and some strings do not. Parts of the matching pattern can be marked for use in operations such as substitution. This is a powerful tool for processing text, especially when producing text-based reports. Many UNIX utilities use a form of regular expressions as a pattern matching mechanism (for example, egrep) and Perl has adopted this concept, almost as its own.

Like arithmetic expressions, regular expressions are made up of a sequence of legal symbols linked with legal operators. Table 11.1 lists all of these operators and symbols in one table for easy reference. If you are new to regular expressions you may find the description in Chapter 7, "Perl Overview," informative.

Table 11.1   Regular Expression Meta-Characters, Meta-Brackets, and Meta-Sequences

Expression	Description
Meta-Characters	
^	This meta-character—the caret—will match the beginning of a string or, if the /m option is used, match the beginning of a line. It is one of two pattern anchors—the other anchor is the $.
.	This meta-character will match any single character except for the newline unless the /s option is specified. If the /s option is specified, then the newline will also be matched.
$	This meta-character will match the end of a string or, if the /m option is used, match the end of a line. It is one of two pattern anchors—the other anchor is the ^.
¦	This meta-character—called *alternation*—lets you specify two values that can cause the match to succeed. For instance, m/a¦b/ means that the $_ variable must contain the "a" or "b" character for the match to succeed.
*	This meta-character indicates that the thing immediately to the left should be matched zero or more times in order to be evaluated as true; thus, .* matches any number of character.

(continues)

Table 11.1 Continued	
Expression	**Description**
Meta-Characters	
+	This meta-character indicates that the thing immediately to the left should be matched one or more times in order to be evaluated as true.
?	This meta-character indicates that the thing immediately to the left should be matched zero or one times in order to be evaluated as true. When used in conjunction with the +, ?, or {n, m} meta-characters and brackets, it means that the regular expression should be non-greedy and match the smallest possible string.
Meta-Brackets	
()	The parentheses let you affect the order of pattern evaluation and act as a form of pattern memory. See Chapter 8, "Perl Special Variables," for more details.
(?...)	If a question mark immediately follows the left parentheses, it indicates that an extended mode component is being specified (new to Perl 5).
(?#comment)	Extension: comment is any text.
(?:regx)	Extension: regx is any regular expression, but parentheses are not saved as a backreference.
(?=regx)	Extension: allows matching of zero-width positive lookahead characters (that is, the regular expression is matched but not returned as being matched).
(?!regx)	Extension: allows matching of zero-width negative lookahead characters (that is, negated form of (=regx)).
(?options)	Extension: applies the specified options to the pattern bypassing the need for the option to specified in the normal way. Valid options are: i (case-insensitive), m (treat as multiple lines), s (treat as single line), x (allow whitespace and comments).
{n, m}	The braces let you specify how many times the thing immediately to the left should be matched. {n} means that it should be matched exactly n times. {n,} means it must be matched at least n times. {n, m} means that it must be matched at least n times but not more than m times.
[]	The square brackets let you create a character class. For instance, m/[abc]/ will evaluate to true if any of a, b, or c is contained in $_. The square brackets are a more readable alternative to the alternation meta-character.
Meta-Sequences	**Description**
\	This meta-character "escapes" the character that follows. This means that any special meaning normally attached to that character is ignored. For instance, if you need to include a dollar sign in a pattern, you must use \$ to avoid Perl's variable interpolation. Use \\ to specify the backslash character in your pattern.
\nnn	Any octal byte (where nnn represents the octal number—this allows any character to be specified by its octal number).
\a	The alarm character (this is a special character that, when printed, produces a warning bell sound).

Expression	Description
Meta-Sequences	
\A	This meta-sequence represents the beginning of the string. Its meaning is not affected by the /m option.
\b	This meta-sequence represents the backspace character inside a character class, otherwise it represents a word boundary. A word boundary is the spot between word (\w) and non-word (\W) characters. Perl thinks that the W meta-sequence matches the imaginary characters of the end of the string.
\B	Match a non-word boundary.
\cn	Any control character (where *n* is the character, for example, \cY for Ctrl+Y).
\d	Match a single digit character.
\D	Match a single non-digit character.
\e	The escape character.
\E	Terminate the \L or \U sequence.
\f	The form feed character.
\G	Match only where the previous m//g left off.
\l	Change the next character to lowercase.
\L	Change the following characters to lowercase until a \E sequence is encountered.
\n	The newline character.
\Q	Quote regular expression meta-characters literally until the \E sequence is encountered.
\r	The carriage return character.
\s	Match a single whitespace character.
\S	Match a single non-whitespace character.
\t	The tab character.
\u	Change the next character to uppercase.
\U	Change the following characters to uppercase until a \E sequence is encountered.
\v	The vertical tab character.
\w	Match a single word character. Word characters are the alphanumeric and underscore characters.
\W	Match a single non-word character.
\xnn	Any hexadecimal byte.
\Z	This meta-sequence represents the end of the string. Its meaning is not affected by the /m option.
\$	The dollar sign character.
\@	The ampersand character.
\%	The percent character.

II

Perl

Chapter 12

Perl Reference Tables

This chapter includes tables for two important areas of Perl programming. First, although regular expressions are explained in Chapter 7, "Perl Overview," it is useful to have a quick reference table for the various symbols and their meanings in regular expressions. Secondly, a list of the Perl 5 standard modules is included.

Regular Expressions

A regular expression is a way of specifying a pattern so that some strings match the pattern and some strings do not. Parts of the matching pattern can be marked for use in operations such as substitution. This is a powerful tool for processing text, especially when producing text-based reports. Many UNIX utilities, such as egrep, use a form of regular expressions as a pattern-matching mechanism, and Perl has adopted this concept, almost as its own.

Like arithmetic expressions, regular expressions are made up of a sequence of legal symbols linked with legal operators. Table 12.1 lists all of these operators and symbols in one table for easy reference. If you are new to regular expressions, you may find the description in Chapter 7 informative.

Table 12.1   Regular Expression Meta-Characters, Meta-Brackets, and Meta-Sequences

Expression	Description
Meta-Characters	
^	This meta-character, the caret, matches the beginning of a string or, if the /m option is used, matches the beginning of a line. It is one of two pattern anchors; the other anchor is the $.
.	This meta-character will match any single character except for the newline character unless the /s option is specified. If the /s option is specified, then the newline will also be matched.
$	This meta-character will match the end of a string or, if the /m option is used, match the end of a line. It is one of two pattern anchors; the other anchor is the ^.
¦	This meta-character, called *alternation*, lets you specify two values that can cause the match to succeed. For instance, m/a¦b/ means that the $ variable must contain the "a" or "b" character for the match to succeed.
*	This meta-character indicates that the "thing" immediately to the left should be matched zero or more times in order to be evaluated as true (thus, .* matches any number of characters).
+	This meta-character indicates that the "thing" immediately to the left should be matched one or more times in order to be evaluated as true.
?	This meta-character indicates that the "thing" immediately to the left should be matched zero or one times to be evaluated as true. When used in conjunction with the +, ?, or {n, m} meta-characters and -brackets, it means that the regular expression should be non-greedy and match the smallest possible string.
Meta-Brackets	
()	The parentheses let you affect the order of pattern evaluation and act as a form of pattern memory. See Chapter 8, "Perl Special Variables," for more details.
(?...)	If a question mark immediately follows the left parentheses, it indicates that an extended mode component is being specified; this is new to Perl 5.
(?#comment)	Extension: comment is any text.
(?:regx)	Extension: regx is any regular expression but () are not saved as a backreference.
(?=regx)	Extension: Allows matching of zero-width positive lookahead characters (that is, the regular expression is matched but not returned as being matched).
(?!regx)	Extension: Allows matching of zero-width negative lookahead characters (that is, negated form of (=regx)).
(?options)	Extension: Applies the specified options to the pattern bypassing the need for the option to specified in the normal way. Valid options are: i (case-insensitive), m (treat as multiple lines), s (treat as single line), and x (allow whitespace and comments).

Expression	Description
Meta-Brackets	
{n, m}	Braces let you specify how many times the "thing" immediately to the left should be matched. {n} means that it should be matched exactly *n* times. {n,} means it must be matched at least *n* times. {n, m} means that it must be matched at least *n* times but not more than *m* times.
[]	Square brackets let you create a character class. For instance, m/[abc]/ evaluates to true if any of a, b, or c is contained in $_. The square brackets are a more readable alternative to the alternation meta-character.
Meta-Sequences	
\	This meta-character "escapes" the character which follows. This means that any special meaning normally attached to that character is ignored. For instance, if you need to include a dollar sign in a pattern, you must use \$ to avoid Perl's variable interpolation. Use \\ to specify the backslash character in your pattern.
\nnn	Any octal byte where *nnn* represents the octal number; this allows any character to be specified by its octal number.
\a	The alarm character; this is a special character which, when printed, produces a warning bell sound.
\A	This meta-sequence represents the beginning of the string. Its meaning is not affected by the /m option.
\b	This meta-sequence represents the backspace character inside a character class; otherwise, it represents a word boundary. A word boundary is the spot between word (\w) and non-word (\W) characters. Perl thinks that the \W meta-sequence matches the imaginary characters of the end of the string.
\B	Match a non-word boundary.
\cn	Any control character where n is the character (for example, \cY for Ctrl+Y).
\d	Match a single digit character.
\D	Match a single non-digit character.
\e	The escape character.
\E	Terminate the \L or \U sequence.
\f	The form feed character.
\G	Match only where the previous m//g left off.
\l	Change the next character to lowercase.
\L	Change the following characters to lowercase until a \E sequence is encountered.
\n	The newline character.
\Q	Quote regular expression meta-characters literally until the \E sequence is encountered.
\r	The carriage return character.
\s	Match a single whitespace character.

(continues)

Table 12.1 Continued	
Expression	**Description**
Meta-Sequences	
\S	Match a single non-whitespace character.
\t	The tab character.
\u	Change the next character to uppercase.
\U	Change the following characters to uppercase until a \E sequence is encountered.
\v	The vertical tab character.
\w	Match a single word character. Word characters are the alphanumeric and underscore characters.
\W	Match a single non-word character.
\xnn	Any hexadecimal byte.
\Z	This meta-sequence represents the end of the string. Its meaning is not affected by the /m option.
\$	The dollar sign character.
\@	The ampersand character.
\%	The percent character.

Perl 5 Standard Modules

This is a list of the standard modules that come with Perl 5 along with a brief description.

For a list of all current modules, including many extra non-standard modules other than those listed here, see the CPAN archive. The contents of the Perl Module List are at **ftp://ftp.funet.fi/pub/languages/perl/CPAN/modules/00modlist.long.html**. The modules of the Perl Module List sorted by authors are at **ftp://ftp.funet.fi/pub/languages/perl/CPAN/modules/by-authors**. The modules of the Perl Module List sorted by category are at **ftp://ftp.funet.fi/pub/languages/perl/CPAN/modules/by-category**. The modules of the Perl Module List sorted by module are at **ftp://ftp.funet.fi/pub/languages/perl/CPAN/modules/by-module**.

Module Name	**Description**
AnyDBM_File	Accesses external databases.
AutoLoader	Special way of loading subroutines on demand.
AutoSplit	Special way to set up modules for use of AutoLoader.
Benchmark	Time code for benchmarking.
Carp	Reports errors across modules.
Config	Reports compiler options used when Perl installed.
Cwd	Functions to manipulate current directory.

Module Name	Description
DB_File	Accesses Berkley DB files.
Devel::SelfStubber	Allows correct inheritance autoloaded methods.
diagnostics	pragma; enables diagnostic warnings.
DynaLoader	Used by modules which link to C libraries.
English	pragma; allows the use of long special variable names.
Env	Allows access to environment variables.
Exporter	Standard way for modules to export subroutines.
ExtUtils::Liblist	Examines C libraries.
ExtUtils::MakeMaker	Creates makefiles for extension modules.
ExtUtils::Manifest	Helps maintain a MANIFEST file.
ExtUtils::Miniperl	Used by makefiles generated by ExtUtils::MakeMaker.
ExtUtils::Mkbootstrap	Used by makefiles generated by ExtUtils::MakeMaker.
Fcntl	Accesses to C Fcntl.h.
File::Basename	Parses filenames according to various operating system rules.
File::CheckTree	Multiple file tests.
File::Find	Finds files according to criteria.
File::Path	Creates/deletes directories.
FileHandle	Allows object syntax for file handles.
Getopt::Long	Uses POSIX style command line options.
Getopt::Std	Uses single letter command line options.
I18N::Collate	Uses POSIX local rules for sorting 8-bit strings.
integer	pragma; uses integer arithmetic.
IPC::Open2	Inter-Process Communications (process with read/write).
IPC::Open3	Inter-Process Communications (process with read/write/error).
less	pragma; unimplemented.
Net::Ping	Tests network node.
overload	Allows overloading of operators (that is, special behavior depending on object type).
POSIX	Uses POSIX standard identifiers.
Safe	Can evaluate Perl code in safe memory compartments.
SelfLoader	Allows specification of code to be autoloaded in module (alternative to the AutoLoader procedure).
sigtrap	pragma; initializes some signal handlers.
Socket	Accesses to C Socket.h.
strict	pragma; forces safe code.
subs	pragma; predeclares specified subroutine names.
Test::Harness	Runs the standard Perl tests.
Text::Abbrev	Creates abbreviation table.

Perl

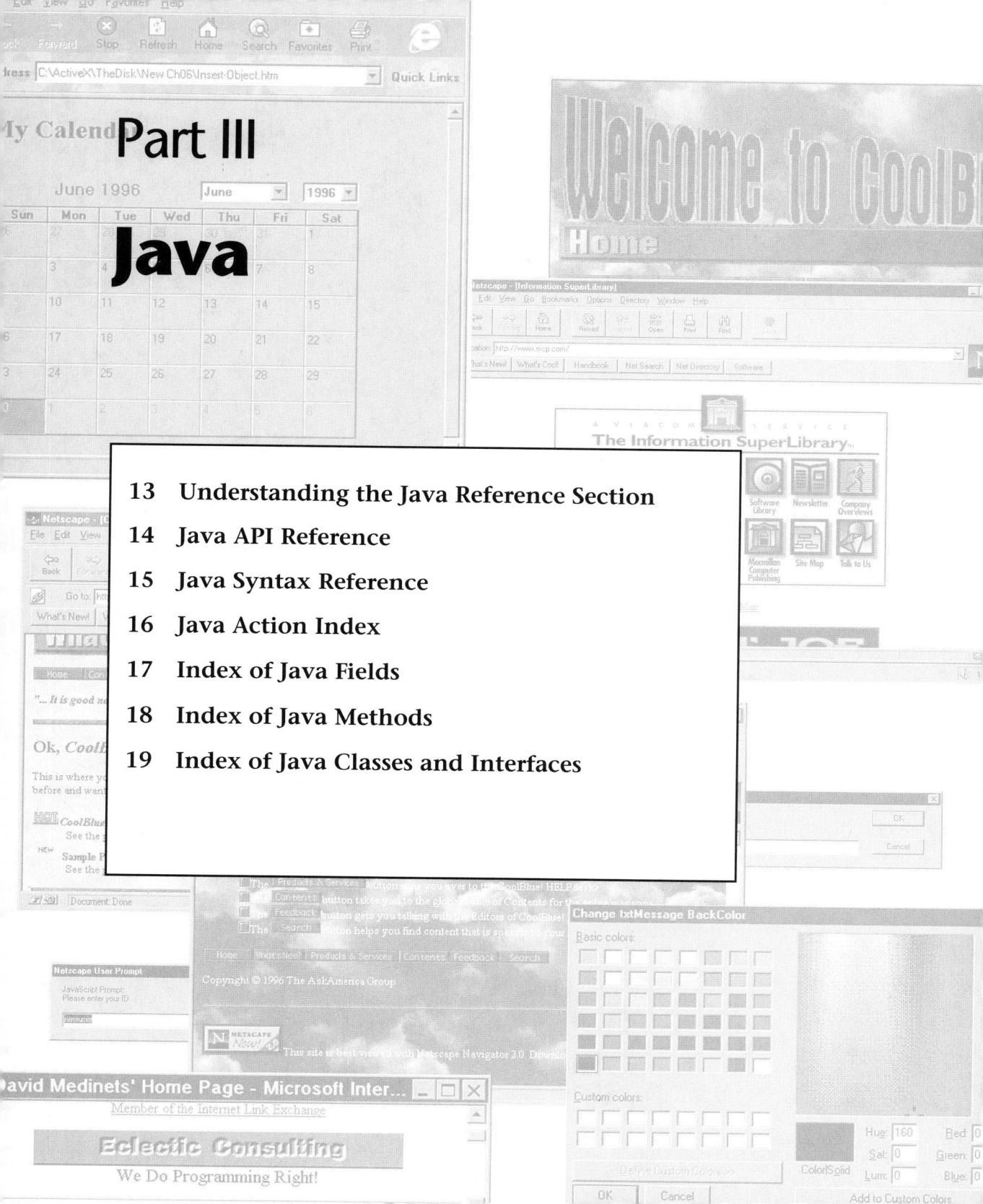

Part III

Java

Chapter 13

Understanding the Java Reference Section

What Does This Section Contain?

The Java language consists of two parts: the *syntax* and the *libraries*. The Java syntax closely resembles that of C++ as it defines the structure of your programs. The Java API libraries are the resources that you, as a programmer, have to work with. By using the libraries according to the rules of the Java syntax, you are able to develop programs.

The API

The largest part of this section is devoted to the Java API libraries. These libraries were written by the developers of Java to enable you to create full-bodied applets and applications.

The API libraries are made up of several packages, each containing several classes that are grouped by functionality. These classes are composed of *fields* and *methods*.

This section lists and explains every *class* and *interface* as well as their respective fields and methods. The classes are in alphabetical order by package, and the summaries of many classes include examples of their use as well as the output of the code. In addition, every component has a figure, so you know how your interface will look before you even begin!

Indexes

To make this section easy to use, there are several indexes that organize the "API Reference" chapter in various manners. At the end of this section, you will find indexes of all classes, methods, and fields. Each entry provides you with the full package and class name as well as the page number directing you to a detailed summary of the class.

Furthermore, you will also find at the middle of this section the "Action Index," which not only lists several of the major tasks that Java is used for, but also lists those classes necessary to accomplish those tasks.

III

Java

How to Use This Section

Designed as a handy reference, this section can be used in a myriad of ways as described in the following sections.

API Reference

This chapter serves as the primary source of information for the section. Each class, interface, exception, and error used in Java programming is listed here and explained in depth. In addition, every method and field within these classes and interfaces is also explained in detail. For easy reference, they are in alphabetical order and grouped by package. Furthermore, to give you a jump start on your task, several classes have complete applets that serve as code examples.

Due to their unique natures, *exceptions* and *errors* are listed separately after the classes and interfaces. They too are in alphabetical order and grouped by package.

Syntax Reference

Even the most experienced programmer sometimes forgets the exact usage of a certain keyword or construct. Arranged alphabetically, this chapter provides you not only with an explanation of each keyword in the Java language, but also a general definition of the syntax and a specific example.

Action Index

Few programs can be written using only one class. The task-related "Action Index" provides you with a list of the several common uses of Java along with the packages, classes, and methods necessary to accomplish these tasks and the page numbers for finding these packages, classes, and methods in the "API Reference" section. Therefore, the "Action Index" enables you to learn not only what classes you need to use, but also how to use them.

Index of Fields

Similar to methods, it is not always clear which package a field belongs to. This index enables you not only to find the page on which the field is explained, but also the class to which it belongs.

Index of Methods

Just because you know of a method doesn't mean that you know where it came from. This index enables you to look up a method based on its name and find its class as well as its page number.

Index of Classes and Interfaces

Because you may not always know the package of a class based solely on its name, this index lists all classes in alphabetical order and provides their complete names and their page numbers. Conveniently located at the end of the section, this index can also be used even if you do know the package of a class.

Chapter 14

Java API Reference

This reference presents and explains the entire Java API. The API, which stands for *Application Programming Interfaces*, is a set of classes and interfaces that outline a set of platform-independent behaviors that establish the foundation of all Java applets and applications. Although any program depends on the strategies of the programmer, these classes and interfaces are the tools that all programmers use in creating Java applications.

java.applet

The java.applet class provides you with only one class and three interfaces, but it is one of the most used packages because it lays the foundation for all applets. The Applet class is most important because it is required when you create an applet. Also useful is the AppletContext interface, which is employed to interact with the browser.

Classes

Applet Extends *java.awt.Panel*. This class is the heart of every Java applet. Derived from the java.awt.Pannel class, the Applet class possesses all the methods found in the java.awt.Container class that enable you to create a powerful and appealing user interface. Every applet that you create *must* extend the Applet class.

As stated above, in order to create a Java applet, you must create a class that extends the java.applet.Applet class. However, to run the applet, you must embed it in an HTML page. This is done with the <APPLET> tag, which must specify the name, height, and width of the applet. You may also specify additional parameters: information that the applet can obtain. The HTML page shown in specifies two parameters: NAME and KEY (see Listing 14.1).

Listing 14.1   Sample HTML Page for an Applet

```
<HEAD>
<TITLE>Applet Example</TITLE>
<BODY>
This text is above the applet.<P>

<applet code="examp.class" width=500 height=100 >
<param name=NAME value="Mike">
<param name=KEY value = "j">
</applet>
<P>This text is below the applet.<P>
</BODY>
```

This document will load the examp class that will be stored in a file named examp.class. Listing 14.2 is the complete source code for that class.

Listing 14.2   Sample Applet

```
import java.applet.Applet;
import java.awt.*;

public class ExampleApplet extends Applet
{
   String userName;
   char favoriteKey;
   int appletWidth, appletHeight, fontHeight;
   Font fontToUse;
   FontMetrics fm;

   /* This class will be called before the applet is
      started.  As a result, it can be used to perform
      preparatory operations. */

   public void init() {
     userName = new String();// creates a new, empty string
     appletWidth = this.size().width - 2; // uses
                                      //Component.size()
     appletHeight = this.size().height - 2;
     fontToUse = new Font("TimesRoman", Font.PLAIN, 20);
                            // creates a new Font object
     fm = getFontMetrics(fontToUse);     // obtains the
                                 //FontMetrics for the font
     fontHeight = fm.getMaxAscent(); /* maximum size that
                           one of the font's characters may
                                      extend upwards     */
     getInfo();      // gets info from HTML tag   }


   /* This method uses the getParameter() method to obtain
       the information passed to the applet in the applet
       tag.  This method assumes that there will be two
       tags, titled "NAME" and "KEY" in the HTML page. */

   void getInfo() {
     userName = getParameter("NAME");
```

```
      favoriteKey = getParameter("KEY").charAt(0);
       // we want the first character in the returned string
       }

       /* This method is automatically called whenever the
          mouse is depressed within the applet */

   public boolean mouseDown(Event evt, int x, int y) {
     showStatus("Mouse Click at ("+x+","+y+")" );
     return true;
   }

       /* This method is automatically called whenever a key is
          depressed within the applet */
   public boolean keyDown(Event evt, int key) {
     if (key == favoriteKey) {
       showStatus("You pressed " + favoriteKey +
                                    ", my favorite key!");
       return true;
     }
     return false;
   }

   /* This method is automatically called whenever the
      applet needs to be drawn */

   public void paint(Graphics g) {
     g.setFont(fontToUse);
     g.drawRect(0,0,appletWidth, appletHeight);
     g.drawString("Hello " + userName +
        ".  Welcome to the world of Java!",10,fontHeight + 3);
   }
 }
```

The classes used in this example, `Font`, `FontMetrics`, and `Graphics`, are explained in the AWT package section. However, you should note that of the five methods in this applet, only one, `getInfo()`, is explicitly called by the applet. The others will be called by either the browser or by one of the classes on which the `java.applet.Applet` class is based. Methods, such as `init()`, are called by the browser itself at particular times. Methods, including `keyDown()` and `mouseDown()`, are called to handle specific user events within the applet. More such methods can be found in the `java.awt.Component` class.

Methods

- **void destroy( )**
  This method may be used to perform any cleanup necessary after execution of the applet. It is empty by default; thus, you must override it if you want the method to do anything. The method is automatically called by the browser when the applet is stopped.

- **AppletContext getAppletContext( )**
  Returns the `AppletContext` of the applet. This is the browser (i.e., Netscape or Appletviewer) used to view the applet.

III

Java

- **String getAppletInfo( )**
  This can be used to return such information as version number or the author's name. If you do not override it, a null string is returned.

- **AudioClip getAudioClip(URL url)**
  Loads the audio clip residing at the specified URL.

- **AudioClip getAudioClip(URL url, String clipname)**
  Loads an audio clip with the specified URL and name.

- **URL getCodeBase( )**
  Returns the URL of the applet, and is usually the URL of the page containing the current applet without the document name.

- **URL getDocumentBase( )**
  Returns the URL of the page on which the current applet resides.

- **Image getImage(URL url)**
  Loads the specified image, which may not be an immediate process inasmuch as it may take some time to actually load the image.

- **Image getImage(URL url, String imagename)**
  Loads the specified image, which may not be an immediate process inasmuch as it may take some time to actually load the image.

- **String getParameter(String labelname)**
  Returns the parameter specified in the HTML page.

- **String[ ] [ ] getParameterInfo( )**
  Returns all parameters from the HTML page.

- **void init( )**
  This method may be used to perform some preparatory actions. While the method is naturally empty, this method is usually used to perform preparatory tasks—such as to create streams and to load information. This method is always called by the browser.

- **boolean isActive( )**
  Returns true if the applet is currently running.

- **void play(URL url)**
  Plays the specified audio clip.

- **void play(URL url, String audioClipName)**
  Plays the specified audio clip.

- **void resize(int width, int height)**
  Resizes the applet to the specified dimensions. In Netscape, this method has no effect. To set the size of an applet, use the width and height parameters in the applet HTML tag.

- **void resize(Dimension d)**
  Resizes the applet to the specified dimensions. In Netscape, this method has no effect. To set the size of an applet, use the `width` and `height` parameters in the applet HTML tag.

- **void setStub(AppletStub stub)**
  Sets the `AppletStub` of the applet. This task is performed automatically by the browser. Therefore, you should have no reason to use this method.

- **void showStatus(String msg)**
  Displays a message at the bottom of the browser. This is usually the simplest way to communicate with the user.

- **void start( )**
  By overriding this method, you can perform some tasks immediately after the applet is created. This method is automatically called by the runtime system.

- **void stop( )**
  By overriding this method, you can perform tasks once the applet is stopped. This method is automatically called by the runtime system. It is not used often, but can be harnessed to perform some cleanup operations.

Interfaces

AppletContext. The `AppletContext` interface provides you with a means to interact with the browser. Every applet can obtain its `AppletContext` through the `getAppletContext( )` method. Although the inner workings of the `AppletContext` depends on the browser, you are guaranteed that it will be capable of performing the following tasks.

▶▶ See Listing 14.18, "Runnable Example—HTML," p. 550

Methods

- **Applet getApplet(String name)**
  Returns the applet with the given name.

- **Enumeration getApplets( )**
  Returns a set of all applets on the given page.

- **AudioClip getAudioClip(URL url)**
  Returns the specified audio clip.

- **Image getImage(URL url)**
  Returns the specified image.

- **void showDocument(URL url)**
  Shows the specified document in the current context.

- **void showDocument(URL url, String target)**
  Requests that the browser show the specified document in a particular location—either a browser window or a Netscape frame.

III

Java

Options for `target` are shown in the following table:

Value	Document Display
`"_self"`	Current Frame.
`"_parent"`	Parent Frame.
`"_top"`	Top-most Frame.
`"_blank"`	In a new and unnamed browser window.
`"aNameofYourChoice"`	Creates a new browser window with the specified name. You may later display other documents in this window by using the same name as the target.

- **void showStatus(String mesg)**
  Displays a string at the bottom of the browser.

AppletStub. The `AppletStub` interface is primarily used when creating an applet viewer. However, it is used by the `Applet` class to retrieve information and interact with the browser. Because all of this interaction is already handled by the `Applet` class, there is generally no need for you to use the `AppletStub` class.

Methods

- **void appletResize(int width, int height)**
  This method is called when the applet wants to be resized.

- **AppletContext getAppletContext( )**
  Returns the applet context.

- **URL getCodeBase( )**
  Returns the base URL without the document name.

- **URL getDocumentBase( )**
  Returns the current URL.

- **String getParameter(String name)**
  Returns the specified parameter.

- **boolean isActive( )**
  Returns `true` whenever the applet is running.

AudioClip. The `AudioClip` interface is a high-level representation of the behavior of an audio clip. While interface objects cannot be created, objects that extend the `AudioClip` interface may be handled through this interface. Consequently, while the `getAudioClip()` in the `Applet` class returns an object we know little about, knowing that it implements the `AudioClip` interface enables us to make use of the `loop()`, `play()`, and `stop()` methods.

Methods

- **void loop( )**
  Begins to play the audio clip and loops to the beginning upon reaching the end of the clip.

- **void play( )**
  Plays the audio clip.

- **void stop( )**
  Halts playing of the audio clip.

java.awt

The Java Abstract Window Toolkit (AWT) consists of resources to enable you to create rich, attractive, and useful interfaces in your applets. Possessing managing tools, such as `LayoutManager` and `Container`, the AWT also has several concrete interactive tools, such as `Button` and `TextField`.

Classes

BorderLayout Implements LayoutManager. A `BorderLayout` is a class that may be used for designing and managing components within your user interface. A `BorderLayout` is a landscape onto which you may place up to five components. Components may be anchored by specifying either "North," "South," "East," "West," or "Center" when adding the component to the layout.

Methods

- **BorderLayout( )**
  Creates a new `BorderLayout` with a `hgap` and a `vgap` of 0. The `hgap` and `vgap` fields determine the amount of padding between components in the layout.

- **BorderLayout(int hgap, int vgap)**
  Creates a new `BorderLayout` with the specified `hgap` and `vgap`. The `hgap` and `vgap` fields determine the amount of padding between components in the layout.

- **void addLayoutComponent(String location, Component comp)**
  Adds a component to the layout at the specified location.

Options for `location` are as follows:

```
"North"
"South"
"West"
"East"
"Center"
```

- **void layoutContainer(Container target)**
  Reshapes the components in the `target` container in accordance with a `BorderLayout`.

- **Dimension minimumLayoutSize(Container target)**
  Returns the minimum size necessary for the components in the specified container. This value is based on the minimum sizes of the components added to the amount of spacing for the container.

- **Dimension preferredLayoutSize(Container target)**
  Returns the "preferred size" of the container. This is based on the preferred size of each component as well as the amount of spacing specified.

- **void removeLayoutComponent(Component comp)**
  Removes the specified component from the layout.

- **String toString( )**
  Returns a string detailing the hgap and the vgap.

Button Extends Component. The Button class creates a standard button for use in your interfaces. A Button is a standard component that may be added to any of the layout manager classes. The label string for each button serves not only to identify the button to the user, but to the programmer as well. Whenever a button is depressed, an ACTION_EVENT will be posted to the container in which the button resides. To distinguish between the various buttons on the screen, the Event will contain an arg string containing the label of the button that was depressed.

▶▶ See Listing 14.6, "GridbagLayout Example," p. 446

Methods
- **Button( )**
  Creates an unlabeled button.

- **Button(String label)**
  Creates a button with the specified label. This will also serve as the arg value in the Event created when the button is depressed.

- **synchronized void addNotify( )**
  Creates a peer for the button.

- **String getLabel( )**
  Returns the label of the button.

- **protected String paramString( )**
  Returns a string specifying the label of the button.

- **void setLabel(String label)**
  Sets the label of the button.

Canvas Extends Component. The Canvas class provides you with a simple background on which you can build. The Canvas class establishes a peer and paints a simple gray background. However, if you choose to extend the Canvas class, you are able to create your own custom components—something very useful.

Methods
- **Canvas( )**
  Creates a new canvas.

- **synchronized void addNotify( )**
  Creates the canvas's peer.

- **void paint(Graphics g)**
  Paints the canvas. By default, this method simply paints a blank background having the same color as the background.

CardLayout Implements LayoutManager. A CardLayout enables you to scroll through a series of components. Generally, the "cards" are containers—each with a specific theme. Each card is referred to by a title and is furthermore sequentially indexed. Therefore, you are to scroll through the cards either in order or by selecting a specific card by name.

The code in Listing 14.3 was used to create the applet. As you can see, the applet uses a Choice component to enable the user to scroll through the various cards.

Listing 14.3 CardLayout **Example Source Code**

```
import java.awt.*;
import java.applet.Applet;

public class CardLayoutExample extends Applet {

    Frame sidecard;
    private static String LINKS = "Links from Here";
    private static String ORDERFORM = "Order Form";

    public CardLayoutExample() {
      Choice selector = new Choice();  // creates a selector
                                       // on the original page
      selector.addItem(LINKS);
      selector.addItem(ORDERFORM);
      add(selector);

      sidecard = new Frame("Multi-Purpose Window");
                            // creates the side frame
      sidecard.setLayout(new CardLayout());

      Panel p = new Panel();  // create the individual panels
      p.add(new Button("Our Homepage"));
      p.add(new Button("Other Products") );
      sidecard.add(LINKS, p);

      p = new Panel();
      p.setLayout( new FlowLayout() );
      p.add(new TextField("Name", 20));
      p.add(new TextField("Address", 50) );
      p.add(new TextField("Phone", 20) );
      p.add(new Button("Order") );
      sidecard.add(ORDERFORM, p);

      sidecard.show();        // shows the side frame
    }

    public boolean action(Event evt, Object arg) {
```

(continues)

Listing 14.3   Continued

```
        CardLayout display;

        if (evt.target instanceof Choice) { /* if the event
                                    occurred in a Choice */
          display = (CardLayout)sidecard.getLayout();
                          // obtains control of the frame
          display.show(sidecard,arg.toString());
              // displays the panel with the corresponding title
          return true;
        }
        return false;
      }

      public synchronized boolean handleEvent(Event evt) {
        if (evt.id == Event.WINDOW_DESTROY) {
          this.hide();
              return true;
        }
        return super.handleEvent(evt);
      }
    }
```

Methods

- **CardLayout( )**
  Creates a new CardLayout manager.

- **CardLayout(int hgap, int vgap)**
  Creates a new CardLayout manager with the specified hgap and vgap—the spacing between components.

- **void addLayoutComponent(String name, Component comp)**
  Adds the component to the container with the specified name.

- **void first(Container parent)**
  Displays the first card in the layout.

- **void last(Container parent)**
  Displays the last card in the layout.

- **void layoutContainer(Container parent)**
  Arranges the parent container based on the CardLayout parameters.

- **Dimension minimumLayoutSize(Container parent)**
  Returns the minimum size necessary for this layout. This value is based on the minimum size of the parameters.

- **void next(Container parent)**
  Displays the next card.

- **Dimension preferredLayoutSize(Container parent)**
  Returns the preferred size of the layout in the parent container. This is based on the preferred size of the components in the container.

- **void previous(Container parent)**
  Displays the previous card.

- **void removeLayoutComponen(Component comp)**
  Removes the specified component from the layout.

- **void show(Container parent, String cardname)**
  Shows the specified card in the parent container.

- **String toString( )**
  Returns a string detailing the hgap and vgap values for this layout.

Checkbox Extends Component. A checkbox provides you with an easy way of obtaining input from the user. It resembles a standard checkbox: a text label and a box on the client's machine.

▶▶ See "CheckboxGroup," p. 416
▶▶ See "CheckboxMenuItem Extends MenuItem," p. 416
▶▶ See Listing 14.6, "GridbagLayout Example," p. 446

Methods

- **Checkbox( )**
  Creates an non-labeled checkbox.

- **Checkbox(String label)**
  Creates a checkbox with the specified label.

- **Checkbox(String label, CheckboxGroup group, boolean state)**
  Creates a checkbox with the specified label and places it in a CheckboxGroup. The state parameter determines whether or not it is initially checked.

- **synchronized void addNotify( )**
  Creates the peer of the checkbox

- **CheckboxGroup getCheckboxGroup( )**
  Returns the CheckboxGroup of which the current checkbox is a member.

- **String getLabel( )**
  Returns the label of the checkbox.

- **boolean getState( )**
  Returns the state of the checkbox (true if checked, false if not).

- **protected String paramString( )**
  Returns a string detailing the checkbox's parameters—such as its status and location.

- **void setCheckboxGroup(CheckboxGroup g)**
  Sets the CheckboxGroup for the current checkbox.

III

Java

- **void setLabel(String label)**
  Sets the label of the checkbox.

- **void setState(boolean state)**
  Sets the state of the checkbox (checked or unchecked).

CheckboxGroup. By employing a CheckboxGroup, you are able to create a radio button group: a set of Checkboxes, only one of which can be selected at a time. This is useful for exclusive choices (the user can only choose one of the options), such as "How do you want to pay for your purchase?"

To employ a CheckboxGroup, first create and layout your checkboxes as you normally would. Then assign them to the CheckboxGroup by using the setCheckboxGroup( ) method.

 ▶▶ See "Checkbox Extends Component," p. 415

Methods

- **CheckboxGroup( )**
  Creates a new Checkbox group.

- **Checkbox getCurrent( )**
  Returns the currently selected checkbox.

- **synchronized void setCurrent(Checkbox box)**
  Sets the specified checkbox to be the selected checkbox.

- **String toString( )**
  Returns a string detailing the currently selected checkbox.

CheckboxMenuItem Extends MenuItem. A CheckboxMenuItem is a MenuItem whose status may be toggled. Placed within a Menu column, a CheckboxMenuItem will display a check mark when selected.

 ▶▶ See "Checkbox Extends Component," p. 415

Methods

- **CheckboxMenuItem(String label)**
  Creates a new checkbox menu item with the specified label.

- **synchronized void addNotify( )**
  Creates the checkbox menu item's peer.

- **boolean getState( )**
  Returns the current state of the checkbox.

- **String paramString( )**
  Returns a string detailing the checkbox's value.

- **void setState(boolean state)**
  Sets the state of the checkbox.

Choice Extends Component. The `Choice` component creates a standard pop-up menu from which the user can select one item.

▶▶ See Listing 14.6, "*GridbagLayout* Example," p. 446

Methods

- **Choice( )**
  Creates a new choice component.

- **synchronized void addItem(String label)**
  Adds a selection to the choice listing with the specified label.

- **synchronized void addNotify( )**
  Creates the choice's peer.

- **int countItems( )**
  Returns the number of items currently existing in the choice's listing.

- **String getItem(int pos)**
  Returns the label of the choice in the specified position in the choice list.

- **int getSelectedIndex( )**
  Returns the index of the currently selected item.

- **String getSelectedItem( )**
  Returns the label of the currently selected item.

- **protected String paramString( )**
  Returns a string including the label of the currently selected item.

- **void select(String label)**
  Selects the item with the specified label.

- **synchronized void select(int pos)**
  Selects the item at the specified position.

Final Color. The `Color` class provides you with the various colors that you can employ in your programs as well as the capability to create and customize your own colors.

▶▶ See "*Abstract* Graphics," p. 438

Fields

- **final static Color black**
- **final static Color blue**
- **final static Color cyan**
- **final static Color darkGray**

- **final static Color gray**
- **final static Color green**
- **final static Color light gray**
- **final static Color magenta**
- **final static Color orange**
- **final static Color pink**
- **final static Color red**
- **final static Color white**
- **final static Color yellow**

Methods

- **Color(int rgb)**

  Creates a new color represented by the passed integer. Bits 0–7 represent the blue component, 8–15 the green component, and 16–23 the red component.

- **Color(float red_value, float green_value, float blue_value)**

  Creates a new color with the specified values ranging from 0 to 1.0.

- **Color(int red_value, int green_value, int blue_value)**

  Creates a new color with the specified values ranging from 0 to 255.

- **Color brighter( )**

  Returns a brighter version of the current color by dividing each integral component of the color by 0.7.

- **Color darker( )**

  Returns a darker version of the current color by multiplying each integral component of the color by 0.7.

- **boolean equals(Object otherObject)**

  Compares a `Color` to another `Object`. They can only be equal if the other object is also a `Color`.

- **int getBlue( )**

  Returns the blue component of the color.

- **static Color getColor(String name)**

  Returns a Color assuming that `name` refers to a color specified in the system properties. If the property is not found, the method returns `null`.

- **static Color getColor(String name, int default)**

  Returns a Color assuming that `name` refers to a color specified in the system properties. If the property is not found, the method returns the color represented by `default`.

- **static Color getColor(String name, Color default)**

  Returns a Color assuming that `name` refers to a color specified in the system properties. If the property is not found, the method returns `default`.

- **int getGreen( )**

  Returns the green component of the color.

- **static Color getHSBColor(float hue, float saturation, float brightness)**
  Creates a `Color` based on the specified HSB (hue, saturation, and brightness) values ranging from 0.0 to 1.0

- **int getRed( )**
  Returns the red component of the current color.

- **int getRGB( )**
  Returns the rgb value of the current color as one integer. Bits 0–7 are blue, 8–15 are green, and 16–23 are red.

- **int hashCode( )**
  Returns the `hashcode` for the current color. This value is the same as the integer returned from `getRGB()`.

- **static int HSBtoRGB(float hue, float saturation, float brightness)**
  Creates a single integer representation of the color defined by the specified hue, saturation, and brightness. In the integer, bits 0–7 are blue, 8–15 are green, and 16–23 are red.

- **static float[ ] RGBtoHSB(int red, int green, int blue, float hsbvals[ ])**
  Returns hue, saturation, and brightness values for the color defined by the red, green, and blue values. In the array, `hsbvals[0]` = hue, `hsbvals[1]` = saturation, and `hsbvals[2]` = brightness.

- **String toString( )**
  Returns a string, including the red, green, and blue components of the color.

***Abstract* Component Implements ImageObserver.** The `Component` class is the basis for the various components in the AWT that may be employed, such as `Button` and `Scrollbar`. While the specific components posses methods pertinent to their function, the `Component` class provides them with a myriad of methods designed to facilitate a base functionality—such as event handling.

You will also note that the `Component` class relies heavily on the `java.awt.peer` classes for much of its implementation because the system commands to create a component on UNIX machines are different from those to create the component on Windows-based machines. Instead of directly interacting with these methods, the peers serve as intermediaries, translating your Java-based code into platform-dependent commands.

Methods

- **boolean action(Event evt, Object what)**
  Called by `handleEvent( )` when an action occurs in the component. This method should be overridden if you want to gain more control over events occurring in components or containers. It returns `true` if the event is handled successfully.

- **void addNotify( )**
  "Notifies" the component that it must create a peer.

- **Rectangle bounds( )**
  Returns the boundaries of the component.

- **int checkImage(Image image, ImageObserver observer)**
  Returns the status of an image being displayed on the screen. This value is either obtained from the component's peer or the current Toolkit. The specified ImageObserver will be notified of the status of the Image.

- **int checkImage(Image image, int width, int height, ImageObserver observer)**
  Returns the status of an scaled image being displayed on the screen. This value is either obtained from the component's peer or the current Toolkit. The specified ImageObserver will be notified of the status of the Image.

- **Image createImage(int width, int height)**
  Creates an off-screen image with the specified width and height.

- **Image createImage(ImageProducer producer)**
  Creates an image from the information supplied by the specific ImageProducer.

- **void deliverEvent(Event e)**
  "Delivers" an event to the component.

- **synchronized void disable( )**
  Disables the current component. The component will not be able to respond to user events.

- **void enable(boolean cond)**
  If cond is true, this method enables the component. Otherwise, it disables the component.

- **synchronized void enable( )**
  Enables the component.

- **Color getBackground( )**
  Returns the current background color.

- **synchronized ColorModel getColorModel( )**
  Returns the ColorModel used when creating the component.

- **Font getFont( )**
  Returns the font of the component. If the component does not have a font, this method returns the font of the parent container.

- **FontMetrics getFontMetrics(Font font)**
  Returns the FontMetrics of the component. Returns null if the component currently is not available.

- **Color getForeground( )**
  Returns the foreground color of the component. If none exists, this method defaults to the foreground color of the parent container.

- **Graphics getGraphics( )**
  Returns the graphics context used in creating this component. As of the 1.0 JDK release, this method was only implemented for Canvas components.

- **Container getParent( )**
  Returns the parent container in which the `Component` resides.

- **ComponentPeer getPeer( )**
  Returns the peer of the component.

- **Toolkit getToolkit( )**
  Returns the component's `Toolkit`.

- **boolean gotFocus(Event evt, Object what)**
  This method is called whenever the component receives the input focus (usually the result of a mouse movement). The `what` parameter represents the argument of the event. (`what` is equal to `evt.arg`.)

- **boolean handleEvent(Event evt)**
  This method is called whenever an `Event` is posted to the component. By default, it calls a series of more specific methods, such as `mouseDown( )` and `keyUp( )`.

  This method returns `true` if the event has been handled successfully. If you override this method but still want to employ the component's default method handling abilities, call `super.handleEvent(evt)`.

- **synchronized boolean inside(int x, int y)**
  Determines if the specified coordinates are inside the current component.

- **synchronized void hide( )**
  "Hides" the component by making it no longer visible.

- **boolean imageUpdate(Image img, int flags, int x, int y, int width, int height)**
  Repaints the specified image if and when the image is changed. The `flags` are constants, such as `FRAMEBITS` and `ALLBITS` found in the `java.awt.image.ImageObserver` interface.

  This method will be called by the system when more information becomes available about the `Image`. Therefore, this method should only be used if you want to add some functionality to the method.

- **void invalidate( )**
  A component is invalid if it needs to be laid out. This method makes the current component invalid, forcing it to be laid out again.

- **boolean isEnabled( )**
  Enables a component to interact with the user. This method returns `true` if the component is enabled and `false` otherwise.

- **boolean isShowing( )**
  Returns `true` if the component is visible to the user. This requires that the component be visible in a container that is also visible.

III

Java

- **boolean isValid( )**
  A component is invalid if it needs to be laid out. This method returns `false` if the component is invalid and `true` if it is valid.

- **boolean isVisible( )**
  Returns `true` if the component is visible.

- **boolean keyDown(Event evt, int key)**
  Called by `handleEvent()` when a key is depressed. The `event` parameter is the complete event posted. The `key` parameter is the key depressed.

- **boolean keyUp(Event evt, int key)**
  Called by `handleEvent()` when a key is released. The `event` parameter is the complete event posted. The `key` parameter is the key released.

- **void layout( )**
  Correctly positions the component in the layout.

- **void list( )**
  Prints out the current parameters to the standard output stream.

- **void list(PrintStream out)**
  Prints out the current parameters to the specified `PrintStream`.

- **void list(PrintStream out, int indent)**
  Prints out the current parameters to the specified `PrintStream`, starting from the specified indentation.

- **Component locate(int x, int y)**
  Returns the component occupying the specified location.

- **Point location( )**
  Returns a `Point` containing the x- and y-coordinates of the component in its container.

- **boolean lostFocus(Event evt, Object what)**
  Called by `handleEvent()` when the component looses the input focus.

- **boolean mouseDown(Event evt, int x, int y)**
  Called by `handleEvent()` when the mouse is depressed in the component.

- **boolean mouseDrag(Event evt, int x, int y)**
  Called by `handleEvent()` when the mouse is dragged in the component. (A *drag* is considered a mouse movement while the mouse button is down.)

- **boolean mouseEnter(Event evt, int x, int y)**
  Called by `handleEvent()` when the mouse enters the component.

- **boolean mouseExit(Event evt, int x, int y)**
  Called by `handleEvent()` when the mouse leaves the component.

- **boolean mouseMove(Event evt, int x, int y)**
  Called by `handleEvent()` when the component loses the input focus. (A *move* is a mouse movement while the mouse button is up.)

- **boolean mouseUp(Event evt, int x, int y)**
  Called by `handleEvent()` when the component loses the input focus.

- **Dimension minimumSize( )**
  Returns the minimum size necessary to display the component.

- **void move(int x, int y)**
  Moves the component to the new location and causes the component to become invalidated.

- **void nextFocus( )**
  Advances the focus to the next component. This is useful in such applications as forms in which the user wants to go from one component to the next.

- **void paint(Graphics g)**
  Paints the component.

- **void paintAll(Graphics g)**
  Paints the component and all its subcomponents.

- **protected String paramString( )**
  Returns a string containing information about the component including its location, and whether it is visible, valid, and/or enabled.

- **boolean postEvent(Event e)**
  Posts the specified event to the component, resulting in a call to `handleEvent()`. If the component does not successfully handle the event, the event will be passed to the component's parent container.

- **Dimension preferredSize( )**
  Returns the preferred size of this component. This value is supplied by the component's peer.

- **boolean prepareImage(Image image, int width, int height, ImageObserver observer)**
  This method "prepares" a scaled image to be displayed. This process includes loading the image and preparing the screen where the image is to be displayed. The `imageUpdate()` method in the specified `ImageObserver` will be informed of the status of this process.

- **boolean prepareImage(Image image, ImageObserver observer)**
  This method "prepares" and image to be displayed. This process includes loading the image and preparing the screen where the image is to be displayed. The specified `ImageObserver` will be informed of the status of this process through the `imageUpdate()` method.

III

Java

- **void print(Graphics g)**
  "Prints" the component. By default, this method simply calls the paint() method.

- **void printAll(Graphics g)**
  "Prints" the component and its subcomponents. By default, this method paints the component and its subcomponents.

- **synchronized void removeNotify( )**
  Disposes of the component's peer.

- **void repaint(int x, int y, int width, int height)**
  Repaints a portion of the component.

- **void repaint(long delay, int x, int y, int width,**
  Repaints a portion of the component after waiting the specified number of milliseconds.

- **void repaint(long time)**
  Repaints the entire component after waiting the specified number of milliseconds.

- **void repaint( )**
  Repaints the entire component.

- **void requestFocus( )**
  Requests the input focus.

- **synchronized void reshape(int x, int y, int width, int height)**
  Moves the component to the specified coordinates and reshapes it to the specified size. This will cause the component to become invalidated.

- **void resize(Dimension d)**
  Resizes the component to the specified dimensions—width and height. This will cause the component to become invalidated.

- **void resize(int width, int height)**
  Resizes the component to the specified width and height. This will cause the component to become invalidated.

- **synchronized void setBackground(Color c)**
  Sets the background color for the component.

- **synchronized void setFont(Font f)**
  Sets the font for the component.

- **synchronized void setForeground(Color c)**
  Sets the background color for the component.

- **void show(boolean cond)**
  Displays the component if the cond parameter is true. If the cond parameter is false, the component is hidden.

- **synchronized void show( )**
  Displays the component.

- **Dimension size( )**
  Returns the size of the component.

- **String toString( )**
  Returns a string containing the component's parameters. This consists of the name of the component as well as the values returned by paramString( ).

- **void update(Graphics g)**
  This method is called as a result of a call to repaint( ). It can be used to perform management tasks associated with updating the component.

- **void validate( )**
  Makes the component valid. This means that it does not need to be laid out.

Abstract **Container Extends Component.** The Container class is a basic class that may hold other Components. The Container class serves as the basis for the other container-type classes such as Frame, Panel, and FileDialog. Note that you cannot create a Container explicitly, but rather must either use one of the derived classes or create your own Container class.

Methods

- **synchronized Component add(String info, Component comp)**
  Adds the component to the container. The use of the information supplied in the string depends on the LayoutManager for the Container.

- **synchronized Component add(Component comp, int pos)**
  Adds the component to the container at the specified position.

- **Component add(Component comp)**
  Adds the component to the end of the container.

- **synchronized void addNotify( )**
  Creates the container's peer.

- **int countComponents( )**
  Returns the number of components in the container.

- **void deliverEvent(Event evt)**
  Delivers the specified event to the appropriate component. If the event does not occur in one of the components belonging to the container, the event is handed over to the java.awt.Component.postEvent( ) method.

- **synchronized Component getComponent(int num) throws ArrayIndexOutOfBoundsException**
  Returns the component at the specified index. Throws an ArrayIndexOutOfBoundsException if there are fewer than num components in the container.

- **synchronized Component[ ] getComponents( )**
  Returns an array containing the components residing in the Container.

III

Java

- **LayoutManager getLayout( )**
  Returns the layout manager used in creating this container.

- **synchronized void layout( )**
  Organizes the components in the container according to the conventions of the layout manager.

- **void list(PrintStream out, int indent)**
  Displays the standard component information (name and parameters) as well as the components within the container. Begins printing at the specified indentation point.

- **Component locate(int x, int y)**
  Returns the component that occupies the specified coordinates.

- **synchronized Dimension minimumSize( )**
  Returns the minimum size necessary for this component. This value is based on the minimum sizes for the individual components.

- **void paintComponents(Graphics g)**
  Paints the components in the container. Identical to the `printComponents()` method in this class.

- **protected String paramString( )**
  Returns the information supplied by the `java.awt.Component.paramString()` method in addition to the layout manager of the component.

- **synchronized Dimension preferredSize( )**
  Returns the preferred size of the container. This is based on the values returned from the `preferredSize()` methods for the individual components.

- **void printComponents(Graphics g)**
  Displays the components in the container. Identical to the `printComponents()` method in this class.

- **synchronized void remove(Component comp)**
  Removes the specified component from the container.

- **synchronized void removeNotify( )**
  Removes the container's peer.

- **void setLayout(LayoutManager mgr)**
  Sets the layout manager for the component.

- **synchronized void validate( )**
  Valid components do not need to be laid out. This method makes the container and all its components valid.

Dialog Extends Window. A `Dialog` is a type of `Window` that is used to accept user input. A `Dialog` must exist in a `Frame` object. A modal `Dialog` is a type of `Dialog` that will capture all the input from the user.

Methods

- **Dialog(Frame parent, String title, boolean modal)**
  Creates a new Dialog in the specified Frame and with the specified title. If the modal parameter is true, the Dialog will be modal.

- **Dialog(Frame parent, boolean modal)**
  Creates a new Dialog in the specified Frame that will have no title. If the modal parameter is true, the Dialog will be modal.

- **synchronized void addNotify( )**
  Creates the Dialog's peer.

- **boolean isModal( )**
  Returns true if the Dialog is modal.

- **boolean isResizable( )**
  Returns true if the Dialog is resizable.

- **protected String paramString( )**
  Returns a string containing the parameters of the Dialog, including its title whether or not it is modal.

- **void setTitle(String title)**
  Sets the title for the Dialog.

Dimension. The Dimension class provides you with a simple way of handling the dimensions of graphical tools. Most often, the Dimension class is used to enable a single method to return two values: width and height.

Fields
- **int height**
- **int width**

Methods
- **Dimension( )**
  Creates a new Dimension object.

- **Dimension(Dimension d)**
  Creates a new Dimension object with the same values as an already created Dimension object.

- **Dimension(int width, int height)**
  Creates a new Dimension object with the specified width and height.

- **String toString( )**
  Returns the width and height of the Dimension in the form of a string.

Event. The Event class, used as a means of responding to user interactions, delivers a lot of information about a user event in a single object. Through its constants and instance variables, each Event object is capable of providing you with many specific details regarding each event.

III

Java

All final fields serve as constants against which you may compare information contained in the Event objects that you receive. In general, the fields fall into two categories: those that represent certain keys (e.g., F1 and HOME) and those that represent certain events (e.g., GOT_FOCUS and KEY_PRESS).

▶▶ See Listing 14.3, "CardLayout Example Source Code," p. 413
▶▶ See Listing 14.7, "Menu Example," p. 458

Fields

- **final static int ACTION_EVENT**
  A flag representing a broad umbrella of event types. An ACTION_EVENT will cause a call to action().

- **final static int ALT_MASK**
  Will be placed in the modifiers field if the ALT key is down. It should be tested for using the AND operator.

- **Object arg**
  An optional argument dependent on the type of event. Most components set the arg equal to their titles.

- **int clickCount**
  Tracks the number of consecutive mouse clicks.

- **final static int CTRL_MASK**
  Will be placed in the modifiers field if the CTRL key is down. Should be tested for using the AND operator.

- **final static int DOWN**
- **Event evt**
  A reference to another Event object. This can be used to create a linked list of Event objects.

- **final static int F1**
  A possible value for the key field.

- **final static int F2**
- **final static int F3**
- **final static int F4**
- **final static int F5**
- **final static int F6**
- **final static int F7**
- **final static int F8**
- **final static int F9**
- **final static int F10**
- **final static int F11**
- **final static int F12**

- **final static int GOT_FOCUS**
  Created when the Component gets the input focus. It calls gotFocus().

- **final static int HOME**
  A possible value for the key field.

- **int id**
  The ID of the event. It can be compared to such static constants as ACTION_EVENT or MOUSE_DOWN.

- **int key**
  Contains the key that was depressed.

- **final static int KEY_ACTION**
  Created when the user presses a function key. It causes a call to keyDown().

- **final static int KEY_ACTION_RELEASE**
  Created when the user releases a function key. It causes a call to keyUp().

- **final static int KEY_PRESS**
  Created when the user presses a standard ASCII key. It causes a call to keyDown().

- **final static int KEY_RELEASE**
  Created when the user releases a standard ASCII key. It causes a call to keyUp().

- **final static int LEFT**
  A possible value for the key field. It represents the left-arrow key.

- **final static int LIST_DESELECT**
  Called when the user deselects an item on a List. The Event will also contain an Integer as its arg field representing the item that was deselected.

- **final static int LIST_SELECT**
  Called when the user deselects an item on a List. The Event will also contain an Integer as its arg field representing the item that was deselected.

- **final static int LOAD_FILE**
  Created when a file is loaded.

- **final static int LOST_FOCUS**
  Created when the Component looses the input focus. It causes a call to lostFocus().

- **final static int META_MASK**
  Will be placed in the modifiers field if the META key is down. It should be tested for using the AND operator.

- **int modifiers**
  Represents the status of the modifier keys: Alt, Ctrl, Meta, and Shift. It can be compared against the static constants defined within the class using the AND operator.

- **final static int MOUSE_DOWN**
  Created by a mouse click. It causes a call to mouseDown().

III

Java

- **final static int MOUSE_DRAG**
- **final static int MOUSE_ENTER**
- **final static int MOUSE_EXIT**
- **final static int MOUSE_MOVE**
- **final static int MOUSE_UP**
- **final static int PGDN**
- **final static int PGUP**
- **final static int RIGHT**
- **final static int SAVE_FILE**
- **final static int SCROLL_ABSOLUTE**
  Created when the user moves a scrollbar marker to a specific location within the scrollbar.

- **final static int SCROLL_LINE_DOWN**
  Created when the user clicks on the down arrow in a scrollbar.

- **final static int SCROLL_LINE_UP**
- **final static int SCROLL_PAGE_DOWN**
- **final static int SCROLL_PAGE_UP**
- **final static int SHIFT_MASK**
  Will be placed in the `modifiers` field if the Shift key is down or if Caps Lock is on. It should be tested for using the `AND` operator.

- **Object target**
  The object at which the event was directed.

- **final static int UP**
- **long when**
  The time at which the event occurred.

- **final static int WINDOW_DEICONIFY**
  A possible value of the `id` field.

- **final static int WINDOW_DESTROY**
  A possible value of the `id` field. It is used when the user tries to close a `Window`.

- **final static int WINDOW_EXPOSE**
  A possible value of the `id` field.

- **final static int WINDOW_ICONIFY**
  A possible value of the `id` field.

- **final static int WINDOW_MOVED**
  A possible value of the `id` field.

- **int x**
  The x-coordinate of a mouse click.

- **int y**
  The y-coordinate of a mouse click.

Methods

- **Event(Object target, int id, Object arg)**
  Creates a new Event with the specified target, ID, and arg values.

- **Event(Object target, long when, int id, int x, int y, int key, int modifiers)**
  Creates a new Event with the specified target, time stamp (when), ID, x, y, key, and modifier values.

- **Event(Object target, long when, int id, int x, int y, int key, int modifiers, Object arg)**
  Creates a new Event with the specified target, time stamp (when), ID, x, y, key, modifiers, and arg values.

- **boolean controlDown( )**
  Returns true if the Control key is down.

- **boolean metaDown( )**
  Returns meta if the Control key is down.

- **protected String paramString( )**
  Returns a string containing the values of all the Event's instance variables.

- **boolean shiftDown( )**
  Returns true if the shift key is down.

- **String toString( )**
  Returns the Event object's name as well as the information returned from the paramString() method.

- **void translate(int x, int y)**

FileDialog Extends Dialog. A FileDialog creates a window to provide the user with a selection of files. The FileDialog itself will resemble the appearance of file dialog boxes on the client's machine.

The FileDialog was created with the code in Listing 14.4. Although the code is obviously too simple to serve as a complete applet, it nevertheless demonstrates the technique for creating a FileDialog.

Listing 14.4 FileDialog **Example**

```
import java.applet.Applet;
import java.awt.*;

public class FDialogExample extends Applet {

    public void init() {
        Frame f;
        f = new Frame();

        Dialog d;
```

(continues)

Listing 14.4   Continued

```
        d = new FileDialog(f,"FileDialogExample");

        f.show();
        d.show();
    }
}
```

Fields

- **final static LOAD**
  This constant is used to define the mode of the `FileDialog`. If the mode equals `LOAD`, then the `FileDialog` is designed to load files.

- **final static SAVE**
  This constant is used to define the mode of the `FileDialog`. If the mode equals `SAVE`, then the `FileDialog` is designed to save files.

Methods

- **FileDialog(Frame parent, String title, int mode)**
  Creates a `FileDialog` with the specified mode.

- **FileDialog(Frame parent, String title)**
  Creates a `FileDialog`, setting the mode to `LOAD`.

- **synchronized void addNotify( )**
  Creates the `FileDialog`'s peer.

- **String getDirectory( )**
  Returns the current directory.

- **String getFile( )**
  Returns the file name selected by the user.

- **FilenameFilter getFilenameFilter( )**
  Returns the `FilenameFilter` used by the user in selecting the file.

- **int getMode( )**
  Returns the mode of the `FileDialog`—either `LOAD` or `SAVE`.

- **protected String paramString( )**
  Returns the attributes of the component including the directory and the mode.

- **void setDirectory(String dir)**
  Sets the directory in the `FileDialog`.

- **void setFile(String file)**
  Highlights the specific file in the `FileDialog`.

- **public void setFilenameFilter(FilenameFilter filter)**
  Sets the filter for the dialog to be employed by the user in selecting the file.

FlowLayout Implements LayoutManager. The `FlowLayout` class is a relatively simple layout manager. It places components in rows and continues on the next line when the current line becomes full.

Fields

- **final static int CENTER**
  Aligns the components with the center.

- **final static int LEFT**
  Aligns the components on the left.

- **final static int RIGHT**
  Aligns the components on the right.

Methods

- **FlowLayout( )**
  Creates a new `FlowLayout` with an alignment of `CENTER`.

- **FlowLayout(int align)**
  Creates a new `FlowLayout` with the specified alignment.

- **FlowLayout(int align, int hgap, int vgap)**
  Creates a new `FlowLayout` with the specified alignment. `hgap` and `vgap` specify the amount of spacing around the component.

- **void addLayoutComponent(String name, Component comp)**
  This method is required inasmuch as this class implements the `LayoutManager` interface. However, it does absolutely nothing.

- **void layoutContainer(Container target)**
  Arranges the specified container according to its `FlowLayout` parameters.

- **Dimension minimumLayoutSize(Container target)**
  Returns the minimum size necessary for the components in the specified container. This value is based on the minimum sizes of the components added to the amount of spacing for the container.

- **Dimension preferredLayoutSize(Container target)**
  Returns the preferred size necessary for the components in the specified container. This value is based on the preferred sizes of the components added to the amount of spacing for the container.

- **void removeLayoutComponent(Component comp)**
  Removes the specified component from the layout manager.

- **String toString( )**
  Returns a string containing the layout's name, the alignment, the `hgap`, and the `vgap`.

Font. The `Font` class serves as an intermediary between your code and the client's machine, providing you with specific styles for your text. Although it will not affect the appearance of the output to the output streams (e.g., `System.out`), the current font will determine the appearance of any text created in displaying a `Component`—particularly an `Applet`.

 ▶▶ See Listing 14.2, "Sample Applet," p. 406

> **Note**
>
> To actually change the display font, you must first create a new `Font` and then set the current font. This is done using either the `java.awt.Component.setFont( )` or `java.awt.Graphics.setFont( )` method.

Fields

- **final static int BOLD**
  A possible value for `style` indicating a bold font.

- **final static int ITALIC**
  A possible value for `style` indicating an italic font.

- **protected String name**
  The name of the font.

- **final static int PLAIN**
  A possible value for `style` indicating the standard font.

- **protected int size**
  The size of the font.

- **protected int style**
  The style of the font.

Methods

- **Font(String name, int style, int size)**
  Creates a new font with the specified name, style, and size.

- **boolean equals(Object anotherobject)**
  Compares two fonts for equality. The return value will always be `false` if the second object is not a `Font`.

- **String getFamily( )**
  Returns the name of the family to which the font belongs. This value depends on the system itself.

- **static Font getFont(String name)**
  Returns the font possessing the system-dependent font name.

- **static Font getFont(String name, Font defaultfont)**
  Returns the font possessing the system-dependent font name. If the font cannot be found, the method returns the `defaultfont`.

- **String getName( )**
  Returns the name of the font.

- **int getSize( )**
  Returns the size of the font.

- **int getStyle( )**
  Returns the style of the font.

- **int hashCode( )**
  Returns the hashcode of the font, a value dependent on the font name, style, and size. Returns the name of the font.

- **boolean isBold( )**
  Returns true if the font is bold.

- **boolean isItalic( )**
  Returns true if the font is italic.

- **boolean isPlain( )**
  Returns true if the font is plain (neither bold nor italic).

- **String toString( )**
  Returns a string containing information on the font, including its name, style, and size.

FontMetrics. The FontMetrics class provides you with information regarding a given font. This class is very useful for such tasks as animation of text because it is often necessary to know exactly where each character will be. By creating a FontMetrics for the font and then using the accessor methods to obtain information, you can determine the exact size of your characters and strings.

▶▶ See "Font," p. 433

> **Note**
>
> To employ a FontMetrics in your program, declare an instance of a FontMetrics and then use the java.awt.getFontMetrics( ) method to provide the FontMetrics with information.

Field

- **protected Font font**
  The font on which the FontMetrics is based.

Methods

- **protected FontMetrics(Font font)**
  Creates a new FontMetrics.

III

Java

- **int bytesWidth(byte data[ ], int offset, int len)**
  Returns the width of a set of bytes. The offset parameter specifies the index at which the measurement begins and the len parameter specifies the number of terms to be considered in the measurement.

- **int charsWidth(char data[ ], int offset, int len)**
  Returns the width of a set of characters. The offset parameter specifies the index at which the measurement begins, and the len parameter specifies the number of terms to be considered in the measurement.

- **int charWidth(char ch)**
  Returns the width of a single character.

- **int charWidth(int ch)**
  Returns the width of a single character.

- **int getAscent( )**
  Returns the amount of space between the x-height (the height of the main body of lowercase letters) and the top of a character in the font.

- **int getDescent( )**
  Returns the amount of space between the baseline (the imaginary line on which the type sits) and the bottom of a character in the font.

- **Font getFont( )**
  Returns the font.

- **int getHeight( )**
  Returns the amount of space between the top and bottom of a character in this font.

- **int getMaxAdvance( )**
  The advance is defined as the space between two characters (actually between the bottom of one character and the top of the next). This method returns the maximum advance for any character in this font.

- **int getMaxAscent( )**
  The ascent is the distance from the x-height to the top of the letter. This method returns the maximum ascent for any character in the font.

- **int getMaxDescent( )**
  The descent is the distance from the baseline to the bottom of the letter. This method returns the maximum descent for any character in the font.

- **int[ ] getWidths( )**
  Returns an array containing the width of the first 256 characters of the font.

- **int stringWidth(String str)**
  Returns an integer representing the width of the specified string.

- **String toString( )**
  Returns a string containing information about the class, including the class name, font name, ascent, descent, and height.

Frame Extends Window Implements MenuContainer. A `Frame` is a `Window` that has added capabilities. In terms of appearance, a `Frame` possesses a border and a title. In terms of functionality, you can add a menu to a `Frame` and specify the image that appears when the `Frame` is minimized.

▶▶ See "MenuBar Extends MenuComponent Implements MenuContainer," p. 457
▶▶ See "Window Extends Container," p. 471

Tip

When using a `Frame`, remember to invoke the `show( )` method. Otherwise, your frame will be invisible!

Fields
- **final static int CROSSHAIR_CURSOR**
- **final static int DEFAULT_CURSOR**
- **final static int E_RESIZE_CURSOR**
- **final static int HAND_CURSOR**
- **final static int MOVE_CURSOR**
- **final static int NE_RESIZE_CURSOR**
- **final static int NW_RESIZE_CURSOR**
- **final static int N_RESIZE_CURSOR**
- **final static int SE_RESIZE_CURSOR**
- **final static int SW_RESIZE_CURSOR**
- **final static int S_RESIZE_CURSOR**
- **final static int TEXT_CURSOR**
- **final static int WAIT_CURSOR**
- **final static int W_RESIZE_CURSOR**

Methods
- **Frame( )**
  Creates a new Frame without a title.

- **Frame(String title)**
  Creates a new frame with the specified title.

- **synchronized void addNotify( )**
  Creates the `Frame`'s peer.

- **synchronized void dispose( )**
  Disposes the resources used by the `Frame`.

III

Java

- **int getCursorType( )**
  Returns the cursor type for this `Frame`.

- **Image getIconImage( )**
  Returns the `icon` for this frame. The `icon` is an inaccessible variable that defines the appearance of the `Frame` when it is minimized.

- **MenuBar getMenuBar( )**
  Returns the current `MenuBar` for this `Frame`.

- **String getTitle( )**
  Returns the title of this `Frame`.

- **boolean isResizable( )**
  Returns `true` if the `Frame` can be resized.

- **protected String paramString( )**
  Returns a string, including the title of the `Frame` and the word *resizable* if the `Frame` is resizable.

- **synchronized void remove(MenuComponent m)**
  Removes the specified `MenuBar` from this `Frame`.

- **void setCursor(int cursorType)**
  Sets the appearance of the cursor for this `Frame`. The parameter value may be any one of the above listed constants.

- **void setIconImage(Image image)**
  Sets the icon for this `Frame`. The icon will be displayed when the `Frame` is minimized.

- **synchronized void setMenuBar(MenuBar mb)**
  Sets the `MenuBar` for this `Frame`.

- **void setResizable(boolean resizable)**
  Makes the `Frame` either resizable (`true`) or not resizable (`false`). All `Frames` are initially resizable.

- **void setTitle(String title)**
  Sets the title for the `Frame`.

***Abstract* Graphics.** The Graphics class provides you with a wide variety of graphical tools, ranging from the generic drawing tools, such as `drawLine()`, to editing tools, such as `clipRect()`.

If you are creating an applet, the creation of a graphics object will be done for you by the browser environment. Therefore, you can use the `Graphics` objects passed as parameters to the `paint()` and `update()` methods without worrying about how `drawLine()` actually does its chore.

 ▶▶ See Listing 14.2, "Sample Applet," p. 406

The Graphics class provides you with a wide variety of graphical tools to create attractive interfaces. Listing 14.5 gives a brief sample of these tools and demonstrates the form for creating graphics.

Listing 14.5 Graphics **Example**

```
import java.applet.Applet;
import java.awt.*;


public class GraphicsExample extends Applet
{

    public void paint(Graphics g) {

    g.setFont( new Font("TimesRoman", Font.PLAIN, 14) );
            // sets the font for the drawString() statement
    g.drawString("This is a sample of what the Graphics class can do!",30,20);

       g.setColor(Color.red);

       g.fill3DRect(10,60,20,10,true);
       g.fill3DRect(50,60,20,10,false);
       int xpoints[ ] = {120,130, 150, 140, 180 };
                       // x-coordinates for polygon
       int ypoints[ ] = {60,50, 90, 170, 60};
       g.fillPolygon( xpoints, ypoints, 5);

       g.fillRoundRect(200,80,100,100,10,5);
       g.setColor(Color.blue);
       g.fillArc(10,150,100,100,0,360);

       g.setColor(Color.white);
       g.fillArc(35,175,50,50,0,270);

       g.setColor(Color.magenta);
       g.drawLine(300,180,350,180);
       g.drawLine(300,180,300,220);
       g.drawLine(300,220,350,180);
    }
}
```

Methods

- **protected Graphics( )**
  Creates a new Graphics object.

- **abstract void clearRect(int x, int y, int width, int height)**
  Clears the specified rectangle with the background color.

- **abstract void clipRect(int x, int y, int width, int height)**
  Sets the clipping rectangle for the graphical operations. Only those graphics within the specified area will be displayed.

> **Tip**
>
> Be careful when setting the clipping area. Once this is done, it cannot be undone! There-
> fore, it is often wise to create a temporary Graphics object with the create( ) method.
> You can set the clipping area and paint with this new object. When you want to display on
> the full screen again, you can revert to the original Graphics object.

- **abstract void copyArea(int x, int y, int width, int width, int height, int dx, int dy)**
  Copies the area defined by the x- and y-coordinates and the width and height dimensions. This region will then be moved dx pixels horizontally and dy pixels vertically.

- **Graphics create(int x, int y, int width, int height)**
  Creates a new Graphics object. This object will be identical to the current Graphics
  object except for the fact that its clipping area will be set to the specified coordinates and dimensions. This is useful inasmuch as once the clipping area is set it
  cannot be reset. Therefore, by creating a new Graphics object, you are able to employ a clipping area without destroying the original Graphics object.

- **abstract Graphics create( )**
  Creates a new Graphics object identical to the current object. Because both the
  original and the new copy may paint to the same region, this is often useful when
  you are making temporary yet irrevocable changes to the Graphics object—such as
  setting the clipping area.

- **abstract void dispose( )**
  Disposes of the resources used by the graphics context.

- **void draw3DRect(int x, int y, int width, int height, boolean raised)**
  Creates a 3-D rectangle with the specified location and size. Setting the raised
  parameter to a value of true gives the rectangle a brighter color—making it appear
  three-dimensional.

- **abstract void drawArc(int x, int y, int width, int height, int startAngle, int arcAngle)**
  Draws the outline of an arc at the specified coordinates with the given size. The
  startAngle and arcAngle are measured in degrees and represent the angle at which
  the arc begins and ends (i.e., an arc from 0 to 360 is a complete circle)

- **void drawBytes(byte data[ ], int offset, int length, int x, int y)**
  Displays bytes from the data[ ] array. The offset value represents the index of the
  first byte to be drawn; length is the number of bytes to be drawn; and x and y are
  the coordinates at which the bytes will be drawn on the screen.

- **void drawChars(char data[ ], int offset, int length, int x, int y)**
  Displays characters from the data[] array. The offset value represents the index of
  the first character to be drawn; length is the number of characters to be drawn; and
  x and y are the coordinates at which the characters will be drawn.

- **abstract boolean drawImage(Image img, int x, int y, int width, int height, Color bgcolor, ImageObserver observer)**
  Draws an image at the specified location with the specified size. bgcolor is the color that will be drawn "behind" the image—visible if there are any transparent pixels in the image. observer is the ImageObserver that monitors the progress of the image.

> **Note**
>
> The java.awtComponent class implements the ImageObserver interface. Therefore, in most applets, you may use the this keyword as the ImageObserver.

- **abstract boolean drawImage(Image img, int x, int y, Color bgcolor, ImageObserver observer)**
  Draws an image at the specified location with its normal size. bgcolor is the color that will be drawn "behind" the applet—visible if there are any transparent pixels in the image. observer is the ImageObserver that monitors the progress of the image.

- **abstract boolean drawImage(Image img, int x, int y, int width, int height, ImageObserver observer)**
  Draws an image at the specified location with the specified size. observer is the ImageObserver that monitors the progress of the image.

- **abstract boolean drawImage(Image img, int x, int y, ImageObserver observer)**
  Draws an image at the specified location with its normal size. observer is the ImageObserver that will monitor the progress of the image.

- **abstract void drawLine(int x1, int y1, int x2, int y2)**
  Draws a line between the given points.

- **abstract void drawOval(int x, int y, int width, int height)**
  Draws the outline of an oval at the specified coordinates with the specified size.

- **void drawRect(int x, int y, int width, int height)**
  Draws the outline of a rectangle at the specified coordinates with the specified size.

- **abstract void drawRoundRect(int x, int y, int width, int height, int arcWidth, int arcHeight)**
  Draws the outline of a rectangle at the specified coordinates having the specified size. arcWidth and arcHeight determine the size and shape of the corners of the rectangle.

- **void drawPolygon(Polygon p)**
  Draws the polygon defined by the specified java.awt.Polygon object.

- **abstract void drawPolygon(int xPoints[ ], int yPoints[ ], int nPoints)**
  Draws the polygon defined by the specified set of points. nPoints represents the

number of vertices on the polygon. Java will pair the first *n* coordinates of the arrays to create *n* ordered pairs that will serve as the vertices of the polygon.

- **abstract void drawString(String str, int x, int y)**
  Draws a string at the specified coordinates using the current font.

- **void fill3DRect(int x, int y, int width, int height, boolean raised)**
  Fills a rectangle at the specified coordinates that has the specified size. The `raised` variable will change the darkness of the rectangle—making it appear three-dimensional if `true`.

- **abstract void fillOval(int x, int y, int width, int height)**
  Fills an oval defined by the x- and y-coordinates that will have the specified size.

- **abstract void fillRect(int x, int y, int width, int height)**
  Fills a rectangle at the given coordinates with the specified size.

- **abstract void fillRoundRect(int x, int y, int width, int height, int arcWidth, int arcHeight)**
  Fills in a rectangle at the specified coordinates having the specified size. `arcWidth` and `arcHeight` determine the size and shape of the corners of the rectangle.

- **abstract void fillArc(int x, int y, int width, int height, int startAngle, int arcAngle)**
  Fills an arc at the given coordinates with the specified size. The arc will extend from the `startAngle` to the `arcAngle`, measured in degrees.

- **void fillPolygon(Polygon p)**
  Fills the polygon defined by the particular `Polygon` object.

- **abstract void fillPolygon(int xPoints[ ], int yPoints[ ], int nPoints)**
  Fills the polygon defined by the specified set of points. `nPoints` represents the number of vertices on the polygon. Java will pair the first *n* coordinates of the arrays to create *n* ordered pairs that will serve as the vertices of the polygon.

- **void finalize( )**
  Disposes of the specific `Graphics` object.

- **abstract Rectangle getClipRect( )**
  Returns the clipping rectangle set by the `clipRect()` method.

- **abstract Color getColor( )**
  Returns the current color used by graphical operations.

- **abstract Font getFont( )**
  Returns the font used by all text-related operations.

- **abstract FontMetrics getFontMetrics(Font f)**
  Returns the `FontMetrics` for the specified `Font`.

- **FontMetrics getFontMetrics( )**
  Returns the `FontMetrics` for the current font.

- **abstract void setColor(Color c)**
  Sets the color to be used by all graphical operations.

- **abstract void setFont(Font font)**
  Sets the font for all graphical operations.

- **abstract void setPaintMode( )**
  Causes subsequent graphical commands to cover the locations with the current color.

- **abstract void setXORMode(Color otherColor)**
  This method will cause the Graphics object to XOR mode using the current color and the specified otherColor. When painting graphics, all figures in the current color will be painted with the otherColor and vice versa. Any figures not in either color will be displayed in a different, random color.

- **abstract void translate(int x, int y)**
  Makes the specified coordinates the new origin for graphical operations. As a result, all operations will be relative to this new origin.

- **String toString( )**
  Returns a string containing information about the Graphics object, including the current color and font.

GridBagConstraints Implements java.lang.Cloneable. The GridBagConstraint class enables you to customize the layout attributes of each component in a GridBagLayout. By first creating a GridBagConstraint and setting its fields, you are able specify the shape, size, and behavior of the component once added to the layout.

▶▶ See "GridBagLayout Implements LayoutManager," p. 445

Fields

- **int anchor**
  Describes the location at which the component will be placed.

- **final static int BOTH**
  A possible fill value. The component will fill as much space as allowed, both horizontally and vertically.

- **final static int CENTER**
  A possible anchor value.

- **final static int EAST**
  A possible anchor value.

- **int fill**
  Determines how the component will behave if the container is resized. The component may expand horizontally, vertically, or in both directions.

III

Java

- **int gridheight**
  Sets the height of the component.

- **int gridwidth**
  Sets the width of the component.

- **int gridx**
  The x-coordinate of the component.

- **int gridy**
  The y-coordinate of the component.

- **final static int HORIZONTAL**
  A value for `fill`. Causes the component to expand horizontally when the area available for the component exceeds the size of the component.

- **Insets insets**
  Defines the amount of space to be placed around the outside of any components on the edge of the layout.

- **int ipadx**
  The amount of horizontal space to be placed between components.

- **int ipady**
  The amount of vertical space to be placed between components.

- **final static int NONE**
  A value for `fill`. The component will not expand in any direction.

- **final static int NORTH**
  A value for `anchor`.

- **final static int NORTHEAST**
  A value for `anchor`.

- **final static int NORTHWEST**
  A value for `anchor`.

- **final static int RELATIVE**
  A value for `gridx` or `gridy`. The component will be placed just after the previous component. For `gridx` this means to the left. For `gridy`, this means directly beneath.

- **final static int REMAINDER**
  A value for `gridwidth` or `gridheight`. The component will take up the remainder of the row or column, respectively.

- **final static int SOUTH**
  A value for `anchor`.

- **final static int SOUTHEAST**
  A value for `anchor`.

- **final static int SOUTHWEST**
  A value for anchor.

- **final static int VERTICAL**
  A value for fill. The component will expand vertically to fill the available area.

- **double weightx**
  Defines the relative importance of the component. This attribute is used when resizing the container in which the component resides.

- **double weighty**
  Defines the relative importance of the component. This attribute is used when resizing the container in which the component resides.

- **final static int WEST**
  A value for anchor.

Methods

- **GridBagConstraints( )**
  Creates a new GridBagConstraints object.

- **Object clone( )**
  Returns a copy of the GridBagConstraints object.

GridBagLayout Implements LayoutManager. The GridBagLayout is the most versatile and commonly used layout manager for components. A GridBagLayout enables you to place any number of components in virtually any layout that you can imagine.

To control the layout of components in a GridBagLayout, you must employ the GridBagConstraints class. After setting the values of the GridBagConstraints class, you can add a component to the layout using the constraints. This flexibility enables you to specify a great deal of information about how the components will be laid out.

▶▶ See "GridBagConstraints Implements java.lang.Cloneable," p. 443

The constraints for a GridBagLayout are set through the fields in the GridBagLayout, as described in the following table:

Fields	Purpose
anchor	Can be used to place the component in a particular region of the container (for example, SOUTHWEST).
fill	Determines how the component will act if the container provides it with room to grow. Valid values are NONE, HORIZONTAL, VERTICAL, and BOTH.
insets	Specifies the amount of space between components on the side of the container and the container edge.
ipadx, ipady	Specifies the amount of space between components.

III

Java

(continues)

(continued)

Fields	Purpose
gridx, gridy	Defines the upper lefthand corner of the component.
gridwidth, gridheight	Defines the size of the component.
weightx, weighty	Defines the relative importance of the components; to be used only when the container is resized.

Listing 14.6 GridbagLayout **Example**

```
import java.applet.Applet;
import java.awt.*;

public class GridBagExample extends Applet
{
    GridBagLayout gridbag;
    GridBagConstraints c;

    public void init() {
        Button button;
        Checkbox checkbox;
        TextArea textarea;
        TextField textfield;
        Choice choice;

        gridbag = new GridBagLayout();
        c = new GridBagConstraints();
        setLayout(gridbag);

        c.ipadx=2;c.ipady=2;   // padding between components
        c.insets=new Insets(5,5,5,5);      /* padding
        between the components and the edge of the container*/

        button = new Button("Button One");
        gridbag.setConstraints(button,c);
        add(button);

        c.gridwidth = GridBagConstraints.REMAINDER;
        /* Button will occupy the remainder of this row.
           Forces the next component onto the next row.    */

        button = new Button("Button Two");
        gridbag.setConstraints(button,c);
        add(button);

        c.gridwidth = 1;
        // back to defaults - components continue on same row


        checkbox = new Checkbox("Checkbox");
        gridbag.setConstraints(checkbox,c);
        add(checkbox);

        c.gridwidth = GridBagConstraints.REMAINDER;
        textfield = new TextField("This is a TextField");
```

```
        gridbag.setConstraints(textfield,c);
        add(textfield);

        c.gridwidth = 1;
        c.gridheight = GridBagConstraints.REMAINDER;
        choice = new Choice();
        choice.addItem("Selection One");
        choice.addItem("Selection Two");
        gridbag.setConstraints(choice,c);
        add(choice);

        textarea = new TextArea("This is a Text Area",10,3);
        gridbag.setConstraints(textarea,c);
        add(textarea);
    }
}
```

Fields

- **double columnWeights[ ]**
  Stores the horizontal weights of the components in each column.

- **int columnWidths[ ]**
  Stores the horizontal sizes of the components in each column.

- **protected Hashtable comptable**
  A Hashtable to store the components.

- **protected GridBagConstraints defaultConstraints**
  The default constraints for a component.

- **protected GridBagLayoutInfo layoutInfo**
  The GridBagLayoutInfo class is a restricted class that facilitates management of the layout for the GridBagLayout class. It tracks the size of the layout, the minimum dimensions of the components, and the weights.

  The class consists only of the following fields and one constructor method. Unless you are creating a new class in the java.awt package that extends the GridbagLayout class, you will not need to use this class—nor will you be able to.

  ```
  int width, height;   // number of cells in each direction
  int startx, starty;  // start of layout
  int minWidth[ ];     // largest minWidth for each column
  int minHeight[ ];    // largest minHeight for each row
  double weightX[ ];   // largest weight for each column
  double weightY[ ];   // largest weight for each row
  ```

- **protected final static int MAXGRIDSIZE**
  The maximum number of rows or columns. Set to 128.

- **protected final static int MINSIZE**
  The minimum number of rows or columns. Set to 1.

- **protected final static int PREFERREDSIZE**
  The preferred size of a component. Set to 2.

- **int rowHeights[ ]**
  Tracks the heights of the components in each row.

- **double rowWeights[ ]**
  Tracks the weights of the components in each row.

Methods

- **GridBagLayout( )**
  Creates a new GridBagLayout.

- **void addLayoutComponent(String name, Component comp)**
  This function is required inasmuch as the GridBagLayout class implements the LayoutManager interface. It however has no function in this class.

- **protected void AdjustForGravity(GridBagConstraints constraints, Rectangle r)**
  Adjusts the components according to their attributes within the specified Rectangle. This method is called by ArrangeGrid().

- **protected void ArrangeGrid(Container parent)**
  Arranges the parent container.

- **protected void DumpConstraints(GridBagConstraints constraints)**
  Prints out the current constraints.

- **protected void DumpLayoutInfo(GridBagLayoutInfo string)**
  Prints out the current layout information.

- **GridBagConstraints getConstraints(Component comp)**
  Returns the current constraints.

- **int[ ][ ] getLayoutDimensions( )**
  Returns an array of integers obtained for the arrays in the LayoutInfo object. If the returned array is named arr, then arr[0] is the array of minimum widths for each column and arr[1] is the array of minimum heights for each row.

- **protected GridBagLayoutInfo GetLayoutInfo(Container parent, int sizeflag)**
  Returns the GridBagLayoutInfo object for the GridBagLayout.

- **Point getLayoutOrigin( )**
  Returns the origin for the layout. This may not always be (0,0).

- **double[ ][ ] getLayoutWeights( )**
  Returns the maximum weights of the components in each row and column. arr[0] is an array of the maximum weight in each column. arr[1] is an array of the maximum weight in each row.

- **protected Dimension GetMinSize(Container parent, GridBagLayoutInfo info)**
  Returns the minimum size required for this layout. This value is based on the size of the components and the insets values for the parent container. This method is

called by `perferredLayoutSize()` and `minimumLayoutSize()`, each with a different `info` parameter.

- **void layoutContainer(Container parent)**
  Arranges the container in accordance with the `GridBagLayout` parameters.

- **Point location(int x, int y)**
  Returns the size of the rectangle occupied by all components above and to the left of the point (x,y) on the grid. This value is created by summing the minimum widths and minimum heights for each component having a x-coordinate less than or equal to x and a y-coordinate less than or equal to y.

- **protected GridBagConstraints lookupConstraints(Component comp)**
  Returns the constraints for the particular component.

- **Dimension minimumLayoutSize(Container parent)**
  Returns the minimum layout size required for the container. It is based on the minimum sizes for the components within the layout.

- **Dimension preferredLayoutSize(Container parent)**
  Returns the preferred size of the container. It is based on the preferred sizes for the components within the layout.

- **void removeLayoutComponent(Component comp)**
  Removes the specified component from the layout.

- **void setConstraints(Component comp, GridBagConstraints constraints)**
  Assigns the given component a new set of constraints.

- **String toString( )**
  Returns the string, "java.awt.GridBagLayout."

GridLayout Implements LayoutManager. A `GridLayout` provides you with slightly less control over the layout than the `GridBagLayout` class. A `GridLayout` is created by specifying a number of rows and columns. Each subsequent `add()` statement will place the specified component in the layout, adjusting the size of all components. As a result, all components in a `GridLayout` are of the same size.

Methods

- **GridLayout(int rows, int cols)**
  Constructs a `GridLayout` with the specified number of rows and columns. The `hgap` and `vgap` will be set to 0.

- **GridLayout(int rows, int cols, int hgap, int vgap)**
  Constructs a `GridLayout` with the specified number of rows and columns, `hgap`, and `vgap`.

- **void addLayoutComponent(String name, Component comp)**
  This method has no function.

- **void layoutContainer(Container parent)**
  Arranges the container in accordance with the `GridLayout` model.

III

Java

- **Dimension minimumLayoutSize(Container parent)**
  Returns the minimum layout size required for the container. It is based on the preferred sizes for the components within the layout.

- **Dimension preferredLayoutSize(Container parent)**
  Returns the preferred layout size requested for the container. Based on the preferred sizes for the components within the layout.

- **void removeLayoutComponent(Component comp)**
  Removes the specified component.

- **String toString( )**
  Returns a string containing the layout's name, hgap, vgaps, and the number of rows and columns.

Abstract **Image.** The Image class provides you with an platform-independent manner of handling images. Regardless of the source of the image or the platform, all the following methods may be used on all Images.

One problem often encountered with images is that they often take some time to completely load. As a result, in all methods where this could be problematic, it is necessary to specify an ImageObserver (an object that implements the ImageObserver interface). If the method is unable to return the requested information, it will return a value of –1 or a null string. However, once the information does become available, the information will be sent along to the imageUpdate() method of the specified ImageObserver.

 ▶▶ See "java.awt.Image," p. 472

Field
- **final static Object UndefinedProperty**
  This field is returned whenever you request a property not defined for the particular Image.

Methods
- **Image( )**
  Creates a new Image.

- **abstract Graphics getGraphics( )**
  Returns the Graphics object for this Image.

- **abstract int getHeight(ImageObserver observer)**
  Returns the height of the Image. If the height is not currently known, this method will return a value of –1 and will inform the specified ImageObserver at a later time though the imageUpdate() method.

- **abstract Object getProperty(String propertyname, ImageObserver observer)**
  Returns the requested property for this `Image`. If this property is undefined, the `UndefinedProperty` object will be returned. If the property is currently unknown, the method will return a value of `null`, and will later inform the `ImageObserver`.

- **abstract void flush( )**
  Disposes of all memory being used by the `Image`. This contains cached information. If the `Image` is to be displayed again, it will be re-created for you, but this will take longer than if it were still cached.

- **abstract ImageProducer getSource( )**
  Returns the source of the `Image` in the form of a class implementing the `ImageProducer` interface.

  This method is useful when using `ImageFilters`. By first invoking this method, you can obtain the source of the `Image` to be used when creating a new `java.awt.image.FilteredImageSource`.

- **abstract int getWidth(ImageObserver observer)**
  Returns the width of the `Image`. If the height is not currently known, this method will return a value of –1 and will later inform the specified `ImageObserver`.

Insets Implements Cloneable. The `Insets` class is a tool to be used by layout managers, particularly `GridBagLayoutManager`. An `Inset` may be used to set and track the amount of space that will be inserted between the components of the layout and the border of the container.

▶▶ See Listing 14.6, "GridbagLayout Example," p. 446

Fields
- **int bottom**
- **int left**
- **int right**
- **int top**

Methods
- **Insets(int top, int left, int bottom, int right)**
  Creates a new `Insets` object with the specified spacing values.

- **Object clone( )**
  Creates a copy of the `Insets` object.

- **String toString( )**
  Returns a string containing the class name and the four spacing values.

Label Extends Component. A `Label` is a convenient way of placing a single line of text on the screen. Because it is a `Component`, it may be placed in a layout manager.

Fields

- **final static int CENTER**
  An alignment value for the text in the Label.

- **final static int LEFT**
  An alignment value for the text in the Label.

- **final static int RIGHT**
  An alignment value for the text in the Label.

Methods

- **Label( )**
  Constructs a new, empty label whose text will be left justified.

- **Label(String label)**
  Constructs a new label with the specified text. The text will be left justified.

- **Label(String label, int alignment)**
  Constructs a new label with the specified text and alignment. The alignment value may be either LEFT, CENTER, or RIGHT.

- **synchronized void addNotify( )**
  Creates the Label's peer.

- **int getAlignment( )**
  Returns the alignment for the Label.

- **String getText( )**
  Returns the current text for the Label.

- **protected String paramString( )**
  Returns a string containing the parameters for the Label including the alignment and the text.

- **void setAlignment(int alignment)**
  Sets the alignment for the displayed text. The parameter may be either LEFT, CENTER, or RIGHT.

- **void setText(String label)**
  Sets the text for the Label.

List Extends Component. A List is a useful scrollable index of textual headers. When using a List, you may not only add items to the end of the list, but may also insert them within the list. Furthermore, during execution, you can query the list for information regarding the user's actions or even scroll the list yourself using the makeVisible( ) method.

Methods

- **List( )**
  Creates a new List that contains no rows and does not allow multiple selections.

- **List(int rows, boolean multipleSelections)**
  Creates a new `List` with the specified number of rows. If the `multipleSelection` argument is `true`, then more than one item in the list can be selected at a given time.

- **synchronized void addItem(String itemTitle, int index)**
  Adds an new item to the list at the specified index. `itemTitle` specifies the title that will be displayed. If the index is –1 or greater than the number of the items in the `List`, the item will be added to the end of the `List`.

- **synchronized void addItem(String itemTitle)**
  Adds an item with the specified title to the end of the `List`.

- **synchronized void addNotify( )**
  Creates the `List`'s peer.

- **boolean allowsMultipleSelections( )**
  Returns `true` if the user may select more than one item in this list.

- **synchronized void clear( )**
  Clears the list. All items are erased.

- **int countItems( )**
  Returns the number of items in the list.

- **String getItem(int index)**
  Returns the title of the item at the specified index.

- **synchronized void delItem(int index)**
  Deletes the item at the specified index.

- **synchronized void delItems(int start, int end)**
  Deletes all items between and including the `start` and `end` parameters.

- **synchronized void deselect(int index)**
  Deselects the specified index. No item will be selected.

- **int getRows( )**
  Returns the number of items that can be seen by the user.

- **synchronized int getSelectedIndex( )**
  Returns the index of the currently selected item. Returns –1 if none is selected at the time.

- **synchronized int[ ] getSelectedIndexes( )**
  Returns an array containing the indexes of all selected items. This is only useful when multiple selections are permitted.

- **synchronized String getSelectedItem( )**
  Returns the title of the currently selected item. Returns –1 if none is selected at the time.

III

Java

- **synchronized String[ ] getSelectedItems( )**
  Returns an array containing the titles of all selected items. This is only useful when multiple selections are permitted.

- **int getVisibleIndex( )**
  Returns the index of the item that was made visible by the last call to `makeVisible()`.

- **synchronized boolean isSelected(int index)**
  Returns `true` if the specified item is visible.

- **void makeVisible(int index)**
  Scrolls the list to make the specified index visible.

- **Dimension minimumSize( )**
  Returns the minimum size required to properly display the entire list. This value is based on either the size returned from the `List`'s peer or the `Component` class.

- **Dimension minimumSize(int rows)**
  Returns the minimum size required to properly display the specified number of rows in this list. This value is based on either the size returned from the `List`'s peer or the `Component` class.

- **protected String paramString( )**
  Returns a string containing information on the `List` including the title of the selected item.

- **Dimension preferredSize( )**
  Returns the size desired to display the entire list. This value is based on either the size returned from the `List`'s peer or the `Component` class.

- **Dimension preferredSize(int rows)**
  Returns the size desired to display the specified number of rows in the list. This value is based on either the size returned from the `List`'s peer or the `Component` class.

- **synchronized void removeNotify( )**
  Removes the `List`'s peer.

- **synchronized void replaceItem(String newValue, int index)**
  Changes the value of the item at the specified index. This is done by deleting the item at the specified index and then creating a new item with the specified title and index.

- **synchronized void select(int index)**
  Selects the specified item.

- **void setMultipleSelections(boolean multipleSelections)**
  If the `multipleSelections` parameter is `true`, then more than one item in the list can be selected at a time. If this is `false`, then only one item can be selected at a given moment.

MediaTracker. A MediaTracker is a means of managing a number of media objects, such as images and audio clips. (However, as of the 1.0 JDK, only Images were supported.) Somewhat like an array, the MediaTracker assigns each a reference number. However, it also keeps track of the status of each image, allowing you to determine the status of each or lock up the tracker until all images have been loaded.

Fields

- **final static int ABORTED**
  A flag indicating the loading of the media has been aborted.

- **final static int COMPLETE**
  A flag indicating the loading of the media has been successfully completed.

- **final static int ERRORED**
  A flag indicating an error has been encountered while loading the media.

Methods

- **MediaTracker(Component comp)**
  Creates a new MediaTracker to report on the media in the specified component.

- **void addImage(Image image, int id)**
  Adds an item to the MediaTracker with the specified id. This id value can later be used as a reference to a set of media items.

- **synchronized void addImage(Image image, int id, int width, int height)**
  Adds an image with the specified dimensions to the MediaTracker with the specified id. This can later be used as a reference to a set of media items.

- **synchronized boolean checkAll(boolean load)**
  Returns true if all media items have been successfully loaded, false otherwise. If the load parameter is true, this method will also load any non-loaded images.

- **boolean checkAll( )**
  Returns true if all media items have been successfully loaded, false otherwise. This method will not affect non-loaded images.

- **synchronized boolean checkID(int id, boolean load)**
  Returns true if all media items with the specified id have been successfully loaded, false otherwise. If the load parameter is true, this method will also load any non-loaded images.

- **boolean checkID(int id)**
  Returns true if all media items with the specified id have been successfully loaded, false otherwise. This method has no effect on unloaded images.

- **synchronized Object[ ] getErrorsAny( )**
  Returns an array of all media items that have encountered an error.

- **synchronized Object[ ] getErrorsID(int id)**
  Returns an array of all media items with the specified id that have encountered an error.

- **synchronized boolean isErrorAny( )**
  Returns true if any media items have encountered an error.

- **synchronized boolean isErrorID(int id)**
  Returns true if any media items with the specified id have encountered an error.

- **int statusAll(boolean load)**
  Returns the status for all media items in the MediaTracker. If the load parameter is true, any unloaded images will be loaded.

- **int statusID(int id, boolean load)**
  Returns the status for all media items with the specified id. If the load parameter is true, all unloaded items will be loaded.

- **void waitForAll( ) throws InterruptedException**
  Begins to load all media items and does not return until this process is complete. *Note that this method does not guarantee that these items will be loaded successfully,* and thus you are strongly encouraged to check for any errors.

- **synchronized boolean waitForAll(long ms) throws InterruptedException**
  Locks up the MediaTracker object and loads all media items. This method relinquishes control of the MediaTracker only when the loading is complete or the specified number of milliseconds has expired. *Note that this method does not guarantee that these items will be loaded successfully,* and thus you are strongly encouraged to check for any errors.

- **void waitForID(int id) throws InterruptedException**
  Begins to load all media items with the specified id and does not return until this process is complete. *Note that this method does not guarantee that these items will be loaded successfully,* and thus you are strongly encouraged to check for any errors.

- **synchronized boolean waitForID(int id, long ms) throws InterruptedException**
  Begins to load all media items and does not return until this process is complete or the specified number of milliseconds has expired. *Note that this method does not guarantee that these items will be loaded successfully,* and thus you are strongly encouraged to check for any errors.

Menu Extends MenuItem Implements MenuContainer. A Menu is a column in a MenuBar. Like the standard "File" and "Help" headers in most applications, a Menu defines the title on the MenuBar as well as the headings in the column. When creating a menu, you must first create Menu items and then add them to your MenuBar.

▶▶ See the following section, "MenuBar Extends MenuComponent Implements MenuContainer"

▶▶ See "Frame Extends Window Implements MenuContainer," p. 437

Methods

- **Menu(String title)**

  Creates a new Menu with the specified title.

- **Menu(String title, boolean tearOff)**

  Creates a new Menu with the specified title. The effects of the tearOff parameter are platform-dependent. However, the idea of a tear-off menu is that it will remain as a separate window until the user selects an item from it.

- **void add(String label)**

  Adds a selection with the specified label to the Menu listing.

- **synchronized MenuItem add(MenuItem mitem)**

  Adds a MenuItem to the Menu listing.

- **synchronized void addNotify( )**

  Creates the Menu's peer.

- **void addSeparator( )**

  Inserts a line between the already added items in the Menu and any later items that you add.

- **int countItems( )**

  Returns the number of items in the menu listing.

- **MenuItem getItem(int index)**

  Returns the item at the specified index.

- **boolean isTearOff( )**

  Returns true if the menu is a tear-off menu.

- **synchronized void remove(MenuComponent item)**

  Removes the specified item from the menu listing.

- **synchronized void remove(int index)**

  Removes the item at the specified index from the menu listing.

- **synchronized void removeNotify( )**

  Removes the Menu's peer.

MenuBar Extends MenuComponent Implements MenuContainer. A MenuBar is a container for Menu items and serves as the head of the menu when displayed. In order to create a menu in your program, you must first create Menu items, and then add them to a MenuBar. By adding a MenuBar to the Frame, you are able to make the menu visible to the user.

III

Java

▶▶ See "Menu Extends MenuItem Implements MenuContainer," p. 456
▶▶ See "Frame Extends Window Implements MenuContainer," p. 437

Also note the use of the `Display` class to enable the applet to monitor the user's selections.

Listing 14.7 Menu **Example**

```java
import java.applet.Applet;
import java.awt.*;

public class MenuExample extends Applet
{
   private Menu category;
   private MenuBar bar;
   private Display picture;

   public void init() {
      bar = new MenuBar();
      category = new Menu("Document");
      category.add("Option One");
      category.add("Option Two");
      category.add("Option Three");
      bar.add(category);

      category = new Menu("Session");
      category.add("Reset");
      category.add("Restart");
      bar.add(category);

      category = new Menu("Screen");
      category.add("Change colors");
      category.add("Display Titles");
      bar.add(category);


      picture = new Display();
      picture.setMenuBar(bar);
      picture.setTitle("Menu Example");
      picture.show();
   }
}

class Display extends Frame {
   public boolean action(Event evt, Object arg) {
      if(arg.equals("Option Two")) {
        System.out.println("Option Two was Selected");
      return true;
      }
      return super.handleEvent(evt);
   }

   public boolean handleEvent(Event evt) {
      if (evt.id == Event.WINDOW_DESTROY) {
         hide();   // closes the frame when appropriate
```

```
        return true;
      }
    return super.handleEvent(evt);
    }
  }
```

Methods

- **MenuBar( )**
  Creates a new MenuBar.

- **synchronized Menu add(Menu m)**
  Adds a Menu to the MenuBar.

- **synchronized void addNotify( )**
  Creates the MenuBar's peer.

- **int countMenus( )**
  Returns the number of Menus in this MenuBar.

- **Menu getHelpMenu( )**
  Returns the Help menu from this MenuBar.

- **Menu getMenu(int index)**
  Returns the Menu at the specified index.

- **synchronized void remove(MenuComponent m)**
  Removes the specified MenuComponent.

- **synchronized void remove(int index)**
  Removes the MenuComponent at the specified index.

- **void removeNotify( )**
  Removes the MenuBar's peer.

- **synchronized void setHelpMenu(Menu m)**
  Makes the specified Menu the Help menu for the MenuBar.

Abstract **MenuComponent.** MenuComponent is the superclass for all classes dealing with menu related components.

▶▶ See "Menu Extends MenuItem Implements MenuContainer," p. 456

Methods

- **MenuComponent( )**
  Creates a new MenuComponent.

- **MenuContainer getParent( )**
  Returns the container of this MenuComponent. This most likely will be the Menu in which the MenuComponent resides.

- **MenuComponentPeer getPeer( )**
  Returns the peer of the MenuComponent.

III

Java

- **Font getFont( )**
  Returns the font of this MenuComponent.

- **protected String paramString( )**
  Returns a string containing information on the MenuComponent. Although overridden in subclasses, this method returns an empty string.

- **boolean postEvent(Event evt)**
  Posts the specified Event to the MenuComponent.

- **void removeNotify( )**
  Removes the MenuComponent's peer.

- **void setFont(Font f)**
  Sets the font for the MenuComponent.

- **String toString( )**
  Returns the object's name in addition to the information returned by paramString().

MenuItem Extends MenuComponent. A MenuItem is a class that contains a string representation of an option on a menu. It is used and extended by the more useful menu classes.

 ▶▶ See "CheckboxMenuItem Extends MenuItem," p. 416

Methods
- **MenuItem(String label)**
  Creates a new MenuItem with the specified text label.

- **synchronized void addNotify( )**
  Creates the MenuItem's peer.

- **void disable( )**
  Prevents the user from selecting the MenuItem.

- **void enable(boolean cond)**
  If cond is true, the user will be able to select the MenuItem. If cond is false, the user will be unable to select the item.

- **void enable( )**
  Enables the user to select the MenuItem.

- **String getLabel( )**
  Returns the textual label of this MenuItem.

- **boolean isEnabled( )**
  Returns true if the MenuItem is enabled, meaning that the user will be able to select it.

- **String paramString( )**
  Returns a string containing the item's label.

- **void setLabel(String label)**
  Sets the label of this `MenuItem`.

Panel Extends Container. `Panel` is a simple container class that may be extended to create richer subclasses. `java.applet.Applet` is a subclass of `Panel`.

▶▶ See Listing 14.3, "CardLayout Example Source Code," p. 413

Methods

- **Panel( )**
  Creates a new `Panel`.

- **synchronized void addNotify( )**
  Creates the Panel's peer.

Point. `Point` is a simple class to keep track of and manage an ordered pair.

Fields

- **int x**
- **int y**

Methods

- **Point (int x, int y)**
  Creates a new `Point` with the specified x and y values.

- **boolean equals(Object anotherobject)**
  Compares a `Point` to another object. Two points are equal if their x and y values are equal.

- **int hashCode( )**
  Returns the `hashcode` for the `Point` object. This value is dependent on the values of x and y.

- **void move(int x, int y)**
  Sets the coordinates of the `Point` to the specified x and y.

- **String toString( )**
  Returns a string containing the class name and the x and y values.

- **void translate(int x, int y)**
  Increments the x- and y-coordinates of the point by the specified amounts.

Polygon. A `Polygon` is a class that enables you to define an arbitrary polygon. This class does not draw a polygon on the screen, but rather specifies the coordinates that can be used by the methods in the `Graphics` class.

To track the vertices, the class maintains two parallel arrays (xpoints[] and ypoints[]). For example, if point #2 is (4,5), then xpoints[3] will equal 4 and ypoints[3] will equal 5.

▶▶ See Listing 14.5, "Graphics Example," p. 439

Fields

- **int npoints**
  The number of points in the Polygon. Regardless of the number of values in the xpoints[] and ypoints[] arrays, this value will be used in defining the polygon.

- **int xpoints[ ]**
  The x-coordinates of the vertices of the polygon. These values are paired with the corresponding values in the ypoints[] array to create the vertices of the polygon.

- **int ypoints[ ]**
  The y-coordinates of the vertices of the polygon. These values are paired with the corresponding values in the xpoints[] array to create the vertices of the polygon.

Methods

- **Polygon( )**
  Creates a new Polygon.

- **Polygon(int xpoints[ ], int ypoints[ ], int npoints)**
  Creates a new Polygon with the specified points. npoints specifies the number of points that will be taken from the arrays.

- **void addPoint(int x, int y)**
  Adds a point to the polygon.

- **Rectangle getBoundingBox( )**
  Returns a Rectangle that encloses the polygon.

- **boolean inside(int x, int y)**
  Returns true if the given point lies within the polygon.

Rectangle. The Rectangle class defines the vertices of a rectangle. While it does not actually draw the rectangle on the screen, it does enable you to create and track rectangular objects.

Fields

- **int height**
- **int width**
- **int x**
- **int y**

Methods

- **Rectangle( )**
  Creates a new Rectangle.

- **Rectangle(Dimension d)**
  Creates a new Rectangle with the specified dimensions.

- **Rectangle(int x, int y, int width, int height)**
  Creates a new Rectangle with the specified coordinates and dimensions.

- **Rectangle(int width, int height)**
  Creates a new Rectangle with the specified coordinates.

- **Rectangle(Point p)**
  Creates a new Rectangle with the specified coordinates.

- **Rectangle(Point p, Dimension d)**
  Creates a new Rectangle with the specified coordinates and dimensions.

- **void add(Rectangle r)**
  Causes the current Rectangle to expand to enclose the specified Rectangle.

- **void add(Point pt)**
  Causes the current Rectangle to expand to enclose the specified Point.

- **void add(int newx, int newy)**
  Causes the current Rectangle to expand to enclose the specified coordinates.

- **boolean equals(Object anotherobject)**
  Compares the Rectangle to another object. Two Rectangles are equal if they have the same x- and y-coordinates and dimensions.

- **void grow(int h, int v)**
  Increases the size of the rectangle by the specified amount.

- **int hashCode( )**
  Returns the hashcode for this Rectangle. This value is dependent on the coordinates and dimensions of the Rectangle.

- **boolean inside(int x, int y)**
  Returns true if the coordinates lie within the rectangle.

- **Rectangle intersection(Rectangle r)**
  Returns the Rectangle representing the intersection of the rectangle and another specified rectangle.

- **boolean intersects(Rectangle r)**
  Returns true if the rectangle intersects the specified rectangle.

- **boolean isEmpty( )**
  Returns true if both the width and the height of the Rectangle are zero.

- **void move(int x, int y)**
  Moves the rectangle to the specified location.

- **void reshape(int x, int y, int width, int height)**
  Specifies a new set of coordinates and dimensions for the rectangle.

III

Java

- **void resize(int width, int height)**
  Changes the dimensions of the Rectangle.

- **String toString( )**
  Returns a string containing the class name, the coordinates, and the dimensions of the rectangle.

- **void translate(int x, int y)**
  Increments the coordinates of the rectangle by the specified x and y values.

- **Rectangle union(Rectangle r)**
  Creates a new Rectangle object containing both the current and another Rectangle.

Scrollbar Extends Component. A Scrollbar is a versatile component used to create scrollbars in your programs. The Scrollbar class enables you to create both vertical and horizontal scrollbars and to set the value range for the scrollbar. Like any other Component, a Scrollbar can be placed by a layout manager.

The code in Listing 14.8 creates a very simple calculator that uses scrollbars to facilitate input. Although the scrollbars adjust themselves automatically, note how the Calculate button updates the TextField.

Listing 14.8 Scrollbar **Example**

```
import java.applet.Applet;
import java.awt.*;


public class ScrollbarExample extends Applet
{
    Scrollbar sb1, sb2;
    TextField info;
    Button trigger;

    public void init() {

      setLayout(null); // won't use one of the layout managers
      add(sb1);
      sb1.reshape(10,10,100,20);

      sb2 = new Scrollbar(Scrollbar.HORIZONTAL,30,20,0,100);
      add(sb2);
      sb2.reshape(10,70,100,20);

      trigger = new Button("Calculate");
      add(trigger);
      trigger.reshape(200,105,80,50);

      info = new TextField("0");
      add(info);
      info.reshape(10,150,75,75);

      refresh();
    }
```

```
    void refresh() {
      int sum = sb1.getValue() + sb2.getValue();
      info.setText("" + sum);
    }

    public boolean action(Event evt, Object arg) {
      if(arg.equals("Calculate")) {
        refresh();
        return true;
      }
      return false;
    }
  }
```

Fields

- **final static int HORIZONTAL**

  A possible value for the orientation of the Scrollbar. Produces a horizontal Scrollbar.

- **final static int VERTICAL**

  A possible value for the orientation of the Scrollbar. Produces a vertical Scrollbar.

Methods

- **Scrollbar( )**

  Creates a new Scrollbar with an orientation set to VERTICAL.

- **Scrollbar(int orientation)**

  Creates a new Scrollbar with the specified orientation.

- **Scrollbar(int orientation, int value, int visible, int minimum, int maximum)**

  Creates a new Scrollbar with the specified orientation. value is the initial value of the Scrollbar. visible is the amount of the Scrollbar that will be visible—a property considered when the applet screen is scrolled. minimum and maximum specify the minimum and maximum values for the Scrollbar.

- **synchronized void addNotify( )**

  Creates the Scrollbar's peer.

- **int getLineIncrement( )**

  Returns the amount that the scrollbar's value will change when the scrollbar is moved a "line." A request to move the scrollbar a line is created by a mouse click on one of the directional arrows at either end of the scrollbar.

- **int getMaximum( )**

  Returns the maximum value for the scrollbar.

- **int getMinimum( )**

  Returns the minimum value for the scrollbar.

- **int getOrientation( )**

  Returns the orientation of the scrollbar—either HORIZONTAL or VERTICAL.

- **int getPageIncrement( )**
  Returns the amount that the scrollbar's value will change when the scrollbar is moved a "page." A request to move the scrollbar a page is created by a mouse click within the scrollbar and to the side of the marker.

- **int getValue( )**
  Returns the value of the scrollbar.

- **int getVisible( )**
  Returns the amount of the scrollbar that is visible.

- **protected String paramString( )**
  Returns a string containing information about the Scrollbar, including its value, visibility, maximum, and minimum values.

- **void setLineIncrement(int l)**
  Sets amount that the scrollbar's value will change when the scrollbar is moved a "line." A request to move the scrollbar a line is created by a mouse click on one of the directional arrows at either side of the scrollbar.

- **void setPageIncrement(int l)**
  Sets the amount that the scrollbar's value will change when the scrollbar is moved a "page." A request to move the scrollbar a page is created by a mouse click within the scrollbar and to the side of the marker.

- **void setValue(int value)**
  Sets the value of the scrollbar. If the value parameter is out of range, the value of the scrollbar will be set to either the maximum or the minimum value of the scrollbar.

- **void setValues(int value, int visible, int minimum, int maximum)**
  Sets the parameters for the scrollbar. orientation, either VERTICAL or HORIZONTAL, determines the appearance of the Scrollbar. value is the initial value of the Scrollbar. visible is the amount of the Scrollbar that will be visible—a property considered when the applet screen is scrolled. minimum and maximum specify the minimum and maximum values for the Scrollbar.

TextArea Extends TextComponent. A TextArea is used for displaying and editing multiple lines of text. Because of this, a TextArea is created with the capability of being scrolled.

 ▶▶ See Listing 14.6, "GridbagLayout Example," p. 446

Methods

- **TextArea( )**
  Creates a new TextArea that is empty.

- **TextArea(int rows, int cols)**
  Creates a new TextArea with the specified number of rows and columns.

- **TextArea(String text)**
  Creates a new TextArea with the specified text.

- **TextArea(String text, int rows, int cols)**
  Creates a new TextArea with the specified number of rows and columns and specified text.

- **synchronized void addNotify( )**
  Creates the TextArea's peer.

- **void appendText(String newText)**
  Adds the specified text to the end of the current text displayed.

- **int getColumns( )**
  Returns the number of columns in the TextArea.

- **int getRows( )**
  Returns the number of columns in the TextArea.

- **void insertText(String str, int pos)**
  Inserts the text into the TextArea at the specified position.

- **Dimension minimumSize( )**
  Returns the minimum size required by this entire component.

- **Dimension minimumSize(int rows, int cols)**
  Returns the minimum size required by the specified number of rows and columns.

- **protected String paramString( )**
  Returns a string that includes the text and the dimensions of the TextArea.

- **Dimension preferredSize( )**
  Returns the minimum size requested by the entire component.

- **Dimension preferredSize(int rows, int cols)**
  Returns the minimum size desired by the specified number of rows and columns.

- **void replaceText(String newText, int start, int end)**
  Replaces the text from start to end with the newText. The length of newText does not need to equal the length of the text being replaced.

TextComponent Extends Component. TextComponent is the basic building block for the text displaying components, TextArea and TextField. Nevertheless, its constructor method has a restricted level of access—preventing you from making use of it unless you are developing within the java.awt package. Therefore, while establishing several useful methods, this class is not usually used directly.

Methods

- **String getSelectedText( )**
  Returns the text that is currently highlighted by the user.

- **int getSelectionEnd( )**
  Returns the index of the last character in the highlighted section.

- **int getSelectionStart( )**
  Returns the index of the first character in the highlighted section.

- **boolean isEditable( )**
  Returns true if the text displayed can be changed.

- **protected String paramString( )**
  Returns a string including the text displayed, the beginning and ending indexes of the highlighted text, and whether or not the text can be edited.

- **void select(int start, int end)**
  Selects all text between the specified indexes.

- **void selectAll( )**
  Selects all text.

- **void setEditable(boolean editable)**
  If editable is true, then the text can be changed by the user. If editable is false, then the text cannot be changed by the user.

TextField Extends TextComponent. A TextField is a simple component that is used to display and edit a single line of text.

Methods

- **TextField( )**
  Creates a new TextField.

- **TextField(int cols)**
  Creates a new TextField with the specified number of columns.

- **TextField(String text)**
  Creates a new TextField with the specified text.

- **TextField(String text, int cols)**
  Creates a new TextField with the specified text and having the specified number of columns.

- **synchronized void addNotify( )**
  Creates the peer of the TextField.

- **boolean echoCharIsSet( )**
  Returns true if an echo character has been set for this TextField. An echo character is a character that will be displayed instead of the characters input by the user. This feature is commonly used for TextFields that accept passwords.

- **int getColumns( )**
  Returns the number of columns in the TextField.

- **char getEchoChar( )**
  Returns the echo character. The echo character is a character displayed as a substitute for the characters entered by the user.

- **Dimension minimumSize( )**
  Returns the minimum size required by this component.

- **Dimension minimumSize(int cols)**
  Returns the minimum size required by the specified number of columns.

- **protected String paramString( )**
  Returns a string containing the current text and the echo character.

- **Dimension preferredSize( )**
  Returns the size requested by this component.

- **Dimension preferredSize(int cols)**
  Returns the size requested by the specified number of columns.

- **void setEchoCharacter(char c)**
  Sets the echo character. This character will be displayed instead of the characters entered by the user.

Toolkit. The Toolkit class serves as the link between the abstract methods of the AWT and the platform-specific native implementation of these methods. Generally, you will not have to interact with the Toolkit. However, it is occasionally convenient to use some of the Toolkit methods, such as getImage(). In such cases, you must employ the getToolkit() method in the Component class to obtain the current Toolkit. Note that the getToolkit() method returns the Toolkit of the Frame in which the component resides.

Methods

- **Toolkit( )**
  Creates a new Toolkit.

- **protected abstract ButtonPeer createButton(Button target)**
  Creates the specified Button and returns its peer.

- **protected abstract CanvasPeer createCanvas(Canvas target)**
  Creates the specified Canvas and returns its peer.

- **abstract int checkImage(Image image, int width, int height, ImageObserver observer)**
  Returns the status of the specified image whose status will be updated through the imageUpdate() method in the specified ImageObserver.

- **abstract CheckboxPeer createCheckbox(Checkbox target)**
  Creates the specified Checkbox and returns its peer.

- **abstract Image createImage(ImageProducer producer)**
  Returns an Image created from the information supplied by the ImageProducer.

- **protected abstract CheckboxMenuItemPeer createCheckboxMenuItem(CheckboxMenuItem target)**
  Creates the specified CheckboxMenuItem and returns its peer.

- **protected abstract ChoicePeer createChoice(Choice target)**
  Creates the specified Choice and returns its peer.

III

Java

- **protected abstract DialogPeer createDialog(Dialog target)**
  Creates the specified `Dialog` and returns its peer.

- **protected abstract FileDialogPeer createFileDialog(FileDialog target)**
  Creates the specified `FileDialog` and returns its peer.

- **protected abstract FramePeer createFrame(Frame target)**
  Creates the specified `Frame` and returns its peer.

- **protected abstract LabelPeer createLabel(Label target)**
  Creates the specified `Label` and returns its peer.

- **protected abstract ListPeer createList(List target)**
  Creates the specified `List` and returns its peer.

- **protected abstract MenuPeer createMenu(Menu target)**
  Creates the specified `Menu` and returns its peer.

- **protected abstract MenuBarPeer createMenuBar(MenuBar target)**
  Creates the specified `MenuBar` and returns its peer.

- **protected abstract MenuItemPeer createMenuItem(MenuItem target)**
  Creates the specified `MenuItem` and returns its peer.

- **protected abstract PanelPeer createPanel(Panel target)**
  Creates the specified `Panel` and returns its peer.

- **protected abstract ScrollbarPeer createScrollbar(Scrollbar target)**
  Creates the specified `Scrollbar` and returns its peer.

- **protected abstract TextAreaPeer createTextArea(TextArea target)**
  Creates the specified `TextArea` and returns its peer.

- **protected abstract TextFieldPeer createTextField(TextField target)**
  Creates the specified `TextField` and returns its peer.

- **protected abstract WindowPeer createWindow(Window target)**
  Creates the specified `Window` and returns its peer.

- **abstract ColorModel getColorModel( )**
  Returns the `ColorModel` used when displaying the screen.

- **static synchronized Toolkit getDefaultToolkit( )**
  Returns the standard `Toolkit` used in this implementation.

- **abstract String[ ] getFontList( )**
  Returns an array containing all possible fonts in this implementation.

- **abstract FontMetrics getFontMetrics(Font font)**
  Returns the `FontMetrics` for the current font based on native information.

- **abstract Image getImage(URL url)**
  Returns the specified `Image`.

- **abstract Image getImage(String filename)**
  Returns the specified `Image`.

- **abstract int getScreenResolution( )**
  Returns the resolution of the screen in dots per inch.

- **abstract Dimension getScreenSize( )**
  Returns the size of the screen in pixels.

- **abstract boolean prepareImage(Image image, int width, int height, ImageObserver observer)**
  Prepares the specified image to be displayed with the specified width and height. The `ImageObserver` will be notified of the success or failure of this method.

- **abstract void sync( )**
  Synchronizes some graphical operations.

Window Extends Container. A `Window` is a simple container that serves as a pop-up window spawned from a `Frame`. Because the `Frame` class extends the `Window` class and builds upon it, you may want to use a `Frame` instead of a `Window`.

Methods
- **Window(Frame parent)**
  Creates a `Window` belonging to the specified `parent`.

- **synchronized void addNotify( )**
  Creates the `Window`'s peer.

- **synchronized void dispose( )**
  Disposes the `Window`'s peer.

- **Toolkit getToolkit( )**
  Returns the `Toolkit` for the `Window`.

- **final String getWarningString( )**
  Returns the string warning to be displayed to the user. In Netscape, this string is "Untrusted Java Window."

- **synchronized void pack( )**
  Shrinks the `Window` to the smallest size that will still display all components.

- **synchronized void show( )**
  Makes the `Window` visible.

- **void toBack( )**
  Places the `Window` behind its parent `Frame`.

- **void toFront( )**
  Places the `Window` in front of its parent `Frame`.

Interfaces

LayoutManager. The `LayoutManager` defines a behavior that is implemented by all layout managers.

- **void addLayoutComponent(String name, Component comp)**
  Adds the specified Component to the layout. The name parameter can be used to supply the layout manager with information regarding the component. The use of this parameter is different for each manager.

- **void layoutContainer(Container parent)**
  Arranges the specified Container.

- **Dimension minimumLayoutSize(Container parent)**
  Returns the minimum size required by the specified Container based on its Components.

- **Dimension preferredLayoutSize(Container parent)**
  Returns the size requested by the specified Container based on its Components.

- **void removeLayoutComponent(Component comp)**
  Removes the specified Component from the layout.

MenuContainer. The MenuContainer interface is implemented by all containers that deal with menus.

Methods

- **Font getFont( )**
  Returns the Font used in displaying the MenuContainer.

- **boolean postEvent(Event evt)**
  Posts an event to the MenuContainer.

- **void remove(MenuComponent comp)**
  Removes the specified Component from the MenuContainer.

java.awt.image

Although related to the java.awt package, this package consists of tools designed to handle images coming across a network. Because all classes and interfaces in this package are closely related, you will see that many of the methods appear multiple times.

Classes

Abstract ColorModel. This abstract class declares the functionality necessary for any ColorModel—a class that translates a color identifier (red, green, blue, or alpha) into the actual color to be displayed.

Field

- **protected int pixel_bits**
  The number of bits per pixel.

Methods

- **ColorModel(int bits)**
  Creates a new `ColorModel` with the specified number of bits per pixel.

- **abstract int getAlpha(int pixel)**
  Returns the alpha value of the specified pixel.

- **abstract int getBlue(int pixel)**
  Returns the blue value of the specified pixel.

- **abstract int getGreen(int pixel)**
  Returns the green value of the specified pixel.

- **int getPixelSize( )**
  Returns the number of bits per pixel for this `ColorModel`.

- **abstract int getRed(int pixel)**
  Returns the red value of the specified pixel.

- **int getRGB(int pixel)**
  Returns the color of the pixel in the default RGB `ColorModel`.

- **static ColorModel getRGBdefault( )**
  Returns the default `ColorModel` used in displaying pixels defined by RGB values.

CropImageFilter Extends ImageFilter. The `CropImageFilter` class is an image filter that enables you to create a new image based on a portion of another image.

The image in the upper left-hand corner of the applet was created by extracting a portion of the larger image in the middle using the `CropImageFilter` class in Listing 14.9. Although each image filter is different, the steps taken here are the general steps to make use of *any* image filter.

Listing 14.9 `CropImageFilter` **Example**

```
import java.applet.*;
import java.awt.*;
import java.awt.image.*;

public class CropImageFilterExample extends Applet {

    Image newimage, image;

    public void init() {

        image = getImage(getCodeBase(), "fract.jpg");
        ImageFilter filter = new CropImageFilter(0,0,50,50);
                        // set the properties for the filer

        /* The following statement creates an ImageProducer.
           producer will be able to produce a new image using
           the source of the old image and the specified filter*/
```

(continues)

III

Java

Listing 14.9   Continued

```
    ImageProducer producer = new FilteredImageSource(image.getSource(),
    filter);

    newimage = createImage(producer);
  }

  public void paint (Graphics g) {
    g.drawImage(newimage,10,10,50,50,this);
    g.drawImage(image,200,85,100,100,this);
  }
}
```

Methods

- **CropImageFilter(int x, int y, int w, int h)**
  Creates a new CropImageFilter. The specified values do not pertain to a specific Image, but will be the values used when filter is later employed to crop an Image.

- **void setDimensions(int width, int height)**
  Sets the dimensions for the filter to be used when producing a cropped image.

- **void setPixels(int x, int y, int w, int h, ColorModel model, int pixels[ ], int offset, int scansize)**
  A method used internally to create the desired Image.

- **void setPixels(int x, int y, int w, int h, ColorModel model, byte pixels[ ], int offset, int scansize)**
  A method used internally to create the desired Image.

- **void setProperties(Hashtable props)**
  Used to supply the ImageFilter.setProperties() method with information regarding the cropped region.

DirectColorModel Extends ColorModel. This class is used to translate machine-dependent pixel values into their alpha, red, green, and blue components.

Methods

- **DirectColorModel(int bits, int rmask, int gmask, int bmask)**
  Creates a new DirectColorModel that will handle pixels with the specified number of bits. rmask, gmask, and bmask represent the location of the bits specifying the red, green, and blue components, respectively.

- **DirectColorModel(int bits, int rmask, int gmask, int bmask, int amask)**
  Creates a new DirectColorModel that will handle pixels with the specified number of bits. rmask, gmask, bmask, and amask represent the location of the bits specifying the red, green, blue, and alpha components, respectively.

- **final int getAlpha(int pixel)**
  Returns the alpha component of the specified pixel.

- **final int getAlphaMask( )**
  Returns the alpha mask for the `DirectColorModel`.

- **final int getBlue(int pixel)**
  Returns the blue component of the specified pixel.

- **final int getBlueMask( )**
  Returns the blue mask for the `DirectColorModel`.

- **final int getGreen(int pixel)**
  Returns the green component of the specified pixel.

- **final int getGreenMask( )**
  Returns the green mask for the `DirectColorModel`.

- **final int getRed(int pixel)**
  Returns the red component of the specified pixel.

- **final int getRedMask( )**
  Returns the red mask for the `DirectColorModel`.

- **final int getRGB(int pixel)**
  Obtains the color of the pixel according to the default RBG color model.

FilteredImageSource Extends Object Implements ImageProducer. A
`FilterImageSource` enables you to pass the information that defines an image through a
filter—somehow changing the appearance of the image. In most cases, the only method
of this class that you will use is its constructor in conjunction with the `createImage()`
method from the `java.awt.Component` class.

▶▶ See Listing 14.9, "CropImageFilter Example," p. 473
▶▶ See Listing 14.10, "MyImageFilter Example," p. 476

Methods
- **FilteredImageSource(ImageProducer source, ImageFilter filter)**
  Creates a new `FilteredImageSource`. The information will be supplied by the
  `ImageProducer` and filtered by the specified `ImageFilter`.

- **synchronized void addConsumer(ImageConsumer ic)**
  Adds a consumer to the objects retrieving information from this `ImageProducer`.

- **synchronized boolean isConsumer(ImageConsumer ic)**
  Returns `true` if the specified `ImageConsumer` is a consumer of the information supplied by this `ImageProducer`.

- **void startProduction(ImageConsumer ic)**
  Begins the process of delivering information to its consumers. The consumers notified include, but are not limited to, the specified `ImageConsumer`.

III

Java

- **synchronized void removeConsumer(ImageConsumer ic)**
  Removes the specified consumer from the list of objects obtaining information from this `ImageProducer`.

- **void requestTopDownLeftRightResend(ImageConsumer ic)**
  Handles a request to send the pixels of the `Image` to the consumer in a top-down, left-right order.

ImageFilter Implements ImageConsumer, Cloneable. The `ImageFilter` class, as it is, does essentially nothing. It receives information from an `ImageProducer` and sends the same information on to an `ImageConsumer`. If you are simply loading and displaying images, you have no reason to explicitly use this class. However, the `ImageFilter` class also provides you with the framework on which you can build your own image filters: objects that will somehow transform the image after it is created by an `ImageProducer` and before it is received by an `ImageConsumer`.

To create your own image filter, you must extend the `ImageFilter` class and override at least one of its methods. The six methods that provide you with access to the image data are `setColorModel()`, `setDimensions()`, `setHints()`, `setPixels()` (two versions), `setProperties()`, and `imageComplete()`.

 ▶▶ See Listing 14.9, "CropImageFilter Example," p. 473

The two images in the applet were both created from the same source file. However, as you can see, the image in the upper left-hand corner has been transposed and shifted somewhat. This transformation was achieved with the code in Listing 14.10.

Listing 14.10 `MyImageFilter` **Example**

```
import java.applet.*;
import java.awt.*;
import java.awt.image.*;

public class MyFilterExample extends Applet {

    Image newimage, image;

    public void init() {
      image = getImage(getCodeBase(), "fract.jpg");

      ImageFilter filter = new MyImageFilter(100);
      ImageProducer producer = new
      FilteredImageSource(image.getSource(), filter);
      newimage = createImage(producer);
    }

    public void paint (Graphics g) {
      g.drawImage(newimage,10,10,100,100,this);
      g.drawImage(image,200,85,100,100,this);
    }
```

```
    }

    public class MyImageFilter extends ImageFilter {
      private int width ;
      private int shift;

      public MyImageFilter (int translation ) {
        shift = translation;
      }

      public void setDimensions(int width, int height) {
        consumer.setDimensions(width, height);
        this.width = width;
      }

/* This implementation of setPixels() shifts all columns
   over by the value of the shift field.  All columns that
   are pushed off the screen (to the left) are displayed on
   the right

 To do this, the method scrolls through each column on
    the screen.  If the column still fits once shifted, it is
    displayed in its new position.  If it is pushed off the
    screen, it is wrapped around relative to its original
    position.   */

    public void setPixels(int x, int y, int w, int h,
    ColorModel model, byte pixels[ ], int off, int scansize) {
      for (int line = x; line < (x+w); line++) {
        if ( (line + shift) <= width)
          consumer.setPixels(line, y, 1, h, model, pixels,
          off+shift, scansize);
        else
          consumer.setPixels(line, y, 1, h, model, pixels,
          off -width + shift, scansize);
      }
    }

/* Shifts all columns over by the value of the shift field.
   All columns that are pushed off the screen (to the left)
   are displayed on the right */

    public void setPixels(int x, int y, int w, int h,
    ColorModel model, int pixels[ ], int off, int scansize) {
      for (int line = x; line < (x+w); line++) {
        if ( (line + shift) <= width)
          consumer.setPixels(line, y, 1, h, model, pixels,
          off+shift, scansize);
       else
          consumer.setPixels(line, y, 1, h, model, pixels,
          off -width + shift, scansize);
      }
    }
  }
```

You will note that this image filter only uses three of the six available methods. In general, the most important method is the `setPixels()` method inasmuch as it assigns each pixel a location. All other methods may be useful, but are not as important as the `setPixels()` method.

Note

The shifting of pixels is the result of placing them in a different position in the array (`pixels[]`) that contains the image. As a rule, pixel (u,v) is stored in `pixels[ v * scansize + u + off]`. If you wanted to store (u,v) in (u,v), you could simply substitute the following statement in Listing 14.10:

```
consumer.setPixels(line, y, 1, h, model, pixels, off, scansize);
```

However, in this example you want to shift the pixels in the *x* direction. To advance each pixel to the left, use the following statement:

```
consumer.setPixels(line, y, 1, h, model, pixels, off + shift, scansize);
```

Field

- **protected ImageConsumer consumer**
  The `ImageConsumer` receiving information from this filter.

Methods

- **ImageFilter( )**
  Creates a new `ImageFilter`.

- **Object clone( )**
  Creates a copy of the `ImageFilter`.

- **ImageFilter getFilterInstance(ImageConsumer ic)**
  Returns a copy of the `ImageFilter` that will provide information to the `ImageConsumer`.

- **void imageComplete(int status)**
  Receives the information supplied by the `ImageProducer` before it is passed to the `ImageConsumer`. By default, this method simply passes the information along, but it may be overridden to do more.

- **void resendTopDownLeftRight(ImageProducer ip)**
  Requests that the `ImageProducer` send the pixel information regarding the `Image` in a top-down, left-right order.

- **void setColorModel(ColorModel model)**
  Receives the information supplied by the `setColorModel()` method of the `ImageConsumer` interface and provides you with an opportunity to make use of this information.

- **void setDimensions(int width, int height)**
  Receives the information supplied by the `setDimensions()` method in the `ImageConsumer` interface.

- **void setHints(int hints)**
  Receives the information supplied by the `setDimensions()` method in the `ImageConsumer` interface.

- **void setPixels(int x, int y, int width, int height, ColorModel model, int pixels[ ], int offset, int scansize)**
  Enables you to manipulate the pixels of the `Image`. This is one of the more useful methods in this class.

- **void setPixels(int x, int y, int w, int h, ColorModel model, byte pixels[ ], int offset, int scansize)**
  Enables you to manipulate the pixels of the `Image`. This is one of the more useful methods in this class.

- **void setProperties(Hashtable props)**
  Adds information regarding the filter to the set of properties before passing them along to the `ImageConsumer`.

IndexColorModel Extends ColorModel. This class enables you to create a lookup table for a set of colors. The table will contain information regarding the individual components of the colors.

Methods

- **IndexColorModel(int bits, int size, byte r[ ], byte g[ ], byte b[ ])**
  Creates a new `IndexColorModel` with the specified `size`. `bits` represents the number of bits per pixel representation. `r[]`, `g[]`, and `b[]` are the arrays of red, green, and blue values.

- **IndexColorModel(int bits, int size, byte r[ ], byte g[ ], byte b[ ], int trans)**
  Creates a new `IndexColorModel` with the specified `size`. `bits` represents the number of bits per pixel representation. `r[]`, `g[]`, and `b[]` are the arrays of red, green, and blue values. `trans` is the index in which the transparent color is stored.

- **IndexColorModel(int bits, int size, byte r[ ], byte g[ ], byte b[ ], byte a[ ])**
  Creates a new `IndexColorModel` with the specified `size`. `bits` represents the number of bits per pixel representation. `r[]`, `g[]`, `b[]`, and `a[]` are the arrays of red, green, blue, and alpha values.

- **final int getAlpha(int index)**
  Returns the alpha value for the pixel having the specified index.

- **final void getAlphas(byte a[ ])**
  Returns the array of alpha values.

- **final int getBlue(int index)**
  Returns the blue value for the pixel having the specified index.

- **final void getBlues(byte b[ ])**
  Returns the array of blue values.

III

Java

- **final int getGreen(int index)**
  Returns the alpha value for the pixel having the specified index.

- **final void getGreens(byte g[ ])**
  Returns the array of green values.

- **final int getMapSize( )**
  Returns the number of values contained in each array.

- **final int getRed(int index)**
  Returns the red value for the pixel having the specified index.

- **final void getReds(byte r[ ])**
  Returns the array of red values.

- **final int getRGB(int index)**
  Returns an integer representation of the pixel value at the specified index based on the current RGB color model.

- **final int getTransparentPixel( )**
  Returns the index of the transparent pixel. Returns –1 if none is defined.

MemoryImageSource Implements ImageProducer. A `MemoryImageSource` enables you to create your own images. After storing the "picture" in an array of either bytes or integers, you are able to load the image from that array—not a saved file.

Methods

- **MemoryImageSource(int w, int h, ColorModel cm, byte pix[ ], int offset, int scansize)**
  Creates a `MemoryImageSource` with the specified dimensions and `ColorModel`. `pix[]` is the source of the image. `offset` is the index at which the image begins. `scansize` is the number of bytes that each row occupies in the array.

- **MemoryImageSource(int w, int h, ColorModel cm, byte pix[ ], int offset, int scansize, Hashtable props)**
  Creates a `MemoryImageSource` with the specified dimensions and `ColorModel`. `pix[]` is the source of the image. `offset` is the index at which the image begins. `scansize` is the number of bytes that each row occupies in the array. `props` is a `Hashtable` of properties with which the image will be created.

- **MemoryImageSource(int w, int h, ColorModel cm, int pix[ ], int offset, int scan)**
  Creates a `MemoryImageSource` with the specified dimensions and `ColorModel`. `pix[]` is the source of the image. `offset` is the index at which the image begins. `scansize` is the number of bytes that each row occupies in the array.

- **MemoryImageSource(int w, int h, ColorModel cm, int pix[ ], int offset, int scan, Hashtable props)**
  Creates a `MemoryImageSource` with the specified dimensions and `ColorModel`. `pix[]` is the source of the image. `offset` is the index at which the image begins. `scansize` is

the number of bytes that each row occupies in the array. props is a Hashtable of properties with which the image will be created.

- **MemoryImageSource(int w, int h, int pix[ ], int offset, int scan)**
  Creates a MemoryImageSource with the specified dimensions of the default RGB color model. pix[] is the source of the image. offset is the index at which the image begins. scansize is the number of bytes that each row occupies in the array.

- **MemoryImageSource(int w, int h, int pix[ ], int offset, int scan, Hashtable props)**
  Creates a MemoryImageSource with the specified dimensions the default RGB color model. pix[] is the source of the image. offset is the index at which the image begins. scansize is the number of bytes that each row occupies in the array. props is a Hashtable of properties with which the image will be created.

- **synchronized void addConsumer(ImageConsumer ic)**
  Adds a consumer to the list of objects retrieving information from this ImageProducer.

- **synchronized boolean isConsumer(ImageConsumer ic)**
  Returns true if the ImageConsumer receives information from this ImageProducer.

- **void startProduction(ImageConsumer ic)**
  Begins the process of delivering information to its consumers. The consumers notified include, but are not limited to, the specified ImageConsumer.

- **synchronized void removeConsumer(ImageConsumer ic)**
  Removes the specified consumer from the list of objects obtaining information from this ImageProducer.

- **void requestTopDownLeftRightResend(ImageConsumer ic)**
  Handles a request to send the pixels of the Image to the consumer in a top-down, left-right order.

PixelGrabber Implements ImageConsumer. The PixelGrabber class is a special type of ImageConsumer designed to "grab" a rectangle of pixels belonging to an image. Note that you may grab pixels from either an ImageProducer or an already loaded image.

To grab a set of pixels, first create a pixel grabber, specifying what rectangle of pixels you want as well as the array in which you would like to store them. To actually grab the pixels, you must invoke the grabPixels() method.

Methods

- **PixelGrabber(Image img, int x, int y, int w, int h, int pix[ ], int offset, int scansize)**
  Creates a new PixelGrabber object to capture the specified pixels from the Image. The pixels will be stored in the pix[] array, using the specified offset and scansize.

- **PixelGrabber(ImageProducer ip, int x, int y, int w, int h, int pix[ ], int offset, int scansize)**

Creates a new `PixelGrabber` object to capture the specified pixels from the `Image`. The pixels will be stored in the `pix[]` array, using the specified `offset` and `scansize`.

- **synchronized boolean grabPixels(long ms) throws InterruptedException**
  Locks up the `PixelGrabber` object in requesting to grab the set of pixels. It returns when successful or after the specified number of milliseconds has expired.

- **boolean grabPixels( ) throws InterruptedException**
  Requests the predetermined set of pixels from the image.

- **void setColorModel(ColorModel model)**
  Required to implement the `ImageConsumer` interface. However, by default it does nothing.

- **void setDimensions(int width, int height)**
  Required to implement the `ImageConsumer` interface. However, by default it does nothing.

- **void setHints(int hints)**
  Required to implement the `ImageConsumer` interface. However, by default it does nothing.

- **void setPixels(int srcX, int srcY, int srcW, int srcH, ColorModel model, byte pixels[ ], int srcOff, int srcScan)**
  The `PixelGrabber` class uses this method to place the desired pixels into the array specified in either the constructor method or the `setPixels()` method.

- **void setPixels(int srcX, int srcY, int srcW, int srcH, ColorModel model, int pixels[ ], int srcOff, int srcScan)**
  The `PixelGrabber` class uses this method to place the desired pixels into the array specified in the constructor method.

- **void setProperties(Hashtable props)**
  Required to implement the `ImageConsumer` interface. However, by default it does nothing.

- **synchronized int status( )**
  Returns any flags produced in the lifetime of the `PixelGrabber`.

- **synchronized void imageComplete(int status)**
  Updates the internal `flags` field to reflect specified `status`. These flags may be returned via the `status()` method.

Abstract RGBImageFilter Extends ImageFilter. The `RGBImageFilter` class provides you with a very convenient way to manipulate the appearance of an image by changing the colors of individual pixels. To use the `RGBImageFilter` class, you must override the class, creating a new class and defining the `filterRGB()` method. This method can be used to adjust the display of the pixels by manipulating the individual color components.

What happened? As you can see, the appearance of the image in the upper left-hand corner has been changed. This was done with the code in Listing 14.11.

You will see that the only important method in the `RGBFilterClass` is the `filterRGB()` method. Implementing it in the `MYRGBImageFilter` class not only makes this class non-abstract, but also performs the actual chore of changing the value of the pixels.

Listing 14.11 `MyRGBImageFilter` **Example**

```
public class ImageFilterExample extends Applet {

    Image newimage, image;

    public void init() {

        image = getImage(getCodeBase(), "fract.jpg");
        ImageFilter filter = new MyRGBFilter();
        ImageProducer producer = new
        FilteredImageSource(image.getSource(), filter);
        newimage = createImage(producer);
    }

    public void paint (Graphics g) {
        g.drawImage(newimage,10,10,100,100,this);
        g.drawImage(image,200,85,100,100,this);
    }
}

public class MYRGBFilter extends RGBImageFilter {
    private int width;
    private int shift;

    public int filterRGB(int x, int y, int rgb) {
        return( rgb >> 1);
    }
}
```

Fields

- **protected boolean canFilterIndexColorModel**
  If `true`, enables the filter to handle pixels values from `IndexColorModel` tables. If your `filterRGB()` method is independent of the coordinates of the pixel, this field should be `true`.

- **protected ColorModel newmodel**
  Set by the `substituteColorModel( )` method.

- **protected ColorModel origmodel**
  Set by the `substituteColorModel( )` method.

Methods

- **RGBImageFilter( )**
  Creates a new `RGBImageFilter`.

- **IndexColorModel filterIndexColorModel(IndexColorModel icm)**
Filters the specified `IndexColorModel` tables, returning a modified version of the model.

- **void filterRGBPixels(int x, int y, int w, int h, int pixels[ ], int offset, int scansize)**
Filters a portion of the `pixel[]` array by passing each pixel through the `filterRGB()` method. `offset` defines the beginning of the portion to be filtered. `x` and `y` define the coordinates of this pixel. `w` and `h` specify the size of the area to be filtered. `scansize` defines the number of pixels per row.

- **void setColorModel(ColorModel model)**
If this filter class can handle `IndexColorModels` and the specified `ColorModel` is an `IndexColorModel`, this method will cause the specified `model` to be replaced by its filtered version whenever encountered in the `setPixels()` methods.

- **void substituteColorModel(ColorModel oldcm, ColorModel newcm)**
Causes the `oldcm` to be substituted for the `newcm` whenever it is encountered in the `setPixels()` methods.

- **void setPixels(int x, int y, int width, int height, ColorModel model, int pixels[ ], int offset, int scansize)**
Passes the pixels through to the `ImageConsumer` after first filtering the pixels with the `filterRGB()` method.

- **void setPixels(int x, int y, int width, int height, ColorModel model, byte pixels[ ], int offset, int scansize)**
Passes the pixels through to the `ImageConsumer` after first filtering the pixels with the `filterRGB()` method.

- **abstract int filterRGB(int x, int y, int rgbpixel)**
This method is the most important method in the class. It must be overridden to create a functional `RGBColorModel`. To change the appearance of the specified `rgbpixel` that will be displayed at (x,y), create and return a new pixel value.

  If x and y are equal to –1, the given pixel was obtained from an `IndexColorModel`.

Interfaces

ImageConsumer. The `ImageConsumer` interface defines a set of behaviors to be implemented by classes that will load ("consume") images. In addition to establishing the behavior of these classes, this class can also be used as a reference-type variable to refer to the following methods and fields that must be defined in *any* `ImageConsumer` class.

Fields
- **final static int COMPLETESCANLINES**
A hint value sent to `setHints()` to indicate that the pixels will be delivered in complete lines.

- **final static int IMAGEABORTED**

  A status value sent to `imageComplete()` to indicate that the creation of the image was aborted.

- **final static int IMAGEERROR**

  A status value sent to `imageComplete()` to indicate that the creation encountered an error.

- **final static int RANDOMPIXELORDER**

  A value sent to `setHints()` to indicate that the pixels will be delivered in a random order.

- **final static int SINGLEFRAME**

  A hint value sent to `setHints()` to indicate that the image contains a single frame.

- **final static int SINGLEFRAMEDONE**

  A status value sent to `imageComplete()` to indicate that a frame of an image has been completely sent but more frames are yet to come.

- **final static int SINGLEPASS**

  A value sent to `setHints()` to indicate that the image has been completely delivered.

- **final static int STATICIMAGEDONE**

  A status value sent to `imageComplete()` to indicate that the entire image has been completely sent.

- **final static int TOPDOWNLEFTRIGHT**

  A hint value sent to `setHints()` to indicate that the image will be delivered in a top-down, left-right manner.

Methods

- **abstract void imageComplete(int status)**

  Called by the `ImageProducer` to indicate that the current image is complete. The status value will supply the `ImageConsumer` with more detailed information.

- **abstract void setColorModel(ColorModel model)**

  Employed by the `ImageProducer` to set the default `ColorModel` for the pixels sent to this `ImageConsumer`.

- **abstract void setDimensions(int width, int height)**

  Employed by the `ImageProducer` to set the dimensions for the image being sent.

- **abstract void setHints(int hintflags)**

  Employed by the `ImageProducer` to inform `ImageConsumer` about various properties of the image about to be sent.

- **abstract void setPixels(int x, int y, int w, int h, ColorModel model, byte pixels[ ], int offset, int scansize)**

  Employed by the `ImageProducer` to set the pixel values.

III

Java

- **abstract void setPixels(int x, int y, int w, int h, ColorModel model, int pixels[ ], int offset, int scansize)**
  Employed by the `ImageProducer` to set the pixel values.

ImageObserver. The `ImageObserver` interface defines a set of behaviors that are implemented by classes that deal with images, and provides for asynchronous updates of an `Image`. This is necessary because not all information pertaining to an `Image` may be available when it is first used. Specifying an `ImageObserver` in such methods as `Graphics.drawImage()` will cause that `Object` to receive updated information on the `Image` as it arrives.

Fields

- **final static int ABORT**
  A value sent to `imageUpdate()` to denote that the loading of the image has been aborted.

- **final static int ALLBITS**
  A value sent to `imageUpdate()` to denote that a previously drawn image is now complete.

- **final static int ERROR**
  A value sent to `imageUpdate()` to denote that an error has been encountered in the loading of the image.

- **final static int FRAMEBITS**
  A value sent to `imageUpdate()` to denote that a complete frame of an image has been received.

- **final static int HEIGHT**
  A value sent to `imageUpdate()` to denote that the height of the image cannot be obtained from the height parameter in the `imageUpdate()` method.

- **final static int PROPERTIES**
  A value sent to `imageUpdate()` to denote that the properties of the image cannot be obtained from the parameters in the `imageUpdate()` method.

- **final static int SOMEBITS**
  A value sent to `imageUpdate()` to denote that more pixels of the image are available.

- **final static int WIDTH**
  A value sent to `imageUpdate()` to denote that the height of the image may not be obtained from the height parameter in the `imageUpdate()` method.

Method

- **abstract boolean imageUpdate(Image img, int infoflags, int x, int y, int width)**
  This method is called when more information regarding an image being loaded becomes available. The `x`, `y`, `width`, and `height` values depend on the `infoflags` supplied. This method should return `true` if more updates are needed and `false` if all required information has been received.

ImageProducer. The `ImageProducer` class declares a set of behaviors common to any class that will produce an image, such as `FilteredImageSource` or `MemoryImageSource`.

▶▶ See Listing 14.9, "CropImageFilter Example," p. 473
▶▶ See Listing 14.11, "MyRGBImageFilter Example," p. 483

Methods

- **abstract void addConsumer(ImageConsumer ic)**
  Records the specified `ImageConsumer` as one interested in the information supplied by this `ImageProducer`.

- **abstract boolean isConsumer(ImageConsumer ic)**
  Returns `true` if the specified `ImageConsumer` is a registered consumer of this `ImageProducer` object.

- **abstract void removeConsumer(ImageConsumer ic)**
  Removes the `ImageConsumer` from the list of consumers. This should be done once all necessary information has been received to prevent the consumer from receiving more copies of the information.

- **abstract void**
- **requestTopDownLeftRightResend(ImageConsumer ic)**
  Requests that the `ImageProducer` send the pixels in a top-down, left-right order.

- **abstract void startProduction(ImageConsumer ic)**
  Adds the specified `ImageConsumer` to the list of consumers and sends pixel information to all registered consumers.

java.io

The java.io package serves as the standard input/output library for the Java language. Providing you with types as simple as a `StringBufferInputStream` or as complex as a `RandomAccessFile`, this package enables a virtually unlimited number of communication possibilities.

The java.io package is composed primarily of two types of classes: those that create streams and those that manage them. The following table is a summary showing where these classes fit into this model:

Stream Creators	Stream Managers
ByteArrayInputStream	BufferedInputStream
ByteArrayOutputStream	BufferedOutputStream
FileInputStream	DataInputStream
FileOutputStream	DataOutputStream

(continues)

(continued)

Stream Creators	Stream Managers
PipedInputStream	FilterInputStream
PipedOutputStream	FilterOutputStream
StringBufferInputStream	LineNumberInputStream
	PrintStream
	PushbackInputStream
	RandomAccessFile
	SequenceInputStream
	StreamTokenizer
	StringBufferInputStream

In general, a stream manager may be created using the syntax:

```
StreamManagerType    instanceofManager   = new StreamManagerType(
StreamCreatorType);
```

where `StreamManagerType` and `StreamCreatorType` are both the names of classes.

Classes

BufferedInputStream Extends FilterInputStream. The buffered stream classes provide you with a more efficient way of reading information from an `InputStream`. Instead of allowing information to pile up on the stream and wait for you to read it, the `BufferedInputStream` will read in all data on the stream and place it in a buffer every time you invoke one of the `read()` methods. Therefore, subsequent information may come from the buffer, not the stream—saving you time.

The `BufferedInputStream` will continue to read from the buffer until it becomes empty. If you attempt to read from an empty buffer, the `BufferedInputStream` will block it until there is sufficient data from the stream to satisfy your request. Any additional data waiting in the stream will be stored in the buffer.

Fields

- **protected byte buf[ ]**
  The buffer in which the data is stored.

- **protected int count**
  The number of bytes in the buffer.

- **protected int marklimit**
  The limit on the number of bytes that you can advance before the `BufferedInputStream` looses track of your mark.

- **protected int markpos**
  The marked position.

- **protected int pos**
  The current position in the buffer.

Methods

- **BufferedInputStream(InputStream in)**
  Creates a new `BufferedInputStream` based on the specified `InputStream`.

- **BufferedInputStream(InputStream in, int size)**
  Creates a new `BufferedInputStream` based on the specified `InputStream`, specifying the buffer size.

- **synchronized int available( ) throws IOException**
  Returns the number of available bytes that can be currently read. This value will include both the number of unread bytes in the buffer and the number of available bytes in the `InputStream`.

- **synchronized void mark(int readlimit)**
  Marks the current position in the stream. By calling the `reset()` method, you will be able to return to this spot and read the same byte again. `readlimit` sets a boundary on the number of bytes that may be read before you call `reset()`. Although larger values for `readlimit` give you more flexibility, they also cause the storage buffer to grow quite large.

- **boolean markSupported( )**
  Because this is a `FilterInputStream`, this method returns a `boolean` indicating whether or not this class supports marks. For this class, this method simply returns `true`.

- **synchronized int read(byte b[ ], int offset, int len) throws IOException**
  In addition to filling the storage buffer, this method places the number of bytes specified by the `len` parameter in the `b[]` array, beginning at the `offset` index.

- **synchronized int read( ) throws IOException**
  Reads a byte of data.

- **synchronized void reset( ) throws IOException**
  Returns to the last marked position, enabling you to read from this point on. Note that you lose your current position in the stream. If you have exceeded the `marklimit` (specified in `mark()`) or if no mark has been specified, then a `IOException` will be thrown.

- **synchronized long skip(long num) throws IOException**
  Skips the specified number of bytes in the stream.

BufferedOutputStream Extends FilterOutputStream. A `BufferedOutputStream` is an `OutputStream` manager that enables you to write to the stream in a more efficient manner. Instead of writing to the stream in small pieces every time you invoke a `write()` method, a `BufferedOutputStream` will write your information to a temporary buffer. This information is then written to the stream either when the buffer becomes filled or when you invoke the `flush()` method.

> ### Caution
>
> Make sure that you invoke the `flush()` method before closing the `OutputStream`! If you fail to
> do so, some of your information may be caught in limbo—left in the buffer and never sent.

Fields

- **protected byte buf[ ]**
  The temporary storage buffer.

- **protected int count**
  The number of bytes currently in the buffer.

Methods

- **BufferedOutputStream(OutputStream out)**
  Creates a new `BufferedOutputStream` that will use the specified `OutputStream`.

- **BufferedOutputStream(OutputStream out, int size)**
  Creates a new `BufferedOutputStream` that will use the specified `OutputStream`. `size`
  specifies the size of the buffer array.

- **synchronized void flush( ) throws IOException**
  Flushes the buffer, writing all bytes in the buffer to the `OutputStream`.

- **synchronized void write(byte b[ ], int offset, int len) throws
  IOException**
  Writes the specified bytes to the buffer. The information written will begin at
  `b[offset]` and contain `len` bytes. If the buffer cannot contain the specified number
  of bytes, then both the buffer and the specified bytes will be written to the
  `OutputStream`.

- **synchronized void write(int b) throws IOException**
  Writes the byte to the buffer. If the buffer has no room, the buffer will first be written to the stream. The specified byte will then be placed in the buffer.

ByteArrayInputStream Extends InputStream. A `ByteArrayInputStream` is a type
of `InputStream` and thus can be handled like any other `InputStream`. However, a
`ByteArrayInputStream` does not receive its information from a standard stream, but
rather from an array that you have already created.

When you create a `ByteArrayInputStream`, you must specify the contents of the buffer
that you want to use. This `InputStream` will then read from this buffer when read commands are invoked.

Fields

- **protected byte buf[ ]**
  The buffer from which the information will be read. Note that this is not a copy of
  the array specified in the constructor, but rather a reference (much like a C pointer)
  to the specified array.

- **protected int count**
  The maximum number of bytes that should be read from the buffer.

- **protected int pos**
  The current position in the buffer.

Methods

- **ByteArrayInputStream(byte buf[ ])**
  Creates a new ByteArrayInputStream that will read from the specified buffer. The current position (pos) is set to zero, and the maximum number of bytes to be read is set to the length of the array.

- **ByteArrayInputStream(byte buf[ ], int offset, int length)**
  Creates a new ByteArrayInputStream that will read from the specified buffer. The pos and count are set to the specified values.

- **synchronized int available( )**
  Returns the number of available bytes to be read. This is equal to the total number of bytes minus the current position (count-pos).

- **synchronized int read(byte b[ ], int offset, int len)**
  Reads up to len bytes from the array input stream, placing the read bytes in the b[] buffer beginning at the offset index.

- **synchronized int read( )**
  Reads one byte from the buffer.

- **synchronized void reset( )**
  Sets the current position to the beginning of the input buffer.

- **synchronized long skip(long num)**
  Skips the specified number of bytes in the buffer.

ByteArrayOutputStream Extends OutputStream. A ByteArrayOuputStream is a special OutputStream that can be used to accumulate data. Instead of writing directly to a stream, the ByteArrayOutputStream will write to a temporary buffer that will grow as needed to accommodate your data.

After you have written your data to the buffer, you can

- Write the entire buffer to an OutputStream using the writeTo() method.

- Retrieve all information in the buffer, storing it in a new array with the toByteArray() method.

- Convert the buffer to a string using the toString() method.

Fields

- **protected byte buf[ ]**
  The temporary buffer used to store the data.

- **protected int count**
  The number of bytes in the buffer.

Methods

- **ByteArrayOutputStream( )**
  Creates a new ByteArrayOutputStream with a capacity of 32 bytes.

- **ByteArrayOutputStream(int size)**
  Creates a new ByteArrayOutputStream with the specified capacity.

- **synchronized byte[ ] toByteArray( )**
  Returns a copy of the buffer.

- **synchronized void reset( )**
- **int size( )**
  Returns the number of bytes stored in the buffer.

- **String toString( )**
  Returns the buffer as a string. (This is the same as using the following method with a hibyte value of zero.)

- **String toString(int hibyte)**
  Returns the buffer as a string, setting the first eight bits of each character to hibyte.

- **synchronized void write(int b)**
  Writes the specified byte to the temporary buffer, increasing its size if necessary.

- **synchronized void write(byte b[ ], int offset, int len)**
  Writes the specified byte array to the temporary buffer, increasing its size if necessary.

- **synchronized void writeTo(OutputStream out) throws IOException**
  Writes the entire buffer to the specified OutputStream.

DataInputStream Extends FilterInputStream Implements DataInput. A DataInputStream allows you to read basic data types from a stream. For example, instead of reading a string from a stream byte by byte, you may use the readLine(), which will read until a newline character is encountered.

 ▶▶ See "DataOutputStream Extends FilterOutputStream Implements DataOutput," p. 494

Methods

- **DataInputStream(InputStream in)**
  Creates a new DataInputStream to handle the specified InputStream.

- **final int read(byte b[ ], int offset, int len) throws IOException**
  Reads `len` bytes from the stream, storing them in the `b[]` buffer beginning at `b[offset]`.

- **final int read(byte b[ ]) throws IOException**
  Reads data from the stream into the specified buffer, returning the number of bytes read.

- **final boolean readBoolean( ) throws IOException**
  Reads the next byte from the stream assuming that it represents a `boolean` value.

- **final byte readByte( ) throws IOException**
  Reads and returns a single byte from the stream.

- **final char readChar( ) throws IOException**
  Reads and returns a character from the stream by combining the next two bytes to produce a 16-bit `char`.

- **final double readDouble( ) throws IOException**
  Reads and returns a `double` value from the stream by combining the next eight bytes to produce a 64-bit `double`.

- **final float readFloat( ) throws IOException**
  Reads and returns a `float` from the stream by combining the next four bytes to produce a 32-bit `char`.

- **final void readFully(byte b[ ], int offset, int len) throws IOException**
  Reads from the stream, and does not return until the entire range (`offset` to `len`) in the buffer has been filled with new data.

- **final void readFully(byte b[ ]) throws IOException**
  Reads from the stream and does not return until the entire buffer has been filled.

- **final int readInt( ) throws IOException**
  Reads and returns a integer from the stream by combining the next four bytes to produce a 32-bit `int`.

- **final String readLine( ) throws IOException**
  Reads a series of characters until encountering `\n`, `\r`, `\r\n`, or `EOF`. Returns this complete string afterwards.

- **final long readLong( ) throws IOException**
  Reads and returns a `long` from the stream by combining the next eight bytes to produce a 64-bit `char`.

- **final short readShort( ) throws IOException**
  Reads and returns a short from the stream by combining the next four bytes to produce a 32-bit short.

- **final int readUnsignedByte( ) throws IOException**
  Reads and returns a byte from the stream.

III

Java

- **final int readUnsignedShort( ) throws IOException**
  Reads and returns a unsigned short from the stream by combining the next two bytes to produce a 16-bit char.

- **final String readUTF( ) throws IOException**
  Reads and returns a UTF string from the stream.

- **final static String readUTF(DataInput in) throws IOException**
  Reads and returns a UTF string from the specified DataInput.

- **final int skipBytes(int num) throws IOException**
  Skips the specified number of bytes.

DataOutputStream Extends FilterOutputStream Implements DataOutput. The counterpart of the DataInputStream class, the DataOutputStream class, enables you to write data to a stream in the form of basic data types, such as characters or doubles rather than a series of bytes.

 ▶▶ See "DataInputStream Extends FilterInputStream Implements DataInput," p. 492

Field

- **protected int written**
  The number of bytes written to the stream.

Methods

- **DataOutputStream(OutputStream out)**
  Creates a new DataOutputStream to handle the specified OutputStream.

- **void flush( ) throws IOException**
  Flushes the stream. This only produces an action if the stream has been buffering output.

- **final int size( )**
  Returns the number of bytes written thus far to the stream—the written field.

- **synchronized void write(byte b[ ], int offset, int len) throws IOException**
  Writes the number of bytes specified by len to the stream. These bytes will be drawn from the specified array starting at the offset index.

- **synchronized void write(int b) throws IOException**
  Writes the byte to the stream.

- **final void writeBoolean(boolean v) throws IOException**
  Writes the boolean to the stream.

- **final void writeByte(int v) throws IOException**
  Writes the boolean to the stream—calls write().

- **final void writeBytes(String s) throws IOException**
  Writes the string as a series of bytes.

- **final void writeChar(int v) throws IOException**
  Writes the character to the stream.

- **final void writeChars(String s) throws IOException**
  Writes the string to the stream as a series of characters.

- **final void writeDouble(double v) throws IOException**
  Writes the double to the stream.

- **final void writeFloat(float v) throws IOException**
  Writes the float to the stream.

- **final void writeInt(int v) throws IOException**
  Writes the int value to the stream.

- **final void writeLong(long v) throws IOException**
  Writes the long to the stream.

- **final void writeShort(int v) throws IOException**
  Writes the short to the stream.

- **final void writeUTF(String str) throws IOException**
  Writes the string to the steam in UTF format.

File. The File class provides you with a means of performing basic file management operations. Although it does not provide you with direct access to the information contained in the files, it does enable to you perform "housekeeping" operations, such as making directories, finding the length of a file, or comparing the versions of two separate files. Because of the nature of its operations, this class relies heavily on native methods.

▶▶ See "DataInputStream Extends FilterInputStream Implements DataInput," p. 492
▶▶ See "DataOutputStream Extends FilterOutputStream Implements DataOutput," p. 494
▶▶ See "FileDialog Extends Dialog," p. 431

Caution

Although Java per se has no problems with the functionality in the class, many of the tasks performed by the methods in this class raise several security concerns. Therefore, while your code compiles, you may not be able to perform many of these tasks if you are running your code as an applet in either the appletviewer or Netscape.

Fields

- **final static String pathSeparator**
  The system dependent path separator (";" for Windows-based machines).

- **final static char pathSeparatorChar**
  The system dependent path separator as a character.

- **final static String separator**
  The system dependent file separator ("\" for Windows-based machines).

- **final static char separatorChar**
  The system dependent file separator as a single character.

Methods

- **File(String path)**
  Creates a new `File` object based on the file at the specified path.

- **File(File dir, String name)**
  Creates a new `File` object based on the file in the given directory having the specified name. The directory will be specified through another `File` object.

- **File(String path, String name)**
  Creates a new `File` object based on the file in the given directory with the specified name.

- **boolean canRead( )**
  Returns `true` if the program can read from the given file.

- **boolean canWrite( )**
  Returns `true` if the program can write to the given file.

- **boolean delete( )**
  Deletes the file. It returns `true` if successful.

- **boolean equals(Object anotherObject)**
  Compares the `File` object to another object. It returns `true` if the other object is a `File` having the same path.

- **boolean exists( )**
  Returns `true` if the file exists.

- **String getAbsolutePath( )**
  Returns the absolute path of the file.

- **String getName( )**
  Returns the name of the file—the string following the last separator character in the path string.

- **String getParent( )**
  Returns the name of the parent directory—everything but the file name.

- **String getPath( )**
  Returns the entire path string consisting of the parent directory and the file name.

- **int hashCode( )**
  Returns the `hashcode` for this `File` object. This value is based on the path string.

- **boolean isAbsolute( )**
  Returns `true` if the path is absolute.

- **boolean isDirectory( )**
  Returns `true` if a directory file exists.

- **boolean isFile( )**
  Returns `true` if a file exists at the path.

- **long lastModified( )**
  Returns the time last modified. The returned value has no meaning and should only be used when comparing two files.

- **long length( )**
  Returns the length of the file.

- **String[ ] list( )**
  Returns an array of the names of the files in the current path.

- **String[ ] list(FilenameFilter filter)**
  Returns an array of the names of the files in the current path that meet the filter requirements.

- **boolean mkdir( )**
  Creates the current directory. It returns `true` if successful.

- **boolean mkdirs( )**
  Creates the current directory path. It returns `true` if successful.

- **boolean renameTo(File newName)**
  Renames the current file.

- **String toString( )**
  Returns the path of the file.

FileDescriptor. The `FileDescriptor` class is used internally by Java classes that deal with files. This class encapsulates the machine-based view of a file—describing each file as an integer. Uses of the `FileDescriptor` object, therefore, can be found in the `FileInputStream` and `FileOutputStream`. Due to the nature of the class, all fields and method are based on native properties.

Fields
- **final static FileDescriptor err**
  A descriptor for the standard error output file.

- **final static FileDescriptor in**
  A descriptor for the standard input file.

- **final static FileDescriptor out**
  A descriptor for the standard output file.

Methods

- **FileDescriptor( )**
  Creates a new FileDescriptor.

- **boolean valid( )**
  Returns true if the FileDescriptor is valid.

FileInputStream Extends InputStream. A FileInputStream, as its name implies, is a specialized InputStream designed to obtain input from a file. In contrast to a standard InputStream, a FileInputStream does nothing more—save the capability to direct the input stream to a file.

Due to this limited capacity, FileInputStreams are generally managed with more robust input stream managers, such as DataInputStream. A DataInputStream can be created from a FileInputStream simply by specifying the FileInputStream as the parameter in the DataInputStream constructor.

▶▶ See "DataInputStream Extends FilterInputStream Implements DataInput," p. 492

Methods

- **FileInputStream(File file) throws FileNotFoundException**
  Creates a FileInputStream that reads from the physical file managed by the specified File object.

- **FileInputStream(String name) throws FileNotFoundException**
  Creates a FileInputStream that reads from the file with the specified name.

- **FileInputStream(FileDescriptor descriptorObject)**
  Creates a FileInputStream that reads from the file referred to by the specified FileDescriptor.

- **int available( ) throws IOException**
  Returns the number of available bytes.

- **void close( ) throws IOException**
  Closes the file.

- **protected void finalize( ) throws IOException**
  Automatically called before the FileInputStream is destroyed. It closes the file.

- **final FileDescriptor getFD( ) throws IOException**
  Returns the file descriptor for the file from which the FileInputStream is reading.

- **int read( ) throws IOException**
  Reads and returns a single byte from the stream. It returns –1 if the end of the file is reached.

- **int read(byte b[ ]) throws IOException**
  Reads into the specified array. It returns the number of bytes read or –1 if the end of the file is reached.

- **int read(byte b[ ], int offset, int len) throws IOException**
  Reads at most `len` bytes into the specified buffer beginning at the `offset` index.
  It returns the number of bytes read or –1 if the end of the file is reached.

- **long skip(long num) throws IOException**
  Skips the specified number of bytes in the stream.

FileOutputStream Extends OutputStream. A `FileOutputStream` is a simple extension
of the `OutputStream` class than enables you to write data to a file. Like `FileInputStream`,
`FileOutputStreams` are generally managed with a more robust stream manager, such as
`DataOutputStream`.

▶▶ See "DataOutputStream Extends FilterOutputStream Implements DataOutput," p. 494

Methods

- **FileOutputStream(String name) throws IOException**
  Creates a `FileOutputStream` that writes to the file with the specified name.

- **FileOutputStream(FileDescriptor fdObj)**
  Creates a `FileOutputStream` that writes to the file referred to by the specified
  `FileDescriptor`.

- **FileOutputStream(File file) throws IOException**
  Creates a `FileOutputStream` that writes to the physical file managed by the specified
  `File` object.

- **void close( ) throws IOException**
  Closes the file.

- **protected void finalize( ) throws IOException**
  This method is called just before the `FileOutputStream` is destroyed. It closes the
  file.

- **final FileDescriptor getFD( ) throws IOException**
  Returns the `FileDescriptor` object for the output file.

- **void write(int b) throws IOException**
  Writes a single byte.

- **void write(byte b[ ]) throws IOException**
  Write all bytes in the buffer.

- **void write(byte b[ ], int offset, int len) throws IOException**
  Writes `len` bytes from the specified array beginning at the `offset` index.

FilterInputStream Extends InputStream. A `FilterInputStream` is a non-abstract version of `InputStream`. It may be used to handle any input stream in a basic, yet useful,
manner. Unfortunately, a `FilterInputStream` requires you to read your information as a
series of bytes—complicating matters if you are reading more complex data types, such

as `doubles` or even `Strings`. Therefore, `FilterInputStreams` are usually managed with more powerful stream managers, such as `DataInputStream`. `FilterInputStream` is also the basis for all other `InputStream` managers, such as `DataInputStream` and `PushBackInputStream`.

How does FilterInputStream Differ from InputStream?

Why can you create an instance of a `FilterInputStream`, but not an `InputStream`? You cannot create an instance of an `InputStream` because it is abstract—its `read()` method is not defined. However, when creating a `FilterInputStream`, you must specify an `InputStream` that you want to manage, such as `FileInputStream` or `ByteArrayInputStream`. Because these classes have defined `read()` methods, the `FilterInputStream` manager employs the methods of the `InputStream` class in accomplishing its tasks.

Field

- **protected InputStream in**
  The `InputStream` that will be read from.

Methods

- **FilterInputStream(InputStream in)**
  Creates a `FilterInputStream` to manage the specified `InputStream`.

- **int available( ) throws IOException**
  Returns the number of bytes available on the stream.

- **void close( ) throws IOException**
  Closes the stream and calls the `close()` method in the managed `InputStream`.

- **synchronized void mark(int readlimit)**
  Places a mark at the current position in the `InputStream`. By invoking the `reset()` method, you can return to the current position in the stream. `readlimit` specifies the number of bytes that can be read beyond the marked position before the mark is lost.

- **boolean markSupported( )**
  Returns `true` if the current `InputStream` supports marking.

- **int read( ) throws IOException**
  Reads and returns a single byte from the stream. It returns –1 if the end of the file is reached.

- **int read(byte b[ ]) throws IOException**
  Reads into the specified array. It returns the number of bytes read or –1 if the end of the file is reached.

- **int read(byte b[ ], int offset, int len) throws IOException**
  Reads at most `len` bytes into the specified buffer beginning at the `offset` index. It returns the number of bytes read or –1 if the end of the file is reached.

- **synchronized void reset( ) throws IOException**
  Returns to the marked position in the stream.

- **long skip(long num) throws IOException**
  Skips the specified number of bytes in the stream.

FilterOutputStream Extends OutputStream. The FilterOutputStream class provides you with a simple but effective manner of managing OutputStreams. This class is the basis for all other classes designed to manage OutputStreams, such as BufferedOutputStream and DataOutputStream.

▶▶ See "FilterInputStream Extends InputStream," p. 499

Field

- **protected OutputStream out**
  The OutputStream that is being managed.

Methods

- **FilterOutputStream(OutputStream out)**
  Creates a new FilterOutputStream to manage the specified OutputStream.

- **void close( ) throws IOException**
  Closes the OutputStream.

- **void flush( ) throws IOException**
  Flushes any buffered information to the stream. This only produces a result in those OutputStreams that buffer information before writing it to the stream.

- **void write(int b) throws IOException**
  Writes a single byte.

- **void write(byte b[ ]) throws IOException**
  Write all bytes in the buffer.

- **void write(byte b[ ], int offset, int len) throws IOException**
  Writes len bytes from the specified array beginning at the offset index.

Abstract **InputStream.** The InputStream class is a basic class for handling input across a stream. While it serves as the basis for all input stream classes, it is nevertheless abstract—which means that you cannot create an instance of an InputStream. However, because all input stream classes derive from the InputStream class, you can handle all InputStreams by using the methods found in the InputStream class.

You will see that the input stream handlers (such as DataInputStream) accept an InputStream as a parameter. Although it is impossible to supply these handlers with a pure InputStream, the stream that you do pass to a handler will be derived from the InputStream class and thus may be treated as a type of InputStream.

III

Java

Methods

- **InputStream( )**
  Creates a new InputStream.

- **int available( ) throws IOException**
  Returns the number of bytes available on the stream.

- **void close( ) throws IOException**
  Closes the stream. It calls the close() method in the managed InputStream.

- **synchronized void mark(int readlimit)**
  Places a mark at the current position in the InputStream. By invoking the reset() method, you may return to the current position in the stream. readlimit specifies the number of bytes that may be read beyond the marked position before the mark is lost.

- **boolean markSupported( )**
  Returns true if the current InputStream supports marking.

- **int read( ) throws IOException**
  Reads and returns a single byte from the stream. It returns –1 if the end of the file is reached.

- **int read(byte b[ ]) throws IOException**
  Reads into the specified array. It returns the number of bytes read or –1 if the end of the file is reached.

- **int read(byte b[ ], int offset, int len) throws IOException**
  Reads at most len bytes into the specified buffer beginning at the offset index. It returns the number of bytes read or –1 if the end of the file is reached.

- **synchronized void reset( ) throws IOException**
  Returns to the marked position in the stream.

- **long skip(long num) throws IOException**
  Skips the specified number of bytes in the stream.

LineNumberInputStream Extends FilterInputStream. A LineNumberInputStream is a input stream manager. Slightly elaborating upon the FilterInputStream, it allows you not only to read information from the stream, but also to keep track of the number of lines that you have read from this stream.

Methods

- **LineNumberInputStream(InputStream in)**
  Creates a new LineNumberInputStream to manage the specified InputStream.

- **int available( ) throws IOException**
  Returns the number of available bytes.

- **int getLineNumber( )**
  Returns the current line number.

- **void mark(int readlimit)**
  Places a mark at the current position in the InputStream. By invoking the reset() method, you can return to the current position in the stream. readlimit specifies the number of bytes that may be read beyond the marked position before the mark is lost.

- **int read( ) throws IOException**
  Reads and returns a byte from the stream.

- **int read(byte b[ ], int offset, int len) throws IOException**
  Reads len bytes to the array beginning at the offset index. It returns the number of bytes read.

- **void reset( ) throws IOException**
  Returns to the marked position in the stream.

- **void setLineNumber(int lineNumber)**
  Sets the current line number to the specified value.

- **long skip(long num) throws IOException**
  Skips the specified number of bytes. It returns the number of bytes actually skipped.

Abstract OutputStream. The OutputStream class is an abstract class that establishes the foundation for all types of OutputStream classes. Although you cannot create an instance of an OutputStream—because all output streams are based on this class—it provides you with a convenient means of handling all types of output streams.

Methods

- **OutputStream( )**
  Creates a new OutputStream.

- **void close( ) throws IOException**
  Closes the OutputStream.

- **void flush( ) throws IOException**
  In subclasses, this method may be used to write any buffered bytes to the stream. However, in this class, the method is empty.

- **abstract void write(int b) throws IOException**
  Writes a single byte. This is the *essence* of the class that must be overridden by any non-abstract subclasses.

- **void write(byte b[ ]) throws IOException**
  Writes the array to the stream.

- **void write(byte b[ ], int offset, int len) throws IOException**
  Writes len bytes from the array beginning at the offset index.

PipedInputStream Extends InputStream. The PipedInputStream class works in conjunction with the PipedOutputStream class. By connecting a PipedInputStream to a

`PipedOutputStream`, you are able to create two separate threads—each running independently—with the capability to send information to each other in an extremely convenient manner.

▶▶ See "PipedOutputStream Extends OutputStream," p. 506

The output was produced by linking instances of the `PipedInputStream` and `PipedOutputStream` classes—each being managed by a separate thread (see Listing 14.12). Due to the idiosyncrasies of thread management, the `sleep()` statement in the `Writer` class is necessary to shift control to the `Reader` class. Without the `sleep()` statement, the `Reader` class would first write all of its data, relinquish control to the `Reader` class, and then allow it to read in all the data.

Also note that in this example, I use the error handling of the `Reader` class to exit the program. Once the `Writer` class completes its task, the output pipe is shut down. This causes an exception in the `Reader` class—causing the entire program to terminate.

Listing 14.22   An Example of `PipedInputStream` and `PipedOutputStream`

```
class Reader extends Thread {

    PipedInputStream in;
    boolean running;

    Reader(PipedOutputStream out) {
      try {
        in = new PipedInputStream(out);
        running = true;
      }
      catch (Exception e)
        System.out.println(e.toString() );
    }

    PipedInputStream getStream() {
        return (in);
    }

    public void run() {
      while (running) {
        try {
          System.out.println("Reading " +in.read());
        }
        catch(Exception e) {
          System.out.println("Done");
          System.exit(1);
        }
      }
    }
}


class Writer extends Thread {
    public PipedOutputStream out;
```

```
    boolean running;

    Writer() {
      out = new PipedOutputStream();
      running = true;
    }

    PipedOutputStream getStream() {
      return (out);
    }

    void connectTo(PipedInputStream in) {
      try {
        out.connect(in);
      }
      catch (Exception e) {
        System.out.println(e.toString() );
        running = false;
      }
    }

    public void run() {
      try {
        for (int i = 1; i <= 10; i++)     {
          out.write(i);
          System.out.println("Wrote " + i + "  ");
          yield();
          sleep(2000);
        }
      }
      catch(Exception e) {
        System.out.println(e.toString() );
      }
    }
}


public class PipedExample {
    public static void main(String args[ ]) {
      Writer w = new Writer();
      Reader r = new Reader( w.getStream() );
      w.connectTo( r.getStream() );
      r.start();
      w.start();
    }
}
```

Methods

- **PipedInputStream( )**

  Creates a PipedInputStream. This stream must be connected to a PipedOutputStream before it can be used.

- **PipedInputStream(PipedOutputStream src) throws IOException**

  Creates a PipedInputStream and connects it to the specified PipedOutputStream.

- **void close( ) throws IOException**

  Closes the stream by instructing it to no longer read from the PipedOutputStream.

- **void connect(PipedOutputStream src) throws IOException**
  Connects the PipedInputStream to the specified PipedOutputStream.

- **synchronized int read( ) throws IOException**
  Reads and returns a byte from the stream.

- **synchronized int read(byte b[ ], int offset, int len) throws IOException**
  Reads len bytes from the stream, storing them in the specified array beginning at the offset index.

PipedOutputStream Extends OutputStream. Working with a PipedInputStream, a PipedOutputStream enables two concurrently running Threads to communicate via a stream.

▶▶ See "PipedInputStream Extends InputStream," p. 504

Methods

- **PipedOutputStream( )**
  Creates a new PipedOutputStream. This must be connected to a PipedInputStream in order to function.

- **PipedOutputStream(PipedInputStream dest) throws IOException**
  Creates a new PipedOutputStream and connects it to the specified PipedInputStream.

- **void close( ) throws IOException**
  Informs the PipedInputStream that it has received its last byte—effectively closing the stream.

- **void connect(PipedInputStream dest) throws IOException**
  Connects the PipedOutputStream to the specified PipedInputStream.

- **void write(int b) throws IOException**
  Writes a single byte to the stream.

- **void write(byte b[ ], int offset, int len) throws IOException**
  Writes len bytes from the specified buffer, beginning at the offset index.

PrintStream Extends FilterOutputStream. A PrintStream is a very straightforward stream manager that prints out all types of data as strings.

Caution

Because a PrintStream prints everything as a String, all data types—even integers and doubles—will be printed as a string. Consequently, be careful when later reading this information. All data types except strings and characters must be first read as strings or bytes and then converted to their natural data types.

Methods

- **PrintStream(OutputStream out)**
  Creates a new PrintStream to manage the specified OutputStream.

- **PrintStream(OutputStream out, boolean autoflush)**
  Creates a new PrintStream to manage the specified OutputStream. If autoflush is true, the stream will be flushed every time a newline character ('\n') is written.

- **boolean checkError( )**
  Returns true if an error has been encountered in writing to the stream. Once an error has occurred, this method will continue to return a value of true.

- **void close( )**
  Closes the stream.

- **void flush( )**
  Flushes any information being buffered by the OutputStream.

- **void print(boolean b)**
  Prints a boolean.

- **void print(double d)**
  Prints a double.

- **void print(float f)**
  Prints a float.

- **void print(long l)**
  Prints a long.

- **void print(int i)**
  Prints an int.

- **void print(char c)**
  Prints a char.

- **synchronized void print(char s[ ])**
  Prints the array of characters.

- **synchronized void print(String s)**
  Prints the string.

- **void print(Object obj)**
  Prints the value returned by String.valueOf(obj).

- **synchronized void println(boolean b)**
  Prints a boolean followed by a newline character.

- **synchronized void println(double d)**
  Prints a double followed by a newline character.

- **synchronized void println(float f)**
  Prints a float followed by a newline character.

III

Java

- **synchronized void println(long l)**
  Prints a `long` followed by a newline character.

- **synchronized void println(int i)**
  Prints an `int` followed by a newline character.

- **synchronized void println(char c)**
  Prints a `char` followed by a newline character.

- **synchronized void println(char s[ ])**
  Prints the array of `chars` followed by a newline character.

- **synchronized void println(String s)**
  Prints a string followed by a newline character.

- **synchronized void println(Object obj)**
  Prints the value returned by `String.valueOf(obj)` followed by a newline character.

- **void println( )**
  Prints a newline character.

- **void write(int b)**
  Writes a single byte.

- **void write(byte b[ ], int offset, int len)**
  Writes all bytes in the specified array from `len` to `len + offset` .

PushbackInputStream Extends FilterInputStream. A `PushbackInputStream` is a stream manager that is quite useful when parsing a stream. It enables you to "take a peek" at the next byte in the stream without completely removing the byte from the stream. If you decide that you don't want the specific byte, you may return it to the stream via the `unread()` method. This will "push" the specified byte back onto the stream, making it the next character to be returned by any future `read()` statements.

How Do You Place a Character Back on a Stream?

You don't. A `PushBackInputStream` does not actually place the character back on the stream. However, it stores it in a protected field named `pushBack`. The next time you read from the stream, it will return the `pushBack` byte—not the next byte from the stream.

Field

- **protected int pushBack**
  The byte that has been "pushed back."

Methods

- **PushbackInputStream(InputStream in)**
  Creates a new `PushBackInputStream` to manage the specified stream.

- **int available( ) throws IOException**
  Returns the number of bytes available on the stream.

- **boolean markSupported( )**
  Returns `false` because this `InputStream` handler does not support the mark/reset procedure.

- **int read( ) throws IOException**
  Reads and returns a single byte.

- **int read(byte b[ ], int offset, int len) throws IOException**
  Reads `len` bytes from the array and places them in the specified buffer beginning at `b[offset]`.

- **void unread(int ch) throws IOException**
  Places the specified byte back on the stream.

RandomAccessFile Implements DataOutput DataInput. Closely resembling a random access file in C, the `RandomAccessFile` class provides you with an extremely flexible tool for file input and output. Furthermore, by enabling you to specify the type of access allowed—either read-only or read and write—this class supplies you with a degree of security.

Methods

- **RandomAccessFile(File file, String mode) throws IOException**
  Creates a new `RandomAccessFile` object to handle the physical file managed by the `File` object. `mode` specifies the type of file access permitted. `"r"` allows read-only and `"rw"` allows both reading and writing.

- **RandomAccessFile(String name, String mode) throws IOException**
  Creates a new `RandomAccessFile` object to handle the file with the specified name. `mode` specifies the type of file access permitted. `"r"` allows read-only and `"rw"` allows both reading and writing.

- **void close( ) throws IOException**
  Closes the file.

- **final FileDescriptor getFD( ) throws IOException**
  Returns the `FileDescriptor` of the file being accessed.

- **long getFilePointer( ) throws IOException**
  Returns the current location of the file pointer in the file.

- **long length( ) throws IOException**
  Returns the length of the file.

- **int read( ) throws IOException**
  Reads and returns a single byte.

- **int read(byte b[ ]) throws IOException**
  Reads to the specified byte array, returning the number of bytes read.

- **int read(byte b[ ], int offset, int len) throws IOException**
  Reads `len` bytes and places them in the array beginning at the `offset` index. It returns the actual number of bytes read.

III

Java

- **final boolean readBoolean( ) throws IOException**
  Reads a `boolean` from the file.

- **final byte readByte( ) throws IOException**
  Reads a `byte` from the file.

- **final char readChar( ) throws IOException**
  Reads a `char` from the file.

- **final double readDouble( ) throws IOException**
  Reads a `double` from the file.

- **final float readFloat( ) throws IOException**
  Reads a `float` from the file.

- **final void readFully(byte b[ ], int offset, int len) throws IOException**
  Reads from the stream, waiting until `len` bytes have been read from the stream. The bytes will be written to the array beginning at the specified `offset`.

- **final void readFully(byte b[ ]) throws IOException**
  Reads from the stream, placing bytes in the specified array until the array is full.

- **final int readInt( ) throws IOException**
  Reads and returns an `int` from the stream.

- **final String readLine( ) throws IOException**
  Reads and returns a string from the stream terminated by `'\n'` or `EOF`.

- **final long readLong( ) throws IOException**
  Reads and returns a `long` from the stream.

- **final short readShort( ) throws IOException**
  Reads and returns a short from the stream.

- **final int readUnsignedByte( ) throws IOException**
  Reads and returns an unsigned byte from the stream.

- **final int readUnsignedShort( ) throws IOException**
  Reads and returns an unsigned short from the stream.

- **final String readUTF( ) throws IOException**
  Reads and returns a string in UTF format from the stream.

- **void seek(long pos) throws IOException**
  Places the file pointer at the specified location in the file.

- **int skipBytes(int num) throws IOException**
  Advances the file pointer the specified number of bytes.

- **void write(byte b[ ]) throws IOException**
  Writes the specified buffer to the file.

- **void write(byte b[ ], int offset, int len) throws IOException**
  Writes `len` bytes from the buffer to the file beginning at the `offset`.

- **final void writeBoolean(boolean v) throws IOException**
Writes the `boolean` to the file.

- **final void writeByte(int v) throws IOException**
Writes the `byte` to the file.

- **final void writeBytes(String s) throws IOException**
Writes the `string` to the file as a series of bytes.

- **final void writeChar(int v) throws IOException**
Writes the `char` to the file.

- **final void writeChars(String s) throws IOException**
Writes the `string` to the file as a sequence of `chars`.

- **final void writeDouble(double v) throws IOException**
Writes the `double` to the file.

- **final void writeFloat(float v) throws IOException**
Writes the `float` to the file.

- **final void writeInt(int v) throws IOException**
Writes the `int` to the file.

- **final void writeLong(long v) throws IOException**
Writes the `long` to the file.

- **final void writeShort(int v) throws IOException**
Writes the `short` to the file.

- **final void writeUTF(String str) throws IOException**
Writes the `string` to the file in UTF format.

SequenceInputStream Extends InputStream. A `SequenceInputStream` enables you to link multiple `InputStreams` to form one pseudo-stream. The `SequenceInputStream` will read from one stream until completion, at which time it will read from the next stream.

Methods

- **SequenceInputStream(InputStream s1, InputStream s2)**
Creates a new `SequenceInputStream`, linking the specified `InputStream`.

- **SequenceInputStream(Enumeration e)**
Creates a `SequenceInputStream`, linking all `InputStreams` in the specified `Enumeration`.

- **void close( ) throws IOException**
Effectively closes the stream by scrolling through all remaining streams until the last stream has been marked as read.

- **int read( ) throws IOException**
Reads and returns a byte from the current stream.

- **int read(byte b[ ], int offset, int len) throws IOException**
  Reads `len` bytes from the sequence of streams, placing them in the array (`b[ ]`) be-ginning at the specified `offset`.

StreamTokenizer. A `StreamTokenizer` is a heavy-duty tool used for parsing streams. Using the `nextToken()` method, you are able to scan the stream for any *tokens—* characters defined by you to be important. When such a character is encountered, the `StreamTokenizer` will return a flag. The flag will either be the character itself or a special flag, such as `TT_EOF` (which signifies the end of the stream).

Fields

- **double nval**
  If `TT_NUMBER` is the returned token, this is the recently read number.

- **String sval**
  If `TT_WORD` is the returned token, this is the recently read string.

- **final static int TT_EOF**
  The end of file token.

- **final static int TT_EOL**
  The end of line token.

- **final static int TT_NUMBER**
  A token indicating a number has just been read.

- **final static int TT_WORD**
  A token indicating a word (string) has just been read.

Methods

- **StreamTokenizer(InputStream in)**
  Creates a `StreamTokenizer` to manage the specified `InputStream`.

- **void commentChar(int ch)**
  Sets the comment character.

- **void eolIsSignificant(boolean flag)**
  If `flag` is `true`, then end-of-line characters will be returned as tokens.

- **int lineno( )**
  Returns the current line number. This is useful when end-of-line tokens are not significant.

- **void lowerCaseMode(boolean flag)**
  If `flag` is `true`, then the string placed in `sval` will be converted to lowercase characters.

- **int nextToken( ) throws IOException**
  Advances in the stream until the next token is reached. It returns this token.

- **void ordinaryChar(int ch)**
  Makes the specified character an *ordinary* character. This means that it will not be returned as a token.

- **void ordinaryChars(int low, int hi)**
  The range of characters from `low` to `hi` are now considered ordinary. They will not be returned as tokens.

- **void parseNumbers( )**
  Forces parsing of numbers. This method is called by default when a `StreamTokenizer` is created, but if you reset the syntax, you must call this method again. This task is accomplished by making the numeric characters (0–9), the period (.), and the hyphen (-) special characters that will be handled differently by the `tokenizer`.

- **void pushBack( )**
  Effectively returns the current token to the stream. As a result, the next call to `nextToken( )` will return the same token with the same `nval` or `sval` if appropriate.

- **void quoteChar(int ch)**
  Sets the quote character.

- **void resetSyntax( )**
  Resets the syntax for the `tokenizer`. All characters are set to ordinary status.

- **void slashSlashComments(boolean flag)**
  If `flag` is `true`, the slash-slash flag (//) will denote comments.

- **void slashStarComments(boolean flag)**
  If `flag` is `true`, the slash-star flag (/* to */) denotes comments.

- **String toString( )**
  Returns a string containing the current token and `sval` or `nval` if appropriate.

- **void whitespaceChars(int low, int hi)**
  All characters between `low` and `hi` are considered whitespace. By default, characters 0 to 32 are considered whitespace.

- **void wordChars(int low, int hi)**
  All characters between `low` and `hi` are considered a part of a word.

StringBufferInputStream Extends InputStream. A `StringBufferInputStream` enables you to read information from a `String` as if it were an `InputStream`.

▶▶ See "PushbackInputStream Extends FilterInputStream," p. 508

Fields

- **protected String buffer**
  A reference to the String specified in the constructor method.

- **protected int count**
  The length of the buffer.

- **protected int pos**
  The current position in the buffer.

Methods

- **StringBufferInputStream(String s)**
  Creates a new StringBufferInputStream to read from the specified string.

- **synchronized int available( )**
  Returns the number of bytes remaining in the string buffer.

- **synchronized int read( )**
  Reads and returns a single byte. It returns –1 if no bytes remain.

- **synchronized int read(byte b[ ], int offset, int len)**
  Reads at most len bytes from string buffer, storing them in the array beginning at the offset index. It returns the number of bytes read and –1 if no bytes remain.

- **synchronized void reset( )**
  Returns to the beginning of the buffer.

- **synchronized long skip(long num)**
  Skips at most num bytes in the stream. It returns the number of bytes skipped.

Interfaces

DataInput. This interface declares a set of methods defining the behavior of a machine-independent input stream. It is implemented by the DataInputStream class.

Methods

- **abstract boolean readBoolean( ) throws IOException**
  Reads and returns a boolean from the stream.

- **abstract byte readByte( ) throws IOException**
  Reads and returns a byte from the stream.

- **abstract char readChar( ) throws IOException**
  Reads and returns a char from the stream.

- **abstract double readDouble( ) throws IOException**
  Reads and returns a double from the stream.

- **abstract float readFloat( ) throws IOException**
  Reads and returns a float from the stream.

- **abstract void readFully(byte b[ ]) throws IOException**
  Reads from the stream, waiting until the entire array is filled.

- **abstract void readFully(byte b[ ], int offset, int len) throws IOException**
  Reads from the stream, waiting until `len` bytes have been read. It places the bytes in the array, beginning at the specified `offset`.

- **abstract int readInt( ) throws IOException**
  Reads and returns an `int` from the stream.

- **abstract long readLong( ) throws IOException**
  Reads and returns a `long` from the stream.

- **abstract short readShort( ) throws IOException**
  Reads and returns a `short` from the stream.

- **abstract int readUnsignedByte( ) throws IOException**
  Reads and returns an unsigned `byte` from the stream.

- **abstract int readUnsignedShort( ) throws IOException**
  Reads and returns an unsigned `short` from the stream.

- **abstract String readUTF( ) throws IOException**
  Reads and returns a `string` from the stream in UTF format.

- **abstract int skipBytes(int num) throws IOException**
  Skips at most `num` bytes in the stream. It returns the actual number of bytes skipped.

DataOutput. This class declares a set of methods that enable machine-independent output of data. It is implemented by the `DataOutputStream` class.

Methods

- **abstract void write(byte b[ ], int offset, int len) throws IOException**
  Writes bytes from the array to the stream, beginning at `b[offset]` and continuing to `b[offset + len]`.

- **abstract void write(byte b[ ]) throws IOException**
  Writes the entire array to the stream.

- **abstract void write(int b) throws IOException**
  Writes an `int` to the stream.

- **abstract void writeBoolean(boolean v) throws IOException**
  Writes a `boolean` to the stream.

- **abstract void writeByte(int v) throws IOException**
  Writes a `byte` to the stream.

- **abstract void writeBytes(String s) throws IOException**
  Writes a `string` to the stream as a series of bytes.

- **abstract void writeChar(int v) throws IOException**
  Writes a `char` to the stream.

- **abstract void writeChars(String s) throws IOException**
  Writes a `string` to the stream as a series of `chars`.

- **abstract void writeDouble(double v) throws IOException**
  Writes a `double` to the stream.

- **abstract void writeFloat(float v) throws IOException**
  Writes a `float` to the stream.

- **abstract void writeInt(int v) throws IOException**
  Writes an `int` to the stream.

- **abstract void writeLong(long v) throws IOException**
  Writes a `long` to the stream.

- **abstract void writeShort(int v) throws IOException**
  Writes a `short` to the stream.

- **abstract void writeUTF(String str) throws IOException**
  Writes a `string` to the stream in UTF format.

FilenameFilter. A `FilenameFilter` is a tool to be used when screening directories. It is used in the `File` and `java.awt.FileDialog` classes.

Method

- **abstract boolean accept(File dir, String name)**
  Returns `true` if the specified file satisfies the requirements of the filter.

java.lang

These classes are essentially the *heart* of the java language. This package includes not only wrappers for the basic data types, such as `Integer` and `String`, but also a means of handling errors through the `Throwable` and `Error` classes. Furthermore, the `SecurityManager` and `System` classes supply you with some degree of control over the client's system, albeit the command prompt or the Java Console in Netscape.

Classes

Boolean. While a `boolean` is a primitive data type, the `Boolean` class serves as a wrapper class—providing you with a means of better handling `boolean` values. Wrapper classes for primitive data types are also useful in using `hashtables`, which only accept objects—not primitive data types.

Fields

- **final static Boolean FALSE**
  A `Boolean` object created with a value of `false`.

- **final static char MAX_VALUE**
  The maximum value of a character: 65535. These values were accidentally placed in the `Boolean` class.

- **final static char MIN_VALUE**
  The minimum value of a character: 0. These values were accidentally placed in the `Boolean` class.

- **final static Boolean TRUE**
  A `Boolean` object created with a value of `true`.

Methods

- **Boolean(String s)**
  Creates a `Boolean` object with the specified value: `true` if s equals `true` and `false` otherwise.

- **Boolean(boolean value)**
  Creates a `Boolean` object with the specified `boolean` value.

- **boolean booleanValue( )**
  Returns the value of the `Boolean` object.

- **boolean equals(Object anotherObject)**
  Returns `true` if the `anotherObject` is a `boolean` with the same value.

- **static boolean getBoolean(String s)**
  Returns `true` if s equals `true`. Otherwise, it returns `false`.

- **int hashCode( )**
  Returns the `hashcode` for the `Boolean` object—a value dependent on the `boolean` value of the object.

- **String toString( )**
  Returns either `true` or `false` depending on the value of the `boolean` value of the object.

- **static Boolean valueOf(String s)**
  Returns a `Boolean` object whose value is the value of the specified string.

Character. The `Character` class serves as a wrapper class for handling `char` values.

Fields

- **final static int MAX_RADIX**
  The maximum radix that can be used in converting a number, represented by a character, to an `int`. The radix refers to the mathematical *base* of the number, denoting the value of each position. `MAX_RADIX` is 36.

- **final static int MIN_RADIX**
  The minimum radix that can be used in converting a number, represented by a character, to an `int`. The radix refers to the mathematical *base* of the number, denoting the value of each position. `MIN_RADIX` is 2.

Methods

- **Character(char value)**

  Creates a `Character` object with the specified character value.

- **char charValue( )**

  Returns the value of the `Character` object.

- **static int digit(char ch, int base)**

  Converts a number, represented by `ch`, to an `int` value in the specified base.

- **boolean equals(Object anotherObject)**

  Returns `true` if `anotherObject` is a `Character` object with the same `char` value.

- **static char forDigit(int digit, int base)**

  Returns a `char` representing the value of the `digit` in the specified `base`.

- **int hashCode( )**

  Returns the `hashcode` of the `Character` object—the `char` value casted to an `int`.

- **static boolean isDigit(char ch)**

  Returns `true` if the `char` value is between 0 and 9.

- **static boolean isJavaLetter(char ch)**

  Returns `true` if `ch` is a *Java letter*—meaning that it can be used as the first letter of an identifier. This includes all characters, the dollar sign ('$'), and the underscore character ('_').

- **static boolean isJavaLetterOrDigit(char ch)**

  Returns `true` if `ch` is a valid character within a Java identifier. This includes all letters and digits as well as the dollar sign ('$'), and the underscore character ('_'). It will return `true` if `ch` equals '$', '_', or if `isLetterOrDigit(ch)` is true.

- **static boolean isLetter(char ch)**

  Returns `true` if `ch` is a letter.

- **static boolean isLetterOrDigit(char ch)**

  Returns `true` if `ch` is a letter or a digit.

- **static boolean isLowerCase(char ch)**

  Returns `true` if the `char` value is a lowercase letter.

- **static boolean isSpace(char ch)**

  Returns `true` if the `char` value is ' ', '\t', '\f', '\n', or '\r'.

- **static boolean isSpace(char ch)**

  Returns `true` if `ch` is one of the five white space characters: ' ', '\t', '\f', '\n', or '\r'.

- **static boolean isTitleCase(char ch)**

  Returns `true` if `ch` is one of four special Unicode characters. These characters are special because they resemble two ASCII characters together, such as *Lj*. This method will return `true` only if `ch` is one of these four characters and its first letter is capitalized.

- **static boolean isUpperCase(char ch)**
  Returns `true` if the `char` value is an uppercase letter.

- **static char toLowerCase(char ch)**
  Returns the lowercase value of the specified `char`.

- **String toString( )**
  Returns the `char` value as a string.

- **static char toTitleCase(char ch)**
  Returns the title case of a `ch`. For all but four characters, this is simply their upper-case form. For the four special Latin Unicode characters resembling two ASCII characters, this capitalizes the first letter and leaves the second unchanged.

- **static char toUpperCase(char ch)**
  Returns the uppercase value of the specified `char`.

Class. To the Virtual Machine, every class is an `Object`. However, within the Virtual Machine, every class (and interface) is handled with the `Class` class. While the `Object` class gives you information regarding an instance of the class (the actual object), this class gives you information regarding the code used in creating the class. Because you cannot create an instance of a `Class`, you must use the `forName()` method to return a `Class` object.

Methods

- **static Class forName(String className) throws ClassNotFoundException**
  Returns the `Class` object descriptor for the specified class.

- **ClassLoader getClassLoader( )**
  Returns the `ClassLoader` for this class.

- **Class[ ] getInterfaces( )**
  Returns an array containing the interfaces implemented by this class.

- **String getName( )**
  Returns the name of this class.

- **Class getSuperclass( )**
  Returns the `Class` object for the superclass of this class.

- **boolean isInterface( )**
  Returns `true` if this "class" is actually an interface.

- **Object newInstance( ) throws InstantiationException, IllegalAccessException**
  Creates a instance of the class described by this `Class` object.

- **String toString( )**
  Returns a string containing either the word *class* or *interface* along with the class/interface name.

III

Java

Abstract **ClassLoader.** A class loader can be used to load a class from a source other than the current server—such as a network. Because the process depends heavily on your particular circumstances, the actual loading of the class is left up to you.

Because the ClassLoader class is abstract, you must first extend the class and override the loadClass() method if you want to use a ClassLoader. Once this is done, you must employ the defineClass() method to create a Class object describing the class—which also enables you to create an instance of the class.

Methods

- **protected ClassLoader( )**
  Creates a new ClassLoader.

- **abstract Class loadClass(String name, boolean resolve) throws ClassNotFoundException**
  This method must be overridden in your own class. resolve represents the need to "resolve" the class: loading all classes referred to by the newly loaded class.

- **final Class defineClass(byte data[ ], int offset, int length)**
  Returns a Class object describing the class created from the specified set of bytes. The class will be created from the bytes beginning at data[offset] and continuing to data[offset + length].

- **final Class findSystemClass(String name) throws ClassNotFoundException**
  Loads a class from the system. This employs the default (null) class loader.

- **final void resolveClass(Class c)**
  Resolves the specified class by loading all classes referred to by the specified class. This must be done before the class can be used.

Compiler. This class is designed to provide an interface with future Java technology that will provide you with more control over the Java compiler. However, there is no complete set of libraries or means of creating a Compiler object as of the 1.0 JDK.

Methods

- **static Object command(Object any)**
  Executes the specified command.

- **static boolean compileClass(Class class)**
  Compiles the specified class.

- **static boolean compileClasses(String string)**
  Compiles the specified classes.

- **static void disable( )**
  Disables the compiler.

- **static void enable( )**
  Enables the compiler.

Double Extends Number. Double is a wrapper class designed to handle double values.

Fields

- **final static double MAX_VALUE**
  The maximum value of a double is 1.79769313486231570 * 10^{308}.

- **final static double MIN_VALUE**
  The minimum value of a double is 4.94065645841246544e * 10^{324}.

- **final static double NaN**
  This special value represents a double that is *Not a Number*. It is set equal to 0.0 / 0.0. It is not equal to *anything*—even itself.

- **final static double NEGATIVE_INFINITY**
  Negative infinity: –1.0/0.0.

- **final static double POSITIVE_INFINITY**
  Positive infinity: 1.0/0.0.

Methods

- **Double(double value)**
  Creates a new Double object based on the specified double value.

- **Double(String s) throws NumberFormatException**
  Creates a new Double object, assuming s represents a valid double value.

- **static long doubleToLongBits(double value)**
  Returns a bit representation of the specified value.

- **double doubleValue( )**
  Returns the value of the Double object.

- **boolean equals(Object anotherObject)**
  Returns true if anotherObject is a Double with the same value.

- **float floatValue( )**
  Returns the double value of the object as a float.

- **int hashCode( )**
  Returns the hashcode of the Double object—the double value casted to an int.

- **int intValue( )**
  Returns the double value casted to an int.

- **boolean isInfinite( )**
  Returns true if the double value equals either POSITIVE_INFINITY or NEGATIVE_INFINITY.

- **static boolean isInfinite(double v)**
  Returns true if the specified double value equals either POSITIVE_INFINITY or NEGATIVE_INFINITY.

- **boolean isNaN( )**
  Returns true if the double value is equal to the special NaN value.

- **static boolean isNaN(double v)**
  Returns `true` if the specified `double` value is equal to the special `NaN` value.

- **static double longBitsToDouble(long bits)**
  Returns the `double` representation of a given bit representation.

- **long longValue( )**
  Returns the `double` value as a `long`.

- **String toString( )**
  Returns the `double` value as a string.

- **static String toString(double d)**
  Converts the specified `double` to a string.

- **static Double valueOf(String s) throws NumberFormatException**
  Converts the specified string into a `Double` object.

Float Extends Number. `Float` is a wrapper class designed to handle float values.

Fields

- **final static float MAX_VALUE**
  The maximum value for a `float` is $3.40282346638528860 * 10^{38}$.

- **final static float MIN_VALUE**
  The minimum value of a `float` is $1.40129846432481707 * 10^{-45}$.

- **final static float NaN**
  This special value represents a `double` that is *Not a* Number. It is set equal to 0.0 / 0.0. It is not equal to *anything*—even itself.

- **final static float NEGATIVE_INFINITY**
  Negative infinity: –1.0/0.0.

- **final static float POSITIVE_INFINITY**
  Positive infinity: 1.0/0.0.

Methods

- **Float(String s) throws NumberFormatException**
  Creates a `Float` object whose `float` value will be that of the specified string.

- **Float(double value)**
  Creates a `Float` object whose initial value will be the value of the specified `double`.

- **Float(float value)**
  Creates a `Float` object whose initial value will be the value of the specified `float`.

- **double doubleValue( )**
  Returns the `float` value as a `double`.

- **boolean equals(Object anotherObject)**
  Returns `true` if `anotherObject` is a `Float` with the same value.

- **static int floatToIntBits(float value)**
  Returns a bit representation of the specified `float`.

- **float floatValue( )**
  Returns the `float` value of the `Float`.

- **int hashCode( )**
  Returns the `hashcode` of the `Float`: the `float` value casted to an `int`.

- **static float intBitsToFloat(int bits)**
  Returns the `float` value of the bit representation.

- **int intValue( )**
  Returns the `float` value as a `float`.

- **boolean isInfinite( )**
  Returns `true` if the `float` value is equal to either `POSITIVE_INFINITY` or `NEGATIVE_INFINITY`.

- **static boolean isInfinite(float v)**
  Returns `true` if the specified `float` is equal to positive or negative infinity.

- **boolean isNaN( )**
  Returns `true` if the `float` value is not a number.

- **static boolean isNaN(float v)**
  Returns `true` if the specified `float` is not a number.

- **long longValue( )**
  Returns the `float` value as a `long`.

- **String toString( )**
  Returns the `float` value in a string.

- **static String toString(float f)**
  Converts the specified `float` into a string.

- **static Float valueOf(String s) throws NumberFormatException**
  Returns a `Float` object whose initial value is equal to the `float` contained in the string.

Integer Extends Number. `Integer` is a wrapper class designed to handle `int` values. Often, `Integer` objects are returned by methods in the API as a means of providing you with a number and a means to manage it.

Fields

- **final static int MAX_VALUE**
  The maximum value for an `Integer` is 2147483647.

- **final static int MIN_VALUE**
  The minimum value for an `Integer` is –2147483648.

Methods

- **Integer(int value)**
  Creates a new Integer object with the specified value.

- **Integer(String s) throws NumberFormatException**
  Creates a new Integer object whose initial value will be equal to the int contained in the specified string.

- **double doubleValue( )**
  Returns the int value as a double.

- **boolean equals(Object anotherObject)**
  Returns true if anotherObject is an Integer with the same int value.

- **float floatValue( )**
  Returns the int value as a float.

- **static Integer getInteger(String propName)**
  Returns a system property whose value is an int that may be stored in hexadecimal or octal format.

- **static Integer getInteger(String propName, int val)**
  Returns a system property whose value is an int that may be stored in hexadecimal or octal format. If this process fails, the method returns an Integer with the value of val.

- **static Integer getInteger(String propName, Integer val)**
  Returns a system property whose value is an int that may be stored in hexadecimal or octal format. If this process fails, the method returns val.

- **int hashCode( )**
  Returns the hashcode of the Integer: its int value.

- **int intValue( )**
  Returns the int value.

- **long longValue( )**
  Returns the int value as a long.

- **static int parseInt(String s) throws NumberFormatException**
  Returns the int represented by the specified string.

- **static int parseInt(String s, int base) throws NumberFormatException**
  Returns the int specified by the string in base base—for example, parseInt("101",2) = 5 and parseInt("101",10) = 10.

- **static String toBinaryString(int)**
  Returns a String representing num as an unsigned binary number.

- **static String toHexString(int)**
  Returns a String representing num as an unsigned hexadecimal number.

- **static String toOctalString(int)**
  Returns a `String` representing num as an unsigned octal number.

- **String toString( )**
  Returns the `int` value in a string.

- **static String toString(int i)**
  Returns a string containing the specified `int`.

- **static String toString(int i, int base)**
  Returns the string represented by i in the specified `base`—for example,
  `toString(5,2)` = 101 and `toString(5,10)` = 5.

- **static Integer valueOf(String s) throws NumberFormatException**
  Returns an `Integer` object with a value equal to the `int` contained in the string.

- **static Integer valueOf(String s, int base) throws NumberFormatException**
  Returns the value of the string in the specified base.

long Extends Number. `long` is a wrapper class designed to handle `long` values.

Fields

- **final static long MAX_VALUE**
  The maximum value for a `Long` is 9223372036854775807.

- **final static long MIN_VALUE**
  The minimum value for a `Long` is –9223372036854775808.

Methods

- **long(String s) throws NumberFormatException**
  Creates a `Long` object with an initial value of the `long` contained in the string.

- **long(long value)**
  Creates a new `long` with the specified initial value.

- **double doubleValue( )**
  Returns the `long` value as a `double`.

- **boolean equals(Object anotherObject)**
  Returns `true` if anotherObject is a `Long` with the same `long` value.

- **float floatValue( )**
  Returns the `long` value of the object as a `float`.

- **static Long getLong(String name)**
  Returns a system property represented by name.

- **static Long getLong(String name, long val)**
  Returns a system property represented by name. If unable to do so, returns a `Long` object with a value of val.

- **static Long getLong(String name, Long val)**
  Returns a system property represented by name. If unable to do so, returns val.

- **int hashCode( )**
  Returns the hashcode of the Long—its value casted to an int.

- **int intValue( )**
  Returns the long value as an int.

- **long longValue( )**
  Returns the long value of the object.

- **static long parseLong(String s) throws NumberFormatException**
  Returns the long value contained in the string.

- **static long parseLong(String s, int base) throws NumberFormatException**
  Returns a long with a value equal to the number in s. base specifies the base in which the number is written. Thus, if you want to parse a string containing a long in base 10, use a base value of 10.

- **static String toBinaryString(long num)**
  Returns a String representing num as an unsigned binary number.

- **static String toHexString(long num)**
  Returns a String representing num as an unsigned hexadecimal number.

- **static String toOctalString(long num)**
  Returns a String representing num as an unsigned octal number.

- **String toString( )**
  Returns the long value as a string.

- **static String toString(long val)**
  Converts the specified long to a string.

- **static String toString(long val, int base)**
  Returns a string containing the specified long stored in the specified base.

- **static Long valueOf(String s) throws NumberFormatException**
  Returns a Long object with a value determined by the number contained in the specified string.

- **static Long valueOf(String s, int base) throws NumberFormatException**
  Returns a Long containing the value of the string assuming that the string contains a number in the specified base.

Math. The Math class provides you with a wide variety of mathematical methods, as well as some handy constants, such as e and Pi.

Fields

- **final static double E**
  The constant e: 2.7182818284590452354.

- **final static double PI**
  The constant Pi: 3.14159265358979323846.

Methods

- **static double abs(double val)**
  Returns the absolute value of a `double`.

- **static float abs(float val)**
  Returns the absolute value of a `float`.

- **static long abs(long val)**
  Returns the absolute value of a `long`.

- **static int abs(int val)**
  Returns the absolute value of an `int`.

- **static double acos(double val)**
  Returns the inverse cosine of the specified number.

- **static double asin(double val)**
  Returns the inverse sin of the specified angle in radians.

- **static double atan(double val)**
  Returns the inverse tangent of the specified number.

- **static double atan2(double u, double v)**
  Returns the angle defined by the rectangular coordinates (`u`,`v`).

- **static double ceil(double val)**
  Returns the smallest integer greater than or equal to val. (This is the "Least-Integer Function" $\lceil val \rceil$.)

- **static double cos(double val)**
  Returns the cosine of the specified angle in radians.

- **static double exp(double x)**
  Returns $e^{\wedge X}$.

- **static double floor(double val)**
  Returns the greatest integer less than or equal to val. (This is the "Greatest-Integer Function" $\lfloor val \rfloor$.)

- **static double IEEEremainder(double v1, double v2)**
  Returns the remainder of the operation v1/v2.

- **static double log(double val) throws ArithmeticException**
  Returns the mathematical log of the specified value.

- **static double max(double v1, double v2)**
  Returns the maximum value: either v1 or v2.

- **static float max(float v1, float v2)**
  Returns the maximum value: either v1 or v2.

- **static long max(long v2, long v2)**
  Returns the maximum value: either v1 or v2.

- **static int max(int v1, int v2)**
  Returns the maximum value: either v1 or v2.

- **static double min(double v1, double v2)**
  Returns the minimum value: either v1 or v2.

- **static float min(float v1, float v2)**
  Returns the minimum value: either v1 or v2.

- **static long min(long v1, long v2)**
  Returns the minimum value: either v1 or v2.

- **static int min(int v1, int v2)**
  Returns the minimum value: either v1 or v2.

- **static double pow(double base, double exp) throws ArithmeticException**
  Returns the value of base^{exp}.

- **static synchronized double random( )**
  Returns a random number by using the `java.util.Random` class.

- **static double rint(double val)**
  Rounds val to the nearest integer, returning the value as a `double`. (e.g., `rint(5.3)` = 5.0).

- **static long round(double val)**
  Rounds the `double`, returning it as a `float`.

- **static int round(float val)**
  Rounds the specified number.

- **static double sin(double val)**
  Returns the sine of the specified angle in radians.

- **static double sqrt(double val) throws ArithmeticException**
  Returns the square root of the number.

- **static double tan(double val)**
  Returns the tangent of the specified angle in radians.

Abstract **Number.** The `Number` class serves as the basis for all wrapper classes designed to handle number data types, such as `Integer`, `Float`, and `Double`.

Although `int`, `double`, and `float` are data types in their own right, they are considered *primitive data types* because they are much more basic that the richer objects used in Java. Although these primitive types facilitate more efficient code, they are often not robust enough for certain circumstances, such as hashtables, where it is necessary to treat each item as a full Object. Furthermore, each of these Number-type classes provides you with a means of handing data in a class-dependent nature. This gives you a very simple means of obtaining primitive values from more complex objects, such as Strings.

Methods

- **Number( )**
  Creates a new Number.

- **abstract double doubleValue( )**
  Returns the Number's value as a double.

- **abstract float floatValue( )**
  Returns the Number's value as a float.

- **abstract int intValue( )**
  Returns the Number's value as an int.

- **abstract long longValue( )**
  Returns the Number's value as a long.

Object. The Object class is the basis for all classes in the Java programming language. Every class, even if you don't declare a superclass, will be derived from the Object class. Therefore, *all* methods in this class are accessible to all classes. However, this is not to say that you will ever have need to actually work with these methods.

Methods

- **Object( )**
  Creates a new Object.

- **protected Object clone( ) throws CloneNotSupportedException**
  Creates a copy of the Object.

- **boolean equals(Object anotherObject)**
  Returns true if the two Objects are equal.

- **protected void finalize( ) throws Throwable**
  This method will be called before the Object is collected by the Java environment. Empty by default, *any* class may override this method to add functionality. Throwing an exception from this method will halt garbage collection.

- **final Class getClass( )**
  Returns the class of the Object as a Class object.

- **int hashCode( )**
  Returns the hashcode of the Object. This value is dependent on the specific object.

- **final void notify( )**
  Notifies a thread (paused with wait()) that it may regain control.

III

Java

- **final void notifyAll( )**
  Notifies all threads (paused with `wait()`) that they may regain control.

- **String toString( )**
  Returns the class name and its *uniqufier:* a special integer tag used to distinguish separate instances of the same class.

- **final void wait( ) throws InterruptedException**
  Causes a thread to wait indefinitely until it is notified.

- **final void wait(long millisec) throws InterruptedException**
  Causes a thread to wait the specified number of milliseconds, or until notified.

- **final void wait(long millisec, int nanos) throws InterruptedException**
  Causes a thread to wait the specified number of milliseconds and nanoseconds, or until notified.

Abstract **Process.** The `Process` class provides a handle for managing operations begun by Java programs. Returned by the `exec()` methods in the `Runtime` class, the `Process` class is generally used to monitor—not to control—the ongoing operation.

 ▶▶ See the following section, "Runtime"

Methods

- **Process( )**
  Creates a new `Process`.

- **abstract void destroy( )**
  Destroys the sub-process.

- **abstract int exitValue( )**
  Returns the exit value of the `Process`. It throws an `IllegalThreadStateException` if the `Process` has not completed.

- **abstract InputStream getErrorStream( )**
  Returns the stream used by the `Process` for standard error output.

- **abstract InputStream getInputStream( )**
  Returns the stream used by the `Process` for standard input.

- **abstract OutputStream getOutputStream( )**
  Returns the stream used by the `Process` for standard output.

- **abstract int waitFor( ) throws InterruptedException**
  Waits until the `Process` is completed and returns its exit value.

Runtime. The `Runtime` class enables you to interface with the system on which your program is running, as well as the Java Virtual Machine.

The Runtime class enables you to perform tasks normally associated with the prompt, such as starting a file. The Runtime class is used to begin a game of Solitaire.

▶▶ See "*Abstract* Process," p. 530

Listing 14.13 Runtime **Example**

```
public class RuntimeExample  {
    public static void main(String argv[ ]) {
      Runtime r=java.lang.Runtime.getRuntime();
      try{
        r.exec("\\winnt\\system32\\sol.exe");
      }
      catch (Exception e) {
        {System.out.println(e.toString() );
      }
    }
  }
```

Methods

- **Process exec(String command) throws IOException**
  Executes the specified command.

- **Process exec(String cmdarray[ ]) throws IOException**
  Executes the commands found in the cmdarray.

- **Process exec(String cmdarray[ ], String envp[ ]) throws IOException**
  Executes the commands in the cmdarray using the environment parameters specified in the envp array. The parameters should be specified in the format parameter = value .

- **Process exec(String command, String envp[ ]) throws IOException**
  Executes the command using the environment parameters specified in the envp array. The parameters should be specified in the format, parameter = value .

- **void exit(int status)**
  Terminates all code and exists the Java Virtual Machine. status is the exit code for the entire operation.

- **long freeMemory( )**
  Returns the number of free bytes in memory.

III

Java

- **void gc( )**
  Calls the garbage collector. This method frees any objects in memory that are no longer in use—no references to the objects remain. Garbage collection is automatically done by the system during lulls in activity or as you run out of memory.

- **InputStream getLocalizedInputStream(InputStream in)**
  The purpose of this method is to return an InputStream that will translate input into UNICODE format. However, this method simply returns the in parameter.

- **OutputStream getLocalizedOutputStream(OutputStream out)**
  The purpose of this method is to return an OutputStream that will translate to UNICODE format. However, this method simply returns the out parameter.

- **static Runtime getRuntime( )**
  Returns the current Runtime object. This method must be used to obtain a Runtime object inasmuch as the constructor method for this class is not public.

- **synchronized void load(String filename)**
  Loads a dynamic library.

- **synchronized void loadLibrary(String libname)**
  Loads a dynamic library.

- **void runFinalization( )**
  Runs the finalize() method in any object being collected. The finalize() methods are automatically called during garbage collection.

- **long totalMemory( )**
  Returns the total number of bytes in memory.

- **void traceInstructions(boolean on)**
  If on is true, instructions will be traced.

- **void traceMethodCalls(boolean on)**
  If on is true, method calls will be traced.

Abstract **SecurityManager.** The SecurityManager provides you with a means of instituting and configuring many security inspections that monitor the power of your programs. These checks are necessary when you consider that Java applets have the ability to run on both intranets and the Internet—networks where security and privacy are important issues.

To create your own security restrictions, it is necessary to subclass this class and define those methods that are important to your program. You will note that most methods in this class that check the validity of an action do not return any data types. Instead, they throw SecurityExceptions when the action is not allowed.

Field

- **protected boolean inCheck**
  True only if the SecurityManager is in the middle of a security check.

Methods

- **protected SecurityManager( )**
  Creates a new SecurityManager.

- **void checkAccept(String host, int port)**
  Determines the success of an attempted connection to the specified host at the given port.

- **void checkAccess(ThreadGroup g)**
  Checks if the current Thread can modify the specified ThreadGroup.

- **void checkAccess(Thread t)**
  Checks to see if the specified Thread can modify the current ThreadGroup, throwing an exception if it cannot.

- **void checkConnect(String host, int port)**
  Checks to see if a socket has connected to the specified port on the specified host, throwing an exception if it has not.

- **void checkConnect(String host, int port, Object executionContext)**
  Checks to see if the current executing code and the specified executionContext can connect to the specified port on the specified host, throwing an exception if it cannot.

- **void checkCreateClassLoader( )**
  Checks to see if the ClassLoader has been created, throwing an exception if not.

- **void checkDelete(String file)**
  Checks to see if the specified file can be deleted, throwing an exception if it cannot.

- **void checkExec(String cmd)**
  Checks to see if the specified command will be run by trusted code, throwing an exception if not.

- **void checkExit(int status)**
  Checks to see if the runtime system has exited with the specified exit code, throwing an exception if not.

- **void checkLink(String lib)**
  Checks to see if the library exists, throwing an exception if not.

- **void checkListen(int port)**
  Checks to see if the server socket on the specified port is listening, throwing an exception if not.

- **void checkPackageAccess(String packageName)**
  Checks to see if the applet can access the specified package, throwing an exception if not.

- **void checkPackageDefinition(String packageName)**
  Checks to see if the applet can create classes in the specified package, throwing an exception if not.

- **void checkPropertiesAccess( )**
  Checks to see if the program has access to the set of system properties, throwing an exception if not.

- **void checkPropertyAccess(String property)**
  Checks to see if the applet can access the specified system property, throwing an exception if not.

- **void checkPropertyAccess(String property, String default)**
  Checks to see if the applet can access the specified system property, throwing an exception if not. default is used when subclassing this class to specify a value that should be used if the value of property is unattainable.

- **void checkRead(String file)**
  Checks to see if the applet can read from the specified file, throwing an exception if not.

- **void checkRead(FileDescriptor fd)**
  Checks to see if the applet can read from the specified file, throwing an exception if not.

- **void checkRead(String file, Object executionContext)**
  Checks to see if the applet and the specified executionContext can read from the specified file, throwing an exception if not.

- **void checkSetFactory( )**
  Checks to see if the applet can set an object factory, throwing an exception if not.

- **boolean checkTopLevelWindow(Object window)**
  Checks to see if the applet can create trusted top-level windows. A return value of false means that a warning message should be displayed along with the window.

- **void checkWrite(String file)**
  Checks to see if the applet can write to the specified file, throwing an exception if not.

- **void checkWrite(FileDescriptor fd)**
  Checks to see if the applet can write to the specified file, throwing an exception if not.

- **protected int classDepth(String name)**
  Returns the first position in the stack frame of the specified class name.

- **protected int classLoaderDepth( )**
  Returns the first position in the stack frame of the specified class loader.

- **protected ClassLoader currentClassLoader( )**
  Returns the current class loader on top of the execution stack.

- **protected Class[ ] getClassContext( )**
  Returns the context of the class.

- **boolean getInCheck( )**
  Returns true if a security check is underway.

- **Object getSecurityContext( )**
  Returns an Object containing information regarding the current context that may be used for later security checks. Currently, this method returns a null string.

- **protected boolean inClass(String className)**
  Returns true if the specified className can be found in the execution stack.

- **protected boolean inClassLoader( )**
  Returns true if the current ClassLoader is not null.

String. The String class provides the basic nature and functionality for a string. Because the value of a String cannot change once created, this class is therefore primarily used for parsing, handling, and obtaining string values—not creating them. Although there are some methods that enable you to somewhat modify and add to the value of the string, these methods do not modify the String itself, but rather return a new String with the desired value.

Methods

- **String( )**
  Creates a new String.

- **String(StringBuffer buffer)**
  Creates a new String, copying the contents of the buffer.

- **String(byte ascii[ ], int hibyte)**
  Creates a new String based on the specified array. hibyte will be the top byte of each character.

- **String(byte ascii[ ], int hibyte, int offset, int count)**
  Creates a new String based on the specified array. offset specifies the first element to be added to the String; count is the number of bytes to be added; and hibyte will be the top byte of each character.

- **String(char value[ ], int offset, int count)**
  Creates a new String based on the specified array. offset specifies the first element to be added to the String, and count is the number of bytes to be added.

- **String(char value[ ])**
  Creates a new String based on the specified array.

- **String(String value)**
  Creates a new String with the specified value.

- **char charAt(int index)**
  Returns the character at the specified index.

- **int compareTo(String anotherString)**
  Returns an integer indicating whether the String is less than, equal to, or greater than another String. If the return value is less than 0, the String is less than anotherString. If it is zero, the String is equal to anotherString. If the return value is greater than zero, the String is greater than anotherString.

- **String concat(String str)**
  Returns the combination of this String and str.

- **boolean equals(Object anotherObject)**
  Returns true if anotherObject is a String with the same value.

- **boolean equalsIgnoreCase(String anotherString)**
  Compares the String with anotherString without case sensitivity. It returns true if they are equal.

- **void getBytes(int srcBegin, int srcEnd, byte dst[ ], int dstBegin)**
  Copies characters between srcBegin and srcEnd in the String to the specified array beginning at dstBegin.

- **void getChars(int srcBegin, int srcEnd, char dst[ ], int dstBegin)**
  Copies characters between srcBegin and srcEnd in the String to the specified array beginning at dstBegin.

- **int length( )**
  Returns the length of the String.

- **static String copyValueOf(char data[ ])**
  Returns a String equal to the specified characters.

- **static String copyValueOf(char data[ ], int offset, int count)**
  Returns a String equal to the characters in data[] between offset and offset + count .

- **boolean endsWith(String suffix)**
  Returns true if the String ends with the specified suffix.

- **int hashCode( )**
  Returns the hashcode of the String—a value based on some (but not necessarily all) characters of the String.

- **int indexOf(String str)**
  Returns the first index of str within this String.

- **int indexOf(String str, int fromIndex)**
  Returns the first index of str within this String after fromIndex.

- **int indexOf(int ch)**
  Returns the first index of the ch in this String.

- **int indexOf(int ch, int fromIndex)**
  Returns the first index of the ch in this String following fromIndex.

- **String intern( )**
  Returns a String equal to this String. The new String will be taken from a Hashtable pool based on the value of the String.

- **int lastIndexOf(String str)**
  Returns the last index of str in this String.

- **int lastIndexOf(String str, int fromIndex)**
  Returns the last index of str in this String that is before fromIndex.

- **int lastIndexOf(int ch)**
  Returns the last index of ch in this String.

- **int lastIndexOf(int ch, int fromIndex)**
  Returns the last index of ch in this String that is before fromIndex.

- **boolean regionMatches(boolean ignoreCase, int toffset, String another, int offset, int len)**
  Compares a portion of this string with an equally sized portion of another. If ignoreCase is true, the case of the characters will be ignored. len is the number of characters to be compared; toffset is the first character to be checked in this String; and offset is the first character to be checked in another.

- **boolean regionMatches(int toffset, String other, int offset, int len)**
  Compares a portion of this string with an equally sized portion of another with case sensitivity. len is the number of characters to be compared; toffset is the first character to be checked in this String; and offset is the first character to be checked in another.

- **String replace(char oldChar, char newChar)**
  Replaces all instances of oldChar in the String with newChar.

- **boolean startsWith(String prefix)**
  Returns true if the String begins with the specified prefix string.

- **boolean startsWith(String prefix, int toffset)**
  Returns true if the substring following toffset is equal to prefix.

- **String substring(int beginIndex, int endIndex)**
  Returns the substring of this String from beginIndex to endIndex.

- **String substring(int beginIndex)**
  Returns the portion of the String extending from beginIndex to the end.

- **char[ ] toCharArray( )**
  Returns the String as an array of characters.

- **String toLowerCase( )**
  Returns a copy of this String in which all characters are in lowercase.

- **String toString( )**
  Returns the String.

- **String toUpperCase( )**
  Returns a copy of this String in which all characters are in uppercase.

- **String trim( )**
  Returns a copy of this String in which any leading or trailing whitespace is removed.

- **static String valueOf(double d)**
  Returns a String containing the double.

- **static String valueOf(float f)**
  Returns a String containing the float.

- **static String valueOf(long l)**
  Returns a String containing the long.

- **static String valueOf(int i)**
  Returns a String containing the int.

- **static String valueOf(char c)**
  Returns a String containing the char.

- **static String valueOf(boolean b)**
  Returns a String containing the boolean.

- **static String valueOf(char data[ ], int offset, int num)**
  Returns a String containing num characters from data[] array beginning at offset.

- **static String valueOf(char data[ ])**
  Returns a String containing characters in the array.

- **static String valueOf(Object obj)**
  Returns a String containing string representation of the Object. This value is obtained using obj.toString().

StringBuffer. A StringBuffer is a dynamic string class that enables you to modify and add to string values. Extremely flexible, this class is used in creating string values—especially those obtained from a separate source, such as a socket connection or the applet tag parameters, as shown in Listings 14.14 and 14.15.

Listing 14.14 StringBuffer **Example Using Applet Tag Parameters—HTML**

```
<HEAD>
<TITLE>StringBuffer Example</TITLE>

<BODY>

<applet code="sbufe.class" width=300 height=300 >
<param name=linenum0 value="This is the">
<param name=linenum1 value="message I'm">
<param name=linenum2 value="trying to show.">
</applet>
</BODY>
```

Listing 14.15 `StringBuffer` **Example**

```java
import java.applet.Applet;
import java.awt.Graphics;

public class StringBufferExample extends Applet {
    String message;

    /* This method parses the applet parameters, and returns
       them in one string separated by spaces */
    public  void init() {
        StringBuffer mes;
        String val;
        int i = 0;

        mes = new StringBuffer();

        do {
            String paramName = "linenum" + i++;
            val = getParameter(paramName);
            if (val != null) {       // continues until end
                mes.append(val);         // adds the message
                mes.append(' ');         // adds the space
            }
        } while (val != null);
        message = mes.toString();  // saves the message
                                   // as a String
    }

    public void paint(Graphics g) {
        g.drawString(message,10,10);
    }
}
```

Methods

- **StringBuffer(String str)**

  Creates a `StringBuffer` based on the specified `String`.

- **StringBuffer(int length)**

  Creates a `StringBuffer` with the specified length.

- **StringBuffer( )**

  Creates a `StringBuffer` initially 16 characters in size.

- **int capacity( )**

  Returns the number of characters that can be added to the `StringBuffer` without requiring additional memory.

- **synchronized char charAt(int index)**

  Returns the character at the specified index.

- **synchronized void ensureCapacity(int minimumCapacity)**

  Increases the size of the `StringBuffer` if necessary to make sure that at least `minimumCapacity` characters can be added.

III

Java

- **synchronized void getChars(int srcBegin, int srcEnd, char dst[ ], int dstBegin)**
Copies all characters between the srcBegin and srcEnd indexes. It places them in the dest array, beginning at dstBegin.

- **synchronized void setLength(int newLength)**
Sets the length of the StringBuffer.

> **Caution**
>
> If the length is reduced, data may be lost.

- **StringBuffer append(double d)**
Appends a double to the StringBuffer, increasing its size if necessary.

- **StringBuffer append(float f)**
Appends a float to the StringBuffer, increasing its size if necessary.

- **StringBuffer append(long l)**
Appends a long to the StringBuffer, increasing its size if necessary.

- **StringBuffer append(int i)**
Appends an int to the StringBuffer, increasing its size if necessary.

- **synchronized StringBuffer append(char c)**
Appends a char to the StringBuffer, increasing its size if necessary.

- **StringBuffer append(boolean b)**
Appends a boolean to the StringBuffer, increasing its size if necessary.

- **synchronized StringBuffer append(char str[ ], int offset, int len)**
Appends a series of characters to the StringBuffer, increasing its size if necessary.

- **synchronized StringBuffer append(char str[ ])**
Appends an array of characters to the StringBuffer, increasing its size if necessary.

- **synchronized StringBuffer append(String str)**
Appends a String to the StringBuffer, increasing its size if necessary.

- **synchronized StringBuffer append(Object obj)**
Appends an Object to the StringBuffer, increasing its size if necessary. The actual string appended will be equal to the value returned by the String.valueOf(obj) method.

- **StringBuffer insert(int offset, double d)**
Inserts a double into the StringBuffer at the specified offset, increasing the size of the buffer if necessary.

- **StringBuffer insert(int offset, float f)**
Inserts a float into the StringBuffer at the specified offset, increasing the size of the buffer if necessary.

- **StringBuffer insert(int offset, long l)**
  Inserts a `long` into the `StringBuffer` at the specified `offset`, increasing the size of the buffer if necessary.

- **StringBuffer insert(int offset, int i)**
  Inserts an `int` into the `StringBuffer` at the specified `offset`, increasing the size of the buffer if necessary.

- **synchronized StringBuffer insert(int offset, char c)**
  Inserts a character into the `StringBuffer` at the specified `offset`, increasing the size of the buffer if necessary.

- **StringBuffer insert(int offset, boolean b)**
  Inserts a `boolean` into the `StringBuffer` at the specified `offset`, increasing the size of the buffer if necessary.

- **synchronized StringBuffer insert(int offset, char str[ ])**
  Inserts an array of characters into the `StringBuffer` at the specified `offset`, increasing the size of the buffer if necessary.

- **synchronized StringBuffer insert(int offset, Object obj)**
  Inserts a `double` into the `StringBuffer` at the specified `offset`, increasing the size of the buffer if necessary. The string added will be equal to the value returned by the `String.valueOf(obj)` method.

- **synchronized StringBuffer insert(int offset, String str)**
  Inserts a `String` into the `StringBuffer` at the specified `offset`, increasing the size of the buffer if necessary.

- **int length( )**
  Returns the length of the `StringBuffer`.

- **synchronized void setCharAt(int index, char ch)**
  Sets the character at the specified `index` to `ch`.

- **String toString( )**
  Returns the contents of the `StringBuffer` as a `String`.

System. Java programs, especially applets, are handled by the Java Virtual Machine in a manner that hides a great deal of functionality from you, the programmer. This is primarily the result of Java's aim to be completely platform-independent. However, in conjunction with the `Runtime` class, the `System` class enables you gain control of some system-related functions—such as garbage collection—all in a system-independent manner.

To use the `System` class, it is not necessary (and is in fact impossible) to create a `System` object. However, because all methods in the class are static, you may use the methods shown in Listing 14.16.

III

Java

Listing 14.16 System **Example**

```
public class SystemExample  {

   public static void main(String argv[ ]) {

      System.out.print("This is an example of the standard");
      System.out.println("output stream.");

      String s = System.getProperty("java.version");
      System.out.println("I am using Java " + s + ".");
   }
}
```

Fields

- **static PrintStream err**
  The standard stream for printing error messages. This is usually the same as out.

- **static InputStream in**
  The standard input stream.

- **static PrintStream out**
  The standard output stream. This is generally the prompt, or Java Console in Netscape.

Methods

- **static void arraycopy(Object src, int src_position, Object dst, int dst_posistion, int length)**
  Copies length elements beginning at src[src_position] and places them in dst[dst_position].

- **static SecurityManager getSecurityManager( )**
  Returns the security manager object for this context. This object can be handled via the SecurityManager interface.

- **static void setSecurityManager(SecurityManager s)**
  Sets the security manager. This method can be invoked only once.

- **static void exit(int status)**
  Causes the Virtual Machine to exit using the specified exit code.

- **static void gc( )**
  Begins the garbage collection process. This does not cause immediate garbage collection.

- **static String getenv(String name)**
  This method is no longer supported.

- **static Properties getProperties( )**

  Returns a `Properties` object containing the properties of the system.

- **static String getProperty(String propName, String def)**

  Returns the property specified by `propName`. If the property is undefined, the `String` `def` will be returned instead.

- **static String getProperty(String key)**

  Returns the property specified by `propName`. If the property is not found, a null string will be returned instead.

- **static void load(String filename)**

  Loads the specified library. `filename` represents the complete path and file name of the library.

- **static void loadLibrary(String libname)**

  Loads the specified library. `libname` represents the library name.

- **static void runFinalization( )**

  Runs the `finalize()` methods in any `Objects` pending garbage collection. The `finalize()` methods are automatically called before the `Objects` are collected. This method forces them all to be called at once.

- **static void setProperties(Properties props)**

  Sets the system properties to the specified set of `Properties`.

Thread Implements Runnable. Threads are one of the most important topics in the Java language. Threads are individual processes that can run at the same time. By creating multiple threads, you are thus able to perform several tasks at once.

Threads are particularly useful in programs that deal with multiple sources of input. For example, you can create an applet that will accept input from both the user and a separate input stream, such as a networked socket. To do so, create the applet to deal with user input as you would normally, and then create a separate thread that reads and parses information from the stream.

Listing 14.17 demonstrates the use of a simple threaded class: `Counter`. While the `threadex` class is waiting for user input, the `Counter` class is counting in the background. Therefore, when the user presses the enter key, the value returned by the `getCount()` method has grown tremendously.

In particular, note the process used to create and begin the `Counter` class. To start execution of a thread, you must invoke the `start()` method. Furthermore, only the `run()` method of the threaded class has the ability to run concurrently.

▶▶ See "Runnable," p. 550

Listing 14.17   Thread Example

```java
public class ThreadEx  {

    public static void main(String argv[ ]) {
      Counter c = new Counter();
      c.start();                        // starts the counter

      for (int i = 1; i <= 5; i++) {
        try {
          System.in.read();
        }
        catch (Exception e) {
            System.out.println( e.toString() );
        }
        System.out.println(c.getCount() );
      }  // end for loop

      c.stop();
      System.exit(1);
    }
}


class Counter extends Thread {
    private int count;

    public void run() {
      count = 0;
      while(true)              // creates a continual loop
        count++;
    }
    public int getCount() {
      return count;
    }
}
```

Fields

- **final static int MAX_PRIORITY**

  The maximum priority of the Thread, which affects the amount of time that it receives to run.

- **final static int MIN_PRIORITY**

  The minimum priority of the Thread, which affects the amount of time that it receives to run.

- **final static int NORM_PRIORITY**

  The normal priority of the Thread, which affects the amount of time that it receives to run.

Methods

- **Thread( )**

  Creates a new Thread.

- **Thread(Runnable target)**
  Creates a new Thread that will use the run() method of the specified (target) class. This class must implement the Runnable interface.

- **Thread(Runnable target, String name)**
  Creates a new Thread with the specified name that will use the run() method of the specified (target) class. This class must implement the Runnable interface.

- **Thread(ThreadGroup group, Runnable target)**
  Creates a new Thread that will use the run() method of the specified (target) class. This class must implement the Runnable interface. The new Thread will be placed in the specified thread group.

- **Thread(ThreadGroup group, Runnable target, String name)**
  Creates a new Thread with the specified name that will use the run() method of the specified (target) class. This class must implement the Runnable interface. The new Thread will be placed in the specified thread group.

- **Thread(ThreadGroup group, String name)**
  Creates a new Thread with the specified name and places it in the specified thread group.

- **Thread(String name)**
  Creates a new Thread with the specified name.

- **static int activeCount( )**
  Returns the number of active threads in the current ThreadGroup.

- **void checkAccess( )**
  Returns true if you are able to modify the Thread. Based on a value returned from the SecurityManager.

- **int countStackFrames( )**
  Returns the number of stack frames in the thread.

- **static Thread currentThread( )**
  Returns a reference to the executing Thread object.

- **void destroy( )**
  Destroys the Thread without performing any cleanup.

- **static void dumpStack( )**
- **static int enumerate(Thread tarray[ ])**
  Places in the array every active Thread in the ThreadGroup of this Thread. It returns the number of Threads placed in the array.

- **final String getName( )**
  Returns the name of this thread.

- **final int getPriority( )**
  Returns the priority of this Thread.

- **final ThreadGroup getThreadGroup( )**
  Returns the `ThreadGroup` to which this `Thread` belongs.

- **void interrupt( )**
  Interrupts the thread. This method must be overridden, or it will return a `NoSuchMethodException`.

- **static boolean interrupted( )**
  Used to determine if this `Thread` has been interrupted. This method must be overridden, or it will return a `NoSuchMethodException`.

- **boolean isInterrupted( )**
  Used to determine if another `Thread` has been interrupted. This method must be overridden, or it will return a `NoSuchMethodException`.

- **final boolean isDaemon( )**
  Returns `true` if the `Thread` is a daemon.

- **final void join( ) throws InterruptedException**
  Waits an unlimited amount of time for the thread to die.

- **final synchronized void join(long millis, int nanos) throws InterruptedException**
  Waits the specified amount of time for the thread to die. It uses `java.lang.wait()`.

- **final synchronized void join(long millis) throws InterruptedException**
  Waits the specified amount of time for the thread to die. It uses `java.lang.wait()`.

- **final void resume( )**
  Used to restart a thread after it has been suspended.

- **void run( )**
  The body of execution for the thread. Although the `run()` method can use other methods, it is the only method that can run concurrently with other operations. Any method in the thread intended to run while another operation is occurring must be called from the `run()` method.

- **final void setDaemon(boolean on)**
  If `on` is `true`, the `Thread` is "daemonized," allowing it to run in the background independently from Java operations.

- **final void setName(String name)**
  Sets the name of the `Thread`.

- **final void setPriority(int newPriority)**
  Sets the priority of the `Thread`.

- **static void sleep(long millis, int nanos) throws InterruptedException**
  Causes the `Thread` to pause for the specified amount of time.

- **static void sleep(long millis) throws InterruptedException**
  Causes the `Thread` to pause for the specified amount of time.

- **synchronized void start( )**
  Causes the `run()` method to begin.

- **final synchronized void stop(Throwable obj)**
  Stops the thread, specifying a `Throwable` object as a reason for termination.

- **final void stop( )**
  Calls the `stop(Throwable)` method with an instance of `ThreadDeath` as the argument.

- **final void suspend( )**
  Suspends the current thread. To restart it, use the `resume()` method.

- **static void yield( )**
  Yields time to any waiting `Threads`.

- **String toString( )**
  Returns a string containing the `Thread`'s name, priority, and `ThreadGroup`.

ThreadGroup. Because threads are somewhat independent processes, it is often advantageous to place some constraints on them in order to manage them better. The `ThreadGroup` class enables you to create collections of `Threads`. Furthermore, it enables you to create a hierarchy of `ThreadGroups` in which a `Thread` can access all `Threads` in the same group, but no `Threads` above it in the current hierarchy.

Methods

- **ThreadGroup(String name)**
  Creates a `ThreadGroup` with the specified name. The current `ThreadGroup` will become the parent of the new `ThreadGroup`.

- **ThreadGroup(ThreadGroup parent, String name)**
  Creates a new `ThreadGroup` with the specified name and parent.

- **synchronized int activeCount( )**
  Returns the number of active threads in this group.

- **synchronized int activeGroupCount( )**
  Returns the number of active thread groups in this group.

- **final void checkAccess( )**
  Sees if the current thread can modify this `ThreadGroup`. Uses the `checkAccess()` method in the current `SecurityManager`.

- **final synchronized void destroy( )**
  Destroys the `ThreadGroup`, but does not harm the individual threads.

- **int enumerate(Thread list[ ])**
  Places a reference to every active `Thread` in this group in the `list[]` array. It returns the number of elements in the array.

- **int enumerate(Thread list[ ], boolean recurse)**
  Places a reference to every active `Thread` in this group in the `list[]` array. If `recurse` is `true`, this method also transverses and adds all `Threads` in all `ThreadGroups` that are in this group. It returns the number of elements in the array.

- **int enumerate(ThreadGroup list[ ])**
  Places a reference to every active `ThreadGroup` in this group in the `list[]` array. It returns the number of elements in the array.

- **int enumerate(ThreadGroup list[ ], boolean recurse)**
  Places a reference to every active `Thread` in this group in the `list[]` array. If `recurse` is `true`, this method also transverses and adds the `ThreadsGroups` in all `ThreadGroups` that are in this group. It returns the number of elements in the array.

- **final int getMaxPriority( )**
  Returns the maximum priority of all the methods in this group.

- **final String getName( )**
  Returns the name of the group.

- **final ThreadGroup getParent( )**
  Returns the parent of the group.

- **final boolean isDaemon( )**
  Returns the value of the `daemon` flag in this `ThreadGroup`. All `Threads` created by a `Thread` in this `ThreadGroup` will inherit the same flag.

- **synchronized void list( )**
  Prints all `Threads` and `ThreadGroups` in this `ThreadGroup` to `System.out`.

- **final boolean parentOf(ThreadGroup anotherGroup)**
  Returns `true` if this `ThreadGroup` is the parent of, or equal to, `anotherGroup`.

- **final synchronized void resume( )**
  Invokes the `resume()` method in all `Threads` belonging to this `ThreadGroup` and any of its child `ThreadGroups`.

- **final void setDaemon(boolean daemon)**
  Sets the `daemon` flag for this `ThreadGroup`.

- **final synchronized void setMaxPriority(int level)**
  Sets the maximum priority level for any new `Threads` created in this group.

- **final synchronized void stop( )**
  Invokes the `stop()` method in all `Threads` belonging to this `ThreadGroup` and any of its child `ThreadGroups`.

- **final synchronized void suspend( )**
  Invokes the `suspend()` method in all `Threads` belonging to this `ThreadGroup` and any of its child `ThreadGroups`.

- **String toString( )**
  Returns a string containing the name of this group and its maximum priority level.

- **void uncaughtException(Thread t, Throwable e)**
  Called by the system to handle uncaught exceptions.

Throwable. A `Throwable` object can be thrown by a method. The `Throwable` class defines a common set of behaviors for all objects that are thrown from methods. All exceptions and errors are derived from the `Throwable` class.

▶▶ See "Exceptions," p. 579
▶▶ See "Errors," p. 581

Methods
- **Throwable( )**
  Creates a new `Throwable` object.

- **Throwable(String message)**
  Creates a new `Throwable` object with the specified error message.

- **Throwable fillInStackTrace( )**
  Fills the stack trace for this `Throwable` object.

- **String getMessage( )**
  Returns the `detailmessage` message of the object. This can only be set in the constructor method.

- **void printStackTrace( )**
  Prints the stack trace to the standard error output stream (`System.err`). This is the error message that is displayed by the browser when you fail to catch an exception. It is useful in finding the source of your errors, and looks something like the following:

  ```
  java.lang.ArithmeticException: / by zero
          at appletname.init(appletname.java:6)
          at sun.applet.AppletPanel.run(AppletPanel.java:243)
          at java.lang.Thread.run(Thread.java:289)
  ```

- **void printStackTrace(PrintStream s)**
  Prints the stack trace to the specified `PrintStream`.

- **String toString( )**
  Returns a string, including the name of the `Throwable` object and its error message (if any).

Interfaces

Cloneable. Although this interface consists of no methods, it nevertheless provides you with a lot of flexibility. It serves as a flag to the `Object` class. If a class used implements the `Cloneable` interface, you can create a copy of such an object.

III

Java

Runnable. The Runnable interface is a chief example of the power of interfaces. By implementing the Runnable interface, you can create a class—most often an applet—that can also serve as a thread.

In Listing 14.18 and Listing 14.19, a simple applet class is created that serves as a message scroller. Using the status bar at the bottom of the browser screen, you are able to scroll through a series of messages that have been obtained from the applet tag parameters.

 ▶▶ See "Thread Implements Runnable," p. 543

Listing 14.18 Runnable **Example—HTML**

```
<HTML>
<HEAD>


<TITLE>Power Computers Inc. Homepage</TITLE>
</HEAD>


<center>
<h2>Power Computers Inc.<br>
How Computers Should be Built</h2>

<hr width=45%>

<a href="\products.html">Our Products</a><P>
<a href="\stocks.html">Investment Information</a><P>
<a href="\operators.html">Consumer Support</a><P>
</center>

<applet code="runne.class" width=0 height=0 >
<param name=linenum0 value="This is the message.">
<param name=linenum1 value="It keeps going,">
<param name=linenum2 value="and going...">
<param name=linenum3 value="...and going.">
</applet>
<hr width=45%>
</BODY>
</HTML>
```

Listing 14.19 Runnable **Example—Java Code**

```
import java.applet.Applet;

public class RunnableEx extends Applet implements Runnable
{
    Thread display;
    int pos, max_mes;
    String message[ ];

    /* This method obtains the applet parameters and stores
       them in message[ ].  It also sets the max_mes value */
```

```java
  public void init() {
    String val;
    int i = 0;

    message = new String[30];
                            // can accept up to 30 messages
    do {
      String paramName = "linenum" + i;
      val = getParameter(paramName);
      if (val != null) {
        message[i] = val;
       i++;
      }
    } while (val != null);

    max_mes = i-1;     /* we don't want to display the null
            message that caused the do loop to terminate */
    pos = 0;

    for (int j = 0; j <= max_mes; j++)
    System.out.println(j+message[j]);
  }

  /* This method creates and begins the thread. */
  public void start() {
    if (display == null)
      display = new Thread(this);
      display.start();
  }

  public void stop() {
    if (display != null) {
      display.stop();
      display = null;
    }
  }

  public void run() {
/* We don't want the scroller to receive too
  much attention. */
  Thread.currentThread().setPriority(Thread.MIN_PRIORITY);

  while (display != null) {
    getAppletContext().showStatus( message[pos++]);
    if (pos > max_mes)
      pos = 0;

      try {
        Thread.sleep(1000);     // pauses
      }
      catch (Exception e) {
        System.out.println( e.toString() );
      }  // end catch
    }  // end while
  }  // end method
}  // end class
```

For the sake of simplicity, an array of Strings is used to store the lines of text. To create a more efficient and flexible model, it would be advisable to use a more adaptive construct, such as a Vector.

Method

- **abstract void run( )**

java.net

Because Java is a network-based language, this comparatively small package is very useful. Most importantly, it provides you with the capability to communicate with other sources of information by creating or connecting to sockets or making use of URLs and Internet addresses.

Classes

***Abstract* ContentHandler.** This class is used to return a specific type of Object from an URL. It is called by the ContentHandlerFactory when an appropriate object is found in an URL.

Methods

- **ContentHandler( )**
  Creates a new ContentHandler object.

- **abstract Object getContent(URLConnection contentSource) throws IOException**
  Assuming that the contentSource contains a particular MIME type, this method parses the information from the contentSource and returns the particular Object.

DatagramPacket. A DatagramPacket is a bundle of information that can be transmitted across a networking stream. Such an object encapsulates a lot of information about the bundle, including the information contained, its length, and the host from which it was sent.

The following are private fields within the class:

```
private byte[ ] buf;
private int length;
private InetAddress address;
private int port;
```

These fields cannot be accessed explicitly in your code; however, it is advantageous to know what a DatagramPacket does and does not contain.

▶▶ See "DatagramSocket," p. 553

Methods

- **DatagramPacket(byte buf[ ], int length)**

  Creates a DatagramPacket that will receive information. The data of the packet will be stored in the buf[] array. length specifies the number of bytes to be received. The address will be set to null and the port to –1.

- **DatagramPacket(byte buf[ ], int length, InetAddress destAddr, int destPort)**

  Creates a DatagramPacket to send information. The information packet will consist of the first length bytes of the buf[] array. destAddr and destPort specify the recipient of the packet.

- **InetAddress getAddress( )**

  Returns address field: the host to which the information will be sent or the host from which the information was received.

- **byte[ ] getData( )**

  Returns information contained in the packet: either the information that has been received or that will be sent.

- **int getLength( )**

  Returns the length field set in the constructor method.

- **int getPort( )**

  Returns the port field to which the packet will be sent or from which the packet was received.

DatagramSocket. A DatagramSocket is a socket that is used in transmitting a DatagramPacket. A DatagramSocket is different from a standard Socket in that it implements no means of error checking. It does not ensure that all packets are sent or received in their entirety. Therefore, it is referred to as *unreliable*.

▶▶ See "DatagramPacket," p. 552

Methods

- **DatagramSocket(int port) throws SocketException**

  Creates a DatagramSocket to listen to a given port.

- **DatagramSocket( ) throws SocketException**

  Creates a DatagramSocket whose port number will be assigned by the system.

- **protected synchronized void finalize( )**

  Used to perform cleanup. As is, this method closes the socket.

- **int getLocalPort( )**

  Returns the port to which the socket is bound on the system.

III

Java

- **synchronized void receive(DatagramPacket p) throws IOException**
  Reads a `DatagramPacket` from the stream, waiting until one is available.

- **void send(DatagramPacket p) throws IOException**
  Sends a `DatagramPacket` across the stream.

Final **InetAddress.** An `InetAddress` is a convenient manner of handling Internet addresses. It can be used to store both raw IP addresses, as well as more friendly host names.

Methods

- **static synchronized InetAddress[ ] getAllByName(String hostName) throws UnknownHostException**
  Returns all addresses for the specified `hostName`

- **static InetAddress getLocalHost( ) throws UnknownHostException**
  Returns an `InetAddress` object representing the local host.

- **boolean equals(Object anotherObject)**
  Returns `true` if `anotherObject` is an `InetAddress` with the same address as this `InetAddress`.

- **byte[ ] getAddress( )**
  Returns the raw IP address of this `InetAddress`. The returned array will consist of four bytes.

- **static synchronized InetAddress getByName(String hostName) throws UnknownHostExction**
  Returns a single address for the specified `hostName`.

- **String getHostName( )**
  Returns the host name of this `InetAddress`.

- **int hashCode( )**
  Returns the `hashcode` value of this `InetAddress`: the IP address.

- **String toString( )**
  Returns a string containing the host name and the IP address of this `InetAddress`.

ServerSocket. `ServerSocket` creates a server-side socket to be used in communications. By default, it is created based on the `PlainSocket SocketImpl`, which performs no security checks. However, you can specify the `socketImpl` for the `ServerSocket` to enhance security restrictions.

Methods

- **ServerSocket(int port) throws IOException**
  Creates a new socket on the specified `port` using the current `SocketImplFactory`.

- **ServerSocket(int port, int count) throws IOException**
  Creates a new socket on the specified `port` using the current `SocketImplFactory`. `count` specifies the amount of time that the socket will wait for a connection.

- **Socket accept( ) throws IOException**
  Waits for a request and then properly handles a request for a connection. It returns the `Socket` that contains the actual connection.

- **void close( ) throws IOException**
  Closes the socket connection.

- **InetAddress getInetAddress( )**
  Returns the `InetAddress` to which the socket is connected.

- **int getLocalPort( )**
  Returns the port number to which the socket is listening.

- **String toString( )**
  Returns a string containing the address and port to which the socket is bound, as well as the local port number.

- **static synchronized void setSocketFactory(SocketImplFactory fac) throws IOException**
  Sets the `SocketImplFactory` for this `ServerSocket` object. All future sockets that are created with this `ServerSocket` object will employ the specified `SocketImplFactory`. This method can be used only once on a `ServerSocket` object.

Socket. `Socket` creates a client-side socket to be used in communications. By default, it is based on the `PlainSocket SocketImpl`, which performs no security checks. However, you can specify the `socketImpl` for the `ServerSocket` to enhance security.

When using a `Socket`, you must consider *whom* you will be speaking to. In general, you will communicate with a socket server residing on a specific port. In such a case, will you be writing the server? What protocol will be used? Will the host name and port be fixed?

Furthermore, you must remember to use the `getInputStream()` and `getOutputStream()` methods to communicate with the socket, inasmuch as these streams are not accessible outside of the sun packages.

The code in Listing 14.20 lays the foundation for a standard socket communication. The `DataInputStream` in and the `OutputStream` out will enable you to freely communicate over the socket if the connection has been successful.

Listing 14.20 Socket **Example**

```
import java.net.Socket;
import java.io.*;
public class Client {
    String host = "host.name.com";
    int port = 1500;

    try {
      me = new Socket(host,port);
      in = new DataInputStream(me.getInputStream());
      out = me.getOutputStream();
```

(continues)

Listing 14.20   Continued

```
    }
    catch (Exception e) {
        System.out.prinln( e.toString()  );
    }
     .
      .
       .
    }
```

Methods

- **Socket(String host, int port) throws UnknownHostException, IOException**
  Creates a Socket and attempts to connect it to the specified port on the specified host.

- **Socket(InetAddress host, int port) throws IOException**
  Creates a Socket and attempts to connect it to the specified port on the specified host.

- **Socket(String host, int port, boolean stream) throws IOException**
  Creates a Socket and attempts to connect it to the specified port on the specified host. If stream is true, then the information will be read as a stream. If stream is false, then it will be read in packets as a DatagramSocket would.

- **Socket(InetAddress address, int port, boolean stream) throws IOException**
  Creates a Socket and attempts to connect it to the specified port on the specified host. If stream is true, then the information will be read as a stream. If stream is false, then it will be read in packets as a DatagramSocket would.

- **synchronized void close( ) throws IOException**
  Closes the socket.

- **InetAddress getInetAddress( )**
  Returns the InetAddress of the host to which the Socket is connected.

- **InputStream getInputStream( ) throws IOException**
  Returns the InputStream for this Socket. This method is necessary if you want to read from the stream.

- **int getLocalPort( )**
  Returns the local port to which the socket is connected.

- **OutputStream getOutputStream( ) throws IOException**
  Returns the OutputStream for this Socket. This method is necessary if you want to write to the stream.

- **int getPort( )**
  Returns the port to which the socket is connected on the remote machine.

- **static synchronized void setSocketImplFactory(SocketImplFactory fac) throws IOException**
  Sets the `SocketImplFactory` for this object. Future `Sockets` created by this object will be based on this factory. This method can be called only once.

- **String toString( )**
  Returns a string containing the host and the port to which the socket is connected, as well as the local port.

Abstract **SocketImpl.** The `SocketImpl` class defines a set of behaviors necessary for communication between sockets. This functionality is integral to socket communication and is used by the `Socket` and `ServerSocket` classes. However, most programmers find little need to use it explicitly.

Fields

- **protected InetAddress address**
  The address to which the socket is connected.

- **protected FileDescriptor fd**
  A `FileDescriptor` object used internally when reading and writing from a socket. This is because the socket interface is based on the `FileInputStream` and `FileOutputStream` classes.

- **protected int localport**
  The local port used by the socket.

- **protected int port**
  The port on the remote system to which the socket is connected.

Methods

- **SocketImpl( )**
  Creates a new `SocketImpl`.

- **protected abstract void accept(SocketImpl connection) throws IOException**
  Accepts the specified connection.

- **protected abstract int available( ) throws IOException**
  Returns the number of bytes available in the stream.

- **protected abstract void bind(InetAddress host, int port) throws IOException**
  Binds the socket to the specified `host` and `port`.

- **protected abstract void close( ) throws IOException**
  Closes the socket.

- **protected abstract void connect(InetAddress host, int port) throws IOException**
  Connects the socket to the specified `host` and `port`.

III

Java

- **protected abstract void connect(String host, int port) throws IOException**
  Connects the socket to the specified host and port.

- **protected abstract void create(boolean stream) throws IOException**
  Creates a socket. If stream is true, then the socket will read information as a stream. If it is false, then information will be read in packets.

- **FileDescriptor getFileDescriptor( )**
  Returns the FileDescriptor object for this socket. This descriptor is used in creating the stream interaction.

- **protected InetAddress getInetAddress( )**
  Returns the InetAddress to which the socket is connected.

- **protected abstract InputStream getInputStream( ) throws IOException**
  Returns the InputStream that will obtain information from the socket stream.

- **protected int getLocalPort( )**
  Returns the local port number connected to the socket.

- **protected abstract OutputStream getOutputStream( ) throws IOException**
  Returns the OutputStream that will write information to the socket stream.

- **protected int getPort( )**
  Returns the port number to which the socket is connected.

- **protected abstract void listen(int time) throws IOException**
  Listens to the socket for the specified amount of time, awaiting requests for connections.

- **String toString( )**
  Returns a string containing the host and the port to which the socket is connected, as well as the local port.

URL. The function of the URL class is twofold. Most simply, it enables you to handle the semantic operations of URL, such as parsing out the file or host name of the URL. More importantly, however, it also serves as a handle for the retrieval of the information stored at the specific URL.

Methods

- **URL(String link) throws MalformedURLException**
  Creates an URL object from the specified string containing a complete URL.

- **URL(URL context, String fileName) throws MalformedURLException**
  Creates an URL object with the same host name and protocol as context, but using the fileName specified.

For example, examine the following code:

```
URL u1 = new URL("http","www.xyz.com",1500,"/foo.html#abc");
URL u = new URL(u1, "funny.html");
System.out.println( u1.toString() );
System.out.println( u.toString() );
```

The output will look as follows:

```
http://www.xyz.com:1500/foo.html#abc
http://www.xyz.com:1500/funny.html
```

- **URL(String protocol, String host, String file) throws MalformedURLException**
  Creates a new URL that will use the specified protocol to interact with the specified host. file is the name of the file to which the URL pertains, such as an HTML document or a file to be received via FTP.

- **URL(String protocol, String host, int port, String file) throws MalformedURLException**
  Creates a new URL that will use the specified protocol to interact with the specified host on the specified port. file is the name of the file to which the URL pertains, such as an HTML document or a file to be received via FTP.

- **int getPort( )**
  Returns the port from which the URL will obtain its information.

- **String getProtocol( )**
  Returns the port from which the URL will obtain its information.

- **boolean equals(Object anotherObject)**
  Returns true if anotherObject is an URL object expressing an interest in the same file, in the same manner. This means that anotherObject must have the same protocol, host, port, and file. However, any "#ref" fields at the end of the URL are ignored. (This is the value that is returned by the sameFile() method.)

- **final Object getContent( ) throws IOException**
- **String getFile( )**
  Returns the name of the file that the URL is interested in.

- **String getHost( )**
  Returns the host from which the URL will obtain its information.

- **String getRef( )**
  Returns the ref of the URL—anything following the pound sign (#).

- **int hashCode( )**
  Returns the hashcode of the URL object—a value dependent on the hashcode of the protocol, host, and file name.

- **URLConnection openConnection( ) throws IOException**
  Opens a connection to obtain the information contained in the file specified by the URL. It returns an appropriate URLConnection based on the current URLStreamHandler.

- **final InputStream openStream( ) throws IOException**
  Opens an InputStream to the URL. This is done by first creating an URLConnection object and then obtaining the InputStream via the URLConnection.getInputStream( ) method.

- **boolean sameFile(URL otherURL)**
  Returns true if the otherURL refers to the same file in the same manner. This means that otherURL must have the same protocol, host, port, and file. However, any "#ref" fields at the end of the URL are ignored.

- **protected void set(String protocol, String host, int port, String file, String ref)**
  Sets the fields of the URL. This method is protected to enable only URLStreamHandlers to change these fields.

- **static synchronized void setURLStreamHandlerFactory(URLStreamHandlerFactory fac)**
  Sets the URLStreamHandlerFactory for this URL. The URLStreamHandlerFactory will determine how to handle the content of the URL's document.

- **String toExternalForm( )**
  Combines the various fields to create an URL in *standard* format.

- **String toString( )**
  Combines the various fields to create an URL in *standard* format.

***Abstract* URLConnection.** The URLConnection class is an abstract class that can be used to assist in managing a connection based on an URL object.

Fields

- **protected boolean allowUserInteraction**
  Some URLs require user input—such as in filling out a password box. It is initially set to false, meaning any requests to obtain user interaction will cause an exception.

- **protected boolean connected**
  Tracks the status of the URLConnection—connected or not.

- **protected boolean doInput**
  True if the URLConnection is to be used as a source of input. It is initially set as true.

- **protected boolean doOutput**
  True if the URLConnection is to be used as a source of input. It is initially set as false.

- **protected long ifModifiedSince**

  This field may be used to make the connection more efficient by not loading old information. It is initially set to zero and further requires you to implement it yourself in any subclasses.

- **protected URL url**

  The URL with which the connection has been made.

- **protected boolean useCaches**

  If useCaches is true, the connection will make use of cached information whenever possible. This field is initially true.

Methods

- **protected URLConnection(URL url)**

  Creates an URLConnection to the specified URL.

- **abstract void connect( ) throws IOException**

  Creates a connection to the specified URL of this object.

- **boolean getAllowUserInteraction( )**

  Returns the allowUserInteraction flag.

- **Object getContent( ) throws IOException**

  Returns the object referred to by the URL.

- **String getContentEncoding( )**

  Returns the "content encoding" field from the headers of this URL.

- **int getContentLength( )**

  Returns the "content length" from the headers of the URL.

- **String getContentType( )**

  Returns the "content type" field from the list of headers of this URL.

- **long getDate( )**

  Returns the "date" field from the list of headers of this URL.

- **boolean getDoInput( )**

  Returns the doInput field of this object.

- **boolean getDoOutput( )**

  Returns the doOutput field of this object.

- **long getExpiration( )**

  Returns the "expires" field from the headers of the URL.

- **String getHeaderField(int n)**

  Returns the title of the nth field from the header list. Returns null if there are fewer than n headers. Currently returns a null string.

- **String getHeaderField(String name)**

  Returns the value of the header with the specified name.

- **long getHeaderFieldDate(String name, long Default)**
  Returns the value of the header with the specified name as a date.

- **int getHeaderFieldInt(String name, int Default)**
  Returns the value of the specified header field as an int.

- **String getHeaderFieldKey(int n)**
  Returns the value of the nth field in the header list. It returns null if there are fewer than n headers.

- **InputStream getInputStream( ) throws IOException**
  Returns the InputStream for this URLConnection.

- **long getLastModified( )**
  Returns the value of the "last modified" field, or zero if undefined.

- **OutputStream getOutputStream( ) throws IOException**
  Returns the OutputStream for this URLConnection.

- **URL getURL( )**
  Returns the URL from which this URLConnection is obtaining its information.

- **void setAllowUserInteraction(boolean allow)**
  Sets the allowUserInteraction field to the specified allow value.

- **static void setDefaultAllowUserInteraction(boolean default)**
  Sets the default value for the allowUserInteraction field.

- **void setDoInput(boolean doinput)**
  Sets the value of the doInput field.

- **void setDoOutput(boolean dooutput)**
  Sets the value of the doOutput field.

- **String toString( )**
  Returns a string containing the class name and the name of the URL to which this URLConnection is connected.

- **static boolean getDefaultAllowUserInteraction( )**
  Returns the default value for the allowUserInteraction field.

- **static String getDefaultRequestProperty(String key)**
  Returns the default value for the allowUserInteraction field. By default, this returns a null string and thus must be overridden.

- **boolean getDefaultUseCaches( )**
  Returns the default value for the useCaches field.

- **long getIfModifiedSince( )**
  Returns the isModifiedSince field.

- **String getRequestProperty(String key)**
  Returns the general request property whose name is key.

- **boolean getUseCaches( )**
  Returns the useCaches field.

- **static synchronized void setContentHandlerFactory(ContentHandlerFactory fac)**
  Specifies the ContentHandlerFactory for this object.

- **static void setDefaultRequestProperty(String key, String value)**
  This method can be used to set the default value of a request property for the URLConnection. Unless overridden this method does nothing.

- **void setDefaultUseCaches(boolean defaultusecaches)**
  Sets the default value for the useCaches field.

- **void setIfModifiedSince(long ifmodifiedsince)**
  Sets the value of the ifModifiedSince field.

- **void setRequestProperty(String key, String value)**
  This method can be used to set a request property to be used by this URLConnection. Currently, the method does nothing.

- **void setUseCaches(boolean usecaches)**
  Sets the value for the useCaches field.

- **static String guessContentTypeFromName(String fileName)**
  Returns a string containing the MIME type that is most likely contained in the file with the specified fileName. This method is already implemented for you and recognizes a total of 39 content-type-specifying extensions, including .exe, .zip, .gif, and .html.

- **static String guessContentTypeFromStream(InputStream is) throws IOException**
  This method can be used to guess at the content type based on the first six bytes of the stream. This method recognizes image/gif, image/jpg, image/x-bitmap, and text/html data MIME types.

URLEncoder. This class is simply a means of translating standard strings into x-www-form-urlencoded format. This process involves such conversions as changing spaces to '+' symbols and representing non-alphanumeric characters with hexadecimal numbers. This is the format that you will see used in standard URLs when passing information to CGI scripts.

Method

- **static String encode(String s)**
  Translates a string in standard format to one in x-www-form-urlencoded format. All spaces become '+' symbols and all characters except digits, characters, and the underscore character '_' are translated into numerical representations in hex format.

Abstract URLStreamHandler. An URLStreamHandler is a rather simple class used to transform an URL into an URLConnection.

Methods

- **URLStreamHandler( )**

  Creates a new URLStreamHandler.

- **abstract URLConnection openConnection(URL url) throws IOException**

  This method creates an InputStream to receive information from the specified URL. It must be overridden to make the class non-abstract.

- **void parseURL(URL url, String spec, int start, int limit)**

  Parses the spec string between (and including) characters start and limit and stores their values in the URL object. Note that although no new URL is returned, the fields in the specified URL will change inasmuch as this method sets the internal fields of the URL.

- **void setURL(URL url, String protocol, String host, int port, String file, String ref)**

  Sets the fields of the specified URL object. Note that although no new URL is returned, the fields in the specified URL will change inasmuch as this method sets the internal fields of the URL.

- **String toExternalForm(URL url)**

  Returns a string representing the specified URL from which this object is retrieving its information.

Interfaces

ContentHandlerFactory. A ContentHandlerFactory can be used to create a manager that will return the appropriate ContentHandler for a specified MIME type. Such classes are used by the URLConnection class to correctly handle incoming data.

Method

- **abstract ContentHandler createContentHandler(String mimetype)**

  Returns the ContentHandler specific for the distinct MIME type.

SocketImplFactory. The SocketImplFactory enables you to make use of the SocketImpl class. The SocketImplFactory class will return a SocketImpl in response to a request to create a socket. By using the setSocketFactory in the java.net.severSocket class, you can specify which SocketImplFactory you want to use and thus which SocketImpl will be employed.

- **abstract SocketImpl createSocketImpl( )**

  Creates a new SocketImpl object to be used in creating a socket.

URLStreamHandlerFactory. By means of the CreateURLStreamHandler() method, the URLStreamHandlerFactory class creates URLStreamHandlers for specific types of data streams. This class is generally not explicilty used in programs.

Method

- **abstract URLStreamHandler CreateURLStreamHandler(String protocol)**

  Creates an URLStreamHandler to handle an URL with the specified protocol.

java.util

This package is essentially a smorgasbord of useful classes that do not truly fit into any of the other packages. Among these handy classes are the Date class, designed to manage and handle operations with dates; the Hashtable class; and ADTs, such as Stack and Vector.

Classes

BitSet Implements java.lang.Cloneable. A Bitset is a dynamic collection of bits that has the added capability of basic logical operations. Although you may perform some logical operations on a BitSet, the methods do not return a new BitSet, but rather modify the current BitSet. As shown in Listing 14.21, the logical operation will result in a change of the original BitSet.

Listing 14.21   BitSet **Example**

```java
import java.util.BitSet;

public class BitsetExample {
    public static void main(String argv[ ]) {

        BitSet a = new BitSet();
        BitSet b = new BitSet();

        a.set(0);
        a.set(1);
        a.set(2);

        b.set(0);
        b.set(1);
        b.set(8);
        b.set(9);

        System.out.println("This is the first set: " + a);
        System.out.println("This is the second set: " + b);
        a.and(b);      // places all elements in both sets into a
        System.out.print("The following elements are in both");
        System.our.println(" sets: " + a );
    }
}
```

Methods

- **BitSet( )**
  Creates a new BitSet with a size of 64.

- **BitSet(int nbits)**
  Creates a new BitSet with the specified size.

- **void and(BitSet set)**
  Places all elements of both sets into the original set—the logical intersection of the two.

- **void clear(int bit)**
  Removes all instances of the specified bit from the set.

- **Object clone( )**
  Creates a copy of the current set.

- **boolean equals(Object anotherObject)**
  Returns `true` if `anotherObject` is a `BitSet` with the same elements.

- **boolean get(int bit)**
  Returns `true` if the specified bit can be found in this `BitSet`.

- **int hashCode( )**
  Returns the `hashcode` of the set—a value based on its elements.

- **void or(BitSet set)**
  Places all elements of either this `BitSet` or the specified `set` into this set—the logical union.

- **void set(int bit)**
  Places the specified bit in the set.

- **int size( )**
  Returns the size of the set.

- **String toString( )**
  Returns a string containing the set in standard set notation (e.g., {1, 2, 3}).

- **void xor(BitSet set)**
  Places all elements of one, but not both sets into the current set. This contains all elements in the union but not the intersection.

Date. The `Date` class provides you with a convenient means of managing dates and times. Rather flexible, this class enables you to set and manipulate the date in a number of ways, and can handle time zone and daylight-saving time conversions.

Methods

- **Date( )**
  Creates a `Date` based on the current time.

- **Data(long date)**
  Creates a `Date` based on the specified `date`, representing the number of milliseconds since 00:00:00 GMT, January 1, 1970. Although this may seem a rather abstruse manner of specifying a time, this compacted format is extremely efficient.

  To obtain the current time in milliseconds since 00:00:00 GMT, January 1, 1970, use the `System.currentTimeMillis()`.

- **Date(int year, int month, int date)**
  Creates a `Date` with the specified `year`, `month`, and `date`. The year must be later than 1900.

- **Date(int year, int month, int date, int hours, int min)**
  Creates a `Date` with the specified `year`, `month`, `date`, `hours`, and `min` values. The year must be later than 1900.

- **Date(String dateString)**
  Creates a `Date` with values specified in `dateString`. This relies on `parse()`, which accepts dates in such formats as `"Tue, 26 Mar 1996 04:05:00 GMT+1900"`.

- **Date(int year, int month, int date, int hrs, int min, int sec)**
  Creates a `Date` with the specified values.

- **boolean after(Date when)**
  Returns `true` if this `Date` is chronologically after `when`.

- **boolean before(Date when)**
  Returns `true` if this `Date` is chronologically before `when`.

- **boolean equals(Object anotherObject)**
  Returns `true` if `anotherObject` is a `Date` with the same `value` field (the number of milliseconds since 1/1/70).

- **int getDate( )**
  Returns the date of the `Date`: an `int` between 1 and 31.

- **int getDay( )**
  Returns the weekday of the `Date`: an `int` between 0 and 6 with 0 representing Sunday.

- **int getHours( )**
  Returns the hour value of the `Date`: an `int` between 0 and 23.

- **int getMinutes( )**
  Returns the minute value of the `Date`: an `int` between 0 and 59.

- **int getMonth( )**
  Returns the month value of the `Date`: an `int` between 1 and 12.

- **int getSeconds( )**
  Returns the seconds value of the `Date`: an `int` between 0 and 59.

- **long getTime( )**
  Returns the date specified by this `Date` object as a `long` representing the number of milliseconds since 00:00:00 GMT, January 1, 1970.

- **int getTimezoneOffset( )**
  Returns the offset of this time zone as the number of minutes from Greenwich mean time.

III

Java

- **int getYear( )**
  Returns the year value of this Date offset from 1900. (Thus, 100 would represent 2000.)

- **int hashCode( )**
  Returns the hashcode of the Date: a value based on the number of elapsed seconds since 00:00:00 GMT, January 1, 1970.

- **static long parse(String s)**
  Parses a string representing a date, returning the number of seconds between that time and 00:00:00 GMT, January 1, 1970.

- **void setDate(int date)**
  Sets the date (the day of the month) of this Date object.

- **void setHours(int hours)**
  Sets the hour value of this Date object.

- **void setMinutes(int minutes)**
  Sets the minutes value of this Date object.

- **void setMonth(int month)**
  Sets the month value of this Date object.

- **void setSeconds(int seconds)**
  Sets the seconds value of this Date object.

- **void setTime(long time)**
  Sets the value of this Date object by specifying a time in milliseconds relative to 00:00:00 GMT, January 1, 1970.

- **void setYear(int year)**
  Sets the year value for this Date.

- **String toGMTString( )**
  Returns a string containing the date in GMT format, adjusted for the specified time zone (e.g., 25 Mar 1996 09:05:00 GMT).

- **String toLocaleString( )**
  Returns a string containing the date in *locale* format, not adjusting for the time zone (e.g., 03/25/96 04:05:00).

- **String toString( )**
  Returns a string representing the time in a system dependent format.

- **static long UTC(int year, int month, int date, int hrs, int min, int sec)**
  Returns the time in milliseconds between 00:00:00 GMT, January 1, 1970 and the specified time.

Abstract **Dictionary.** This class defines the behavior of a Hashtable. While all of its methods serve a purpose in a Hashtable, they are all abstract in this class.

Methods

- **Dictionary( )**
  Creates a new Dictionary.

- **abstract Enumeration elements( )**
  Returns an Enumeration of the elements for sequential viewing.

- **abstract Object get(Object key)**
  Returns the element with the specified key.

- **abstract boolean isEmpty( )**
  Returns true if the Dictionary is empty.

- **abstract Enumeration keys( )**
  Returns an Enumeration of the keys for sequential viewing.

- **abstract Object put(Object key, Object element)**
  Places the specified element in the Dictionary under the specified key.

- **abstract Object remove(Object key)**
  Removes the key and its corresponding element.

- **abstract int size( )**
  Returns the number of elements in the Dictionary.

Hashtable Extends Dictionary Implements java.lang.Cloneable. The Hashtable class is a simple implementation of a hashtable ADT. A hashtable provides you with a convenient and efficient means of storing information based on a distinct relationship. Like an array, whose elements are each paired with a specific index, each element in a hashtable is paired with a specific *key*. By using this key, you are able to retrieve the information stored in the table.

One important consideration when using the Hashtable class is that every key and element *must* be an Object. As you can see, this is not a problem when dealing with strings (see Listing 14.22).

Listing 14.22 Hashtable **Example Using** String **Objects**

```
import java.util.*;
import java.io.DataInputStream;

public class HashtableExample  {

    public static void main(String argv[ ]) {
        Hashtable phones = new Hashtable();
        String name = null;
        String phone = null;

        phones.put("Danny", "555-0718"  );
        phones.put("Jason", "555-0031"  );
        phones.put("Jaime", "555-2191" );
        phones.put("Jeff",  "555-1391" );
```

(continues)

Listing 14.22 Continued

```
        System.out.print("Please enter a name ==> ");
        System.out.flush(); // forces the prompt to be displayed
        DataInputStream din = new DataInputStream(System.in);

        try {
          name = din.readLine();
        }
        catch (Exception e) {
          System.out.println( e.toString() );
        }

        if (phones.containsKey(name)) {     /* checks to see if
                                            the name is valid */
          phone = (String)phones.get(name);
          System.out.println(name + "'s phone number is " +phone + "." );
        }
        else {
          System.out.print("Sorry.  I don't know who ");
          System.out.println(name + " is.");
        }
    }
```

The requirement to use full-blown Objects poses a slight problem when dealing with primitive data types, such as an int or a float. As shown in Listing 14.23, it is necessary to create a wrapper Object to handle such primitive data types. This wrapper must be used initially to store the value and again used when retrieving the information.

Listing 14.23 Hashtable Example Using Integer Objects

```
import java.util.*;
import java.io.DataInputStream;

public class HashtableExample2  {

    public static void main(String argv[ ]) {
      Hashtable ages = new Hashtable();
      String name = null;
      Integer age = null;

      ages.put("Danny", new Integer(13) );
      ages.put("Jason", new Integer(7)  );
      ages.put("Jaime", new Integer(39) );
      ages.put("Jeff", new Integer(54)  );

      System.out.print("Please enter a name ==> ");
      System.out.flush();
       DataInputStream din = new DataInputStream(System.in);


      try {
        name = din.readLine();
      }
```

```
    catch (Exception e) {
      System.out.println( e.toString() );
    }

    if (ages.containsKey(name)) {
      age = (Integer)ages.get(name);
      System.out.print(name + "is " +age.intValue())';
      System.out.println(" years old." );              }
    }
    else {
      System.out.print("Sorry.  I don't know who ");
      System.out.println(name + " is.");
    }
  }
}
```

Methods

- **Hashtable( )**
  Creates a new Hashtable. The capacity will be set to 101 and the loadFactor will be set to 0.75.

- **Hashtable(int initialCapacity)**
  Creates a new Hashtable with the specified capacity and a loadFactor of 0.75.

- **Hashtable(int initialCapacity, float loadFactor)**
  Creates a new Hashtable. initialCapacity is the number of entries that the Hashtable will be able to contain and loadFactor is a number between 0.0 and 1.0 that represents the percentage of the hashtable that may be filled before it is resized via the rehash() method.

- **synchronized void clear( )**
  Clears the Hashtable, removing all keys and elements.

- **synchronized Object clone( )**
  Creates a clone of the Hashtable. However, the contents of the new table will be references to the old objects, not new objects.

- **synchronized boolean contains(Object value)**
  Returns true if value is an element in the hashtable.

- **synchronized boolean containsKey(Object key)**
  Returns true if key is a key in the hashtable.

- **synchronized Enumeration elements( )**
  Returns an Enumeration of the elements for sequential viewing.

- **synchronized Object get(Object key)**
  Returns the element with the specified key.

- **boolean isEmpty( )**
  Returns true if the hashtable is empty.

- **synchronized Enumeration keys( )**
  Returns an `Enumeration` of the keys for sequential viewing.

- **synchronized Object put(Object key, Object element)**
  Places the specified `element` into the `hashtable` with the specified `key`.

- **protected void rehash( )**
  Resizes the `hashtable`. This is automatically triggered when the size of the `hashtable` exceeds the threshold specified in the `constructor` method. The new `hashtable` will be one more than twice the current size.

- **synchronized Object remove(Object key)**
  Removes the `key` and its corresponding element. Returns the `key` if properly removed, or `null` if it could not be found.

- **int size( )**
  Returns the number of elements in the `hashtable`.

- **synchronized String toString( )**
  Returns a string containing all key-element pairs.

Observable. The `Observable` class enables you to create an `Object` containing data that will be manipulated in close connection with other objects. To use this class, you must extend it to create your own "observable" class. This class will have the ability to communicate with a number of `Observer` classes via the `notifyObservers()` method. As a result, any change in the `Observable` class can trigger an appropriate response in all `Observers`.

 ▶▶ See "Observer," p. 578

Methods

- **Observable( )**
  Creates a new `Observable` object.

- **synchronized void addObserver(Observer o)**
  Adds an observer to the list of observers of this object.

- **protected synchronized void clearChanged( )**
  Sets the `changed` flag to `false`.

- **synchronized int countObservers( )**
  Returns the number of observers.

- **synchronized void deleteObserver(Observer o)**
  Removes the specified `Observer` from the list of observers.

- **synchronized void deleteObservers( )**
  Removes all observers from the observer list.

- **synchronized boolean hasChanged( )**
  Returns the value of the `changed` flag.

- **synchronized void notifyObservers(Object information)**
  Sends the specified information object to all observers.

- **void notifyObservers( )**
  Sends a null object to all observers.

- **protected synchronized void setChanged( )**
  Sets the changed flag to true.

Properties Extends Hashtable. The Properties class is a Hashtable that may be saved and/or loaded. It is generally used to handle system properties, inasmuch as it is often necessary to retrieve these properties and sometimes convenient to be able to store them.

▶▶ See "System," p. 541

Field

- **protected Properties defaults**
  A set of properties that will be used when a property cannot be found in the new Properties set.

Methods

- **Properties( )**
  Creates a new Properties object with no set of defaults.

- **Properties(Properties defaults)**
  Creates a new Properties object with the specified set of defaults.

- **String getProperty(String key, String defaultValue)**
  Returns the property element with the specified key. If it cannot be found, the method will then check the default Properties. If it is still unable to find the specified key, it will return the defaultValue.

- **String getProperty(String key)**
  Returns the property element with the specified key. If it cannot be found, the method will then check the default Properties.

- **void list(PrintStream out)**
  Prints out the properties to the specified PrintStream.

- **synchronized void load(InputStream in) throws IOException**
  Retrieves a set of Properties from the specified InputStream.

- **Enumeration propertyNames( )**
  Returns an Enumeration of all the keys in this Properties table.

- **synchronized void save(OutputStream out, String header)**
  Saves the Properties table to the specified OutputStream using the header.

Random. The Random class encapsulates the behavior necessary for creating random numbers.

Methods

- **Random( )**
  Creates a new Random object using the current time in milliseconds as the seed.

- **Random(long seed)**
  Creates a new Random object using the specified seed.

- **double nextDouble( )**
  Returns a random number between 0.0 and 1.0.

- **float nextFloat( )**
  Returns a random number between 0.0 and 1.0.

- **synchronized double nextGaussian( )**
  Returns a randomly generated double centered around zero but with a standard deviation of 1.0. This means that you will get some numbers above one.

- **int nextInt( )**
  Returns a random int value.

- **long nextLong( )**
  Returns a randomly generated long value.

- **synchronized void setSeed(long seed)**
  Sets the seed used in generating the random numbers.

Stack Extends Vector. The Stack class implements a standard stack ADT. A stack follows the Last In First Out (LIFO) algorithm in which new items are placed on top of the stack—thereby making them the first items removed. In Java, each *item* in a stack must be a full-blown Object.

Methods

- **Stack( )**
  Creates an empty Stack.

- **boolean empty( )**
  Returns true if the stack is empty.

- **Object peek( )**
  Returns the top item in the stack without removing it.

- **Object pop( )**
  Returns the top item in the stack and removes it from the stack.

- **Object push(Object item)**
  Places the specified item at the top of the stack.

- **int search(Object item)**
  Returns the position of the item relative to the top of the stack, or –1 if it is not in the stack.

StringTokenizer Implements Enumeration. The `StringTokenizer` class enables you to parse a string consisting of several sub-strings.

In using a `StringTokenizer`, there are two internal fields that may be altered: the `delimiters` string and the value `retTokens`. The `delimiters` string contains all tokens that are important. When parsing the string, the `StringTokenizer` will return a string if the current characters are in `delimiters`. `retTokens` is a flag that specifies whether or not to return the delimiter characters as separate tokens.

Methods

- **StringTokenizer(String str)**
  Creates a new `StringTokenizer`. By default, `" \t\n\r"` will be used as the delimiter string (making `' '`, `'\t'`, `'\n'`, and `'\r'` token delimiters), and the `retTokens` flag will be set to `false`.

- **StringTokenizer(String str, String delim)**
  Creates a new `StringTokenizer` with the specified set of delimiting characters.

- **StringTokenizer(String str, String delim, boolean returnTokens)**
  Creates a new `StringTokenizer` with the specified set of delimiting characters. If `returnTokens` is `true`, all tokens will be returned, as well as the separate strings.

- **int countTokens( )**
  Counts the number of tokens in this string.

- **boolean hasMoreElements( )**
  Returns `true` if elements remain in the string. By default, it simply returns the value of `hasMoreTokens()`. This method is necessary to satisfy the requirements of implementing the `Enumeration` interface.

- **boolean hasMoreTokens( )**
  Returns `true` if more tokens exist in the string.

- **Object nextElement( )**
  Returns the string returned by `nextToken()`. This method is necessary to satisfy the requirements of implementing the `Enumeration` interface.

- **String nextToken(String delim)**
  Makes `delim` the new set of delimiters and then returns the next token.

- **String nextToken( )**
  Returns the next token in the string.

Vector Implements java.lang.Cloneable. A `Vector` is a dynamic array, most useful when dealing with an unknown quantity of data that will be changed frequently. Although based on the structure of an array, a `Vector` will automatically grow to provide new memory when needed. Furthermore, this capability enables you to perform more manipulative tasks, such as removing an element from a `Vector` or inserting an element into the middle of the `Vector`.

When using a Vector, keep in mind that—like a Hashtable—all elements must be Objects. Therefore, if you want to store simple data, such as an int or float, you must use the wrapper classes in the java.lang package.

Fields

- **protected int capacityIncrement**
  The amount that the Vector array will grow each time that expansion is required. If capacityIncrement is zero, then the array will double in size.

- **protected int elementCount**
  The number of elements in the Vector.

- **protected Object elementData[ ]**
  The array of the stored elements.

Methods

- **Vector( )**
  Creates a new Vector object with an initial capacity of 10. When the Vector needs to grow, it will double in size.

- **Vector(int initialCapacity)**
  Creates a new Vector object with the specified initalCapacity. When the Vector needs to grow, it will double in size.

- **Vector(int initialCapacity, int capacityIncrement)**
  Creates a new Vector object with the specified initalCapacity. When the Vector needs to grow, it will do so by the specified amount.

- **final synchronized void addElement(Object element)**
  Adds the specified element to the end of the Vector array, growing in size as required.

- **final int capacity( )**
  Returns the total capacity of the Vector: the length of the elementData[] array.

- **synchronized Object clone( )**
  Clones the Vector object itself, but not its elements. This means that the elements of both the new and the old Vector objects will be references to the same objects.

- **final boolean contains(Object element)**
  Returns true if the Vector contains the specified element.

- **final synchronized void copyInto(Object anArray[ ])**
  Copies the elements in the Vector into a static (standard) array.

- **final synchronized Object elementAt(int index)**
  Returns the element at the specified index.

- **final synchronized Enumeration elements( )**
  Returns an Enumeration of the elements in the Vector.

- **final synchronized void ensureCapacity(int elements)**
  Checks to see if the Vector can contain at least the specified number of elements.

- **final synchronized Object firstElement( )**
  Returns the first element in the Vector array.

- **final int indexOf(Object element)**
  Returns the first index at which the specified element is located. It returns –1 if the element was not found.

- **final synchronized int indexOf(Object elem, int start)**
  Returns the first index at which the specified element is located. It begins searching at the specified start and returns –1 if the element is not found.

- **final synchronized void insertElementAt(Object object, int index)**
  Inserts the specified object at the specified index.

- **final boolean isEmpty( )**
  Returns true if the Vector array is empty.

- **final synchronized Object lastElement( )**
  Returns the last element at the last index in the array.

- **final int lastIndexOf(Object elem)**
  Returns the last index at which the specified element is located. It returns –1 if the element is not found.

- **final synchronized int lastIndexOf(Object elem, int start)**
  Returns the first index at which the specified element is located. It begins the backwards search at the specified start and returns –1 if the element is not found.

- **final synchronized void removeAllElements( )**
  Erases all elements in the Vector.

- **final synchronized boolean removeElement(Object element)**
  Removes the first instance of the specified element from the Vector array.

- **final synchronized void removeElementAt(int index)**
  Removes the element at the specified index from the Vector array.

- **final synchronized void setElementAt(Object obj, int index)**
  Sets the element at the specified index, overwriting any value previously stored at the index.

- **final synchronized void setSize(int newSize)**
  Sets the size of the Vector array. If newSize is greater than the current size, the array will be shrunk to the newSize. If newSize is larger than the current size, the array will be enlarged to the newSize.

- **final int size( )**
  Returns the size of the Vector array.

III

Java

- **final synchronized String toString( )**
  Returns a string containing all the elements in the `Vector` array.

- **final synchronized void trimToSize( )**
  Shrinks the array to the minimum size that is capable of containing all the elements in the `Vector`.

Interfaces

Enumeration. An `Enumeration` is a simple way to handle a set of items without having to worry about the number of items contained in the set. This is necessary when dealing with many groups of data that do not provide you with a simple manner of dealing with each element in a sequential manner, such as `Hashtables` and the applets in an `AppletContext`. By using an `Enumeration`, you are able to scroll through the items—such as the keys in a set of `Properties`, the applets in an `AppletContext`, or the sub-strings in a `StringTokenizer`—in a very simple manner.

Listing 14.24 Enumeration **Example**

```
import java.util.Enumeration;
import java.util.Properties;

public class EnumerationExample {

    public static void main(String args[ ]) {

        Enumeration propNames = System.getProperties().propertyNames();
        int index = 1;

         while (propNames.hasMoreElements() )
           System.out.print("Property " + (index++) + ": ");
           System.out.println(propNames.nextElement() );
        }
    }
}
```

Methods

- **abstract boolean hasMoreElements( )**
  Returns `true` if the `Enumeration` contains more elements.

- **abstract Object nextElement( )**
  Returns the next element in the `Enumeration`.

Observer. The `Observer` interface is used in conjunction with an `Observable` class. By adding an `Observer` to the `Observable` class list of observers, the `Observable` class will be informed of any important changes in the `Observable` class. (This communication transpires whenever the `notifyObservers()` method is invoked in the `Observable` class.)

Method

- **abstract void update(Observable o, Object arg)**

▶▶ See "Observable," p. 572

Exceptions

Exceptions provide you with a means of managing the ordinary runtime problems that may be encountered during execution of your program. All exceptions are derived from the `java.lang.Exception` class and most consist only of two constructor methods. Consequently, only the constructor methods for the `java.lang.Exception` class are listed here.

Unless otherwise noted, all exceptions may be created with no parameters or with a descriptive string as a parameter. Exceptions are handled by using the `try...catch` construct. Once an exception has been caught, it may be dealt with or thrown to the calling method. Listing 14.25 is an example of a simple division method that sets the result equal to zero if division by zero occurs.

Listing 14.25   Catching an Exception

```
int divide(int a, int b) {
    int val;
    try {
        val = a / b;
    }
    catch(ArithmeticException e) {
        System.out.println("Invalid data.  val set to 0.");
        val = 0;
    }
    return (val);
}
```

To throw an exception, you must use the `throw` statement, as shown in Listing 14.26 and Listing 14.27.

Listing 14.26   Throwing a Caught Exception

```
void connect(String host, int port) throws IOException {
    try {
        s = new Socket(host,port);
    }
    catch(IOException e) {
        throw e;
    }
}
```

Listing 14.27   Throwing a New Exception

```
static void connect(String host, int port) throws IOException {
    /* Makes sure the port satisfies our system policy */
    if (port < 1600)
        throw new SocketException("Port under 1600");

    try {
        s = new Socket(host,port);
    }
    catch(IOException e) {
        throw e;
    }
}
```

III

Java

java.awt

AWTException
AWTException(String message)

java.io

EOFException Extends IOException

FileNotFoundException Extends IOException

IOException Extends java.lang.Exception

InterruptedIOException Extends IOException

UTFDataFormatException Extends IOException

java.lang

ArithmeticException Extends RuntimeException

ArrayIndexOutOfBoundsException Extends IndexOutOfBoundsException
Constructors

> ArrayIndexOutOfBoundsException( )

> ArrayIndexOutOfBoundsException(int invalid_index)

> ArrayIndexOutOfBoundsException(String message)

ArrayStoreException Extends RuntimeException

ClassCastException Extends RuntimeException

ClassNotFoundException Extends Exception

CloneNotSupportedException Extends Exception

Exception Extends Throwable

Methods
- **Exception(String message)**
- **Exception( )**

IllegalAccessException Extends Exception

IllegalArgumentException Extends RuntimeException

IllegalMonitorStateException Extends RuntimeException

IllegalThreadStateException Extends RuntimeException

IndexOutOfBoundsException Extends RuntimeException

InstantiationException Extends Exception

InterruptedException Extends Exception

NegativeArraySizeException Extends RuntimeException

NoSuchMethodException Extends Exception

NullPointerException Extends RuntimeException

NumberFormatException Extends IllegalArgumentException

RuntimeException Extends Exception

SecurityException Extends RuntimeException

StringIndexOutOfBoundsException Extends IndexOutOfBoundsException

Constructors

> StringIndexOutOfBoundsException( )
>
> StringIndexOutOfBoundsException(int invalid_index)
>
> StringIndexOutOfBoundsException(String)

java.net

MalformedURLException Extends java.lang.IOException

ProtocolException Extends java.lang.IOException

SocketException Extends java.lang.IOException

UnknownHostException Extends java.lang.IOException

UnknownServiceException Extends java.lang.IOException

java.util

EmptyStackException Extends java.lang.RuntimeException

Constructors

> EmptyStackException( )

NoSuchElementException Extends java.lang.RuntimeException

Errors

Although errors and exceptions are both based on the java.lang.Throwable class, errors are designed to manage more critical runtime errors. Errors may be handled in a similar manner to exceptions. However, unless you clearly understand the problem and have devised a suitable way of resolving it, error handling is not something that should be used in your code.

Similar to exceptions, all errors are derived from java.lang.Error. All errors contain only constructor methods and most contain only two: ErrorName() and ErrorName(String message). Although all errors are listed here, only those errors whose constructors conform to the above pattern are listed in detail.

III

Java

java.awt

AWTError Extends java.lang.Error

Constructors

AWTError( )

java.lang

AbstractMethodError Extends IncompatibleClassChangeError

ClassCircularityError Extends LinkageError

ClassFormatError Extends LinkageError

Error Extends Throwable

Methods

- **Error(String message)**
- **Error( )**

IllegalAccessError Extends IncompatibleClassChangeError

IncompatibleClassChangeError Extends LinkageError

InstantiationError Extends IncompatibleClassChangeError

InternalError Extends VirtualMachineError

LinkageError Extends Error

NoClassDefFoundError Extends LinkageError

NoSuchFieldError Extends IncompatibleClassChangeError

NoSuchMethodError Extends IncompatibleClassChangeError

OutOfMemoryError Extends VirtualMachineError

StackOverflowError Extends VirtualMachineError

ThreadDeath Extends Error

Constructors

ThreadDeath( )

UnknownError Extends VirtualMachineError

UnsatisfiedLinkError Extends LinkageError

VerifyError Extends LinkageError

VirtualMachineError Extends Error

Chapter 15

Java Syntax Reference

This section serves as a reference for the Java language itself. All keywords and operators in the language are listed in alphabetical order, each followed by a complete explanation of the term, its syntax, and an example of how it might be used in actual code. Further, for ease of identification, the terms are set in bold in the code samples.

abstract

An abstract class or method is one that is not complete. Interfaces are automatically abstract.

Syntax:

```
abstract class className {
    abstract returnType methodName(optionalParameters);
}
```

Example:

```
abstract class Grapher

abstract void displayImage(Image im);
```

break

This is used to exit a loop.

Syntax:

```
break;
```

Example:

```
while (true) {
    if ( connection.isClosed() )
```

```
        break;
    else
      // code goes here
    }
```

---

catch

The catch statement is used to handle any exceptions thrown by code within a try block.

Syntax:

```
try {
    statement(s)
}
catch(Exception list) {
    statement(s)
}
```

Example:

```
InputStream in;
int val;
...
try {
    val = in.read() / in.read();
}
catch(ArithmeticException e) {
    System.out.println("Invalid data.  val set to 0.");
    val = 0;
    }
catch(Exception e) {
    System.out.println("Exception encountered, but not handled.");
    }
```

---

class

This is used in a class declaration to denote that the following code defines a class.

Syntax:

```
modifiers class className extends SuperClassName implements InterfaceNames
```

Example:

```
class MyClass
```

```
public class GraphAnimator extends Applet
```

```
public class Calculator implements Runnable, Cloneable
```

continue

This returns the program to the top of a loop.

Syntax:

```
continue;
```

Example:

```
Enumeration enum;
Object value;
...
while ( enum.hasMoreElements() ) {
    value = enum.nextElement();
    if ( value.equals("Invalid") )
        continue;
    else
        System.out.println( value);
}
```

do...while

This is used to perform operations while a condition is met. The loop body will be executed at least once.

Syntax:

```
do
  statement(s)
while (booleanVariable);

do
  statement(s)
while (booleanExpression);
```

Example:

```
do {
    val = in.readByte();
    System.out.println(val);
} while (val != '\n');

boolean valid = true;
do {
    val = in.readByte();
    if (val == '\n')
        valid = false;
    else
        System.out.println(val);
} while (valid);
```

else

This is used in conjunction with the `if` statement to perform operations only when the requirements of the `if` statement are not met.

Syntax:

```
if (booleanVariable)
    statement(s)
else
    statement(s)

if (booleanExpression)
    statement(s)
else
    statement(s)
```

Example:

```
if (stillRunning) {
    System.out.println("Still Running");
    advanceCounter();
}
else {
    System.out.println("We're all done.");
    closeConnection();
}
if (size >= 5)
    System.out.println("Too big");
else
    System.out.println("Just Right");
```

extends

This is used to make the current class or interface a subclass of another class or interface.

Syntax:

```
modifiers class className extends superClassName

interface interfaceName extends superInterfaceName
```

Example:

```
public class Clock extends Applet

public interface carefulObserver extends Observer
```

final

The `final` modifier makes a class or method final, meaning that it cannot be changed in a subclass. Interfaces cannot be final.

Syntax:

```
final class className

final returnType methodName(optionalParameters)
```

Example:

```
final class LogoAnimator

final Color getCurrentColor()
```

finally

The `finally` statement is used in error handling to ensure the execution of a section of code. Regardless of whether an exception is thrown within a `try` statement, the code in the finally block will be executed.

Syntax:

```
try {
    statement(s)
    }
finally {
    cleanUpStatement(s)
    }

try {
    statement(s)
    }
catch (Exception) {
    exceptionHanldingStatement(s)
    }
finally {
    cleanUpStatement(s)
    }
```

Example:

```
public static void testMath(int numerator, int divisor) throws
ArithmeticException {
try {
        if (divisor == 0)
            throw new ArithmeticException("Division by Zero.");
        }
        finally {
```

III

Java

```
                System.out.println("The fraction was " + numerator + "/" + divisor);
        }

    }
    try {
        percent_over = quantity / number_ordered * 100;        // could cause
    division by 0
        }
    catch (ArithmeticException e) {
        percent_over = 0;
        }
    finally {   // regardless of the success of the try, we still need to print
    the info
        System.out.println("Quantity = " + quantity);
        System.out.println("Ordered = " + ordered);
        System.out.println("Percent Over = " + percent_over);
        }
```

for

This is used to execute a block of code a specific number of times.

Syntax:

```
for (counterInitialization ; counterCheck    ; counterChange)
    statement(s)
```

Example:

```
String name;
...
for (pos = 0; pos < name.length(); I++)
    System.out.println(name.charAt(i));
```

if

This is used to perform operations only if a certain condition is met.

Syntax:

```
if (booleanVariable)
    statement(s)

if (booleanExpression)
    statement(s)
```

Example:

```
if (ValidNumbersOnly)
    checkInput(Answer);
```

```
if (area >= 2*PI) {
  System.out.println("The size of the loop is still too big.");
  reduceSize(area);
}
```

implements

This is used to force a class to implement the methods defined in an interface.

Syntax:

```
modifiers class className implements interfaceName
```

Example:

```
public class Clock implements Runnable, Cloneable
```

import

This is used to include other libraries.

Syntax:

```
import packageName;
```

```
import className;
```

```
import interfaceName;
```

Example:

```
import java.io.*;
```

```
import java.applet.Applet;
```

```
import java.applet.AppletContext;
```

instanceof

The instanceof operator returns true if the object to the left of the expression is an instance of the class to the right of the expression.

Syntax:

```
object instanceof ClassName
```

III

Java

Example:

```
void testType(Object instance) {
    if (instance instanceof String) {
        System.out.println("This is a string.")
        System.out.println("It is " + ((String)i).length() );   // casts the
Object to a String first
```

Modifiers

Access modifiers are used to control the accessibility and behavior of classes, interfaces, methods, and fields.

Modifier	Effect on Classes	Effect on Methods	Effect on Fields
none (friendly)	Visible to subclasses and classes within the same package.	Can be called by methods belonging to classes within the same package.	Accessible only to classes within the same package.
public	Visible to subclasses and other classes regardless of their package.	Can be called by methods in subclasses and all classes regardless of their package.	Accessible to subclasses and all classes regardless of their package.
private	Classes cannot be private.	Can only be called by methods within the current class.	Accessible only to methods within the current class.
static	Not applicable to classes.	Method is shared by all instances of the current class.	Field is shared by all instances of the current class.
abstract	Some methods are not defined. These methods must be implemented in subclasses.	Contains no body and must be overridden in subclasses.	Not applicable to fields.
final	The class cannot be used as a superclass.	The method cannot be overridden in any subclasses.	Variable's value cannot be changed.
native	Not applicable to classes.	This method's implementation will be defined by code written in another language.	Not applicable to fields.
synchronized	Not applicable to classes.	This method will seize control of the class while running. If another method has already seized control, it will wait until the first has completed.	Not applicable to fields.

native

A `native` method will be defined by code written in another language.

Syntax:

```
native returnType methodName(optionlParameters)
```

Example:

```
native long sumSeries();
```

new

The `new` operator allocates memory for an object, such as a `String`, a `Socket`, an array, or an instance of any other class.

Syntax:

```
dataType arrayName[] = new dataType[ number ];
dataType fieldName = new dataType( constructor parameters)
```

Example:

```
int sizes[] = new int[9];
String name = new String("Hello");
```

package

This is used to place the current class within the specified package.

Syntax:

```
package packageName;
```

Example:

```
package java.lang;
package mytools;
```

public

`public` makes the class, method, or field accessible to all classes.

Syntax:

```
public class className;
public interface interfaceName;
public returnType methodName(optionalParameters)
public dataType fieldName;
```

Example:

```
public class GraphicsExample;
public interface Graph;
public boolean checkStatus(int x, int y)
public int size;
```

private

The `private` modifier makes the method or field accessible only to methods in the current class.

Syntax:

```
private returnType methodName(optionalParameters)
private dataType fieldName;
```

Example:

```
private int changeStatus(int index);
private int count;
```

return

The `return` statement is used to return a value from a method. The data type returned must correspond to the data type specified in the method declaration.

Syntax:

```
return value;
```

Example:

```
float calculateArea(float circumference) {
    float radius, area;
    radius = circumference / (2 * PI);
    area = radius * radius * PI;
    return(area);
}
```

static

The static modifier makes a method or field static. Regardless of the number of instances that are created of a given class, only one copy of a static method or field will be created.

Syntax:

```
static returnType methodName(optionalParameters)

static dataType fieldName;
```

Example:

```
static void haltChanges(optionalParameters)

static Color backgroundColor;
```

A static block is a set of code that is executed immediately after object creation. It can only handle static methods and static fields.

Syntax:

```
static
    statement(s)
```

Example:

```
static {
        type = prepare();
        size = 25;
    }
```

super

This is used to refer to the superclass of this class.

Syntax:

```
super

super.methodName()

super.fieldName
```

III

Java

Example:

```
class FloorManager extends Manager {
    FloorManager() {
        type = floor;
        super();          // calls the Manager constructor
        }
    void organize() {
        size = name.getSize();
        super.organize(size);  // calls the organize method in the Manager
method
        ....      }
}
```

switch

The switch statement is a conditional statement with many options.

Syntax:

```
switch (variableName) {
   case (valueExpression1)  :   statement(s)
   case (valueExpression2)  :   statement(s)
   default  :  statement(s)
   }
```

Example:

```
char ans;
...
switch (ans) {
    case 'Y'   :   startOver();
                   break;
    case 'n'   ;
    case 'N'   :   cleanUp();
    default    :   System.out.println("Invalid response.");
}
```

synchronized

Every object has a "lock" that can be seized by an operation. Any synchronized operation seizes this lock, preventing other synchronized processes from beginning until it has finished.

Syntax:

Synchronized Method:

synchronized returnType methodName(optionalParameters)

synchronized (objectName)
    statement(s)

Example:

```
synchronized void changeValues(int size, int shape, String name)

synchronized (runningThread) {
    runningThread.name = newName;
}
```

this

this is used to refer to the current class.

Syntax:

```
this

this.methodName()

this.fieldName
```

Example:

```
ticker = new Thread(this);
```

throw

The throw statement is used to throw an exception within the body of a method. The exception must be a subclass of one of the exceptions declared with the throws statement in the method declaration.

Syntax:

```
throw exceptionObject
```

Example:

```
float calculateArea(float radius) throws IllegalArgumentException {
    if (radius < 0)
        throw(new IllegalArgumentException("Radius less than 0."));
    else
        return(radius*radius*PI);
}
```

III

Java

throws

The throws keyword specifies the types of exceptions that can be thrown from a method.

Syntax:

```
modifiers returnType methodName(optionalParameters) throws ExceptionNames
```

Example:

```
String getName(InputStream in) throws IOException
```

try

The try statement is used to enclose code that can throw an exception. It should be used with the catch() statement and may be used with the finally statement.

Syntax:

```
try
    statement(s)
catch(Exception list)
   statement(s)
finally
   statement(s)
```

Example:

```
InputStream in;
int val;
...
try
  val = in.read() / in.read();
catch(ArithmeticException e) {
    System.out.println("Invalid data.  val set to 0.");
    val = 0;
  }
catch(Exception e)
    System.out.println("Exception encountered, but not handled.");
finally {
    in.close();
    System.out.println("Stream closed.");
  }
```

while

This is used to perform a loop operation while a certain condition is met.

Syntax:

```
while (booleanVariable)
    statement(s)
```

```
while (booleanExpression)
    statement(s)
```

Example:

```
FileInputStream din;
byte info;

while (info = din.read() != -1) // End of File
    System.out.println(info);

while (stillValidData) {
    info = din.read();
    stillValidData = checkData(info);  // returns false if data is not valid
}
```

Chapter 16

Java Action Index

This is a table for problem solving. Common questions are posed in the first column below, while the second column tells you what Java command will help you with the solution. The page numbers refer you to a detailed explanation for each entry.

Animation

Question	Solution	See
How do I display my graphics?	Graphics	p.438
How do I enable my applet to run on its own?	Runnable	p.550
How do I begin the animation?	Thread	p.543
Is there an animation example in this manual?	Runnable	p.550
How do I reduce flickering?	Override the update() method in the Applet class	

Applets

Question	Solution	See
How do I create an applet?	Applet	p.409
How do I interact with the browser?	AppletContext	p.409
How do I handle user interactions?	Event	p.431
Which methods catch user interactions?	Component	p.419

III

Java

Applications

Question	Solution	See
How do I display text on the screen?	System.out	p.508
How do I start other programs on the client's side?	Runtime	p.530
How do I handle files?	File	p.495
How do I read from a file?	FileInputStream	p.498
How do I write to a file?	FileOutputStream	p.499

Communication

Question	Solution	See
How do I display an URL?	AppletContext.showDocument()	p.409
How do I handle URLs?	URL	p.558
How do I load information from an URL?	URLConnection	p.560
How do I communicate with a server?	Socket	p.555
How do I create a TCP socket?	ServerSocket	p.554
How can I continually communicate with a socket?	Thread	p.543

Image Processing

Question	Solution	See
How do I load an image in an applet?	Applet.getImage()	p.408
How do I load an image in an application?	Toolkit.getImage()	p.471
How do I manipulate an image?	ImageFilter	p.476
How do I crop an image?	CropImageFilter	p.473
How do I create an image from pixel data?	MemoryImageSource	p.480

Input and Output

Question	Solution	See
Is there a class that's like printf() in C?	Printstream	p.506
Is there any easy way to parse streams?	StreamTokenizer	p.512

Question	Solution	See
How do I read doubles, strings, etc., from a stream?	DataInputStream	p.492
How do I write doubles, strings, etc., to a stream?	DataOutputStream	p.494
How do I link InputStreams together?	SequenceInputStream	p.511
How do I interact with the environment (either the prompt of the Java console or a browser)?	System	p.541

Math

Question	Solution	See
How do I perform standard mathematical functions?	Math	p.526
How do I create random numbers?	Random	p.574
How do I handle a char as an Object?	Character	p.517
How do I handle an int as an Object?	Integer	p.523

User Interfaces

Question	Solution	See
Where can I find the window components?	java.awt package	p.411
How do I create a pop-up menu?	Frame	p.437
How do I position components on the screen?	GridBagLayout	p.445
How do I handle user interactions?	Event	p.427
Which methods catch user interactions?	Component	p.419
How do I scroll through a series of screens?	CardLayout	p.413

III

Java

Chapter 17

Index of Java Fields

This is a complete alphabetical listing of all public and protected fields in the Java API. For a thorough explanation of each field, refer to the specified page number. Note that all field names set in italics are *protected* fields.

Field	Class	Turn to...
ABORT	java.awt.image.ImageObserver	p. 486
ABORTED	java.awt.MediaTracker	p. 455
ACTION_EVENT	java.awt.Event	p. 419
ALLBITS	java.awt.image.ImageObserver	p. 486
allowUserInteraction	java.net.URLConnection	p. 560
ALT_MASK	java.awt.Event	p. 428
anchor	java.awt.GridBagConstraints	p. 443
arg	java.awt.Event	p. 428
black	java.awt.Color	p. 417
blue	java.awt.Color	p. 417
BOLD	java.awt.Font	p. 434
BOTH	java.awt.GridBagConstraints	p. 434
bottom	java.awt.Insets	p. 451
buffer	java.io.StringBufferInputStream	p. 514
buf[]	java.io.BufferedInputStream	p. 488
buf[]	java.io.BufferedOutputStream	p. 490
buf[]	java.io.ByteArrayInputStream	p. 490
buf[]	java.io.ByteArrayOutputStream	p. 492
canFilterIndexColorModel	java.awt.Image.RGBImageFilter	p. 483
capacityIncrement	java.util.Vector	p. 576
CENTER	java.awt.FlowLayout	p. 433
CENTER	java.awt.GridBagConstraints	p. 433

(continues)

III

Java

(continued)

Field	Class	Turn to...
CENTER	java.awt.Label	p. 452
clickCount	java.awt.Event	p. 428
columnWeights[]	java.awt.GridBagLayout	p. 447
columnWidths[]	java.awt.GridBagLayout	p. 447
COMPLETE	java.awt.MediaTracker	p. 455
COMPLETESCANLINES	java.awt.image.ImageConsumer	p. 484
comptable	java.awt.GridBagLayout	p. 447
connected	java.net.URLConnection	p. 560
consumer	java.awt.Image.ImageFilter	p. 478
count	java.io.BufferedInputStream	p. 488
count	java.io.BufferedOutputStream	p. 490
count	java.io.ByteArrayInputStream	p. 491
count	java.io.ByteArrayOutputStream	p. 492
count	java.io.StringBufferInputStream	p. 514
CROSSHAIR_CURSOR	java.awt.Frame	p. 437
CTRL_MASK	java.awt.Event	p. 428
cyan	java.awt.Color	p. 417
darkGray	java.awt.Color	p. 417
defaultConstraints	java.awt.GridBagLayout	p. 447
defaults	java.util.Properties	p. 573
DEFAULT_CURSOR	java.awt.Frame	p. 437
doInput	java.net.URLConnection	p. 560
doOutput	java.net.URLConnection	p. 560
DOWN	java.awt.Event	p. 428
E	java.lang.Math	p. 526
EAST	java.awt.GridBagConstraints	p. 443
elementCount	java.util.Vector	p. 576
elementData[]	java.util.Vector	p. 576
err	java.io.FileDescriptor	p. 497
ERROR	java.awt.image.ImageObserver	p. 486
ERRORED	java.awt.MediaTracker	p. 455
evt	java.awt.Event	p. 428
E_RESIZE_CURSOR	java.awt.Frame	p. 437
F1	java.awt.Event	p. 428
F2	java.awt.Event	p. 428
F3	java.awt.Event	p. 428
F4	java.awt.Event	p. 428

Field	Class	Turn to...
F5	java.awt.Event	p. 428
F6	java.awt.Event	p. 428
F7	java.awt.Event	p. 428
F8	java.awt.Event	p. 428
F9	java.awt.Event	p. 428
F10	java.awt.Event	p. 428
F11	java.awt.Event	p. 428
F12	java.awt.Event	p. 428
FALSE	java.lang.Boolean	p. 428
fill	java.awt.GridBagConstraints	p. 443
font	java.awt.Font	p. 433
FRAMEBITS	java.awt.image.ImageObserver	p. 486
GOT_FOCUS	java.awt.Event	p. 429
gray	java.awt.Color	p. 418
green	java.awt.Color	p. 418
gridheight	java.awt.GridBagConstraints	p. 444
gridwidth	java.awt.GridBagConstraints	p. 444
gridx	java.awt.GridBagConstraints	p. 444
gridy	java.awt.GridBagConstraints	p. 444
HAND_CURSOR	java.awt.Frame	p. 437
height	java.awt.Dimension	p. 427
HEIGHT	java.awt.image.ImageObserver	p. 486
height	java.awt.Rectangle	p. 462
HOME	java.awt.Event	p. 429
HORIZONTAL	java.awt.GridBagConstraints	p. 444
HORIZONTAL	java.awt.Scrollbar	p. 465
id	java.awt.Event	p. 429
ifModifiedSince	java.net.URLConnection	p. 561
IMAGEABORTED	java.awt.image.ImageConsumer	p. 485
IMAGEERROR	java.awt.image.ImageConsumer	p. 485
in	java.io.FileDescriptor	p. 497
in	java.io.FilterInputStream	p. 499-500
insets	java.awt.GridBagConstraints	p. 444
ipadx	java.awt.GridBagConstraints	p. 444
ipady	java.awt.GridBagConstraints	p. 444
ITALIC	java.awt.Font	p. 434

(continues)

III

Java

(continued)

Field	Class	Turn to...
key	java.awt.Event	p. 429
KEY_ACTION	java.awt.Event	p. 429
KEY_ACTION_RELEASE	java.awt.Event	p. 429
KEY_PRESS	java.awt.Event	p. 429
KEY_RELEASE	java.awt.Event	p. 429
layoutInfo	java.awt.GridBagLayout	p. 447
LEFT	java.awt.Event	p. 429
LEFT	java.awt.FlowLayout	p. 433
left	java.awt.Insets	p. 451
LEFT	java.awt.Label	p. 452
lightGray	java.awt.Color	p. 418
LIST_DESELECT	java.awt.Event	p. 429
LIST_SELECT	java.awt.Event	p. 429
LOAD	java.awt.FileDialog	p. 432
LOAD_FILE	java.awt.Event	p. 429
LOST_FOCUS	java.awt.Event	p. 429
magenta	java.awt.Color	p. 418
marklimit	java.io.BufferedInputStream	p. 488
markpos	java.io.BufferedInputStream	p. 488
MAXGRIDSIZE	java.awt.GridBagLayout	p. 447
MAXGRIDSIZE	java.awt.GridBagLayout	p. 447
MAX_PRIORITY	java.lang.Thread	p. 544
MAX_RADIX	java.lang.Character	p. 517
MAX_VALUE	java.lang.Boolean	p. 517
MAX_VALUE	java.lang.Double	p. 521
MAX_VALUE	java.lang.Float	p. 522
MAX_VALUE	java.lang.Integer	p. 523
MAX_VALUE	java.lang.Long	p. 525
META_MASK	java.awt.Event	p. 429
MINSIZE	java.awt.GridBagLayout	p. 447
MINSIZE	java.awt.GridBagLayout	p. 447
MIN_PRIORITY	java.lang.Thread	p. 544
MIN_RADIX	java.lang.Character	p. 517
MIN_VALUE	java.lang.Boolean	p. 517
MIN_VALUE	java.lang.Double	p. 521
MIN_VALUE	java.lang.Float	p. 522
MIN_VALUE	java.lang.Integer	p. 523

Field	Class	Turn to...
MIN_VALUE	java.lang.Long	p. 525
modifiers	java.awt.Event	p. 429
MOUSE_DOWN	java.awt.Event	p. 429
MOUSE_DRAG	java.awt.Event	p. 430
MOUSE_ENTER	java.awt.Event	p. 430
MOUSE_EXIT	java.awt.Event	p. 430
MOUSE_MOVE	java.awt.Event	p. 430
MOUSE_UP	java.awt.Event	p. 430
MOVE_CURSOR	java.awt.Frame	p. 437
name	java.awt.Font	p. 434
NaN	java.lang.Double	p. 521
NaN	java.lang.Float	p. 522
NEGATIVE_INFINITY	java.lang.Double	p. 521
NEGATIVE_INFINITY	java.lang.Float	p. 522
newmodel	java.awt.Image.RGBImageFilter	p. 483
NE_RESIZE_CURSOR	java.awt.Frame	p. 437
NONE	java.awt.GridBagConstraints	p. 444
NORM_PRIORITY	java.lang.Thread	p. 544
NORTH	java.awt.GridBagConstraints	p. 444
NORTHEAST	java.awt.GridBagConstraints	p. 444
NORTHWEST	java.awt.GridBagConstraints	p. 444
npoints	java.awt.Polygon	p. 461
nval	java.io.StreamTokenizer	p. 512
NW_RESIZE_CURSOR	java.awt.Frame	p. 437
N_RESIZE_CURSOR	java.awt.Frame	p. 437
orange	java.awt.Color	p. 418
origmodel	java.awt.Image.RGBImageFilter	p. 483
out	java.io.FileDescriptor	p. 497
out	java.io.FilterOutputStream	p. 501
pathSeparator	java.io.File	p. 495
pathSeparatorChar	java.io.File	p. 496
PGDN	java.awt.Event	p. 430
PGUP	java.awt.Event	p. 430
PI	java.lang.Math	p. 527
pink	java.awt.Color	p. 418
pixel_bits	java.awt.Image.ColorModel	p. 472
PLAIN	java.awt.Font	p. 434
port	java.net.SocketImp	p. 368

III

Java

(continues)

(continued)

Field	Class	Turn to...
pos	java.io.BufferedInputStream	p. 488
pos	java.io.ByteArrayInputStream	p. 491
pos	java.io.StringBufferInputStream	p. 514
POSITIVE_INFINITY	java.lang.Double	p. 521
POSITIVE_INFINITY	java.lang.Float	p. 522
PREFERREDSIZE	java.awt.GridBagLayout	p. 447
PROPERTIES	java.awt.image.ImageObserver	p. 486
pushBack	java.io.PushBackInputStream	p. 508
RANDOMPIXELORDER	java.awt.image.ImageConsumer	p. 485
red	java.awt.Color	p. 418
RELATIVE	java.awt.GridBagConstraints	p. 444
REMAINDER	java.awt.GridBagConstraints	p. 444
RIGHT	java.awt.Event	p. 430
RIGHT	java.awt.FlowLayout	p. 433
right	java.awt.Insets	p. 451
RIGHT	java.awt.Label	p. 452
SAVE	java.awt.FileDialog	p. 432
SAVE_FILE	java.awt.Event	p. 430
SCROLL_ABSOLUTE	java.awt.Event	p. 430
SCROLL_LINE_DOWN	java.awt.Event	p. 430
SCROLL_LINE_UP	java.awt.Event	p. 430
SCROLL_PAGE_DOWN	java.awt.Event	p. 430
SCROLL_PAGE_UP	java.awt.Event	p. 430
separator	java.io.File	p. 496
separatorChar	java.io.File	p. 496
SE_RESIZE_CURSOR	java.awt.Frame	p. 437
SHIFT_MASK	java.awt.Event	p. 430
SINGLEFRAME	java.awt.image.ImageConsumer	p. 485
SINGLEFRAMEDONE	java.awt.image.ImageConsumer	p. 485
SINGLEPASS	java.awt.image.ImageConsumer	p. 485
size	java.awt.Font	p. 434
SOMEBITS	java.awt.image.ImageObserver	p. 486
SOUTH	java.awt.GridBagConstraints	p. 444
SOUTHEAST	java.awt.GridBagConstraints	p. 444
SOUTHWEST	java.awt.GridBagConstraints	p. 445
STATICIMAGEDONE	java.awt.image.ImageConsumer	p. 485
style	java.awt.Font	p. 434
sval	java.io.StreamTokenizer	p. 512
SW_RESIZE_CURSOR	java.awt.Frame	p. 437

Field	Class	Turn to...
S_RESIZE_CURSOR	java.awt.Frame	p. 437
target	java.awt.Event	p. 430
TEXT_CURSOR	java.awt.Frame	p. 437
top	java.awt.Insets	p. 451
TOPDOWNLEFTRIGHT	java.awt.image.ImageConsumer	p. 485
TRUE	java.lang.Boolean	p. 517
TT_EOF	java.io.StreamTokenizer	p. 512
TT_EOL	java.io.StreamTokenizer	p. 512
TT_NUMBER	java.io.StreamTokenizer	p. 512
TT_WORD	java.io.StreamTokenizer	p. 512
UndefinedProperty	java.awt.Image	p. 450
UP	java.awt.Event	p. 430
useCaches	java.net.URLConnection	p. 561
VERTICAL	java.awt.GridBagConstraints	p. 445
VERTICAL	java.awt.Scrollbar	p. 465
WAIT_CURSOR	java.awt.Frame	p. 437
weightx	java.awt.GridBagConstraints	p. 447
weighty	java.awt.GridBagConstraints	p. 447
WEST	java.awt.GridBagConstraints	p. 445
white	java.awt.Color	p. 418
width	java.awt.Dimension	p. 427
WIDTH	java.awt.image.ImageObserver	p. 486
width	java.awt.Rectangle	p. 462
WINDOW_DEICONIFY	java.awt.Event	p. 430
WINDOW_DESTROY	java.awt.Event	p. 430
WINDOW_EXPOSE	java.awt.Event	p. 430
WINDOW_ICONIFY	java.awt.Event	p. 430
WINDOW_MOVED	java.awt.Event	p. 430
W_RESIZE_CURSOR	java.awt.Frame	p. 437
x	java.awt.Event	p. 430
x	java.awt.Point	p. 461
x	java.awt.Rectangle	p. 462
xpoints[]	java.awt.Polygon	p. 461-462
y	java.awt.Event	p. 430
y	java.awt.Point	p. 461
y	java.awt.Rectangle	p. 462
yellow	java.awt.Color	p. 418
ypoints[]	java.awt.Polygon	p. 461-462

Chapter 18

Index of Java Methods

This index is an alphabetical listing of all methods found in the Java API. The page numbers refer you to the complete explanations of the methods and their classes.

Method	Class	Turn to Page...
abs(double)	java.lang.Math	p.527
abs(float)	java.lang.Math	p.527
abs(int)	java.lang.Math	p.527
abs(long)	java.lang.Math	p.527
accept()	java.net.ServerSocket	p.555
accept(File, String)	java.io.FilenameFilter	p.516
accept(SocketImpl)	java.net.SocketImpl	p.557
acos(double)	java.lang.Math	p.527
action(Event, Object)	java.awt.Component	p.419
activeCount()	java.lang.Thread	p.545
activeCount()	java.lang.ThreadGroup	p.547
activeGroupCount()	java.lang.ThreadGroup	p.547
add(Component)	java.awt.Container	p.425
add(Component, int)	java.awt.Container	p.425
add(int, int)	java.awt.Rectangle	p.463
add(Menu)	java.awt.MenuBar	p.459
add(MenuItem)	java.awt.Menu	p.457
add(Point)	java.awt.Rectangle	p.463
add(Rectangle)	java.awt.Rectangle	p.463
add(String)	java.awt.Menu	p.425
add(String, Component)	java.awt.Container	p.425

(continues)

(continued)

Method	Class	Turn to Page...
addConsumer(ImageConsumer)	java.awt.image.FilteredImageSource	p.475
addConsumer(ImageConsumer)	java.awt.image.ImageProducer	p.487
addConsumer(ImageConsumer)	java.awt.image.MemoryImageSource	p.481
addElement(Object)	java.util.Vector	p.576
addImage(Image, int)	java.awt.MediaTracker	p.455
addImage(Image, int, int, int)	java.awt.MediaTracker	p.455
addItem(String)	java.awt.Choice	p.417
addItem(String)	java.awt.List	p.453
addItem(String, int)	java.awt.List	p.453
addLayoutComponent(String, Component)	java.awt.BorderLayout	p.411
addLayoutComponent(String, Component)	java.awt.CardLayout	p.414
addLayoutComponent(String, Component)	java.awt.FlowLayout	p.433
addLayoutComponent(String, Component)	java.awt.GridBagLayout	p.448
addLayoutComponent(String, Component)	java.awt.GridLayout	p.449
addLayoutComponent(String, Component)	java.awt.LayoutManager	p.472
addNotify()	java.awt.Button	p.412
addNotify()	java.awt.Canvas	p.413
addNotify()	java.awt.Checkbox	p.415
addNotify()	java.awt.CheckboxMenuItem	p.416
addNotify()	java.awt.Choice	p.417
addNotify()	java.awt.Component	p.419
addNotify()	java.awt.Container	p.425
addNotify()	java.awt.Dialog	p.427
addNotify()	java.awt.FileDialog	p.432
addNotify()	java.awt.Frame	p.437
addNotify()	java.awt.Label	p.452
addNotify()	java.awt.List	p.453
addNotify()	java.awt.Menu	p.457
addNotify()	java.awt.MenuBar	p.459
addNotify()	java.awt.MenuItem	p.460
addNotify()	java.awt.Panel	p.461
addNotify()	java.awt.Scrollbar	p.465
addNotify()	java.awt.TextArea	p.467

Method	Class	Turn to Page...
addNotify()	java.awt.TextField	p.468
addNotify()	java.awt.Window	p.471
addObserver(Observer)	java.util.Observable	p.572
addPoint(int, int)	java.awt.Polygon	p.462
addSeparator()	java.awt.Menu	p.457
AdjustForGravity (GridBagConstraints, Rectangle)	java.awt.GridBaglayout	p.448
after(Date)	java.util.Date	p.567
allowsMultipleSelections()	java.awt.List	p.453
and(BitSet)	java.util.BitSet	p.566
append(boolean)	java.lang.StringBuffer	p.540
append(char)	java.lang.StringBuffer	p.540
append(char[])	java.lang.StringBuffer	p.540
append(char[], int, int)	java.lang.StringBuffer	p.540
append(double)	java.lang.StringBuffer	p.540
append(float)	java.lang.StringBuffer	p.540
append(int)	java.lang.StringBuffer	p.540
append(long)	java.lang.StringBuffer	p.540
append(Object)	java.lang.StringBuffer	p.540
append(String)	java.lang.StringBuffer	p.540
appendText(String)	java.awt.TextArea	p.467
appletResize(int, int)	java.applet.AppletStub	p.410
ArrangeGrid(Container)	java.awt.GridBagLayout	p.448
arraycopy(Object, int, Object,int, int)	java.lang.System	p.542
asin(double)	java.lang.Math	p.527
atan(double)	java.lang.Math	p.527
atan2(double, double)	java.lang.Math	p.527
available()	java.io.BufferedInputStream	p.489
available()	java.io.ByteArrayInputStream	p.491
available()	java.io.FileInputStream	p.498, 500
available()	java.io.FilterInputStream	p.499
available()	java.io.InputStream	p.502
available()	java.io.LineNumberInputStream	p.502

(continues)

III

Java

(continued)

Method	Class	Turn to Page...
available()	java.io.PushbackInputStream	p.508
available()	java.io.StringBufferInputStream	p.514
before(Date)	java.util.Date	p.567
bind(InetAddress, int)	java.net.SocketImpl	p.557
BitSet()	java.util.BitSet	p.565
BitSet(int)	java.util.BitSet	p.565
Boolean(boolean)	java.lang.Boolean	p.517
Boolean(String)	java.lang.Boolean	p.517
booleanValue()	java.lang.Boolean	p.517
BorderLayout()	java.awt.BorderLayout	p.411
BorderLayout(int, int)	java.awt.BorderLayout	p.411
bounds()	java.awt.Component	p.419
brighter()	java.awt.Color	p.418
BufferedInputStream(InputStream)	java.io.BufferedInputStream	p.489
BufferedInputStream(InputStream, int)	java.io.BufferedInputStream	p.488
BufferedOutputStream(OutputStream)	java.io.BufferedOutputStream	p.490
BufferedOutputStream(OutputStream, int)	java.io.BufferedOutputStream	p.490
Button()	java.awt.Button	p.412
Button(String)	java.awt.Button	p.412
ByteArrayInputStream(byte[])	java.io.ByteArrayInputStream	p.490-491
ByteArrayInputStream(byte[], int, int)	java.io.ByteArrayInputStream	p.490-491
ByteArrayOutputStream()	java.io.ByteArrayOutputStream	p.492
ByteArrayOutputStream(int)	java.io.ByteArrayOutputStream	p.492
bytesWidth(byte[], int, int)	java.awt.FontMetrics	p.436
canRead()	java.io.File	p.496
Canvas()	java.awt.Canvas	p.412
canWrite()	java.io.File	p.496
capacity()	java.lang.StringBuffer	p.539
capacity()	java.util.Vector	p.576
CardLayout()	java.awt.CardLayout	p.414
CardLayout(int, int)	java.awt.CardLayout	p.414
ceil(double)	java.lang.Math	p.527
Character(char)	java.lang.Character	p.517
charAt(int)	java.lang.String	p.535
charAt(int)	java.lang.StringBuffer	p.539
charsWidth(char[], int, int)	java.awt.FontMetrics	p.436

Method	Class	Turn to Page...
charValue()	java.lang.Character	p.518
charWidth(char)	java.awt.FontMetrics	p.436
charWidth(int)	java.awt.FontMetrics	p.436
checkAccept(String, int)	java.lang.SecurityManager	p.533
checkAccess()	java.lang.Thread	p.545
checkAccess()	java.lang.ThreadGroup	p.547
checkAccess(Thread)	java.lang.SecurityManager	p.533
checkAccess(ThreadGroup)	java.lang.SecurityManager	p.533
checkAll()	java.awt.MediaTracker	p.455
checkAll(boolean)	java.awt.MediaTracker	p.455
Checkbox()	java.awt.Checkbox	p.415
Checkbox(String)	java.awt.Checkbox	p.415
Checkbox (String, CheckboxGroup, boolean)	java.awt.Checkbox	p.415
CheckboxGroup()	java.awt.CheckboxGroup	p.416
CheckboxMenuItem(String)	java.awt.CheckboxMenuItem	p.416
checkConnect(String, int)	java.lang.SecurityManager	p.533
checkConnect(String, int, Object)	java.lang.SecurityManager	p.533
checkCreateClassLoader()	java.lang.SecurityManager	p.533
checkDelete(String)	java.lang.SecurityManager	p.533
checkError()	java.io.PrintStream	p.507
checkExec(String)	java.lang.SecurityManager	p.533
checkExit(int)	java.lang.SecurityManager	p.533
checkID(int)	java.awt.MediaTracker	p.455
checkID(int, boolean)	java.awt.MediaTracker	p.455
checkImage(Image, ImageObserver)	java.awt.Component	p.420
checkImage (Image, int, int, ImageObserver)	java.awt.Component	p.420
checkImage (Image, int, int, ImageObserver)	java.awt.Toolkit	p.420
checkLink(String)	java.lang.SecurityManager	p.533
checkListen(int)	java.lang.SecurityManager	p.533
checkPackageAccess(String)	java.lang.SecurityManager	p.533
checkPackageDefinition(String)	java.lang.SecurityManager	p.534
checkPropertiesAccess()	java.lang.SecurityManager	p.534
checkPropertyAccess(String)	java.lang.SecurityManager	p.534
checkPropertyAccess(String, String)	java.lang.SecurityManager	p.534
checkRead(FileDescriptor)	java.lang.SecurityManager	p.534
checkRead(String)	java.lang.SecurityManager	p.534
checkRead(String, Object)	java.lang.SecurityManager	p.534

III

Java

(continues)

(continued)

Method	Class	Turn to Page...
checkSetFactory()	java.lang.SecurityManager	p.534
checkTopLevelWindow(Object)	java.lang.SecurityManager	p.534
checkWrite(FileDescriptor)	java.lang.SecurityManager	p.534
checkWrite(String)	java.lang.SecurityManager	p.534
Choice()	java.awt.Choice	p.417
ClassLoader()	java.lang.ClassLoader	p.520
classLoaderDepth()	java.lang.SecurityManager	p.534
clear()	java.util.Hashtable	p.571
clear()	java.awt.List	p.453
clear(int)	java.util.BitSet	p.566
clearChanged()	java.util.Observable	p.572
clearRect(int, int, int, int)	java.awt.Graphics	p.439
clipRect(int, int, int, int)	java.awt.Graphics	p.439
clone()	java.util.BitSet	p.566
clone()	java.awt.GridBagConstraints	p.445
clone()	java.util.Hashtable	p.571
clone()	java.util.Vector	p.576
close()	java.io.FileInputStream	p.498, 500
close()	java.io.FileOutputStream	p.499-501
close()	java.io.InputStream	p.502
close()	java.io.OutputStream	p.503
close()	java.io.PipedInputStream	p.505, 506
close()	java.io.PipedOutputStream	p.505, 506
close()	java.io.PrintStream	p.507
close()	java.io.RandomAccessFile	p.509
close()	java.io.SequenceInputStream	p.511
close()	java.net.Socket	p.555
close()	java.net.SocketImpl	p.557
Color(float, float, float)	java.awt.Color	p.418
Color(int)	java.awt.Color	p.418

Method	Class	Turn to Page...
Color(int, int, int)	java.awt.Color	p.418
ColorModel(int)	java.awt.image.ColorModel	p.473
command(Object)	java.lang.Compiler	p.520
commentChar(int)	java.io.StreamTokenizer	p.520
compareTo(String)	java.lang.String	p.536
compileClass(Class)	java.lang.Compiler	p.520
compileClasses(String)	java.lang.Compiler	p.520
concat(String)	java.lang.String	p.536
connect()	java.net.URLConnection	p.561
connect(InetAddress, int)	java.net.SocketImpl	p.557
connect(PipedInputStream)	java.io.PipedOutputStream	p.506
connect(PipedOutputStream)	java.io.PipedInputStream	p.506
connect(String, int)	java.net.SocketImpl	p.558
contains(Object)	java.util.Hashtable	p.571
contains(Object)	java.util.Vector	p.576
containsKey(Object)	java.util.Hashtable	p.571
ContentHandler()	java.net.ContentHandler	p.552
controlDown()	java.awt.Event	p.431
copyArea(int, int, int, int, int, int)	java.awt.Graphics	p.440
copyInto(Object[])	java.util.Vector	p.576
copyValueOf(char[])	java.lang.String	p.536
copyValueOf(char[], int, int)	java.lang.String	p.536
cos(double)	java.lang.Math	p.527
countComponents()	java.awt.Container	p.425
countItems()	java.awt.Choice	p.417
countItems()	java.awt.List	p.453
countItems()	java.awt.Menu	p.457
countMenus()	java.awt.MenuBar	p.459
countObservers()	java.util.Observable	p.572
countStackFrames()	java.lang.Thread	p.545

(continues)

III

Java

(continued)

Method	Class	Turn to Page...
countTokens()	java.util.StringTokenizer	p.575
create()	java.awt.Graphics	p.440
create(boolean)	java.net.SocketImpl	p.440
create(int, int, int, int)	java.awt.Graphics	p.440
createButton(Button)	java.awt.Toolkit	p.469
createCanvas(Canvas)	java.awt.Toolkit	p.469
createCheckbox(Checkbox)	java.awt.Toolkit	p.469
createCheckboxMenuItem (CheckboxMenuItem)	java.awt.Toolkit	p.469
createChoice(Choice)	java.awt.Toolkit	p.469
createContentHandler(String)	java.net.ContentHandlerFactory	p.564
createDialog(Dialog)	java.awt.Toolkit	p.470
createFileDialog(FileDialog)	java.awt.Toolkit	p.470
createFrame(Frame)	java.awt.Toolkit	p.470
createImage(ImageProducer)	java.awt.Component	p.420
createImage(ImageProducer)	java.awt.Toolkit	p.469
createImage(int, int)	java.awt.Component	p.420
createLabel(Label)	java.awt.Toolkit	p.470
createList(List)	java.awt.Toolkit	p.470
createMenu(Menu)	java.awt.Toolkit	p.470
createMenuBar(MenuBar)	java.awt.Toolkit	p.470
createMenuItem(MenuItem)	java.awt.Toolkit	p.470
createPanel(Panel)	java.awt.Toolkit	p.470
createScrollbar(Scrollbar)	java.awt.Toolkit	p.470
createSocketImpl()	java.net.SocketImplFactory	p.470
createTextArea(TextArea)	java.awt.Toolkit	p.470
createTextField(TextField)	java.awt.Toolkit	p.470
createURLStreamHandler(String)	java.net.URLStreamHandlerFactory	p.470
createWindow(Window)	java.awt.Toolkit	p.470
CropImageFilter(int, int, int, int)	java.awt.image.CropImageFilter	p.473
currentClassLoader()	java.lang.SecurityManager	p.534
currentThread()	java.lang.Thread	p.545
darker()	java.awt.Color	p.418
DatagramPacket(byte[], int)	java.net.DatagramPacket	p.553
DatagramPacket (byte[], int,InetAddress, int)	java.net.DatagramPacket	p.553
DatagramSocket()	java.net.DatagramSocket	p.553
DatagramSocket(int)	java.net.DatagramSocket	p.553

Method	Class	Turn to Page...
DataInputStream(InputStream)	java.io.DataInputStream	p.492
DataOutputStream(OutputStream)	java.io.DataOutputStream	p.492
Date()	java.util.Date	p.566
Date(int, int, int)	java.util.Date	p.567
Date(int, int, int, int, int)	java.util.Date	p.567
Date(int, int, int, int, int, int)	java.util.Date	p.567
Date(long)	java.util.Date	p.566
Date(String)	java.util.Date	p.567
defineClass(byte[], int, int)	java.lang.ClassLoader	p.520
delete()	java.io.File	p.496
deleteObserver(Observer)	java.util.Observable	p.572
deleteObservers()	java.util.Observable	p.572
delItem(int)	java.awt.List	p.453
delItems(int, int)	java.awt.List	p.453
deliverEvent(Event)	java.awt.Component	p.420
deliverEvent(Event)	java.awt.Container	p.425
deselect(int)	java.awt.List	p.453
destroy()	java.lang.Process	p.530
destroy()	java.lang.Thread	p.545
destroy()	java.lang.ThreadGroup	p.547
Dialog(Frame, boolean)	java.awt.Dialog	p.427
Dialog(Frame, String, boolean)	java.awt.Dialog	p.427
Dictionary()	java.util.Dictionary	p.569
digit(char, int)	java.lang.Character	p.518
Dimension()	java.awt.Dimension	p.427
Dimension(Dimension)	java.awt.Dimension	p.427
Dimension(int, int)	java.awt.Dimension	p.427
DirectColorModel(int, int, int, int)	java.awt.image.DirectColorModel	p.474
DirectColorModel (int, int, int, int, int)	java.awt.image.DirectColorModel	p.474
disable()	java.lang.Compiler	p.520
disable()	java.awt.Component	p.420
disable()	java.awt.MenuItem	p.460
dispose()	java.awt.Frame	p.437
dispose()	java.awt.Graphics	p.440
dispose()	java.awt.Window	p.471
Double(double)	java.lang.Double	p.521
Double(String)	java.lang.Double	p.521

III

Java

(continues)

(continued)

Method	Class	Turn to Page...
doubleToLongBits(double)	java.lang.Double	p.521
doubleValue()	java.lang.Double	p.521
doubleValue()	java.lang.Float	p.522
doubleValue()	java.lang.Integer	p.524
doubleValue()	java.lang.Long	p.525
doubleValue()	java.lang.Number	p.529
draw3DRect(int, int, int, int, boolean)	java.awt.Graphics	p.440
drawArc(int, int, int, int, int, int)	java.awt.Graphics	p.440
drawBytes(byte[], int, int, int, int)	java.awt.Graphics	p.440
drawChars(char[], int, int, int, int)	java.awt.Graphics	p.440
drawImage (Image, int, int, Color, ImageObserver)	java.awt.Graphics	p.441
drawImage (Image, int, int, ImageObserver)	java.awt.Graphics	p.441
drawImage (Image, int, int, int, int, Color, ImageObserver)	java.awt.Graphics	p.441
drawImage(Image, int, int, int, int, ImageObserver)	java.awt.Graphics	p.441
drawLine(int, int, int, int)	java.awt.Graphics	p.441
drawOval(int, int, int, int)	java.awt.Graphics	p.441
drawPolygon(int[], int[], int)	java.awt.Graphics	p.441
drawPolygon(Polygon)	java.awt.Graphics	p.441
drawRect(int, int, int, int)	java.awt.Graphics	p.441
drawRoundRect (int, int, int, int, int, int)	java.awt.Graphics	p.441
drawString(String, int, int)	java.awt.Graphics	p.442
DumpConstraints(GridBagConstraints)	java.awt.GridBagLayout	p.448
DumpLayoutInfo(GridBagLayoutInfo)	java.awt.GridBagLayout	p.488
echoCharIsSet()	java.awt.TextField	p.468
elementAt(int)	java.util.Vector	p.576
elements()	java.util.Dictionary	p.569
elements()	java.util.Hashtable	p.571
elements()	java.util.Vector	p.576
empty()	java.util.Stack	p.574
enable()	java.lang.Compiler	p.520
enable()	java.awt.Component	p.420
enable()	java.awt.MenuItem	p.460
enable(boolean)	java.awt.Component	p.420

Method	Class	Turn to Page...
enable(boolean)	java.awt.MenuItem	p.460
encode(String)	java.net.URLEncoder	p.563
endsWith(String)	java.lang.String	p.536
ensureCapacity(int)	java.lang.StringBuffer	p.539
ensureCapacity(int)	java.util.Vector	p.577
enumerate(Thread[])	java.lang.Thread	p.547-548
enumerate(Thread[])	java.lang.ThreadGroup	p.548
enumerate(Thread[], boolean)	java.lang.ThreadGroup	p.548
enumerate(ThreadGroup[])	java.lang.ThreadGroup	p.548
enumerate(ThreadGroup[], boolean)	java.lang.ThreadGroup	p.548
eolIsSignificant(boolean)	java.io.StreamTokenizer	p.512
equals(Object)	java.util.BitSet	p.566
equals(Object)	java.lang.Boolean	p.517
equals(Object)	java.lang.Character	p.518
equals(Object)	java.awt.Color	p.418
equals(Object)	java.util.Date	p.567
equals(Object)	java.lang.Double	p.521
equals(Object)	java.io.File	p.496
equals(Object)	java.lang.Float	p.522
equals(Object)	java.awt.Font	p.434
equals(Object)	java.lang.Integer	p.524
equals(Object)	java.lang.Long	p.525
equals(Object)	java.lang.Object	p.529
equals(Object)	java.awt.Point	p.461
equals(Object)	java.awt.Rectangle	p.463
equals(Object)	java.lang.String	p.536
equals(Object)	java.net.URL	p.559
equalsIgnoreCase(String)	java.lang.String	p.536
Error()	java.lang.Error	p.582
Error(String)	java.lang.Error	p.582
Event(Object, int, Object)	java.awt.Event	p.431
Event(Object, long, int, int, int, int, int)	java.awt.Event	p.4331
Event(Object, long, int, int, int, int, int, Object)	java.awt.Event	p.431
Exception()	java.lang.Exception	p.579

(continues)

Java

(continued)

Method	Class	Turn to Page...
exec(String)	java.lang.Runtime	p.531
exec(String, String[])	java.lang.Runtime	p.531
exec(String[])	java.lang.Runtime	p.531
exec(String[], String[])	java.lang.Runtime	p.531
exists()	java.io.File	p.496
exit(int)	java.lang.Runtime	p.531
exit(int)	java.lang.System	p.542
exitValue()	java.lang.Process	p.530
exp(double)	java.lang.Math	p.527
File(File, String)	java.io.File	p.496
File(String)	java.io.File	p.496
File(String, String)	java.io.File	p.496
FileDescriptor()	java.io.FileDescriptor	p.497
FileDialog(Frame, String)	java.awt.FileDialog	p.432
FileDialog(Frame, String, int)	java.awt.FileDialog	p.432
FileInputStream(File)	java.io.FileInputStream	p.498
FileInputStream(FileDescriptor)	java.io.FileInputStream	p.498
FileInputStream(String)	java.io.FileInputStream	p.498
FileOutputStream(File)	java.io.FileOutputStream	p.499
FileOutputStream(FileDescriptor)	java.io.FileOutputStream	p.499
FileOutputStream(String)	java.io.FileOutputStream	p.499
fill3DRect(int, int, int, int, boolean)	java.awt.Graphics	p.442
fillArc(int, int, int, int, int, int)	java.awt.Graphics	p.442
fillOval(int, int, int, int)	java.awt.Graphics	p.442
fillPolygon(int[], int[], int)	java.awt.Graphics	p.442
fillPolygon(Polygon)	java.awt.Graphics	p.442
fillRect(int, int, int, int)	java.awt.Graphics	p.442
fillRoundRect (int, int, int, int, int, int)	java.awt.Graphics	p.442
FilteredImageSource (ImageProducer, ImageFilter)	java.awt.FilteredImageSource	p.475
filterIndexColorModel(IndexColorModel)	java.awt.image.RGBImage	p.484
FilterInputStream(InputStream)	java.io.FilterInputStream	p.590
FilterOutputStream(OutputStream)	java.io.FilterOutputStream	p.591
filterRGB(int, int, int)	java.awt.image.RGBImageFilter	p.484
filterRGBPixels (int, int, int, int, int[], int, int)	java.awt.image.RGBImageFilter	p.484

Method	Class	Turn to Page...
finalize()	java.net.DatagramSocket	p.553
finalize()	java.io.FileInputStream	p.498
finalize()	java.io.FileOutputStream	p.499
finalize()	java.awt.Graphics	p.422
finalize()	java.lang.Object	p.529
first(Container)	java.awt.CardLayout	p.414
firstElement()	java.util.Vector	p.577
Float(double)	java.lang.Float	p.522
Float(float)	java.lang.Float	p.522
Float(String)	java.lang.Float	p.522
floatToIntBits(float)	java.lang.Float	p.523
floatValue()	java.lang.Double	p.521
floatValue()	java.lang.Float	p.523
floatValue()	java.lang.Integer	p.524
floatValue()	java.lang.Long	p.525
floatValue()	java.lang.Number	p.529
floor(double)	java.lang.Math	p.527
FlowLayout()	java.awt.FlowLayout	p.433
FlowLayout(int)	java.awt.FlowLayout	p.433
FlowLayout(int, int, int)	java.awt.FlowLayout	p.433
flush()	java.io.BufferedOutputStream	p.490
flush()	java.io.DataOutputStream	p.494
flush()	java.io.FilterOutputStream	p.501
flush()	java.io.OutputStream	p.503
flush()	java.io.PrintStream	p.507
Font(String, int, int)	java.awt.Font	p.434
FontMetrics(Font)	java.awt.FontMetrics	p.435
forDigit(int, int)	java.lang.Character	p.518
forName(String)	java.lang.Class	p.519
Frame()	java.awt.Frame	p.437
Frame(String)	java.awt.Frame	p.437
freeMemory()	java.lang.Runtime	p.531
gc()	java.lang.Runtime	p.532
gc()	java.lang.System	p.542
get(int)	java.util.BitSet	p.566
get(Object)	java.util.Dictionary	p.569
get(Object)	java.util.Hashtable	p.571

III

Java

(continues)

(continued)

Method	Class	Turn to Page...
getAbsolutePath()	java.io.File	p.496
getAddress()	java.net.DatagramPacket	p.553
getAddress()	java.net.InetAddress	p.544
getAlignment()	java.awt.Label	p.452
getAllowUserInteraction()	java.net.URLConnection	p.561
getAlpha(int)	java.awt.image.DirectColorModel	p.474
getAlpha(int)	java.awt.image.IndexColorModel	p.479
getAlphaMask()	java.awt.image.DirectColorModel	p.475
getAlphas(byte[])	java.awt.image.IndexColorModel	p.479
getApplet(String)	java.applet.AppletContext	p.409
getAppletContext()	java.applet.Applet	p.410
getAppletContext()	java.applet.AppletStub	p.410
getAppletInfo()	java.applet.Applet	p.408-409
getApplets()	java.applet.AppletContext	p.409
getAscent()	java.awt.FontMetrics	p.436
getAudioClip(URL)	java.applet.Applet	p.409
getAudioClip(URL)	java.applet.AppletContext	p.409
getAudioClip(URL, String)	java.applet.Applet	p.408
getBackground()	java.awt.Component	p.420
getBlue()	java.awt.Color	p.418
getBlue(int)	java.awt.image.ColorModel	p.473
getBlue(int)	java.awt.image.DirectColorModel	p.475
getBlue(int)	java.awt.image.IndexColorModel	p.479
getBlueMask()	java.awt.image.DirectColorModel	p.475
getBlues(byte[])	java.awt.image.IndexColorModel	p.479
getBoolean(String)	java.lang.Boolean	p.517
getBoundingBox()	java.awt.Polygon	p.462
getBytes(int, int, byte[], int)	java.lang.String	p.536
getChars(int, int, char[], int)	java.lang.String	p.536
getChars(int, int, char[], int)	java.lang.StringBuffer	p.536
getClass()	java.lang.Object	p.529
getClassContext()	java.lang.SecurityManager	p.535
getClassLoader()	java.lang.Class	p.519
getClipRect()	java.awt.Graphics	p.442
getCodeBase()	java.applet.Applet	p.410
getCodeBase()	java.applet.AppletStub	p.410

Method	Class	Turn to Page...
getColor()	java.awt.Graphics	p.442
getColor(String)	java.awt.Color	p.418
getColor(String, Color)	java.awt.Color	p.418
getColor(String, int)	java.awt.Color	p.418
getColorModel()	java.awt.Component	p.420
getColorModel()	java.awt.Toolkit	p.470
getColumns()	java.awt.TextArea	p.467
getColumns()	java.awt.TextField	p.468
getComponent(int)	java.awt.Container	p.425
getComponents()	java.awt.Container	p.425
getConstraints(Component)	java.awt.GridBagLayout	p.448
getContent()	java.net.URL	p.561
getContent()	java.net.URLConnection	p.561
getContent(URLConnection)	java.net.ContentHandler	p.552
getContentEncoding()	java.net.URLConnection	p.561
getContentLength()	java.net.URLConnection	p.561
getContentType()	java.net.URLConnection	p.561
getCurrent()	java.awt.CheckboxGroup	p.416
getCursorType()	java.awt.Frame	p.438
getData()	java.net.DatagramPacket	p.553
getDate()	java.util.Date	p.567
getDate()	java.net.URLConnection	p.561
getDay()	java.util.Date	p.567
getDefaultAllowUserInteraction()	java.net.URLConnection	p.562
getDefaultRequestProperty(String)	java.net.URLConnection	p.562
getDefaultToolkit()	java.awt.Toolkit	p.470
getDefaultUseCaches()	java.net.URLConnection	p.562
getDescent()	java.awt.FontMetrics	p.436
getDirectory()	java.awt.FileDialog	p.432
getDocumentBase()	java.applet.AppletStub	p.410
getDoInput()	java.net.URLConnection	p.561
getDoOutput()	java.net.URLConnection	p.561
getEchoChar()	java.awt.TextField	p.468
getenv(String)	java.lang.System	p.542
getErrorsAny()	java.awt.MediaTracker	p.455
getErrorsID(int)	java.awt.MediaTracker	p.455
getErrorStream()	java.lang.Process	p.456
getExpiration()	java.net.URLConnection	p.561

(continues)

III

Java

(continued)

Method	Class	Turn to Page...
getFamily()	java.awt.Font	p.434
getFD()	java.io.FileInputStream	p.498
getFD()	java.io.FileOutputStream	p.499
getFile()	java.awt.FileDialog	p.432
getFile()	java.net.URL	p.559
getFileDescriptor()	java.net.SocketImpl	p.558
getFilenameFilter()	java.awt.FileDialog	p.432
getFilePointer()	java.io.RandomAccessFile	p.509
getFont()	java.awt.Component	p.420
getFont()	java.awt.FontMetrics	p.436
getFont()	java.awt.Graphics	p.442
getFont()	java.awt.MenuComponent	p.460
getFont()	java.awt.MenuContainer	p.472
getFont(String)	java.awt.Font	p.434
getFont(String, Font)	java.awt.Font	p.434
getFontList()	java.awt.Toolkit	p.470
getFontMetrics()	java.awt.Graphics	p.442
getFontMetrics(Font)	java.awt.Component	p.442
getFontMetrics(Font)	java.awt.Graphics	p.442
getFontMetrics(Font)	java.awt.Toolkit	p.470
getForeground()	java.awt.Component	p.420
getGraphics()	java.awt.Component	p.420
getGreen()	java.awt.Color	p.418
getGreen(int)	java.awt.image.ColorModel	p.473
getGreen(int)	java.awt.image.DirectColorModel	p.475
getGreen(int)	java.awt.image.IndexColorModel	p.480
getGreenMask()	java.awt.image.DirectColorModel	p.475
getGreens(byte[])	java.awt.image.IndexColorModel	p.480
getHeaderField(int)	java.net.URLConnection	p.561
getHeaderField(String)	java.net.URLConnection	p.561
getHeaderFieldDate(String, long)	java.net.URLConnection	p.562
getHeaderFieldInt(String, int)	java.net.URLConnection	p.562
getHeaderFieldKey(int)	java.net.URLConnection	p.562
getHeight()	java.awt.FontMetrics	p.436
getHelpMenu()	java.awt.MenuBar	p.459

Method	Class	Turn to Page...
getHost()	java.net.URL	p.559
getHours()	java.util.Date	p.567
getHSBColor(float, float, float)	java.awt.Color	p.419
getIconImage()	java.awt.Frame	p.438
getIfModifiedSince()	java.net.URLConnection	p.562
getImage(String)	java.awt.Toolkit	p.471
getImage(URL)	java.applet.Applet	p.408
getImage(URL)	java.applet.AppletContext	p.409
getImage(URL)	java.awt.Toolkit	p.471
getInCheck()	java.lang.SecurityManager	p.535
getInetAddress()	java.net.ServerSocket	p.555
getInetAddress()	java.net.Socket	p.556
getInetAddress()	java.net.SocketImpl	p.558
getInputStream()	java.lang.Process	p.530
getInputStream()	java.net.Socket	p.556
getInputStream()	java.net.SocketImpl	p.558
getInputStream()	java.net.URLConnection	p.562
getInteger(String)	java.lang.Integer	p.524
getInteger(String, int)	java.lang.Integer	p.524
getInteger(String, Integer)	java.lang.Integer	p.524
getInterfaces()	java.lang.Class	p.519
getItem(int)	java.awt.Choice	p.417
getItem(int)	java.awt.List	p.453
getItem(int)	java.awt.Menu	p.457
getLabel()	java.awt.Button	p.412
getLabel()	java.awt.Checkbox	p.415
getLabel()	java.awt.MenuItem	p.460
getLastModified()	java.net.URLConnection	p.562
getLayout()	java.awt.Container	p.426
getLayoutDimensions()	java.awt.GridBagLayout	p.448
GetLayoutInfo(Container, int)	java.awt.GridBagLayout	p.448
getLayoutOrigin()	java.awt.GridBagLayout	p.448
getLayoutWeights()	java.awt.GridBagLayout	p.488
getLength()	java.net.DatagramPacket	p.553
getLineIncrement()	java.awt.Scrollbar	p.465
getLineNumber()	java.io.LineNumberInputStream	p.502

(continues)

III

Java

(continued)

Method	Class	Turn to Page...
getLocalizedInputStream(InputStream)	java.lang.Runtime	p.532
getLocalizedOutputStream(OutputStream)	java.lang.Runtime	p.532
getLocalPort()	java.net.DatagramSocket	p.553
getLocalPort()	java.net.ServerSocket	p.555
getLocalPort()	java.net.Socket	p.556
getLocalPort()	java.net.SocketImpl	p.558
getLong(String)	java.lang.Long	p.525
getLong(String, Long)	java.lang.Long	p.526
getLong(String, long)	java.lang.Long	p.525
getMapSize()	java.awt.image.IndexColorModel	p.480
getMaxAdvance()	java.awt.FontMetrics	p.436
getMaxAscent()	java.awt.FontMetrics	p.436
getMaxDecent()	java.awt.FontMetrics	p.436
getMaxDescent()	java.awt.FontMetrics	p.436
getMaximum()	java.awt.Scrollbar	p.465
getMaxPriority()	java.lang.ThreadGroup	p.548
getMenu(int)	java.awt.MenuBar	p.459
getMenuBar()	java.awt.Frame	p.438
getMessage()	java.lang.Throwable	p.549
getMinimum()	java.awt.Scrollbar	p.465
GetMinSize (Container, GridBagLayoutInfo)	java.awt.GridBagLayout	p.448
getMinutes()	java.util.Date	p.567
getMode()	java.awt.FileDialog	p.432
getMonth()	java.util.Date	p.567
getName()	java.lang.Class	p.519
getName()	java.io.File	p.496
getName()	java.awt.Font	p.435
getName()	java.lang.Thread	p.545
getName()	java.lang.ThreadGroup	p.548
getOrientation()	java.awt.Scrollbar	p.465
getOutputStream()	java.lang.Process	p.530
getOutputStream()	java.net.Socket	p.558
getOutputStream()	java.net.URLConnection	p.562
getPageIncrement()	java.awt.Scrollbar	p.466
getParameter(String)	java.applet.AppletStub	p.410

Method	Class	Turn to Page...
getParameterInfo()	java.applet.Applet	p.408
getParent()	java.awt.Component	p.421
getParent()	java.io.File	p.496
getParent()	java.awt.MenuComponent	p.459
getParent()	java.lang.ThreadGroup	p.548
getPath()	java.io.File	p.496
getPeer()	java.awt.Component	p.421
getPeer()	java.awt.MenuComponent	p.459
getPixelSize()	java.awt.image.ColorModel	p.473
getPort()	java.net.DatagramPacket	p.553
getPort()	java.net.Socket	p.556
getPort()	java.net.SocketImpl	p.558
getPort()	java.net.URL	p.559
getPriority()	java.lang.Thread	p.545
getProperties()	java.lang.System	p.543
getProperty(String)	java.util.Properties	p.573
getProperty(String)	java.lang.System	p.543
getProperty(String, ImageObserver)	java.awt.Image	p.451
getProperty(String, String)	java.util.Properties	p.573
getProperty(String, String)	java.lang.System	p.543
getProtocol()	java.net.URL	p.559
getRed()	java.awt.Color	p.419
getRed(int)	java.awt.image.ColorModel	p.473
getRed(int)	java.awt.image.DirectColorModel	p.475
getRed(int)	java.awt.image.IndexColorModel	p.480
getRedMask()	java.awt.image.DirectColorModel	p.475
getReds(byte[])	java.awt.image.IndexColorModel	p.480
getRef()	java.net.URL	p.559
getRequestProperty(String)	java.net.URLConnection	p.562
getRGB()	java.awt.Color	p.419
getRGB(int)	java.awt.image.ColorModel	p.473
getRGB(int)	java.awt.image.DirectColorModel	p.475
getRGB(int)	java.awt.image.IndexColorModel	p.480
getRGBdefault()	java.awt.image.ColorModel	p.473
getRows()	java.awt.List	p.453
getRows()	java.awt.TextArea	p.467
getRuntime()	java.lang.Runtime	p.532
getScreenResolution()	java.awt.Toolkit	p.471
getScreenSize()	java.awt.Toolkit	p.471

III

Java

(continues)

(continued)

Method	Class	Turn to Page...
getSeconds()	java.util.Date	p.567
getSecurityContext()	java.lang.SecurityManager	p.535
getSecurityManager()	java.lang.System	p.542
getSelectedIndex()	java.awt.Choice	p.417
getSelectedIndex()	java.awt.List	p.453
getSelectedIndexes()	java.awt.List	p.453
getSelectedItem()	java.awt.Choice	p.417
getSelectedItem()	java.awt.List	p.453
getSelectedItems()	java.awt.List	p.454
getSelectedText()	java.awt.TextComponent	p.467
getSelectionEnd()	java.awt.TextComponent	p.467
getSelectionStart()	java.awt.TextComponent	p.468
getSize()	java.awt.Font	p.435
getState()	java.awt.Checkbox	p.415
getState()	java.awt.CheckboxMenuItem	p.416
getStyle()	java.awt.Font	p.435
getSuperclass()	java.lang.Class	p.519
getText()	java.awt.Label	p.452
getThreadGroup()	java.lang.Thread	p.546
getTime()	java.util.Date	p.567
getTimezoneOffset()	java.util.Date	p.567
getTitle()	java.awt.Frame	p.438
getToolkit()	java.awt.Component	p.421
getToolkit()	java.awt.Window	p.471
getTransparentPixel()	java.awt.image.IndexColorModel	p.480
getURL()	java.net.URLConnection	p.562
getUseCaches()	java.net.URLConnection	p.563
getValue()	java.awt.Scrollbar	p.466
getVisible()	java.awt.Scrollbar	p.466
getVisibleIndex()	java.awt.List	p.454
getWarningString()	java.awt.Window	p.471
getWidth(ImageObserver)	java.awt.Image	p.451
getWidths()	java.awt.FontMetrics	p.436
gotFocus(Event, Object)	java.awt.Component	p.421
grabPixels()	java.awt.image.PixelGrabber	p.482

Method	Class	Turn to Page...
grabPixels(long)	java.awt.image.PixelGrabber	p.482
Graphics()	java.awt.Graphics	p.439
GridBagConstraints()	java.awt.GridBagConstraints	p.445
GridBagLayout()	java.awt.GridBagLayout	p.449
GridLayout(int, int)	java.awt.GridLayout	p.449
GridLayout(int, int, int, int)	java.awt.GridLayout	p.463
grow(int, int)	java.awt.Rectangle	p.463
guessContentTypeFromName(String)	java.net.URLConnection	p.563
guessContentTypeFromStream(InputStream)	java.net.URLConnection	p.563
handleEvent(Event)	java.awt.Component	p.421
hasChanged()	java.util.Observable	p.572
hashCode()	java.util.BitSet	p.566
hashCode()	java.lang.Boolean	p.517
hashCode()	java.lang.Character	p.518
hashCode()	java.util.Date	p.568
hashCode()	java.lang.Double	p.521
hashCode()	java.io.File	p.496
hashCode()	java.lang.Float	p.523
hashCode()	java.awt.Font	p.435
hashCode()	java.lang.Integer	p.524
hashCode()	java.lang.Long	p.526
hashCode()	java.lang.Object	p.529
hashCode()	java.awt.Point	p.461
hashCode()	java.awt.Rectangle	p.463
hashCode()	java.lang.String	p.536
hashCode()	java.net.URL	p.559
Hashtable()	java.util.Hashtable	p.571
Hashtable(int)	java.util.Hashtable	p.571
Hashtable(int, float)	java.util.Hashtable	p.571
hasMoreElements()	java.util.Enumeration	p.578
hasMoreElements()	java.util.StringTokenizer	p.575
hasMoreTokens()	java.util.StringTokenizer	p.595
hide()	java.awt.Component	p.421
HSBtoRGB(float, float, float)	java.awt.Color	p.419
IEEEremainder(double, double)	java.lang.Math	p.527

(continues)

III

Java

(continued)

Method	Class	Turn to Page...
Image()	java.awt.Image	p.450
imageComplete(int)	java.awt.image.ImageConsumer	p.485
imageComplete(int)	java.awt.image.ImageFilter	p.478
imageComplete(int)	java.awt.image.PixelGrabber	p.482
ImageFilter()	java.awt.image.ImageFilter	p.478
imageUpdate (Image, int, int, int, int, int)	java.awt.Component	p.421
imageUpdate (Image, int, int, int, int, int)	java.awt.image.ImageObserver	p.486
inClass(String)	java.lang.SecurityManager	p.535
inClassLoader()	java.lang.SecurityManager	p.535
IndexColorModel (int, int, byte[], byte[], byte[])	java.lang.IndexColorModel	p.479
IndexColorModel(int, int, byte[], byte[], byte[], byte[])	java.lang.IndexColorModel	p.479
IndexColorModel(int, int, byte[], byte[], byte[], int)	java.lang.IndexColorModel	p.479
IndexColorModel (int, int, byte[], int, boolean)	java.lang.IndexColorModel	p.479
IndexColorModel (int, int, byte[], int, boolean, int)	java.lang.IndexColorModel	p.479
indexOf(int)	java.lang.String	p.536
indexOf(int, int)	java.lang.String	p.536
indexOf(Object)	java.util.Vector	p.577
indexOf(Object, int)	java.util.Vector	p.577
indexOf(String)	java.lang.String	p.536
indexOf(String, int)	java.lang.String	p.536

Method	Class	Turn to Page...
InputStream()	java.io.InputStream	p.502
insert(int, boolean)	java.lang.StringBuffer	p.541
insert(int, char)	java.lang.StringBuffer	p.541
insert(int, char[])	java.lang.StringBuffer	p.541
insert(int, double)	java.lang.StringBuffer	p.540
insert(int, float)	java.lang.StringBuffer	p.540
insert(int, int)	java.lang.StringBuffer	p.541
insert(int, long)	java.lang.StringBuffer	p.541
insert(int, Object)	java.lang.StringBuffer	p.541
insert(int, String)	java.lang.StringBuffer	p.541
insertElementAt(Object, int)	java.util.Vector	p.577
insertText(String, int)	java.awt.TextArea	p.467
Insets(int, int, int, int)	java.awt.Insets	p.451
inside(int, int)	java.awt.Component	p.421
inside(int, int)	java.awt.Polygon	p.462
inside(int, int)	java.awt.Rectangle	p.463
intBitsToFloat(int)	java.lang.Float	
Integer(int)	java.lang.Integer	p.524
Integer(String)	java.lang.Integer	p.524
intern()	java.lang.String	p.537
interrupt()	java.lang.Thread	p.546
interrupted()	java.lang.Thread	p.546
intersection(Rectangle)	java.awt.Rectangle	p.463
intersects(Rectangle)	java.awt.Rectangle	p.463
intValue()	java.lang.Double	p.521
intValue()	java.lang.Float	p.523

(continues)

III

Java

(continued)

Method	Class	Turn to Page...
intValue()	java.lang.Integer	p.524
intValue()	java.lang.Long	p.526
intValue()	java.lang.Number	p.529
invalidate()	java.awt.Component	p.421
isAbsolute()	java.io.File	p.497
isActive()	java.applet.Applet	p.410
isActive()	java.applet.AppletStub	p.410
isBold()	java.awt.Font	p.435
isConsumer(ImageConsumer)	java.awt.image.FilteredImageSource	p.475
isConsumer(ImageConsumer)	java.awt.image.ImageProducer	p.487
isConsumer(ImageConsumer)	java.awt.image.MemoryImageSource	p.481
isDaemon()	java.lang.Thread	p.546
isDaemon()	java.lang.ThreadGroup	p.548
isDigit(char)	java.lang.Character	p.518
isDirectory()	java.io.File	p.497
isEditable()	java.awt.TextComponent	p.468
isEmpty()	java.util.Dictionary	p.569
isEmpty()	java.util.Hashtable	p.571
isEmpty()	java.awt.Rectangle	p.463
isEmpty()	java.util.Vector	p.577
isEnabled()	java.awt.Component	p.421
isEnabled()	java.awt.MenuItem	p.460
isErrorAny()	java.awt.MediaTracker	p.456
isErrorID(int)	java.awt.MediaTracker	p.456
isFile()	java.io.File	p.497
isInfinite()	java.lang.Double	p.521
isInfinite()	java.lang.Float	p.523
isInfinite(double)	java.lang.Double	p.521
isInfinite(float)	java.lang.Float	p.523
isInterface()	java.lang.Class	p.519
isInterrupted()	java.lang.Thread	p.546
isItalic()	java.awt.Font	p.435
isLowerCase(char)	java.lang.Character	p.518
isModal()	java.awt.Dialog	p.427
isNaN()	java.lang.Double	p.521
isNaN()	java.lang.Float	p.523

Method	Class	Turn to Page...
isNaN(double)	java.lang.Double	p.521
isNaN(float)	java.lang.Float	p.523
isPlain()	java.awt.Font	p.435
isResizable()	java.awt.Dialog	p.427
isResizable()	java.awt.Frame	p.438
isSelected(int)	java.awt.List	p.454
isShowing()	java.awt.Component	p.421
isSpace(char)	java.lang.Character	p.518
isTearOff()	java.awt.Menu	p.457
isUpperCase(char)	java.lang.Character	p.519
isValid()	java.awt.Component	p.422
isVisible()	java.awt.Component	p.422
join()	java.lang.Thread	p.546
join(long)	java.lang.Thread	p.546
join(long, int)	java.lang.Thread	p.546
keyDown(Event, int)	java.awt.Component	p.422
keys()	java.util.Dictionary	p.569
keys()	java.util.Hashtable	p.572
keyUp(Event, int)	java.awt.Component	p.422
Label()	java.awt.Label	p.452
Label(String)	java.awt.Label	p.452
Label(String, int)	java.awt.Label	p.452
last(Container)	java.awt.CardLayout	p.414
lastElement()	java.util.Vector	p.577
lastIndexOf(int)	java.lang.String	p.537
lastIndexOf(int, int)	java.lang.String	p.537
lastIndexOf(Object)	java.util.Vector	p.577
lastIndexOf(Object, int)	java.util.Vector	p.577
lastIndexOf(String)	java.lang.String	p.537
lastIndexOf(String, int)	java.lang.String	p.537
lastModified()	java.io.File	p.497
layout()	java.awt.Component	p.422
layout()	java.awt.Container	p.426
layoutContainer(Container)	java.awt.BorderLayout	p.411
layoutContainer(Container)	java.awt.CardLayout	p.414
layoutContainer(Container)	java.awt.FlowLayout	p.433
layoutContainer(Container)	java.awt.GridBagLayout	p.449
layoutContainer(Container)	java.awt.GridLayout	p.449
layoutContainer(Container)	java.awt.LayoutManager	p.472

(continues)

(continued)

Method	Class	Turn to Page...
length()	java.io.File	p.497
length()	java.io.RandomAccessFile	p.509
length()	java.lang.String	p.536
length()	java.lang.StringBuffer	p.541
LineNumberInputStream(InputStream)	java.io.LineNumberInputStream	p.502
list()	java.awt.Component	p.422
list()	java.io.File	p.497
List()	java.awt.List	p.452
list()	java.lang.ThreadGroup	p.548
list(FilenameFilter)	java.io.File	p.497
List(int, boolean)	java.awt.List	p.453
list(PrintStream)	java.awt.Component	p.422
list(PrintStream)	java.util.Properties	p.573
list(PrintStream, int)	java.awt.Component	p.422
list(PrintStream, int)	java.awt.Container	p.426
listen(int)	java.net.SocketImpl	p.422
load(InputStream)	java.util.Properties	p.449
load(String)	java.lang.Runtime	p.532
load(String)	java.lang.System	p.543
loadClass(String, boolean)	java.lang.ClassLoader	p.520
loadLibrary(String)	java.lang.Runtime	p.532
loadLibrary(String)	java.lang.System	p.543
locate(int, int)	java.awt.Component	p.422
locate(int, int)	java.awt.Container	p.426
location()	java.awt.Component	p.422
location(int, int)	java.awt.GridBagLayout	p.449
log(double)	java.lang.Math	p.527
Long(long)	java.lang.Long	p.525
Long(String)	java.lang.Long	p.525
longBitsToDouble(long)	java.lang.Double	p.522
longValue()	java.lang.Double	p.522
longValue()	java.lang.Float	p.523
longValue()	java.lang.Integer	p.524
longValue()	java.lang.Long	p.526
longValue()	java.lang.Number	p.529
lookupConstraints(Component)	java.awt.GridBagLayout	p.449

Method	Class	Turn to Page...
loop()	java.applet.AudioClip	p.410
lostFocus(Event, Object)	java.awt.Component	p.422
lowerCaseMode(boolean)	java.io.StreamTokenizer	p.512
makeVisible(int)	java.awt.List	p.454
mark(int)	java.io.BufferedInputStream	p.489
mark(int)	java.io.FilterInputStream	p.500
mark(int)	java.io.InputStream	p.502
mark(int)	java.io.LineNumberInputStream	p.503
markSupported()	java.io.BufferedInputStream	p.489
markSupported()	java.io.FilterInputStream	p.500
markSupported()	java.io.InputStream	p.502
markSupported()	java.io.PushbackInputStream	p.509
max(double, double)	java.lang.Math	p.527
max(float, float)	java.lang.Math	p.527
max(int, int)	java.lang.Math	p.528
max(long, long)	java.lang.Math	p.528
MediaTracker(Component)	java.awt.MediaTracker	p.455
MemoryImageSource(int, int, ColorModel,byte[], int, int)	java.lang.MemoryImageSource	p.480-481
MemoryImageSource(int, int, ColorModel, byte[], int, int, Hashtable)	java.lang.MemoryImageSource	p.480-481
MemoryImageSource(int, int, ColorModel, int[], int, int)	java.lang.MemoryImageSource	p.480-481
MemoryImageSource(int, int, ColorModel, int[], int, int, Hashtable)	java.lang.MemoryImageSource	p.480-481
MemoryImageSource (int, int, int[], int, int)	java.lang.MemoryImageSource	p.480-481
MemoryImageSource(int, int, int[], int, int, Hashtable)	java.lang.MemoryImageSource	p.480-481
Menu(String)	java.awt.Menu	p.457
Menu(String, boolean)	java.awt.Menu	p.457
MenuBar()	java.awt.MenuBar	p.457
MenuComponent()	java.awt.MenuComponent	p.459
MenuItem(String)	java.awt.MenuItem	p.460
metaDown()	java.awt.Event	p.431
min(double, double)	java.lang.Math	p.528
min(float, float)	java.lang.Math	p.528
min(int, int)	java.lang.Math	p.528

(continues)

III

Java

(continued)

Method	Class	Turn to Page...
min(long, long)	java.lang.Math	p.528
minimumLayoutSize(Container)	java.awt.BorderLayout	p.411
minimumLayoutSize(Container)	java.awt.CardLayout	p.414
minimumLayoutSize(Container)	java.awt.FlowLayout	p.433
minimumLayoutSize(Container)	java.awt.GridBagLayout	p.449
minimumLayoutSize(Container)	java.awt.GridLayout	p.450
minimumLayoutSize(Container)	java.awt.LayoutManager	p.472
minimumSize()	java.awt.Component	p.423
minimumSize()	java.awt.Container	p.426
minimumSize()	java.awt.List	p.454
minimumSize()	java.awt.TextArea	p.467
minimumSize()	java.awt.TextField	p.469
minimumSize(int)	java.awt.List	p.454
minimumSize(int)	java.awt.TextField	p.467
minimumSize(int, int)	java.awt.TextArea	p.469
mkdir()	java.io.File	p.497
mkdirs()	java.io.File	p.497
mouseDown(Event, int, int)	java.awt.Component	p.422
mouseDrag(Event, int, int)	java.awt.Component	p.422
mouseEnter(Event, int, int)	java.awt.Component	p.422
mouseExit(Event, int, int)	java.awt.Component	p.422
mouseMove(Event, int, int)	java.awt.Component	p.423
mouseUp(Event, int, int)	java.awt.Component	p.423
move(int, int)	java.awt.Component	p.423
move(int, int)	java.awt.Point	p.461
move(int, int)	java.awt.Rectangle	p.463
newInstance()	java.lang.Class	p.519
next(Container)	java.awt.CardLayout	p.414
nextDouble()	java.util.Random	p.574

Method	Class	Turn to Page...
nextElement()	java.util.Enumeration	p.578
nextElement()	java.util.StringTokenizer	p.575
nextFloat()	java.util.Random	p.574
nextFocus()	java.awt.Component	p.423
nextGaussian()	java.util.Random	p.574
nextInt()	java.util.Random	p.574
nextLong()	java.util.Random	p.574
nextToken()	java.io.StreamTokenizer	p.513
nextToken()	java.util.StringTokenizer	p.575
nextToken(String)	java.util.StringTokenizer	p.575
notify()	java.lang.Object	p.529
notifyAll()	java.lang.Object	p.530
notifyObservers()	java.util.Observable	p.573
notifyObservers(Object)	java.util.Observable	p.573
Number()	java.lang.Number	p.529
Object()	java.lang.Object	p.529
openConnection()	java.net.URL	p.560
openConnection(URL)	java.net.URLStreamHandler	p.564
openStream()	java.net.URL	p.560
or(BitSet)	java.util.BitSet	p.566
ordinaryChar(int)	java.io.StreamTokenizer	p.513
ordinaryChars(int, int)	java.io.StreamTokenizer	p.513
OutputStream()	java.io.OutputStream	p.503
pack()	java.awt.Window	p.471
paint(Graphics)	java.awt.Canvas	p.413
paint(Graphics)	java.awt.Component	p.423
paintAll(Graphics)	java.awt.Component	p.423
paintComponents(Graphics)	java.awt.Container	p.426
Panel()	java.awt.Panel	p.461
paramString()	java.awt.Button	p.412

(continues)

III

Java

(continued)

Method	Class	Turn to Page...
paramString()	java.awt.Checkbox	p.415
paramString()	java.awt.CheckboxMenuItem	p.416
paramString()	java.awt.Component	p.423
paramString()	java.awt.Container	p.426
paramString()	java.awt.Dialog	p.427
paramString()	java.awt.Event	p.431
paramString()	java.awt.FileDialog	p.432
paramString()	java.awt.Frame	p.438
paramString()	java.awt.Label	p.452
paramString()	java.awt.List	p.454
paramString()	java.awt.MenuComponent	p.460
paramString()	java.awt.MenuItem	p.461
paramString()	java.awt.Scrollbar	p.466
paramString()	java.awt.TextArea	p.467
paramString()	java.awt.TextComponent	p.468
paramString()	java.awt.TextField	p.469
parentOf(ThreadGroup)	java.lang.ThreadGroup	p.548
parse(String)	java.util.Date	p.568
parseInt(String)	java.lang.Integer	p.524
parseInt(String, int)	java.lang.Integer	p.524
parseLong(String)	java.lang.Long	p.526
parseLong(String, int)	java.lang.Long	p.526
parseNumbers()	java.io.StreamTokenizer	p.513
parseURL(URL, String, int, int)	java.net.URLStreamHandler	p.564
peek()	java.util.Stack	p.574
PipedInputStream()	java.io.PipedInputStream	p.506
PipedInputStream(PipedOutputStream)	java.io.PipedInputStream	p.506
PipedOutputStream()	java.io.PipedOutputStream	p.506
PipedOutputStream(PipedInputStream)	java.io.PipedOutputStream	p.506
PixelGrabber(Image, int, int, int, int, int[], int, int)	java.awt.Image.PixelGrabber	p.481
PixelGrabber(ImageProducer, int, int, int, int, int[], int, int)	java.awt.Image.PixelGrabber	p.481
play()	java.applet.AudioClip	p.411
play(URL)	java.applet.Applet	p.408
play(URL, String)	java.applet.Applet	p.408
Point(int, int)	java.awt.Point	p.461
Polygon()	java.awt.Polygon	p.462
Polygon(int[], int[], int)	java.awt.Polygon	p.462

Method	Class	Turn to Page...
pop()	java.util.Stack	p.574
postEvent(Event)	java.awt.Component	p.423
postEvent(Event)	java.awt.MenuComponent	p.460
postEvent(Event)	java.awt.MenuContainer	p.472
preferredLayoutSize(Container)	java.awt.BorderLayout	p.412
preferredLayoutSize(Container)	java.awt.CardLayout	p.414
preferredLayoutSize(Container)	java.awt.FlowLayout	p.433
preferredLayoutSize(Container)	java.awt.GridBagLayout	p.449
preferredLayoutSize(Container)	java.awt.GridLayout	p.450
preferredLayoutSize(Container)	java.awt.LayoutManager	p.472
preferredSize()	java.awt.Component	p.423
preferredSize()	java.awt.Container	p.426
preferredSize()	java.awt.List	p.454
preferredSize()	java.awt.TextArea	p.467
preferredSize()	java.awt.TextField	p.469
preferredSize(int)	java.awt.List	p.454
preferredSize(int)	java.awt.TextField	p.469
preferredSize(int, int)	java.awt.TextArea	p.467
prepareImage(Image, ImageObserver)	java.awt.Component	p.423
prepareImage (Image, int, int, ImageObserver)	java.awt.Component	p.423
prepareImage(Image, int, int, ImageObserver)	java.awt.Toolkit	p.471
previous(Container)	java.awt.CardLayout	p.415
print(boolean)	java.io.PrintStream	p.507
print(char)	java.io.PrintStream	p.507
print(char[])	java.io.PrintStream	p.507
print(double)	java.io.PrintStream	p.507
print(float)	java.io.PrintStream	p.507
print(Graphics)	java.awt.Component	p.424
print(int)	java.io.PrintStream	p.507
print(long)	java.io.PrintStream	p.507
print(Object)	java.io.PrintStream	p.507
print(String)	java.io.PrintStream	p.507
printAll(Graphics)	java.awt.Component	p.424
printComponents(Graphics)	java.awt.Container	p.426
println()	java.io.PrintStream	p.508
println(boolean)	java.io.PrintStream	p.507

(continues)

III

Java

(continued)

Method	Class	Turn to Page...
println(char)	java.io.PrintStream	p.508
println(char[])	java.io.PrintStream	p.508
println(double)	java.io.PrintStream	p.507
println(float)	java.io.PrintStream	p.507
println(int)	java.io.PrintStream	p.508
println(long)	java.io.PrintStream	p.508
println(Object)	java.io.PrintStream	p.508
println(String)	java.io.PrintStream	p.508
printStackTrace()	java.lang.Throwable	p.549
printStackTrace(PrintStream)	java.lang.Throwable	p.549
PrintStream(OutputStream)	java.io.PrintStream	p.507
PrintStream(OutputStream, boolean)	java.io.PrintStream	p.507
Process()	java.lang.Process	p.530
Properties()	java.util.Properties	p.573
Properties(Properties)	java.util.Properties	p.573
propertyNames()	java.util.Properties	p.573
push(Object)	java.util.Stack	p.574
pushBack()	java.io.StreamTokenizer	p.513
PushbackInputStream(InputStream)	java.io.PushbackInputStream	p.508
put(Object, Object)	java.util.Dictionary	p.569
put(Object, Object)	java.util.Hashtable	p.572
quoteChar(int)	java.io.StreamTokenizer	p.513
random()	java.lang.Math	p.528
Random()	java.util.Random	p.574
Random(long)	java.util.Random	p.574
RandomAccessFile(File, String)	java.io.RandomAccessFile	p.509
RandomAccessFile(String, String)	java.io.RandomAccessFile	p.509
read()	java.io.BufferedInputStream	p.489
read()	java.io.ByteArrayInputStream	p.491
read()	java.io.FileInputStream	p.498, 500
read()	java.io.InputStream	p.502
read()	java.io.LineNumberInputStream	p.503
read()	java.io.PipedInputStream	p.506
read()	java.io.PushbackInputStream	p.509
read()	java.io.RandomAccessFile	p.509
read()	java.io.SequenceInputStream	p.512

Method	Class	Turn to Page...
read()	java.io.StringBufferInputStream	p.514
read(byte[])	java.io.DataInputStream	p.493
read(byte[])	java.io.FileInputStream	p.498, 500
read(byte[])	java.io.InputStream	p.502
read(byte[])	java.io.RandomAccessFile	p.509
read(byte[], int, int)	java.io.BufferedInputStream	p.489
read(byte[], int, int)	java.io.ByteArrayInputStream	p.491
read(byte[], int, int)	java.io.DataInputStream	p.493
read(byte[], int, int)	java.io.FileInputStream	p.499-500
read(byte[], int, int)	java.io.InputStream	p.502
read(byte[], int, int)	java.io.LineNumberInputStream	p.503
read(byte[], int, int)	java.io.PipedInputStream	p.506
read(byte[], int, int)	java.io.PushbackInputStream	p.509
read(byte[], int, int)	java.io.RandomAccessFile	p.509
read(byte[], int, int)	java.io.SequenceInputStream	p.512
read(byte[], int, int)	java.io.StringBufferInputStream	p.514
readBoolean()	java.io.DataInput	p.514
readBoolean()	java.io.DataInputStream	p.493
readBoolean()	java.io.RandomAccessFile	p.510
readByte()	java.io.DataInput	p.514
readByte()	java.io.DataInputStream	p.493
readByte()	java.io.RandomAccessFile	p.510
readChar()	java.io.DataInput	p.514
readChar()	java.io.DataInputStream	p.493
readChar()	java.io.RandomAccessFile	p.510
readDouble()	java.io.DataInput	p.514
readDouble()	java.io.DataInputStream	p.493
readDouble()	java.io.RandomAccessFile	p.510
readFloat()	java.io.DataInput	p.514
readFloat()	java.io.DataInputStream	p.493
readFloat()	java.io.RandomAccessFile	p.510
readFully(byte[])	java.io.DataInput	p.515
readFully(byte[])	java.io.DataInputStream	p.493
readFully(byte[])	java.io.RandomAccessFile	p.510
readFully(byte[], int, int)	java.io.DataInput	p.515
readFully(byte[], int, int)	java.io.DataInputStream	p.493
readFully(byte[], int, int)	java.io.RandomAccessFile	p.510

(continues)

III

Java

(continued)

Method	Class	Turn to Page...
readInt()	java.io.DataInput	p.515
readInt()	java.io.DataInputStream	p.493
readInt()	java.io.RandomAccessFile	p.510
readLine()	java.io.DataInput	p.515
readLine()	java.io.DataInputStream	p.493
readLine()	java.io.RandomAccessFile	p.510
readLong()	java.io.DataInput	p.515
readLong()	java.io.DataInputStream	p.493
readLong()	java.io.RandomAccessFile	p.510
readShort()	java.io.DataInput	p.515
readShort()	java.io.DataInputStream	p.493
readShort()	java.io.RandomAccessFile	p.510
readUnsignedByte()	java.io.DataInput	p.515
readUnsignedByte()	java.io.DataInputStream	p.493
readUnsignedByte()	java.io.RandomAccessFile	p.510
readUnsignedShort()	java.io.DataInput	p.515
readUnsignedShort()	java.io.DataInputStream	p.494
readUnsignedShort()	java.io.RandomAccessFile	p.510
readUTF()	java.io.DataInput	p.515
readUTF()	java.io.DataInputStream	p.494
readUTF()	java.io.RandomAccessFile	p.510
readUTF(DataInput)	java.io.DataInputStream	p.515
receive(DatagramPacket)	java.net.DatagramSocket	p.554
Rectangle()	java.awt.Rectangle	p.462
Rectangle(Dimension)	java.awt.Rectangle	p.463
Rectangle(int, int)	java.awt.Rectangle	p.463
Rectangle(int, int, int, int)	java.awt.Rectangle	p.463
Rectangle(Point)	java.awt.Rectangle	p.463
Rectangle(Point, Dimension)	java.awt.Rectangle	p.463
regionMatches (boolean, int, String, int, int)	java.lang.String	p.537
regionMatches(int, String, int, int)	java.lang.String	p.537
rehash()	java.util.Hashtable	p.572
remove(Component)	java.awt.Container	p.426
remove(int)	java.awt.Menu	p.457
remove(int)	java.awt.MenuBar	p.459
remove(MenuComponent)	java.awt.Frame	p.438
remove(MenuComponent)	java.awt.Menu	p.457
remove(MenuComponent)	java.awt.MenuBar	p.459

Method	Class	Turn to Page...
remove(MenuComponent)	java.awt.MenuContainer	p.472
remove(Object)	java.util.Dictionary	p.569
remove(Object)	java.util.Hashtable	p.572
removeAllElements()	java.util.Vector	p.577
removeConsumer(ImageConsumer)	java.awt.image.FilteredImageSource	p.476
removeConsumer(ImageConsumer)	java.awt.image.ImageProducer	p.487
removeConsumer(ImageConsumer)	java.awt.image.MemoryImageSource	p.481
removeElement(Object)	java.util.Vector	p.577
removeElementAt(int)	java.util.Vector	p.577
removeLayoutComponent(Component)	java.awt.BorderLayout	p.412
removeLayoutComponent(Component)	java.awt.CardLayout	p.415
removeLayoutComponent(Component)	java.awt.FlowLayout	p.433
removeLayoutComponent(Component)	java.awt.GridBagLayout	p.449
removeLayoutComponent(Component)	java.awt.GridLayout	p.450
removeLayoutComponent(Component)	java.awt.LayoutManager	p.472
removeNotify()	java.awt.Component	p.424
removeNotify()	java.awt.Container	p.426
removeNotify()	java.awt.List	p.454
removeNotify()	java.awt.Menu	p.457
removeNotify()	java.awt.MenuBar	p.459
removeNotify()	java.awt.MenuComponent	p.460
renameTo(File)	java.io.File	p.497
repaint()	java.awt.Component	p.424
repaint(int, int, int, int)	java.awt.Component	p.424
repaint(long)	java.awt.Component	p.424
repaint(long, int, int, int, int)	java.awt.Component	p.424
replace(char, char)	java.lang.String	p.537
replaceItem(String, int)	java.awt.List	p.454
replaceText(String, int, int)	java.awt.TextArea	p.467
requestFocus()	java.awt.Component	p.424
requestTopDownLeftRightResend(ImageConsumer)	java.awt.image.FilteredImageSource	p.476
requestTopDownLeftRightResend(ImageConsumer)	java.awt.image.ImageProducer	p.487
requestTopDownLeftRightResend(ImageConsumer)	java.awt.image.MemoryImageSource	p.481
resendTopDownLeftRight(ImageProducer)	java.awt.image.ImageFilter	p.487
reset()	java.io.BufferedInputStream	p.489

(continues)

III

Java

(continued)

Method	Class	Turn to Page...
reset()	java.io.ByteArrayInputStream	p.491
reset()	java.io.ByteArrayOutputStream	p.492
reset()	java.io.FilterInputStream	p.501
reset()	java.io.InputStream	p.502
reset()	java.io.LineNumberInputStream	p.503
reset()	java.io.StringBufferInputStream	p.514
resetSyntax()	java.io.StreamTokenizer	p.513
reshape(int, int, int, int)	java.awt.Component	p.424
reshape(int, int, int, int)	java.awt.Rectangle	p.463
resize(Dimension)	java.awt.Component	p.409, 424
resize(int, int)	java.awt.Component	p.408, 424
resize(int, int)	java.awt.Rectangle	p.464
resolveClass(Class)	java.lang.ClassLoader	p.520
resume()	java.lang.Thread	p.546
resume()	java.lang.ThreadGroup	p.548
RGBImageFilter()	java.awt.image.RGBImageFilter	p.483
RGBtoHSB(int, int, int, float[])	java.awt.Color	p.483
rint(double)	java.lang.Math	p.528
round(double)	java.lang.Math	p.528
round(float)	java.lang.Math	p.528
run()	java.lang.Thread	p.546
runFinalization()	java.lang.Runtime	p.532
runFinalization()	java.lang.System	p.543
sameFile(URL)	java.net.URL	p.560
Scrollbar()	java.awt.Scrollbar	p.465
Scrollbar(int)	java.awt.Scrollbar	p.465
Scrollbar(int, int, int, int, int)	java.awt.Scrollbar	p.465
search(Object)	java.util.Stack	p.574
SecurityManager()	java.lang.SecurityManager	p.533
seek(long)	java.io.RandomAccessFile	p.510
select(int)	java.awt.Choice	p.417
select(int)	java.awt.List	p.454
select(int, int)	java.awt.TextComponent	p.468
select(String)	java.awt.Choice	p.417

Method	Class	Turn to Page...
selectAll()	java.awt.TextComponent	p.468
send(DatagramPacket)	java.net.DatagramSocket	p.554
SequenceInputStream(Enumeration)	java.io.SequenceInputStream	p.511
SequenceInputStream (InputStream, InputStream)	java.io.SequenceInputStream	p.511
ServerSocket(int)	java.net.ServerSocket	p.554
ServerSocket(int, int)	java.net.ServerSocket	p.554
set(int)	java.util.BitSet	p.566
set (String, String, int, String, String)	java.net.URL	p.560
setAlignment(int)	java.awt.Label	p.452
setAllowUserInteraction(boolean)	java.net.URLConnection	p.562
setBackground(Color)	java.awt.Component	p.424
setChanged()	java.util.Observable	p.573
setCharAt(int, char)	java.lang.StringBuffer	p.541
setCheckboxGroup(CheckboxGroup)	java.awt.Checkbox	p.415
setColor(Color)	java.awt.Graphics	p.443
setColorModel(ColorModel)	java.awt.image.ImageConsumer	p.485
setColorModel(ColorModel)	java.awt.image.ImageFilter	p.478
setColorModel(ColorModel)	java.awt.image.PixelGrabber	p.482
setColorModel(ColorModel)	java.awt.image.RGBImageFilter	p.484
setConstraints (Component, GridBagConstraints)	java.awt.GridBagLayout	p.449
setContentHandlerFactory (ContentHandlerFactory)	java.net.URLConnection	p.563
setCurrent(Checkbox)	java.awt.CheckboxGroup	p.416
setCursor(int)	java.awt.Frame	p.438
setDaemon(boolean)	java.lang.Thread	p.546
setDaemon(boolean)	java.lang.ThreadGroup	p.548
setDate(int)	java.util.Date	p.568
setDefaultAllowUserInteraction(boolean)	java.net.URLConnection	p.562
setDefaultRequestProperty (String, String)	java.net.URLConnection	p.563
setDefaultUseCaches(boolean)	java.net.URLConnection	p.563
setDimensions(int, int)	java.awt.image.CropImageFilter	p.474
setDimensions(int, int)	java.awt.image.ImageConsumer	p.485
setDimensions(int, int)	java.awt.image.ImageFilter	p.478

(continues)

III

Java

(continued)

Method	Class	Turn to Page...
setDimensions(int, int)	java.awt.image.PixelGrabber	p.482
setDirectory(String)	java.awt.FileDialog	p.432
setDoInput(boolean)	java.net.URLConnection	p.562
setDoOutput(boolean)	java.net.URLConnection	p.562
setEchoCharacter(char)	java.awt.TextField	p.469
setEditable(boolean)	java.awt.TextComponent	p.468
setElementAt(Object, int)	java.util.Vector	p.577
setFile(String)	java.awt.FileDialog	p.432
setFilenameFilter(FilenameFilter)	java.awt.FileDialog	p.432
setFont(Font)	java.awt.Component	p.424
setFont(Font)	java.awt.Graphics	p.443
setFont(Font)	java.awt.MenuComponent	p.460
setForeground(Color)	java.awt.Component	p.424
setHelpMenu(Menu)	java.awt.MenuBar	p.459
setHints(int)	java.awt.image.ImageConsumer	p.485
setHints(int)	java.awt.image.ImageFilter	p.479
setHints(int)	java.awt.image.PixelGrabber	p.482
setHours(int)	java.util.Date	p.568
setIconImage(Image)	java.awt.Frame	p.438
setIfModifiedSince(long)	java.net.URLConnection	p.563
setLabel(String)	java.awt.Button	p.412
setLabel(String)	java.awt.Checkbox	p.416
setLabel(String)	java.awt.MenuItem	p.461
setLayout(LayoutManager)	java.awt.Container	p.426
setLength(int)	java.lang.StringBuffer	p.540
setLineIncrement(int)	java.awt.Scrollbar	p.466
setLineNumber(int)	java.io.LineNumberInputStream	p.503
setMaxPriority(int)	java.lang.ThreadGroup	p.548

Method	Class	Turn to Page...
setMenuBar(MenuBar)	java.awt.Frame	p.438
setMinutes(int)	java.util.Date	p.568
setMonth(int)	java.util.Date	p.568
setMultipleSelections(boolean)	java.awt.List	p.454
setName(String)	java.lang.Thread	p.546
setPageIncrement(int)	java.awt.Scrollbar	p.466
setPaintMode()	java.awt.Graphics	p.443
setPixels(int, int, int, int, ColorModel, byte[], int, int)	java.awt.image.RGBImageFilter	p.484
setPriority(int)	java.lang.Thread	p.546
setProperties(Hashtable)	java.awt.image.CropImageFilter	p.474
setProperties(Hashtable)	java.awt.image.ImageFilter	p.479
setProperties(Hashtable)	java.awt.image.PixelGrabber	p.482
setRequestProperty(String, String)	java.net.URLConnection	p.563
setResizable(boolean)	java.awt.Frame	p.438
setSeconds(int)	java.util.Date	p.568
setSecurityManager(SecurityManager)	java.lang.System	p.542
setSeed(long)	java.util.Random	p.574
setSize(int)	java.util.Vector	p.577
setSocketFactory(SocketImplFactory)	java.net.ServerSocket	p.555
setSocketImplFactory(SocketImplFactory)	java.net.Socket	p.557
setState(boolean)	java.awt.Checkbox	p.416
setState(boolean)	java.awt.CheckboxMenuItem	p.417
setText(String)	java.awt.Label	p.452
setText(String)	java.awt.TextComponent	p.452
setTime(long)	java.util.Date	p.568
setTitle(String)	java.awt.Dialog	p.427
setTitle(String)	java.awt.Frame	p.438
setURL(URL, String, String, int, String, String)	java.net.URLStreamHandler	p.564

(continues)

III

Java

(continued)

Method	Class	Turn to Page...
setURLStreamHandlerFactory (URLStreamHandlerFactory)	java.net.URL	p.560
setUseCaches(boolean)	java.net.URLConnection	p.563
setValue(int)	java.awt.Scrollbar	p.466
setValues(int, int, int, int)	java.awt.Scrollbar	p.466
setXORMode(Color)	java.awt.Graphics	p.443
setYear(int)	java.util.Date	p.568
shiftDown()	java.awt.Event	p.431
show()	java.awt.Component	p.424
show()	java.awt.Window	p.471
show(boolean)	java.awt.Component	p.424
show(Container, String)	java.awt.CardLayout	p.415
showDocument(URL)	java.applet.AppletContext	p.409
showDocument(URL, String)	java.applet.AppletContext	p.409
showStatus(String)	java.applet.Applet	p.409
showStatus(String)	java.applet.AppletContext	p.410
sin(double)	java.lang.Math	p.528
size()	java.util.BitSet	p.566
size()	java.io.ByteArrayOutputStream	p.492
size()	java.awt.Component	p.425
size()	java.io.DataOutputStream	p.494
size()	java.util.Dictionary	p.569
size()	java.util.Hashtable	p.572
size()	java.util.Vector	p.577
skip(long)	java.io.BufferedInputStream	p.489
skip(long)	java.io.ByteArrayInputStream	p.491
skip(long)	java.io.FileInputStream	p.499, 501
skip(long)	java.io.InputStream	p.502
skip(long)	java.io.LineNumberInputStream	p.503
skip(long)	java.io.StringBufferInputStream	p.514
skipBytes(int)	java.io.DataInput	p.515
skipBytes(int)	java.io.DataInputStream	p.494
skipBytes(int)	java.io.RandomAccessFile	p.510
slashSlashComments(boolean)	java.io.StreamTokenizer	p.513
slashStarComments(boolean)	java.io.StreamTokenizer	p.513

Method	Class	Turn to Page...
sleep(long)	java.lang.Thread	p.546
sleep(long, int)	java.lang.Thread	p.546
Socket(InetAddress, int)	java.net.Socket	p.556
Socket(InetAddress, int, boolean)	java.net.Socket	p.556
Socket(String, int)	java.net.Socket	p.556
Socket(String, int, boolean)	java.net.Socket	p.556
SocketImpl()	java.net.SocketImpl	p.557
sqrt(double)	java.lang.Math	p.528
Stack()	java.util.Stack	p.574
start()	java.applet.Applet	p.409
start()	java.lang.Thread	p.547
startProduction(ImageConsumer)	java.awt.image.FilteredImageSource	p.475
startProduction(ImageConsumer)	java.awt.image.ImageProducer	p.487
startProduction(ImageConsumer)	java.awt.image.MemoryImageSource	p.481
startsWith(String)	java.lang.String	p.537
startsWith(String, int)	java.lang.String	p.537
status()	java.awt.image.PixelGrabber	p.482
statusAll(boolean)	java.awt.MediaTracker	p.456
statusID(int, boolean)	java.awt.MediaTracker	p.456
stop()	java.applet.Applet	p.411
stop()	java.applet.AudioClip	p.411
stop()	java.lang.Thread	p.547
stop()	java.lang.ThreadGroup	p.548
stop(Throwable)	java.lang.Thread	p.547
String()	java.lang.String	p.535
String(byte[], int)	java.lang.String	p.535
String(byte[], int, int, int)	java.lang.String	p.535
String(char[])	java.lang.String	p.535
String(char[], int, int)	java.lang.String	p.535
String(String)	java.lang.String	p.535
String(StringBuffer)	java.lang.String	p.535
StringBuffer()	java.lang.StringBuffer	p.539
StringBuffer(int)	java.lang.StringBuffer	p.539
StringBuffer(String)	java.lang.StringBuffer	p.539
StringBufferInputStream(String)	java.io.StringBufferInputStream	p.514

(continues)

III

Java

(continued)

Method	Class	Turn to Page...
StringTokenizer(String)	java.util.StringTokenizer	p.575
StringTokenizer(String, String)	java.util.StringTokenizer	p.575
StringTokenizer (String, String, boolean)	java.util.String	p.575
stringWidth(String)	java.awt.FontMetrics	p.436
substituteColorModel (ColorModel, ColorModel)	java.awt.image.RGBImageFilter	p.484
substring(int)	java.lang.String	p.537
substring(int, int)	java.lang.String	p.537
suspend()	java.lang.Thread	p.547
suspend()	java.lang.ThreadGroup	p.548
sync()	java.awt.Toolkit	p.471
tan(double)	java.lang.Math	p.528
TextArea()	java.awt.TextArea	p.467
TextArea(int, int)	java.awt.TextArea	p.466
TextArea(String)	java.awt.TextArea	p.467
TextArea(String, int, int)	java.awt.TextArea	p.467
TextField()	java.awt.TextField	p.468
TextField(int)	java.awt.TextField	p.468
TextField(String)	java.awt.TextField	p.468
TextField(String, int)	java.awt.TextField	p.468
Thread()	java.lang.Thread	p.544
Thread(Runnable)	java.lang.Thread	p.545
Thread(Runnable, String)	java.lang.Thread	p.545
Thread(String)	java.lang.Thread	p.545
Thread(ThreadGroup, Runnable)	java.lang.Thread	p.545
Thread(ThreadGroup, Runnable, String)	java.lang.Thread	p.545
Thread(ThreadGroup, String)	java.lang.Thread	p.545
ThreadGroup(String)	java.lang.ThreadGroup	p.547
ThreadGroup(ThreadGroup, String)	java.lang.ThreadGroup	p.547
Throwable()	java.lang.Throwable	p.549
Throwable(String)	java.lang.Throwable	p.549
toBack()	java.awt.Window	p.471

Method	Class	Turn to Page...
toByteArray()	java.io.ByteArrayOutputStream	p.492
toCharArray()	java.lang.String	p.537
toExternalForm()	java.net.URL	p.560
toExternalForm(URL)	java.net.URLStreamHandler	p.564
toFront()	java.awt.Window	p.471
toGMTString()	java.util.Date	p.568
toLocaleString()	java.util.Date	p.568
toLowerCase()	java.lang.String	p.537
toLowerCase(char)	java.lang.Character	p.519
Toolkit()	java.awt.Toolkit	p.469
toString()	java.util.BitSet	p.566
toString()	java.lang.Boolean	p.517
toString()	java.awt.BorderLayout	p.412
toString()	java.io.ByteArrayOutputStream	p.492
toString()	java.awt.CardLayout	p.415
toString()	java.lang.Character	p.519
toString()	java.awt.CheckboxGroup	p.416
toString()	java.lang.Class	p.519
toString()	java.awt.Color	p.419
toString()	java.awt.Component	p.425
toString()	java.util.Date	p.568
toString()	java.awt.Dimension	p.427
toString()	java.lang.Double	p.522
toString()	java.awt.Event	p.431
toString()	java.io.File	p.497
toString()	java.lang.Float	p.523
toString()	java.awt.FlowLayout	p.433
toString()	java.awt.Font	p.435
toString()	java.awt.FontMetrics	p.437
toString()	java.awt.Graphics	p.443
toString()	java.awt.GridBagLayout	p.449
toString()	java.awt.GridLayout	p.449
toString()	java.util.Hashtable	p.572
toString()	java.lang.Integer	p.525
toString()	java.lang.Long	p.526
toString()	java.awt.MenuComponent	p.460
toString()	java.lang.Object	p.530

(continues)

III

Java

(continued)

Method	Class	Turn to Page...
toString()	java.awt.Point	p.461
toString()	java.awt.Rectangle	p.464
toString()	java.net.ServerSocket	p.555
toString()	java.net.Socket	p.557
toString()	java.net.SocketImpl	p.558
toString()	java.io.StreamTokenizer	p.513
toString()	java.lang.String	p.537
toString()	java.lang.StringBuffer	p.541
toString()	java.lang.Thread	p.547
toString()	java.lang.ThreadGroup	p.549
toString()	java.lang.Throwable	p.549
toString()	java.net.URL	p.560
toString()	java.net.URLConnection	p.562
toString()	java.util.Vector	p.578
toString(double)	java.lang.Double	p.522
toString(float)	java.lang.Float	p.523
toString(int)	java.io.ByteArrayOutputStream	p.492
toString(int)	java.lang.Integer	p.525
toString(int, int)	java.lang.Integer	p.525
toString(long)	java.lang.Long	p.526
toString(long, int)	java.lang.Long	p.526
totalMemory()	java.lang.Runtime	p.532
toUpperCase()	java.lang.String	p.538
toUpperCase(char)	java.lang.Character	p.519
traceInstructions(boolean)	java.lang.Runtime	p.532
traceMethodCalls(boolean)	java.lang.Runtime	p.532
translate(int, int)	java.awt.Event	p.431
translate(int, int)	java.awt.Graphics	p.443
translate(int, int)	java.awt.Point	p.461
translate(int, int)	java.awt.Rectangle	p.464
trim()	java.lang.String	p.538
trimToSize()	java.util.Vector	p.578
uncaughtException(Thread, Throwable)	java.lang.ThreadGroup	p.549
union(Rectangle)	java.awt.Rectangle	p.464

Method	Class	Turn to Page...
unread(int)	java.io.PushbackInputStream	p.509
update(Graphics)	java.awt.Component	p.425
URL(String)	java.net.URL	p.558
URL(String, String, int, String)	java.net.URL	p.559
URL(String, String, String)	java.net.URL	p.559
URL(URL, String)	java.net.URL	p.558
URLConnection(URL)	java.net.URLConnection	p.561
URLStreamHandler()	java.net.URLStreamHandler	p.564
UTC(int, int, int, int, int, int)	java.util.Date	p.568
valid()	java.io.FileDescriptor	p.498
validate()	java.awt.Component	p.425
validate()	java.awt.Container	p.426
valueOf(boolean)	java.lang.String	p.538
valueOf(char)	java.lang.String	p.538
valueOf(char[])	java.lang.String	p.538
valueOf(char[], int, int)	java.lang.String	p.538
valueOf(double)	java.lang.String	p.538
valueOf(float)	java.lang.String	p.538
valueOf(int)	java.lang.String	p.538
valueOf(long)	java.lang.String	p.538
valueOf(Object)	java.lang.String	p.538
valueOf(String)	java.lang.Boolean	p.517
valueOf(String)	java.lang.Double	p.522
valueOf(String)	java.lang.Float	p.523
valueOf(String)	java.lang.Integer	p.525
valueOf(String)	java.lang.Long	p.526
valueOf(String, int)	java.lang.Integer	p.525
valueOf(String, int)	java.lang.Long	p.526
Vector()	java.util.Vector	p.576
Vector(int)	java.util.Vector	p.576
Vector(int, int)	java.util.Vector	p.576

(continues)

III

Java

(continued)

Method	Class	Turn to Page...
wait()	java.lang.Object	p.530
wait(long)	java.lang.Object	p.530
wait(long, int)	java.lang.Object	p.530
waitFor()	java.lang.Process	p.530
waitForAll()	java.awt.MediaTracker	p.456
waitForAll(long)	java.awt.MediaTracker	p.456
waitForID(int)	java.awt.MediaTracker	p.456
waitForID(int, long)	java.awt.MediaTracker	p.456
whitespaceChars(int, int)	java.io.StreamTokenizer	p.513
Window(Frame)	java.awt.Window	p.471
wordChars(int, int)	java.io.StreamTokenizer	p.513
write(byte[])	java.io.DataOutput	p.515
write(byte[])	java.io.FileOutputStream	p.499, 501
write(byte[])	java.io.OutputStream	p.503
write(byte[])	java.io.RandomAccessFile	p.510
write(byte[], int, int)	java.io.BufferedOutputStream	p.490
write(byte[], int, int)	java.io.ByteArrayOutputStream	p.492
write(byte[], int, int)	java.io.DataOutput	p.515
write(byte[], int, int)	java.io.DataOutputStream	p.494
write(byte[], int, int)	java.io.FileOutputStream	p.499, 501
write(byte[], int, int)	java.io.OutputStream	p.503
write(byte[], int, int)	java.io.PipedOutputStream	p.506
write(byte[], int, int)	java.io.PrintStream	p.508
write(byte[], int, int)	java.io.RandomAccessFile	p.510
write(int)	java.io.BufferedOutputStream	p.490
write(int)	java.io.ByteArrayOutputStream	p.492
write(int)	java.io.DataOutput	p.515
write(int)	java.io.DataOutputStream	p.494
write(int)	java.io.FileOutputStream	p.499, 501
write(int)	java.io.OutputStream	p.503
write(int)	java.io.PipedOutputStream	p.506
write(int)	java.io.PrintStream	p.508
write(int)	java.io.RandomAccessFile	p.510
writeBoolean(boolean)	java.io.DataOutput	p.515

Method	Class	Turn to Page...
writeBoolean(boolean)	java.io.DataOutputStream	p.494
writeBoolean(boolean)	java.io.RandomAccessFile	p.511
writeByte(int)	java.io.DataOutput	p.515
writeByte(int)	java.io.DataOutputStream	p.494
writeByte(int)	java.io.RandomAccessFile	p.511
writeBytes(String)	java.io.DataOutput	p.515
writeBytes(String)	java.io.DataOutputStream	p.495
writeBytes(String)	java.io.RandomAccessFile	p.511
writeChar(int)	java.io.DataOutput	p.516
writeChar(int)	java.io.DataOutputStream	p.495
writeChar(int)	java.io.RandomAccessFile	p.511
writeChars(String)	java.io.DataOutput	p.516
writeChars(String)	java.io.DataOutputStream	p.495
writeChars(String)	java.io.RandomAccessFile	p.511
writeDouble(double)	java.io.DataOutput	p.516
writeDouble(double)	java.io.DataOutputStream	p.495
writeDouble(double)	java.io.RandomAccessFile	p.511
writeFloat(float)	java.io.DataOutput	p.516
writeFloat(float)	java.io.DataOutputStream	p.495
writeFloat(float)	java.io.RandomAccessFile	p.511
writeInt(int)	java.io.DataOutput	p.516
writeInt(int)	java.io.DataOutputStream	p.495
writeInt(int)	java.io.RandomAccessFile	p.511
writeLong(long)	java.io.DataOutput	p.516
writeLong(long)	java.io.DataOutputStream	p.495
writeLong(long)	java.io.RandomAccessFile	p.511
writeShort(int)	java.io.DataOutput	p.516
writeShort(int)	java.io.DataOutputStream	p.495
writeShort(int)	java.io.RandomAccessFile	p.511
writeTo(OutputStream)	java.io.ByteArrayOutputStream	p.492
writeUTF(String)	java.io.DataOutput	p.516
writeUTF(String)	java.io.DataOutputStream	p.495
writeUTF(String)	java.io.RandomAccessFile	p.511
xor(BitSet)	java.util.BitSet	p.566
yield()	java.lang.Thread	p.547

III

Java

Chapter 19

Index of Java Classes and Interfaces

This is a complete alphabetical listing of all classes and interfaces found in this section of the book. The page numbers refer you to the complete documentation for each entry. Each interface is indicated by an asterisk (*).

III

Java

Part IV

JavaScript

Chapter 20

Understanding the JavaScript Reference Section

JavaScript is a scripting language used with HTML pages to increase functionality and interaction with the end user. It was developed by Netscape with Sun's Java language.

Finding information on programming in JavaScript can be a bit like looking for the Holy Grail. Among Netscape's site, online tutorials, and examples, information seems to be everywhere but at your fingertips. So here is the information you're looking for in one place, including statements, operators, and color values.

JavaScript and Java

It's important to note that JavaScript is a completely different beast from Java. Java is an object-oriented programming language developed by Sun Microsystems, and needs a variety of compilers and support files to function. It is useful for programmers and developers who have prior programming experience with languages like C++.

Programs developed under the Java development kit can work as full-fledged, stand-alone applications or as *applets* embedded in HTML pages. Even though applets are embedded in HTML pages, they still arrive on the client's computer as separate files.

JavaScript was developed by Netscape. It is a cousin to Java, containing a smaller and simpler set of commands that vary slightly in their implementation.

JavaScript's structure and syntax are similar to Java's but JavaScript is only functional when included as part of an HTML page. You can't develop applets or stand-alone applications with JavaScript—it can only reside within an HTML script and function when loaded on a compatible browser such as Netscape 2.0.

Using This Section

Several conventions used in this section make finding information easier.

Each entry has the same basic structure. Following the term and its type (object, property, or method) is a brief description of its use. This is followed by the syntax of the command.

Some items, especially those relating to forms, have a variety of implementations. The basic variations are listed as part of the syntax. *Italicized* items need to be replaced with actual values or variable names. Given the following syntax:

```
document.formName
```

a form called `userInfo` would be implemented this way:

```
document.userInfo
```

Methods with an asterisk are built-in methods and don't need association with an object to function.

A detailed description of use and programming examples is next, followed by a cross-reference to related items in the book.

When you see the term *URL*, it refers to a complete Uniform Resource Locator, including type and machine address, plus path and hash if applicable.

General Terms

Although they are not necessarily JavaScript objects or keywords, these terms can help you to understand JavaScript and how it works. These include general terms used in most discussions about JavaScript and its implementations.

Event Handlers

Event handlers are special items in JavaScript that give it much of its power. They allow the programmer to look for specific user behavior in relation to the HTML page, such as clicking a form button or moving the mouse pointer over an anchor.

Event handlers are embedded in HTML tags, typically used as part of forms, but are also included as a part of some anchors and links.

Virtually anything a user can do to interact with a page is covered with the event handlers, from moving the mouse to leaving the current page. For example, the following line displays "Netscape's Home Page" in the status bar instead of the link's URL when the mouse is placed over the anchor:

```
<A HREF="home.netscape.com" onMouseOver="window.status='Netscape's Home
Page'; return true">
```

Functions

A function is a user-defined or built-in method that performs a task. It can also return a value when used with the `return` statement. Functions are universal and do not need to be associated with an object to run, while methods are integrated with objects.

As a general rule, it's best to place function definitions within the `<HEAD>` tags of a document. This practice ensures that any functions are loaded and ready before the user has a chance to interact with the rest of the page.

Hierarchies

In a hierarchy, objects exist in a set relation to each other. For example, Navigator objects have a structure that reflects the construction of an HTML page. This is called *instance hierarchy* because it only works with specific instances of objects rather than with general classes.

The `window` object is the parent of all other Navigator objects. Underneath the `window` object, `location`, `history`, and `document` all share precedence. Under `document` are other objects such as forms, links, and anchors.

Each object is a descendant of a higher object. A form called `orderForm` is an object and it is also a property of `document`. As such, it is called `document.orderForm`.

Another way to think about a hierarchy is the relationship items in the real world have to each other. Spokes, handlebars, and pedals are all objects that belong to a bicycle. A bicycle is an object that belongs to ground transportation. Ground transportation is an object that belongs to modes of travel.

If represented as JavaScript objects, these relationships could be expressed this way:

```
travelMode.groundTransport.bicycle.handleBars
```

The highest and most nonspecific object is on the left and it gains specificity as it moves to the right and its descendants begin to branch out.

Java

In the words of Sun Microsystems, "Java is a simple, robust, object-oriented, platform-independent multithreaded, dynamic, general-purpose programming environment." What all these buzz-words mean is that Java is ideally suited for creating applets and applications for the Internet, for intranets, and for any other complex, distributed network.

Once compiled, it is possible for a single piece of Java source code to run on any machine—Windows 95, Solaris, Macintosh, or any other—that is equipped with a Java interpreter. Programming in Java requires a Java Developer's Kit with compiler and core classes provided by Sun or a third-party vendor, such as Symantec.

JavaScript

JavaScript is a scripting language for HTML documents developed by Netscape in cooperation with Sun Microsystems. Scripts are performed after specific user-triggered events. Creating JavaScript Web documents requires a text editor and compatible browser. Netscape Gold also includes an editor within the browser itself, so an external text editor isn't necessary.

Although not directly related to Java, JavaScript can interact with the exposed properties and methods of Java applets embedded on an HTML page. The difference boils down to this—Java applets exist outside the browser, whereas JavaScript only exists within a browser.

Literals

A literal is a value that can be assigned to a variable. Literals are what they are and do not change. Examples include 1, 3.1415927, "Bob," and `true`.

Several types of literals in JavaScript correspond to the variable types.

Integers

Integers are whole numbers such as 1, 16, and 25,896. They can be expressed in decimal (base 10), hexadecimal (base 16), or octal (base 8) form.

Hexadecimal numbers include 0–9 and A–F, and are represented in JavaScript by preceding the number with 0x (zero–x). Octal numbers only include 0–7 and are preceded by 0 (zero).

For example, decimal 23 is represented in hexadecimal by 0x17 and in octal by 027.

Floating-Point Numbers

Floating-point numbers are fractional portions of integers and must include at least one digit, and a decimal point or exponent symbol ("e" or "E").

The following are all ways of expressing the same floating-point number:

```
3.1415927

3145927e-7

.3141527E1
```

Boolean Literals

Boolean literals have only two values, `true` or `false`. In some implementations of JavaScript, 0 (`false`) and 1 (`true`) cannot be substituted for Boolean values. The current versions of Netscape Navigator and Gold both support 0 and 1 as Boolean `false` and `true`.

Strings

Strings are defined by any number of characters within single or double quotation marks. Use the backslash (\) to escape the quotation marks to print special characters. For example, the following:

```
document.write("Doc said, \"Festus, you need a bath,\" and wrinkled his
nose.")
```

results in:

```
Doc said, "Festus, you need a bath," and wrinkled his nose.
```

Methods

A method is a function assigned to an object. For example, `userName.toUpperCase()` returns an uppercase version of the string contained in `userName`.

Objects

An object is a construct with properties that are JavaScript variables or other objects. Functions associated with an object are called the *object's methods*. You access the properties and methods of an object with a simple notation:

```
objectName.propertyName
objectName.methodName
```

All names are case-sensitive.

If an object called `house` has the properties of `bedrooms`, `bathrooms`, `floors`, and `squareFeet`, you could access its values by using the object notation:

```
house.bedrooms
house.bathrooms
house.floors
house.squareFeet
```

Another way of thinking of objects is an array using the following array notation:

```
house["bedrooms"]
house["bathrooms"]
house["floors"]
house["squareFeet"]
```

The same object is also represented in JavaScript by a traditional array:

```
house[0]
house[1]
house[2]
house[3]
```

This type of relationship between indexes and strings is called an *associative array*.

Creating a new object requires a function that *instantiates* (creates an instance of) the object. Using the house example, the following function would create a new instance of a house object:

```
function House(bedrooms, bathrooms, floors, squareFeet) {
        this.bedrooms = bedrooms;
        this.bathrooms = bathrooms;
        this.floors = floors;
        this.squareFeet = squareFeet
}
```

Now that the object is defined, an instance is created by using the new directive:

```
500South5th = new House(2, 1, 1, 1700)
```

Other objects can be included as part of the object definition. For example, an object called owner has properties called name, age, mortgageLength:

```
function Owner(name, age, mortgageLength) {
        this.name = name;
        this.age = age;
        this.mortgageLength = mortgageLength
}
```

Adding an additional argument and line to the House function adds an owner to the house:

```
function House(bedrooms, bathrooms, floors, squareFeet, owner) {
        this.bedrooms = bedrooms;
        this.bathrooms = bathrooms;
        this.floors = floors;
        this.squareFeet = squareFeet;
        this.owner = owner
}
```

Now, owner Glenn Woodson, 38, with a 20-year mortgage, represented by G_Woodson, is included with the house:

```
G_Woodson = new Owner("Glenn Woodson",38,20);
500South5th = new House(2, 1, 1, 1700, G_Woodson)
```

The properties of G_Woodson are included as part of 500South5th:

```
500South5th.bedrooms
500South5th.bathrooms
500South5th.floors
500South5th.squareFeet
500South5th.G_Woodson.name
500South5th.G_Woodson.age
500South5th.G_Woodson.mortgageLength
```

Operators

An operator performs a function on one or more operands or variables. Operators are divided into two basic classes: *binary* and *unary*. Binary operators need two operands and unary operators need a single operand.

For example, addition is a binary operand:

```
sum = 1 + 5
```

Unary operands are often used to update counters. The following example increases the `counter` variable by 1:

```
counter++
```

Properties

Properties are used to describe an object or its current state. A property is defined by assigning it a value. The value can be assigned by the browser, the program, or as the user interacts with the page.

Several properties in JavaScript contain *constants*—values that never change. These are items such as the value of Pi (Π) or Euler's constant (E). Other items change from page to page but can't be changed, such as form elements.

Scripts

One or more JavaScript commands can be enclosed in a `<SCRIPT>` tag. The advent of several scripting languages has made it necessary to identify for the browser which language is being used. For JavaScript, the syntax is:

```
<SCRIPT LANGUAGE="JavaScript">
<!--
...Statements...
// -->
</SCRIPT>
```

The use of the `LANGUAGE` attribute is still optional in Netscape browsers, but this could change if other languages, such as Microsoft's VBScript, are implemented.

Note the use of HTML comment tags, `<!--` and `-->`. If the page containing the script is used on a browser that is not compatible with the scripting languages, the script statements are displayed as any other text on the page, adding clutter and trash to the screen.

If you use the comment tags, an incompatible browser ignores the script portion of the document. The double slashes that precede the closing HTML comment tag ensure that the tag won't be mistaken for a JavaScript statement.

Type Casting

A variable's type depends on the kind of information it contains (see the earlier section, "Literals"). JavaScript is loosely typed, meaning it does not need variables to declare what kind of type they are when created. The type is automatically assigned depending on the literal assigned to the variable.

By the same token, the type can change depending on the operation. Take the following statements:

```
//example 1
var oneString = "1"
var oneInt = 1
var oneConcatenate = oneString + oneInt //Results in "11"
var oneAddition = oneInt + oneString //Results in 2
```

In the first addition statement, the first operator is a string. JavaScript assumes that the operation is to join two strings. When JavaScript encounters an integer in the second operator, it converts the variable to a string to meet its own expectations.

Since JavaScript does not maintain any methods or properties to determine the current type for a variable, it is important to monitor the use of variables closely to avoid unexpected results.

Chapter 21

JavaScript Reference

JavaScript syntax and commands are divided into several categories depending on their use and function.

Objects are the building blocks of JavaScript. They are used to return and modify the status of forms, pages, the browser, and programmer-defined variables. An easy way to think about an object is as a noun. Cat, car, house, computer, and form are all nouns and could all be represented as an object.

You use *properties* to differentiate between objects of the same class—for example, all objects that are a cat. Properties are adjectives and refer to items that might make the object different from other objects. In the cat example, this could be weight, color, breed, disposition, current activity.

You use *methods* to pass messages to the object and sometimes to change its properties. For example, one method could be used to change the cats current activity from eating to sleeping, whereas another could be used to change its weight from heavy to really heavy.

Following is a listing of the building blocks of JavaScript.

abs

(Method)

Returns the absolute (unsigned) value of its argument.

```
Math.abs(argument)
```

Usage

The following example returns 10 and 12.5, respectively.

```
document.writeln(Math.abs(-10));
John.age.value = 12.5
document.writeln(Math.abs(John.age.value))
```

Related Items
Method of `Math`.

---

acos

(Method)

Returns the arc cosine (from zero to pi] radians) of its argument.

```
Math.acos(argument)
```

Usage

The argument should be a number between –1 and 1. If the value is outside the valid range, a zero is returned.

Related Items
Method of `Math`.

See the `asin`, `atan`, `cos`, `sin`, and `tan` methods.

---

action

(Property)

A reflection of the action attribute in an HTML `<form>` tag.

```
document.formName.action
document.forms[index].action
```

Usage

`action` returns a string consisting of a destination URL for data submitted from a form. This value can be set or changed before or after the document has been loaded and formatted.

In this example, the `action` for a form called `outlineForm` is set to the URL in the variable `outlineURL`.

```
outlineURL = "http://www.wossamottau.edu/cgi-bin/outline.cgi"
outlineForm.action=outlineURL
```

Related Items
Property of `form`.

See the `encoding`, `method`, and `target` properties.

alert

(Method)

Displays a JavaScript alert dialog box with an OK button and a user-defined message (see Figure 21.1).

```
[window.]alert(AlertMessage)
```

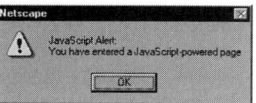

Fig. 21.1 Users must click the OK button in a JavaScript alert box before they can return to the document.

Usage

Before users can continue with an operation, they must press the OK button in the alert box.

Related Items

Method of window.

See the confirm and prompt methods.

alinkColor

(Property)

The color of a link after the mouse button is pressed but before it's released.

```
document.alinkColor
```

Usage

Like all colors in JavaScript, alinkColor is expressed as a hexadecimal RGB triplet or string literal. It cannot be changed after the HTML source document is processed. Both of these examples set the color to alice blue.

```
document.alinkColor="aliceblue"
document.alinkColor="F0F8FF"
```

Related Items

Property of document.

See the bgColor, fgColor, linkColor, and vlinkColor properties.

anchors array

(Object)

An array containing information about possible targets of a hypertext link in a document.

```
[windowName.]document.anchors[index]
```

Usage

anchors array is a read-only object that is set in HTML with <A> tags.

```
<A [HREF=URL] NAME="anchor name" [TARGET="windowName"]>
anchor text
</A>
```

Including a value for HREF also makes the anchor a link and adds it to the links array. New anchors are defined with JavaScript by using the anchor method.

To determine how many anchors are included in a document, use the length property.

```
document.anchors.length
```

The value of document.anchor[index] returns null. For example, the value of document.anchor[0] returns null even though it was the first anchor created with <A NAME="bob">All about Bob</A>.

Related Items

Property of document.

See the link object and the anchor method.

anchor

(Method)

Creates and displays an HTML hypertext target.

```
textString.anchor(anchorName)
```

Usage

Used with write or writeln methods, anchor creates an HTML anchor in the current document, where textString is what the user sees and anchorName is equivalent to the name attribute of an HTML <anchor> tag.

```
anchorString = "Louie's Place";
document.writeln(anchorString.anchor("louies_place")
```

Related Items

Method of `string`.

See the `link` method.

anchors

(Property)

An array of all defined anchors in the current document. See the `anchor` object for a detailed description.

```
document.anchors[index]
```

Usage

If the length of an anchor array in a document is 5, then the `anchors` array is represented as `document.anchors[0]` through `document.anchors[4]`.

Related Items

Property of `document`.

See the `anchor` object.

See the `length` and `links` properties.

appCodeName

(Property)

Returns a read-only string with the code name of the browser.

```
navigator.appCodeName
```

Usage

To display the code name for the current browser, use the following line:

```
document.write("The code name of your browser is " + navigator.appCodeName +
".")
```

For Netscape Navigator 2.0, this returns:

```
The name of your browser is Mozilla.
```

Related Items

Property of `navigator`.

See the `appName`, `appVersion`, and `userAgent` properties.

appName

(Property)

Returns a read-only string with the name of the browser.

```
navigator.appName
```

Usage

To display the application name for the current browser, use the following line:

```
document.write("The name of your browser is " + navigator.appName + ".")
```

For Netscape Navigator 2.0, this returns:

```
The code name of your browser is Netscape.
```

Related Items

Property of `navigator`.

See the `appCodeName`, `appVersion`, and `userAgent` properties.

appVersion

(Property)

Returns a string with the browser version information.

```
navigator.appVersion
```

Usage

`appVersion` is used to check which browser version the client is using. It returns in the *releaseNumber (platform; country)* format. For a Windows 95 release of Netscape 2.0:

```
document.write("The version of your browser is: " + navigator.appVersion +
".")
```

returns

```
The version of your browser is: 2.0 (Win95; I).
```

This specifies an international release of Navigator 2.0 running on Windows 95. The U country code specifies a U.S. release, whereas an I indicates an international release.

Related Items

Property of `navigator`.

See the `appName`, `appCodeName`, and `userAgent` properties.

asin

(Method)

Returns the arc sine of its argument.

```
Math.asin(argument)
```

Usage

Passing a number between –1 and 1 to asin returns the arcsine (between – /2 and /2 radians). If the number is outside the range, a zero is returned.

Related Items

Method of Math.

See the acos, atan, cos, sin, and tan methods.

atan

(Method)

Returns the arc tangent of its argument.

```
Math.(argument)
```

Usage

atan returns a number between between –pi/2 and pi/2 radians, representing the size of an angle in radians. Its argument is a number between –1 and 1, representing the tangent.

Related Items

Method of Math.

See the acos, asin, cos, sin, and tan methods.

back

(Method)

Recalls the previous URL from the history list.

```
history.back()
```

Usage

The usage for back is the same as for history.go(-1).

Related Items

Method of `history`.

See the `forward` and `go` methods.

bgColor

(Property)

The document background color.

```
document.bgColor
```

Usage

The usage for `bgColor` overrides the background color set in the browser preferences. It is expressed as a hexadecimal RGB triplet or string literal. It can be changed at any time. The following example allows users to use radio buttons to set their own background color.

```
function newColor(colorString) {
        document.bgColor = colorString
}
...
<FORM NAME="colors">
<INPUT TYPE="radio" NAME="color" VALUE="F0F8FF"
onClick="newColor(this.value)">Alice Blue
<INPUT TYPE="radio" NAME="color" VALUE="FF4500"
onClick="newColor(this.value)">Ochre
<INPUT TYPE="radio" NAME="color" VALUE="FFEFD5"
onClick="newColor(this.value)">Papaya Whip
</FORM>
```

Related Items

Property of `document`.

See the `alinkColor`, `fgColor`, `linkColor`, and `vlinkColor` properties.

big

(Method)

Formats a string object as a big font.

```
stringName.big()
```

Usage

Functionally, the usage for big is the same as encasing text with HTML <BIG> tags. Both of the following examples result in the same output: displaying the message "Welcome to my home page" in a big font:

```
var welcomeMessage = "Welcome to my home page."
document.write(welcomeMessage.big())

<BIG> Welcome to my home page.</BIG>
```

Related Items

Method of string.

See the fontsize and small methods.

---

blink

(Method)

Formats a string object as a blinking line.

```
stringname.blink()
```

Usage

The usage for blink same as encasing text with HTML <BLINK> tags. Both of the following examples produce a flashing line that says "Notice:"

```
var attentionMessage = "Notice"
document.write(attentionMessage.blink())

<BLINK>Notice</BLINK>
```

Related Items

Method of string.

See the bold, italics, and strike methods.

---

blur

(Method)

Removes focus from the specified form element.

```
document.formName.elementName.blur()
document.forms[index].elements[index].blur()
```

Usage

For example, the following line removes focus from the feedback element:

```
feedback.blur()
```

assuming that feedback is defined as:

```
<INPUT TYPE="text" NAME="feedback">
```

Related Items

Method of password, select, text, and textarea.

See the focus and select methods.

bold

(Method)

Formats a string object in bold text.

```
stringName.bold()
```

Usage

The usage for bold is same as encasing text with HTML <B> tags.

Related Items

Method of string.

See the blink, italics, and strike methods.

button

(Object)

A pushbutton on a form.

```
formName.buttonName
forms[index].elements[index]
```

Usage

Buttons must be defined within a <FORM> tag and can be used to perform an action.

```
<INPUT TYPE="button" NAME="buttonName" VALUE="textOnButton"
[onClick="eventHandler"]>
```

When accessed from within a form, the form name is understood. To avoid confusion and create clearer code, it's preferred to use the form name with form elements. Used with an `onClick` event handler, a button becomes a custom item that can initiate events and activities beyond the basic submit and reset.

The following button invokes the `validateForm` function when the button is pressed.

```
<INPUT TYPE="button" NAME="validate" VALUE="Check for Accuracy"
onClick="validateForm(this.form)">
```

Related Items
Property of `form`.

See the `reset` and `submit` objects.

See the `name` and `value` properties.

See the `click` method.

See the `onClick` event handler.

ceil

(Method)

Returns the next integer larger than the argument.

```
Math.ceil(argument)
```

Usage
`ceil` returns the smallest integer greater than or equal to the integer or floating-point decimal passed to it as an argument. For example:

```
Math.ceil(1.01)
```

returns a 2.

Related Items
Method of `Math`.

See the `floor` method.

charAt

(Method)

Returns a character from a string.

```
stringName.charAt(index)
```

Usage

This method accepts an index as its argument and returns the character at that position in the string. The first character is at position 0 and the last at length –1.

```
var userName = "Bobba Louie"
document.write(userName.charAt(4))
```

returns an "a."

Related Items

Method of string.

See the indexOf and lastIndexOf methods.

checkbox

(Object)

A form element that the user sets to *on* or *off* by clicking it.

```
formName.checkboxName
forms[index].elements[index]
```

Usage

checkboxes are defined within a <FORM> tag.

```
<INPUT TYPE="checkbox" NAME="checkboxName" VALUE="checkboxValue"
[CHECKED] [onClick="eventHandler"]> textToDisplay
```

The properties and methods of checkboxes are used in a variety of ways.

Use the checked value of checkbox to see if it is currently selected (true) or not (false). If the CHECKED option is used as part of the definition, defaultChecked also returns true.

Related Items

Property of form.

See the radio object.

See the checked, defaultChecked, name, and value properties.

See the click method.

See the onClick event handler.

checked

(Property)

Returns a Boolean flag representing an individual checkbox or radio button status.

```
formName.checkboxName.checked
formName.radioButtonName[index].checked
forms[index].elements[index].checked
```

Usage

checked returns a Boolean value (true or false) indicating whether a checkbox or radio button is selected. The value is updated immediately when an item is checked. Used with the for...in statement, it can check the status of buttons:

```
function whichOneChecked() {
        var checkedValue = ""
        for (var i in document.formName.radioName) {
            if (document.formName.radioName[i].checked==true)
            checkedValue=document.formName.radioName[i].value
    }
}
```

Related Items

Property of checkbox and radio.

See the defaultChecked property.

clear

(Method)

Clears window contents, as a clear screen does.

```
document.clear()
```

Usage

clear erases the contents of a window, regardless of how the window was filled.

Related Items

Method of document.

See the close, open, write, and writeln methods.

clearTimeout

(Method)

Cancels a timeout.

```
[windowName.]clearTimeout(argument)
parent.[frameName.]clearTimeout(argument)
```

Usage

clearTimeout removes a timeout that was previously set using the setTimeout method. A timeout is set using a unique timeout ID that must be used to clear it:

```
clearTimeout(waitTime)
```

Related Items

Method of frame and window.

See the setTimeout method.

click

(Method)

Simulates a mouse click.

```
formName.elementName.click()
forms[index].elements[index].click()
```

Usage

The effect of a click depends on the type of form element that is referenced.

Table 21.1   The Click Method and its Effect on Form Elements

Form Element	Action
Button, Reset, and Submit	Same as clicking button
Radio	Selects radio button
Checkbox	Marks checkbox and sets value to *on*

Related Items

Method of button, checkbox, radio, reset, and submit.

close

(Method)

For a document object, closes the current stream of output and forces its display.

For a window object, closes the current window.

```
document.close()
window.close()
[windowName.]close()
```

Usage

For documents, close stops the winsock browser's animation and displays "Document: Done" in the status bar.

For windows, as with all window commands, the window object is assumed. For example:

```
window.close()
close()
self.close()
```

all close the current window.

Related Items

Method of document and window.

See the clear, open, write, and writeln methods.

confirm

(Method)

Displays a JavaScript confirmation dialog box (see Figure 21.2).

```
window.confirm()
[windowName.]confirm()
```

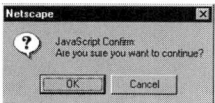

Fig. 21.2   The JavaScript confirmation box allows a user to continue or to cancel out of an operation.

Usage

Similar to an alert with the addition of a Cancel button, confirm displays a message and a button to continue. confirm returns a true if the user selects OK and a false for Cancel. The following example loads a new window if the user presses OK:

```
if (confirm("Are you sure you want to enter.") {
    tourWindow = window.open("http:\\www.haunted.com\","hauntedhouse")
}
```

Related Items

Method of `window`.

See the `alert` and `prompt` methods.

cookie

(Property)

String value of a small piece of information stored by Navigator in a client-side cookies.txt file.

```
document.cookie
```

Usage

The value stored in the `cookie` is found using substring `charAt`, `IndexOf`, and `lastIndexOf`.

The cookie is a special property containing state/status information about the client that can be accessed by the server. Included in that `state` is a description of the range of URLs for which that state is valid.

Future HTTP requests from the client falling within a range of URLs described within the state object will include transmission of the current value of the state object from the client back to the server.

This simple form of data storage allows the server to provide personalized service to the client. Online merchants can store information about items currently in an electronic shopping basket, services can post registration information and automate functions such as typing a user ID.

User preferences can be saved on the client and retrieved by the server when the site is contacted. For limited-use information such as shopping services, you can also set a time limit on the life of the cookie information.

To post and view cookie settings within an HTML script, assign a value to the property.

```
document.cookie = "string"
```

CGI scripts are also used to set and retrieve cookie values. Generating the cookie requires sending an HTTP header in the format:

```
Set-Cookie: NAME=Value; [EXPIRES=date;] [PATH=pathname;] [DOMAIN=domainname;]
[SECURE]
```

When a request for cookie information is made, the list of cookie information is searched for all URLs that match the current URL. Any matches are returned in this format:

```
cookie: NAME1=string1; NAME2=string2; ...
```

Cookie was an arbitrarily assigned name. For more information about the cookie and its function, see Netscape's Cookie Specification at **http://home.netscape.com/ newsref/std/cookie_spec.html**.

Related Items
Property of document.

See the hidden object.

cos

(Method)

Returns the cosine of the argument.

    Math.cos(*argument*)

Usage
Angle size must be expressed in radians and the result is from –1 to 1.

Related Items
Method of Math.

See the acos, asin, atan, sin, and tan methods.

Date

(Object)

Provides a set of methods for working with dates and times.

    Date.*method(parameters)*

Usage
The built-in Date object replaces a normal date type. Although it does not have any properties, the built-in Date object is equipped with a range of methods to set and change the values of its values.

Although date values are returned in standard form and syntax, the actual value is stored as the number of milliseconds since midnight on 1/1/70. The use of this convention prohibits the use of dates before 1/1/70.

To create a new Date object, use one of the following syntax conventions:

```
objectName = new Date() //Creates object with current date and time
objectName = new Date("month day, year [hours:minutes:seconds]")
        //Creates date object with date and time values in string variable or
        constant
objectName = new Date(year, month, day [, hours, minutes, seconds])
        //Creates date object with integer values
```

If you omit the time component when you create a Date object, it defaults to midnight (00:00:00). Methods for getting and setting time and date information are divided into four classes: set, get, to, and parse/UTC.

Except for the day of the month, all numerical representations of date components begin numbering with 0. This should not present a problem except with months, which are represented by 0 (January) through 11 (December).

The standard date syntax is "Thu, 11 Jan 1996 06:20:00 GMT". U.S. time zone abbreviations are also understood; but for universal use, specify the time zone offset. For example, "Thu, 11 Jan 1996 06:20:00 GMT+0530" is a place 5 hours and 30 minutes west of the Greenwich meridian.

Related Items

See the getDate, getDay, getHours, getMinutes, getMonth, getSeconds, getTime, getTimezoneOffset, getYear, parse, setDate, setHours, setMinutes, setMonth, setSeconds, setTime, setYear, toGMTString, toLocaleString, and toUTC methods.

defaultChecked

(Property)

A Boolean value (true or false) indicating whether a checkbox or radio button is checked by default.

```
formName.elementName.defaultChecked
forms[index].elements[index].defaultChecked
```

Usage

Setting a value to defaultChecked can override the checked attribute of a form element. The following section of code resets a group of radio buttons to their original state by finding and setting the default button:

```
for (var i in menuForm.choices) {
   if (menuForm.choices[i].defaultChecked) {
      menuForm.choices[i].defaultChecked = true
   }
}
```

The button display is not affected with a change in the defaultChecked even if the status of other buttons are affected.

Related Items

Property of checkbox and radio.

See the form object.

See the checked property.

defaultSelected

(Property)

Default state of an item in a form select element.

```
formName.elementName.defaultSelected
forms[index].elements[index].defaultSelected
```

Usage

defaultSelected returns a true or a false, depending on whether or not the CHECKED option was used with a select form element. Setting a value with this property can override the selected attribute of an <option> tag. The syntax and behavior are identical to those of defaultChecked.

Related Items

Property of options.

See the index, selected, and selectedIndex properties.

defaultStatus

(Property)

The default message displayed in the status bar at the bottom of a Navigator window (see Figure 21.3).

```
[windowName.]defaultStatus
```

Usage

Sets the message in the status bar when nothing else is displayed. This is preempted by a priority or transient message such as a mouseOver event with an anchor. For example:

```
window.defaultStatus = "Welcome to my home page"
```

displays the welcome message while the mouse is not over a link or Netscape is not performing an action that it needs to notify the user about.

Related Items

Property of window.

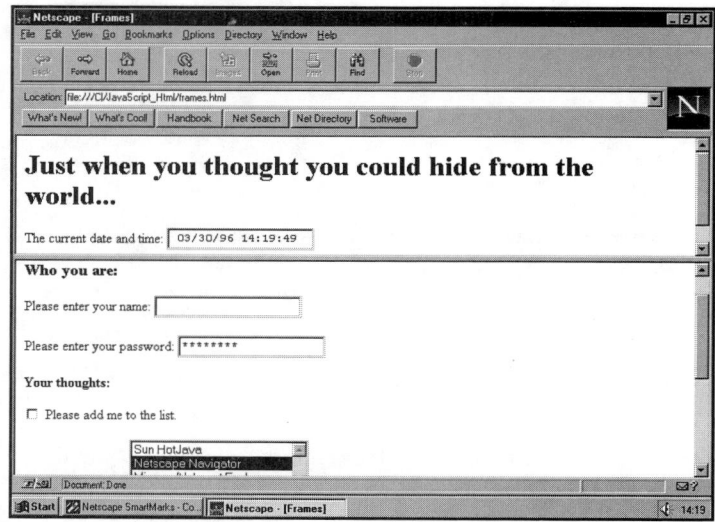

Fig. 21.3 The window status bar, which can hold predefined text other than a link URL.
See the status property.

defaultValue

(Property)

The initial contents of text-type form elements.

```
formName.elementName.defaultValue
forms[index].elements[index].defaultValue
```

Usage

For any of the standard HTML text form fields—hidden, password, text, textarea (between the <TEXTAREA> tags), and string—defaultValue returns the initial contents, regardless of the current value. For password elements, this property is initially set to null for security reasons, regardless of any set value.

Related Items

Property of hidden, password, text, and textarea.

See the value property.

document

(Object)

An object created by Navigator when a page is loaded.

```
document.propertyOrMethod
document.objectName.propertyOrMethod
```

Usage

document is one of the base objects of JavaScript and contains information on the current document such as title, background color, and forms. These properties are defined within <body> tags. Through write and writeln, document also provides methods for displaying HTML text to the user.

You can reference the anchors, forms, and links of a document by using the appropriate arrays of the document object. These arrays contain an entry for each anchor, form, or link in a document.

Related Items

Property of window.

See the frame object.

See the alinkColor, anchors, bgColor, cookie, fgColor, forms, lastModified, linkColor, links, location, referrer, title, and vlinkColor properties.

See the clear, close, open, write, and writeln methods.

See the onLoad and onUnload event handlers.

E

(Property)

The base of natural logarithms.

```
Math.E
```

Usage

Also called *Euler's constant*, this value is approximately 2.71828.

Related Items

Property of Math.

See the LN2, LN10, LOG2E, LOG10E, PI, SQRT1_2, and SQRT2 properties.

elements array

(Object)

An array of `form` elements in source order.

```
formName.elements[index]
forms[index].elements[index]
```

Usage

All elements of a form are included in this array, which is accessible through the form name or the `forms` array. Form elements include buttons, checkboxes, radio buttons, text, and textarea objects. The elements can be referenced by their index.

For example, if a form contains two text fields, three radio buttons, and two push buttons, they are referenced in the `elements` array as `formName.elements[0]` through `formName.elements[6]`. Note that numbering begins with 0 and not 1.

To find the number of elements in a form, use the `length` property. The value of a member of the element array is the complete HTML text used to create it.

Elements can also be referenced by the element name. For example, a password element called newPassword is the second form element on an HTML page. Its value is accessed in three ways:

```
formName.elements[1].value
formName.elements["newPassword"].value
formName.newPassword.value
```

Values cannot be set or changed using the read-only `elements` array.

Related Items

Property of `form`.

See the `length` property.

elements

(Property)

An array of objects containing form elements in HTML source order.

```
formName.elements[index]
forms[index].elements[index]
```

Usage

The array index begins with 0 and ends with the number of `form` elements –1. For a complete discussion on `elements`, see the `elements` object.

Related Items

Property of `form`.

See the `elements` object.

---

encoding

(Property)

Returns a string reflecting the MIME encoding type.

```
formName.encoding
forms[index].encoding
```

Usage

MIME encoding types are set in the `enctype` attribute of an HTML `<FORM>` tag. The standards for MIME encoding in HTML are not established, but progress and draft documents are located at the University of California-Irvine Information and Computer Sciences Department, found on the Web at **http://www.ics.uci.edu/pub/ietf/html/**.

Related Items

Property of `form`.

See the `action`, `method`, and `target` properties.

---

*escape**

(Method)

Returns the ASCII code of its argument.

```
escape(argument)
```

Usage

HTML ASCII codes are based on the ISO Latin –1 character set in the form %xxx where xxx is the decimal ASCII code. This method is not associated with any other object but is actually a native part of the JavaScript language. Alphanumeric characters (letters and numbers) will return as themselves, while symbols are returned as their ASCII code.

```
document.write(escape("Hi!"))
```

returns

```
Hi%21
```

Related Items

See the `unescape` method.

eval

(Method)

Evaluates a string as a numeric expression.

```
eval(string)
```

Usage

This built-in function takes a string or numeric expression as its argument. If a string, eval tries to convert it to a numeric expression, then evaluates the expression and returns the value.

```
var x = 10
var y = 20
document.write(eval("x + y"))
```

This method can also be used to perform JavaScript commands included as part of a string.

```
var doThis = "if (x==10) { alert('Your maximum has been reached') }
function checkMax () {
   x++;
   eval(doThis)
}
```

This can be useful when converting a date from a form (always a string) into a numerical expression or number.

exp

(Method)

Returns a natural logarithm.

```
Math.exp(argument)
```

Usage

exp returns the argument raised to the power of E (Euler's constant) to compute a natural logarithm.

Related Items

Method of Math.

See the log and pow methods.

See the E property.

fgColor

(Property)

The color of foreground text.

```
document.fgColor
```

Usage

Colors in JavaScript are represented as a hexadecimal RGB triplet or a sting literal. This value cannot be changed after a document is processed, although it can be changed for individual sections of text with the fontcolor method.

fgColor takes two forms:

```
document.fgColor="aliceblue"
document.fgColor="F0F8FF"
```

which has the same effect as the TEXT attribute in the <BODY> tag:

```
<BODY TEXT="aliceblue">
```

Related Items

Property of document.

See the alinkColor, bgColor, linkColor, and vlinkColor properties.

See the fontcolor method.

fixed

(Method)

Formats the calling string into a fixed-pitch font.

```
stringName.fixed()
```

Usage

Using fixed is identical to encasing a string argument in HTML <tt> tags.

Related Items

Method of string.

floor

(Method)

Returns the next integer smaller than the argument.

```
Math.floor(argument)
```

Usage
Passing an integer or floating-point decimal to this method returns an integer less than or equal to its argument. For example:

```
Math.floor(2.99)
```

returns a 2.

Related Items
Method of Math.

See the ceil method.

focus

(Method)

Gives focus to a specific form element.

```
formName.elementName.focus()
forms[index].elements[index].focus()
```

Usage
Using the name of the form and the element, focus gives the element focus. From that point, a value can be entered by JavaScript commands or the user can complete the entry.

Related Items
Method of password, select, text, and textarea.

See the blur and select methods.

fontcolor

(Method)

Overrides the default foreground color for a string object.

```
stringName.fontcolor()
```

Usage

`fontcolor` formats the string object to a specific color expressed in the argument as a hexadecimal RGB triplet or a string literal. Using `fontcolor` is like using `<FONT COLOR=COLOR>`.

```
myDog = "Brown";
document.write(myDog.fontcolor("sienna"))
```

Related Items

Method of `string`.

---

fontsize

(Method)

Formats the string object to a specific font size.

```
stringName.fontsize(argument)
```

Usage

This method uses one of seven defined sizes using an integer through the `<FONTSIZE=SIZE>` tag. If a string is passed, then the size is changed relative to the value set in the `<BASEFONT>` tag.

The argument represents the size. If it is an integer, it is the size of the font and must be a number ranging from 1 to 7. If it is a string, it changes the size of the font relative to the base font.

Related Items

Method of `string`.

See the `big` and `small` methods.

---

form (forms array)

(Object)

An object representing a form on a page.

```
document.formName
document.forms[index]
```

Usage

`form` is a property of the `document` object. Each form in a document is a separate and distinct object that can be referenced using the name of the form as the form object. The form object is also represented as an array created as forms are defined through HTML tags.

If the first form in a document is named `orderForm`, then it could be referenced as `document.orderForm` or `document.forms[0]`. If no name is given to the form, it can only be referenced by its index in the forms array. The number of individual forms on a page is available by using the `length` property.

```
document.forms.length
```

Individual elements of the form are referenced by their name or by using the `elements` array.

```
document.formName.elements[index]
```

The forms array is a read-only object. Attempts to set the value through statements such as:

```
document.forms[1]="OldGuestBook"
```

have no effect.

The value of an item in the forms array is presented in syntax similar to the syntax of HTML tags. For example, the value of the `form` object for a form with the name `userInfo` is `<object userInfo>`.

Related Items
Property of `document`.

See the `hidden` object, the `action`, `elements`, `encoding`, `forms`, `method`, `name`, and `target` properties.

See the `submit` method.

See the `onSubmit` event handler.

forms

(Property)

An array of objects corresponding to named forms in HTML source order.

```
document.forms
```

Usage
`forms` are a property of the `document` object and contain an entry for each `form` object in a document. For a detailed discussion, see the `form` object.

Related Items
Property of `document`.

See the `form` object.

See the `length` property.

forward

(Method)

Loads the next document on the URL history list.

```
history.forward()
```

Usage

This method is the same as `history.go(1)`.

Related Items

Method of `history`.

See the `back` and `go` methods.

frame

(Object)

A window containing HTML subdocuments that are independently scrollable.

```
[windowName.][parent.]frameName
[windowName.][parent.]frames[index]
```

Usage

Frames can point to different URLs and be targeted by other frames—all in the same window. Each `frame` is a `window` object defined using the `<frameset>` tag to define the layout that makes up the page. The page is defined from a parent HTML document. All subdocuments are children of the parent.

If a `frame` contains definitions for `SRC` and `NAME` attributes, then the `frame` can be identified from a sibling by using the `parent` object as `parent.frameName` or `parent.frames[index]`.

Related Items

Property of `window`.

See the `document` and `window` objects.

See the `defaultStatus`, `frames`, `parent`, `self`, `status`, `top`, and `window` properties.

See the `setTimeout` and `clearTimeout` methods.

frames

(Property)

An array corresponding to child frame windows created using the <frameset> tag.

```
[windowName.][parent.]frameName
[windowName.][parent.]frames[index]
```

Usage

To obtain the number of child frames in a window, use the length property. For more information on the frames array, see the frame object.

Related Items

Property of window.

See the frame object.

See the length property.

getDate

(Method)

Returns the day of the month.

```
Date.getDate()
```

Usage

One of the few items in JavaScript that doesn't begin with a 0, this method returns a number between 1 and 31 representing the day of the month.

```
endOfTheWorld = new Date("January 11, 1996 06:18:00")
document.write(endOfTheWorld.getDate()) //Returns 11
```

Related Items

Method of Date.

See the setDate method.

getDay

(Method)

Returns the day of the week as an integer from 0 (Sunday) to 6 (Saturday).

```
Date.getDay()
dateName.getDay()
```

Usage

There is no corresponding setDay command because the day is automatically computed when the date value is assigned.

Related Items

Method of Date.

getHours

(Method)

Returns the hour of the day.

```
Date.getHours()
dateName.getHours()
```

Usage

The value is returned in 24-hour format, from 0 (midnight) to 23 (11 PM).

Related Items

Method of Date.

See the setHours method.

getMinutes

(Method)

Returns the minutes with an integer from 0 to 59.

```
Date.getMinutes()
dateName.getMinutes()
```

Usage

Like the other date functions, getMinutes is a straightforward matter of returning one element of the time.

```
endOfTheWorld = new Date("January 11, 1996 06:18:00")
document.write(endOfTheWorld.getMinutes()) //Returns 18
```

Related Items

Method of Date.

See the setMinutes method.

---

getMonth

(Method)

Returns the month of the year.

```
Math.getMonth()
dateName.getMonth()
```

Usage

The month is returned as an integer between 0 (January) and 11 (December), not as a string. The value can be confusing since it doesn't follow conventional numbering for months of the year. When sending the value to the screen or prompting it from the user, be sure to make the conversion.

```
function toReality() { //converts month to 1-12 numbering system
     this += 1
}

function toConvention() { //converts month to 0-11 numbering system
     this -= 1
}
```

Related Items

Method of `Date`.

See the `setMonth` method.

---

getSeconds

(Method)

Returns the seconds.

```
Date.getSeconds()
dateName.getSeconds()
```

Usage

Seconds are returned as an integer from 0 to 59.

Related Items

Method of `Date`.

See the `setSeconds` method.

getTime

(Method)

Returns an integer representing the current value of the date object.

```
Date.getTime()
dateName.getTime()
```

Usage

The value is the number of milliseconds since midnight, Jan. 1, 1970. This value can be used to compare the length of time between two date values.

For functions involving computation of dates, it is useful to create a set of variables defining minutes, hours, and days in milliseconds:

```
var dayMillisec = 1000 * 60 * 60 * 24  //1,000 milliseconds x 60 sec x 60 min
x 24 hrs
var hourMillisec = 1000 * 60 * 60  //1,000 milliseconds x 60 sec x 60 min
var minuteMillisec = 1000 * 60  //1,000 milliseconds x 60 sec
```

Related Items

Method of Date.

See the setTime method.

getTimezoneOffset

(Method)

Returns the difference in minutes between the client machine and Greenwich mean time (GMT).

```
Date.getTimezoneOffset()
dateName.getTimezoneOffset()
```

Usage

This value is a constant except for daylight savings time.

Related Items

Method of Date.

getYear

(Method)

Returns the year of the date object minus 1900.

```
Date.getYear()
dateName.getYear()
```

Usage

Although the year can be passed to a date object as a 4-digit number in a string, the value is returned from getYear as a 2-digit number. For example, 1996 is returned as 96.

Related Items

Method of Date.

See the setYear method.

go

(Method)

Loads a document specified in the history list.

```
history.go(argumentOrURL)
```

Usage

This method can reference documents in the history list by URL or relative to the current position on the list. If the URL is incomplete, then the closest match is used. The search is not case-sensitive.

Related Items

Method of history.

See the back and forward methods.

hash

(Property)

Returns a string with the portion of a URL beginning with a hash mark (#).

```
document.linkName.hash
document.links[index].hash
document.location.hash
```

Usage

Hashes denote an anchor name fragment. They can be used to set a hash property, although it is safest to set the entire URL as a href property. An error is returned if the hash isn't found in the current location.

Related Items

Property of link and location.

See the anchor object.

See the host, hostname, href, pathname, port, protocol, and search properties.

hidden

(Object)

A text object suppressed from appearing on an HTML form.

```
document.formName.hiddenName
document.forms[index].elements[index].propertyOrMethod
```

Usage

The hidden object can be used in addition to cookies to pass name/value pairs for client/server communication. The difference between the two is that cookies are persistent on the client between session, whereas the hidden object is specific to the form.

The initial contents of the hidden object can be changed within a function by assigning new contents to its value property.

```
<INPUT TYPE="hidden" NAME="failedTries" VALUE="0">
     ... statements ...
     function setRetry() {
     document.userPasswordForm.failedTries.value++
}
```

Each time the setRetry function is called, the value of the hidden object named failedTries is incremented by 1. This is also an example of the loose typecasting in JavaScript. Even though the value is initially a string, when the script sees the mathematical operator, it attempts to convert the value to an integer.

Related Items

Property of form.

See the cookie, defaultValue, name, and value properties.

history

(Object)

A list of previously visited URLs, identical to the browser's Go menu.

```
document.history
```

Usage

This object is derived from the Go menu and contains the URL information for previously visited pages. Its methods are used to navigate to any point on the list.

To determine the number of items on the list, use the `length` property:

```
document.history.length
```

Navigation is possible with relative movements on the list using the `forward` and `back` methods, similar to using the menu bar navigation buttons.

```
document.history.forward()
document.history.back()
```

The go method allows jumps on the list beyond simple forward and back movement, similar to selecting an address directly from the Go menu.

```
document.history.go(-2) //loads the page two links ago
```

When you specify a window, the navigation in other windows or frames is controllable. The following example loads a new page from the `history` list in the `content` frame. Note that the name of the frame replaces the `document` notation.

```
parent.content.history.back() //loads the previous page in the frame
```

Related Items

Property of `document`.

See the `location` object.

See the `length` property.

See the `back`, `forward`, and go methods.

host

(Property)

Returns a string formed by combining the `hostname` and `port` properties of a URL:

```
location.host
linkName.host
links[index].host
```

Usage

Provides a method for viewing and changing URL host properties of location-type objects. If a port is not specified, the `host` property is the same as the `hostname` property.

```
location.host = "www.montana.com:80"
```

Related Items

Property of `link` and `location`.

See the `hash`, `hostname`, `href`, `pathname`, `port`, `protocol`, and `search` properties.

hostname

(Property)

Returns or changes a string with the domain name or IP address of a URL.

```
location.hostname
linkName.hostname
links[index].hostname
```

Usage

This property is similar to the `host` property except that it doesn't include the port information. When the port property is null, the `host` and `hostname` properties are identical.

Although `hostname` can be changed at any time, it is recommended to change the entire URL at once. If the `hostname` can't be found, an error is returned.

Related Items

Property of `link` and `location`.

See the `hash`, `host`, `href`, `pathname`, `port`, `protocol`, and `search` properties.

href

(Property)

Returns a string with the entire URL of the current document.

```
location.href
linkName.href
links[index].href
```

Usage

All other `location` and `link` properties are substrings of `href`, which can be changed at any time.

The URL of the current document is reflected to the screen using `document.write`.

```
document.write("You are here: " + window.location.href)
```

Related Items

Property of `link` and `location`.

See the `hash`, `host`, `hostname`, `pathname`, `port`, `protocol`, and `search` properties.

index

(Property)

Returns the index of a select element option.

```
formName.selectName.options[index].index
forms[index].elements[index].options[index].index
```

Usage

The position of the option in the select object, with numbering beginning at 0.

Related Items

Property of `select` (options array).

See the `defaultSelected`, `selected`, and `selectedIndex` properties.

indexOf

(Method)

Returns the location of a specific character or string.

```
stringName.indexOf(character¦string, startingPoint)
```

Usage

The search starts from a specific location. The first character of the string is specified as zero and the last is the string's `length` –1. If the string is not found, the method returns a –1.

The `startingPoint` is zero by default.

```
if (navigator.appVersion.indexOf('Unix') != -1)
        return true
```

Related Items

Method of `string`.

See the `charAt` and `lastIndexof` methods.

*isNaN**

(Method)

Checks to see if an argument is not a number.

```
isNaN(argument)
```

Usage

For UNIX platforms only, this stand-alone function returns `true` if the argument is not a number. On all platforms except Windows, the `parseFloat` and `parseInt` return `NaN` when the argument is not a number.

Related Items

See the `parseFloat` and `parseInt` methods.

italics

(Method)

Formats a string object into italics.

```
stringName.italics()
```

Usage

`italics` are the same as encasing a string in HTML `<I>` tags.

Related Items

Method of `string`.

See the `blink`, `bold`, and `strike` methods.

lastIndexOf

(Method)

Returns the index of a character or string in a `string` by searching from the end.

```
stringName.lastIndexOf()
```

Usage

Returns the index of a character or string in a `string` object by looking backwards from the end of the string or a user-specified index. It returns a –1 if the string is not found.

```
if (navigator.appVersion.lastIndexOf('Win') != -1)
     return true
```

IV

JavaScript

Related Items

Method of string.

See the charAt and indexOf methods.

---

lastModified

(Property)

A read-only string containing the date that the current document was last changed.

```
document.lastModified
```

Usage

This property is based on the attributes of the source file. The string is formatted in the standard form used by JavaScript (see the Date object). A common usage is:

```
dateModified = "This page last modified on " + document.lastModified
document.write(dateModified.small())
```

Related Items

Property of document.

---

length

(Property)

An integer reflecting a length- or size-related property of an object.

```
formName.length
forms.length
formName.elements.length
forms[index].length
[windowName.]frameName.length
frameRef.frames.length
history.length
radioName.length
selectName.length
selectName.options.length
stringName.length
windowName.length
anchors.length
links.length
```

Usage

The meaning of the value returned by length is determined by the array or object to which it's applied (see Table 21.2).

Table 21.2 Length Property Results	
Object/Array	**Property Measured**
history	Length of the history list
string	Integer length of the string; zero for a null string
radio	Number of radio buttons
anchors, forms, frames, links, options	Number of elements in the array

Related Items

Property of anchors, elements, forms, frame, frames, history, links, options, radio, string, and window.

link (links array)

(Object)

Text or an image defined as a hypertext link to another URL.

```
document.linkName
document.links[index]
```

Usage

A link is a location object and, as such, has the same properties and methods as a location object.

If a name is defined for the object, it is also defined as an anchor and given an entry in the anchors array.

```
<A HREF='http://www.cnet.com/'>c¦net's front door</A>
<A HREF='http://www.cnet.com/' NAME='cnet'>c¦net's front door</A>
```

In the previous example, the first line only creates an entry in the links array. With the addition of the NAME attribute, an additional entry is created in the anchors array.

The link object is read-only. To create a new hypertext link, use the link method (method of string).

Related Items

Property of document.

See the anchor object.

See the hash, host, hostname, href, length, pathname, port, protocol, search, and target properties.

See the link method.

See the onClick and onMouseOver event handlers.

link

(Method)

Creates a hypertext link to another URL.

```
stringName.link(argument)
```

Usage

Creates a new hyperlink by defining the <HREF> attribute and the text representing the link to the user.

```
linkText = "Wossamatta University";
linkURL = "http://www.wossammotta.edu/";
document.write("Rocky's alma mater is " + linkText.link(linkURL))
```

Related Items

Method of string.

See the anchor method.

linkColor

(Property)

The hyperlink color displayed in the document.

```
document.linkColor
```

Usage

Colors are expressed as a hexadecimal RGB triplet or as a string literal. The color corresponds to the link attribute in the HTML <BODY> tag and cannot be changed after the document is processed.

```
document.write("The current link color is " + document.linkColor)
```

Related Items

Property of document.

See the alinkColor, bgColor, fgColor, and vlinkColor properties.

links

(Property)

An array representing link objects.

```
document.links[index]
```

Usage

Links are defined in HTML using <A HREF=URL> tags. These are reflected in the links property with the first link identified as document.links[0]. For a more detailed description, see the link object.

Related Items

See the link object.

See the anchors and length properties.

LN2

(Property)

A constant representing the natural logarithm of 2.

```
Math.LN2
```

Usage

This value is approximately 0.69315.

Related Items

Property of Math.

See the E, LN10, LOG2E, LOG10E, PI, SQRT1_2, and SQRT2 properties.

LN10

(Property)

A constant representing the natural logarithm of 10.

```
Math.LN10
```

Usage

This value is approximately 2.30259.

Related Items

Property of Math.

See the E, LN2, LOG2E, LOG10E, PI, SQRT1_2, and SQRT2 properties.

location

(Object)

Complete URL information for the current document.

```
[WindowName.][frameName.]location.propertyName
parent.[frameName.]location.propertyName
```

Usage

location is used to determine the URL for any active document, including those in other browser windows or frames. If the window object is omitted, the current window is assumed.

Each property of location contains a different portion of the URL. There are six parts of the URL reflected in the location object:

protocol://hostname:port/pathname search#hash

Protocols include the initial portion of the address (http, mailto, ftp, etc.) up to and including the colon. Several additional protocols are included for JavaScript.

The javascript protocol evaluates the expression after the colon and tries to load the string value of its result. If there is no result or it is undefined, the current page remains.

```
javascript:parent.content.history.go(-1)
```

The about protocol provides three methods to view information about the browser. By itself, it is the same as selecting Help, About. The other two methods, cache and plugins, reflect the current status of the cache and information about installed plug-in applications.

```
about:cache
about:plugins
```

Don't confuse this object, which is a property of window, with the location property of document. Generally, they reflect the same value but the property can't be changed, whereas the properties of the object can be changed.

Related Items

Property of window.

See the history object.

See the hash, host, hostname, href, location, pathname, port, protocol, search, and target properties.

location

(Property)

Returns a string with the URL of the current document.

```
document.location
```

Usage

This read-only property (`document.location`) is different from the location `object` properties (`window.location.propertyName`), which can be changed.

Related Items

Property of `document`.

See the `location` object.

log

(Method)

Returns the natural logarithm (base E) of a positive numeric expression greater than 0.

```
Math.log(expression)
```

Usage

An out-of-range number always returns $-1.797693134862316e+308$.

Related Items

Method of `Math`.

See the `exp` and `pow` methods.

LOG2E

(Property)

A constant representing the base-2 logarithm of E.

```
Math.LOG2E
```

Usage

The value is approximately 1.44270.

Related Items
Property of `Math`.

See the `E`, `LN2`, `LN10`, `LOG10E`, `PI`, `SQRT1_2`, and `SQRT2` properties.

LOG10E

(Property)

A constant representing the base-10 logarithm of E.

```
Math.LOG10E
```

Usage
The value is approximately .43429.

Related Items
Property of `Math`.

See the `E`, `LN2`, `LN10`, `LOG2E`, `SQRT1_2`, and `SQRT2` properties.

Math

(Object)

A built-in object providing constants and mathematical functions.

```
Math.property
Math.method(arguments)
```

Usage
The `Math` object is divided into two parts—properties containing constants and methods for implementing functions. For example, to access the value of pi in an equation, use:

```
Math.PI
```

Standard trigonometric, logarithmic, and exponential functions are also included. All arguments in trigonometric functions are limited to radians. Several comparison operations are provided, such as `max` for determining the greater of two numbers.

Because the purpose of the `Math` object is to provide a vehicle for math operations, there are no provisions for a constructor to create a duplicate math object.

For functions needing extensive use of JavaScripts math functions and constants, it is tedious to include `Math` as part of each equation. The `with` statement simplifies the syntax for this type of situation. Note the difference in the following to sections of code. Both perform the same operations.

```
function Hard() {
      circleArea = Math.PI*(radius^2);
      radians = (degrees/360)*Math.PI;
      result = Math.cos(radians);
}
function Easy() {
      with Math {
          circleArea = PI*(radius^2);
          radians = (degrees/360)*PI;
          result = cos(radians);
      }
}
```

Related Items

See the E, LN10, LN2, PI, SQRT1_2, and SQRT2 properties.

See the abs, acos, asin, atan, ceil, cos, exp, floor, log, max, min, pow, random, round, sin, sqrt, and tan methods.

max

(Method)

Returns the greater of its two arguments.

```
Math.max(argument1, argument2)
```

Usage

Can accept any combination of numeric literals or variables, and returns the value of the largest. For example:

```
firstNum = 1
secondNum = 100
Math.max(firstNum,secondNum)
```

returns 100.

Related Items

Method of Math.

See the min method.

method

(Property)

Reflects the method attribute of an HTML <FORM> tag.

```
formName.method
forms[index].method
```

Usage

The returned value is either get or post. It can be set to a new value at any time.

The first function returns the current value of the form object, whereas the second function sets the method to the contents of newMethod.

```
function getMethod(formObj) {
    return formObj.method
}

function setMethod(formObj,newMethod) {
    formObj.method = newMethod
}
```

Related Items

Property of form.

See the action, encoding, and target properties.

min

(Method)

Returns the lesser of its two arguments.

```
Math.min(argument1, argument2)
```

Usage

Can accept any combination of literals and variables as its argument, and returns the smaller number. For example:

```
firstNum = 1
secondNum = 100
Math.min(firstNum,secondNum)
```

returns 1.

Related Items

Method of Math.

See the max method.

name

(Property)

Returns a string with the name attribute of the object.

```
objectName.name
frameRef.name
frameRef.frames.name
radioName[index].name
selectName.options.name
windowRef.name
windowRef.frames.name
```

Usage

The attribute of this property depends on the object it is applied to. It can be changed at any time.

This property refers to the internal name for the `button`, `reset`, and `submit` objects, not the on-screen label.

For example, after opening a new window with:

```
indexOutline = window.open("http://www.wossamotta.com/
outline.html","MenuPage")
```

and issuing the command

```
document.write(indexOutline.name)
```

JavaScript returns `MenuPage`, which was specified as the name attribute.

For radio buttons, the name is the same for each button in the group, whereas individual buttons are identified by their position in the index.

Related Items

Property of `button`, `checkbox`, `frame`, `password`, `radio`, `reset`, `select`, `submit`, `text`, `textarea`, and `window`.

See the `value` property.

navigator

(Object)

Contains information on the client's current browser.

```
navigator
```

Usage

The `navigator` object returns version information about the browser, such as version number, name, and user-agent header. One common use is to determine the type of platform in use by the client so browser-specific features, such as newline characters and random numbers, are correctly used.

```
function UnixMachine() {
        if (navigator.appVersion.lastIndexOf('Unix') != -1)
            return true
        else
            return false
}
```

Related Items

See the `link` and `anchors` objects.

See the `appName`, `appCodeName`, `appVersion`, and `userAgent` properties.

onBlur

(Event Handler)

Occurs when a `select`, `text`, or `textarea` form element loses focus.

```
<INPUT TYPE="elementType" onBlur="function">
```

Usage

A blur event can check input as a user leaves the element. This is different from `onChange`, which only occurs if the contents of the field have changed.

```
<INPUT TYPE="textarea" VALUE="" NAME="feedback"
onBlur="checkSignature(this.value)">
```

Related Items

Event handler of `select`, `text`, `textarea`.

See the `focus` and `blur` methods.

See the `onChange` and `onFocus` event handlers.

onChange

(Event Handler)

Occurs when the value of a `select`, `text`, or `textarea` form element changes and loses focus.

```
<INPUT TYPE="elementType" onChange="function">
```

Usage

This event is especially useful for validating user form input.

```
<INPUT TYPE="text" VALUE="MT" NAME="state"
onChange="checkAvailability(this.value)">
```

Related Items

Event handler of `select`, `text`, `textarea`.

See the `onBlur` and `onFocus` event handlers.

---

onClick

(Event Handler)

Occurs when a clickable object is selected with the mouse.

```
<INPUT TYPE="elementType" onClick="function">
```

Usage

`onClick` offers a variety of functionality to buttons and other objects on a page. Buttons can be used to validate input before submitting or to compute the results of a form or equation. Clicking other objects, such as checkboxes and radio buttons, can trigger the capture of other information.

The following example sends the contents of the `overtime` form to the `howRich` function.

```
<FORM NAME="overtime">
Full days worked: <INPUT TYPE="text" VALUE="0" NAME="days" SIZE=3>
Hours worked: <INPUT TYPE="text" VALUE="0" NAME="hours" SIZE=30>
<INPUT TYPE="button" VALUE="Compute" NAME="computeWage"
onClick="howRich(this.form)">
</FORM>
```

Related Items

Event handler of `button`, `checkbox`, `radio`, `link`, `reset`, and `submit`.

---

onFocus

(Event Handler)

Occurs when the user chooses a `select`, `text`, or `textarea` for input.

```
<INPUT TYPE="inputType" onFocus="function">
```

Usage

A form element receives focus when the user tabs to or clicks the input area with the mouse. Selecting within a field results in a `select` event.

One use of the `onFocus` function is for pop-up help when an item is selected for the first time.

Related Items

Event handler of `select`, `text`, and `textarea`.

See the `onBlur` and `onChange` event handlers.

onLoad

(Event Handler)

Occurs when a document finishes loading into a window or frameset.

```
<BODY onLoad="function">
<FRAMESET onLoad="function">
```

Usage

A load event is created when the browser finishes loading a window or all the frames within a `<frameset>` tag.

Related Items

Event handler of `window`.

See the `onUnload` event handler.

onMouseOver

(Event Handler)

Occurs when a mouse is placed over a hyperlink.

```
<A HREF="URL" onMouseOver="function">linkText</A>
```

Usage

`onMouseOver` occurs when the mouse pointer is placed over a `link` object. To function with the `status` or `defaultStatus` properties, the event handler must return `true`.

```
<A HREF="http://home.netscape.com/"
 onMouseOver="window.status='Netscape Home'; return true">
Netscape</A>
```

Related Items

Event handler of `link`.

onSelect

(Event Handler)

onSelect occurs when text is highlighted within a form element.

```
<INPUT TYPE="textType" onSelect="function">
```

Usage

A select event is triggered by selecting some or all of the text in a text or textarea field.

Related Items

Event handler of text and textarea.

onSubmit

(Event Handler)

Occurs when a form is submitted by the user with the submit button.

```
<TAG onSubmit="function">
```

Usage

onSubmit is triggered when the user submits a form. Any return value other than false, including omitting the return statement, submits the form. To clarify the code, it is recommended to add return statements for both options.

```
<FORM onSubmit="feedbackSubmit()">
...form elements...
</FORM>

function feedbackSubmit () {
...statements...
if (!validData) {
   return true }
else {
   return false; }
}
```

Related Items

Event handler of form.

See the submit object.

See the submit method.

onUnload

(Event Handler)

Occurs when the user exits a document.

```
<BODY onUnload="function">
<FRAMESET onUnload="function">
```

Usage

When several unload events are included in a frame relationship, the order of operation proceeds from child to parent.

For example, an unload event is included with two documents and the parent `<FRAMESET>` tag that loaded them. When the child document changes, its unload event is triggered but the frameset unload is not affected. When the user selects an option that preempts the parent document for a new source, the top unload event is triggered.

Related Items

Event handler of `window`.

See the `onLoad` event handler.

open

(Method)

Creates a new document or window instance.

```
document.open([MIMEtype])
window.open("URL", "windowName" [,"windowFeatures"]
```

Usage

For a document, `open` opens a stream to collect the output of `write` or `writeln` methods. If the MIME type is a version of `text` or `image` such as `text/html` or `image/gif`, the document is opened for layout. Otherwise, the stream is routed to a plug-in. If a document already exists in the target window, then the open method clears it. The stream is ended by using the `document.close()` method.

For a window, `open` opens a new browser window in a similar fashion to choosing File, New Web Browser from the browser menu. Using the URL argument, it loads a document into the new window; otherwise, the new window is blank. When used as part of an event handler, the form must include the window object; otherwise, the document is assumed.

Window features are defined by a comma-separated list of options with `=1` or `=yes` to enable and `=0` or `=no` to disable. Window features include toolbar, location, directories, status, menubar, scrollbars, resizable, copyhistory, width, and height.

Related Items

Method of `document` and `window`.

See the `clear`, `close`, `write`, and `writeln` methods.

options

(Property)

This array of options is a property of a `select` form element. The array is created by using `<OPTION>` tags within a set of `<SELECT>` tags.

```
formName.selectName.options[index]
forms[index].elements[index].options[index]
```

Usage

The first option's index is zero, the second is 1, and so on. For more detailed information, see the `select` object.

Related Items

See `select` object.

parent

(Property)

Refers to the calling document in the current frame created by a `<frameset>` tag.

```
parent
parent.frameName
parent.frames[index]
parent.property
```

Usage

Using `parent` allows access to other frames created by the same `<FRAMESET>` tag. For example, two frames invoked are called *index* and *contents*. The index frame can write to the contents frame using the syntax:

```
parent.contents.document.write("Kilroy was here.")
```

Related Items

Property of `frame` and `window`.

parse

(Method)

Takes a date string, such as Jan. 11, 1996, and returns the number of milliseconds since midnight, Jan. 1, 1970.

Usage

This function can be used to set date values based on string values. When passed a string with a time, it returns the time value.

Because parse is a static function of Date, it is always used as Date.parse() rather than as a method of a created Date object.

```
Date.parse("Jan 11, 1996");
Today = new Date();
Date.parse(Today.toLocaleString())
```

Related Items

Method of Date.

See the UTC method.

*parseFloat**

(Method)

```
parseFloat(string)
```

Usage

parseFloat parses a string argument and returns a floating-point number if the first character is a plus sign, minus sign, decimal point, exponent, or a numeral.

If parseFloat encounters a character other than one of the valid choices after that point, it returns the value up to that location and ignores all succeeding characters. If the first character is not a valid character, parseFloat returns one of two values based on the platform:

Windows   0

Non-Windows   NaN

Related Items

See methods isNaN and parseInt.

*parseInt**

(Method)

Parses a string argument and returns an integer based on a specified radix or base.

```
parseInt(string [,radix])
```

Usage

A radix of 10 converts the value to a decimal, whereas 8 converts to octal and 16 to hexadecimal. Values greater than 10 for bases above 10 are represented with letters A through F in place of numbers. Using a radix of 2 is used for binary number conversions.

Floating-point values are converted to integers. The rules for evaluating the string are identical to those for parseFloat.

If the radix is omitted or a radix which contradicts the initial characters, JavaScript assumes the radix based on the first characters of the string (see Table 21.3).

Table 21.3   Default Radix Based on the Initial String Characters

Characters	Radix
0	8 (octal)
0x	16 (hexadecimal)
Any other	10 (decimal)

Related Items

See the isNaN and parseFloat methods.

password

(Object)

A password element in an HTML form (see Figure 21.4).

```
document.formName.passwordName
document.forms[index].element[index]
```

Usage

A password is a text field that for security is masked with asterisks when entered by the user.

Any default values included as part of the HTML definition are cleared when the page is loaded. This prevents inadvertent or intentional security breaches. Even though the defaultValue property is valid for password, it always returns a null value.

The value of a `password` object can be evaluated programmatically within a script but it is recommended not to use a literal for obvious security reasons.

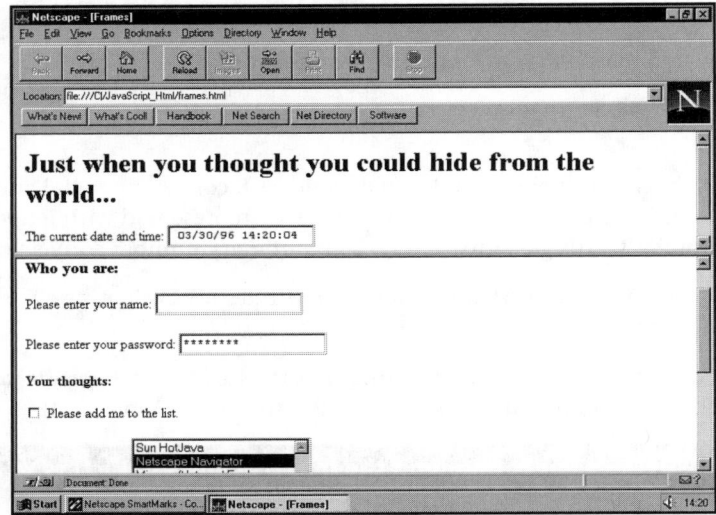

Fig. 21.4   A password element is masked with asterisks for security.

Related Items

Property of `form`.

See the `text` object.

See the `defaultValue`, `name`, and `value` properties.

See the `focus`, `blur`, and `select` methods.

pathname

(Property)

Returns the path portion from an URL.

```
location.pathname
link.pathname
links[index].pathname
```

Usage

Although the `pathname` can be changed at any time, it is always safer to change the entire URL at once using the `href` property.

Related Items

Property of `link` and `location`.

See the `hash`, `host`, `hostname`, `href`, `port`, `protocol`, and `search` properties.

PI

(Property)

Returns the value of pi.

```
Math.PI
```

Usage

The value of `Math.PI` is approximately 3.14159. This is the ratio of the circumference of a circle to its diameter.

```
circumference = 2 * Math.PI * radius
area = Math.PI * Math.pow(radius,2)
```

Related Items

Property of `Math`.

See the `E`, `LN2`, `LN10`, `LOG2E`, `LOG10E`, `SQRT1_2`, and `SQRT2` properties.

port

(Property)

Returns the port number of a URL address.

```
location.port
link.port
links[index].port
```

Usage

The port value is a substring of the `host` property in `href`.

Related Items

Property of `link` and `location`.

See the `hash`, `host`, `hostname`, `href`, `pathname`, `protocol`, and `search` properties.

pow

(Method)

Returns a base raised to an exponent.

```
Math.pow(argument)
```

Usage

Many languages use the caret operator (^) to calculate an exponent. JavaScript includes its own method to do this. The caret is used in JavaScript to calculate a bitwise XOR operation.

Related Items

Method of Math.

See the exp and log methods.

prompt

(Method)

Displays a prompt dialog box that accepts user input (see Figure 21.5).

```
[windowName.]prompt(message [inputDefault])
```

Usage

If an initial value is not specified for inputDefault, the dialog box displays the <undefined> value. Generating the prompt in Figure 21.5 required one line of code:

```
var userid = prompt("Please enter your ID","")
```

Fig. 21.5 The prompt dialog box is used to get user input outside of a form.

Related Items

Method of window.

See the alert and confirm methods.

protocol

(Property)

Returns the file access method.

```
location.protocol
link.protocol
links[index].protocol
```

Usage

The string returned by this property is the initial portion of a URL, up to and including the colon. This is the part of the URL that indicates the access method (http, ftp, mailto, etc.).

about	Information about the client browser.
ftpA	File transfer protocol address for downloading files.
http	Hypertext transfer address that is the basis of the World Wide Web.
mailto	An e-mail address.
news	A usenet news site.
file	Refers to a file on the local machine.
javascript	Precedes a set of JavaScript commands.

Related Items

Property of link and location.

See the hash, host, hostname, href, pathname, port, and search properties.

radio

(Object)

A set of radio buttons.

```
formName.radioName[index]
forms[index].elements[index]
```

Usage

radio objects are created within HTML <form> tags and represent radio buttons. A set of radio buttons enables the user to select one item from a group of options.

When referencing the object using the radio button name, the index is comprised of the buttons with the same name property. When referring to a radio button using the elements array, each button is a separate item in the index.

Related Items

Property of `form`.

See the `checkbox` and `select` objects.

See the `checked`, `defaultChecked`, `index`, `length`, `name`, and `value` properties.

See the `click` method.

See the `onClick` event handler.

random

(Method)

Returns a random number between 0 and 1 (UNIX only).

```
Math.random()
```

Usage

The `random` method is only enabled on UNIX platforms—Windows and Macintosh users need to use an alternative form of generating a random number. An example of this type of usage is included in the Task Reference at the end of this book.

Related Items

Method of `Math`.

referrer

(Property)

URL of the document which led to the current document.

```
document.referrer
```

Usage

Returns a read-only string containing the complete URL of the document that called the current document. It can be used with a CGI script to keep track of how users are linked to a page.

```
document.write("Click <A HREF=\''"+document.referrer+"\'>here</A> to go back
from whence you came.">
```

Related Items

Property of `document`.

reset

(Object)

Button to return a form to its default values.

```
formName.resetButtonName
forms[index].elements[index]
```

Usage

This button correlates with an HTML reset button, which resets all `form` objects to their default values.

A `reset` object must be created within a `<form>` tag and cannot be controlled through the `onClick` event handler. When the button is clicked, the form is reset. However, the event handler can invoke other actions with the reset.

Related Items

Property of `form`.

See the `button` and `submit` objects.

See the `name` and `value` properties.

See the `click` method.

See the `onClick` event handler.

round

(Method)

Rounds a number to the nearest integer.

```
Math.round(argument)
```

Usage

Returns the value of a floating-point argument rounded to the next highest integer if the decimal portion is greater than or equal to .5, or the next lowest integer if less than .5.

```
Math.round(2.1)   //Returns 2
Math.round(2.9)   //Returns 3
```

Related Items

Method of `Math`.

search

(Property)

Returns any query information attached to a URL.

```
location.search
linkName.search
links[index].search
```

Usage

Returns a string containing any query information appended to a URL. Query data is preceded by a question mark and is the last item included in the document URL. Information in the string is formatted this way:

```
?elementName=element+value
```

Like all substrings of the href property, search can be changed at any time.

Related Items

Property of link and location.

See the hash, host, hostname, href, pathname, port, and protocol properties.

select (options array)

(Object)

A selection list or scrolling list on an HTML form (see Figure 21.6).

```
formName.selectName
forms[index].elements[index]
formName.selectName[index].options[index]
forms[index].elements[index].options[index]
```

Usage

A selection list enables the user to choose one item from a list. A scrolling list enables the choice of one or more items from a list, enabled using the MULTIPLE attribute in the input tag.

When used without the options array, the select object refers to the entire list, using options such as length and name. The value and selectedIndex indicate the currently selected option in a selection list or the first selected item of a scrolling list.

Related Items

Property of form.

See the radio object.

See the length, name, options, and selectedIndex properties.

See the blur and focus methods.

See the onBlur, onChange, and onFocus event handlers.

For the options property of select, see the defaultSelected, index, selected, text, and value properties.

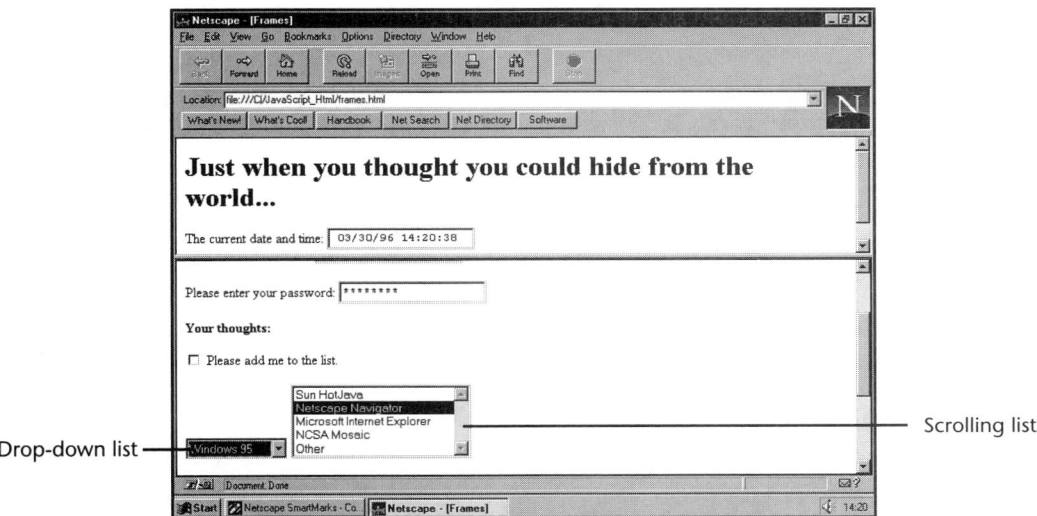

Fig. 21.6   A drop-down selection list from an HTML form allows one choice, whereas a scrolling list allows multiple choices.

select

(Method)

Selects the input area of a specified form element.

```
formName.elementName.select()
forms[index].elements[index].select()
```

Usage
Used with the focus method, JavaScript can highlight a field and position the cursor for user input.

Related Items
Method of password, text, and textarea.

See the blur and focus methods.

selected

(Property)

Returns a Boolean value (`true` or `false`) indicating the current state of an option in a select object.

```
formName.elementName.[options[index].]selected
forms[index].elements[index].[options[index].]selected
```

Usage

The selected property can be changed at any time and the display will immediately update to reflect the new value. The selected property is useful for `select` elements that are created using the `multiple` attribute.

Using the `select` property, you can view or change the value of any element in an `options` array without changing the value of any other element in the array.

Related Items

Property of `options`.

See the `defaultSelected`, `index`, and `selectedIndex` properties.

selectedIndex

(Property)

Returns an integer specifying the index of a selected item.

```
formName.elementName.[options[index].]selected
forms[index].elements[index].[options[index].]selected
```

Usage

The `selectedIndex` property is useful for `select` elements that are created without using the `MULTIPLE` attribute in the `<SELECT>` tag. If `selectedIndex` is evaluated when the `MULTIPLE` attribute is set, the property returns the index of the first option only. Setting the property clears any other options that are selected in the element.

Related Items

Property of `select`, `options`.

See the `defaultSelected`, `index`, and `selected` properties.

self

(Property)

Refers to the current window or form.

```
self
```

Usage

The `self` property is useful for removing ambiguity when dealing with `window` and `form` properties of the same name.

Related Items

Property of `frame` and `window`.

See the `window` property.

setDate

(Method)

Sets the day of the month.

```
Date.setDate(argument)
dateName.setDate(argument)
```

Usage

setDate uses an integer from 1 to 31 to set the day of the month for a Date object.

```
endOfTheWorld = new Date("January 11, 1996 06:18:00")
endOfTheWorld.setDate(26)
document.write(endOfTheWorld.getDate()) //Returns 26
```

Related Items

Method of `Date`.

See the `getDate` method.

setHours

(Method)

Sets the hour for the current time.

```
Date.setHours(argument)
dateName.setHours(argument)
```

Usage

setHours uses an integer from 0 (midnight) to 23 (11 p.m.) to set the hour of the day using military time.

Related Items

Method of Date.

See the getHours method.

setMinutes

(Method)

Sets the minutes for the current time.

```
Date.setMinutes(argument)
dateName.setMinutes(argument)
```

Usage

Uses an integer from 0 to 59 to set the minutes of a date object.

Related Items

Method of Date.

See the getMinutes method.

setMonth

(Method)

Sets the month value of a date object.

```
Date.setMonth(argument)
dateName.setMonth(argument)
```

Usage

Uses an integer from 0 (January) to 11 (December). This is the one item of the Date object that doesn't follow normal numbering conventions. Be sure to make the adjustment when transferring values from the JavaScript month to a form understandable by the user.

Related Items

Method of Date.

See the getMonth method.

setSeconds

(Method)

Sets the seconds.

```
Date.setSeconds(argument)
dateName.setSeconds(argument)
```

Usage

Uses an integer from 0 to 59 to set the seconds of a date object. Although the Date object uses milliseconds to track time, seconds are the greatest level of detail allowed when entering a specific time.

Related Items

Method of Date.

See the getSeconds method.

setTime

(Method)

Sets the value of a date object.

```
dateName.setTime(argument)
```

Usage

This is the base form of a Date object. It returns the number of milliseconds since midnight on Jan. 1, 1970. Although it is not necessary to know this number, it can be used as a simple method of copying the value of one date object to another.

```
endOfTheWorld = new Date(userGuess)
checkDate = new Date()
checkDate.setTime(endOfTheWorld.getTime())
```

Related Items

Method of Date.

See the getTime method.

setTimeout

(Method)

Evaluates an expression after a specified amount of time, expressed in milliseconds.

```
[window.]setTimeout(timerID)
[windowName.]setTimeout(timerID)
```

Usage

Timeouts are not repeated indefinitely. For example, setting a timeout to 3 seconds evaluates the expression once after 3 seconds—not every 3 seconds.

To call setTimeout recursively, reset the timeout as part of the function invoked by the method. Calling the function startclock in the following example sets a loop in motion that clears the timeout, displays the current time, and sets the timeout to redisplay the time in 1 second.

```
<SCRIPT>
var timerID = null;
var timerRunning = false;

function stopclock () {
  if(timerRunning) clearTimeout(timerID);
  timerRunning=false;
}
function startclock () {
  stopclock();
  showtime();
}
function showtime () {
  var now = new Date();
  document.clock.display.value = now.toLocaleString();
  timerID = setTimeout("startclock()",1000);
  timerRunning = true;
}
</SCRIPT>

<BODY onLoad="startclock()">
<FORM NAME="clock">
<INPUT ITEM=text NAME="display" VALUE="Standby for the time">
</FORM>
</BODY>
```

Related Items

Method of window.

See the clearTimeout method.

setYear

(Method)

Sets the year in the current date.

```
Date.setYear(argument)
dateName.setYear(argument)
```

Usage

setYear needs a 2-digit integer representing the year minus 1900.

Related Items

Method of Date.

See the getYear method.

sin

(Method)

Returns the sine of an argument.

```
Math.sin(argument)
```

Usage

The argument is the size of an angle expressed in radians and the returned value is from −1 to 1.

Related Items

Method of Math.

See the acos, asin, atan, cos, and tan methods.

small

(Method)

```
stringName.small()
```

Usage

small formats a string object into a small font using the HTML <small> tags.

Related Items

Method of string.

See the big and fontsize methods.

sqrt

(Method)

Returns the square root of a positive numeric expression.

```
Math.sqrt(argument)
```

Usage

If the argument's value is outside the range, the returned value is 0.

SQRT1_2

(Property)

The square root of 1/2.

```
Math.SQRT1_2
```

Usage

The square root of 1/2 is also expressed as the inverse of the square root of 2 (approximately 0.707).

Related Items

Property of Math.

See the E, LN2, LN10, LOG2E, LOG10E, PI, and SQRT2 properties.

SQRT2

(Property)

The square root of 2.

```
Math.SQRT2
```

Usage

The value of this constant is approximately 1.414.

Related Items

Property of Math.

See the E, LN2, LN10, LOG2E, LOG10E, PI, and SQRT1_2 properties.

status

(Property)

Specifies a priority or transient message to display in the status bar.

```
window.status
[windowName].status
```

Usage

The status bar is located at the bottom of the window. A user status message is usually triggered by a `mouseOver` event from an `anchor`. To display a message in the status bar when the mouse pointer is placed over a link, the usage is:

```
<A anchorDefinition onMouseOver="window.status='Your message.'; return
true">link</A>
```

Note the use of nested quotes and use of `return true`, needed for operation.

Once invoked, the message remains until the mouse is placed over another link.

Related Items

Property of `window`.

See the `defaultStatus` property.

string

(Object)

A series of characters defined by double or single quotation marks.

```
stringName
```

Usage

For example:

```
myDog = "Brittany Spaniel"
```

returns a string object called `myDog` with the `Brittany Spaniel` value. Quotation marks are not a part of the string's value—they are only used to delimit the string.

The object's value is manipulated using methods that return a variation on the string—for example `myDog.toUpperCase()` returns BRITTANY SPANIEL. A string object also includes methods that return HTML versions of the string, such as `bold` and `italics`.

Related Items

See the `text` and `textarea` objects.

See the `length` property.

See the `anchor`, `big`, `blink`, `bold`, `charAt`, `fixed`, `fontcolor`, `fontsize`, `indexOf`, `italics`, `lastIndexOf`, `link`, `small`, `strike`, `sub`, `substring`, `sup`, `toLowerCase`, and `toUpperCase` methods.

strike

(Method)

Formats a string object as strikeout text.

> *stringName*.strike()

Usage

Using `strike` is identical to using HTML <strike> tags.

Related Items

Method of `string`.

See the `blink`, `bold`, and `italics` methods.

sub

(Method)

Formats a string object into subscript text.

> *stringName*.sub()

Usage

Using `sub` is identical to using HTML <sub> tags.

Related Items

Method of `string`.

See the `sup` method.

submit

(Object)

A submit button on an HTML page.

> *formName.buttonName*
> forms[*index*].elements[*index*]

Usage

Clicking the button causes the form to be submitted to the program specified by the `action` property. The button is created within an HTML <form> tag, and always loads a new page, which may be the same as the current page if an action isn't specified.

Related Items

Property of form.

See the button and reset objects.

See the name and value properties.

See the click method.

See the onClick event handler.

submit

(Method)

Performs the same action as clicking a submit button.

```
formName.submit()
forms[index].submit()
```

Usage

The information from the form is submitted depending on the attribute of the METHOD attribute—get or post.

Related Items

Method of form.

See the submit object.

See the onSubmit event handler.

substring

(Method)

Returns a subset of a string object based on two indexes.

```
stringName.substring(index1, index2)
```

Usage

If the indexes are equal, an empty string is returned. Regardless of order, the substring is built from the smallest index to the largest.

Related Items

Method of string.

sup

(Method)

Formats a string object into superscript text.

```
stringName.sup()
```

Usage
Using sup is identical to using HTML <sup> tags.

Related Items
Method of string.

See the sub method.

tan

(Method)

Returns the tangent of an argument.

```
Math.tan(argument)
```

Usage
The argument is the size of an angle expressed in radians.

Related Items
Method of Math.

See the acos, asin, atan, cos, sin methods.

target

(Property)

A string specifying the name of a window for posting responses to after a form is submitted.

```
formName.target
forms[index].target
location.target
link.target
links[index].target
```

Usage

Normally used to view the destination for a form submission, `target` can also be used to view or change a link's destination. For a link, `target` returns a string specifying the name of the window that displays the content of a selected hypertext link.

```
homePage.target = "http://www.wossamotta.edu/"
```

You must use a literal to set the `target` property. JavaScript expressions and variables are invalid entries.

Related Items

Property of `form`, `link`, and `location`.

See the `action`, `encoding`, and `method` properties.

text

(Object)

A one-line input field on an HTML form (see Figure 21.7).

```
formName.textName
forms[index].elements[index]
```

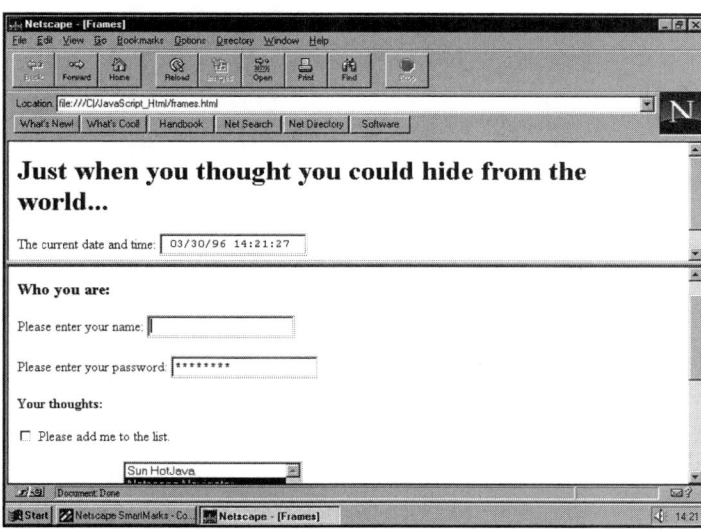

Fig. 21.7   Text input boxes are objects within the form.

Usage

`text` objects accept characters or numbers. A `text` object can be updated by assigning new contents to its value.

Related Items

Property of `form`.

See the `password`, `string`, and `textarea` objects.

See the `defaultValue`, `name`, and `value` properties.

See the `focus`, `blur`, and `select` methods.

See the `onBlur`, `onChange`, `onFocus`, and `onSelect` event handlers.

text

(Property)

Returns the value of text following the `<option>` tag in a `select` object.

```
formName.selectName.options[index].text
forms[index].elements[index].options[index].text
```

Usage

`text` can also be used to change the value of the option, with an important limitation: although the value is changed, its appearance on-screen is not.

Related Items

Property of `options`.

textarea

(Object)

`textarea` is similar to a `text` object, with the addition of multiple lines (see Figure 21.8).

```
formName.textAreaName
forms[index].elements[index]
```

Usage

A `textarea` object can also be updated by assigning new contents to its value. The screen is updated immediately after the new value is assigned.

```
<FORM>
<ITEM INPUT=textarea NAME="sponsorMessage" VALUE="And now a brief message
from our sponsor.">
</FORM>
...
<SCRIPT>
sponsorMessage.value = "Now is the time \r\nfor everybody to get up \r\nand
run away."
</SCRIPT>
```

Note the use of the newline character \n. The implementation of a new line depends on the platform. For Windows, it's the combination \r\n; for Macintosh and UNIX, it's \n.

When defining a textarea in a form, you can load a default value by including text between the <TEXTAREA> tags. The following example loads three lines of text and a blank line into a textarea element.

```
<BR><TEXTAREA NAME="user_comments" ROWS=4 COLS=40>
Enter your comments here.

Or just press the submit button to let us
know you liked what you saw.
</TEXTAREA>
```

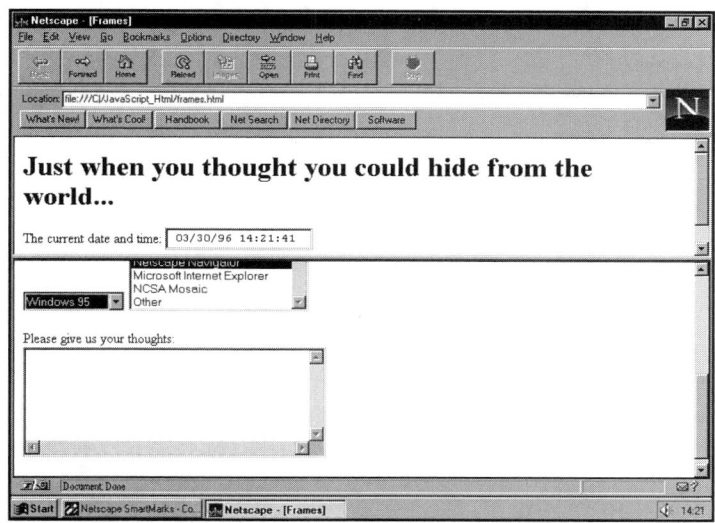

Fig. 21.8 The textarea object can accept multiple lines of text from the user.

Related Items

Property of form.

See the password, string, and text objects.

See the defaultValue, name, and value properties.

See the focus, blur, and select methods.

See the onBlur, onChange, onFocus, and onSelect event handlers.

---
title

(Property)

Returns the read-only value set within HTML `<title>` tags.

```
document.title
```

Usage
If a document doesn't include a title, the value is `null`.

Related Items
Property of `document`.

---
toGMTString

(Method)

Converts a date object to a string using the Internet GMT conventions.

```
Date.toGMTString()
dateName.toGMTString()
```

Usage
This string conversion returns a string containing the time in a GMT format, which can vary depending on the platform.

For example, if `today` is a date object:

```
today.toGMTString()
```

then the string "Thu, 11 Jan 1996 06:05:15" is returned. Actual formatting may vary from platform to platform. The time and date are based on the client machine.

Related Items
Method of `Date`.

See `toLocaleString` method.

---
toLocaleString

(Method)

Converts a date object to a string using the local conventions.

```
Date.toLocaleString()
dateName.toLocaleString()
```

Usage

The date string returned by this method depends on the preferences defined on the client machine, such as *mm/dd/yy hh:mm:ss*.

Related Items

Method of Date.

See the toGMTString method.

toLowerCase

(Method)

Converts all characters in a string to lowercase.

```
stringName.toLowerCase()
```

Usage

The results of the toLowerCase method are displayed entirely in lowercase characters although the actual contents of the string are not changed.

Related Items

Method of string.

See the toUpperCase method.

top

(Property)

The top-most browser window.

```
top
top.frameName
top.frames[index]
```

Usage

Also called an *ancestor* or *Web browser window*, the top property refers to the highest precedence window that contains frames or nested framesets.

Related Items

Property of window.

toUpperCase

(Method)

Converts all characters in a string to uppercase.

    stringName.toUpperCase()

Usage
Although it affects the immediate display of the string, toUpperCase does not affect the value of its object.

Related Items
Method of string.

See the toLowerCase method.

*unescape**

(Method)

Returns a character based on its ASCII value.

    unescape(*string*)

Usage
The value returned is expressed as a string in the format %xxx where xxx is a decimal number between zero and 255, or 0x0 to 0xFF in hex.

Related Items
See the escape method.

userAgent

(Property)

Header sent as part of HTTP protocol from client to server to identify the type of client.

    navigator.userAgent

Usage
The syntax of the returned value is the same as for appVersion, with the addition of the browser application code name.

    codename/releaseNumber (platform; country)

Related Items

Property of navigator.

See the appName, appVersion, and appCodeName properties.

UTC

(Method)

Returns the number of milliseconds for a universal coordinated time (UTC) date since midnight, January 1, 1970.

```
Date.UTC(year, month, day [, hrs] [, min] [, sec])
```

Usage

UTC is always calculated from the same date, and therefore, always used as Date.UTC(), not with a created date object. When including the value for the month, don't forget that JavaScript numbers the months from 0 to 11.

Related Items

Method of Date.

See the parse method.

value

(Property)

Returns the value of an object.

```
formName.buttonName.value
formName.resetName.value
formName.submit.value
formName.checkboxName.value
formName.radioName.value
formName.hiddenName.value
formName.textName.value
formName.textareaName.value
formName.selectName.value
formName.passwordName.value
forms[index].elements[index].value
```

Usage

The value of an object depends on the type of object it is applied to (see Table 21.4).

Table 21.4	Values of Various Form Objects
Object	**Value Attribute**
button, reset, submit	Value attribute that appears on-screen, not the button name
checkbox	On if item is selected, off if not
radio	String reflection of value
hidden, text, textarea	Contents of the field
select	Reflection of option value
password	Returns a valid default value, but an encrypted version if modified by the user

Changing the value of a text or textarea object results in an immediate update to the screen. All other form objects are not graphically updated when changed.

Related Items
Property of button, checkbox, hidden, options, password, radio, reset, submit, text, and textarea.

For password, text, and textarea, see the defaultValue property.

For button, reset, and submit, see the name property.

For options, see the defaultSelected, selected, selectedIndex, and text properties.

For checkbox and radio, see the checked and defaultChecked properties.

vlinkColor

(Property)

Returns or sets the color of visited links.

```
document.vlinkColor
```

Usage
Like all colors, vlinkColor uses hexadecimal RGB triplets or a string literal. The property cannot be set after the document has been formatted. To override the browser defaults, color settings are used with the onLoad event handler in the <BODY> tag:

```
<BODY onLoad="document.vlinkColor='aliceblue'">
```

Related Items
Property of document.

See the alinkColor, bgColor, fgColor, and linkColor properties.

window

(Object)

The highest precedence object accessible by JavaScript relating to an open Navigator window.

```
window
self
top
parent
windowName
propertyName
methodName(parameters)
```

Usage

`window` is created by Navigator when a page is loaded containing properties that apply to the whole window. It is the top-level object for each `document`, `location`, and `history` object. Because its existence is assumed, you do not have to reference the name of the window when referring to its objects, properties, or methods.

For example, the following two lines have the same result (printing a message to the status line):

```
status="Go away from here."
window.status="Go away from here."
```

There are numerous ways of referencing a window, depending on its relation to the current location as outlined in Table 21.5.

Table 21.5 Window Aliases	
Window Name	**Reference**
`window`, `self`	The window containing the current document. When these aliases are omitted, the current document is still assumed. The exception is in scripting event handlers, where methods such as open and `close` must be used with specific windows or frames.
`top`	Refers to the top most window. Useful for parent-child-child relationships created with multiple <FRAMESET> tags.
`parent`	The window containing the <FRAMESET> tag that created the current window.
`windowName`	Used to reference the window in HTML tags. When using properties and methods of a window, use the name of the window variable.

A new window is created using the `open` method:

```
aNewWindow = window.open("URL","Window_Name"[,"windowFeatures"])
```

The variable name is used to refer to the window's properties and methods. The window name is used in the target argument of a `form` or `anchor` tag. The list of features (shown in Table 21.6) controls the appearance and functionality of the browser (see Figure 21.9).

Table 21.6 Window Feature Attributes

Option	Use
toolbar	Includes standard toolbar, including forward, back, home, and print buttons.
location	Creates a location object.
directories	In Netscape, includes the list of buttons for standard links, such as What's New, What's Cool, and Handbook.
status	Creates a status bar at the bottom of the screen.
menubar	Includes the menubar at the top of the screen, including items such as File, Edit, and View.
scrollbars	Adds scrollbars if the document extends beyond the size of the screen.
resizable	Allows the user to modify the size of the window.
width	Initial window width, in pixels.
height	Initial window height, in pixels.

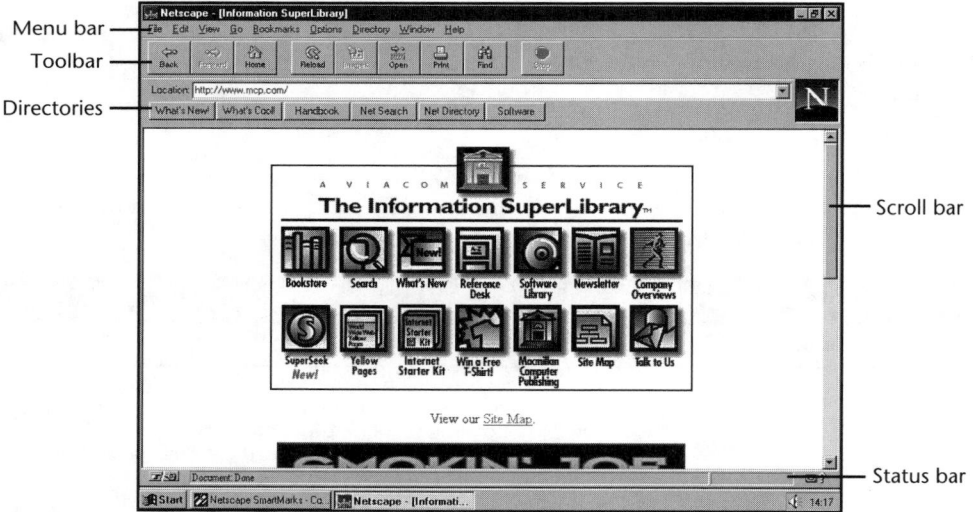

Fig. 21.9 Some of the various features of a Navigator window are controlled through the window.open method.

If no features are listed, all are included by default. If any feature is explicitly defined, any not included in the feature list are excluded by default.

Related Items

See the document and frame objects.

See the defaultStatus, frames, parent, self, status, top, and window properties.

See the `alert`, `close`, `confirm`, `open`, `prompt`, `setTimeout`, and `clearTimeout` methods.

See the `onLoad` and `onUnload` event handlers.

window

(Property)

A synonym for the current window.

```
frameName.window
[windowName.]window
```

Usage
The `window` property is used to remove ambiguity between a `window` and `form` object of the same name. Although `window` also applies to the current frame, it is less ambiguous to use the `self` property.

Related Items
Property of `frame` and `window`.

See `self` property.

write

(Method)

Writes one or more lines to a document window.

```
document.write(string)
```

Usage
Strings written to a window can include HTML tags and JavaScript expressions, including numeric, string, and logical values. The `write` method does not add a new line (`<br>` or `/n`) character to the end of the output. If `write` is called from an event handler, the current document is cleared if a new window is not created for the output.

Related Items
Method of `document`.

See the `close`, `clear`, `open`, and `writeln` methods.

---

writeln

(Method)

Writes one or more lines to a document window, followed by a newline character.

```
document.writeln(string)
```

Usage

Like its cousin `write`, `writeln` can include HTML tags and JavaScript expressions, including numeric, string, and logical values. If `writein` is called from an event handler, the current document is cleared if a new window is not created for the output.

HTML ignores the newline character, unless it is used within <PRE> tags.

Related Items

Method of `document`.

See the `close`, `clear`, `open`, and `write` methods.

Chapter 22

JavaScript Statements

The statements used to control program flow in JavaScript are similar to those used in Java and C. A statement can span several lines if needed or several statements can be placed on the same line.

There are a couple of important items to remember. First, blocks of statements, such as a function definition, must be enclosed in curly braces. This is how JavaScript delineates blocks of code. Second, a semicolon must be placed between all statements. Without a semicolon, script behavior is unpredictable.

Since JavaScript is not strict in its formatting, you must provide the line breaks and indentation to make sure the code is readable and easy to understand later.

break

break terminates the current for or while loop and passes control to the first statement after the loop.

Usage

The following example adds elements on a form, assuming that all the elements contain numeric values. If a 0 is encountered, the adding stops:

```
function checkValues(form) {
      var total
      for (I=0; I<=form.elements.length; I++) {
            if (element[I].value = "0") {
                  break; }
            else {
                  total += I;
                  document.write("The running total is "+ttal); }
      }
      return total
}
```

comment

These are notes from the script author that are ignored by the interpreter. Single line comments are preceded by //. Multiple line comments begin with /* and end with */.

Usage

```
/* These comments could start here
and
end
down here. */
...statements...
// This comment is limited to this line only.
```

continue

continue passes control to the condition in a while loop and to the update expression in a for loop. The important difference from break is that the loop is not terminated.

Usage

The following example adds elements on a form, assuming that all the elements contain numeric values. If a value less than 0 is encountered, it is not included in the running total:

```
function checkValues(form) {
        var total
        for (I=0; I<=form.elements.length; I++) {
                if (element[I].value < 0) {
                        continue; }
                else {
                        total += I;
                        document.write("The running total is "+total); }
        }
        return total

}
```

for

for creates a loop with three optional expressions enclosed in parentheses and separated by semicolons, followed by a set of statements to be executed during the loop:

```
for (initialExpression; condition; updateExpression) {
        ...statements...
}
```

The `initial` expression is used to initialize the counter variable, which can be a new variable declared with `var`.

The `condition` expression is evaluated on each pass through the loop. If the condition is `true`, the loop statements are executed. If the condition is omitted, then it defaults to `true`, and the loop continues until an error or `break` is reached.

The `update` expression is used to increment the counter variable. It is also optional and can be updated programatically within the loop statements.

Usage

`for` creates a loop that continues until an error occurs or a `break` statement is executed. The `increment` variable is increased by two each time through the loop:

```
for (var increment=0; ; increment+=2) {
   ...statements...
}
```

The following example is a loop that does not update its counter. If the counter is never updated in the course of the statements, then the value will remain ten:

```
for (var increment=10; increment<101; ) {
   ...statements...
}
```

for...in

This iterates a variable for all of properties of an object. For each property, `for...in` executes the statement block:

```
for (objectVariable) {
...statements...
}
```

Usage

`for...in` is a useful function for debugging because of its ability to display all of the properties of an object in one loop:

```
function objectDisplay (obj) {
      var displayLine;
      for (var prop in obj) {
            displayLine = obj.name + "." + prop + " = " + obj[prop];
            document.write(displayLine + "<BR>")
      }
      document.write("End of object " + obj.name)
}
```

function

This declares a JavaScript function with a name and parameters. To return a value, the `function` must include a `return` statement. A function definition cannot be nested within another function:

```
function name ([parameter [...,parameter]]) {
        ...statements...
}
```

if...else

A conditional statement that executes the first set of statements if the condition is `true` and the statements following `else` if `false`. `if...else` statements can be nested to any level. If single statements are used after the statements, curly braces are not needed:

```
if (condition) {
        ...statements...
} [else {
        ...statements...
}]
```

Usage

The following example converts minutes to a two-digit number for use in a clock display:

```
function makeMinutes() {
   var minString = "";
   var now = new Date();
   var min = Date.getMinutes();
   if (min < 10) {
        minString += ":0" + min; }
   else {
        minString += ":" + min; }
   return minString
}
```

return

`return` specifies a value to be returned by a function:

```
return expression;
```

Usage

The following example takes three strings and puts them together, separated by commas:

```
function stringAssemble (string1, string2, string3) {
      return string1 + ", " + string2 + ", " + string3
}
```

var

var declares a variable and optionally initializes it to a value. The scope of a variable is the current function or—when declared outside a function—the current document:

```
var variableName [=value] [..., variableName [=value]]
```

Usage

The `globalString` variable can be used in any function or script in the current document, whereas the variable `localString` can only be used within the `bracket` function:

```
var globalString
function bracket() {
   var localString = "[" + globalString + "]";
   document.write(localString);
}
```

while

while repeats a loop while an expression is `true`. If the condition is no longer true, execution drops to the first statement after the `while` statements:

```
while (condition) {
   ...statements...
}
```

Usage

The following example examines a string for a specific character and stops its search when it finds it or runs out of characters to look for:

```
var found = false
n = 0
while (n <= searchString.length || !found) {
   if (searchString.charAt[n] == "?")
           found = true
   else
           n++;
}
```

with

`with` establishes a default object for a set of statements. Any property references without an object are assumed to use the default object:

```
with (object) {
statements...
}
```

Usage

The `with` statement is especially useful when applied to the `Math` object for a set of calculations. For example:

```
with (Math) {
var Value1 = cos(angle);
var Value2 = sin(angle);
}
```

replaces:

```
var Value1 = Math.cos(angle);
var Value2 = Math.sin(angle);
```

CHAPTER 23

JavaScript Operators

The two types of operations in JavaScript are those that assign a value to a variable and those that create a value without an assignment.

The following expression

```
x = 1 + 1
```

has two parts. First, the expression on the right is evaluated, resulting in 2. Then, the result is assigned to the variable on the left, x. On the other hand,

```
1 + 1
```

evaluates to 2. The expression is completed but since there is no assignment operator, no assignment is made. When the rest of the expression, such as a method or function call is completed, the value is abandoned.

JavaScript includes a null value for variables that have not been assigned another value. Any attempt to use a null variable in an equation results in an error, unless it is an assignment for initializing a variable, such as timerID = null.

Special Operators

```
.         //call
[]        //index
()        //member
```

The period is used to separate objects from their properties and methods.

Brackets are used for denoting indexes in arrays, such as form and elements.

Parentheses have two uses. First, they contain the parameters and arguments for functions and methods. Second, they are used to give order to complex equations. Although the following two equations appear to be the same, the results are different:

```
I = 5 * 5 + 10   //Result: 35
I = 5 * (5 + 10)  //Result: 75
```

Usage

When processing an equation, JavaScript begins with any operators inside parentheses and works its way out until all operations are completed. For the first example, the multiplication symbol has higher precedence than the addition symbol, so JavaScript multiplies 5 times 5 and then adds 10. In the second example, the parentheses force the computation of 5 plus 10 and the result is multiplied times 5.

Unary Operators

```
++        //increment
—         //decrement
!         //complement
-         //unary negation
```

The double-plus and double-minus are used to increment or decrement single variables and can be used prefix or postfix.

Usage

When the double operator is placed in front of the variable (prefix), the operation is completed before the assignment is made. When the double operator is placed after the variable (postfix), the assignment is made to the variable on the left and then the operation is completed:

```
J = 1
I = J++ //I=1, J=2
I = ++J  //I=3, J=3
```

The complement operator is used for Boolean values to reverse the value although the variable itself is not changed:

```
testResult = true
document.write(testResult)   //"true"
document.write(!testResult)  //"false"
```

Unary negation changes the sign of the variable, just as multiplying the number times -1 does.

Binary Operators

```
+         //addition
-         //subtraction
*         //multiplication
/         //division
%         //modulus
```

Binary operators need two operands. Addition, subtraction, multiplication, and division are the standard versions of these operators.

Usage

Modulus is a special division operator that only returns the remainder of the operation. For example:

```
I2 = 8 % 2  //returns 0
I3 = 8 % 3  //returns 2
```

Bitwise Operators

```
~       //bitwise complement
<<      //left shift
>>      //right shift
>>>     //right shift with zero fill
&       //and
^       //xor
¦       //or
```

Bitwise operators work on variables at their lowest level: bits (0 and 1). Shift operators convert the operand on the left to a 32-bit integer, which is shifted by the number of bits specified on the right side. The logical bitwise operators convert both values to 32-bit integers before comparing them.

Usage

Bitwise complements are similar to the regular complement, only at the bit level. All bits with a 1 are changed to 0 and a 0 is changed to 1.

Left shift moves all bits to the left by the number of places on the right side of the equation filling in with 0s behind, whereas the zero-fill right shift works in the same way in the opposite direction. The standard right shift propagates the leftmost bit:

```
function bitShift() {
        I = -1
        for (increment = 0; increment<9; increment++) {
                document.write(I)
                I = I << 1
        }
}
```

The bitwise logical operators work in a slightly different way. When compared with another value, they return a value based on a bit-by-bit comparison based on Tables 4.7, 4.8, and 4.9.

Table 4.7   Boolean Operations—*And* (&)

Bit1	Bit2	Result
1	1	1
0	1	0
1	0	0
0	0	0

Table 4.8   Boolean Operations—*Xor* (^)

Bit1	Bit2	Result
1	1	0
0	1	1
1	0	1
0	0	0

Table 4.9	Boolean Operations—*Or*:	
Bit1	**Bit2**	**Result**
1	1	1
0	1	1
1	0	1
0	0	0

For example, the 4-bit binary value of 13 is represented as 1101. The results of binary operations with 15 (binary 1111) and 0 (binary 0000) would return the following values:

```
bin13 = 13; //1101
bin15 = 15; //1111
bin0 = 0; //0000
document.writeln(bin13 & bin15); //results in 13 (1101)
document.writeln(bin13 & bin0); //results in 0 (0000)
document.writeln(bin13 ^ bin15); //results in 2 (0010)
document.writeln(bin13 ^ bin0); //results in 13 (1101)
document.writeln(bin13 ¦ bin15); //results in 15 (1111)
document.writeln(bin13 ¦ bin0); //results in 13 (1101)
```

Relational/Equality

```
<       //less than
>       //greater than
<=      //less than or equal to
>=      //greater than or equal to
==      //equal to
!=      //not equal to
?:      //conditional
```

A Boolean value is returned when using variables or literals with the relational/equality operators.

Usage

It is important to note the last two operators in the example above: equal to and not equal to.

A double-equal is needed so JavaScript doesn't confuse the comparison for an assignment. For not equal to, a common convention is opposing arrows (<>). In JavaScript, however, the implementation is formed by adding the complement operator.

The conditional operation is a special type of comparison that is only used with the assignment operator. It functions as an if-then statement for assigning a value:

```
underAge = (age=>21) ? "no" : "yes"
```

If the expression in the parentheses evaluates to true, then the first value is assigned to the variable. If it evaluates to false, the value after the colon is assigned.

Logical

```
&&      //and
¦¦      //or
```

The logical operators are for comparing two Boolean values, typically other relational/equality expressions.

Usage

The logical operators work in the same manner as the bitwise and and or, only at the variable level.

In the following example, if the variable age is greater than or equal to 21 and the variable hasID is a Boolean true, then the block of statements will be executed:

```
if ( (age>=21) && (hasID) ) {
      ...statements...
}
```

Logical comparisons short-circuit before completing the right half of the expression, depending on the comparison being made:

```
false && anyExpression  //Shorts to false
true ¦¦ anyExpression  //Shorts to true
```

Assignment

```
=       //assign
+=      //addition, concatenate
-=      //subtraction
*=      //multiplication
/=      //division
%=      //modulus
<<=     //bitwise left shift
>>=     //bitwise right shift
>>>=    //bitwise zero fill right shift
&=      //bitwise and
^=      //bitwise xor
¦=      //bitwise or
```

When combined with one of the other binary operators, the assignment operator offers a convenient shorthand for updating variables.

Usage

For example, the following two statements do the same task (adding 5 to the variable shipping):

```
shipping = shipping + 5;
shipping += 5;
```

The += operator can also be used to concatenate strings:

```
sentence = "";
subject = "The dog";
predicate = " walked home.";
sentence += subject;
sentence += predicate;
document.write(sentence);  //results in "The dog walked home."
```

Operator Precedence

Precedence refers to the order in which compound operations are computed. Operators on the same level have equal precedence. Calculations are computed from left to right on all binary operations, beginning with the operators at the top of the list and working down.

call, member	. [] ()
negation/increment	++ — ! ~ -
multiply/divide	* / %
addition/subtraction	+ -
bitwise shift	<< >> >>>
relational	< > <= >=
equality	== !=
bitwise and	&
bitwise xor	^
bitwise or	¦
logical and	&&
logical or	¦¦
conditional	?:
assignment	= += -= *= /= %= <<= >>= >>>= &= ^= ¦=
comma	,

Chapter 24

JavaScript Reference Tables

ISO Latin Character Set

When using methods such as escape and unescape, the returned values relate to the ISO Latin character set. In Table 24.1, you can see a listing of the values and characters for this set.

Table 24.1 ISO Latin Characters		
Decimal Value	**Character**	**Entity Reference**
0	NUL	
1	SOH	
2	STX	
3	ETX	
4	EOT	
5	ENQ	
6	ACK	
7	BEL	
8	BS	
9	HT	
10	NL	
11	VT	
12	NP	
13	CR	
14	SO	
15	SI	
16	DLE	
17	DC1	
18	DC2	
19	DC3	
20	DC4	

(continues)

Table 24.1 Continued		
Decimal Value	**Character**	**Entity Reference**
21	NAK	
22	SYN	
23	ETB	
24	CAN	
25	EM	
26	SUB	
27	ESC	
28	FS	
29	GS	
30	RS	
31	US	
32	SP	
33	!	
34	"	&quot;
35	#	
36	$	
37	%	
38	&	&amp
39	`	
40	(	
41	)	
42	*	
43	+	
44	,	
45	-	
46	.	
47	/	
48	0	
49	1	
50	2	
51	3	
52	4	
53	5	
54	6	
55	7	
56	8	
57	9	
58	:	
59	;	

Decimal Value	Character	Entity Reference
60	<	&lt
61	=	
62	>	&gt
63	?	
64	@	
65	A	
66	B	
67	C	
68	D	
69	E	
70	F	
71	G	
72	H	
73	I	
74	J	
75	K	
76	L	
77	M	
78	N	
79	O	
80	P	
81	Q	
82	R	
83	S	
84	T	
85	U	
86	V	
87	W	
88	X	
89	Y	
90	Z	
91	[	
92	\	
93	]	
94	^	
95	_	
96	`	
97	a	
98	b	
99	c	

(continues)

Table 24.1   Continued

Decimal Value	Character	Entity Reference
100	d	
101	e	
102	f	
103	g	
104	h	
105	i	
106	j	
107	k	
108	l	
109	m	
110	n	
111	o	
112	p	
113	q	
114	r	
115	s	
116	t	
117	u	
118	v	
119	w	
120	x	
121	y	
122	z	
123	{	
124	|	
125	}	
126	~	
127	DEL	
128–159	- -	
160		
161	¡	
162	¢	
163	£	
164	¤	
165	¥	
166	¦	
167	§	
168	¨	
169	©	

IV

JavaScript

Decimal Value	Character	Entity Reference
170	ª	
171	«	
172	¬	
173	–	
174	®	
175	‾	
176	°	
177	±	
178	²	
179	³	
180	´	
181	µ	
182	¶	
183	·	
184	¸	
185	¹	
186	º	
187	»	
188	¼	
189	½	
190	¾	
191	¿	
192	À	À
193	Á	Á
194	Â	Â
195	Ã	Ã
196	Ä	Ä
197	Å	Å
198	Æ	Æ
199	Ç	Ç
200	È	È
201	É	É
202	Ê	Ê
203	Ë	Ë
204	Ì	Ì
205	Í	Í
206	Î	Î
207	Ï	Ï
208	Ð	

(continues)

Table 24.1 Continued		
Decimal Value	**Character**	**Entity Reference**
209	Ñ	&Ntilde;
210	Ò	&Ograve;
211	Ó	&Oacute;
212	Ô	&Ocirc;
213	Õ	&Otilde;
214	Ö	&Ouml;
215	×	
216	Ø	&Oslash;
217	Ù	&Ugrave;
218	Ú	&Uacute;
219	Û	&Ucirc;
220	Ü	&Uuml;
221	Ý	&Yacute;
222	Þ	&THORN;
223	ß	&szlig;
224	à	&agrave;
225	á	&aacute;
226	â	&acirc;
227	ã	&atilde;
228	ä	&auml;
229	å	&aring;
230	æ	&aelig;
231	ç	&ccedil;
232	è	&egrave;
233	é	&eacute;
234	ê	&ecirc;
235	ë	&euml;
236	ì	&igrave;
237	í	&iacute;
238	î	&icirc;
239	ï	&iuml;
240	ð	&eth;
241	ñ	&ntilde;
242	ò	&ograve;
243	ó	&oacute;
244	ô	&ocirc;
245	õ	&otilde;
246	ö	&ouml;
247	÷	

Decimal Value	Character	Entity Reference
248	ø	&oslash;
249	ù	&ugrave;
250	ú	&uacute;
251	û	&ucirc;
252	ü	&uuml;
253	ý	&yacute;
254	þ	&thorn;
255	ÿ	&yuml;

Color Values

Colors can be referenced in a variety of properties in two ways. The first is by using the string literal, which is the color's name. The second is by using an RGB hexadecimal triplet formed by combining the three color values. For example, a specific shade of blue is represented by the string literal `aliceblue` and the triplet `F0F8FF`. The actual color displayed by the browser is determined by the range of colors supported by the client machine—a VGA monitor with 16 colors is going to be much less dramatic than an SVGA with 16 million colors.

Color/String Literal	Red	Green	Blue
aliceblue	F0	F8	FF
antiquewhite	FA	EB	D7
aqua	00	FF	FF
aquamarine	7F	FF	D4
azure	F0	FF	FF
beige	F5	F5	DC
bisque	FF	E4	C4
black	00	00	00
blanchedalmond	FF	EB	CD
blue	00	00	FF
blueviolet	8A	2B	E2
brown	A5	2A	2A
burlywood	DE	B8	87
cadetblue	5F	9E	A0
chartreuse	7F	FF	00

(continues)

(continued)

Color/String Literal	Red	Green	Blue
chocolate	D2	69	1E
coral	FF	7F	50
cornflowerblue	64	95	ED
cornsilk	FF	F8	DC
crimson	DC	14	3C
cyan	00	FF	FF
darkblue	00	00	8B
darkcyan	00	8B	8B
darkgoldenrod	B8	86	0B
darkgray	A9	A9	A9
darkgreen	00	64	00
darkkhaki	BD	B7	6B
darkmagenta	8B	00	8B
darkolivegreen	55	6B	2F
darkorange	FF	8C	00
darkorchid	99	32	CC
darkred	8B	00	00
darksalmon	E9	96	7A
darkseagreen	8F	BC	8F
darkslateblue	48	3D	8B
darkslategray	2F	4F	4F
darkturquoise	00	CE	D1
darkviolet	94	00	D3
deeppink	FF	14	93
deepskyblue	00	BF	FF
dimgray	69	69	69
dodgerblue	1E	90	FF

Color/String Literal	Red	Green	Blue
firebrick	B2	22	22
floralwhite	FF	FA	F0
forestgreen	22	8B	22
fuchsia	FF	00	FF
gainsboro	DC	DC	DC
ghostwhite	F8	F8	FF
gold	FF	D7	00
goldenrod	DA	A5	20
gray	80	80	80
green	00	80	00
greenyellow	AD	FF	2F
honeydew	F0	FF	F0
hotpink	FF	69	B4
indianred	CD	5C	5C
indigo	4B	00	82
ivory	FF	FF	F0
khaki	F0	E6	8C
lavender	E6	E6	FA
lavenderblush	FF	F0	F5
lawngreen	7C	FC	00
lemonchiffon	FF	FA	CD
lightblue	AD	D8	E6
lightcoral	F0	80	80
lightcyan	E0	FF	FF
lightgoldenrodyellow FA	FA	D2	
lightgreen	90	EE	90
lightgrey	D3	D3	D3
lightpink	FF	B6	C1

(continues)

(continued)

Color/String Literal	Red	Green	Blue
lightsalmon	FF	A0	7A
lightseagreen	20	B2	AA
lightskyblue	87	CE	FA
lightslategray	77	88	99
lightsteelblue	B0	C4	DE
lightyellow	FF	FF	E0
lime	00	FF	00
limegreen	32	CD	32
linen	FA	F0	E6
magenta	FF	00	FF
maroon	80	00	00
mediumaquamarine	66	CD	AA
mediumblue	00	00	CD
mediumorchid	BA	55	D3
mediumpurple	93	70	DB
mediumseagreen	3C	B3	71
mediumslateblue	7B	68	EE
mediumspringgreen	00	FA	9A
mediumturquoise	48	D1	CC
mediumvioletred	C7	15	85
midnightblue	19	19	70
mintcream	F5	FF	FA
mistyrose	FF	E4	E1
moccasin	FF	E4	B5
navajowhite	FF	DE	AD
navy	00	00	80
oldlace	FD	F5	E6
olive	80	80	00

Color/String Literal	Red	Green	Blue
olivedrab	6B	8E	23
orange	FF	A5	00
orangered	FF	45	00
orchid	DA	70	D6
palegoldenrod	EE	E8	AA
palegreen	98	FB	98
paleturquoise	AF	EE	EE
palevioletred	DB	70	93
papayawhip	FF	EF	D5
peachpuff	FF	DA	B9
peru	CD	85	3F
pink	FF	C0	CB
plum	DD	A0	DD
powderblue	B0	E0	E6
purple	80	00	80
red	FF	00	00
rosybrown	BC	8F	8F
royalblue	41	69	E1
saddlebrown	8B	45	13
salmon	FA	80	72
sandybrown	F4	A4	60
seagreen	2E	8B	57
seashell	FF	F5	EE
sienna	A0	52	2D
silver	C0	C0	C0
skyblue	87	CE	EB
slateblue	6A	5A	CD
slategray	70	80	90

IV

JavaScript

(continues)

(continued)

Color/String Literal	Red	Green	Blue
snow	FF	FA	FA
springgreen	00	FF	7F
steelblue	46	82	B4
tan	D2	B4	8C
teal	00	80	80
thistle	D8	BF	D8
tomato	FF	63	47
turquoise	40	E0	D0
violet	EE	82	EE
wheat	F5	DE	B3
white	FF	FF	FF
whitesmoke	F5	F5	F5
yellow	FF	FF	00
yellowgreen	9A	CD	32

Reserved Words

The following words cannot be used as user objects or variables in coding JavaScript. Not all are currently in use by JavaScript—they are reserved for future use.

abstract	do	if
boolean	double	implements
break	else	import
byte	extends	in
case	false	instanceof
catch	final	int
char	finally	interface
class	float	long
const	for	native
continue	function	new
default	goto	null

package	super	true
private	switch	try
protected	synchronized	var
public	this	void
return	throw	while
short	throws	with
static	transient	

Chapter 25

JavaScript Task Reference

JavaScript provides tools to perform a variety of tasks in an HTML document without the need to interact with the server.

New Browser

One of the powerful features of JavaScript that makes it useful for implementing demonstrations and tours is its ability to spawn new versions of the client browser with controllable levels of functionality.

The basic command to create a new browser is:

```
windowVar = window.open("URL", "windowName" [, "windowFeatures"])
```

To open a plain window with hotlink-only navigation:

```
//Note: Setting one feature automatically sets all non-mentioned
features to false.
window.open("URL", "windowName", "toolbar=no")
```

To open a window without the directories or menubar:

```
window.open("URL", "windowName",
"toolbar=yes,location=yes,directories=no,status=yes,menubar=no,scrollbars=yes,
resizable=yes")
```

For more information, see:

window object

open method

Creating a Custom Navigation Web Site

One of the powerful capabilities of JavaScript is its ability to control the functionality of the browser (see the previous section "New Browser"). This is useful for creating guided-tour or demonstration programs. To create a site requires a front door that generates the rest of the application:

```
<FORM>
<INPUT TYPE="button" NAME="tour" VALUE="Start Tour"
   onClick="window.open('tourframes.html','tourWindow','toolbar=no')">
</FORM>
```

The `tourframes.html` file creates the frames containing a starting page and navigation bar:

```
<FRAMESET COLS="%10,%90">
   <FRAME SRC="navbar.html">
   <FRAME SRC="tourstart.html" NAME="contentWin">
</FRAMESET>
```

The `navBar` file is a simple set of buttons with custom `onClick` event handlers to direct the browser:

```
<FORM NAME = "navBar">
<INPUT TYPE="button" NAME="back" VALUE="  <-- Back "
onClick="contentWin.document.history.back()">
<INPUT TYPE="button" NAME="forw" VALUE="Forward -->"
onClick="contentWin.document.history.forward()">
<INPUT TYPE="button" NAME="home" VALUE="Home"
onClick="contentWin.document.history.go(0)">
<INPUT TYPE="button" NAME="quit" VALUE="Quit the Tour"
onClick="parent.close()">
</FORM>
```

To prevent premature escapes, the quit button could also call a function that confirms the user's choice before closing the window.

For more information, see:

> `button`, `document`, `form`, `history`, and `window` objects
>
> `back`, `close`, `forward`, and `go` methods
>
> `top` and `parent` properties
>
> `onClick` event handler

Self-Resetting Status Messages

A sometimes annoying side effect of the `window.status` property is its persistence. Once set, it doesn't change unless another `window.status` assignment is encountered.

You can overcome this attribute using the `setTimeout` method:

```
timeDelay = 1500 //1.5 seconds
```

```
function eraseStatus () {
   window.status = "" //This can also be set to a 'default' message.
};

function setStatus (statusText) {
   window.status = statusText;
   setTimeout("eraseStatus()",timeDelay)
}
```

Using these two functions is a simple matter of including the setStatus function in the onMouseOver event:

```
<A HREF=URL onMouseOver="setStatus('Your message here.'); return
true">linkText</A>
```

For more information, see:

window object

status property

setTimeout method

onMouseOver event handler

Platform-Specific Newline Characters

Which version of the newline character to use depends on the platform used by the client. Windows needs an /r in addition to the /n needed for all other platforms. Since it's impossible to control which platforms access your page, a simple function can ensure that the proper form of the newline character is used:

```
function brk() {
   if (navigator.appVersion.lastIndexOf('Win') != -1)
           return "\r\n"
   else
           return "\n"
}
```

For more information, see:

navigator object

appVersion property

lastIndexOf method

Validating Form Information

Validating information through CGI scripts is a time-consuming process. Not only is there the added communication between the client and server, but time and expertise are also needed to develop the actual CGI script.

Including form validation with JavaScript directly on the HTML page increases the speed and localizes the process to the end user. This makes it much harder for end users to send incompatible data that could cause damage to the server.

There are several ways to do form validation but a basic tenet is adding a JavaScript function to a true submit button. The HTML definition of the submit button could look like this:

```
<INPUT TYPE="BUTTON" NAME="SUBMIT" VALUE="SUBMIT"
onClick="checkInformation(this.form)">
```

`checkInformation` provides for verifying that the information meets CGI script expectations. If not, it should at least return to the document without submitting or return focus to the offending items. If everything passes muster, then the function can also submit the form:

```
function checkInformation(form) {
   ...validation statements ...;
   if (validationPassed) {
           form.submit(); }
   return;
}
```

For more information, see:

`form` and `button` objects

`focus` methods

`onClick` event handlers

Creating Arrays

Although JavaScript uses arrays for several of its objects (forms, elements, etc.), it doesn't provide a straightforward method to create user-defined arrays—one of the staples of data processing.

Here is a function to create a new array by initializing the elements. This is useful for small arrays but is unwieldy for larger implementations:

```
function arrayCreator() {
   this.length = initArray.arguments.length;
   //counts the number of arguments included when the function is called
   for (var I=0; I<this.length; I==) {
           this[I+1] = userArray.arguments[I] //load the new values into the
           array
   }
}
```

To initialize a new array, use the function with this syntax:

```
var arrayName = new userArray(argument1[,argument2][,argument3][etc.])
```

Generating a Random Number (Non-UNIX)

At present, the `random` method works only with UNIX versions of Netscape. There is another way of generating pseudo-random numbers without using the built-in method. This is called a *calculated random number* and, if accessed repeatedly over a short time, reveals its biases and true nonrandom nature.

To ensure compatibility for a script across platforms, any script depending on random numbers should not use the `random` method and instead should rely on a user-defined function like the following one:

```
function UnixMachine() {
   if (navigator.appVersion.lastIndexOf('Unix') != -1)
           return true
   else
           return false
}

function randomNumber() {
   if (UnixMachine()) {
           num = Math.random() }
   else {
           num = Math.abs(Math.sin(Date.getTime())); }
   return num;
}
```

This generates a number between 0 and 1, and works well for applications needing random numbers every few seconds. If random numbers are needed with greater frequency, you need to add more variation into the equation, such as a different computation (`cos`, `tan`, `log`) every third division of time or something similar.

For more information, see:

Date and Math objects

random method

function and return statements

Chapter 26

JavaScript Internet Resources

Because of JavaScript's very specific platform base (it's currently only recognized by Netscape Navigator), the number of "official" online resources that directly address it are few and far between. However, the "unofficial" resources (put up by experimental souls who wish to share their discoveries in this new technology) are growing at a rapid rate.

The World Wide Web

Since JavaScript is *for* the Web, it's only appropriate that the best sources of information on its use are found *on* the Web. As with most other Internet-based sources, the bulk of Java/Script sites are primarily Java-oriented, with JavaScript covered as a subsection.

The following list is by no means comprehensive. To keep up on new offerings on the Web, your best bet is to take advantage of the Other Hot Links pages that many of the sites have.

Navigator was the first browser that supported JavaScript, making Netscape's home site a good place to check periodically, especially for updates/additions to the JavaScript language specification.

Netscape also has its own Development Partners Program, providing subscribers with extended technical and programming support, information on upcoming products, extensions, plug-ins, and access to pre-beta releases of new browsers, servers, and plug-ins.

Also be sure to check out the Netscape ColorCenter at **http:// www.hidaho.com/colorcenter/**. This is a handy place to compare the values of colors against their appearance on the screen.

Voodoo JavaScript Tutorial (http://rummelplatz.uni-mannheim.de/~skoch/ js/script.htm)

Voodoo JavaScript Tutorial is an ongoing tutorial presented in easy-to-digest sections covering the basics of JavaScript. It includes examples built into the page, along with descriptive text and code examples. A good place to get your feet wet.

The Unofficial JavaScript Resource Center (http://www.intercom.net/user/ mecha/java/index.html)

The Unofficial JavaScript Resource Center is a new, well-produced site devoted to JavaScript. At first, it was fairly limited but it promises to grow with more examples and techniques for a range of users.

The idea is to provide a few examples and snippets of code to copy and drop into place. Its organization will make it a useful resource as the content expands.

Danny Goodman's JavaScript Pages (http://www/dannyg.com:80/javascript)

Danny Goodman's JavaScript Pages are a collection of examples covering more advanced concepts in JavaScript, including cookies. Danny Goodman is one of the de facto experts on JavaScript on the Web, and he gives some good examples for learning and adapting other applications.

JavaScript Index (http://www.c2.org/~andreww/javascript/)

JavaScript Index is a solid compendium of JavaScript implementations and experimentations, including a growing list of personal home pages that show off a variety of JavaScript tricks. A subset of the site is the JavaScript Library, a small but expanding collection of source code from around the Web community.

Gamelan (http://www.gamelan.com/)

Called *The On-Line Java Index*, EarthWeb's Gamelan has an extensive collection of links to other sites, examples, tools, utilities, and other interesting things. Although primarily targeting Java, the JavaScript section is quite sizable as well.

Sun Microsystems (http://java.sun.com/)

At Sun Microsystems, the place where it *all* started, Sun hosts the Java home site. Additionally, Sun maintains the Java Users Group (a subgroup inside the Sun Users Group) and several mailing and notification lists to keep developers informed of the latest events.

JavaWorld (http://www.javaworld.com/)

To support its efforts to integrate Java development into Latte, Borland's host site for Java development promises to keep Java developers informed.

Symantec (http://cafe.symantec.com/)

Symantec led the pack when it came to providing a development platform for Java applet creation for Windows and Macintosh. With the first publicly available (for free and for Windows NT/95) java development add-on to their popular C++ package,

Symantec provided the first graphical user interface (GUI)-based development environment for applet creation.

Dimension X (http://www.dnx.com/)

Dimension X is the home of Liquid Reality, a Java applet development platform that merges the capabilities of a 3D modeling package with a Java applet builder.

The Java Developer (http://www.digitalfocus.com/faq/)

Sponsored by Digital Focus, the Java Developer serves as the home site for the Java Developer FAQ. It is one of the more interesting implementations of frames to present search and question submission buttons as you browse the site.

UseNet

Several UseNet newsgroups have sprung up to provide channels for developers looking for guidance with Java, JavaScript, and Web programming in general. These are as follows.

comp.lang.javascript

comp.lang.javascript is dedicated to JavaScript development. A large number of messages are posted to this forum every day, including many from the established gurus of JavaScript. It contains a lot of information if you take the time to peruse all the messages.

netscape.navigator (news://secnews.netscape.com)

It never hurts to have a direct line monitored by the folks who developed JavaScript at Netscape, and **netscape.navigator** is the closest thing there is. JavaScript topics are definitely in the minority in this group but they're there if you look.

Note the different newsserver. The title implies that it's secure, but it seems to be readily available for browsing and posting.

comp.lang.java

comp.lang.java is the group from which the **comp.lang.javascript** group sprang. It deals specifically with Sun's Java language but occasionally has information about JavaScript also.

comp.infosystems.www.authoring.*

The traditional collection of newsgroups for Web-oriented discussion has been **comp.infosystems.www**. As the Web has expanded, so have they, covering everything from browsers to announcements of newly opened Web sites.

Although there is no JavaScript-specific group in the **comp.infosystems** heirarchy, there are several that cover the various facets of Web authoring:

- **comp.infosystems.www.authoring.cgi**
- **comp.infosystems.www.authoring.html**
- **comp.infosystems.www.authoring.images**
- **comp.infosystems.www.authoring.misc**

Mailing Lists

For those who prefer the thrill of receiving e-mail until their inboxes burst, there are mailing lists dedicated to JavaScript that offer similar information to the UseNet newsgroups.

Keep in mind, however, that mailing lists are a lot like a telephone party line and can get rather chatty (the downside being that you have to wade through all the flotsam in your inbox to figure out what you can use).

If you plan to use mailing lists heavily, you might want to look into an e-mail program that enables *threading*, or linking together messages that share the same subject to help keep the volume organized.

A word about mailing lists. Although you post your questions and comments to the list's address (for rebroadcast to the rest of the list's readers), subscribing to and unsubscribing from the list are done through a separate e-mail address, specifically the address of the *listserver*.

The lists discussed below mention both the list address and the listserver address, and sending subscribe requests to the list address (so everyone on the list knows you don't know what you're doing) is a guaranteed way to get branded a "newbie."

If you want more information on how to communicate with the listserver (or on other possible lists of a particular server), you can send a message to the listserver address with "help" in the message body.

javascript@obscure.org

Sponsored by the Obscure Organization (**http://www.obscure.org/**) and TeleGlobal Media, Inc. (**http://www.tgm.com/**), the JavaScript Index is the only mailing list dedicated specifically to JavaScript.

The discussion gets pretty varied and ranges from introductory questions to more involved discussions on how best to handle animations, framing, reloads, and so on.

To subscribe, send a message to **majordomo@obscure.org** with **subscribe javascript** in the message body. Alternatively, you can point your browser at **http://www.obscure.org/javascript/** for further information.

java@borland.com

A companion newsletter that parallels the activity on Borland's JavaWorld site, the Borland Java newsletter keeps you informed about Borland's work on integrating Java technology into their development tools. To subscribe, send a message to **listserv@borland.com** with **subscribe java *{your first name} {your last name}*** in the message body.

java-announce@java.sun.com

Sun Microsystems, the home of Java, has its own collection of mailing lists. The **java-announce** list is primarily for notifications of new Java-related tools. To subscribe, send a message to **majordomo@java.sun.com** with **subscribe java-announce** in the message body.

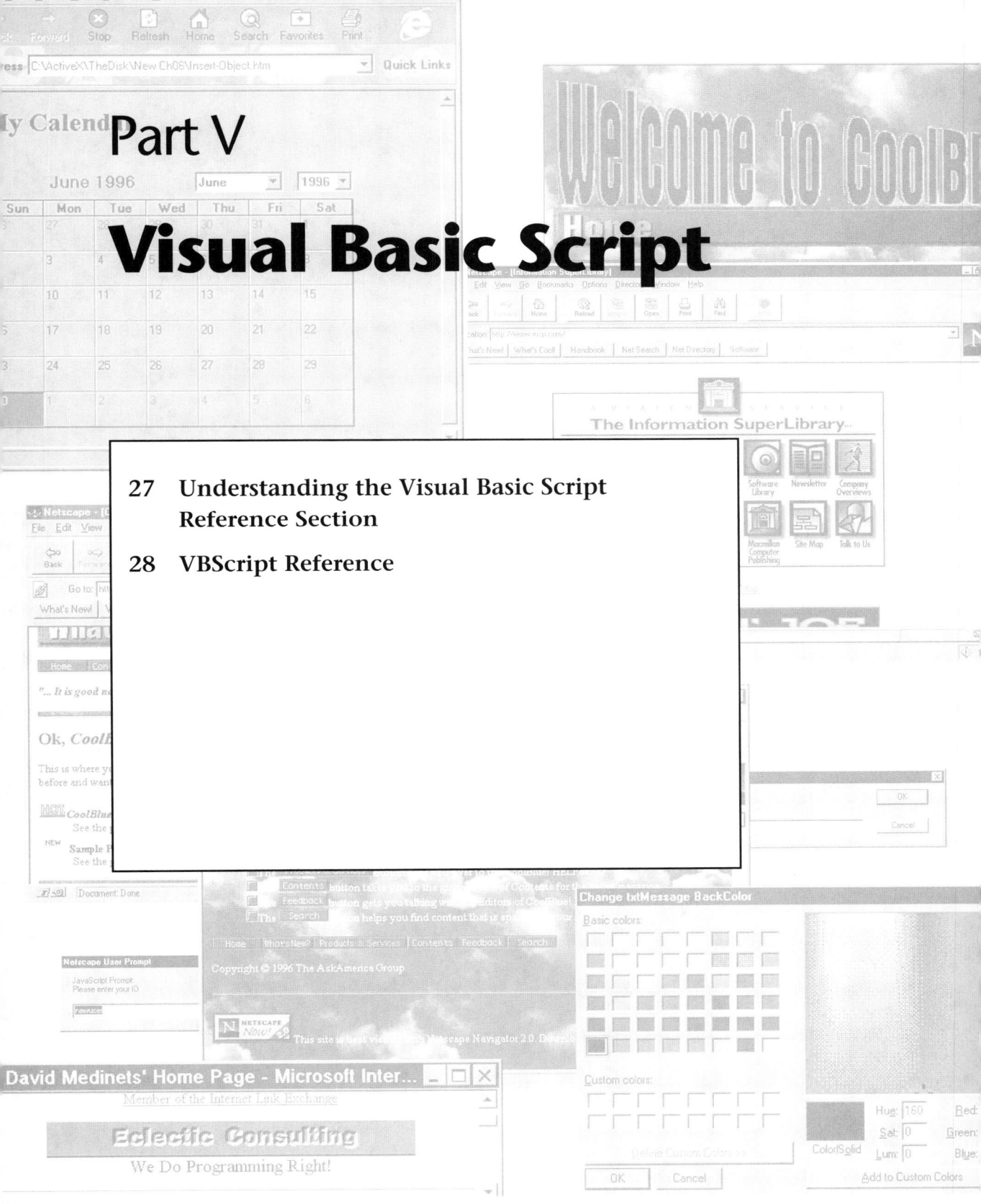

Part V

Visual Basic Script

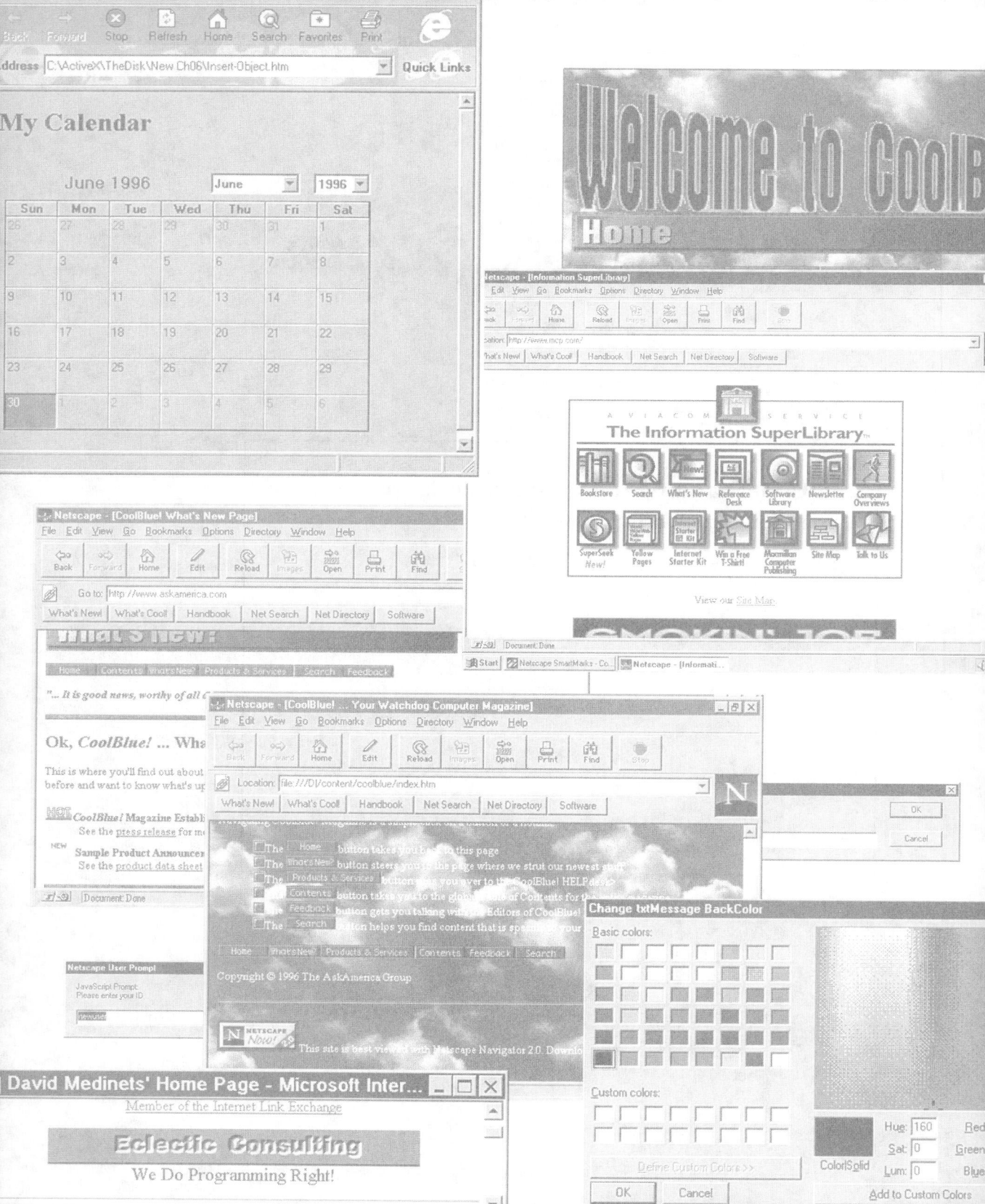

Chapter 27

Understanding the Visual Basic Script Reference Section

This section is a reference guide to the concepts, statements, and objects of Visual Basic Script. It is not an introduction to the language. Quick references are designed to sit on your programming desk so that you can easily look up a forgotten spelling or some procedure's parameter that you are unsure of.

> **Note**
>
> This book assumes that you have a working knowledge of HTML. You need to know HTML because all VBScript programs reside inside HTML documents. If you are not familiar with HTML, please read Que's *HTML by Example*.

Using This Reference

Several conventions used in this book make finding information easier. Several entries contain tables that point you off to other entries. This was done so that the information did not need to be listed twice. For example, the section on variables briefly discusses the nature of variables and then lists the variable types. Each variable type has its own entry.

Each entry has the same basic structure. First, the type and syntax are presented. Then a one-line description (the synopsis) and the parameters are discussed. Next come the description, example, figure, and see also sections. All of these elements are optional and only appear if the entry needs it.

The syntax description follows several guidelines. *Italicized* items need to be replaced with actual values or variable names. Optional items are surrounded by square brackets ([]). If an entry has more than one form of syntax, more than one syntax element will be present. In this case, the syntax elements are numbered to indicate the different forms.

What is VBScript?

This section briefly covers some vital information that you need to know before you can successfully create VB scripts.

VBScript is used with HTML pages to increase functionality and interaction with the end user. The language currently has no other purpose other than to enhance Web documents.

VBScript is essentially a subset of the full Visual Basic language; if you already know Visual Basic, then you can safely say that you know VBScript.

VBScript is not case-sensitive. This means that a function called SendAlert is the same as one called sendAlert.

All VBScript statements are contained inside HTML <SCRIPT> tags or inside form element tags. VBScript statements are executed when the HTML document is loaded or in response to some event that happens in the browser's window.

When the document is loaded, any VBScript statements that are not inside procedures are executed. If you have variables to declare or other initialization statements, place them inside a <SCRIPT> tag inside the header section (the <HEAD> and </HEAD> tags) of the document. Procedures must be defined before they can be used, therefore it's a good idea to place procedure definitions inside the header section also. Placing initialization statement and procedure definitions in the header section makes the body of the document less cluttered.

Listing 27.1 shows a very simple example of how VBScript programs are used. The document.open and VBScript statements in the <SCRIPT> tag are not associated with any events and are executed as soon as the Web browser reads the statements. You can prove this by noticing that the phrase "This is a test." appears *before* the "VB Script Example Page" header in Figure 27.1.

Listing 27.1   A Short Example of a VBScript Program

```
<HTML>
<HEAD>
<TITLE>VB Script Example Page</TITLE>
<SCRIPT LANGUAGE="VBScript">
<!--
document.open
document.write "This is a test."
document.close

Sub sendAlert (msg)
Alert msg
End Sub
-->
</SCRIPT>
```

```
    </HEAD>
    <BODY>
    <H1>VB Script Example Page</H1>
    <FORM>
    <INPUT NAME=btnLaugh OnClick=sendAlert("HA-HA!")
    TYPE=button VALUE="Want a laugh?">
    </FORM>
    </BODY>
    </HTML>
```

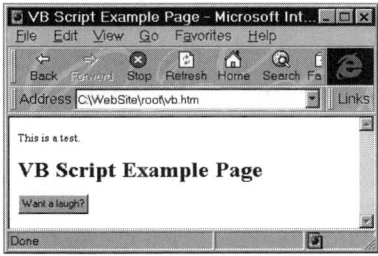

Fig. 27.1   This is what Listing 27.1 looks like when displayed in Internet Explorer.

The reference section has several dictionary-type entries that you may want to look at. These entries are listed in Table 27.1.

Table 27.1   Dictionary Entries

Word	Page
Conversion Functions	p. 829
Date/Time Functions	p. 833
Events	p. 847
Event Handling	p. 847
Hierarchies	p. 858
Literal Values	p. 874
Math Functions	p. 877
Methods	p. 877
Object Variables	p. 886
Operators	p. 894
Operator Precedence	p. 895
Procedures	p. 899
Properties	p. 901
Scope	p. 906
String Functions	p. 912
Type Conversion	p. 918
Variables	p. 920
Variant	p. 922

(continues)

V

Visual Basic Script

Table 27.1 Continued	
Word	**Page**
Variant Testing Functions	p. 923
VBScript Statements	p .925
Whitespace	p. 927

Differences Between VBScript and Visual Basic

There are quite a few differences between VBScript and Visual Basic. The most notable difference is that VBScript needs a Web browser in order to execute, whereas VB programs can be stand-alone executables.

If you don't know Visual Basic, skip this section. However, if you are already proficient in Visual Basic, you need to be aware of VBScript's limitations so that you don't waste time trying to do things that aren't possible. While some of the functionality of Visual Basic forms can be duplicated using HTML forms and ActiveX Controls, you'll find that some aspects of your applications will be hard to implement in VBScript.

Table 27.2 lists the limitations that VBScript has in relation to Visual Basic. Most of the limitations are due to security or memory considerations. In addition, VBScript is designed to enhance HTML documents, not to perform transaction processing or file access.

Table 27.2 VBScript's Limitations	
Feature	**Description**
Array Handling	VBScript does not support the `Array` function, the `Option Base` statement, or declaring arrays with a lower bound different from zero.
Clipboard	Not supported.
Collection	Not supported.
Conditional Compilation	Not supported.
Constants	Not supported. However, you can emulate constants by assigning values to variables in the header section of the HTML document and then not changing them.
Control Flow	The following control statements are not supported: `DoEvents`, `For Each...Next`, `GoSub...Return`, `GoTo`, `On Error GoTo`, `On...GoSub`, `On...GoTo`, `Line Numbers`, `Line Labels`, and `With...End With`.
Data Conversion	The following data conversion functions are not supported: `CCur`, `CVar`, `CVDate`, `Format`, `Str`, and `Val`.
Data Types	VBScript only supports one data type called `Variant`. However, you can use many different subtypes. In addition, the `Type...End Type` statement is not supported.
Date/Time	The `Date` and `Time` statements and the `Timer` function are not supported.

Feature	Description
DDE	Not supported.
Debugging	The Debug, Print, End, and Stop statements are not supported.
Declaration	The Declare, Property Get, Property Let, Property Set, Public, Private, Statement, ParamArray, Option, and New statements are not supported.
Error Handling	Only the On Error Resume Next is supported. The Err object still contains the error code and description if an error occurred.
File Input/Output	Not supported.
Financial	Not supported.
Object Manipulation	The CreateObject, GetObject, and TypeOf functions are not supported.
Operators	The Like operator is not supported.
Strings	Fixed-length strings and the LSet, RSet, Mid, and StrConv functions are not supported.
Using Objects	The TypeName keyword is not supported.
Variables	Public and Private variables do not seem to be supported. There is conflicting information as of September, 1996. In addition, Static variables are not supported.

Chapter 28

VBScript Reference

VBScript syntax and commands are divided into several categories depending on their use and function.

Objects are the building blocks of VBScript. They are used to return and modify the status of forms, pages, the browser, and programmer-defined variables. An easy way to think about an object is as a noun. Cat, car, house, computer, and form are all nouns and could all be represented as an object.

You use *properties* to differentiate between objects of the same class—for example, all objects that are a cat. Properties are adjectives and refer to items that might make the object different from other objects. In the cat example, this could be weight, color, breed, disposition, and current activity.

You use *methods* to pass messages to the object and sometimes to change its properties. For example, one method could be used to change the cat's current activity from eating to sleeping, whereas another could be used to change its weight from heavy to really heavy.

The following is a list of the objects, properties, and methods used in VBScript.

+ (Addition)

Syntax:	*result = operand1 + operand2*
Type:	Arithmetic Operator
Synopsis:	Adds two operands together
Description:	If either operand has the Null value, then *result* is Null. Operands that have the Empty value are equivalent to zero.
See Also:	Operators, Subtraction

/ (Division)

Syntax:	*result = operand1 / operand2*
Type:	Arithmetic Operator
Synopsis:	Divides operand1 by operand2
Description:	If either operand has the Null value, then *result* is Null. Operands that have the Empty value are equivalent to zero. And, of course, division by zero results in a run-time error.
See Also:	On Error, Operators

= (Equality)

Syntax:	*operand1 = operand2*
Type:	Comparison Operator
Synopsis:	Returns True if *operand1* is equal to *operand2*.
Description:	If either operand has the Null value, then *result* is Null. Operands that have the Empty value are equivalent to zero.

The equality operator is frequently used in conditional expression for If, Do, and For statements.

Example:

```
' In this If statement, the equality operator
' is used in the conditional expression.
if intNumPages = 15 Then
 Alert "Ok"
End If

' In the third assignment statement below, the
' equality operator is used to give a value of
' False to intTest.
intA = 10
intB = 5
intTest = (intA = intB) ' intTest equals False.
```

See Also:	Operators

^ *(Exponentiation)*

Syntax:	*result = operand1 ^ operand2*
Type:	Arithmetic Operator
Synopsis:	Raises *operand1* to the power of *operand2*.
Description:	If either operand has the Null value, then *result* is Null. Operands that have the Empty value are equivalent to zero.
See Also:	Operators

> *(Greater Than)*

Syntax:	*operand1 > operand2*
Type:	Comparison Operator
Synopsis:	Returns True if *operand1* is greater than *operand2*.
Description:	If either operand has the Null value, then *result* is Null. Operands that have the Empty value are equivalent to zero.

The greater than operator is frequently used in conditional expression for If, Do, and For statements.

Example:

```
' In this If statement, the greater than operator
' is used in the conditional expression.
if intNumPages > 15 Then
 Alert "Ok"
End If

' In the third assignment statement below, the
' greater than operator is used to give a value of
' True to intTest.
intA = 10
intB = 5
intTest = (intA > intB)
```

See Also:	Operators

>= *(Greater Than Or Equal To)*

Syntax:	*operand1* >= *operand2*
Type:	Comparison Operator
Synopsis:	Returns True if *operand1* is greater than or equal to *operand2*.
Description:	If either operand has the Null value, then *result* is Null. Operands that have the Empty value are equivalent to zero.

The greater than or equal to operator is frequently used in conditional expression for If, Do, and For statements.

Example:

```
' In this If statement, the >= operator
' is used in the conditional expression.
if intNumPages >= 15 Then
 Alert "Ok"
End If

' In the third assignment statement below, the
' >= operator is used to give a value of
' True to intTest.
intA = 10
intB = 5
intTest = (intA >= intB)
```

See Also:	Operators

<> *(Inequality)*

Syntax:	*operand1* <> *operand2*
Type:	Comparison Operator
Synopsis:	Returns True if *operand1* does not equal *operand2*.
Description:	If either operand has the Null value, then *result* is Null. Operands that have the Empty value are equivalent to zero.

The inequality operator is frequently used in conditional expression for If, Do, and For statements.

Example:

```
' In this If statement, the inequality operator
' is used in the conditional expression.
if intNumPages <> 15 Then
 Alert "Ok"
```

```
End If

' In the third assignment statement below, the
' inequality operator is used to give a value of
' True to intTest.
intA = 10
intB = 5
intTest = (intA <> intB)
```

See Also: Operators

\ *(Integer Division)*

Syntax: *result = operand1 \ operand2*

Type: Arithmetic Operator

Synopsis: Divides one number by another and rounds the result to the near-
                     est whole number.

Description: If either operand has the Null value, then *result* is Null. Operands
                     that have the Empty value are equivalent to zero. And, of course,
                     division by zero results in a run-time error.

See Also: On Error, Operators

< *(Less Than)*

Syntax: *operand1 < operand2*

Type: Comparison Operator

Synopsis: Returns True if *operand1* is less than *operand2*.

Description: If either operand has the Null value, then *result* is Null. Operands
                     that have the Empty value are equivalent to zero.

The less than operator is frequently used in conditional expression for If, Do, and For
statements.

Example:

```
' In this If statement, the less than operator
' is used in the conditional expression.
if intNumPages < 15 Then
 Alert "Ok"
End If

' In the third assignment statement below, the
' less than operator is used to give a value of
```

```
' False to intTest.
intA = 10
intB = 5
intTest = (intA < intB)
```

See Also: Operators

<= (Less Than Or Equal To)

Syntax: *operand1 < operand2*

Type: Comparison Operator

Synopsis: Returns True if *operand1* is less than or equal to *operand2*.

Description: If either operand has the Null value, then *result* is Null. Operands
                          that have the Empty value are equivalent to zero.

The less than or equal to operator is frequently used in conditional expression for If, Do,
and For statements.

Example:

```
' In this If statement, the <= operator
' is used in the conditional expression.
if intNumPages <= 15 Then
 Alert "Ok"
End If

' In the third assignment statement below, the
' <= operator is used to give a value of
' False to intTest.
intA = 10
intB = 5
intTest = (intA <= intB)
```

See Also: Operators

* (Multiplication)

Syntax: *result = operand1 * operand2*

Type: Arithmetic Operator

Synopsis: Multiplies one number by another.

Description: If either operand has the Null value, then *result* is Null. Operands
                          that have the Empty value are equivalent to zero.

See Also: Operators

- *(Negation)*

Syntax:	*- operand*
Type:	Arithmetic Operator
Synopsis:	Negates the value of *operand*.

Example:

```
intA = 10 ' intA equals positive 10.
intB = -10 ' intB equals negative 10.
```

See Also:	Operators

- *(Subtraction)*

Syntax:	*result = operand1 - operand2*
Type:	Arithmetic Operator
Synopsis:	Subtracts *operand2* from *operand1*.
Description:	If one of the operands contain the Null value, then the result is Null. If one of the operands contain the Empty value, it is treated as if it were zero.
See Also:	Operators

& *(String Concatenation)*

Syntax:	*result = string1 & string2*
Type:	String Concatenation Operator
Synopsis:	Appends *string2* to *string1*.
Description:	Although you can also use the + operator to concatenate two character strings, you should use the & operator for concatenation instead. The & operator eliminates ambiguity and provides self-documenting code.
See Also:	Operators

Abs

Syntax:	Abs(*number*)
Type:	Intrinsic Conversion and Math Function
Synopsis:	Returns the absolute value of *number*.

Example:

```
intTemp = abs(-2) ' intTemp equals 2.
intTemp = abs(2) ' intTemp equals 2.
```

See Also:	Atn, Conversion Functions, Cos, Exp, Log, Math Functions, Randomize, Rnd, Sin, Sqr, Tan

Action

Syntax 1:	*form*.Action
Syntax 2:	*form*.Action = *string*
Type:	Property
Synopsis:	Gets or sets the address that does the form's action.
Description:	The *string* parameter is usually a URL that represents a CGI script. However, it can also be a script procedure or an e-mail address. If no URL is specified for a form's action, the base URL is used.

Addition (+)

Syntax:	*result = operand1 + operand2*
Type:	Arithmetic Operator
Synopsis:	Adds two operands together
Description:	If either operand has the Null value, then *result* is Null. Operands that have the Empty value are equivalent to zero.
See Also:	Operators, Subtraction

Alert

Syntax: *window*.alert(*string*)

Type: Method

Synopsis: Displays a message dialog box.

Description: If *window* is not specified, then the current window object is used.

Example:

```
<!-- This document shows how to use the
Alert method.
-->
<HTML>
 <HEAD>
 <TITLE>VB Script Example Page</TITLE>
 <SCRIPT LANGUAGE="VBScript">
 <!--
 Alert("This is an Alert message box.")
 -->
 </SCRIPT>
 </HEAD>
 <BODY>
 <H1>VB Script Example Page</H1>
 Did you like the Alert message?<P>
 </BODY>
 </HTML>
```

Picture:

Fig. 28.1 An Alert message box.

aLinkColor

Syntax 1:   *document*.aLinkColor = *rgbValue*

Syntax 2:   *document*.aLinkColor = *string*

Type: Property

Synopsis: Gets or sets *document*'s active link color.

Description: You can set the color by specifying a RGB value in hexadecimal or
                          by specifying a color name. The "Color Names" entry lists all of
                          the color names that you can use.

A link is active when the mouse pointer is positioned over it and the mouse button is
pressed and held down.

You can only set this property while the document is being parsed. An OnLoad event
handler procedure is a good place to set document properties.

> **Caution**
>
> Internet Explorer does not support this feature. It is part of the browser's object module for com-
> patibility reasons.

Anchor

Type: Object

Synopsis: Represents a hyperlink link in a document.

Description: Table 28.3 lists the sole property of an anchor object. See the
                          "Anchors" entry for more information.

Table 28.1	Properties of an Anchor Object	
Property	**Page Number**	**Description**
Name	p. 882	Gets or sets the name of an anchor.

Anchors

Syntax: *document*.Anchors[*index*]

Type: Read-Only Property

Synopsis: Returns an array of anchors, or you can specify an index to re-
                          trieve a single anchor.

Description: You can find out how many anchors *document* has by using the
                          sample code in the Example section. Figure 28.2 shows the results
                          of the example HTML document. Notice that the number of links
                          in the document changes as the document is parsed.

Example:

```
<!-- This document shows how to determine
the number of anchors in a document.
-->
<HTML>
 <HEAD>
 <TITLE>VB Script Example Page</TITLE>
 <SCRIPT language="VBScript">
 <!--
 Sub dispAnchors
 intNumAnchors = Document.Anchors.Length
 Document.Open
 Document.Write "This document has " &
 intNumAnchors &
 " anchors.<P>"
 Document.Clear
 End Sub

 dispAnchors
 -->
 </SCRIPT>
 </HEAD>
 <BODY LANGUAGE="VBScript">
 <H1>VB Script Example Page</H1>
      Visit my home page at
 <A NAME="Home Page">http://www.planet.net/pmedined</A>
 <P>
 <SCRIPT language="VBScript">
 <!--
 dispAnchors
 -->
 </SCRIPT>
 </BODY>
</HTML>
```

Picture:

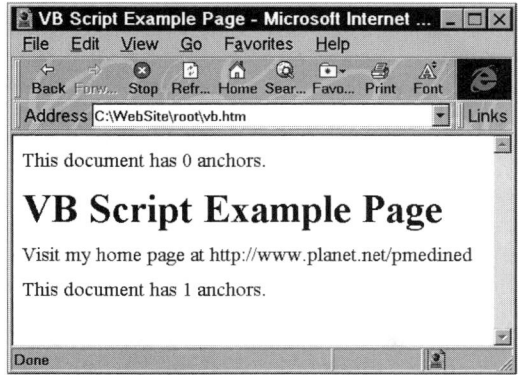

Fig. 28.2   The number of anchors in a document depends a lot on when the anchors are counted.

And

Syntax:	*result = operand1 And operand2*
Type:	Operator
Synopsis:	Returns True if both operands are true.
Description:	If one operand is True and the second is Null or if both operands are Null then the result is Null. If the operands are numeric then a bit-wise comparison is made.

Example:

```
intHasCold = blnFever And blnSniffling
```

See Also:	Operators

AppCodeName

Syntax:	*navigator*.AppCodeName
Type:	Read-Only Property
Synopsis:	The code name of the current application.
Description:	This property returns "Mozilla" when using Microsoft Internet Explorer v3.0 (4.70.1158).

Example:

```
' Display the application code name.
Alert Navigator.AppCodeName
```

AppName

Syntax:	*navigator*.AppName
Type:	Read-Only Property
Synopsis:	The name of the current application.
Description:	This property returns "Microsoft Internet Explorer" when using Microsoft Internet Explorer v3.0 (4.70.1158).

Example:

```
' Display the application name.
Alert Navigator.AppName
```

AppVersion

Syntax:	*navigator*.AppVersion
Type:	Read-Only Property
Synopsis:	The version number of the current application.
Description:	This property returns "2.0 (compatible; MSIE 3.0A; Windows 95)" when using Microsoft Internet Explorer v3.0 (4.70.1158).

Example:

```
' Display the application version
Alert Navigator.AppVersion
```

Array Variables

Type:	Definition
Description:	An array variable can contain a collection or series of values. Array variables can have more than one dimension. For example, you can use a two-dimensional array to hold values generated by the formula: y = .5 + x. Each x, y pair of values is another element in the array. Three-dimensional arrays are also useful when doing mathematics. While VBScript supports up to 60 dimensions, few programmers use more than three or four.

If you don't know in advance how big the array should be, use a *dynamic* array. Dynamic arrays are created by using empty parentheses. When your script knows the correct size, the ReDim keyword is used to resize the array.

The lower bound of an array variable is always zero. This means that an array will always hold one more element than is declared in the Dim statement. The following example should make this concept clear.

Table 28.2	VBScript Array Functions and Keywords
Function	**Description**
Dim	Declares script-level or procedure-level variables.
Erase	Reinitializes fixed-size arrays and frees memory associated with dynamic arrays.
IsArray	Tests a variable to see if it is an array.
LBound	Returns the smallest subscript for a given dimension of an array.
ReDim	Declares or modifies the bounds for dynamic arrays.
UBound	Returns the largest subscript for dimension of an *arrayname*.

Example:

```
<SCRIPT LANGUAGE="VBScript">
<!--
 ' Declare a vector of integer - a one-dimensional
 ' array.
 Dim aryInt_A(20)

 ' assign a value to the 5th element.
 aryInt_A(4) = 23;

 ' retrieve the eighth element of the array.
 lngNumBooks = aryInt_A(7)

 ' Declare a 66-element two-dimensional array of
 ' long integers. It will have 11 rows and 6 columns.
 Dim aryLng_B(10, 5)

 ' assign a value to the first element
 aryLng_B(0, 0) = 2343412

 ' Declare a dynamic array.
 Dim ary_C()

 ' Define the bounds of the dynamic array.
 ReDim ary_C(10, 10)

-->
</SCRIPT>
```

See Also: Dim, IsArray, ReDim

Asc

Syntax: Asc(*string*)

Type: Intrinsic Conversion and String Function

Synopsis: Returns the ANSI code of the first character in *string*.

Description: If *string* contains no characters, a run-time error occurs.

Example:

```
intTemp = Asc("ABCDE") ' intTemp equals 65.
```

See Also: AscB, AscW, Chr, ChrB, ChrW, Conversion Functions, InStr, InStrB, Len, LenB, Left, LeftB, LCase, LTrim, Mid, MidB, Right, RightB, Space, StrComp, String, String Functions, Trim, UCase

---

AscB

Syntax:	AscB(*string*)
Type:	Intrinsic Conversion and String Function
Synopsis:	Returns the first byte in *string*.
Description:	AscB should be used when *string* contains byte data.
See Also:	Asc, AscW, Chr, ChrB, ChrW, Conversion Functions, InStr, InStrB, Len, LenB, Left, LeftB, LCase, LTrim, Mid, MidB, Right, RightB, Space, StrComp, String, String Functions, Trim, UCase

---

AscW

Syntax:	AscW(*string*)
Type:	Intrinsic String Function
Synopsis:	Returns the first Unicode character (32-bits) in *string*.
Description:	AscW should be used when *string* contains Unicode data.
See Also:	Asc, AscB, Chr, ChrB, ChrW, Conversion Functions, InStr, InStrB, Len, LenB, Left, LeftB, LCase, LTrim, Mid, MidB, Right, RightB, Space, StrComp, String, String Functions, Trim, UCase

---

Atn

Syntax:	Atn(*number*)
Type:	Intrinsic Math Function
Synopsis:	Returns the arctangent of *number*.

V

Visual Basic Script

Description:	The *number* parameter is the ratio of two sides of a right triangle. Atn will return the corresponding angle in radians. The range of the result is -pi/2 to pi/2 radians. You can multiply radians to degrees to multiplying radians by 180/pi.
See Also:	Abs, Cos, Exp, Log, Math Functions, Randomize, Rnd, Sin, Sqr, Tan

Back

Syntax:	*history*.Back(*number*)
Type:	Method
Synopsis:	Moves backwards in the history list—exactly as if the browser's back button was clicked.

Example:

```
' Move backwards five times.
History.Back(5)
```

BgColor

Syntax 1:	*document*.BgColor = *rbgValue*
Syntax 1:	*document*.BgColor = *string*
Type:	Method - applies to History objects
Synopsis:	Gets or sets *document*'s background color.
Description:	You can set the color by specifying a RGB value in hexadecimal or by specifying a color name. The "Color Names" entry lists all of the color names that you can use.

You can only set this property while the document is being parsed. An OnLoad event handler procedure is a good place to set document properties.

Example:

```
' Set the background color to gold.
Document.BgColor = &HFFD700
```

See Also:	FgColor

Blur

Syntax:	*element*.Blue
Type:	Method
Synopsis:	Clears the focus from *element*.
Description:	This method causes the OnBlur event.

Boolean Variables

Type:	Definition
Description:	Boolean variables have only two values, True(1) or False(0). If you use the CBool function to convert a variable into the boolean subtype, anything that is not zero will become True.

VBScript functions and Web browser functions sometime handle boolean variables in different ways. The example section highlights these differences. However, in real world usage you rarely display the value of boolean values. They are almost always used to indicate status (did the mail arrive? has the checkbox been selected?).

Example:

```
blnTemp = True ' using a constant
blnTemp = CByte(1) ' using a conversion function
Alert blnTemp ' displays "-1"
MsgBox blnTemp ' displays "True"
```

Byte Variables

Type:	Definition
Description:	Byte variables can have whole number values ranging from 0 to 255, inclusive.

Example:

```
bytTemp = CBool(234)
```

Call

Syntax:	Call *name*([*argumentlist*])
Type:	Keyword
Synopsis:	Runs a Sub or Function procedure.
Description:	In most cases, the Call keyword is optional. However, if you do use it, then you must also surround the procedure parameter's with parentheses. If you don't use Call then you must also omit the surrounding parentheses. Any return value from functions invoked using Call are ignored.

Example:

```
Call myFunction(parameterOne, parameterTwo)
myFunction parameterOne, parameterTwo
```

See Also:	Function, Procedure, Sub

CBool

Syntax:	CBool(*expression*)
Type:	Intrinsic Conversion Function
Synopsis:	Converts *expression* into a Boolean subtype.
Description:	If *expression* is zero, then False is returned, otherwise True is returned. If *expression* is not numeric, a run-time error will occur.

Example:

```
blnBigBook = CBool(numPages > 500)
```

See Also:	CByte, CDate, CDbl, CInt, CLng, Conversion Functions, CSng, CStr

CByte

Syntax:	CByte(*expression*)
Type:	Intrinsic Conversion Function

Synopsis:	Converts *expression* into a Byte subtype.
Description:	If *expression* can't be converted into a Byte value, a run-time error will occur.
See Also:	CBool, CDate, CDbl, CInt, CLng, Conversion Functions, CSng, CStr

CDate

Syntax:	CDate(*expression*)
Type:	Intrinsic Conversion Function
Synopsis:	Converts *expression* into a Date subtype.
Description:	The IsDate function can determine if conversion is possible for *expression*. You can specify date and time literals or a variable as *expression*. When converting a number to a date, the whole number portion is converted to a date. Any fractional part of the number is converted to a time of day, starting at midnight. CDate usually only recognizes date formats that correspond to the locale setting of your system. The correct order of day, month, and year may not be determined if it is provided in a format other than one of the recognized date settings.

Example:

```
myBirthday = CDate("9-20-96")
```

See Also:	CBool, CByte, CDbl, CInt, CLng, Conversion Functions, CSng, CStr

CDbl

Syntax:	CDbl(*expression*)
Type:	Intrinsic Conversion Function
Synopsis:	Converts *expression* into a Double subtype.
See Also:	CBool, CByte, CDate, CInt, CLng, Conversion Functions, CSng, CStr

Checked

Syntax 1:	*element*.Checked
Syntax 2:	*element*.Checked = *status*
Type:	Property
Synopsis:	Gets or sets the checked state of *element*.
Description:	If you are testing the checked state, a 1 is returned if *element* is checked, otherwise a 0 is returned. If you are setting the checked state, *status* can be either 1 or 0.

Chr

Syntax:	Chr(*charcode*)
Type:	Intrinsic Conversion Function
Synopsis:	Returns the character associated with *charcode*.
Description:	The ANSI standard assigns a number to each alphanumeric character. The numbers from 0 to 31 are associated with various control functions. For example, the tab character is 9 and the carriage return character is a 13.
See Also:	Asc, AscB, AscW, ChrB, ChrW, Conversion Functions, InStr, InStrB, Len, LenB, Left, LeftB, LCase, LTrim, Mid, MidB, Right, RightB, Space, StrComp, String, String Functions, Trim, UCase

ChrB

Syntax:	ChrB(*charcode*)
Type:	Intrinsic Conversion Function
Synopsis:	Returns the byte associated with *charcode*.
Description:	ChrB is used for strings with byte data.
See Also:	Asc, AscB, AscW, Chr, ChrW, Conversion Functions, InStr, InStrB, Len, LenB, Left, LeftB, LCase, LTrim, Mid, MidB, Right, RightB, Space, StrComp, String, String Functions, Trim, UCase

ChrW

Syntax:	ChrW(*charcode*)
Type:	Intrinsic Conversion Function
Synopsis:	Returns the Unicode character associated with *charcode*.
Description:	ChrW is used for strings with byte data. Unicode characters are 32-bits wide.
See Also:	Asc, AscB, AscW, Chr, ChrB, Conversion Functions, InStr, InStrB, Len, LenB, Left, LeftB, LCase, LTrim, Mid, MidB, Right, RightB, Space, StrComp, String, String Functions, Trim, UCase

CInt

Syntax:	CInt(expression)
Type:	Intrinsic Conversion Function
Synopsis:	Converts *expression* into a Integer subtype.
Description:	CInt is used when you need to force integer math. If *expression* lies outside the acceptable range for the Integer subtype, an error occurs. The CInt function will round the value of *expression*, not truncate it like Fix and Int. Fractional values of .5 and higher cause CInt to round up to the nearest even number.

Example:

```
a = CInt(0.5) ' a will equal 0
b = CInt(1.5) ' b will equal 2
```

See Also:	CBool, CByte, CDate, CDbl, CLng, Conversion Functions, CSng, CStr

Clear

Syntax 1:	*document*.Clear
Syntax 2:	*err*.Clear
Type:	Method
Synopsis:	Closes *document* and updates the display or clears the property settings for *err*.

Document Object Description:	There seems to be some confusion in the Microsoft documentation about the necessity of calling the Clear method. Most of the documentation refers solely to the Close method; however, the Close method does not actually close the document; it simply updates the display according to that same documentation. My best advice is to ignore the Clear method and solely use Close. Hopefully, this confusing situation will be rectified shortly by Microsoft.
Error Object Description:	The Clear method should be called to clear the Err object when an error has been handled. The Err object is automatically cleared after On Error Resume Next, Exit Sub, and Exit Function statements.

ClearTimeout

Syntax:	*window*.clearTimeout(*timerId*)
Type:	Method - applies to Window objects
Synopsis:	Clears a timeout timer so that it will not go off.
Description:	If *window* is not specified, the current window object is used.

Example:

```
' Setup a time so that the Send button is clicked in
' five seconds.
clickTimer = setTimeout ("btnSend_OnClick", 5000, "VBScript")

' Clear the timer to avoid automatically clicking
' the Send button.
clearTimer(clickTimer)
```

See Also:	setTimeout

Click

Syntax:	*element*.Click
Type:	Method
Synopsis:	Emulates the user clicking *element*.
Description:	This method causes an OnClick event.

CLng

Syntax:	CLng(*expression*)
Type:	Intrinsic Conversion Function
Synopsis:	Converts *expression* into a Long subtype.
Description:	CLng is used when you need to force integer math. The CLng function will round the value of expression, not truncate it like Fix and Int. Fractional values of .5 and higher cause CLng to round up to the nearest even number.

Example:

```
a = CLng(0.5) ' a will equal 0
b = CLng(1.5) ' b will equal 2
```

See Also:	CBool, CByte, CDate, CDbl, CInt, Conversion Functions, CSng, CStr

Close

Syntax 1:	*document*.Close
Syntax 2:	*window*.Close
Type:	Method
Synopsis:	Closes *document* and updates the display or Closes *window*.
Description:	If *window* is not specified, then the current window object is used. This means that if you simply see a Close method without an attached object, it always means that a window is being closed.

Color Names

Type:	Definition
Description:	Table 28.3 lists all of the color names that you can use in VB-Script. While you normally specify the RGB value as one six-digit hexadecimal number, the table displays the numbers as separate red, green, and blue two-digit numbers to make understanding the numbers easier.

V

Visual Basic Script

| Table 28.3   VBScript's Color Names | | | |
Color	Red	Green	Blue

Cookie

Syntax 1:	*result* = *document*.Cookie
Syntax 2:	*document*.Cookie = *string*
Type:	Read-Only Property
Synopsis:	Gets or sets *document*'s cookie.
Description:	Cookies are pieces of information that can be associated with *document*. Setting a cookie overrides any cookie that was previously associated with *document*.

Confirm

Syntax:	*result* = *window*.Confirm(*string*)
Type:	Method - applies to Window objects
Synopsis:	Displays a message box with OK and Cancel buttons.
Description:	If *window* is not specified, then the current window object is used.
Return Value:	Returns True if the OK button was clicked, False otherwise.

Example:

```
<!-- This document shows how to use the
 Confirm method.
 -->
<HTML>
 <HEAD>
 <TITLE>VB Script Example Page</TITLE>
 </HEAD>
 <BODY>
 <H1>VB Script Example Page</H1>
 <SCRIPT language="VBScript">
<!--
If Confirm("Click OK to take a survery.") Then
document.open
document.write "Here is the survey<P>"
Else
document.write "Thanks, anyway.<P>"
```

```
    End If
    document.close
    -->
    </SCRIPT>
    </BODY>
    </HTML>
```

Picture:

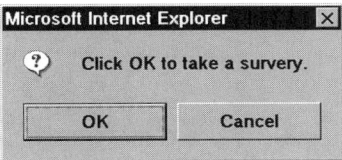

Fig. 28.3 Another Alert message box.

Constants

Type: Definition

Description: VBScript has five built-in constants as shown in Table 28.4. You might notice that the descriptions of True and False do not mention an actual value. This is because their value is irrelevant—just the fact that they are opposites is important.

Table 28.4 **VBScript's Constants**

Constant	Description
Empty	Indicates that a variable has not been initialized.
False	The opposite of True.
Nothing	Indicates that a reference does not refer to anything.
Null	Indicates that a variable has no valid data.
True	The opposite of False.

Conversion Functions

Type: Definition

Description: VBScript has quite a few intrinsic functions designed to convert from one data type to another, from one base to another, or simply from one format to another. Table 28.5 lists the conversion functions available in VBScript.

Table 28.5 VBScript Conversion Functions

Function	Page Number	Description
Abs	p. 812	Returns the absolute value of a number.
Asc	p. 818	Returns the ANSI code of the first character in a string.
AscB	p. 819	Returns the first byte in a string.
AscW	p. 819	Returns the first Unicode character (32-bits) in a string.
CBool	p. 822	Converts a value into a Boolean subtype.
CByte	p. 822	Converts a value into a Byte subtype.
CDate	p. 823	Converts a value into a Date subtype.
CDbl	p. 823	Converts a value into a Double subtype.
Chr	p. 824	Returns the character associated with an ASCI code.
ChrB	p. 824	Returns the byte associated with a character code.
ChrW	p. 825	Returns the Unicode character associated with a character code.
CInt	p. 825	Converts a value into a Integer subtype.
CLng	p. 827	Converts a value into a Long subtype.
CSng	p. 831	Converts a value into a Single subtype.
CStr	p. 831	Converts a value into a String subtype.
DateSerial	p. 834	Returns a string representing the year, month, and year parameters.
DateValue	p. 835	Returns a Date value representing its parameter.
Fix	p. 851	Returns the integer portion of a number.
Hex	p. 858	Converts the value of a string into hexadecimal.
Int	p. 864	Returns the integer half of a number.
Oct	p. 887	Converts the value of a string into hexadecimal.
Sgn	p. 909	Returns 1, -1, or 0 depending on the sign of the parameter.
TimeSerial	p. 916	Returns a Date variable that represents the hour, minute, and second parameters.
TimeValue	p. 917	Returns a Date value representing its parameter.

Cos

Syntax:	Cos(*angle*)
Type:	Intrinsic Math Function
Synopsis:	Returns the cosine of *angle*.
Description:	The cosine is the ratio of the length of a right angle's side adjacent to the angle divided by the length of the hypotenuse. The returned value is in the range -1 to 1.

See Also: Abs, Atn, Exp, Log, Math Functions, Randomize, Rnd, Sin, Sqr, Tan

CSng

Syntax: CSng(*expression*)

Type: Intrinsic Conversion Function

Synopsis: Converts *expression* into a Single subtype.

Description: CSng is used when you need to force single-precision math. If expression lies outside the acceptable range for the Single subtype, an error occurs.

See Also: CBool, CByte, CDate, CDbl, CInt, CLng, Conversion Functions, CStr

CStr

Syntax: CStr(*expression*)

Type: Intrinsic Conversion Function

Synopsis: Converts *expression* into a String subtype.

Description: The CStr function converts *expression* into a string in a manner that depends on the data type of *expression*. Table 28.6 shows how the conversion is performed.

Table 28.6   Return Values From CStr

Data Type of Expression	Return Format
Boolean	"True" or "False".
Date	The date expressed using the short-date format of your system.
Null	Causes a run-time error.
Empty	A zero-length string ("").
Error	A string with the word Error followed by the error number.
Numeric	A string with the number.

See Also: CBool, CByte, CDate, CDbl, CInt, CLng, Conversion Functions, CSng

Date

Syntax: Date

Type: Intrinsic Date/Time Function

Synopsis: Returns the current system date.

Example:

    Alert Date

Picture:

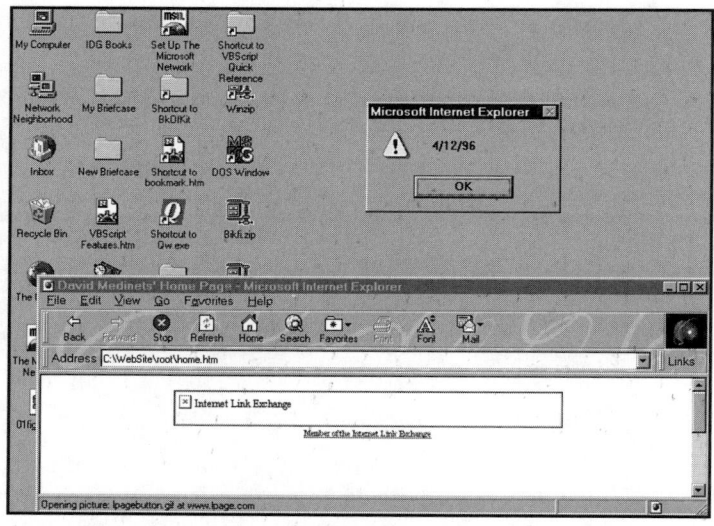

Fig. 28.4   This is what the output from the Date function looks like.

See Also: DateSerial, DateValue, Date/Time Functions, Day, Hour, Minute, Month, Now, Second, Time, TimeSerial, TimeValue, Weekday, Year

Date Variables

Type: Definition

Description: Date variables can range from January 1, 100 to December 31, 9999. Internally, the number one represents the date 1/1/100. Each whole number represents a day and the decimal number represents the time. Negative numbers count back from December 30, 1899 and positive numbers count forward from that date. Decimal values of .0 represent midnight and .5 represents noon.

Literal dates are created by delimiting the date with the # character as shown in the example section below.

Example:

```
dtmFirstDay = CDate(1.234) ' equals 12/31/1899 5:36:58AM
dtmFirstDay = CDate(1) ' equals 12/31/1899
dblFirstday = CDbl(dtmFirstDay) ' equals 1
dtmBirthday = #09-20-96# ' equals 9/20/1996
```

Date/Time Functions

Type: Definition

Description: VBScript has many intrinsic functions that work with date and time values. Table 28.7 lists the date/time functions available in VBScript.

Table 28.7   VBScript Date/Time Functions

Function	Page Number	Description
Date	p. 832	Returns the current system date.
DateSerial	p. 834	Returns a string representing the year, month, and year parameters.
DateValue	p. 835	Returns a Date value representing its parameter.
Day	p. 836	Returns the day of the month of its parameter.
Hour	p. 860	Returns the hour of the day of its parameter.
Minute	p. 878	Returns the minute value of its parameter.
Month	p. 879	Returns the month value of its parameter.
Now	p. 884	Returns the current date and time as a Date value.
Second	p. 907	Returns the seconds value of its parameter.
Time	p. 916	Returns the current system time as a Date value.
TimeSerial	p. 916	Returns a Date value representing its parameters.
TimeValue	p. 917	Returns a Date value representing its parameter.
Weekday	p. 926	Returns the day of the week of its parameter.
Year	p. 929	Returns the year of its parameter.

V

Visual Basic Script

DateSerial

Syntax:	DateSerial(*year, month, day*)
Type:	Intrinsic Conversion and Date/Time Function
Synopsis:	Returns a string representing the year, month, and year parameters.
Description:	The *year* parameter can range from 100 to 9999—the values of 0 to 99 are interpreted as the years 1900 to 1999. The *month* parameter can range from 1-12. And *day* can range from 1-31. You can pass expressions instead of literals to perform some basic date arithmetic. The example shows how to subtract two from a given month. Parameters that are too large to fit into the normal range will carry over into the next larger unit. For instance, a day parameter of 34 will increment the month parameter. If one of the parameters falls outside the range -32,768 to 32,767, or if the date specified by the three arguments falls outside the acceptable range of dates, an error occurs.

Example:

```
intMonth = 6
Alert DateSerial(1996, intMonth - 2, 12)
```

Picture:

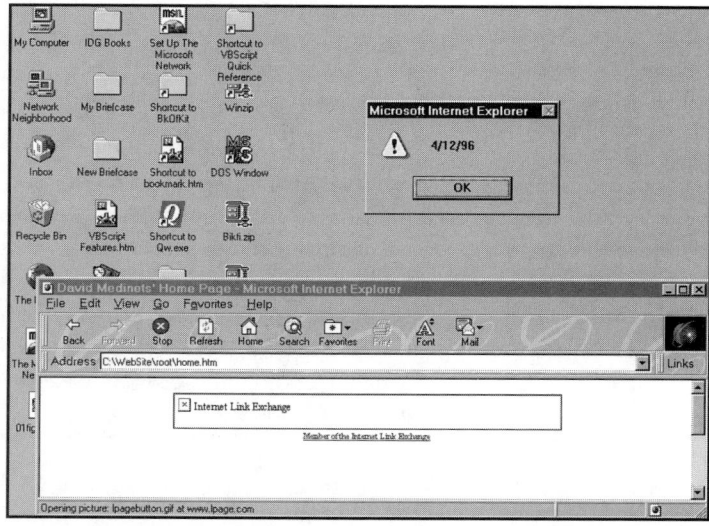

Fig. 28.5 This is what the output from the DateSerial function looks like.

See Also: Date, DateValue, Date/Time Functions, Day, Hour, Minute, Month, Now, Second, Time, TimeSerial, TimeValue, Weekday, Year

DateValue

Syntax: DateValue(*date*)

Type: Intrinsic Date/Time Function

Synopsis: Returns a Date value representing *date*.

Description: The *date* parameter is a literal string or a variable that holds a date string. However, *date* can also be any expression that represents a date value. Time information in *date* is ignored, but incorrect time will cause an error. DateValue can recognize the abbreviated forms of each month name (Jan, Feb, and so on). The current year of your computer's system date will be used if date does not specify a year.

Example:

```
Alert DateValue("April 28, 1995")
```

Picture:

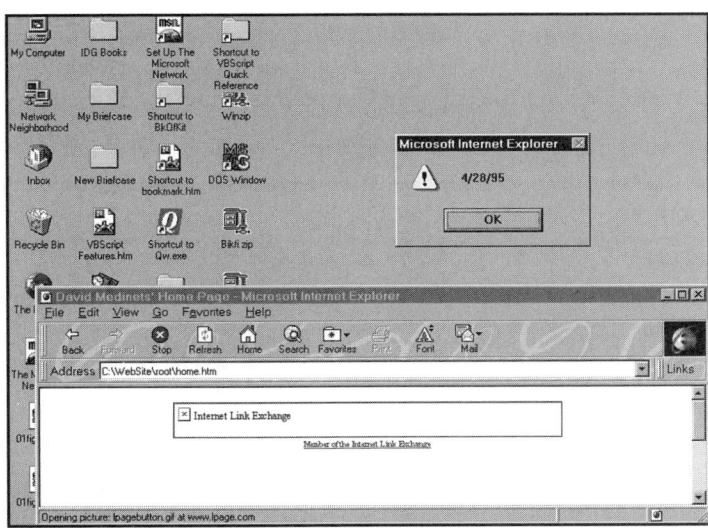

Fig. 28.6   This is what the output from the DateValue function looks like.

See Also: Date, DateSerial, Date/Time Functions, Day, Hour, Minute, Month, Now, Second, Time, TimeSerial, TimeValue, Weekday, Year

Day

Syntax:	Day(*date*)
Type:	Intrinsic Date/Time Function
Synopsis:	Returns the day of the month of *date*—which can range from 1 to 31.
Description:	If *date* contains Null, Null is returned.
See Also:	Date, Date/Time Functions, DateSerial, DateValue, Hour, Minute, Month, Now, Second, Time, TimeSerial, TimeValue, Weekday, Year

DefaultChecked

Syntax 1:	*element*.DefaultChecked
Syntax 2:	*element*.DefaultChecked = *status*
Type:	Property
Synopsis:	Gets or sets the default checked state of *element*.
Description:	If you are testing the default checked state, a 1 is returned if *element* is checked by default, otherwise a 0 is returned. If you are setting the default checked state, *status* can be either 1 or 0.

DefaultStatus

Syntax 1:	*window*.DefaultStatus
Syntax 2:	*window*.DefaultStatus = *string*
Type:	Property - applies to a Window object
Synopsis:	Gets or sets the default status text for the lower left portion of the status bar.

Example:

```
' set the default status text.
self.defaultStatus = "Ready for Input"

' assign the default status text to a variable
strDefaultText = self.defaultStatus
```

DefaultValue

Syntax 1:	*element*.DefaultValue
Syntax 2:	*element*.DefaultValue = *string*
Type:	Property
Synopsis:	Gets or sets the default value of *element*.

Description

Syntax 1:	Err.Description
Syntax 2:	Err.Description = *stringExpression*
Type:	Property
Synopsis:	Gets or sets the description of an error.
Description:	The Description property holds a brief description of the error that the Err object represents. If Err.Number represents a run-time error and the Description property is not explicitly set, then the default error description will be used.

Example:

```
Err.Description = "No more items to process."
Err.Number = 2000
```

Dim

Syntax:	Dim varname[([subscripts])][, varname[([subscripts])]]...
Type:	Keyword
Synopsis:	Declares script-level or procedure-level variables.
Description:	The varname parameter indicates the name of the variable being declared. The subscripts parameter, if used, indicates the dimensions of the associated varname parameter. An array variable can have up to 60 dimensions. For example, Dim aryTemp(10, 15) creates an array of 11x16 elements. You only need to specify the upper bounds of each dimension; the lower bound will always be zero. Dynamic arrays can be created using empty parentheses and the ReDim keyword. An error will occur if a variable is re-dimensioned.

All variables are initialized when declared with Dim. Strings are initialized to a zero-length string ("") and number variables are initialized to zero.

Local variables can be created by using Dim inside Sub or Function procedures. Otherwise, all procedures can access all variables—in other words, variables have a script-level scope by default.

Most programmers place all Dim statements at the beginning of a script or procedure where they are easy to find.

Example:

```
Dim a(10,10,10) ' a is an array with three dimensions.
Dim b(), c() ' b and c are dynamic arrays.
```

See Also: Array Variables, Erase, IsArray, LBound, ReDim, UBound

Division (/)

Syntax:	*result = operand1 / operand2*
Type:	Arithmetic Operator
Synopsis:	Divides operand1 by operand2
Description:	If either operand has the Null value, then *result* is Null. Operands that have the Empty value are equivalent to zero. And, of course, division by zero results in a run-time error.
See Also:	On Error, Operators

Do

Syntax 1:	Do While condition [statements] Loop
Syntax 2:	Do Until condition [statements] Loop
Syntax 3:	Do [statements] Loop While condition

Syntax 4:	Do
	[statements]
	Loop Until condition

Type: Keyword

Synopsis: Repeatedly executes a statement block while a condition is True or until a condition becomes True.

Description: The only difference between the Do While...Loop and the Do Until...Loop is how the conditional expression is tested. The while loop will continue until the condition is false and the until loop will continue until the condition is true. You decide which one to use based on your own program logic.

There are two forms of each Do...Loop statement. The first form tests the conditional expression before executing the statement block and the second checks the conditional statement after the statement block. Again, the choice depends on your program logic. However, the second form implies that the statement block will only be executed at least once—a handy feature to remember when reading and testing information from a data file.

You can use the Exit Do keyword to exit the loop early. You can nest one Do loop inside another.

Example:

```
<SCRIPT LANGUAGE="VBScript">
<!--
 intTemp = 0
 Do While intTemp < 5
 Alert intTemp
 intTemp = intTemp + 1
 Loop

 intTemp = 0
 Do Until intTemp > 5
 Alert intTemp
 intTemp = intTemp + 1
 Loop

 intTemp = 0
 Do
 Alert intTemp
 intTemp = intTemp + 1
 Loop Until intTemp > 5

 intTemp = 0
 Do
 Alert intTemp
 intTemp = intTemp + 1
```

```
    Loop While intTemp < 5
    -->
    </SCRIPT>
```

See Also: Exit Do

Document (Method)

Type: Object

Synopsis: Represents the Document object associated with *window*.

Description: Document objects are directly analogous to HTML pages. You use the document object to access hypertext links and form elements of the HTML page.

If the page has objects created with the <OBJECT> tag, you can refer directly to them by name instead of indirectly using the document object.

If *window* is not specified, the Document object of the current window is returned.

Some of a document's properties can only be set in non-event statements—in other words, the properties can only be set when the HTML document is parsed. You can use an OnLoad event handler to set document properties.

Table 28.8   Methods of Document Objects

Method	Page Number	Description
Clear	p. 825	Closes the document and updates the document's display.
Close	p. 827	Updates the document's display.
Open	p. 892	Opens a document for output.
Write	p. 928	Writes a string into a document.
WriteLn	p. 929	Writes a string into a document with a newline at its end.

Table 28.9   Properties of Document Objects

Property	Page Number	Description
aLinkColor	p. 813	Gets or sets the color of active links.
Anchors	p. 814	An array of a document's anchors.
BgColor	p. 820	Gets or sets a document's background color.
Cookie	p. 828	Gets or sets a document's cookie.
FgColor	p. 850	Gets or sets a document's foreground color.
Forms	p. 854	An array of a document's forms.
LastModified	p. 868	The last modified date of a document.

Property	Page Number	Description
LinkColor	p. 873	Gets or sets the color of hyperlinks.
Links	p. 873	An array of a document's hyperlinks.
Location	p. 875	Gets the document's location object.
Referrer	p. 903	Gets the URL of the referring document.
Title	p. 917	Gets the document's title.
vLinkColor	p. 925	Gets or sets the color of visited links.

Document (Property)

Syntax:	*window*.Document
Type:	Property
Synopsis:	Returns the Document object associated with *window*.
Description:	For more information about Document objects, see the "Document (Object)" Entry.

Double Precision Numbers

Type:	Definition
Description:	Double-precision variables can have over 300 digits—so that can get pretty large.

Example:

```
3.1415297
31415927e-7
.31415297E1
```

Element

Type: Object

Synopsis:	Represents a control or object on an HTML document.
Description:	Information about form elements are accessed through the Elements property of a form object. See the "Elements" entry for more information.

Table 28.10 lists each type of HTML element and the events, methods and properties that you can use with them. ActiveX controls can also be considered form elements, but there are too many of them to describe here. Refer to the documentation that came with the ActiveX controls for more information.

Table 28.10	Element Types		
Type	**Events**	**Methods**	**Properties**
Button	OnClick	Click, Reset, Submit	Form, Name, Value
Checkbox	OnClick	Click	Checked, DefaultChecked, Form, Name, Value
Hidden			Name, Value
Password		Blur, Focus, Select	DefaultValue, Form, Name, Value
Radio	OnClick	Click, Focus	Checked, Form, Name, Value
Select	OnBlur, OnChange, OnFocus	Blur, Focus	Length, Name, Options, SelectedIndex
Text	OnBlur, OnChange, OnFocus, OnSelect	Blur, Focus, Select	DefaultValue, Form, Name, Value
Textarea	OnBlur, OnChange, OnFocus, OnSelect	Blur, Focus, Select	DefaultValue, Form, Name, Value

Table 28.11	Events of an Element Object	
Event	**Page Number**	**Description**
OnBlur	p. 887	Happens when the element loses the focus.
OnChange	p. 887	Happens when the element changes.
OnClick	p. 887	Happens when the element is clicked.
OnFocus	p. 888	Happens when the element gets the focus.
OnSelect	p. 890	Happens when the contents of the element are selected.

Table 28.12	Methods of an Element Object	
Method	**Page Number**	**Description**
Blur	p. 821	Clears the focus from an element.
Click	p. 826	Fires the OnClick event.
Focus	p. 851	Sets the focus to an element.
Select	p. 907	Selects the contents of the element.

Table 28.13	**Properties of an Element Object**	
Property	**Page Number**	**Description**
Checked	p. 824	Gets or sets the checkbox's checked state.
DefaultChecked	p. 836	Gets or sets the checkbox's default checked state.
DefaultValue	p. 837	Gets or sets the element's default value.
Form	p. 852	Gets the form object containing the element.
Length	p. 870	Gets the number of options in a selected element.
Name	p. 882	Gets or sets the element's name.
Options	p. 897	Gets the <OPTIONS> tag for a selected element.
SelectedIndex	p. 908	Gets the index for the selected option.
Value	p. 920	Gets or sets the element's value.

Elements

Syntax:	*form*.Elements[*index*]
Type:	Property
Synopsis:	An array of objects and controls associated with *form*.
Description:	If the form elements are named, you can access them directly by name. Otherwise, use *index* to specify which element in the array you want.

Example:

```
' Find out how many element the form called
' myForm has.
intNumElements = Document.myForm.Elements.Length

' Assign the name of the third element to strName
strName = Document.Forms[2].name
```

Empty

Syntax:	Empty
Type:	Constant
Synopsis:	Indicates that a variable has not been initialized.

Example:

```
numRecords = Empty
```

See Also: IsEmpty, IsNull, Null

Encoding

Syntax 1:	*form*.Encoding
Syntax 2:	*form*.Encoding = *string*
Type:	Property
Synopsis:	Gets or sets the encoding for a form.
Description:	The encoding of a form is its mime type. For example, "text/html."

> **Caution**
>
> In Internet Explorer v3.0, this property has no effect on the operation of the form.

End Function

Type:	Keyword
Synopsis:	Ends a function definition.
See Also:	Function, Procedure

End Sub

Type:	Keyword
Synopsis:	Ends a subroutine definition.
See Also:	Sub, Procedure

Equality (=)

Syntax:	operand1 = operand2
Type:	Comparison Operator
Synopsis:	Returns True if operand1 is equal to operand2.
Description:	If either operand has the Null value, then result is Null. Operands that have the Empty value are equivalent to zero.

The equality operator is frequently used in conditional expression for If, Do, and For statements.

Example:

```
' In this If statement, the equality operator
' is used in the conditional expression.
if intNumPages = 15 Then
 Alert "Ok"
End If

' In the third assignment statement below, the
' equality operator is used to give a value of
' False to intTest.
intA = 10
intB = 5
intTest = (intA = intB) ' intTest equals False.
```

See Also:	Operators

Eqv

Syntax:	result = operand1 Eqv operand2
Type:	Operator
Synopsis:	Returns True when both operands are logically equivalent.
Description:	Both operands need to be equal to True or both operands must be False in order for True to be returned.
	If the operands are numeric, a bitwise comparson of identically placed bits is performed.
See Also:	Operators

Erase

Syntax:	Erase *array*
Type:	Intrinsic Array Function
Synopsis:	Reinitializes fixed-size arrays and frees memory associated with dynamic arrays.
Description:	Each element of a fixed-size array is set to zero if numeric, a zero-length string if string, or the special Nothing value if an object reference. If you need to reuse an erased dynamic array, use ReDim to redeclare the array's dimensions.
See Also:	Array Variables, Dim, IsArray, LBound, ReDim, UBound

Err

Syntax 1:	Err.*property*
Syntax 2:	Err.*method*
Type:	Object
Synopsis:	Holds information about run-time errors.
Properties:	Description, Number, Source
Methods:	Clear, Raise
Description:	The generator an error (the VBScript engine, OLE Objects, or the VBScript script) is responsible for setting the properties of the Err object. The Raise method will generate a run-time error and the Clear method will clear a run-time error.

The Clear method is executed after every On Error Resume Next, Exit Sub, or Exit Function statement.

The Err object is available to all procedures—it has script-level scope.

Table 28.14 Methods of an Err Object		
Methods	**Page Number**	**Description**
Clear	p. 825	Clears property settings for an Err object.
Raise	p. 901	Generates a run-time error.

Table 28.15	Properties of an Err Object	
Property	**Page Number**	**Description**
Description	p. 837	Gets or sets the description of an error.
Number	p. 885	Gets or sets a numeric value specifying an error.
Source	p. 910	Gets or sets the name of the object or application that originally generated the error.

Events

Type: Definition

Description: The <A>, <BODY>, <FORM>, <INPUT>, and <OBJECT> HTML tags all have events associated with them. You can place VBScript statements directly inside the tags or you can create an *event handler* procedure. Both methods of responding to events are covered in the "Event Handling" section.

Table 28.16	VB Script Events	
Event	**Page Number**	**Description**
OnBlur	p. 887	Happens when a control or object loses focus.
OnChange	p. 887	Happens when a control or object has changed.
OnClick	p. 887	Happens when a control, object, or hyperlink is clicked.
OnFocus	p. 888	Happens when a control or object gets the focus.
OnLoad	p. 888	Happens when a document is loaded.
OnMouseMove	p. 889	Happens when the mouse pointer moves while over a link.
OnMouseOver	p. 889	Happens when the mouse pointer moves over a link.
OnSelect	p. 890	Happens when the contents of a control or object are selected.
OnSubmit	p. 890	Happens just before the form's information is sent to the server.
OnUnload	p. 891	Happens when a document is unloaded.

Event Handling

Type: Definition

Description: *Event handlers* are special procedures in VBScript that give it much of its power. They allow the programmer to look for specific user

V

Visual Basic Script

behavior in relation to the HTML page, such as clicking a form
button or moving the mouse pointer over an anchor.

When an event occurs, the browser looks first in the tag for VBScript statements to
handle the event, and then for a procedure named after the form element associated
with the event. For example, if a button called myButton is clicked, then VBScript will
look for a procedure called myButton_OnClick.

When event handlers are embedded in HTML tags, they are typically used in forms, but
some are also used in anchors and links tags. Virtually anything a user can do to interact
with a page is covered with the event handlers, from moving the mouse to leaving the
current page.

The three ways of creating event handlers are shown in the Example section.

Example 1:

```
<!--
  The event handler in this example is placed inside
  the HEAD section of the HTML page. This is a good
  idea of other procedures might call it. Or you want
  to add comments to your scripts.
-->
<HTML><HEAD>
<TITLE>My Test Page</TITLE>
<SCRIPT LANGUAGE="VBScript">
<!--
  Sub maleGender_OnClick
  MsgBox "Thanks for making a selection."
  End Sub
-->
</SCRIPT></HEAD>
<BODY><H1>My Test Page</H1>
<FORM>
<INPUT NAME="maleGender" TYPE="button" VALUE="Male">
</FORM></BODY></HTML>
```

Example 2:

```
<!--
  In this example, the event handler is placed inside
  the form element definition surrounded by single
  quotes. Placing an event handler inside the form
  element should only be done if the hander is very
  small. Otherwise, your HTML page becomes cluttered.
-->
<INPUT NAME="maleGender" TYPE="button" VALUE="Male"
OnClick='MsgBox "Thanks for making a selection."'
LANGUAGE="VBScript">
```

Example 3:

```
<!--
  This example defines the VBScript statements that
  get executed when a specific event happens for a
  specific control. The syntax used in this example
```

```
can be used with any named form element or any
elements defined by the OBJECT tag. Notice that
the Sub keyword is not needed.
-->
<SCRIPT LANGUAGE="VBScript" EVENT="OnClick" FOR="maleGender">
<!--
MsgBox "Thanks for making a selection."
-->
</SCRIPT>
```

Exit

Syntax:	Exit
	Exit Do
	Exit For
	Exit Function
	Exit Sub
Type:	Keyword
Synopsis:	Exits a block of statements or ends the script.
Description:	Exit statements are usually used to alter the flow of program logic in special situations. For example, if the program is inside a loop and the user chooses to cancel the current operation, the Exit Do statement might be used to end the loop.

The Exit Do statement is used to stop all four types of Do...Loop statements.

Each type of Exit statement must be used in the appropriate context. For example, an Exit For statement can't be used to exit from a Do loop.

When an Exit statement is encountered, control is transferred to the statement immediately following the end of the statement block.

Exit Do and Exit For statements are usually combined with an If statement to conditionally exit a statement block. For example, a For loop that counts from 10 to 1,000 might need to be terminated if the user pressed the Esc key.

Example:

```
<SCRIPT LANGUAGE="VBScript">
<!--
' Exit Do
number = 0
Do While number < 100
Print number
If alert = True Then Exit Do
number = number + 1
Loop
```

```
' Exit For
For index = 1 to 10
Print index
If alert = True Then Exit For
Next

-->
</SCRIPT>
```

See Also: Do...Loops, For...Next Loops, Function, Sub

Exp

Syntax: Exp(*number*)

Type: Intrinsic Math Function

Synopsis: Returns e (the base of natural logarithms) raised to a power.

Description: If *number* is greater than roughly 709.782, then an error occurs. The constant e is approximately 2.718282. The Exp function is sometimes called the antologarithm because it complements the Log function.

See Also: Abs, Atn, Cos, Log, Math Functions, Randomize, Rnd, Sin, Sqr, Tan

Exponentiation (^)

Syntax: *result = operand1 ^ operand2*

Type: Arithmetic Operator

Synopsis: Raises *operand1* to the power of *operand2*.

Description: If either operand has the Null value, then *result* is Null. Operands that have the Empty value are equivalent to zero.

See Also: Operators

FgColor

Syntax 1:   *document*.FgColor = *rbgValue*

Syntax 2:   *document*.FgColor = *string*

Type:	Property
Synopsis:	Gets or sets *document*'s foreground color.
Description:	You can set the color by specifying a RGB value in hexadecimal or by specifying a color name. The "Color Names" entry lists all of the color names that you can use.

You can only set this property while the document is being parsed. An OnLoad event handler procedure is a good place to set document properties.

Example:

```
' Set the foreground color to gold.
Document.FgColor = &HFFD700
```

See Also:	BgColor

Fix

Syntax:	Fix(*number*)
Type:	Intrinsic Conversion and Math Function
Synopsis:	Returns the integer portion of *number*.
Description:	If number is negative, Fix returns the first negative number greater than or equal to number. Fix(number) is the same as Sgn(number) * Int(Abs(number)).

Example:

```
a = Fix(-3.37) ' a equals -3.
```

See Also:	CInt, Conversion Functions, Int, Math Functions

Focus

Syntax:	*element*.Focus
Type:	Method
Synopsis:	Sets the focus to *element*.
Description:	This method causes the OnFocus event.

For

Syntax:	For *loopVariable = start* to *end* [STEP *step*] [statements] Next
Type:	Keyword
Synopsis:	Repeatedly executes *statements* for a specific number of times.
Description:	For...Next loops are used to execute a code block a specific number of times. A loop variable is specified for each For...Next statement. The loop variable is initialized to the starting value before the code block is executed. After the execution of the code block, the Step value (*step*) is added to loop variable. If no step is specified, the loop variable is incremented by one.

When For loops are nested, each loop needs to have a unique variable name. See the Example section for a demonstration of nested For loops.

Example:

```
' Count forwards from one to five.
For index = 1 to 5
 Alert index
Next

' Count backwards from five to one.
For index = 5 to 1 Step -1
 Alert index
Next

' Use nested for loop to find row, column pairs.
For row = 0 to 2
 For col = 0 to 2
 Alert "[" & row & "," & col & "]"
 Next
Next
```

See Also:	Do...Loop, Exit

Form

Type:	Object
Synopsis:	Represents an HTML form.

Description: Most HTML form elements have a Form property that references the form containing the element. So if you need to find out which method of data transfer the form that contains the btnYield button uses, then use btnYield.Form.Method.

You can access each element of a form through the form array that is part of the document object. The forms can be accessed by name or by array index. Refer to the Example section to see how this is done.

Note

I believe that accessing forms by form name leads to self-documenting and more robust scripts. Forms are named by using the NAME attribute of the <FORM> HTML tag. By using the form name in a script, you gain the ability to rearrange the HTML forms (move one on top of another or to the end of the document, perhaps) without needing to recalculate the form's index.

If the script tag is defined inside the form tag, then you don't need to specify the document part of the object specification.

Table 28.17   Events of a Form Object

Event	Page Number	Description
OnSubmit	p. 890	Happens just before the form data is sent to the server.

Table 28.18   Methods of a Form Object

Method	Page Number	Description
Submit	p. 915	Sends the form data to the server.

Table 28.19   Properties of a Form Object

Property	Page Number	Description
Action	p. 812	Gets or sets the address that does the form's action.
Elements	p. 841	An array of form objects and controls.
Encoding	p. 844	Gets or sets the encoding for the form.
Method	p. 877	Specifies how data is sent to the server (either GET or POST)
Target	p. 916	Sets the name of the window where the form should be displayed.

Example:

```
<!-- This document shows that the document and
 form names do not need to be specified if
 the script is defined inside the form.
-->
<HTML>
 <HEAD>
```

(continues)

```
<TITLE>VB Script Example Page</TITLE>
</HEAD>
<BODY>
<H1>VB Script Example Page</H1>
<FORM NAME="myForm">
<INPUT NAME=btnLaugh TYPE=button VALUE="Want a laugh?">
<script language="VBScript" for="btnLaugh" event="OnClick">
btnLaugh.value="HA-HA!"
</script>
</FORM>
</BODY>
</HTML>
```

Forms

Syntax:	*document*.Forms[*index*]
Type:	Property
Synopsis:	An array of *document*'s forms.
Description:	See the "Form" entry for more information.

Forward

Syntax:	*history*.Forward(*number*)
Type:	Method
Synopsis:	Moves forwards in the history list—exactly as if the browser's forward button was clicked.

Example:

```
' Move forward five times.
History.Forward(5)
```

Frames

Syntax:	*window*.Frames
Type:	Property - applies to Window objects
Synopsis:	Returns an array of frames contained in *window*.

Example:

```
strURL = Parent.Frames[0].Location.Href
```

> **Caution**
>
> While the Microsoft documentation uses the above example, it generated an error message when I tried it. This problem may be resolved by the time you read this book.

Function

Syntax: Function *name* [(*arglist*)]
             [*statements*]
             [*name = expression*]
             End Function

Type: Keyword

Synopsis: Creates a user-defined function called *name*.

Description: Function statements are used to create user-defined functions. Functions differ from subroutines because they do return a value. Simply assign the return value to a variable with the same name as the function.

All functions should be declared towards the beginning of your script in the HEAD section of your HTML page. This ensures that the functions will be available for use by later VBScript statements.

arglist is an optional list of arguments or parameters that the function can use. Functions always return a value and you specify the value to return by assigning it to a variable named identically to *name*. If you would like the function to assign values to the arguments, use the ByVal keyword inside the parameter list.

Example:

```
' Define a function with one parameter
Function squareIt(intTemp)
 squareIt = intTemp * intTemp
End Function

' Define a function that can modify its
' parameter. This function determines if
' a field's valiue is in the correct range
' and if it is, added the value to an ongoing
' total.
Function IsInValidRange(intField, intMin, intMax, intTotal)
 validate = False
 If intField >= intMin And intField <= intMax Then
 validate = True
 intTotal = intTotal + intField
```

(continues)

```
        End If
    End Function
```

See Also: Procedure, Sub

Go

Syntax: *history*.Go(*number*)

Type: Method

Synopsis: Connects to the URL at position *number* in the history list.

Example:

```
' Connect to the first URL in the
' history list.
history.go(1)
```

Greater Than (>)

Syntax: *operand1* > *operand2*

Type: Comparison Operator

Synopsis: Returns True if *operand1* is greater than *operand2*.

Description: If either operand has the Null value, then *result* is Null. Operands
                        that have the Empty value are equivalent to zero.

The greater than operator is frequently used in conditional expression for If, Do, and For
statements.

Example:

```
' In this If statement, the greater than operator
' is used in the conditional expression.
if intNumPages > 15 Then
 Alert "Ok"
End If

' In the third assignment statement below, the
' greater than operator is used to give a value of
' True to intTest.
intA = 10
intB = 5
intTest = (intA > intB)
```

See Also: Operators

Greater Than Or Equal To (>=)

Syntax: *operand1 >= operand2*

Type: Comparison Operator

Synopsis: Returns True if *operand1* is greater than or equal to *operand2*.

Description: If either operand has the Null value, then *result* is Null. Operands that have the Empty value are equivalent to zero.

The greater than or equal to operator is frequently used in conditional expressions for If, Do, and For statements.

Example:

```
' In this If statement, the >= operator
' is used in the conditional expression.
if intNumPages >= 15 Then
 Alert "Ok"
End If

' In the third assignment statement below, the
' >= operator is used to give a value of
' True to intTest.
intA = 10
intB = 5
intTest = (intA >= intB)
```

See Also: Operators

Hash

Syntax 1:   *link*.Hash

Syntax 2:   *location*.Hash

Syntax 3:   *location*.Hash = *string*

Type: Property

Synopsis: Gets the hash part of *link* or *location*. Sets the hash part of *location*.

Description: The hash part of an URL starts with a hash mark. For example, in http://www.planet.net/trains.htm#Amtrak, the #Amtrak is the hash part of the URL. If the URL has no hash, then Null is returned.

Hex

Syntax:	Hex(*number*)
Type:	Intrinsic Conversion and Math Function
Synopsis:	Returns a string that represents the value of number converted into hexadecimal.
Description:	Only integer values can be converted. If number is not an integer, it is rounded up to the nearest whole number.
See Also:	Conversion Functions, Math Functions

Hierarchies

Type:	Definition
Description:	In an hierarchy, some relationship exists between all objects. For example, Internet Explorer objects have a structure that reflects the construction of an HTML page. The Window object is the parent of all other Internet Explorer objects. The Location, History, and Document objects are all subordinate to the Window object.

Some objects are contained inside other objects. For example, the form called myForm is an object and it is also the property of a Document object. In addition, the Document object is a property of the Window object. Therefore, the form's full specification is Window.Document.myForm.

History (Object)

Type:	Object
Synopsis:	Represents the URLs visited by a window.
Description:	The History object allows access to the browser's history list. You use the object's method in order to select which URL in the history list that you need to connect with.

Table 28.20	Methods of a History Object	
Object	**Page Number**	**Description**
Back	p. 820	Like clicking the browser's back button.
Forward	p. 854	Like clicking the browser's forward button
Go	p. 856	Connects to a specified entry in the history list.

Table 28.21	Properties of a History Object	
Object	**Page Number**	**Description**
Length	p. 870	The number of entries in the list.

History (Property)

Syntax:	*window*.History
Type:	Property
Synopsis:	Returns the History object of *window*.
Description:	If *window* is not specified, the history object of the current window is returned.

Host

Syntax 1:	*link*.Host
Syntax 2:	*location*.Host
Syntax 3:	*location*.Host = *host*
Type:	Property
Synopsis:	Gets the host for *link* or *location*. Sets the host for *location*.
Description:	The *host* parameter is a string of the form, "hostname:port". This property always returns the empty string ("") for the file: protocol.

Hostname

Syntax 1:	*link*.Hostname
Syntax 2:	*location*.Hostname
Syntax 3:	*location*.Hostname = *hostname*
Type:	Property
Synopsis:	Gets the hostname for *link* or *location*. Sets the hostname for *location*.
Description:	The *hostname* parameter can specify either a server name or IP address. This property always returns the empty string ("") for the file: protocol.

Hour

Syntax:	Hour(*time*)
Type:	Intrinsic Time/Date Function
Synopsis:	Returns the hour of the day (from 0 to 23) in *time*.
See Also:	Date, Date/Time Functions, DateSerial, DateValue, Day, Month, Now, Second, Time, TimeSerial, TimeValue, Weekday, Year

Href

Syntax 1:	*link*.Href
Syntax 2:	*location*.Href
Syntax 3:	*location*.Href = *url*
Type:	Property
Synopsis:	Gets the URL for *link* or *location*. Sets the URL for *location*.

If

Syntax 1:	If *condition* Then *statement*

Syntax 2:	If *condition* Then
	[statements]
	End If

Syntax 3:	If *condition* Then
	[statements]
	
	Else
	
	[statements]
	End If

Type:	Keyword
Synopsis:	Optionally Executes statements based on *condition*.
Description:	The Else syntax is optional—only use it when statements need to be executed if *condition* is false.

Example:

```
If maritalStatus = "Married" Then
 MsgBox "Congradulations!"
 moreQuestions = True
Else
 MsgBox "Good Luck!"
End If
```

Imp

Syntax:	*result = operand1* Imp *operand2*
Type:	Operator
Synopsis:	Performs a logical implication on two operands.
Description:	The result of the logical implication can be found using Table 28.22 unless the operands are numeric. If the operands are numeric, a bitwise comparson of identically placed bits is performed using Table 28.23.

Table 28.22   The Results of the Imp Operator

Operand1	Operand2	Result
True	True	True
True	False	False
True	Null	Null
False	True	True
False	False	True
False	Null	True
Null	True	True
Null	False	Null
Null	Null	Null

Table 28.23   The Results of the Imp Operator for Numeric Operands

Bit in Operand1	Bit in Operand2	Result
0	0	1
0	1	1
1	0	0
1	1	1

See Also: Operators

Inequality (<>)

Syntax: *operand1 <> operand2*

Type: Comparison Operator

Synopsis: Returns True if *operand1* does not equal *operand2*.

Description: If either operand has the Null value, then *result* is Null. Operands
                     that have the Empty value are equivalent to zero.

The inequality operator is frequently used in conditional expression for If, Do, and For
statements.

Example:

```
' In this If statement, the inequality operator
' is used in the conditional expression.
if intNumPages <> 15 Then
 Alert "Ok"
End If
```

```
' In the third assignment statement below, the
' inequality operator is used to give a value of
' True to intTest.
intA = 10
intB = 5
intTest = (intA <> intB)
```

See Also: Operators

InputBox

Syntax: InputBox(*prompt* [, *title*][, *default*][, *xpos*][, *ypos*][, *helpfile, context*])

Type: Intrinsic Function

Synopsis: Displays a prompt in a dialog box, waits for the user to enter text or click a button.

Description: The *prompt* parameter will be displayed in the dialog box for the user to read. The *title* parameter will be displayed in the title bar of the dialog box. The *default* parameter will be displayed in the text box where the user entered his input. The *xpos* and *ypos* parameters specify, in twips, the horizontal and vertical distance of the dialog box from the top left edge of the screen. If *xpos* is omitted, the dialog box will be horizontally centered. If *ypos* is omitted, the dialog box will be placed about one-third of the way down the screen. The *helpfile* parameter is the name of a help file that will provide context-sensitive help and context is the ID number of the topic that should be displayed when the user presses the F1 key.

InputBox will return the contents of the text box if the user presses ENTER or clicks the OK button. A zero-length string ("") will be returned if the Cancel button is clicked.

Example:

```
name = InputBox "Please enter your name",
  "Name Entry Phase", "John Doe"
```

InStr

Syntax: InStr([*start,*] *string1, string2* [, *compare*])

Type: Intrinsic String Function

Synopsis: Returns the location of *string2* in *string1*.

Description: The *start* parameter lets you start the search at a position other than beginning of *string1*. The *compare* parameter controls the type of search that is performed. Normally, a binary comparison is performed. However, if you use a *compare* value of 1 then a textual, case-insensitive comparison is performed. If *compare* is Null, an error occurs. The *start* parameter must be specified if the *compare* parameter is specified.

Example:

```
Alert InStr(10, "This is a fine test", "test")
```

See Also: Asc, AscB, AscW, Chr, ChrB, ChrW, InStrB, Len, LenB, Left, LeftB, LCase, LTrim, Mid, MidB, Right, RightB, Space, StrComp, String, String Functions, Trim, UCase

---

InStrB

Syntax: InStrB([*start*,] *string1*, *string2* [, *compare*])

Type: Intrinsic String Function

Synopsis: Returns the byte position of *string2* in *string1*.

Description: InStrB is used for binary data contained in strings.

See Also: Asc, AscB, AscW, Chr, ChrB, ChrW, InStr, Len, LenB, Left, LeftB, LCase, LTrim, Mid, MidB, Right, RightB, Space, StrComp, String, String Functions, Trim, UCase

---

Int

Syntax: Int(*number*)

Type: Intrinsic Conversion and Math Function

Synopsis: Returns the integer half of *number*.

Description: If *number* is negative, the first negative number less than or equal to *number* is returned.

Example:

```
intA = Int(10.34) ' intA equals 10
intB = Int(-4.4) ' intB equal -5
```

See Also: CInt, Conversion Functions, Fix, Math Functions

Integer

Type:	Definition
Description:	Integers are whole numbers such as 1, 16, and 456 and can range from -32,768 to 32,767. They can be expressed in decimal (base 10), hexadecimal (base 16), or octal (base 8) form.

Hexadecimal numbers include 0-9 and a-f, and are represented in VBScript by preceding the number with &H. Octal numbers only include 0-7 and are preceded by &O.

For example, decimal 23 is represented in hexadecimal by &H17 and in octal by &O27.

See Also:	Hex, Oct, Variables

Integer Division (\)

Syntax:	*result = operand1 \ operand2*
Type:	Arithmetic Operator
Synopsis:	Divides one number by another and rounds the result to the nearest whole number.
Description:	If either operand has the Null value, then *result* is Null. Operands that have the Empty value are equivalent to zero. And, of course, division by zero results in a run-time error.
See Also:	On Error, Operators

Is

Syntax:	*result = object1* Is *object2*
Type:	Operator
Synopsis:	Returns True if *object1* and *object2* refer to the same object, otherwise False is returned.
Description:	The Is operator compares two object reference variables. When assigning object references to variables, you must use the Set keyword as shown in the Example section.

Example:

```
Set objA = objCar
Set objB = objCar
intTemp = objA Is objB ' intTemp equals True.
```

See Also: Operators

IsArray

Syntax:	IsArray(*varname*)
Type:	Intrinsic Array and Variant Testing Function
Synopsis:	Returns True if *varname* is an array variable, otherwise False is returned.
See Also:	Array Variables, Array Functions, Dim, Erase, IsDate, IsEmpty, IsNull, IsNumeric, IsObject, LBound, ReDim, UBound, VarType

IsDate

Syntax:	IsDate(*expression*)
Type:	Intrinsic Date/Time and Variant Testing Function
Synopsis:	Returns True if expression represents a date, otherwise False is returned.
Description:	In Microsoft Windows, the range of valid dates is January 1, 100 A.D. through December 31, 9999 A.D.; the ranges vary among operating systems.
See Also:	Date/Time Functions, IsArray, IsEmpty, IsNull, IsNumeric, IsObject, VarType

IsEmpty

Syntax:	IsEmpty(*expression*)
Type:	Intrinsic Variant Testing Function
Synopsis:	Returns True if expression represents an uninitialized variable or has the Empty value, otherwise False is returned.

Description: If expression contains more than one variable, IsEmpty will always return `False`.

See Also: Empty, IsArray, IsDate, IsNull, IsNumeric, IsObject, VarType

---

IsNull

Syntax: IsNull(*expression*)

Type: Intrinsic Variant Testing Function

Synopsis: Returns `True` if expression contains no valid data or has the `Null` value, otherwise `False` is returned.

Description: If expression contains more than one variable, any Null value will cause IsNull to return True.

Example:

```
If IsNull(numRecords) Then
 Alert "No records were available!"
End If
```

See Also: IsArray, IsDate, IsEmpty, IsNumeric, IsObject, Null, VarType

---

IsNumeric

Syntax: IsNumeric(*expression*)

Type: Intrinsic Variant Testing Function

Synopsis: Returns `True` if *expression* contains a number, otherwise `False` is returned.

Description: If *expression* contains a date, `IsNumeric` will return `False`.

Example:

```
If IsNumeric(Document.myForm.myText.Value) Then
    MsgBox "The value is numeric"
Else
    MsgBox "Please enter a number!"
End If
```

See Also: IsArray, IsDate, IsEmpty, IsNull, IsObject, VarType

IsObject

Syntax:	IsObject(*expression*)
Type:	Intrinsic Variant Testing Function
Synopsis:	Returns True if expression references an object, otherwise False is returned.
See Also:	IsArray, IsDate, IsEmpty, IsNull, IsNumeric, VarType

LastModified

Syntax:	*document*.LastModified
Type:	Read-Only Property
Synopsis:	Returns a string containing the date that *document* was last modified.

LBound

Syntax:	LBound(*arrayname* [, *dimension*])
Type:	Intrinsic Array Function
Synopsis:	Returns the smallest available subscript for *dimension*.
Description:	The *dimension* parameter will default to one if not specified. The default lower bound for any dimension is always zero.

Use the LBound function in conjunction with the UBound function to determine an array's size.

See Also:	Array Variables, Dim, Erase, IsArray, ReDim, UBound

LCase

Syntax:	Lcase(*string*)
Type:	Intrinsic String Function

Synopsis:	Returns a copy of *string* with all characters converted to lowercase.
See Also:	Asc, AscB, AscW, Chr, ChrB, ChrW, InStr, InStrB, LeftB, Len, LenB, LTrim, Mid, MidB, Right, RightB, Space, StrComp, String, String Functions, Trim, UCase

Left

Syntax:	Left(*string*, *length*)
Type:	Intrinsic String Function
Synopsis:	Returns a copy of the first length characters of string.
Description:	If length is greater than string's length then the entire string is returned.

Example:

```
' removes the last character from strA
strB = Left(strA, Len(strA) - 1)
```

See Also:	Asc, AscB, AscW, Chr, ChrB, ChrW, InStr, InStrB, LCase, LeftB, Len, LenB, LTrim, Mid, MidB, Right, RightB, Space, StrComp, String, String Functions, Trim, UCase

LeftB

Syntax:	LeftB(*string*, *length*)
Type:	Intrinsic String Function
Synopsis:	Returns a copy of the first *length* bytes of *string*.
Description:	LeftB should be used with binary data. If *length* is greater than *string*'s length then the entire string is returned.

Example:

```
' removes the last byte from strA
strB = Left(strA, Len(strA) - 1)
```

See Also:	Asc, AscB, AscW, Chr, ChrB, ChrW, InStr, InStrB, LCase, Left, Len, LenB, LTrim, Mid, MidB, Right, RightB, Space, StrComp, String, String Functions, Trim, UCase

Len

Syntax:	Len(*string* | *varname*)
Type:	Intrinsic String Function
Synopsis:	Returns the number of characters in *string* or the number of bytes it takes to store *varname*'s value.
Description:	If *string* or *varname* is Null, then Null is returned.
Example:	

```
strA = "12345"
intB = Len(strA) ' intB equals 5
```

See Also:	Asc, AscB, AscW, Chr, ChrB, ChrW, InStr, InStrB, LCase, Left, LeftB, LenB, LTrim, Mid, MidB, Right, RightB, Space, StrComp, String, String Functions, Trim, UCase

LenB

Syntax:	LenB(*expression*)
Type:	Intrinsic String Function
Synopsis:	Returns the length of *expression* in bytes.
Description:	LenB should be used with binary data.
See Also:	Asc, AscB, AscW, Chr, ChrB, ChrW, InStr, InStrB, LCase, Left, LeftB, Len, LTrim, Mid, MidB, Right, RightB, Space, StrComp, String, String Functions, Trim, UCase

Length

Syntax 1:	*element*.Length
Syntax 2:	*history*.Length
Type:	Property
Synopsis:	Gets the number of options in a Select element or gets the number of entries in the browser's history list.
Limitation:	The Length property of History objects always returns zero in Internet Explorer v3.0.

Less Than (<)

Syntax:	operand1 < operand2
Type:	Comparison Operator
Synopsis:	Returns True if operand1 is less than operand2.
Description:	If either operand has the Null value, then result is Null. Operands that have the Empty value are equivalent to zero.

The less than operator is frequently used in a conditional expression for If, Do, and For statements.

Example:

```
' In this If statement, the less than operator
' is used in the conditional expression.
if intNumPages < 15 Then
 Alert "Ok"
End If

' In the third assignment statement below, the
' less than operator is used to give a value of
' False to intTest.
intA = 10
intB = 5
intTest = (intA < intB)
```

See Also:	Operators

Less Than Or Equal To (<=)

Syntax:	*operand1 < operand2*
Type:	Comparison Operator
Synopsis:	Returns True if *operand1* is less than or equal to *operand2*.
Description:	If either operand has the Null value, then *result* is Null. Operands that have the Empty value are equivalent to zero.

The less than or equal to operator is frequently used in a conditional expression for If, Do, and For statements.

Example:

```
' In this If statement, the <= operator
' is used in the conditional expression.
if intNumPages <= 15 Then
 Alert "Ok"
```

(continues)

```
End If

' In the third assignment statement below, the
' <= operator is used to give a value of
' False to intTest.
intA = 10
intB = 5
intTest = (intA <= intB)
```

See Also: Operators

Link

Type: Object

Synopsis: Represents a hyperlink.

Description: Link objects are accessed using the Links property of a document
object. See the "Links" entry for additional information.

Table 28.24	Events of a Link Object	
Event	**Page Number**	**Description**
OnClick	p. 887	Happens when a hyperlink is clicked.
OnMouseMove	p. 889	Happens when the mouse pointer moves and it is over a hyperlink.
OnMouseOver	p. 889	Happens when the mouse pointer moves over a hyperlink.

Table 28.25	Properties of a Link Object	
Property	**Page Number**	**Description**
Hash	p. 857	Gets or sets the hash part of the URL.
Href	p. 860	Gets or sets the whole URL.
Host	p. 859	Gets or sets the host and port part of the URL.
Hostname	p. 860	Gets or sets the hostname part of the URL.
Pathname	p. 899	Gets or sets the pathname part of the URL.
Port	p. 899	Gets or sets the port part of the URL.
Protocol	p. 901	Gets or sets the protocol part of the URL.
Search	p. 906	Gets or sets the search part of the URL.
Target	p. 916	Gets the target of the hyperlink.

See Also: Links

LinkColor

Syntax 1:	*document*.LinkColor = *rgbValue*
Syntax 2:	*document*.LinkColor = *string*
Type:	Property
Synopsis:	Gets or sets *document*'s hyperlink color.
Description:	You can set the color by specifying a RGB value in hexadecimal or by specifying a color name. The "Color Names" entry lists all of the color names that you can use.

You can only set this property while the document is being parsed. An OnLoad event handler procedure is a good place to set document properties.

Links

Syntax:	*document*.Links[*index*]
Type:	Read-Only Property
Synopsis:	Returns an array of links, or you can specify an index to retrieve a single link.
Description:	You can find out how many links *document* has by using the sample code in the example section. Figure 28.7 shows the results of the example HTML document. Notice that the number of links in the document changes as the document is parsed.

Example:

```
<!-- This document shows how to determine
 the number of links in a document.
 -->
<HTML>
 <HEAD>
 <TITLE>VB Script Example Page</TITLE>
 <SCRIPT language="VBScript">
 <!--
 Sub dispLinks
 intNumLinks = Document.Anchors.Length
 Document.Open
 Document.Write "This document has " &
 intNumLinks &
 " links.<P>"
 Document.Clear
 End Sub
```

(continues)

V

Visual Basic Script

```
    dispLinks
    -->
    </SCRIPT>
    </HEAD>
    <BODY LANGUAGE="VBScript">
    <H1>VB Script Example Page</H1>
      Visit my home page at
    <A HREF="http://www.planet.net/pmedined">
    http://www.planet.net/pmedined
    </A>
    <P>
    <SCRIPT language="VBScript">
    <!--
    dispLinks
    -->
    </SCRIPT>
    </BODY>
    </HTML>
```

Picture:

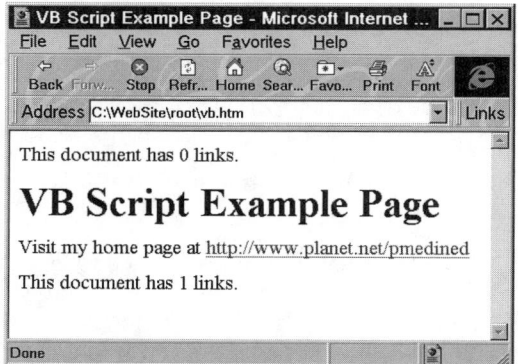

Fig. 28.7 The number of links in a document depends a lot on when the links are counted.

Literal Values

Type: Definition

Description: A literal is a value that is represented "as is" in your source code. VBScript uses several types of literals: boolean, date, floating-point (both single and double precision), integer, and string. Table 28.26 shows an example of each data type. In addition, each data type has its own entry in this book.

Table 28.26	VBScript Literal Values	
Data Type	**Value**	**Page**
Boolean	True or False	p. 821
Date	"01/23/1996" "Jan 23, 1996"	p. 832
Single Precision	12.34	p. 910
Double Precision	34.67	p. 841
Integer	45	p. 865
String	"Hello, World"	p. 912

Location (Object)

Type:	Object
Synopsis:	Represents the URL of a document or window.
Description:	The Location object does not have any events or methods. Table 28.27 lists the Location object's properties.

Table 28.27	Properties of a Location Object	
Property	**Page Number**	**Description**
Hash	p. 857	Gets or sets the hash part of the URL.
Href	p. 860	Gets or sets the whole URL.
Host	p. 859	Gets or sets the host and port part of the URL.
Hostname	p. 860	Gets or sets the hostname part of the URL.
Pathname	p. 899	Gets or sets the pathname part of the URL.
Port	p. 899	Gets or sets the port part of the URL.
Protocol	p. 901	Gets or sets the protocol part of the URL.
Search	p. 906	Gets or sets the search part of the URL.

Location (Property)

Syntax 1:	*document*.Location
Syntax 2:	*window*.Location
Type:	Read-Only Property
Synopsis:	Returns the Location object for *document*, or *window*.
Description:	If *window* is not specified, then Location object of the current window is returned.

V

Visual Basic Script

If you need the location object for a document, you must specify the document object (most of the time, you use document.Location).

See the "Location (Object)" Entry for more information.

Log

Syntax:	Log(*number*)
Type:	Intrinsic Math Function
Synopsis:	Returns the natural logarithm of number.
Description:	The natural logarithm is the logarithm to the base e. The constant e is approximately 2.718282.
See Also:	Abs, Atn, Cos, Exp, Math Functions, Randomize, Rnd, Sin, Sqr, Tan

Long Variables

Type:	Definition
Description:	Long variables are whole numbers that can range from -2,147,483,648 to 2,147,483,647.

Example:

```
lngTemp = 1222333
```

LTrim

Syntax:	LTrim(*string*)
Type:	Intrinsic Math Function
Synopsis:	Returns a copy of string without leading spaces.
See Also:	Asc, AscB, AscW, Chr, ChrB, ChrW, InStr, InStrB, LeftB, Len, LenB, Mid, MidB, Right, RightB, Space, StrComp, String, String Functions, Trim, UCase

Math Functions

Type:	Definition
Description:	VBScript has relatively few math functions and they are listed in Table 28.28.

Table 28.28   VBScript Math Functions

Function	Page Number	Description
Abs	p. 812	Returns the absolute value of a number.
Atn	p. 819	Returns the arctangent of a number.
Cos	p. 830	Returns the cosine of an angle.
Exp	p. 850	Returns *e* raised to a power.
Log	p. 876	Returns the natural logarithm of number.
Randomize	p. 902	Initializes the random-number generator.
Rnd	p. 904	Returns a random number.
Sin	p. 910	Returns the sine of an angle.
Sqr	p. 911	Returns the square root of a number.
Tan	p. 915	Returns the tangent of *angle*.

Method

Syntax 1:	*form*.Method
Syntax 2:	*form*.Method = *string*
Type:	Property
Synopsis:	Gets or sets the method for sending form information to the sever.
Description:	You can send form information to the server using either the GET or POST method.

Methods

Type:	Definition
Description:	A method is a function assigned to an object. For example, document.myForm.Submit( ) will execute the Submit method and send the information from the myForm form to the server.
See Also:	Procedures

V

Visual Basic Script

Mid

Syntax:	Mid(*string*, *start* [, *length*])
Type:	Intrinsic String Function
Synopsis:	Returns a copy of the part of *string* beginning at *start* for *length* characters.
Description:	If *string* contains Null, then Null is returned. If *start* is greater than the length of *string*, then a zero-length string will be returned. If no *length* parameter is specified then all characters from *start* to the end of the string are returned.
See Also:	Asc, AscB, AscW, Chr, ChrB, ChrW, InStr, InStrB, LeftB, Len, LenB, LTrim, MidB, Right, RightB, Space, StrComp, String, String Functions, Trim, UCase

MidB

Syntax:	MidB(*string*, *start* [, *length*])
Type:	Intrinsic String Function
Synopsis:	Returns a copy of the part of *string* beginning at *start* for *length* bytes.
Description:	MidB should be used for binary information.
See Also:	Asc, AscB, AscW, Chr, ChrB, ChrW, InStr, InStrB, LeftB, Len, LenB, LTrim, Mid, Right, RightB, Space, StrComp, String, String Functions, Trim, UCase

Minute

Syntax:	Minute(*time*)
Type:	Intrinsic Date/Time Function
Synopsis:	Returns the minute value in *time*—which can range from 0 to 59, inclusive.
See Also:	Date, Date/Time Functions, DateSerial, DateValue, Day, Month, Now, Second, Time, TimeSerial, TimeValue, Weekday, Year

Mod (Modulus)

Syntax:	*result = operand1* Mod *operand2*
Type:	Operator
Synopsis:	Returns the remainder of *operand1* divided by *operand2*.
Description:	The Modulus operator is a special form of division that only returns the remainder of the operation. If either operand has the Null value, then *result* is Null. Operands that have the Empty value are equivalent to zero.

Example:

```
i = 8 Mod 2 ' returns 0
i = 8 Mod 3 ' returns 2
```

See Also:	Operators

Modulus (Mod)

Syntax:	*result = op1* Mod *op2*
Type:	Operator
Synopsis:	Returns the remainder of operand1 divided by operand2
Description:	The Modulus operator is a special form of division that only returns the remainder of the operation. If either operand has the Null value, then *result* is Null. Operands that have the Empty value are equivalent to zero.

Example:

```
i = 8 Mod 2 ' returns 0
i = 8 Mod 3 ' returns 2
```

See Also:	Operators

Month

Syntax:	Month(*date*)
Type:	Intrinsic Date/Time Function
Synopsis:	Returns the month value in *date*—which can range from 1 to 12, inclusive.

See Also: Date, Date/Time Functions, DateSerial, DateValue, Day, Minute, Now, Second, Time, TimeSerial, TimeValue, Weekday, Year

MouseOver

Type: Event

Synopsis: Happens when the user moves the mouse pointer over an object or control.

MsgBox

Syntax: MsgBox(stringt [, buttons][, title][, helpfile, context])

Type: Intrinsic Function

Synopsis: Displays a message in a dialog box and waits for the user to click a button. Returns an value related to the button that was clicked according to Table 28.29.

Table 28.29	Return Values From MsgBox
Value	**Description**
1	OK button was pressed.
2	Cancel button or the ESC key was pressed.
3	Abort button was pressed.
4	Retry button was pressed.
5	Ignore button was pressed.
6	Yes button was pressed.
7	No button was pressed.

Description: The *string* parameter is displayed inside the dialog box when it appears. You can display about 1,024 characters depending on the font that is used. Multi-line prompts can be created by separating by adding a carriage return character (Chr(13)) into *string* where you want the lines to end.

The *buttons* parameter controls which buttons are displayed in dialog box. It also controls which icon is displayed, the modality, and which button is the default. The default value for *buttons* is zero, which displays the OK button. Use the following table to determine the value of *buttons* that you need:

Table 28.30 The *buttons* Parameter of *MsgBox*	
Value	**Description**
Values Affecting the Number and Type of Buttons	
0	Displays the OK button.
1	Displays the OK and Cancel buttons.
2	Displays the Abort, Retry, and Ignore buttons.
3	Displays the Yes, No, and Cancel buttons.
4.	Displays the Yes and No buttons.
5	Displays the Retry and Cancel buttons.
Values Affecting the Icon Style	
16	Displays the Critical Message icon.
32	Displays the Warning Query icon.
48	Displays the Warning Message icon.
64	Displays the Information Message icon.
Values That Set the Default Button	
0	Makes the first button the default.
256	Makes the second button the default.
512	Makes the third button the default.
768	Makes the fourth button the default.
Values That Set the Modality	
0	Makes the dialog box application modal - user must respond before work can continue in the current application.
4096	Makes the dialog box system modal - user must respond before work can continue in any applications. Use this option with care!

Add together one number from each sub-section of the above table to arrive at the correct value for *buttons*.

The *helpfile* and *context* parameters work together to define what happens if the user presses the F1 key or the question-mark button while the dialog box is active.

Multiplication (*)

Syntax:	*result = operand1 * operand2*
Type:	Arithmetic Operator
Synopsis:	Multiplies one number by another.
Description:	If either operand has the Null value, then *result* is Null. Operands that have the Empty value are equivalent to zero.
See Also:	Operators

V

Visual Basic Script

Name

Syntax 1:	*anchor*.name
Syntax 2:	*element*.name
Syntax 3:	*element*.name = *string*
Syntax 4:	*window*.name
Type:	Read-Only Property
Synopsis:	Gets the name of *anchor*, *element* or *window*. Sets the name of *element*.
Description:	If *window* has no name, then "null" is returned. If *window* is not specified, the name of the current window is returned.

Example:

```
' Assign the current window name to strWindowName.
strWindowName = name
```

Navigate

Syntax:	*window*.Navigate(*url*)
Type:	Method - applies to Window objects
Synopsis:	Connects the current window to a new URL.
Description:	If *window* is not specified, then the current window is used.

Example:

```
' switch the current window to the Microsoft Home Page
Navigate("http://www.microsoft.com")
```

Navigator (Object)

Type:	Object
Synopsis:	Represents the browser.
Description:	The Navigator object lets you access information about the browser.

Table 28.31	Properties of a History Object	
Object	**Page Number**	**Description**
AppCodeName	p. 816	The code name of the browser.
AppName	p. 816	The name of the browser.
AppVersion	p. 817	The version of the browser.
UserAgent	p. 920	The user agent name of the browser.

Navigator (Property)

Syntax: *window*.Navigator

Type: Property

Synopsis: Returns the Navigator object associated with *window*.

Description: See the "Navigator (Object)" entry for more information.

Negation (-)

Syntax: - *operand*

Type: Arithmetic Operator

Synopsis: Negates the value of *operand*.

Example:
```
intA = 10 ' intA equals positive 10.
intB = -10 ' intB equals negative 10.
```

See Also: Operators

Not

Syntax: *result* = Not *operand*

Type: Operator

Synopsis: Returns the logical opposite of expression.

Description: The Not function returns True if *operand* is False and False if *operand* is True. If *operand* is a variable, it returns a copy of the variable with each bit inverted. If *operand* is Null, then Null is returned.

Visual Basic Script

See Also: Operators

Not Equals (<>)

Syntax: *operand1 <> operand2*

Type: Comparison Operator

Synopsis: Returns True if *operand1* does not equal *operand2*.

Description: If either operand has the Null value, then *result* is Null. Operands
                     that have the Empty value are equivalent to zero.

The inequality operator is frequently used in conditional expression for If, Do, and For
statements.

Example:

```
' In this If statement, the inequality operator
' is used in the conditional expression.
if intNumPages <> 15 Then
 Alert "Ok"
End If

' In the third assignment statement below, the
' inequality operator is used to give a value of
' True to intTest.
intA = 10
intB = 5
intTest = (intA <> intB)
```

See Also: Operators

Now

Syntax: Now

Type: Intrinsic Date/Time Function

Synopsis: Returns the current date and time.

See Also: Date, Date/Time Functions, DateSerial, DateValue, Day, Minute,
                     Month, Second, Time, TimeSerial, TimeValue, Weekday, Year

Null

Syntax:	Null
Type:	Constant
Synopsis:	Indicates that a variable has no valid data.
Description:	Typically, Null is assigned to variables to indicate that they have no valid data. For instance, you might assign Null to a variable called numRecords to indicate that a data file could not be opened.

Null is not the same as Empty, which indicates that a variable has not yet been initialized. It is also not the same as a zero-length string, which is sometimes referred to as a null string.

You can't directly test to see if a variable has a Null value because any expression containing Null is itself Null. Therefore, you must use the IsNull function to test for the Null value.

Example:

```
numRecords = Null
```

See Also:	Empty

Number

Syntax 1:	Err.Number
Syntax 2:	Err.Number = *errornumber*
Type:	Property
Synopsis:	Gets or sets a numeric value specifying an error.
Description:	You set Err.Number when returning a user-defined error. Add your error number to the variable vbObjectError when return OLE Automation or ActiveX errors. Normally, you create a list of pseudo-constants that hold error values to avoid re-using numbers.

Example:

```
' Raise an error.
' Notice that I use my initials as a prefix
' for the pseudo-constants. This should avoid
```

(continues)

Visual Basic Script

```
' naming conflicts with another programmer's
' scripts.
dmErrNoFile = 1000
dmErrNoRecords = 1001
Err.Raise Number:= vbObjectError + dmErrNoFile, Source:= "myClass"
```

Objects

Type:	Definition
Description:	An object has properties that are either variables or references to other objects. Functions associated with objects are called the *object's methods*. You access the properties and methods of an object with a simple notation:

```
objectName.propertyName
objectName.methodName
```

All names are case-insensitive. This means that OnClick is the same as onClick, or even ONCLICK.

Table 28.32 lists the predefined objects in VBScript and the page that discusses them:

Table 28.32   Predefined Objects Associated With HTML

Object	Page Number	Description
Anchor	p. 814	Represents a hyperlink link in a document.
Document	p. 840	Represents the Document object associated with a window.
Element	p. 841	Represents a control or object on an HTML document.
Form	p. 852	Represents an HTML form.
History	p. 858	Represents the URLs visited by a window.
Link	p. 872	Represents an hyperlink.
Location	p. 875	Represents the URL of a document or window.
Navigator	p. 882	Represents the browser.
Window	p. 927	Represents a window in the browser.

Object Variables

Syntax:	Definition
Description:	Object variables are really pointers (or references) to a block of memory that holds an OLE Automation object. Both ActiveX and Java controls are considered to be OLE Automation objects.
See Also:	Objects

Oct

Syntax:	Oct(*number*)
Type:	Intrinsic Conversion and Math Function
Synopsis:	Returns a string representing the octal value of *number*.
Description:	If number is Null, then Null is returned. If number is Empty then zero is returned. If number is not an integer, then it is rounded to the nearest whole number.
See Also:	Conversion Functions, Math Functions

OnBlur

Syntax:	*element*.OnBlur
Type:	Event
Synopsis:	Happens when *element* loses the focus.
See Also:	Events, Event Handling, OnChange, OnClick, OnFocus, OnLoad, OnMouseMove, OnMouseOver, OnSelect, OnSubmit, OnUnload

OnChange

Syntax:	*element*.OnChange
Type:	Event
Synopsis:	Happens when *element* has changed.
See Also:	Events, Event Handling, OnBlur, OnClick, OnFocus, OnLoad, OnMouseMove, OnMouseOver, OnSelect, OnSubmit, OnUnload

OnClick

Syntax 1:	*element*.OnClick
Syntax 2:	*link*.OnClick
Type:	Event

Synopsis:	Happens when the user clicks an element or a hyperlink.
See Also:	Events, Event Handling, OnBlur, OnChange, OnFocus, OnLoad, OnMouseMove, OnMouseOver, OnSelect, OnSubmit, OnUnload

OnFocus

Syntax:	*element*.OnFocus
Type:	Event
Synopsis:	Happens when *element* gets the focus.
See Also:	Events, Event Handling, OnBlur, OnChange, OnClick, OnLoad, OnMouseMove, OnMouseOver, OnSelect, OnSubmit, OnUnload

OnLoad

Syntax:	OnLoad = *eventHandler*
Type:	Event
Synopsis:	Happens after all of the HTML for a document has been parsed and processed.
Description:	An OnLoad event handler function is a good place to put initialization statements. Since the OnLoad event handler is defined inside the HTML <BODY> tag, there can be only one function per HTML document.

Example:

```
<!-- This document shows how to use the
 OnLoad event.
-->
<HTML>
 <HEAD>
 <TITLE>VB Script Example Page</TITLE>
 <SCRIPT language="VBScript">
<!--
Sub loadHandler
Alert "The document has loaded!"
End Sub
-->
</SCRIPT>
</HEAD>
<BODY LANGUAGE="VBScript" OnLoad="loadHandler">
```

```
    <H1>VB Script Example Page</H1>
    </BODY>
    </HTML>
```

See Also: Events, Event Handling, OnBlur, OnChange, OnClick, OnFocus,
                       OnMouseMove, OnMouseOver, OnSelect, OnSubmit, OnUnload

OnMouseMove

Syntax: *link*.OnMouseMove(*shift*, *button*, *x*, *y*)

Type: Event

Synopsis: Happens when the mouse pointer moves while over a hyperlink.

Description: The parameters are automatically passed to your event handler
                       routine by the browser. The *shift* parameter holds the status of the
                       shift key. The *button* indicates which button on the mouse is
                       pressed, if any. The *x* and *y* parameters indicate the position of the
                       mouse pointer in pixels.

The Microsoft documentation indicates that the *shift* and *button* parameters are currently
set to zero and are, therefore, not accurate.

The Example section shows one way to create an event handler for this event.

Example:

```
    ' The following script handles the OnMouseMove
    ' event for a single hyperlink named lnkMicrosoftHome.

    <SCRIPT LANGUAGE="VB Script" FOR="lnkMicrosoftHome"
     EVENT="OnMouseMove(shift, button, x, y)">
     <!--
     ' add the event handler statements here.
     -->
    </SCRIPT>
```

See Also: Events, Event Handling, OnBlur, OnChange, OnClick, OnFocus,
                       OnLoad, OnMouseOver, OnSelect, OnSubmit, OnUnload

OnMouseOver

Syntax: *link*.OnMouseOver

Type: Event

Synopsis: Happens when the mouse pointer moves over a hyperlink.

Description:	You can attach a script to this event using the HTML <SCRIPT> tag as shown in the example for the OnMouseMove event. Or you can place VBScript statements directly in an <A> tag using OnMouseOver as an attribute. The Example section shows how this is done.

Example:

```
' The following script handles the OnMouseMove
' event for a single hyperlink named lnkMicrosoftHome.

<SCRIPT LANGUAGE="VB Script" FOR="lnkMicrosoftHome"
 EVENT="OnMouseMove(shift, button, x, y)">
<!--
' add the event handler statements here.
-->
</SCRIPT>
```

See Also:	Events, Event Handling, OnBlur, OnChange, OnClick, OnFocus, OnLoad, OnMouseMove, OnSelect, OnSubmit, OnUnload

OnSelect

Syntax:	*element*.OnSelect
Type:	Event
Synopsis:	Happens when the contents of *element* are selected.
See Also:	Events, Event Handling, OnBlur, OnChange, OnClick, OnFocus, OnLoad, OnMouseMove, OnMouseOver, OnSubmit, OnUnload

OnSubmit

Syntax:	*form*.OnUnload = *eventHandler*
Type:	Event
Synopsis:	Happens just before the form's information is sent to the server.
Description:	You can use this event to perform information validation and prevent the information from being sent if it is not valid. A validation function must return False to prevent submitting the form. The Example section shows how this can be done.

Example:

```
' The Return keyword must be used in order for VB Script
' to pay attention to the return value of a validation
' function. If the Return keyword is not used, the return
' value is ignored.
document.myForm.OnSubmit = "return IsValid()"
```

See Also: Events, Event Handling, OnBlur, OnChange, OnClick, OnFocus, OnLoad, OnMouseMove, OnMouseOver, OnSelect, OnUnload

---

OnUnload

Syntax: OnUnload = *eventHandler*

Type: Event

Synopsis: Happens after the document has been unloaded.

Description: You can see the unload event handler in action by loading the HTML document in the example section and then clicking the browser's refresh button.

Example:

```
<!-- This document shows how to use the
 OnUnload event.
-->
<HTML>
 <HEAD>
 <TITLE>VB Script Example Page</TITLE>
 <SCRIPT language="VBScript">
 <!--
 Sub unloadHandler
 Alert "The document has loaded!"
 End Sub
 -->
 </SCRIPT>
 </HEAD>
 <BODY LANGUAGE="VBScript" OnUnload="unloadHandler">
 <H1>VB Script Example Page</H1>
 </BODY>
</HTML>
```

See Also: Events, Event Handling, OnBlur, OnChange, OnClick, OnFocus, OnLoad, OnMouseMove, OnMouseOver, OnSelect, OnSubmit

V

Visual Basic Script

On Error

Syntax:	On Error Resume Next
Type:	Keyword
Synopsis:	Enables or disables an error-handling routine.
Description:	If an On Error statement is not used, all run-time errors are fatal.

The On Error Resume Next statement essentially causes run-time errors to be ignored. However, you can still examine the Err object to see if an error has occurred. You should check the Err object after each procedure call that has a high-probability of generating a run-time error. Each procedure that you write needs it own On Error Resume Next statement in order to trap errors local to that procedure.

See Also:	Err

Open

Syntax 1:	*document*.open
Syntax 2:	*newWindow* = Window.Open(*url*, *target*, *options*)
Type:	Method
Synopsis:	Opens *document* for output or creates a new browser window.
Document Object Description:	The Open method opens *document* for output. Then Write or WriteLn methods are used to append HTML-based text to the document. After all text has been written, the close or clear method is used to update the browser's window.
Window Object Description:	When the new window has been successfully created, the Window object associated with the new window is returned.

While the Microsoft documentation indicates that using "Window" is optional, when it is not specified, a syntax error is created.

The *url* parameter can be either an absolute or a relative URL.

If *target* names an existing window, that window will be reused. The *target* parameter is directly analogous to the TARGET attribute in HTML.

You can turn the following options on or off using either "yes" or "no" in a comma-delimited list: toolbar, location, directories, status, menubar, scrollbars, and resizeable. You can specify the height and width of the new window in pixels. In addition, you can set the location of the top left corner of the window, by setting the top and left options.

> **Caution**
>
> Some problems seems to exist with this method. The results of the example HTML are shown in the picture for this entry. You'll notice that while the parameters to the Open method indicate that the window should not be resizeable, it is. In addition, even though the Open method works, I received an error message that said, " Microsoft VBScript runtime error [Line: 12] Object doesn't support this property or method". Please test very thoroughly when using this method.

Example:

```
<!-- This document shows how to use the
Confirm method.
-->
<HTML>
 <HEAD>
 <TITLE>VB Script Example Page</TITLE>
 </HEAD>
 <BODY>
 <H1>VB Script Example Page</H1>
 <SCRIPT language="VBScript">
 <!--
 newWin = window.open("C:/WebSite\root\index.htm",
 "", "toolbar=no, menubar=no, resizeable=no")
 -->
 </SCRIPT>
 </BODY>
</HTML>
```

Picture:

Fig. 28.8 Even though the parameters indicate that this window is not resizable, it is.

Opener

Syntax:	*window*.Opener
Type:	Read-Only Property - applies to a Window object
Synopsis:	Returns the Window object that represents the window that opened the current window.

Operators

Type: Definition

Description: Operators are instructions you give to the computer so that it can perform some task or operation. All operators cause actions to be performed on *operands*. An operand can be anything that you perform an operation on. In practical terms, any particular operand will be a literal, a variable, or an expression. VBScript operators can be divided into two basic classes: binary and unary. Binary operators need two operands and unary operators need a single operand.

I like to think about operators in the same way I would give instructions to the driver of a car. I might say "turn left" or "turn right." These commands could be considered directional operators in the same way that + and – mathematical operators that say "add this" or "subtract this." If I yell "stop" while the car is moving, on the other hand, it should supersede the other commands. This means that "stop" has precedence over "turn left" and "turn right."

For example, the subtraction operator is a binary operator:

```
5 - 2
```

Of course, simply subtracting two numbers together doesn't mean much if you don't store the value somewhere. This is where variables play a role. You can assign values to variables using the assignment operator:

```
int_Num = 5 - 2
```

The minus sign can also act as a unary operator when placed in front of a number. For example,

```
int_Num = -34
```

Table 28.33 lists all of VBScript's operators. Some of them will be familiar to you from math class—for others, you might need a description. Operators that have their own entry in this book have the page number indicted in the third column.

Table 28.33   VBScript's Operators

Operator	Name	Page	Description
Arithmetic Operators			
+	Addition	p. 812	Adds two operands together.
/	Division	p. 838	Divides one number by another.
^	Exponentiation	p. 850	Raises one number to the power of another.
\	Integer division	p. 865	Divides one number by another and rounds the result to the nearest whole number.

Operator	Name	Page	Description
Comparison Operators			
Mod	Modulus	p. 882	Returns the remainder of a division operation.
*	Multiplication	p. 885	Multiplies one number by another.
-	Negation	p. 886	Negates a number.
-	Subtraction	p. 915	Subtracts one number from another.
Comparison Operators			
=	Equality	p. 845	Returns True if one number equals another.
>	Greater than	p. 856	Returns True if one number is greater than another.
>=	Greater than or equal to	p. 857	Returns True if one number is greater than or equal to another.
<>	Inequality	p. 862	Returns True if two numbers are not equal.
<	Less than	p. 873	Returns True if one number is greater than another.
<=	Less than or or equal to	p. 874	Returns True if one number is less than equal to another.
Is	Object	p. 805	Returns True if two object references equivalence refer to the same object.
Logical Operators			
And	Conjunction	p. 816	Returns True if its two operands are true.
Eqv	Equivalence	p. 845	Returns True if its two operands are logically equivalent.
Imp	Implication	p. 861	Performs a logical implication on two operands.
Not	Negation	p. 886	Returns the logical opposite of an operand.
Or	Disjunction	p. 897	Returns True if either of its operands is True.
Xor	Exclusion	p. 929	Returns True if only one of its operands is True.
String Concatenation Operator			
&	Concatenation	p. 914	Appends one string to another.

Operator Precedence

Type: Definition

Description: Precedence is very important in every computer language and VBScript is no exception. The *order of precedence* indicates which operator should be evaluated first. However, you can use parentheses to explicitly change the order of evaluation. Expressions inside parentheses are always evaluated before expressions outside the parentheses. Otherwise, regular operator precedence is always used.

Table 28.34 lists the operators in order of precedence. When operators have equal precedence, they are evaluated left to right as they appear in the expression.

Table 28.34   VB Script's Order of Operator Precedence

Operator	Description
Arithmetic Operators	
^	Exponentiation
-	Unary negation
*	Multiplication
/	Division
\	Integer division
Mod	Modulus
+	Addition
-	Subtraction
&	String concatenation
Comparison Operators	
All comparison operators have the same level of precedence.	
Logical Operators	
Not	Negation
And	Conjunction
Or	Disjunction
Xor	Exclusion
Eqv	Equivalence
Imp	Implication

Option Explicit

Syntax:	Option Explicit
Type:	Keyword
Synopsis:	Ensures that all variables are explicitly declared.
Description:	When the Option Explicit statement is placed at the top of your script, an error will be generated by any variable that is not explicitly defined. The error is generated when the web browser reads the HTML document file. Requiring every variable to be explicitly declared means that you can't misspell variables without generating an error message—a great bug prevention feature.

Example:

```
<HTML>
<HEAD>
<SCRIPT>
<!--
 Option Explicit ' must be the first line
 ' in the script.

 Dim lngTemp
-->
</SCRIPT>
</HEAD>
</HTML>
```

See Also: Dim

Options

Syntax:	*element*.Options
Type:	Read-Only Property
Synopsis:	Gets the `<OPTIONS>` tag for *element*.
Description:	The *element* specified must be a Select element. An object with the following properties is returned:

Property	**Description**
DefaultSelected	Gets the currently selected attribute.
Index	Gets the index of an option.
Length	Gets the number of options in the selected object.
Name	Gets the name of the selected object.
Selected	Used to programmatically select an option.
SelectedIndex	Gets the index of the selected option.
Text	Gets the text to be displayed.
Value	Gets the value attribute.

Or

Syntax:	*result = operand1* Or *operand2*
Type:	Operator
Synopsis:	Returns `True` if either operand is `True`.

Description: If either operand is Null, then Null is returned. If the operands are numeric, then a bitwise comparison of identically positioned bits is performed.

See Also: Operators

Parent

Syntax: *window*.Parent

Type: Read-Only Property - applies to a Window object

Synopsis: Returns a reference to the parent window object.

Description: The parent of the current window is the containing frame. If there is no containing frame, then the current window object is returned. Therefore, you can tell if the current document is inside a frame by comparing the current window object with the parent object. If they are the same, then no frame is present. The example section shows how this could be done.

Example:

```
<!-- This document shows how to determine if
 the current document is inside a frame.
-->
<HTML>
 <HEAD>
 <TITLE>VB Script Example Page</TITLE>
 <script language="VBScript">
 <!--
 Function IsFrame
 IsFrame = NOT(window Is window.parent)
 End Function
 -->
 </script>
 </HEAD>
 <BODY>
 <H1>VB Script Example Page</H1>
 <SCRIPT language="VBScript">
 <!--
 Document.Open
 If IsFrame = True Then
 Document.Write "Frames"
 Else
 Document.Write "No Frames"
 End If
 Document.Close
 -->
 </SCRIPT>
 </BODY>
</HTML>
```

Pathname

Syntax 1:	*link*.Pathname
Syntax 2:	*location*.Pathname
Syntax 3:	*location*.Pathname = *path*
Type:	Property
Synopsis:	Gets the path for *link* or *location*. Sets the path for *location*.
Description:	The path part of a URL is between the host part and the search or hash parts.

Port

Syntax 1:	*link*.Port
Syntax 2:	*location*.Port
Syntax 3:	*location*.Port = *portnumber*
Type:	Property
Synopsis:	Gets the port for *link* or *location*. Sets the port for *location*.
Description:	This property always returns the empty string ("") for the file: protocol.

Procedures

Type:	Definiton
Description:	A function is a user-defined or built-in method that performs a task. It can also return a value. Functions are universal and do not need to be associated with an object to run, while methods are integrated with objects.

As a general rule, it's best to place function definitions within the <HEAD> tags of a document. This practice ensures that any functions are loaded and ready before the user has a chance to interact with the rest of the page.

All procedures can accept information in the form of *arguments* or *parameters*. For example, if you have a function that calculates the floor space of a room, you'll need to tell the function the length and width of the room. Parameters are placed inside parentheses immediately after the name of the procedure being called like this:

```
calcSquareFootage(width, length)
```

The parentheses are not required until you also use the Call keyword.

If a procedure needs to change a variable used by another procedure or the calling procedure, the variable needs to have script-level scope. (See "Scope").

Prompt

Syntax:	*result* = *window*.Prompt(*prompt* [, *default*])
Type:	Method - applies to Window objects
Synopsis:	Requests input from the user.
Description:	The Prompt method will return the string that the user entered. The *prompt* parameter is used to display a message, usually a question that indicates what kind of input is needed. The *default* parameter is used to provide a default answer. The Microsoft documentation indicates that both *prompt* and *default* parameters are optional. However, as you can see in Figure 28.9 if they are not specified the string "<undefined>" is used.

Example:

```
<!-- This document shows how to use the
Confirm method.
-->
<HTML>
 <HEAD>
 <TITLE>VB Script Example Page</TITLE>
 </HEAD>
 <BODY>
 <H1>VB Script Example Page</H1>
 <SCRIPT language="VBScript">
 <!--
 result = Prompt()
 -->
 </SCRIPT>
 </BODY>
</HTML>
```

Picture:

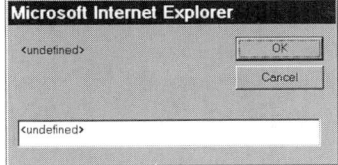

Fig. 28.9   A prompt box with no parameters specified.

Properties

Type:	Definition
Description:	Properties are used to describe an object or its current state. A property is defined by assigning it a value. The value can be assigned by the browser, the program, or as the user interacts with the page.

Protocol

Syntax 1:	*link*.Protocol
Syntax 2:	*location*.Protocol
Syntax 3:	*location*.Protocol = *protocol*
Type:	Property
Synopsis:	Gets the protocol for *link* or *location*. Sets the protocol for *location*.
Description:	The *protocol* parameters is a string that represents the protocol that you need to use. For example, "ftp:" is used for the file transfer protocol.

Raise

Syntax:	Err.Raise(number, [source, [description, [helpfile, contextID]]])
Type:	Method
Synopsis:	Generates a run-time error.

Description:	The number parameter indicates the nature of the run-time error and can range from 0 to 65,535.

The optional *source* parameter is the name of the error generator. If an Automation object generates an error, then *source* should have the form "myProject.myClass." The default value is the programmatic ID of the current VBScript project.

The optional *description* parameter describes the error. It defaults to the internal string associated with `Err.Number` or a generic error message.

The optional *helpfile* and *contextID* parameters are used to specify a topic inside a help file that can be used for context-sensitive help.

Randomize

Syntax:	Randomize [*number*]
Type:	Intrinsic Math Function
Synopsis:	Initializes the random-number generator.
Description:	In order to generate "true" random numbers, the random-number generator needs to be reseeded with a different number each time your script starts. If the number parameter is not specified, a number based on the current date and time is used.
See Also:	Abs, Atn, Cos, Exp, Log, Math Functions, Rnd, Sin, Sqr, Tan

ReDim

Syntax:	ReDim [Preserve] *varname(subscripts)* [, *varname(subscripts)*] ...
Type:	Keyword
Synopsis:	Declares or modifies the bounds for dynamic arrays.
Description:	A ReDim statement can be used to allocate or reallocate space to dynamic arrays. There is no limit to the number of times that you can modify the dimensions of an array. Dynamic arrays are created using the Dim statement and empty parentheses.

The Preserve option will let you change an array's dimension and keep its existing data. However, you are limited to changing only the last array dimension. If you reduce the size of the array, you will lose the data in the freed-up element. Increasing the size of the array will result in elements that are either zero (numeric), have a zero-length string (string), or have the Nothing value (object).

Example:

```
Dim a() ' declare a dynamic array
ReDim a(10, 10) ' allocate memory for a 10x10 array
ReDim Preserve a(10, 15) ' make array larger, but keep the contents.
```

See Also: Array Variables, Dim, Erase, IsArray, LBound, UBound

Referrer

Syntax:	*document*.Referrer
Type:	Read-Only Property
Synopsis:	Returns the URL of the referring document.
Description:	The referring document is the document that contained the hyperlink that the user clicked to get to *document*. If there was no referring document, then Null is returned.

Rem

Syntax 1:	Rem *comment*
Syntax 2:	' *comment*
Type:	Keyword
Synopsis:	Lets you add comments to your scripts.
Description:	Comments are very important. They help you understand the intent behind the simple mechanics of a program. You can use either the Rem keyword or a single quote to create comments. However, most programmers use the single quote syntax. Using the single quote syntax lets you easily add comments to the end of a line of code—as demonstrated in the example.

Example:

```
REM This is a comment.
' This is another comment.
intA = intB ^ 4 ' yet another comment
```

V

Visual Basic Script

Right

Syntax:	Right(*string*, *length*)
Type:	Intrinsic String Function
Synopsis:	Returns a copy of length characters taken from the end of string.
See Also:	Asc, AscB, AscW, Chr, ChrB, ChrW, InStr, InStrB, LeftB, Len, LenB, LTrim, Mid, MidB, RightB, Space, StrComp, String, String Functions, Trim, UCase

---

RightB

Syntax:	RightB(*string*, *length*)
Type:	Intrinsic String Function
Synopsis:	Returns a copy of *length* bytes taken from the end of *string*.
Description:	RightB is used for binary data.
See Also:	Asc, AscB, AscW, Chr, ChrB, ChrW, InStr, InStrB, LeftB, Len, LenB, LTrim, Mid, MidB, Right, Space, StrComp, String, String Functions, Trim, UCase

---

Rnd

Syntax:	Rnd[(*number*)]
Type:	Intrinsic Math Function
Synopsis:	Returns a random number that is greater than or equal to zero but less than one.
Description:	The random numbers are generated using a algorithm that produces a sequence of numbers. If number is not specified or is greater than zero, the next number in the random number sequence is returned. If number is less than zero, then the same number is returned every time. If the number is zero, the previous random number is returned again.

To generate random numbers in a certain range, use this formula: Int((upperbound - lowerbound + 1) * Rnd + lowerbound)

Example:

```
' Simulate a six-sided die—the range is 1 to 6.
intResult = Int((6 - 1 + 1) * Rnd + 1)

' Simulate two six-sided dice—the range is 2 to 12.
intResult = Int((12 - 2 + 1) * Rnd + 2)
```

See Also: Abs, Atn, Cos, Exp, Log, Math Functions, Randomize, Sin, Sqr, Tan

---

RTrim

Syntax: RTrim(*string*)

Type: Intrinsic String Function

Synopsis: Returns a copy of *string* with no trailing spaces.

See Also: Asc, AscB, AscW, Chr, ChrB, ChrW, InStr, InStrB, LeftB, Len, LenB, LTrim, Mid, MidB, Right, RightB, Space, StrComp, String, String Functions, Trim, UCase

---

<Script>

Syntax: <SCRIPT [EVENT=*event*] [FOR=*object*] [LANGUAGE=*lang*]>
...
</SCRIPT>

Type: HTML Tag

Synopsis: Contains script statements inside an HTML document.

Description: The <SCRIPT> tag encloses VBScript statements so that the browser knows that they are executable. If the EVENT attribute is used, it specifies the type of event that the script statements will handle. The FOR attribute is used in conjunction with EVENT and it specifies which object or control the script should be associated with.

One or more VBScript commands can be enclosed in a <SCRIPT> tag. The advent of several scripting languages has made it necessary to identify for the browser which language is being used. For VBScript, the syntax is:

Visual Basic Script

V

```
<SCRIPT LANGUAGE="VBScript">
<!--
 [statements]
-->
</SCRIPT>
```

Note the use of HTML comment tags, `<!--` and `-->`. If the page containing the script is used on a browser that is not compatible with the scripting languages, the script statements are normally displayed as any other text on the page, adding clutter and trash to the screen. If you use the comment tags, an incompatible browser ignores the script portion of the document.

See Also: Events, Event Handling

Scope

Type: Definition

Description: When variables are declared inside a procedure, they can only be used by statements inside that procedure. This limitation is referred to as the *scope* of the variable. Local scope means that a variable has declared inside a procedure. Script-level scope means that a variable was declared outside of all procedures and therefore can be accessed by all of the procedures.

Search

Syntax 1:   *link*.Search

Syntax 2:   *location*.Search

Syntax 3:   *location*.Search = *string*

Type: Property

Synopsis: Gets the search part of *link* or *location*. Sets the search part of *location*.

Description: The search part of a URL starts with a question mark. For example, in http://www.planet.net/search.pl?trains, the ?trains is the search part of the URL. If the URL has no search part, then Null is returned.

Second

Syntax:	Second(*time*)
Type:	Intrinsic Date/Time Function
Synopsis:	Returns the seconds value from *time*—which can range from 0 to 59, inclusive.
See Also:	Date, Date/Time Functions, DateSerial, DateValue, Day, Minute, Month, Now, Time, TimeSerial, TimeValue, Weekday, Year

Select

Syntax:	*element*.Select
Type:	Method
Synopsis:	Selects the contents of *element*.

Select Case

Syntax:	Select Case *testexpression* [Case *expression* [*statements*]] ... [Case Else *expression* [*statements*]] End Select
Type:	Keyword
Synopsis:	Selectively executes a statement block when the expression associated with the statement block equals the testexpression. If no matches are found, then the statement block in the Else clause is executed.
Description:	If *testexpression* matches more than one expression, only the statement block associated with the first matching *expression* is executed. You can use string values in both the *testexpression* and *expression* parts of the Select Case statement.

The Else clause is frequently used to catch unexpected values. For example, if you are processing payroll records by month, the `Else` clause might be used to catch values that are not in the range of 1 to 12.

SelectedIndex

Syntax:	*element*.SelectedIndex
Type:	Read-Only Property
Synopsis:	Gets the index for the selected options.
Description:	If there are multiple selected options, then the index of the first option selected is returned.

Self

Syntax:	*window*.Self
Type:	Read-Only Property - applies to a Window object
Synopsis:	Returns an object reference to *window*.
Description:	If *window* is not specified, the current window object is returned.

Set

Syntax:	Set *objectvar* = { *objectexpression*	Nothing}
Type:	Keyword
Synopsis:	Assigns a value to an object variable.
Description:	You must use the Set keyword when assigning objects to variables or properties. Memory associated with *objectVar* can be freed by assigning the special value Nothing to it.

Generally speaking, the values that get assigned will be object references not copies of the object. This means that more than one variable can reference the same object. The Is operator can be used to determine if two variables point to the same object.

Example:
```
Set index = 0
Set myForm = Document.ValidForm
```
See Also: Is

SetTimeout

Syntax: timerID = window.SetTimeout(expression, msec, language)

Type: Method - applies to Window objects

Synopsis: Executes a procedure after a specified amount of time has elapsed and returns a timer object.

Description: The expression parameter must evaluate to a procedure name or an object's method. The procedure or method will be executed after msec milliseconds (one second = 1,000 milliseconds). This method is an excellent way to create dialog box timeouts. In the example given previously, the Quit button will be clicked after five seconds.

Example:
```
clickTimer = setTimeout ("quitButton.OnClick", 5000).
```
See Also: clearTimeout

Sgn

Syntax: Sgn(*number*)

Type: Intrinsic Conversion or Math Function

Synopsis: Returns 1 if *number* is greater than zero, -1 if *number* is less than zero, and zero if *number* is zero.

Example:
```
intResult = Sgn(-10) ' intResult equals -1
```
See Also: Conversion Functions, Math Functions

Sin

Syntax:	Sin(*angle*)
Type:	Intrinsic Math Function
Synopsis:	Returns the sine of *angle*.
Description:	The Sin function takes an angle and returns the ratio of two sides of a right triangle. The ratio is the length of the side opposite the angle divided by the length of the hypotenuse. The result lies in the range -1 to 1. To convert degrees to radians, multiply degrees by pi/180. To convert radians to degrees, multiply radians by 180/pi.
See Also:	Abs, Atn, Cos, Exp, Log, Math Functions, Randomize, Rnd, Sqr, Tan

Single-Precision Variables

Syntax:	Definition
Description:	Single-precision variables can have around 45 digits of precision—not even half the size of double-precision regardless of the name. However, since single-precision numbers can fit inside 32 bits and double-precision numbers need 64 bits, extensive calculations will perform faster using single-precision.
See Also:	Variables

Source

Syntax 1:	Err.Source
Syntax 2:	Err.Source = *stringexpression*
Type:	Source
Synopsis:	Gets or sets the name of the object or application that originally generated the error.
Description:	Source is usually the class name or programmatic ID of the object that caused the error.

Space

Syntax:	Space(*number*)
Type:	Intrinsic String Function
Synopsis:	Returns a string of *number* spaces.
See Also:	Asc, AscB, AscW, Chr, ChrB, ChrW, InStr, InStrB, LeftB, Len, LenB, LTrim, Mid, MidB, Right, RTrim, StrComp, String, String Functions, Trim, UCase

Sqr

Syntax:	Sqr(*number*)
Type:	Intrinsic Math Function
Synopsis:	Returns the square root of *number*.
See Also:	Abs, Atn, Cos, Exp, Log, Math Functions, Randomize, Rnd, Sin, Tan

Status

Syntax 1:	*window*.Status
Syntax 2:	*window*.Status = *string*
Type:	Property - applies to a Window object
Synopsis:	Returns or sets the status text for the lower left portion of the status bar.

Example:

```
' set the default status text.
self.Status = "Ready for Input"

' assign the default status text to a variable
strText = self.Status
```

V

Visual Basic Script

StrComp

Syntax:	StrComp(*string1*, *string2* [, *compare*])
Type:	Intrinsic String Function
Synopsis:	Returns -1 if *string1* is less than *string2*, 0 if they are equal, 1 if *string1* is greater than *string2*, and Null if either *string1* or *string2* are Null.
See Also:	Asc, AscB, AscW, Chr, ChrB, ChrW, InStr, InStrB, LeftB, Len, LenB, LTrim, Mid, MidB, Right, RTrim, Space, String, String Functions, Trim, UCase

String

Syntax:	String(*number*, *character*)
Type:	Intrinsic String Function
Synopsis:	Returns a string that contains *character* repeated *number* times.
Description:	If *character* is Null, then the Null value is returned. If the value of *character* is greater than 255, then it is turned into a valid character code using the modulus operator (*character* Mod 256).
See Also:	Asc, AscB, AscW, Chr, ChrB, ChrW, InStr, InStrB, LeftB, Len, LenB, LTrim, Mid, MidB, Right, RTrim, Space, StrComp, String Functions, Trim, UCase

String Functions

Type:	Definition
Description:	VBScript's string functions are listed in Table 28.35.

Table 28.35	**VBScript String Functions**	
Function	**Page Number**	**Description**
Asc	p. 818	Returns the ANSI code of the first character in a string.
AscB	p. 819	Returns the first byte in a string.
AscW	p. 819	Returns the first Unicode character (32-bits) in a string.

Function	Page Number	Description
Chr	p. 824	Returns the character associated with a character code.
ChrB	p. 824	Returns the byte associated with a character code.
ChrW	p. 825	Returns the Unicode character associated with a character code.
InStr	p. 863	Returns the location of one string in another.
InStrB	p. 864	Returns the byte position of one string in another.
LCase	p. 868	Returns a copy of a string with all characters converted to lowercase.
Left	p. 869	Returns a copy of the beginning of a string.
LeftB	p. 869	Returns a copy of the beginning of a string.
Len	p. 870	Returns the number of bytes it takes to store a variable's value.
LenB	p. 870	Returns the number of bytes it takes to store an expression's value.
LTrim	p. 876	Returns a copy of string without leading spaces.
Mid	p. 878	Returns a copy of part of a string.
MidB	p. 878	Returns a copy of part of a string.
Right	p. 904	Returns a copy of the end of a string.
RightB	p. 904	Returns a copy of the end of a string.
RTrim	p. 905	Returns a copy of a string with no trailing spaces.
Space	p. 911	Returns a string of a specified number of spaces.
StrComp	p. 912	Compares two strings.
String	p. 912	Returns a string of a specified character repeated a specified number of times.
Trim	p. 918	Returns a copy of a string with no leading or trailing spaces.
UCase	p. 919	Returns a copy of a string with all characters converted into uppercase.

V

Visual Basic Script

String Variables

Syntax: Definition

Description: Strings are defined by a number of characters (up to 2 billion) within double quotes.

Examples:

```
strTemp = "The Doctor said, \"You're Fine.,\" to me."
```

See Also: Variables

String Concatenation (&)

Syntax:	result = string1 & string2
Type:	String Concatenation Operator
Synopsis:	Appends string2 to string1.
Description:	Although you can also use the + operator to concatenate two character strings, you should use the & operator for concatenation instead. The & operator eliminates ambiguity and provides self-documenting code.
See Also:	Operators

Sub

Syntax:	Sub *name* [(*arglist*)] [*statements*] End Sub
Type:	Keyword
Synopsis:	Declares a user-defined subroutine called *name*.
Description:	Sub statements are used to create user-defined subroutines. Subroutines differ from functions because they do not return any value.

All subroutines should be declared towards the beginning of your script in the HEAD section of your HTML page. This ensures that the subroutines will be available for use by later VBScript statements.

arglist is an optional list of arguments or parameters that the subroutine can use. If you would like the subroutine to assign values to the arguments, use the ByVal keyword inside the parameter list.

> **Note**
>
> Subroutines do not return values. Therefore, it seems logical that they should not modify parameters either. If you need to return a value or modify a parameter, try creating a user-defined function instead.

Example:

```
' Define a subroutine with one parameter.
Sub displayIt(strMsg)
```

```
      Alert "Error: " & strMsg
   End Sub
```

See Also: Call, Exit, Function, Scope

Submit

Syntax: *form*.Submit

Type: Method

Synopsis: Sends form information to the server.

See Also: OnSubmit

Subtraction (-)

Syntax: result = operand1 - operand2

Type: Arithmetic Operator

Synopsis: Subtracts operand2 from operand1.

Description: If one of the operands contain the Null value, then the result is
                       Null. If one of the operands contain the Empty value, it is treated
                       as if it were zero.

See Also: Operators

Tan

Syntax: Tan(*angle*)

Type: Intrinsic Math Function

Synopsis: Returns the tangent of *angle*.

Description: Tan takes an angle and returns the ratio of two sides of a right
                       triangle. The ratio is the length of the side opposite the angle
                       divided by the length of the side adjacent to the angle.

See Also: Abs, Atn, Cos, Exp, Log, Math Functions, Randomize, Rnd,
                       Sin, Sqr

Target

Syntax 1:	*form*.Target
Syntax 2:	*form*.Target = *string*
Syntax 3:	*link*.Target
Type:	Property
Form Synopsis:	Gets or sets the name of the window to display form results in.

Caution
In Internet Explorer v3.0, this property has no effect on the operation of the form.

Link Synopsis:	Gets the name of the window—the TARGET attribute of the HTML <A> tag—to display the URL in.

Time

Syntax:	Time
Type:	Intrinsic Date/Time Function
Synopsis:	Returns the current system time.
See Also:	Date, Date/Time Functions, DateSerial, DateValue, Day, Minute, Month, Now, Second, TimeSerial, TimeValue, Weekday, Year

TimeSerial

Syntax:	TimeSerial(*hour*, *minute*, *second*)
Type:	Intrinsic Conversion and Date/Time Function
Synopsis:	Returns a Date variable that represents *hour*, *minute*, and *second*
Description:	The *hour* parameter can range from 0 (midnight) to 23 (11:00 P.M.). The *minute* and *second* parameters can range from 0 to 59. You can pass expressions instead of literals to perform some basic date arithmetic. The example shows how to subtract two from a given month. Parameters that are too large to fit into the normal range will carry-over into the next larger unit. For instance, a *minute* parameter of 70 will increment the *hour* parameter. If one

of the parameters fall outside the range -32,768 to 32,767, or if the date specified by the three arguments falls outside the acceptable range of times, an error occurs.

See Also:	Date, Date/Time Functions, DateSerial, DateValue, Day, Minute, Month, Now, Second, Time, TimeValue, Weekday, Year

TimeValue

Syntax:	TimeValue(*time*)
Type:	Intrinsic Conversion and Date/Time Function
Synopsis:	Returns a Date value representing *time*.
Description:	The *time* parameter can range from 0:00:00 (midnight) to 23:59:59 (11:59:59 P.M.). If *time* is Null, then Null is returned. The DateValue function understands both 12-hour and 24-hour clocks. If *time* contains date information, it is ignored. However, if *time* includes invalid date information, an error occurs.
See Also:	Date, Date/Time Functions, DateSerial, DateValue, Day, Minute, Month, Now, Second, Time, TimeSerial, Weekday, Year

Title

Syntax:	*document*.Title
Type:	Read-Only Property
Synopsis:	Returns a string with *document*'s title.

Top

Syntax:	*window*.Top
Type:	Read-Only Property - applies to a Window object
Synopsis:	Returns a Window object that represents the top-most window.

Trim

Syntax:	Trim(*string*)
Type:	Intrinsic String Function
Synopsis:	Returns a copy of *string* with no leading or trailing spaces.
See Also:	Asc, AscB, AscW, Chr, ChrB, ChrW, InStr, InStrB, LeftB, Len, LenB, LTrim, Mid, MidB, Right, RTrim, Space, StrComp, String, String Functions, UCase

Type Conversion

Type:	Definition
Description:	A variable's type depends on the kind of information it contains (see the "Literals" entry). VBScript is loosely typed, meaning that you don't need to declare what kind of variables you are using. The data type is automatically assigned depending on the value assigned to the variable.

VBScript automatically changes the data type of the variable depending on the operation taking place. The best example of automatic data type conversion involves the string concatenation operator. The follow statements serve to illustrate type conversion.

```
' example 1
var oneString = "1";
var oneInt = 1
var oneConcatenate = oneString + oneInt ' results in "11"
var oneAddition = oneInt + oneString ' results in 2
```

In the first addition statement, the first operand is a string. VBScript assumes that the operation is to join two strings. When VBScript encounters an integer as the second operand, it converts the value of the variable into a string to meet its own expectations.

The "Conversion Functions" entry has a list of functions that can convert from one data type to another.

See Also:	Conversion Functions, Variable Testing

UBound

Syntax:	UBound(*arrayname* [, *dimension*])
Type:	Intrinsic Array Function

Synopsis:	Returns the largest subscript for dimension of an *arrayname*.
Description:	You can use LBound in conjunction with UBound to find out an array's size.

Example:

```
Dim C(50, 10) ' declare an array
d1 = UBound(C, 1) ' d1 equals 49
d2 = UBound(C, 2) ' d2 equals 9
```

See Also:	Array Variables, Dim, Erase, IsArray, LBound, ReDim

UCase

Syntax:	UCase(*string*)
Type:	Intrinsic String Function
Synopsis:	Returns a copy of *string* with all characters converted into uppercase.
Description:	If *string* is Null, then Null is returned.
See Also:	Asc, AscB, AscW, Chr, ChrB, ChrW, InStr, InStrB, LeftB, Len, LenB, LTrim, Mid, MidB, Right, RTrim, Space, StrComp, String, String Functions, Trim

V

Visual Basic Script

Negation (-)

Type:	Operator
Description:	When the unary negation operator is placed in front of an expression, it means that the negative value of the expression is used. The unary negation operation and the subtraction operation both use the - character.

Example:

```
intA = 234 ' intA equals 234.
intB = -intA ' intB equals -234.
```

See Also:	Operators

UserAgent

Syntax:	*navigator*.UserAgent
Type:	Read-Only Property
Synopsis:	The name of the current application user agent.
Description:	This property returns "Mozilla/2.0 (compatible; MSIE 3.0A; Windows 95)" when using Microsoft Internet Explorer v3.0 (4.70.1158).

Example:

```
' Display the application version
Alert Navigator.UserAgent
```

Value

Syntax 1:	*element*.Value
Syntax 2:	*element*.Value = *string*
Type:	Property
Synopsis:	Gets or sets the value of *element*.

Variables

Type:	Definition
Description:	The *variant* data type can hold any type of information and it is the only type of data that VBScript uses. All VBScript functions return variant data types.

If a variable holds a number and is being used in a numeric context, then it behaves like a number. If the variable is used in a string content, VBScript will silently convert the number into a string. Uninitialized variables have the Empty value.

Some property names are reserved words—which means that you can't use them for your own variable names. In order to avoid having to remember which property names are reserved and which are not, the "Variable Naming" section suggests some prefixes that you can use to distinguish your variable names.

VBScript has 12 subtypes that automatically come into play depending on the context:

Table 28.36	VBScript's Variant Subtypes
Subtype	**Description**
Empty	An uninitialized variable.
Null	A variable containing no valid data.
Boolean	The variable can be either `True` or `False`.
Byte	The variable is in the range 0 to 255.
Integer	The variable is in the range -32,768 to 32,767.
Long	The variable is in the range -2,147,483,648 to 2,147,483,647.
Single	The variable is a single-precision floating-point number that can be over 35 digits in length.
Double	The variable is a double-precision floating-point number that can be over 300 digits in length.
Date	The variable contains a date/time between 01/01/0100 and 12/31/9999.
String	The variable contains a sequence of characters that can be up to about two billion characters in length.
Object	The variable contains an object.
Error	The variable contains an error number.

See Also: Boolean Variables, Empty, Null

Variable Naming

Type: Guideline

Description: Because VBScript is so loosely typed, it is critical that you remember what type of data is stored in each of your variables. One way of doing this is to create your own variable naming guidelines. Table 28.37 lists some prefixes that you can use to help get you started on your own guidelines.

Table 28.37	Suggested Variable Naming Guidelines
Prefix	**Data Type**
ani	Animated button control
ary	Array
bln	Boolean
btn	Button control
byt	Byte
cbo	Combo control
chk	Checkbox control
cht	Chart control
cmd	Command button

(continues)

Table 28.37 Continued	
Prefix	**Data Type**
cst	Constant (actually a pseudo-constant)
dlg	Dialog control
dbl	Double-precision
dtm	Date/time
err	Error
fra	Frame object
hsb	Horizontal scrollbar control
img	Image control
int	Integer
lbl	Label control
lin	Line control
lnk	Hyperlink
lst	List control
lng	Long
obj	Object
pnl	Panel control
sld	Slider control
sng	Single-precision
spn	Spin button control
str	String
txt	Text control
vsb	Vertical scrollbar control

Variant

Type: Definition

Description: *Variant* is the single data type that VBScript supports. Each variant variable can contain any type of data. In fact, there are 12 data subtypes (which are described in the "Variables" entry). VBScript normally does an excellent job of automatically converting between the subtypes—matching the subtype to the task at hand. However, if you run into a problem use one of the data type conversion functions (listed in the See Also section)

One of the few times you might have trouble with the variant data type is when using the + sign. The + sign can be used to both add two numbers together and concatenate two strings. VBScript decides between adding and concatenating by checking the subtype of the first operand. If the first operand is numeric, the second operand is converted to a number and added to the first. Otherwise, string concatenation is performed. If you are not careful, you might not get the results you expect.

Tip

Always use the & operator for string concatenation to ensure consistent results.

See Also: Variables

Variant Testing Functions

Type: Definition

Description: VBScript provides several functions that let you determine what type of data is in a Variant variable.

Table 28.38   VBScript's Variant Testing Functions

Function	Page Number	Description
IsArray	p. 866	Returns true if its parameter is an array.
IsDate	p. 866	Returns true if its parameter is a date.
IsEmpty	p. 866	Returns true if its parameter has a Empty value.
IsNull	p. 867	Returns true if its parameter has a Null value.
IsNumeric	p. 867	Returns true if its parameter is numeric.
IsObject	p. 868	Returns true if its parameter is an object reference.
VarType	p. 923	Returns a value representing the data subtype of its parameter.

VarType

Syntax: VarType(*varname*)

Type: Intrinsic Function

Synopsis: Returns a value representing the data subtype of *varname*.

Description: The VarType function never returns the array subtype value by itself. It is always added to some other value to indicate an array of a particular type. The value for Variant is only returned when it has been added to the value for Array to indicate that the argument to the VarType function is an array. For example, the value returned for an array of integers is calculated as 8192 + 2, or 8194. If an object has a default property, VarType (object) returns the type of its default property.

Table 28.39	**Return Values for the VarType Functon**	
Value	**Description**	**Page Number**
0	Empty (uninitialized)	p. 843
1	Null (no valid data)	p. 885
2	Integer	p. 865
3	Long integer	p. 876
4	Single-precision floating-point number	p. 910
5	Double-precision floating-point number	p. 841
6	Currency (not supported by VBScript)	
7	Date	p. 832
8	String	p. 912
9	Automation Object	
10	Error	p. 846
11	Boolean	p. 821
12	Variant (used only with arrays of Variants)	p. 922
13	Non-automation object	p. 886
17	Byte	p. 821
8192	Array	p. 817

Example:

```
' create some pseudo-constants.
cstLong = 3
cstArray = 8192

lngTemp = CLng(324)
If VarType(lngTemp) = cstLong Then
 Alert "It's a long variable"
Else
 Alert "It's not long."
End If


' put the subtype of an array elements into
' the intElementType variable. If the variable
' is not an array, then make the element type
' equal to Null.
If VarType(anyVar) And cstArray Then
 intElementType = VarType(anyVar) - cstArray
Else
 intElementType = Null
End If
```

See Also: IsArray, IsDate, IsEmpty, IsNull, IsNumeric, IsObject, Variables

VBScript Statements

Type: Definition

Description: The statements used to control program flow in VBScript are similar to Visual Basic. A statement can span several lines if needed or several statements can be placed on the same line provided they are separated by a colon character.

Table 28.40	VB Statement Types	
Statement	**Page Number**	**Description**
Call	p. 822	Runs a Sub or Function procedure.
Dim	p. 837	Declares script-level or procedure-level variables.
Do	p. 838	Repeatedly executes a statement block while a condition is True or until a condition becomes True.
End Function	p. 844	Ends a function definition.
End Sub	p. 844	Ends a subroutine definition.
Exit	p. 849	Exits a block of statements or ends the script.
For	p. 852	Repeatedly executes a statement block for a specific number of times.
Function	p. 885	Creates a user-defined function.
If	p. 861	Optionally Executes statements based on a conditional expression.
Option	p. 896	Ensures that all variables are Explicit explicitly declared.
ReDim	p. 902	Declares or modifies the bounds for dynamic arrays.
Set	p. 908	Assigns a value to an object variable.
Sub	p. 914	Creates a user-defined subroutine.
While	p. 926	Not recommended, use Do instead.

V

Visual Basic Script

vLinkColor

Syntax 1:   *document*.vLinkColor = *rgbValue*

Syntax 2:   *document*.vLinkColor = *string*

Type: Property

Synopsis: Gets or sets *document*'s visited link color.

Description: You can set the color by specifying a RGB value in hexadecimal or by specifying a color name. The "Color Names" entry lists all of the color names that you can use.

You can only set this property while the document is being parsed. An OnLoad event handler procedure is a good place to set document properties.

Weekday

Syntax:	Weekday(*date*, [*firstdayofweek*])
Type:	Intrinsic Date/Time Function
Synopsis:	Returns the day of the week (from one for Sunday to seven for Saturday) that *date* falls on.
Description:	You can change the beginning day of the week by providing a *firstdayofweek* parameter.

Table 28.41   Values for the firstdayofweek Parameter

Value	Description
0	Use NLS API setting.
1	Sunday (this is the default value)
2	Monday
3	Tuesday
4	Wednesday
5	Thursday
6	Friday
7	Saturday

See Also:	Date, Date/Time Functions, DateSerial, DateValue, Day, Minute, Month, Now, Second, Time, TimeSerial, TimeValue, Year

While

Type:	Keyword
Synopsis:	The While statement, while supported, is no longer recommended. Use a Do...Loop statement instead.

Whitespace

Type: Definition

Description: Whitespace refers to spaces, tabs, and carriage return characters—
                   in short, any character that can be used to create white space on a
                   piece of paper.

Window

Type: Object

Synopsis: Represents a window in the browser.

Description: You can use "Window" to refer to the object associated with the
                   current window. However, using the "Window" object name is
                   usually not needed because your code will probably be inside the
                   window's scope. Window objects are at the top of the object hier-
                   archy. They are directly analogous to browser windows.

Table 28.42 Objects Contained Inside a Window Object

Object	Page Number	Description
Document	p. 840	Represents the document in the current windows
Frame	p. 854	Each element in this array represents one of the frames of the browser.
History	p. 858	Represents the history list of the browser.
Location	p. 875	Represents the URL of the current document.
Navigator	p. 882	Represents the browser application.
Script	p. 905	Represents all of the scripts in the current window.

Table 28.43 Events of Window Objects

Event	Page Number	Description
OnLoad	p. 888	Happens when a document is loaded.
OnUnload	p. 891	Happens when a document is unloaded.

Table 28.44	Methods of Window Objects	
Method	**Page Number**	**Description**
Alert	p. 813	Displays an alert message box.
ClearTimeout	p. 826	Clears a specified timer that was created by SetTimeout.
Close	p. 827	Closes a browser window.
Confirm	p. 828	Displays a message box with OK and Cancel buttons.
Navigate	p. 882	Opens a new URL in the window.
Open	p. 892	Creates a new browser window.
Prompt	p. 900	Prompts the user for input using a dialog box.
SetTimeout	p. 909	Calls a specified function after a specified amount of time.

Table 28.45	Properties of Window Objects	
Property	**Page Number**	**Description**
DefaultStatus	p. 836	Gets or sets the default status text for the lower left portion of the status bar.
Document	p. 841	Gets the Document object associated with a window.
Frames	p. 854	Gets an array of frames contained in a window.
History	p. 859	Gets the History object of a window.
Location	p. 875	Gets the Location object for a window.
Name	p. 882	Gets the name of a window.
Navigator	p. 883	Gets the Navigator object associated with a window.
Opener	p. 893	Gets the Window object that represents the window that opened the current window.
Parent	p. 898	Gets a reference to the parent window object.
Self	p. 908	Gets an object reference to a window.
Status	p. 911	Gets or sets the status text for the lower left portion of the status bar.
Top	p. 917	Gets a Window object that represents the top-most window.

Write

Syntax:	*document*.Write(*string*)
Type:	Method
Synopsis:	Places *string* into *document*.
Description:	The Write method will append *string* to *document*. Remember that *string* needs to have HTML tags if formatted output is needed.

WriteLn

Syntax:	*document*.WriteLn(*string*)
Type:	Method
Synopsis:	Places *string* into *document* and adds a newline character.
Description:	The WriteLn method will append *string* to *document*. Remember that *string* needs to have HTML tags if formatted output is needed and that the newline character does not show up in the brower's window unless the <PRE> HTML tag is being used.

Xor

Syntax:	*result* = *operand1* Xor *operand2*
Type:	Operator
Synopsis:	Returns True if only one operand is True.
Description:	If either *operand* is Null, then Null is returned. If the operands are numeric, then a bitwise comparison of identically positioned bits is performed.
See Also:	Operators

Year

Syntax:	Year(*date*)
Type:	Intrinsic Date/Time Function
Synopsis:	Returns the year part of *date*.
See Also:	Date, Date/Time Functions, DateSerial, DateValue, Day, Minute, Month, Now, Second, Time, TimeSerial, TimeValue, Weekday

V

Visual Basic Script

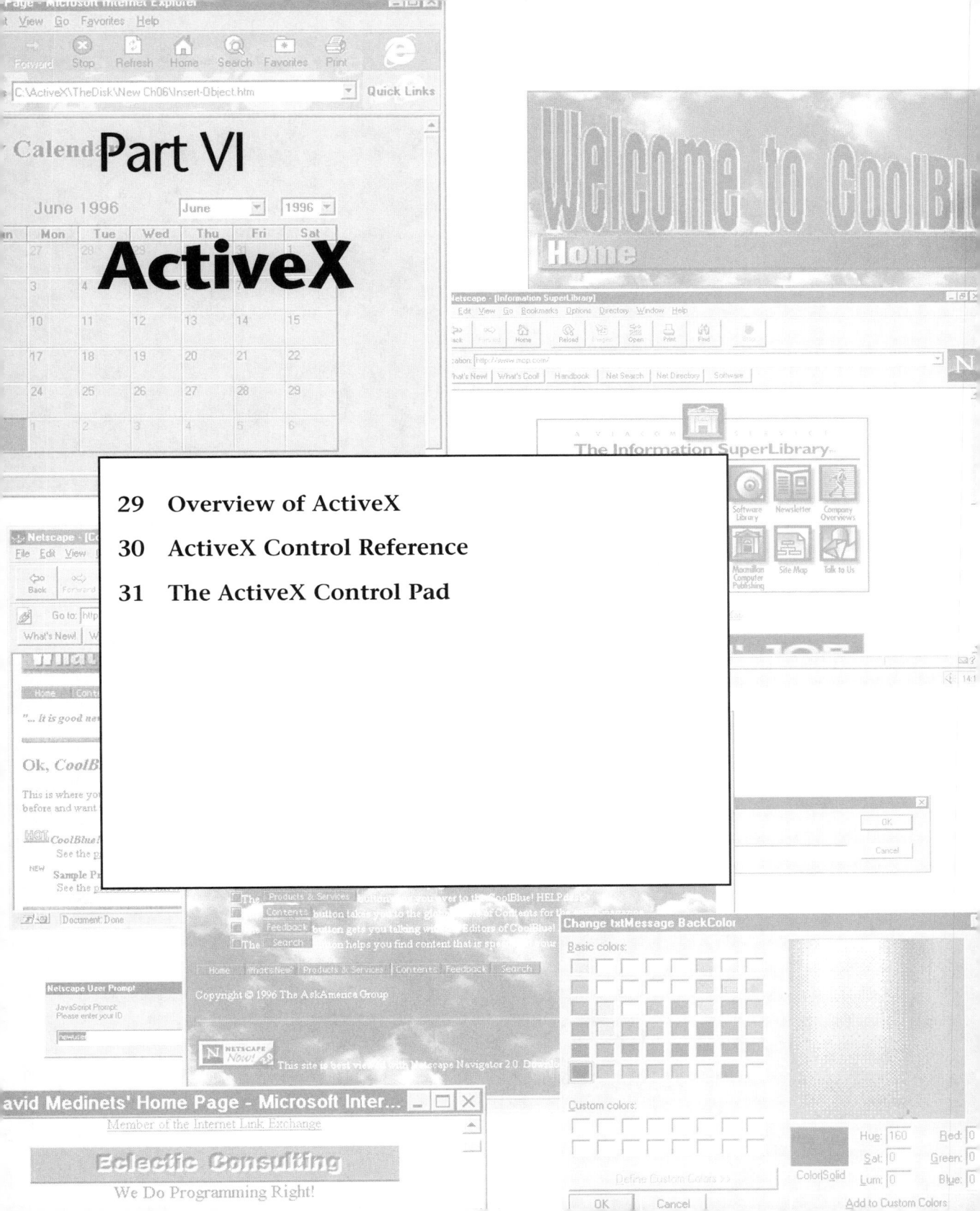

Part VI

ActiveX

Chapter 29

Overview of ActiveX

ActiveX is not a single technological thing. If you've browsed Microsoft's Web site (**http://www.microsoft.com**) you've probably gathered that ActiveX is a centerpiece of Microsoft's overall Internet strategy. ActiveX helps application developers and Web content authors build dynamic Internet tools, content, and sites. That's a pretty tall order.

To achieve this design goal, Microsoft needed to bring together a number of different components. When you're first introduced to a bunch of new items, it's often hard to assimilate all the pieces of information into an overall picture. (The old forest versus the trees problem.) So this chapter will take you through a quick tour of all the major components of ActiveX so that as we slice into the gory details, you won't lose sight of the overall ActiveX design.

ActiveX Controls for the Internet

As the content you consume from the Internet becomes more and more dynamic, the Web browser will be managing more and more of the computing tasks required to render that content. Much has been made of the executable content model for Web content. Sun Microsystem's Java takes early honors in the race for the development standard for executable content. Many Web sites employ simple multimedia widgets provided by Java, such as the Animator class.

> **Note**
>
> You can find a wealth of information about Java and many of the freely available classes for Web page developers at **http://java.sun.com** or **http://www.gamelan.com**.

Netscape helped to push Java into prominence by releasing Navigator 2.0 with support for Java applets. Java provides Web developers a highly sophisticated tool set for interacting with the user and the client machine. Microsoft, not to be outdone, announced support for Java in MSIE 3.0 and a new alternative called ActiveX Controls. ActiveX Controls are based upon the OLE 2.0

standard. ActiveX Controls are to Web pages what the VBX and OCX are to MS-Windows GUI development.

You'll use ActiveX Controls in many of the places you're using Java applets today. ActiveX Controls have several advantages over Java applets, which include the following:

- Built from tools you already know

- Easy to integrate with other applications

- Easy to employ in containers that are not Web pages

Let's take a brief look at each of these advantages.

Built Using Tools You Already Know

Java requires that you learn an entire new language. Although Java and C++ have syntactic similarities, Java requires that you learn a whole new set of class hierarchies. (Of course, Java saves you from being engulfed in the search for "a pointer from hell" as in C++.) When you consider all the methods and properties that you must learn to be proficient, it's quite an undertaking. But, on the other hand, if you've been using C++ and constructed an OCX, then you already know most of the basic concepts. Unfortunately, ActiveX Controls are not constructed using Microsoft Foundation Classes. Instead, Microsoft has made the ActiveX Template Library (ATL) available to help developers build ActiveX Controls.

Integration with Applications

Because ActiveX Controls are based upon the OLE 2.0 specification, the potential for ActiveX Controls to interact with other applications like word processing, spreadsheets, and presentations opens many possibilities. Although stand-alone applications can be constructed using Java, Java does not really offer the same potential interaction with other existing applications yet.

Employing Containers in Web Pages and Other Containers

As mentioned previously, Java can be used to produce other stand-alone applications. However, Java applets are intended to execute in a Web browser and not as controls in other applications. The Internet ActiveX Control Pack demonstrates the value of ActiveX in other development environments like Visual C++, Delphi, Visual Basic, and MS-Access. Microsoft's use of the OLE 2.0 specification as the basis for ActiveX Controls and its use in these other environments provide additional interoperability characteristics.

Of course, there are a couple of problems with the use of ActiveX Controls. You'll want to consider the following concerns:

- Not currently supported in Netscape

- Not currently supported on UNIX platforms

Why are these disadvantages important? Let's take a moment and discuss each problem briefly.

Netscape Support. If Netscape continues to dominate the browser market and ActiveX is slow to take off, there is little advantage for Netscape in supporting ActiveX. Netscape provides support for Java and sees Microsoft as a significant competitive threat. However, Microsoft will probably provide a plug-in to allow support for ActiveX. So it is unlikely that this potential disadvantage will significantly affect the long-run viability of ActiveX.

UNIX Support. Many computers connected to the Internet are UNIX-based machines. Unfortunately, Microsoft has made no significant effort to deploy Microsoft technology to the UNIX platform. The Internet has thrived on the concept of open platform support. That is, most major Internet applications work on a diverse set of platforms. In fact, much of the Internet's recent surge in popularity is due to the platform-independent nature of Web pages. With so many Internet users relying on UNIX machines, failure to support ActiveX on UNIX might seriously hamper market acceptance. However, Microsoft has indicated that ActiveX will be supported in the UNIX environment.

ActiveX Scripting Services

Netscape added another highly useful feature to Navigator called JavaScript. JavaScript provides a simple mechanism for placing conditional logic and user interface elements in Web pages without CGI applications. Basically, the Web browser provides an interpreter platform for this script. ActiveX provides a similar scripting service for MSIE 3.0.

But the ActiveX scripting service is a more general service than that offered by Netscape. The ActiveX scripting service empowers you to add scripting and OLE Automation capabilities to programs. ActiveX scripting provides a platform for developing script engines. The script language, syntax, and execution model can vary based upon the design of the script language developer. There are two types of ActiveX scripting components:

- ActiveX scripting hosts
- ActiveX scripting engines

The following sections take a look at these components.

ActiveX Scripting Hosts

An ActiveX scripting host provides a platform on which to run the ActiveX scripting engine. The principle ActiveX scripting host is MSIE 3.0. However, under ActiveX there are a number of potential script hosts:

- Other Web browsers
- Internet authoring tools
- Web servers (server-based scripting)

ActiveX Scripting Engines

An ActiveX scripting engine is basically the language to be executed on the ActiveX scripting host. The first ActiveX scripting engine is VBScript, a subset of the popular Visual Basic 4.0 development environment. However, ActiveX provides any number of potential script engine environments such as the following:

- Perl
- Lisp
- Delphi
- Scheme

ActiveX Documents

An existing application that doesn't need to be embedded in a Web page can be converted to an ActiveX document. Documents that conform to the ActiveX standard can be opened within other ActiveX document containers including:

- Microsoft Internet Explorer 3.0
- Microsoft Office Binder
- Forthcoming new Windows shell

ActiveX documents are based upon a more general abstraction called *DocObjects*. The DocObjects technology is a set of extensions to OLE documents, the compound document technology of OLE. As with OLE documents, the DocObjects standard requires a container to provide the display space for a DocObject. This technology allows the browser to present documents from Office and Office-compatible applications. Such functionality might allow any kind of document to be displayed within the Web browser.

Recall the OLE convention that an embedded object is displayed within the page of its owner document. Embedded objects do not, however, control the page on which they appear. These types of objects are usually quite small and hold very little persistent data. A spreadsheet with a few columns and rows, for instance, might be included in a Word document.

ActiveX documents, on the other hand, provide a fully functional document space. ActiveX documents also control the page in which they appear (called a *DocObject container*). This means that ActiveX documents can be considerably more feature-rich than the related embedded object.

One of the reasons for the rise of the Internet is the way that the Web has created an environment where every document is viewable in a single application. The ActiveX document standard aims to take those features another step beyond. ActiveX documents make the technology to use the Web as a vehicle for distribution of application specific documents. Microsoft's Internet Explorer 3.0 is an excellent example of an ActiveX document hosting engine.

Internet ActiveX Control Pack

The Internet ActiveX Control Pack (ICP) is not really ActiveX, per se. ICP is, instead, an application of ActiveX. But don't let that stop you. With ICP, it's easy to integrate

ActiveX Controls into your Visual Basic programs. The ICP contains controls for most of the major Internet services you'll want to integrate into your own applications.

The TCP Control

The Transmission Control Protocol (TCP) is the first of two principle methods for transmitting data over the Internet today. TCP is a connection-oriented protocol most often used for transmitting Internet Protocol (IP) packets over a network. Connection-oriented protocols like TCP are responsible for ensuring that a series of data packets sent over a network all arrive at the destination and are properly sequenced. That's why you'll frequently see the moniker "TCP/IP." The ActiveX TCP control allows you to easily handle TCP data packets in your applications without knowing much about the details of the TCP protocol.

The UDP Control

The User Datagram Protocol (UDP) is the second of two principle methods for transmitting data over the Internet today. UDP is a connectionless protocol regularly used for transmitting Internet Protocol (IP) packets over a network. Unlike TCP and other connection-oriented protocols, UDP doesn't care about the sequence of data packets. A UDP packet must stand on its own. The UDP control allows you to handle UDP data packets in your applications without knowing much about the details of the UDP protocol.

The FTP Client Control

The File Transfer Protocol (FTP) is probably the second most popular application used on the Internet today. FTP allows Internet users to upload and download files across the network. FTP also provides a mechanism to obtain filenames, directory names, attributes, and file size information. As with most Internet-based applications, FTP employs the client/server paradigm. The FTP server responds to requests for files from an FTP client. You'll use the FTP client control when your applications need to transfer text and binary files from FTP servers somewhere on the network.

The HTTP Client Control

The HyperText Transfer Protocol (HTTP) is absolutely the most popular application on the Internet. HTTP governs the interaction between an HTTP server and the Web browser. The HTTP client control allows you to directly retrieve HTTP documents. You'll use the HTTP control to create applications like HTML browsers.

The HTML Client Control

Programming Web content requires Hypertext Markup Language (HTML) programming. Typically the job of a Web browser parses and renders the HTML. HTML describes the placement and size of text and graphics. You'll use the HTML control to parse and layout HTML data, as well as provide a scrollable view of the selected HTML page. Unfortunately, the HTML client control only supports HTML 2.0 and not the evolving HTML 3.2 standard. The HTML control lets you implement an HTML viewer, with or without automatic network retrieval of HTML documents, into any application.

VI

ActiveX

The SMTP Control

Many users find e-mail to be a convenient and easy way to exchange personal and corporate information. Electronic mail finds its way over the Internet using the Simple Mail Transfer Protocol (SMTP). The SMTP client control sends Internet mail messages to SMTP servers. The SMTP control supports all SMTP commands used in sending out a mail message. So integrating e-mail directly into new and existing applications is easy.

The POP Client Control

E-mail is typically stored on the SMTP server and then distributed to the actual recipient via the Post Office Protocol (POP). The POP control provides access to Internet mail servers using the POP3 protocol. If your applications need to retrieve and delete messages from Internet mails servers, the POP client control makes it easy.

The NNTP Control

UseNet newsgroups are distributed over the Internet via the Network News Transmission Protocol (NNTP). The NNTP CLIENT control enables interaction with newsgroups on the net. With this control, you'll connect to a news server, retrieve a list of available newsgroups and their descriptions, and view news messages. Newsgroups contain a wealth of information on an extremely diverse set of topics, so you may have many applications that require scanning of news group posts.

ActiveX Server Framework

The ActiveX Server Framework provides an alternative to the Common Gateway Interface method of executing applications on a Web server and interacting with the Web browser dynamically. There are two major types of applications that can be developed using the ActiveX Server Framework:

- ISAPI applications

- ISAPI filters

The following sections take a look at the these types of applications.

ISAPI Applications

Web servers spawn Common Gateway Interface applications in separate processes with a separate environment. The Internet Server Application Programming Interface (ISAPI) specification provides an alternative to CGI programs with potentially higher performance type capabilities for the Microsoft Internet Information Server (IIS). ISAPI allows Web developers to build applications that execute in the same process space as the Web server.

Applications written using ISAPI should be faster simply because the operating system does not have to duplicate the environment and spawn a new process as is required by CGI.

ISAPI applications are actually Dynamic Link Libraries (DLLs). Note that operating in the server's process space carries higher risk while providing somewhat higher performance.

Since the ISAPI application is loaded in the same process as the HTTP server, an access violation by the ISAPI application may crash the HTTP server.

ISAPI Filters

The Internet Survey Application Programming Interface (ISAPI) also provides a mechanism for modifying the behavior of the server in specific ways. You'll employ ISAPI filters in cases where the default behavior of the server is inappropriate for the application. ISAPI filters can modify the behavior of the following server functions:

- Authentication
- Compression
- Encryption
- Logging
- Traffic analysis
- Request analysis

The following sections take a look at these server functions.

Authentication. If you've been surfing the Web, you've probably come across Web sites with pages that require a user name and password. Web site managers may want to control access to Web pages for any number of reasons. For instance, you might want to sell subscriptions to valuable content on your Web site. By default, most Web servers provide a basic authentication scheme. Usually this is a simple user name and password verification step.

With ISAPI, you can replace this basic authentication with a customized authentication process. Perhaps your environment requires that all user names and passwords for all systems be verified with a centralized database (so-called *Single Sign On procedures*). ISAPI filters provide a mechanism to accomplish this goal.

Compression. Sufficient bandwidth is perhaps the greatest inhibitor to complex content on the Internet. With an ISAPI filter, you can provide custom compression filters to improve throughput in high-end custom applications of Web technology.

Encryption. Many believe that commerce, the buying and selling of goods and services, will largely take place over the Internet. Because commerce requires the exchange of information (such as credit card numbers) that creates a tasty target for hackers, encryption is a key enabling technology. Encryption may be important in other applications as well. For instance, a company may want to transmit sensitive data to customers or suppliers. Encryption protects the data while it is in transit from source to destination. You can implement encryption to protect your data using an ISAPI filter.

Logging. When a Web server services a request for a Web page, the server makes an entry in the access log file. The access log file indicates which Web page, CGI, or ISAPI application was accessed. If the user has authenticated via the Web servers built-in authentication, the access log also contains the user name in access record. Date, time, and some other information is also recorded in the log as well.

One of the ways Web site operators make money is through advertising sales. Advertisers buy ad space based upon how many people will see their ad. So reporting information about how and by whom Web pages are accessed is extremely critical. You'll customize logging functionality using ISAPI filters.

Traffic Analysis. You may want to handle requests for a specific URL differently. For instance, you might want to catch all **http://www.yourhost.com/../../etc/passwd** requests and handle them in a certain way. You might want to examine other details of the transactions between Web browsers and your server. You'll use ISAPI filters to engage in traffic analysis.

Under the Hood of ActiveX

Microsoft has consolidated all its OLE and OCX technologies under the heading of "ActiveX." ActiveX defines a new specification for OLE controls which allows them to be much smaller and more efficient. New OLE interfaces are also specified, which addresses the problem of data and property management. Controls that are built using the new ActiveX lightweight control class are smaller than their Visual C++ Control Wizard-generated counterparts, and they can use the new interfaces to function efficiently and cooperatively with control containers in the Internet environment.

The *OLE Control and Control Container Guidelines V2.0* defines a control as a COM software component that is self-registering and implements the IUnknown interface. In order to support self-registration, the control must export the DLLRegisterServer and DLLUnRegisterServer function calls. All the OLE interfaces that were previously mandatory are now optional. Controls are free to implement as many or as few of the standard interfaces as they require.

This leads to the first question with ActiveX Controls. Previously, a control container could depend on functionality being present in the control because of the mandatory OLE interfaces. If a control only implements the IUnknown interface, how does a control container, such as a browser or authoring tool, know or find out what a control's functionality is? The answer is component categories.

Component Categories

Component categories describe different prescribed areas of functionality. Each component category is identified by a Globally Unique Identifier (GUID) and each defines a set of standards that a control must meet in order to be part of that category. Component categories are stored as entries in the system registry with GUIDs and human readable keys.

Previously, when a control was registered on a client machine it also registered the keyword *Control* under its CLSID. This keyword advertised the control's suitability for insertion into container applications like *Access* and *Visual Basic*. The Control keyword is now obsolete, but it remains for the benefit of older applications that do not understand component categories.

Component categories are a natural extension of this process. They allow a control to describe its functionality in far more detail than plain OLE interface signatures. When a control self-registers in the system registry, it adds entries under its CLSID for the GUID for a control, the GUID for each category that it supports, and the GUID of each category that it requires support for from a container in order to function properly. Additionally, it registers its own CLSID under each category registry entry.

Until now, when an application wanted to find out if a particular control supported a piece of functionality, the application had to instantiate the control and use `QueryInterface`. If a valid pointer to a new interface was returned, then the application knew that the control supported the desired functionality.

This is a very expensive and cumbersome operation. Using categories and new OLE interfaces in the OLE libraries that allow categories to be registered/unregistered, enumerated, and queried means that an application does not have to instantiate a control any more. It can get information about controls from the system registry through these new interfaces in one of two ways. If a control's CLSID is known to the application, then the application can retrieve the category GUIDs under the control's registry entry to find out the functionality of the control. If a specific area of functionality is required, then the application can go to the registry entry for the category and retrieve a list of the controls on the machine that have registered support for that functionality. It can then go to each control's registry entry and determine if it can host the control. The list can then be presented to the user of the application via an application or system user interface and the user can choose which control to use.

Management of Data and Properties

The major difference between controls designed for use on the desktop and controls that are Internet-aware is the management of data and properties. A control may have any or all of the following types of data, which needs to be stored such that it can be easily retrieved by a control container when it recreates the control. These types do not imply any form of structure or storage location. A control's properties and BLOB data collectively make up its state. The data types are shown in Table 29.1.

Table 29.1 ActiveX Data Types		
Data Type	**Size**	**Purpose**
Class Identifier (CLSID)	16 bytes	The CLSID of the control class that can read the data that follows.
Properties	Around 10k to 30k	Standard and custom property values.
Binary Large Objects (BLOB)	Arbitrary size	Any number of large binary files. These files may be in any format, e.g. bitmaps, multimedia files, etc.

If a control has no persistent state, then none of the above will be present in an HTML document. The control container will retrieve the CLSID of the control class directly from the `CLSID` attribute of the HTML `<OBJECT>` tag or indirectly from the `CODE` attribute. The control can then be instantiated and no further initialization is required.

VI

ActiveX

When the user of an application that is hosting a control gives the command to save, the control container calls QueryInterface on the control for a persistent storage interface and the control serializes its state through it. Similarly, when a control is recreated, it retrieves its state through a persistent storage interface. Where the application stores the control's state is up to the user of the application that is hosting the control. The control is not concerned. It may be embedded within the HTML document or in a separate file that is linked to the HTML document. This linking and embedding mechanism is familiar territory to anyone with knowledge of OLE compound documents.

Although the control is not concerned with the actual storage of its state, it is concerned with the interfaces through which its state is saved and retrieved. One of the goals Microsoft had when creating the ActiveX specification was to introduce as little new technology as possible. However, the existing persistence interfaces used in the current OLE compound document architecture are potentially unsuitable for Internet-aware controls.

Problems with the Current Implementation of OLE Compound Documents

In OLE compound documents, an object and its native data can be stored in two ways. They can be embedded in the document or linked to the document. In the embedding case, the object's CLSID, its native data, and a presentation cache are stored within the document. In the linking case, a moniker and a presentation cache are stored within the document. The moniker points to a file which contains the object's CLSID and native data.

The problems with this architecture are as follows:

- The compound document usually always contains a presentation cache. This can lead to document sizes which are too large for effective use on the Internet.

- Embedded objects can only use the IPersistStorage interface for saving and loading of data. This interface is a heavy duty interface and is not well suited to small simple controls. Implementing this interface leads to code that is not required and is simply extra baggage for small simple controls.

- When a compound document recreates an object, the object retrieves its native data and properties synchronously. That is, when an object makes a call to a persistence interface to retrieve data, execution control does not return to the object until the data has been completely retrieved. This is not a problem on the desktop as the data is stored locally in files on a high speed disk subsystem. The length of time for which the user interface is frozen while retrieval takes place therefore is usually very small. In a relatively slow environment like the Internet, synchronous retrieval of large amounts of data from a remote site will freeze the user interface for an unacceptably long time.

- If an OLE compound document wants to use linking to save an object's native data and properties, then it must implement the IPersistFile interface for moniker binding. File monikers, however, are designed to work with the Universal Naming Convention (UNC) file and path names. They do not work with the Universal Resource Location (URL) file and path names that are used on the Internet.

- Any references to external data that are contained within the embedded or linked object's native data are known only to the object that created the data. This prohibits the control container from participating in the retrieval of the external data. Asynchronous retrieval of this data may also not be possible.

The problem of the presentation cache was eliminated for the embedding scenario in the first release of the OLE control specification in 1994. Controls could implement a new lightweight interface called `IPersistStreamInit`, which can be used in preference to `IPersistStorage`. `IPersistStreamInit` allows all properties and BLOBs to be channeled into one stream and stored by the application in the document. This eliminated the cache as the data could simply and quickly be reloaded into the control when the document was loaded and the control was instantiated and initialized. In the linking case, because the objects data and properties were stored locally in files and could be retrieved quickly, the presentation cache was also eliminated.

Because of the shortcomings of the existing persistence mechanisms, Microsoft has developed new persistence mechanisms and monikers that extend the concept of linking and embedding beyond the OLE Compound Document architecture. These new mechanisms also allow for asynchronous retrieval of properties and BLOBs from remote sites.

Persistent Embedding. The control's CLSID, properties, and BLOBs are stored within the HTML document itself. This is really only useful where the aggregate size of this information is small. It is not suitable for large amounts of data as the time taken to download the page and make it active would be unacceptable.

Persistent Linking. A single URL moniker is stored in the HTML document. This moniker points to a file on a remote site that contains the CLSID, properties, and BLOBs for the control.

An important point to note is that the specification of embedding and linking in OLE compound documents entails adherence to certain user interface standards. Specifically, linked objects may not be in-place activated. Persistent linking and embedding are not concerned with user interface and the standards are not relevant. Their sole function is for storage management of properties and BLOBs. Controls that are in-place activated, therefore, can still work with persistently linked data.

The persistent interface mechanisms that can now be used by a control are summarized in the Table 29.2.

Table 29.2 Persistent Interface Mechanisms

Use	Mechanism	Comments
Embedding/linking	IPersistStorage	Standard persistence mechanism used in OLE compound documents. The container supplies an IStorage pointer to a storage object. The control may create any data structure within that object for its state.

(continues)

VI

ActiveX

Table 29.2 Continued		
Use	**Mechanism**	**Comments**
Embedding/linking	IPersistStreamInit	This is a lightweight alternative to IPersistStorage. All of the control's state can be serialized into one stream.
Embedding/linking	IPersistMemory	The container defines a fixed size block of memory into which a control saves or retrieves its state. The control must not try to access memory outside the block.
Embedding	IPersistPropertyBag	The container and control exchange property/value pairs in Variant structures.
linking	IPersistFile	The container gives the control a UNC filename and is told to save or retrieve its state from that file.
linking	IPersistMoniker	The control is given a moniker. When the control reads or writes its state, it may choose any storage mechanism (IStorage, IStream, ILockBytes, etc.) it wants. If the storage mechanism chosen by the control is asynchronous, then IPersistMoniker must support asynchronous transfer.

For each mechanism that a control implements, the control container must provide the appropriate support.

A control container that wants to support embedding must provide the appropriate support for the persistence interfaces exposed by the control, as in the following table:

Control Persistence Interface	Container Supplied Support
IPersistStreamInit	IStream
IPersistStorage	IStorage
IPersistMemory	Memory (*void)
IPersistPropertyBag	IPropertyBag

A control container that wants to implement linking must use a moniker that can supply support for the persistence interfaces exposed by the control. At the time of writing, the only available moniker is the URL moniker.

If a control implements the IPersistMemory or the IPersistFile mechanism, then it should also implement one other interface as both of these require that the data be present locally. These mechanisms do not work well with asynchronous downloads of properties and BLOBs.

Controls are free to implement as many of these new persistence mechanisms as the developer of the control sees fit. For maximum flexibility, therefore, a control container should implement support for as many of these interfaces as possible. This will ensure that it can work with a wide range of controls which may not implement all of the new persistence mechanisms.

These new persistence mechanisms define the protocol through which the container and the control exchange information. What happens when an application decides to save a control's state (perhaps in response to a user request) depends on the application's (user's) preferences for storage. It can either be embedded in the HTML document or in a separate file and linked to the document.

When embedding is used, the control container chooses which persistence interface to use. The sequence in which a container looks for persistence interfaces is generally up to the designer of the container. However, IPersistMemory and IPersistStreamInit may be given precedence over IPersistProperyBag and IPersistStorage as they will generally produce the smallest amount of data. Note that it is perfectly acceptable for a container to have a control save its state in one location and then copy it to some other location. All that is required is that the container be able to retrieve the saved state and give it back to the control via the same interface. For example, a container could ask a control to save its state in a memory block. The container may then save the contents of that memory block in a storage location of its choosing. When the control is initialized, the container must retrieve the saved state and give it back to the control via a memory block.

When linking is used, the container is not concerned with any of the persistence interfaces. The container must store and interact with an URL moniker. The moniker takes care of all the interface querying. URL monikers query for persistence interfaces in the following order:

1. IPersistMoniker

2. IPersistStreamInit

3. IPersistStorage

4. IPersistMemory

5. IPersistFile

In both linking and embedding, the container is responsible for the asynchronous transfer of data from the remote site. For more information on this, see the "Compound Files on the Internet" document supplied as part of the Sweeper SDK. All the persistence interfaces with the exception of IPersistMoniker are synchronous in operation. When a control receives a call to the Load member of one of its persistence interfaces, it expects all of the data to be available.

Data Paths. Data paths serve two purposes. They allow a control to store its BLOBs separately from its properties and they solve the problem of embedded links. Controls may have links to BLOBs buried away in their native data that only they know about. This prohibits the container from participating in the retrieval of these BLOBs. One solution to this is data path properties. *Data path properties* are properties that hold text string values. These string values are simply URL file names. Data path properties can be used with either persistent linking or persistent embedding.

VI

ActiveX

In a control's type library, data path properties must be marked as [bindable] and [requestedit]. This allows container applications to update these properties through its own user interface. These properties may also be updated through the control's property sheet. They are also tagged with a special custom attribute which identifies them as data path properties. The custom attribute is called GUID_PathProperty. It has its own GUID. Additionally, a control's coclass entry in its type library is also tagged with a special attribute which signifies that it has data path properties. This attribute is called GUID_HasPathProperties and it too has its own GUID.

> **Note**
>
> Applications such as authoring tools and Web site management tools can query controls for data path properties and use them to perform link management or other tasks.

When a control wants to retrieve the file named by a data path property, it gives the URL to the container and asks it to create a moniker for the URL. The moniker is created in the implementation of the IBindHost interface. This interface is supplied as a service by the container site's IServiceObject implementation. In order for the control to call members of IBindHost, the control must provide a way for the container to pass a pointer that identifies the IServiceObject interface. A control could implement the IOleObject interface in order to achieve this.

This interface has a function called SetClientSite that allows a container to pass the pointer to the control. The IOleObject interface, however, is a large interface. All its functionality may not be required by a small control. A smaller interface called IObjectWithSite can be implemented. It has just two member functions, one of which, SetSite, allows the container to pass the required pointer.

> **Note**
>
> Any control that uses data path properties must support a siting mechanism. Either IOleObject or IOleObjectWithSite. This is a requirement of the specification.

In order to get the IBindHost interface, two steps are required. The control calls QueryInterface on the site pointer for the IServiceProvider interface. Then the control calls QueryService on the IServiceProvider interface for the IBindHost interface.

In order to get a moniker for the file and data path property names, the control calls the ParseDisplayName function of the IBindHost interface. The data path may be either an absolute path name or a path name relative to the location of the document. Either way, a moniker is returned which the control can use to retrieve data.

When downloading data, the control should be as cooperative as possible with the container and other controls by supporting asynchronous retrieval of data. This allows the user interface to remain active while data trickles down in the background.

Before initiating a retrieval operation, a control should check to see if the moniker that it is supplied with is an asynchronous one. It does this by calling QueryInterface on the moniker for the `IMonikerAsynch` interface. If this interface is not present, then the moniker is synchronous and the control has to bind directly to the storage identified by the moniker by creating a bind context and calling the `BindToStorage` member of the moniker.

If the moniker is asynchronous, then the control should get its bind context from the container through the `GetBindCtx` member of `IBindHost`. By obtaining it this way, the container has a chance to register itself as an interested party in the download process. It can monitor the download and display some sort of progress indicator for the user's convenience or perhaps allow the user to cancel the download.

Once a control has the bind context, it registers its own `FORMATETC` enumerator and a pointer to its `IBindStatusCallBack` interface in the bind context. The control initiates an asynchronous download in the `Load` member of a persistence interface. In this function, another asynchronous stream should be obtained so that the moniker and the bind context can be released. This allows the `Load` function to return immediately and execution control can return to the container. When data arrives, the `OnDataAvailable` member of the `IBindStatusCallBack` interface will be called. The control should obtain the data exclusively through this function.

For detailed information on how the control, the container and the moniker interact in asynchronous downloads, see the "Asynchronous Monikers" specification in the Sweeper SDK.

Data transfer may be aborted by a call to the `OnStopBinding` member of the `IBindStatusCallBack` interface. If a control receives such a call, then there are two possibilities. If the control has received all its data, then the call is merely a notification that transfer is complete; otherwise, the data transfer has been aborted for some reason.

A control may abort the data transfer by calling the `Abort` member of the `IBinding` interface. The control receives a pointer to this interface through the `IStartBinding` member of the `IBindStatusCallBack` interface.

Since the container has control and data is trickling down in the background, how does a container know when a control is ready to begin full interaction? One way is to return a new code, `E_PENDING`, from member functions of the control when the control is not yet ready to fully interact. When this code is not returned, the control may be ready to interact. This however does not allow for progressive changes in a control's ability to interact with the application and/or the user. Microsoft solved this problem by defining a new standard property, `ReadyState`, and a new standard event, `OnReadyStateChanged`. When the control's ready state changes, the new standard event is fired with the value of the `ReadyState` property to notify the container. The `ReadyState` property may progressively have the following values:

Uninitialized   The control is waiting to be initialized through the `Load` member of a persistence interface.

VI

ActiveX

Loading	The control is synchronously retrieving its properties. Some may not yet be available.
Loaded/Can Render	The control has retrieved its properties and is able to draw something through the `Draw` member of the `IViewObject2` interface.
Interactive	The control may interact with user in a limited way. It has not yet received all its data from the asynchronous download.
Complete	The control is completely ready.

The control does not have to support all of the previous states. It only has to support as many as it needs.

Object Persistence and Data Path Properties

When a control is requested to save its state by a call to the `Save` member of a persistence interface, it saves all of its properties—including data path properties as strings—through the interface and then saves all the BLOBs referred to by any data path properties. It does this by obtaining a moniker for each data path through the container's `IBindHost` as described previously and synchronously saving the BLOB. When the `Save` function returns, a control is assumed to have saved all of its state.

Instantiation of a Control

The instantiation and initialization sequence for a control is described in the following paragraphs. The assumption is made that the control is already on the client machine and properly registered.

The application obtains the CLSID of the control from the `CLSID` attribute of the HTML `<OBJECT>` tag and instantiates the control.

The `DATA` attribute will contain either the property data encoded in MIME or an URL which names a file on a remote site that contains the property data.

If the `DATA` attribute contains the property data, the container obtains a persistence interface on the control and calls the `Load` member with a stream containing the property data.

If the `DATA` attribute contains an URL, then the container makes an URL moniker and calls the `IBindToObject` member of the `IMoniker` interface in order to retrieve the property data from a remote site. Inside this function, the URL moniker attempts to get an `IPersistMoniker` interface on the control. If it succeeds, it passes a pointer to itself to the `Load` member of this interface. The control then has complete control over retrieval of its properties from the remote site.

> **Note**
>
> Because properties are usually very small amounts of data, measured in hundreds of bytes or so, asynchronous retrieval may not be the best method. Synchronous retrieval may be a better option as it may allow the control to become interactive sooner.

If it cannot get the `IPersistMoniker` interface, it gets another persistence interface. It then retrieves the property data, wraps it up in an `IStream` object if necessary, and calls the `Load` member function of the interface with a pointer to the object. The control then retrieves its property data from the `IStream` object.

Inside the `Load` member of the persistence interface, the control will also initiate any asynchronous download of BLOBs. It asks the container to make URL monikers so that the container may also bind to them and participate in the download process. The control binds to each moniker and registers its `IOnBindStatusCallback` interface in order to receive data. Control is then returned to the container.

As BLOBs trickle down in the background, the control changes the value of the `ReadyState` variable and notifies the container of any change in its state through the `OnReadyStateChange` event. The `ReadyState` variable is passed as a parameter of the event.

Summary of Requirements for Internet-Aware Controls

If a control has no data path properties, then a control need only implement as many of the persistence interfaces as the developer sees fit. The more interfaces a control implements, the more flexibility it has for initialization by control containers and URL monikers.

Controls that have data path properties and BLOBs must meet the following requirements:

- It must support either `IOleObject` or `IObjectWithSite` as a siting mechanism.

- It must mark data path properties with the `[bindable]` and `[requestedit]` attributes, as well as the custom `GUID_PathProperty` attribute.

- It must mark its `coclass` entry in its type information with the `GUID_HasPathProperties` custom attribute.

- It must follow the rules for moniker creation and persistence using the container's `IBindHost` as necessary.

- It must bind with an asynchronous moniker using a container provided bind context from `IBindHost` and receive its data through the `OnDataAvailable` member of the `IBindStatusCallback` interface.

- It must coordinate data retrieval and begin interaction as soon as possible.

Additionally, it should supply a `ReadyState` variable and an `OnReadyStateChange` event if they are required. It should also support `IPersistPropertyBag` for supporting HTML PARAM attributes.

VI

ActiveX

Chapter 30

ActiveX Control Reference

So far in this section you have been given a whirlwind tour of ActiveX, its implementation, and general characteristics. The remainder of this chapter focuses on showing you different ActiveX Controls, their properties, and their methods.

The TCP Control

The Transmission Control Protocol (TCP) is the first of two principle methods for transmitting data over the Internet today. TCP is a connection oriented protocol most often used for transmitting Internet Protocol (IP) packets over a network. Connection oriented protocols like TCP are responsible for ensuring that a series of data packets sent over a network all arrive at the destination and are properly sequenced. The ActiveX TCP control allows you to easily handle TCP data packets in your applications without knowing much about the details of the TCP protocol.

Properties

Table 30.1 summarizes all the properties available in the TCP control. Not suprisingly, all the data elements required to create a TCP connection are included as properties in this control.

Table 30.1	Summary of Properties in the TCP Control
Property	**Purpose**
BytesReceived	The amount of data in the receive buffer.
LocalHostName	The name of the local machine.
LocalIP	The Internet Protocol (IP) address of the local machine.
LocalPort	The TCP port used by the local machine for this communication.
RemoteHost	The name of the remote machine.
RemoteHostIP	The IP address of the remote machine.
RemotePort	The TCP port used by the remote machine for this communication.
SocketHandle	Handle used to communicate with the WinSock layer.
State	Returns the current status of the connection.

Before we dive into the properties themselves, consider the basic components of a TCP connection. A TCP connection requires that both the client and the server have both an IP address and a port.

The specified port must not be used by any other application. Many ports are already defined as standard ports and are therefore off-limits to your application. For instance, Web browsers use port 80 to connect to Web servers. Most books about TCP/IP will contain a good list of port numbers that are already spoken for. A good rule of thumb is to use port numbers higher than 1,000—these are mostly free.

Now let's take a look at a few of these properties in a bit more detail.

The *RemoteHost*, *RemotePort*, and *LocalPort* Properties. RemoteHost, RemotePort, and LocalPort are the properties you'll be setting in your programs most often. If the application you're writing is a client that will initiate connections with another application, you'll set the RemoteHost and RemotePort properties to the appropiate host and port. The RemoteHost should be a string with either a domain name (for example, **ftp.myhost.com**) or a dot format IP address (for example, **198.5.164.222**). Set the RemotePort number equal to the port number that the server listens on.

If the application you're writing is a server that will listen for connections from another application, you'll set LocalPort to the port number you want to listen for connections on. (Note that the combination of an IP address and a host name is sometimes referred to as a *socket*.) The TCP control will take care of setting LocalHost on the client side.

The *State* Property. The State property stores the current state of the TCP connection. Since State is a read-only property, you'll never set the state of the connection. However, you'll want to use the value of State in all sorts of ways. Table 30.2 summarizes the values that State may contain.

Table 30.2   Values That *State* May Contain

Value	Description
sckClosed	Default. The socket is closed.
sckOpen	The socket is open.
sckListening	Listening on the socket.
sckConnectionPending	Connection pending.
sckResolvingHost	Resolving the host name to obtain an IP address.
sckConnecting	Currently connecting.
sckConnected	Connected.
sckClosing	Another application is closing the socket.
sckError	The socket is errored.

Most of the time, your programs will be checking to see if the connection is sckOpen or sckClosed.

Methods

The process of creating a connection involves each of the following steps:

1. Server listens on a specific port.

2. Client requests a connection with the server.

3. Server accepts the connection.

4. Data is transferred between the client and the server.

5. Either the client or the server closes the connection.

As you'll see in Table 30.3, the TCP control has a method for each of these actions.

Table 30.3	Summary of Methods in the TCP Control
Method	**Description**
Accept	Accepts an incoming connection.
Close	Closes a TCP connection.
Connect	Makes a connection request to a distant machine.
GetData	Obtains the current block of data.
Listen	Creates and listens on a socket.
PeekData	Obtains a copy of the current block of data.
SendData	Sends data to a remote machine.

Connecting Clients and Servers

So, to implement the server-side of a TCP connection you'll use the following methods:

- Listen

- Accept

Say you have a TCP control named MyTCPControl. To start the server, your VB code would look something like Listing 30.1.

Listing 30.1   Starting a Server Listening for a Connection

```
MyTCPControl.LocalPort = 1252
MyTCPControl.Listen
```

When a client requests a connection to the server, the server must accept the connection. Your VB code for accepting a connection would look like Listing 30.2.

Listing 30.2   Accepting an Incoming Connection

```
Private Sub MyTCPControl_ConnectionRequest(ByVal requestID As Long)

MyTCPControl.Accept requestID

End Sub
```

Note that you'll use a response function for the ConnectionRequest event to obtain the requestID for the connection.

VI

ActiveX

To implement the client-side of a TCP connection, your VB program will contain code like Listing 30.3. Assume that your client program has a TCP control named `MyOtherTCPControl`.

Listing 30.3 Initiating a Connection with a Server

```
MyOtherTCPControl.RemotePort = 1252
MyOtherTCPControl.RemoteHost = "198.5.164.222"

MyOtherTCPControl.Connect
```

Sending and Receiving Data

Both clients and servers use the data transmission methods the same way. To send data from one to the other, your code will look something like this:

```
MyTCPControl.SendData "This is my message"
```

To obtain received data, you'll usually write a response to the `DataArrival` event (more on the `DataArrival` event in a moment). Your code will look something like Listing 30.4.

Listing 30.4 Getting Data From the Input Buffer

```
Private Sub sktStockServer_DataArrival(ByVal bytesTotal As Long)

Dim A

MyTCPControl.GetData A

    DoSomethingWith A

End Sub
```

Note that calling `GetData` causes the incoming buffer to be emptied. If you want to look at the incoming data without clearing the data, you'll use `PeekData` in a similar manner.

Events

You've already seen how several of the most important events summarized in Table 30.4 are used.

Table 30.4 Summary of Events in the TCP Control

Event	Description
Close	Triggered when the remote machine closes the connection.
Connect	Signals that the connection is ready for data transfer.
ConnectionRequest	Occurs when a distant machine requests a connection.
DataArrival	Fires when new data has arrived in the receive buffer.
Error	Signals a background processing error.
SendProgress	Used to signal progress of data transfers.

The UDP Control

The User Datagram Protocol (UDP) is the second of two principle methods for transmitting data over the Internet. UDP is a connection-less protocol most often used for transmitting Internet Protocol (IP) packets over a network. Connection-less oriented protocols like UDP are typically employed for sending independent data packets over a network where one packet has no relationship to the next sequential packet. UDP is often used for network services that do not require an ongoing conversation between client and server. UDP senders typically don't care whether the receiver actually receives the message. Instead, UDP is used for discrete transmissions of information where the individual requests and replies are unrelated to one another. The best part about the ActiveX UDP control, however, is the ease with which you can implement these sorts of services without knowing much about the details of the UDP protocol.

Properties

Table 30.5 summarizes all the properties available in the UDP control. All the data elements required to create a UDP connection are included as properties in this control.

Table 30.5   Properties of the UDP ActiveX Control

Property	Purpose
LocalHostName	The name of the local machine.
LocalIP	The Internet Protocol (IP) address of the local machine.
LocalPort	The TCP port used by the local machine for this communication.
RemoteHost	The name of the remote machine.
RemoteHostIP	The IP address of the remote machine.
RemotePort	The TCP port used by the remote machine for this communication.
SocketHandle	Handle used to communicate with the WinSock layer.

Consider the basic components of a UDP connection. A UDP connection (like a TCP connection) requires that both the client and the server have both an IP address and a port.

The specified port must not be used by any other application. Many ports are already defined as standard ports and are therefore off limits to your application. For instance, FTP servers use ports 20 and 21 to manage connections between clients and servers. As mentioned in the previous chapter, a good rule of thumb is to use port numbers higher than 1,000 because they are mostly free.

Now let's take a look at a few of these properties in a bit more detail.

The *RemoteHost*, *RemotePort*, and *LocalPort* Properties. Just like the TCP control, the RemoteHost, RemotePort, and LocalPort on the UDP control are the properties you'll be setting in your programs most often. Remember that you'll set the RemoteHost and RemotePort properties to the host and port on which your application will be sending a message. On the receiving application, you'll set LocalPort to the port number you want to receive the message on. (Note that the combination of an IP address and a host name is sometimes referred to as a *socket*.)

VI

ActiveX

Methods

Unlike the TCP control, there are only a couple of methods in the UDP control. This is because the connection-less UDP protocol is less involved. Table 30.6 summarizes these methods.

Table 30.6 Methods for the UDP Control	
Method	**Description**
Connect	Makes a connection request to a distant machine.
GetData	Obtains the current block of data.
SendData	Sends data to a remote machine.

Because the UDP protocol does not involve an ongoing conversation between two computers, there is no need for the Accept, Listen, and Close methods found in the TCP control. The reasons for this will become more obvious in a moment.

Connecting the Sending and Receiving Application

To implement the receiving side of a UDP connection, you'll do the following:

■ Set the LocalHost property.

■ Employ the GetData method when data arrives (for example, when the DataArrival event is triggered).

Say you have a UDP control named MyUDPControl. To program the receiver, your VB code would look something like this:

```
MyUDPControl.LocalPort = 1252
```

You will also need to provide an event handler for the DataArrival event (more on this in a moment) as shown in Listing 30.5.

Listing 30.5 Using *GetData* to Receive UDP Datagrams

```
Private Sub MyUDPControl_DataArrival(ByVal bytesTotal As Long)

    Dim ADatagram

    MyUDPControl.GetData ADatagram
        DoSomethingWith ADatagram

End Sub
```

To implement the sender side of a UDP connection, you'll do the following:

■ Set the RemoteHost property

■ Set the RemotePort property

■ Send data using the SendData method

When a sending application sends data over the network, you'll initialize the RemotePort and RemoteHost properties and then send data using the SendData method (see Listing 30.6). Assume that your sender program has a UDP control named MyOtherUDPControl.

Listing 30.6   Setting the *RemoteHost* and *RemotePort* Properties

```
Dim ADatagram

MyOtherUDPControl.RemoteHost = "198.5.164.222"
MyOtherUDPCOntrol.RemotePort = 1252

MyOtherUDPControl.SendData ADatagram
```

Events

Similar to the method list, the event list for the UDP control is quite sparse. Table 30.7 summarizes the events that are fired by the UDP control.

Table 30.7 Summary of Events in the UDP Control	
Event	**Description**
DataArrival	Fires when new data has arrived in the receive buffer.
Error	Signals a background processing error.

In the UDP control, these events are triggered in the same way as the TCP control.

The FTP Client Control

The File Transfer Protocol (FTP) provides a simple interface for moving text and binary files over the Internet. FTP is one of the most popular applications used on the Internet today. In fact, many Web browsers support the FTP protocol in addition to other more popular protocols like HTTP. Like most of the other Internet protocols, FTP requires both a client and a server to complete file transfers. The technical details of the FTP protocol are a bit more complicated but, fortunately, the ActiveX FTP client control allows us to avoid knowing much about FTP itself.

Properties

Table 30.8 summarizes all the properties available in the FTP Client control. All the data elements required to transfer a file from an FTP server are included as properties in this control.

Table 30.8 Properties of the FTP Client ActiveX Control	
Property	**Purpose**
AppendToFile	Tells whether file operations are appended or not.
Busy	True if a command is currently in progress.
DocInput	Refers to the DocInput object which must be set before invoking the SendDoc method and conveys information about the progress of the data transfer.
DocOutput	Refers to the DocOutput object which must be set before invoking the GetDoc method and conveys information about the progress of the data transfer.

(continues)

VI

ActiveX

Table 30.8 Continued	
Property	**Purpose**
EnableTimer	Tells the kind of timer that is fired by the TimeOut event.
Errors	Refers to a collection of errors detailing the last error.
IsAuthenticated	True if authentication has been successfully completed.
ListItemNotify	Tells how the ListItem event will pass an FTPDirItem object.
LocalFile	The file name to be used in GetFile and PutFile operations.
NotificationMode	Determines how notification of inbound data will be provided.
Password	Sets the password to be used for logging on to an FTP server.
ProtocolState	Indicates whether the FTP client is not connected, waiting for authorization to connect, or connected to an FTP server.
RemoteDir	The current directory on the remote server.
RemoteFile	The file name to be used in GetFile and PutFile operations.
RemoteHost	The host name or IP address of the server to be connected to.
RemotePort	The port number used to connect to the FTP server.
ReplyCode	The reply code sent by the server in response to requests from the client.
ReplyString	The reply string sent by the server in response to requests from the client.
State	Used to report the current state of the FTP connection.
TimeOut	Tells how long to wait before firing the TimeOut event for the type of timer referred to by EnableTimer.
URL	The Uniform Resource Locator such as **ftp://myhost.com/ myfile.txt**.
UserID	Sets the user name to be used for logging on to an FTP server.

Now let's take a look at a few of these properties in a bit more detail.

The *DocInput* and *DocOutput* Properties. DocInput and DocOutput objects allow you to control and monitor the incoming and outgoing documents from client to server. These objects also allow the output of one control to be streamed directly to the input of another control.

The *EnableTimer* Property. Often times, you'll want to take some action after a time-out period has expired. For instance, you might want to ask the user to try again later if a connection took more than 30 seconds to obtain. The EnableTimer property tells what kind of timer is enabled. The kinds of timers that can be enabled are listed in Table 30.9.

Table 30.9 *EnableTimer* Settings

Kind of Timer	Value
prcConnectTimeout	Enables a connect timer. If a connection is not established within the time-out period, the TimeOut event is triggered.
prcReceiveTimeout	Enables a receive timer. If no data arrives within the time-out period, the TimeOut event is triggered.
prcUserTimeout	Provides a mechanism for adding user-defined timers. To implement such a timer, add an integer to prcUserTimeout.

So, to enable a connect timer, your code would look something like Listing 30.8.

Listing 30.8   Enabling Timers

```
...
'-----------------------------------
'-- Define a custom timeout
'-----------------------------------
prcMyCustomTimeout = prcUserTimeout + 1

'-----------------------------------
'--- Enable the connect timeout
'-----------------------------------
MyFTPControl.EnableTimer(prcConnectTimeout) = True

'-----------------------------------
'--- Disable the receive timeout
'-----------------------------------
MyFTPControl.EnableTimer(prcReceiveTimeout) = False

'-----------------------------------
'--- Enable a user define timeout
'-----------------------------------
MyFTPControl.EnableTimer(prcMyCustomTimeout) = True
...
```

As is apparent from Listing 30.8, you can enable all, none, or any number of timers as required for your applications.

The *ListItemNotify* Property. The ListItemNotify property allows you to select whether requests for a directory listing will be passed as an FTPDirItem object through the ListItem event or as data blocks through the DocOutput event. As you'll see in the explanation of the ListItem event, the FTPDirItem makes obtaining details about files and directory entries easy.

The *NotificationMode* Property. When you use the FTP ActiveX control to transfer data, you can select when you will be notified that data has arrived. Table 30.10 shows the available modes.

VI

ActiveX

Table 30.10	*NotificationMode* Settings
Value	**Meaning**
0	Notify when the data transmission has been completed. This is the default setting.
1	The arrival of data causes an event to be continuously fired.

The *ProtocolState* Property. This property provides protocol-specific information about the state of the connection. For the FTP control, there are three states that the protocol can be in. These states are listed in Table 30.11.

Table 30.11	FTP *ProtocolState* Values
Value	**Meaning**
ftpBase	The default state of the protocol prior to connecting to an FTP server.
ftpAuthorization	Authorization using the UserID and Password is currently underway.
ftpTransaction	Authorization has been completed and the FTP client has identified itself to the FTP server.

The *State* Property. The State property stores the current state of the FTP connection. Since State is a read-only property, you'll never set the state of the connection. However, you'll want to use the value of State in all sorts of ways. Table 30.12 summarizes the values that State may contain.

Table 30.12	Values That *State* May Contain
Value	**Description**
prcConnecting	This is the state of the FTP connection after requesting a connection and before receiving acknowlegement of the server.
prcResolvingHost	If the RemoteHost property is a domain name and not an IP address, the connection will reach this state while the host name is obtained.
prcHostResolved	After the host name has been resolved to an IP address, this state is reached.
prcConnected	The connection is established.
prcDisconnecting	The close connection process has been initiated but has not yet completed.
prcDisconnected	When the connection is closed and acknowledgment has been received, the state holds this value. This is also the state of the FTP control when instantiated.

Methods

Most of the action in an FTP session involves sending and receiving files. The methods to accomplish this work are summarized in Table 30.13.

Table 30.13   Methods for the FTP Client Control

Method	Use
Abort	Stops the last request for a data transfer.
Account	Sends account information to the FTP server. Check the reply string to determine the results.
Authentication	Authenticates the user using the UserID and Password properties.
Cancel	Stops a pending request.
ChangeDir	Requests that the directory on the FTP server is changed.
Connect	Issues a request to the FTP server to open a connection. If a connection is established, the State property is set.
CreateDir	Creates the specified directory on the FTP server if the user is permitted.
DeleteDir	Deletes the specified directory on the FTP server if the user is permitted.
DeleteFile	Deletes the specified file on the FTP server if the user is permitted.
Execute	Executes a command directly on the server via the RFC-959 Quote command.
GetDoc	Requests the retrieval of a document identified by a URL and can be used in conjunction with the DocInput and DocOutput objects and events.
GetFile	Obtains a file from the FTP server and places it in the current directory.
Help	Obtains a help listing from the FTP server. The ReplyString property will contain the results of the request.
List	Returns a detailed listing of a FTP server directory. The ListItemNotify property indicates how and when this List is returned.
ListSize	Lists files by size.
Mode	Sets the FTP mode.
NameList	Returns a list of filenames from the FTP server.
NOOP	Causes the FTP server to reply with an OK in the ReplyString property.
ParentDir	Asks the FTP server to change directory to the parent of the current directory.
PrintDir	Asks the FTP server to reply with the current directory.
PutFile	Places a file in server's current directory.
Quit	Closes the connection and fires the Quit event.
ReInitialize	Issues a reinitialize request and obtains a reply in the ReplyString property.
SendDoc	Requests that a document identified by the URL to be sent to the server and can be used in conjunction with the DocInput and DocOutput objects and events.
Site	Obtains the type of file system supported by the remote system. The reply is found in ReplyString.
State	Obtains the state of the connection as defined in RFC-959 Stat command.
System	Requests that the server identify which operating system it requires. Checks ReplyString for the response.
Type	Sets the type of data to be transferred.

Most of these methods are self-explanatory. However, one merits additional discussion.

VI

ActiveX

The *Type* Method. You'll use FTP to transfer files that contain all sorts of data. The FTP protocol requires that you identify the type of data contained in the transfer in order to ensure that data is transferred reliably. The values to be passed to the Type method are shown in Table 30.14.

Table 30.14 Transfer Types for the *Type* Method	
Type	**Meaning**
ftpAscii	Text file transfer. This is the default Type.
ftpEBCDIC	The file to be transferred is an Extended Binary Coded Decimal Interchange file.
ftpImage	For transferring image files.
ftpBinary	Binary files are transferred using this type.

Getting and Putting Files

The primary purpose of the FTP protocol is to transfer files from client to server and back again. The there are two methods to make this happen using the FTP ActiveX control including:

- Using DocInput and DocOutput objects and events with the SendDoc and GetDoc methods

- Using the GetFile and PutFile methods

The DocInput and DocOutput approach is available in a number of different controls from the Internet Control Pack, including the HTTP and NNTP controls. So for variety, you'll use the GetFile and PutFile approach in the example program in this chapter.

To send a file from the client to the server, you'll have take several steps after connecting the FTP server. You'll need to set the LocalFile property to the filename that needs to be transferred. Next, you'll set the RemoteFile to the filename to an appropriate name for the distant system. Finally, you'll invoke the PutFile method to complete the transfer. Your code would look something like Listing 30.9.

Listing 30.9   Sending a File to the Server

```
...
'-------------------------------------
'-- Set the two and from file names
'-------------------------------------
MyFTPControl.LocalFile = "FileToSend.txt"
MyFTPControl.RemoteFile = "SendItHere.txt"

'-------------------------------------
'-- Send the file
'-------------------------------------
MyFTPControl.PutFile
...
```

Getting a file from the server to the client to you, you'll use a very similar approach. You'll need to set the LocalFile and RemoteFile as appropriate and then invoke the

GetFile method to complete the transfer. Your code would look something like
Listing 30.10.

Listing 30.10   Getting a File From the Server

```
...
'............................................
'-- Set the two and from file names
'............................................
MyFTPControl.LocalFile = "SendItHere.txt"
MyFTPControl.RemoteFile = "FileToSend.txt"

'............................................
'-- Get the file
'............................................
MyFTPControl.GetFile
...
```

Events

The FTP Control provides numerous events on which your application can take action.
Table 30.15 summarizes the events that are fired by the FTP control.

Table 30.15   Summary of Events in the FTP Control

Event	Description
Abort	Occurs after the Abort method is invoked.
Account	Fired after the Account method is invoked.
Authenticate	Triggered after the Authentication method is invoked.
Busy	Fires when a command is in progress and when a command is completed.
Cancel	Occurs at the completion of the cancellation of a request.
ChangeDir	Triggered by the execution of a CWD or an invocation of the ChangeDir method.
CreateDir	Occurs after the execution of a MKD or by calling the CreateDir method.
DelDir	Occurs after the execution of a RMD or by calling the DeleteDir method.
DelFile	Triggered by the execution of a DELE or an invocation of the DeleteFile method.
DocInput	Fired when data arrives at the control.
DocOutput	Triggered when data is sent from the control.
Execute	Occurs after the calling the Execute method.
Help	Occurs after the execution of a HELP or by calling the Help method.
ListItem	If ListItemNotify is set to true, this event is triggered by every ListItem in a directory.
Mode	Triggered by calling the Mode method.
NOOP	Fired when the NOOP method is invoked.

(continues)

VI

ActiveX

Table 30.15 Continued	
Event	**Description**
ParentDir	Occurs after the execution of a CDUP or by calling the ParentDir method.
PrintDir	Triggered by the execution of a PWD or an invocation of the PrintDir method.
ProtocolStateChanged	Whenever the state of the FTP session changes this event is fired.
Reinitialize	Occurs after the execution of a REINIT or by calling the ReInitialize method.
Site	Fired by the Site event or by invoking the Site method.
State	Triggered by the execution of the State method.
StateChanged	Occurs anytime the State of the connection changes and therefore the State property changes.
System	Triggered by the execution of a SYST or an invocation of the System method.
TimeOut	Occurs when a given event fails to occur within the time period specified in the TimeOut property.
Type	Fired after the Type method has been called.

Let's take a close look at a few of these events.

The *ListItem* Event. The ListItem event is used to parse directory entries. If you set the ListItemNotify property to true, the ListItem event will fire each time a new entry from a directory entry is returned. The ListItem event has an FTPDirItem passed in as a parameter. Take a moment to look at Table 30.16 where the properties of the FTPDirItem object are summarized.

Table 30.16 Properties of the *FTPDirItem* Object	
Property	**Description**
Attributes	Contains the file system attributes.
Date	Stores the last modified date of the file or directory entry.
Details	Returns details about the file or directory entry.
Filename	Keeps the name of the file.
Size	Keeps the size of the file.

When the ListItem event fires, you'll want to format a text entry for display to the user. Your code might look something like Listing 30.11.

Listing 30.11   Responding to the *ListItem* Event Using the *FTPDirItem* Object

```
Private Sub MyFTPControl_ListItem(ByVal Item As FTPDirItem)
    Dim LineToDisplay As String
    Select Case Item.Attributes
        Case 1                      'If its a directory
            LineToDisplay = Item.Filename & " " Item.Date
        Case 2              'If its a file
        LineToDisplay = Item.Filename & " " Item.Size & " " Item.Date
```

```
        End Select
        ShowDirectoryListing LineToDisplay
    End Sub
```

This listing assumes that there is a `ShowDirectoryListing` procedure which populates a list box or some other control.

The *ProtocolStateChanged* Event. You may want to notify the user of changes to the state of the connection between the client and the server. The `ProtocolStateChanged` event is triggered when changes occur at the protocol level. When the event fires, you'll be passed an integer that represents the current `ProtocolState`. Refer to the discussion of the `ProtocolState` property for a list of possible values. Listing 30.12 provides an example of how this event might be used.

Listing 30.12   Responding to the *ProtocolStateChanged* Event

```
    Private Sub MyFTPControl_ProtocolStateChanged(ByVal ProtocolState As Integer)

        Select Case ProtocolState
            Case ftpAuthorization
                    Status.Panels(1).Text = "Authoru]izatin"
            Case ftpBase
                    Status.Panels(1).Text = "Base"
            Case ftpTransaction
                    Status.Panels(1).Text = "Transaction"
        End Select

    End Sub
```

Of course, you would need to have a StatusBar control named `Status` to use this code.

The HTTP Client Control

The HyperText Transfer Protocol (HTTP) is absolutely the most popular protocol on the Internet today. After all, HTTP is the protocol for the World Wide Web. Like most of the other Internet protocols, HTTP requires both a client and a server to complete document transfers.

Properties

Table 30.17 summarizes all the properties available in the HTTP Client control. All the data elements required to transfer a file from an HTTP server are included as properties in this control.

Table 30.17   Properties of the HTTP Client ActiveX Control

Property	Purpose
Busy	True if a command is currently in progress.
DocInput	Refers to the DocInput object which must be set before invoking the SendDoc method and conveys information about the progress of the data transfer.

(continues)

VI

ActiveX

Table 30.17 Continued	
Property	**Purpose**
DocOutput	Refers to the DocOutput object which must be set before invoking the GetDoc method and conveys information about the progress of the data transfer.
Document	This property plus the RemoteHost identifies the target document.
EnableTimer	Tells the kind of timer that is fired by the TimeOut event.
Errors	Refers to a collection of errors detailing the last error.
Method	Sets the HTTP method to be used to request information from the HTTP server.
NotificationMode	Determines how notification of inbound data will be provided.
ProtocolState	Indicates whether the FTP client is not connected, waiting for authorization to connect, or connected to an FTP server.
RemoteHost	The host name or IP address of the server to be connected to.
RemotePort	The port number used to connect to the FTP server.
ReplyCode	The reply code sent by the server in response to requests from the client.
ReplyString	The reply string sent by the server in response to requests from the client.
State	Used to report the current state of the FTP connection.
TimeOut	Tells how long to wait before firing the TimeOut event for the type of timer referred to by EnableTimer.
URL	The Uniform Resource Locator such as **http://myhost.com/ myfile.htm**.

Now let's take a look at a few of these properties in a bit more detail.

The *DocInput* Property. Controls that have the DocInput property can use properties of the DocInput object. Although it is somewhat counter intuitive, DocInput refers to data that will be sent from your application to a remote machine. As you'll see more clearly through the end of this chapter, the DocInput object is also passed through the DocInput event. With the DocInput object and the corresponding event working together, control and action during document transfer can be quite robust.

Properties of the *DocInput* Object. The DocInput object makes many properties available for dealing with Internet documents. These properties are summarized in Table 30.18.

Table 30.18 Properties of the *DocInput* Object	
Property	**Value**
BytesTotal	Returns either the size of the document to be passed or 0 if the size is not known.
BytesTransferred	Returns the number of bytes already transferred.
DocLink	Allows data sent from a DocOutput object to be connected directly to this DocInput object.

Property	Value
Filename	Source from which DocInput data comes from. Valid only if DocLink is empty.
Headers	A reference to a DocHeaders collection.
State	Stores the current state of a document transfer.
Suspended	True if the document transfer has been suspended.

Let's take a moment and examine the Headers property and the State property a bit more closely.

The Headers property is a reference to a DocHeaders collection. The DocHeaders collection is basically a collection of DocHeader objects. The DocHeader object consists of a name and a value property. The Name property keeps the MIME header label (such as "Content-type") and the value property stores that MIME header's value (such as text/html). You'll find the Headers property to be quite useful in working with the DocOutput object as you'll see in a moment.

> **Note**
>
> MIME stands for Multipurpose Internet Mail Extensions. MIME headers and values are employed in many applications on the Internet. To learn more about MIME headers, you should review RFC 1521 or see **http://www.ncsa.uiuc.edu/SDG/Software/Mosaic/Docs**.

The DocInput object's State property provides information about the current state of the document transfer. There are several possible States that can be achieved; they are summarized in Table 30.19.

Table 30.19 Values for the *State* Property in the *DocInput* Object

State	Meaning
icDocNone	No document transfer is in progress.
icDocBegin	A document transfer is being initiated.
icDocHeaders	Document headers are being transferred.
icDocData	A block of data is being transferred.
icDocError	An error has occurred during the document transfer.
icDocEnd	Document transfer has completed.

During the DocInput event response function, your application can take action based upon this State value.

Methods of the *DocInput* Object. The DocInput object exposes several methods for use in your Visual Basic applications. Table 30.20 summarizes these methods and their function.

VI

ActiveX

Table 30.20	***DocInput* Object Methods**
Method	**Use**
GetData	Retrieves the data currently being transferred when the DocInput event is fired.
SetData	Used to specify the data that will next be transferred when the DocInput event is fired.
Suspend	Suspends a transfer in progress.

The *DocOutput* Property. All controls that have the DocOutput property can access the properties of the DocOutput object. More importantly (as we'll discuss in more detail in a moment), the DocOutput object is passed through the DocOutput event. The DocOutput object and event provides all the necessary tools to do sophisticated processing of document transfer. Even though it seems backwards, DocOutput refers to data that will be received by your application from a remote machine. In the next few sections, you'll be introduced to the key properties and methods of the DocOutput object.

Properties of the *DocOutput* Object. The properties made available by DocOutput are the same as those of the DocInput object with one exception. The DocOutput object does not have a DocLink property. These properties are summarized in Table 30.21.

Table 30.21	**Properties of the *DocOutput* Object**
Property	**Value**
BytesTotal	Returns either the size of the document to be passed or zero if the size is not known.
BytesTransferred	Returns the number of bytes already transferred.
Filename	Source from which data comes from.
Headers	A reference to a DocHeaders collection.
State	Stores the current state of a document transfer.
Suspended	True if the document transfer has been suspended.

The Headers property in DocOutput is exactly the same as in the DocInput object. Using the Headers property in the DocOutput object will be a common task. Listing 30.13 provides a brief demonstration of how to use this important property.

Listing 30.13   Using the *Headers* Property

```
Private Sub http_DocOutput(ByVal DocOutput As DocOutput)

    Dim hdr As DocHeader


    Select Case DocOutput.State

      ...

        Case icDocHeaders
            For Each hdr In DocOutput.Headers
                MsgBox "Name: " & CStr(hdr.Name) & " Value: " &
```

```
        CStr(hdr.Value)
                Next

            . . .

        End Select

    End Sub
```

In this example, each time a new header is received, a message box is presented with the name and value of the header. Not a particularly useful function, but it demonstrates clearly how to use and access the `Headers` collection.

`DocInput` and `DocOutput` both use the same values for the `State` property. So handling the various states of the data transfer will be handled with a `Select Case` statement for each of the states in `DocOutput` in the same manner as for `DocInput`. A simple example of such a statement is provided in Listing 30.14 in the section on the `DocInput` and `DocOutput` events.

Methods of the *DocOutput* Object. The `DocOutput` object exposes the same methods exposed by the `DocInput` object.

The *Method* Property. The `Method` property allows you to set the type of request that will be issued to the Web server. Table 30.22 summarizes the types of requests available.

Table 30.22 *Method* Settings	
Setting	**Meaning**
prcGet	The HTTP GET request is used to obtain a document from the server.
prcHead	The HTTP HEAD request returns only the document header from the server.
prcPost	The HTTP POST request is issued to the server.
prcPut	The HTTP PUT request places a document on the server.

The *ProtocolState* Property. This property provides protocol-specific information about the state of the connection. For the HTTP control, there are two states that the protocol can be in. These states are listed in Table 30.23.

Table 30.23 HTTP *ProtocolState* Values	
Value	**Meaning**
prcBase	The default state of the protocol prior to connecting to an HTTP server.
prcTransaction	Connection with the HTTP server has been obtained.

Methods

Most of the action in an HTTP session involves sending and receiving files. The methods to accomplish this work are summarized in Table 30.24.

Table 30.24 Methods for the HTTP Client Control	
Method	**Use**
Cancel	Stops a pending request.
Connect	Issues a request to the HTTP server to open a connection. If a connection is established, the State property is set.
GetDoc	Requests the retrieval of a document identified by an URL and can be used in conjunction with the DocInput and DocOutput objects and events.
PerformRequest	Like GetDoc, PerformRequest is another way to retrieve a document from the HTTP server.
SendDoc	Requests that a document identified by the URL be sent to the server and can be used in conjunction with the DocInput and DocOutput objects and events.

Most of these methods are self-explanatory. However, a few of them bear additional discussion.

Events

The HTTP control provides numerous events on which your application can take action. Table 30.25 summarizes the events that are fired by the HTTP control.

Table 30.25 Summary of Events in the HTTP Control	
Event	**Description**
Busy	Fires when a command is in progress and when a command is completed.
Cancel	Occurs at the completion of the cancellation of a request.
DocInput	Fired when data is sent from the control.
DocOutput	Triggered when data is sent to the control.
Error	Fires when an error is encountered.
ProtocolStateChanged	Whenever the state of the HTTP session changes, this event is fired.
StateChanged	Occurs anytime the state of the connection changes and therefore the State property changes.
TimeOut	Occurs when a given event fails to occur within the time period specified in the TimeOut property.

The *DocInput* and *DocOutput* Events. The DocInput and DocOutput events provide the programmer with a DocInput and DocOutput object. The properties and methods available in the DocInput and DocOutput objects allow you to control and monitor the incoming and outgoing documents from client to server. The most common way to use a DocInput or DocOutput event is to handle the various States in a Select Case statement. Listing 30.14 provides a basic skeleton for this approach.

Listing 30.14　Using *DocOutput State* Values

```
Private Sub http_DocOutput(ByVal DocOutput As DocOutput)


    Select Case DocOutput.State

        Case icDocBegin

        Case icDocHeaders

        Case icDocData

        Case icDocEnd

        Case icDocError

    End Select

End Sub
```

The *ProtocolStateChanged* Event. You may want to notify the user of changes to the state of the connection between the client and the server. The `ProtocolStateChanged` event is triggered when changes occur at the protocol level. When the event fires, you'll be passed an integer that represents the current `ProtocolState`. Refer to the discussion of the `ProtocolState` property for a list of possible values. Listing 30.15 provides an example of how this event might be used.

Listing 30.15　Responding to the *ProtocolStateChanged* Event

```
Private Sub MyHTTPControl_ProtocolStateChanged(ByVal ProtocolState As
Integer)

    Select Case ProtocolState
                Case prcBase
                        Status.Panels(1).Text = "Base"
                Case prcTransaction
                        Status.Panels(1).Text = "Transaction"
    End Select

End Sub
```

Of course, you would need to have a StatusBar control named `Status` to use this code.

The HTML Control

The HyperText Markup Language (HTML) is the code that describes how Web pages should look. After all, HTML documents are carried via the HTTP protocol over the World Wide Web between client and server.

Properties

Table 30.26 summarizes all the properties available in the HTML control. All the data elements required to transfer and render an HTML document over the World Wide Web are included as properties in this control.

Table 30.26   Properties of the HTML ActiveX Control

Property	Purpose
BackImage	Stores the background image to be used in rendering the page.
BaseURL	Equal to the value of the `<BASE>` tag or URL if there is no base.
DeferRetrieval	`True` if embedded objects are not downloaded. `False` if embedded objects are downloaded.
DocBackColor	Keeps the `BGCOLOR` attribute of the `<BODY>` tag.
DocForeColor	Stores the `TEXT` attribute of the `<BODY>` tag.
DocInput	Refers to the `DocInput` object which must be set before invoking the `SendDoc` method and conveys information about the progress of the data transfer.
DocLinkColor	Equal to the value of the `LINK` attribute of the `<BODY>` tag.
DocOutput	Refers to the `DocOutput` object which must be set before invoking the `GetDoc` method and conveys information about the progress of the data transfer.
DocVisitedColor	Keeps the value of the `VLINK` attribute of the `<BODY>` tag.
ElemNotification	Used to parse each HTML element. Set to `false` unless you're using the HTML control as a parser in another application.
EnableTimer	Tells the kind of timer that is fired by the `TimeOut` event.
FixedFont	Identifies the font to be used for fixed width text.
Forms	Refers to an HTMLForms collection.
Heading1Font	The font is used for text enclosed in H1 tags.
Heading2Font	The font is used for text enclosed in H2 tags.
Heading3Font	The font is used for text enclosed in H3 tags.
Heading4Font	The font is used for text enclosed in H4 tags.
Heading5Font	The font to be used for text enclosed in H5 tags.
Heading6Font	The font to be used for text enclosed in H6 tags.
LayoutDone	`True` when the main HTML document has been rendered but embedded objects have not been downloaded.
LinkColor	The color used for text representing Hypertext links.
ParseDone	True when the HTML has been parsed.
RedrawProperty	Set this property to `false` to make changes to the HTML document and avoid display defects. To cause the HTML control to be redrawn, set this property to true.
RequestURL	The URL that is currently being requested.
RetainSource	Set this to true to keep the source HTML code.
RetrieveBytesDone	Reports the number of bytes retrieved so far.
RetrieveBytesTotal	If available, the total number of bytes to be transferred.
SourceText	The HTML code currently rendered by the HTML control (read-only).
TimeOut	Tells how long to wait before firing the `TimeOut` event for the type of timer referred to by `EnableTimer`.
TotalHeight	The height in pixels of the complete document.
TotalWidth	The width in pixels of the complete document.

Property	Purpose
UnderlineLinks	True if hyptertext links should be underlined.
URL	The URL to be retrieved.
UseDocColors	If this is false, document specific color settings are ignored and the defaults are used.
ViewSource	Determines whether the HTML code should be rendered or shown as text.
VisitedColor	The color to render the text of visited links.

Now let's take a look at a few of these properties in a bit more detail.

URL **versus** *RequestURL.* At first glance, it might seem that these two properties are redundant. But, of course, they are not. The RequestURL property is set by the argument you pass to RequestDoc at execution. The URL property, on the other hand, is set during the process of fulfilling the request and thus may look a bit different from the original address you requested. For instance, the port number might be appended to the domain name. Listing 30.16 shows how these two properties are used.

Listing 30.16   Using *URL* and *RequestURL*

```
...

HTML.RequestDoc txtURL.Text

Status.Panel(2).Text = "Retrieving " & HTML.RequestURL
...
...
Private Sub HTML_EndRetrieval()

        Status.Panels(2).Text = "Document complete"

        txtURL.Text = HTML.URL

End Sub
```

While there are some methods and events you haven't seen yet here, you can see that the RequestURL property is used before the retrieval of the document and the URL property is used after completion of the document retrieval.

HTMLForms Properties and Methods. The Forms property points to an HTMLForms collection. The HTMLForms collection contains a number of HTMLForm objects. Table 30.27 details the properties of the HTMLForm object.

Table 30.27   Properties of the HTMLForm Object

Property	Value
Method	Must be one of prcGet, prcHead, prcPost, or prcPut HTML verbs.
URL	The ACTION URL from the form.
URLEncodedBody	Stores all the values of all of the form fields in text.

VI

ActiveX

The HTMLForm object exposes only one method, the `RequestSubmit` function. `RequestSubmit` is used to send a form for processing. The `RequestURL` property of HTML object is set to the action URL for the form. The `URL` property is updated after processing of the request has successfully begun.

Methods

The HTML control offers very few methods for execution. The three available methods are summarized in Table 30.28.

Table 30.28   Methods for the HTML Control

Method	Use
Cancel	Stops a pending request.
RequestAllEmbedded	Requests all that all the embedded objects in the main document be downloaded.
RequestDoc	Requests that the main document be downloaded.

Most of the time, you'll use `RequestDoc`. However, say that you had a configuration option that allowed the user to turn off the downloading of images and other embedded objects. (This is a common feature in most Web browsers so that you don't have to wait for big graphics to download if you don't want to.) You might then want the user to be able to download embedded objects on demand. This type of scenario would be an excellent situation for using the `RequestAllEmbedded` method.

Events

The HTML control provides numerous events on which your application can take action. Table 30.29 summarizes the events that are fired by the HTML control.

Table 30.29   Summary of Events in the HTML Control

Event	Description
BeginRetrieval	Occurs when the document transfer is initiated.
DocInput	Fired when data is sent from the control.
DocOutput	Triggered when data is sent to the control.
DoNewElement	Fires during HTML parsing when a new element is added.
DoRequestDoc	Triggered by either a call to RequestDoc or a click by the user on a hypertext link.
DoRequestEmbedded	Occurs when an embedded item is to be transferred.
DoRequestSubmit	Triggered by either a call to RequestSubmit or a user submitting a form.
EndRetrieval	Fires when the document and embedded objects have all been transferred.
LayoutComplete	Occurs when the entire main document has been transferred, although embedded objects may still be downloading.
ParseComplete	When the HTML source has been parsed, this event fires.
TimeOut	Occurs when a given event fails to occur within the time period specified in the TimeOut property.

The SMTP Control

The Simple Mail Transport Protocol (SMTP) is responsible for carrying electronic mail messages over the Internet. You'll encounter many cases where your applications need to send e-mail. Consider, for example, an application that copies files at night for use by users in the morning. You might want the application to fire off an e-mail in the event of an error.

Properties

Table 30.30 summarizes all the properties available in the SMTP control. All the data elements required to send e-mail messages to an SMTP server are included as properties in this control.

Table 30.30	Properties of the SMTP Client ActiveX Control
Property	**Purpose**
Busy	True if a command is currently in progress.
DocInput	Refers to the DocInput object which must be set before invoking the SendDoc method and conveys information about the progress of the data transfer.
Errors	Refers to a collection of errors detailing the last error.
NotificationMode	Determines how notification of outbound data will be provided.
ProtocolState	Indicates whether the SMTP client is not connected, waiting for authorization to connect, or connected to an SMTP server.
RemoteHost	The host name or IP address of the SMTP server to be connected to.
RemotePort	The port number used to connect to the SMTP server.
ReplyCode	The reply code sent by the server in response to requests from the client.
ReplyString	The reply string sent by the server in response to requests from the client.
State	Used to report the current state of the SMTP connection.

You have seen all of these properties in previous controls. Note that port 25 is standard for SMTP. Unless you need to run a special SMTP server on another port, the default value will be fine.

Methods

The SMTP control offers a few methods for programmers. The two available methods are summarized in Table 30.31.

Table 30.31	Methods for the SMTP Client Control
Method	**Use**
Cancel	Stops a pending request.
SendDoc	Sends the mail message.

Your applications will make extensive use of SendDoc. To familiarize yourself with the elements of this handy function, take a look at each of the following parameters:

- URL—This optional parameter permits you to identify a remote document for sending.

- Headers—SMTP uses a number of headers to send mail, including things such as the To and From addresses. So the SMTP control accepts a DocHeaders collection for passing these headers. This parameter is optional.

- InputData—An optional parameter for a buffer of data that holds the document to be sent.

- InputFile—A file on the local system that is the document to be sent may optionally be set.

You'll always use the Headers parameter to set up SMTP headers as necessary.

Events

The SMTP Control provides numerous events on which your application can take action. Table 30.32 summarizes the events that are fired by the SMTP client control.

Table 30.32   Summary of Events in the SMTP Client Control

Event	Description
Busy	This event is triggered when commands are in progress.
Cancel	This event is triggered when the Cancel method is executed.
DocInput	Fired when data is sent from the control.
Error	Occurs when an error has been encountered.
ProtocolStateChange	When the state of the protocol changes, this event is fired.
StateChanged	When the State of the SMTP control changes, this event is thrown.
TimeOut	Occurs when a given event fails to occur within the time period specified in the TimeOut property.

The NNTP Control

The Network News Transmission Protocol (NNTP) is used to read from and post to the UseNet news network.

Properties

Table 30.33 details the properties available in the NNTP control. All the data elements required to retrieve and post news articles to an NNTP server are included as properties in this control.

Table 30.33 Properties of the NNTP Client ActiveX Control

Property	Purpose
ArticleNumbersSupported	If this property is true, the GetArticleNumbers method will properly return a list of article numbers.
Busy	True if a command is currently in progress.
DocInput	Refers to the DocInput object which must be set before invoking the SendDoc method and conveys information about the progress of the data transfer.
DocOutput	Refers to the DocOutput object, which must be set before invoking the GetDoc method and conveys information about the progress of the data transfer.
EnableTimer	Tells the kind of timer that is fired by the TimeOut event.
Errors	Refers to a collection of errors detailing the last error.
LastUpdate	The date used by NEWGROUPS and NEWNEWS to decide what is "new."
NotificationMode	Determines how notification of outbound data will be provided.
OverviewSupported	True if the GetOverviewFormat and GetOverview methods will return headers stored in the server's overview database.
PostingAllowed	When the server permits posting of messages, this property is set to true.
ProtocolState	Indicates whether the NNTP client is not connected, waiting for authorization to connect, or connected to an NNTP newsserver.
RemoteHost	The host name or IP address of the NNTP server to be connected to.
RemotePort	The port number used to connect to the NNTP server.
ReplyCode	The reply code sent by the server in response to requests from the client.
ReplyString	The reply string sent by the server in response to requests from the client.
State	Used to report the current state of the NNTP connection.
TimeOut	Tells how long to wait before firing the TimeOut event for the type of timer referred to by EnableTimer.
URL	The URL of the document being retrieved.

Although explaining the details of the NNTP protocol is beyond the scope of this book, you should take note of the LastUpdate property explained in the next section. In addition, you can find RFC 977 which defines the NNTP protocol with the other RFCs at **http://ds.internic.net/ds/rfc-index.html**.

The *LastUpdate* Property. NNTP provides a mechanism for deciding which articles and groups are to be transmitted (for example, what things are new). A call to the ListNewGroups method uses this property as the date the group list was last updated. Say that the LastUpdate property is equal to 7/3/96 and on 7/4/96 a new group **comp.new.group** is added. A call to ListNewgroups made on 7/5/96 in your application can obtain the **comp.new.group** during the DocOutput event.

VI

ActiveX

Methods

The NNTP control offers a number of methods for programmers. These methods are summarized in Table 30.34.

Table 30.34	Methods for the NNTP Client Control
Method	**Use**
Cancel	Stops a pending request.
Connect	Issues a request to the POP server to open a connection. If a connection is established, the State property is set.
GetAdministrationFile	Sends the NNTP XMOTD command and retrieves the server's administrator data.
GetArticleByArticleNumber	Requests an article from the newsserver using the article number. Successful requests fire the DocOutput event.
GetArticleByMessageID	Requests an article from the newsserver using the message ID. The DocOutput event is triggered on success.
GetArticleHeaders	Obtains specific headers from a list of articles.
GetArticleNumbers	Gets a list of article numbers from the newsserver. Triggers the DocOutput event on success.
GetBodyByArticleNumber	Obtains the body of an article based on the article number. Fires the DocOutput event on success.
GetBodyByMessageID	Obtains the body of an article based on the message ID. Causes the DocOutput event to occur on success.
GetDoc	Requests the retrieval of a document identified by an URL and can be used in conjunction with the DocInput and DocOutput objects and events.
GetHeaderByArticleNumber	Obtains the header of an article based on the article number. Fires the DocOutput event on success.
GetHeaderByMessageID	Obtains the header of an article based on the message ID. Causes the DocOutput event to occur on success.
GetOverView	Returns information from the overview database for the specified article.
GetOverViewFormat	Retrieves a list of headers in the order they appear in the overview database.
GetStatByArticleNumber	Requests the stat of an article.
ListGroupDescriptions	Requests a list of group descriptions and triggers the DocOutput event.
ListGroups	Requests a list of groups and fires the DocOutput event.
ListNewGroups	Requests a list of new groups from the NNTP server. The DocOutput event occurs on success.
Quit	Closes the connection and fires the Quit event.
SelectGroup	Requests a list of articles from the newsserver. Triggers the DocOutput event on success.
SendDoc	Requests the transmission of a document identified by an URL and to the server. Used in conjunction with the DocInput event.
SetLastArticle	Selects a newsgroup's last article.
SetNextArticle	Selects a newsgroup's next article.

The NNTP control is rich with methods to make the interface with the newsserver simple and flexible. To fully exploit the power of the NNTP control, you'll need to learn a bit about some of these functions.

Current Article Pointer. The newsserver keeps a "current article pointer" that refers to the article that will be acted on by the server unless an article number is passed. There are several functions that rely on this current article pointer including the following:

- `SetLastArticle`
- `SetNextArticle`
- The `GetArticle` functions

`SetLastArticle` moves the article pointer to the last article in a newsgroup. The `SetNextArticle` advances the article pointer to the next article in the newsgroup. All of the `GetArticle` functions will act on the current article unless an appropriate reference is passed. For instance, take a look at Listing 30.17.

Listing 30.17   The Current Article Pointer

```
    ...
    ...

    '--------------------------------
    '--  Without a parameter the
    '--  current article is retrieved
    '--------------------------------
    MyNNTPControl.GetArticleByArticleNumber

    '--------------------------------
    '--  Retrieves article 903 and moves
    '--  current article pointer
    '--------------------------------
    MyNNTPControl.GetArticleByArticleNumber 903
    ...
    ...
```

Say that the article pointer was referencing article 847. The first call would return article 847, while the second call returns article 903 and advances the current article pointer.

Events

The NNTP Control provides numerous events that your application can handle. Table 30.35 summarizes the events that are thrown by the NNTP client control.

Table 30.35   Summary of Events in the NNTP Client Control

Event	Description
AuthenticateRequest	Triggered when the newsserver requests authentication.
AuthenticateResponse	Occurs after an authentication response is received from the newsserver.
Banner	Fires when the server's welcome banner is received.

(continues)

Table 30.35   Continued

Event	Description
Busy	This event is triggered when commands are in progress.
Cancel	This event is triggered when the Cancel method is executed.
DocInput	Fired when data is sent from the control.
DocOutput	Fired when data arrives at the control.
LastArticle	Occurs when the last article in a list is reached.
NextArticle	Triggered by selecting the next article in the list.
ProtocolStateChange	When the state of the protocol changes, this event is fired.
SelectGroup	Occurs when the SelectGroup method is successful.
StateChanged	When the State of the NNTP control changes, this event is thrown.
TimeOut	Occurs when a given event fails to occur within the time period specified in the TimeOut property.

The POP Control

The Post Office Protocol (POP) is used to retrieve mail from a POP server. Typically, SMTP is used to transport mail to the appropriate POP server. The POP protocol is then used to retrieve and delete messages. The Post Office Protocol will be handy for any applications that need to download mail messages from a server.

Properties

Table 30.36 details the properties available in the POP control. All the data elements required to retrieve e-mail messages from a POP server are included as properties in this control.

Table 30.36   Properties of the POP Client ActiveX Control

Property	Purpose
Busy	True if a command is currently in progress.
DocOutput	Refers to the DocOutput object which must be set before invoking the GetDoc method and conveys information about the progress of the data transfer.
EnableTimer	Tells the kind of timer that is fired by the TimeOut event.
Errors	Refers to a collection of errors detailing the last error.
MessageCount	Stores the number of messages currently available on the POP server.
NotificationMode	Determines how notification of outbound data will be provided.
Password	Sets the password to be used for logging on to a POP server.
ProtocolState	Indicates whether the POP client is not connected, waiting for authorization to connect, or connected to a POP server.
RemoteHost	The host name or IP address of the POP server to be connected to.

Property	Purpose
RemotePort	The port number used to connect to the POP server.
ReplyCode	The reply code sent by the server in response to requests from the client.
ReplyString	The reply string sent by the server in response to requests from the client.
State	Used to report the current state of the POP connection.
TimeOut	Tells how long to wait before firing the TimeOut event for the type of timer referred to by EnableTimer.
TopLines	Keeps the number of lines to be returned in response to a TOP command.
TopSupported	Set to true when the server supports the TOP command.
URL	The URL of the document being retrieved.
UserID	Sets the user name to be used for logging on to an POP server.

Note

Explaining the details of the POP protocol is beyond the scope of this book. However, you can find RFC 1081, which defines the POP protocol, with the other RFCs at **ftp://ds.internic.net/rfc**.

Methods

The POP control offers a few methods for programmers. The available methods are summarized in Table 30.37.

Table 30.37   Methods for the POP Client Control

Method	Use
Authenticate	Authenticates the user using the UserID and Password properties.
Cancel	Stops a pending request.
Connect	Issues a request to the POP server to open a connection. If a connection is established, the State property is set.
Delete	Deletes the specified message on the POP server.
GetDoc	Requests the retrieval of a document identified by an URL and can be used in conjunction with the DocInput and DocOutput objects and events.
Last	Initiates a Last request.
MessageSize	Requests the size of the next message. The MessageSize event is fired when the request is successful.
NOOP	Causes the POP server to reply with an OK in the ReplyString property.
Quit	Closes the connection and fires the Quit event.

(continues)

VI

ActiveX

Table 30.37   Continued

Method	Use
Reset	Issues a RSET command. Any messages marked for deletion are unmarked.
RetrieveMessage	Downloads the passed message number. The message is streamed through a DocOutput object.
TopMessage	Sends a Top of Message request for the message number passed through a DocOutput object.

You've encountered most of these methods in previous chapters. There are a few, however, that are specific to the POP control and deserve a bit more attention.

The *MessageSize* Method. Sometimes you may want to know the size of a mail message before retrieving a message from the POP server. Perhaps you're concerned that some hacker has sent you a 2 GB mail message (yuck!). You might also build a specialized application that waits for a message of a certain size and then replies with a special message. Using MessageSize in your applications is simple. Take a look at Listing 30.18.

Listing 30.18   Using the *MessageSize* Method

```
...
...
Dim SizeOfThisMsg As Integer

Dim MsgOfInterest As Integer

MsgOfInterest = 1

MyPOPControl.MessageSize  MsgOfInterest
```

To act on the size of the message, you'll respond to the MessageSize event.

The *RetrieveMessage* Method. Certainly the most important method exposed by the POP control is RetrieveMessage. Not suprisingly, RetrieveMessage is used to obtain a mail message from the POP server. When the POP control receives the message from the server, you have two options for the output. You can access the POP control's built-in DocOutput object, or you can pass RetrieveMessage your own DocOutput object. In most cases, you'll simply use the DocOutput object in the POP control. Listing 30.19 shows the alternate method of passing your own DocOutput object.

Listing 30.19   Using *RetrieveMessage*

```
Dim MyOwnDocOutput As DocOutput
Dim MsgOfInterest As Integer
...
...
POP.RetrieveMessage MsgOfInterest, MyOwnDocOutput
...
...
```

Events

The POP control provides numerous events that your application can handle. Table 30.38 summarizes the events that are thrown by the POP client control.

Table 30.38   Summary of Events in the POP Client Control

Event	Description
Authenticate	Triggered after the Authentication method is invoked.
Busy	This event is triggered when commands are in progress.
Cancel	This event is triggered when the Cancel method is executed.
DocOutput	Fired when data arrives at the control.
Error	Occurs when an error has been encountered.
Last	Triggered when the Last method is called and passes the last message accessed by the client.
MessageSize	Occurs in response to a call to the MessageSize method. The size of the message is passed.
ProtocolStateChange	When the state of the protocol changes, this event is fired.
Quit	Occurs after a call to the Quit method.
Reset	When a Reset call is successful, this event is triggered.
StateChanged	When the State of the POP control changes, this event is thrown.
TimeOut	Occurs when a given event fails to occur within the time period specified in the TimeOut property.

Chapter 31

The ActiveX Control Pad

While the ActiveX Control Pad has no general support for WYSIWG HTML editing, inserting ActiveX Controls and adding client-side scripting like VBScript is straightforward.

You'll recognize many of the elements of the user interface from other applications you use like Lotus 1-2-3, or Microsoft Word. Most of the common items are there including the File toolbar for saving, creating, and opening new HTML files. However, there are also a couple of elements that you probably haven't seen before. The first of these two new items is found on the toolbar (the second button from the right) that uses a scroll as its icon. Pressing this button will bring up the Script Wizard. The second difference is in the document window. Take a look at the document window in Figure 31.1. Notice the gray vertical bar along the left side of the screen.

Since you'll be inserting objects and scripts into the HTML documents in this window, the margin bar makes keeping track of where objects and scripts are inserted in the document easy. The scroll icon indicates the start of a script. Pressing the scroll button in the margin bar opens the Script Wizard (which you'll use in a moment) and loads the appropriate script. ActiveX objects are indicated in the margin bar by a small cube icon. This kind indicates the start of an <OBJECT> declaration in HTML. Pressing the ActiveX object button in the gray margin bar brings up a window containing the object and a window containing its property sheet. The Control Pad uses a special icon for insertions of HTML layouts. HTML layouts are indicated in the margin bar by a small icon containing the letter A, a circle, and a square. Pressing this button brings up the HTML Layout Editor and its associated toolbar.

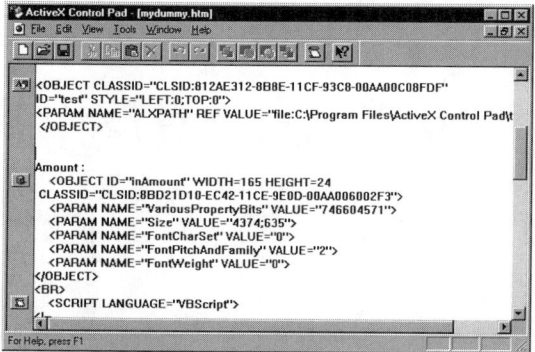

Fig. 31.1 Objects and scripts in the Control Pad margin bar.

Creating an HTML Layout

The ActiveX Control Pad is not an HTML editing environment, per se. There are no built-in tools to make the general HTML coding easier. However, ActiveX includes a control called the HTML Layout control which is used for building forms, laying out toolbars, or making reusable elements in your Web pages. The ActiveX Control Pad provides a Visual Basic-like interface for creating HTML layouts. To create an HTML layout, follow these steps:

1. Start the ActiveX Control Pad.

2. Select File, New HTML Layout from the menu bar. This brings up two windows—the Layout window and the Toolbox windows. Your screen should resemble Figure 31.2.

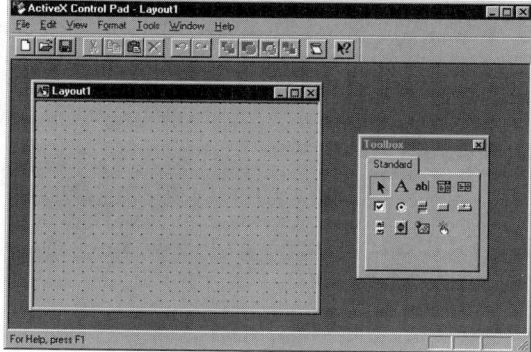

Fig. 31.2 Creating an HTML layout.

3. Try adding a command button to the layout. From the toolbox, select the command button tool. Then place your cursor over the Layout window and it changes

to cross hairs. Press the left mouse button and draw in the control. When you're finished, the screen should resemble Figure 31.3.

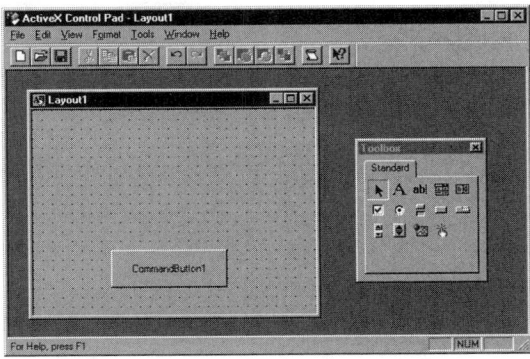

Fig. 31.3   Adding a command button.

4. To edit the properties of this control, select View, Properties. Select the Caption property and place your cursor in the Apply text box. Now type a suitable caption like Press Me. Your screen should resemble Figure 31.4.

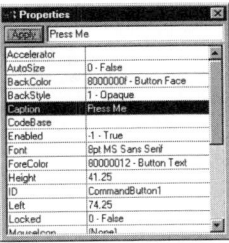

Fig. 31.4   Changing the Caption property.

5. Open the property sheet again, select the ID property, and place your cursor in the Apply text box. Now type a name like cmdPressMe.

6. Now try adding a text box to your layout. Select the Text Control tool from the toolbox. Then place your cursor over the Layout window and it changes to cross hairs. Press the left mouse button and draw in the control. Your screen should look like Figure 31.5.

7. Select View, Properties and change the ID and Text properties. Select the ID property and place your cursor in the Apply text box. Set the ID to something like cmdPressMe. Select the Text property and add some initialization text. When you're finished, your screen should look like Figure 31.6.

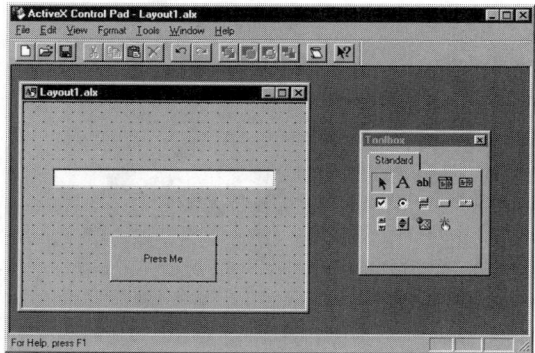

Fig. 31.5 Adding a Text control.

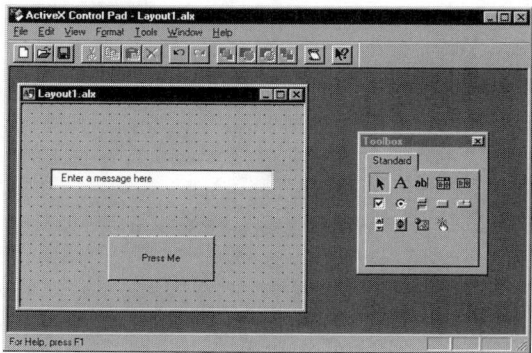

Fig. 31.6 The complete HTML layout.

8. Save your layout to a file. The file extension for an HTML layout is ALX. If you open an ALX file with a text editor, you'll find that the code is itself HTML.

Using the ActiveX Control Pad Script Wizard

The ActiveX Control Pad provides a graphical user interface for adding VBScript to HTML pages and HTML layouts. In this section, you'll add two simple VB scripts to the previously-created HTML layout using the Script Wizard. To add VB scripts using the Script Wizard, follow these steps:

1. Start the ActiveX Control Pad, if it's not already running.

2. Open the HTML layout you created previously.

3. Start the Script Wizard. You can do this in two ways. Press the Script Wizard toolbar button (the one with the scroll icon) or select Tools, Script Wizard from the menu bar. Your screen will look something like Figure 31.7.

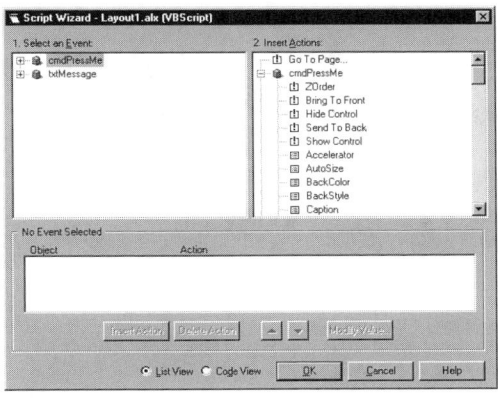

Fig. 31.7   Starting the Script Wizard.

Notice that the Script Wizard has two different views. The List View is a graphical tool for making scripts. The Code View provides a method for entering custom scripts by typing in VBScript syntax.

4. Now let's add a simple script using the List View. Adding a script element in the List View is a three-step process. Select an event to respond to, select an action to take, and (if necessary) provide a value or parameter. Let's take it one step at a time. From the Event list (the list box in the upper left third of the screen), expand the txtMessage item and select the KeyDown event. Your screen will look something like Figure 31.8.

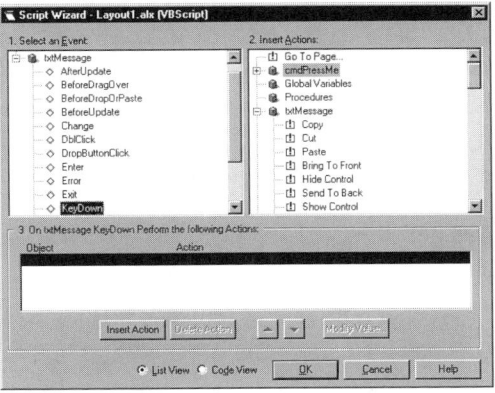

Fig. 31.8   Selecting an event to respond to.

5. Next expand the txtMessage item on the Action list (the list box in the upper right third of the screen). Select the BackColor property and double-click. The color selection window will come forward. Your screen will look something like Figure 31.9.

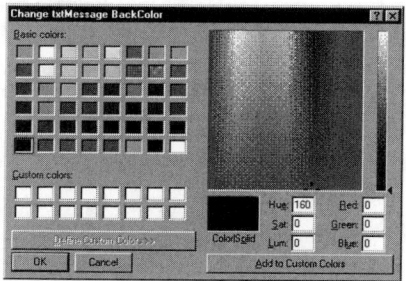

Fig. 31.9 Setting the `BackColor` property.

Go ahead and select the color that you want to change the `txtMessage` box to when a key is pressed, and press OK. You'll see both the object and the action listed in the Script list.

6. Now change the Script Wizard to the Code View by selecting the Code View radio button. From the Event list, expand the `cmdPressMe` object and select the `Click` event. Your screen will look something like Figure 31.10.

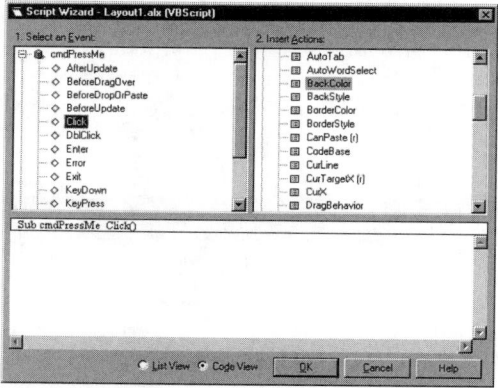

Fig. 31.10 Adding a script in the Code View.

7. Next, add a simple VBScript in the code window. (You learned about VBScript in the previous two chapters.) But for now, enter **MsgBox txtMessage.Text** into the code window. Your screen will look like Figure 31.11.

8. Finally, collapse all of the items in the Action list. You'll notice that there is now a `Procedures` object. Expand the `Procedures` object. You should see an entry for the two events you've now added scripts for (see Figure 31.12).

9. Save the HTML layout to a file.

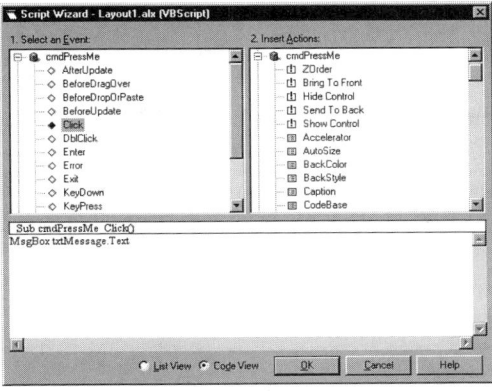

Fig. 31.11 Entering the script.

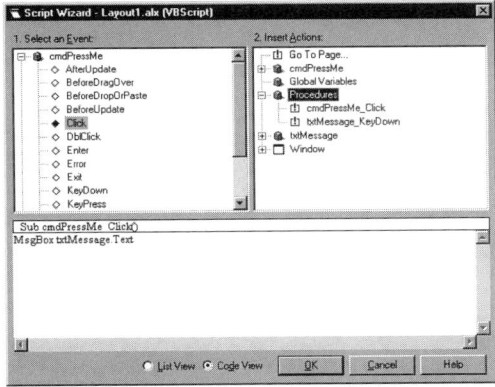

Fig. 31.12 The Procedures object.

The Script Wizard Interface

Now that you've had a quick test drive through the Script Wizard, there are a couple of features that require some additional explanation. This chapter takes the Script Wizard and breaks it down into its components to give you an in depth look at coding scripts using the Script Wizard. Specifically, you'll work through the following processes:

- **Navigating the Event window**—The ActiveX Control Pad uses a number of conventions for identifying events that are fired by the controls in your Web pages. Much of your user interface programming will revolve around responding to these events.

- **Navigating the Action window**—The Action window makes it simple to identify the responses your script will make to various events.

- **Using the List View script editor**—The List View editor provides a friendly interface for editing your scripts. Inserting, deleting, and modifying script actions can be accomplished from here.

- **Using the Code View script editor**—More complicated actions will need to be handled by using the Code View. The Code View basically requires that you type VBScript syntax.

Navigating the Event Window

Many of the objects that you'll use in your Web pages will trigger various events. To make your Web page interactive with the user, you'll select events and assign actions that will execute in response to the selected event. VBScript makes events available to the browser window itself. When you start a new HTML document, you can respond to events that occur to the browser window.

When you add an ActiveX control to your HTML document, the Script Wizard adds an object entry to the Event window. In Figure 31.13, the Event window is shown after a Calendar control was added to the document.

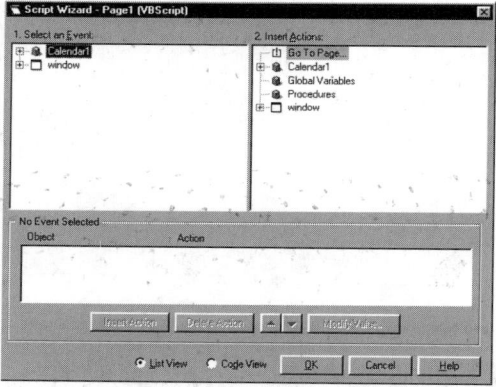

Fig. 31.13   An additional object in the Event window.

Notice that the Calendar control uses a small blue cube as its icon. The document window uses a small replica of a window as its icon. To select an event for creating a response procedure, expand the entry for the Window object in the Event window. The Window object triggers two events—OnLoad and OnUnload. Figure 31.14 shows a selection of the OnLoad event.

Each object that fires events will appear in the Event window. Of course, each object may have any number of different events associated with actions on the object (see Figure 31.15). For instance, the Calendar control fires several events. To add an action for any of these events, simply expand the Calendar1 object entry in the Event window and select the desired event.

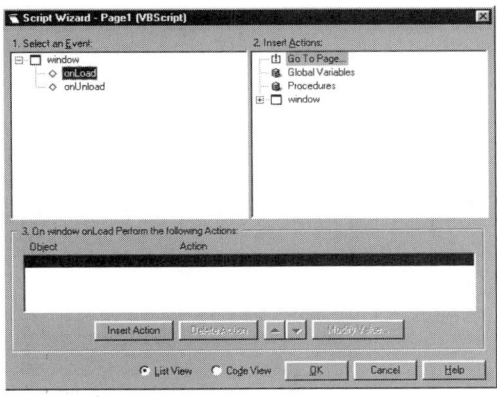

Fig. 31.14 Exposing the Window object's events.

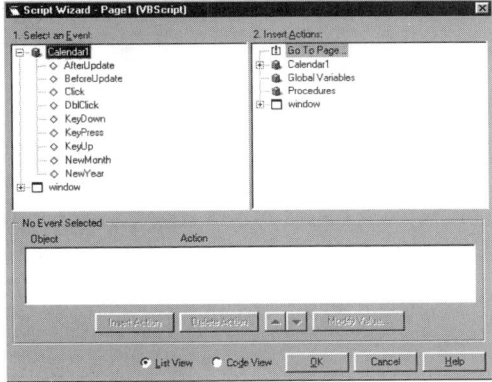

Fig. 31.15 Showing an object's events.

Navigating the Action Window

Once you've selected an object and an event, the next step is to select an action to be executed. The Action window provides an interface for selecting and entering the following actions:

- Invoking methods exposed by ActiveX objects

- Setting properties of ActiveX objects

- Entering and setting global variables

- Invoking procedures

Let's take each of these items in turn.

Invoking the Methods of ActiveX Objects. Many ActiveX objects expose methods. In the Action window, methods are represented by a small exclamation point icon. For

VI

ActiveX

instance, say you placed a Calendar control in a Web page and wanted to invoke a Calendar method in response to some event. After selecting an event in the event window, expand the Calendar object's entry in the Action list. Figure 31.16 shows how the list of methods is displayed.

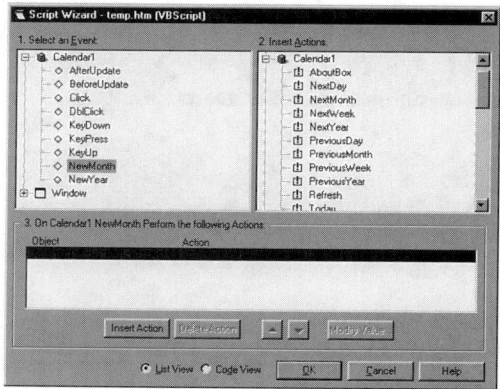

Fig. 31.16 The Calendar object's Action list.

Setting the Properties of ActiveX Objects. ActiveX objects also contain properties. In the Action window, properties are indicated by a small property sheet icon. The process of setting a property for an ActiveX object in the Script Wizard varies depending on the nature of the property itself. However, the process always begins when you double-click the property you want to change. Say you wanted to set the Year property of the Calendar control. Figure 31.17 shows the dialog box that the ActiveX Control Pad supplies in response to the double-click.

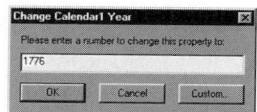

Fig. 31.17 Setting a property.

Depending on the property, the dialog box may differ. Setting the TitleFont property in the Calendar control, for instance, brings forward the standard Windows Fonts dialog box. Any property that requires a color brings forward the standard Windows Color dialog box.

Entering and Setting Global Variables. Many applications require global variables for storing information. Of course, global variables must first be added to the Web page before you can set them to a value. To create a global variable, place the cursor over the Action window and press the right mouse button. Select New Global Variable and you'll be presented with a dialog box something like what's shown in Figure 31.18.

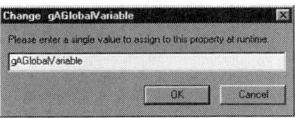

Fig. 31.18 Adding a global variable.

Once you've entered a name for your global variable, press OK. When you're done, expand the Global Variables object in the Action window and you'll see the global variable you just entered similar to that shown in Figure 31.19.

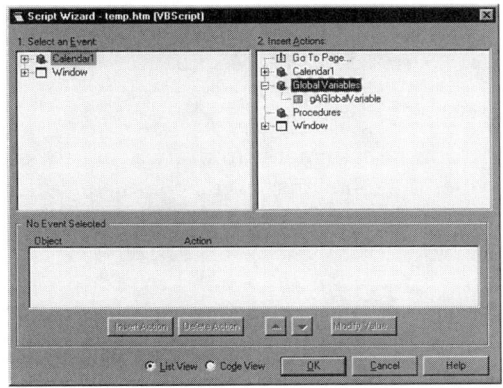

Fig. 31.19 Expanding the Global Variables object in the Action window.

Now your global variable can be set and checked just like the property of an ActiveX control. Say that you wanted to set gAGlobalVariable to 10 when the page is loaded. Select the Window's OnLoad event and then double-click the gAGlobalVariable and enter the number **10** into the text box. The screen will look something like Figure 31.20.

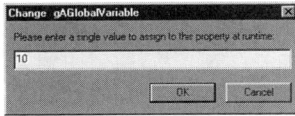

Fig. 31.20 Setting a global variable.

Editing Scripts in the List View

Once you press OK from Figure 31.20, the action will be entered in to the List View's action list as shown in Figure 31.21.

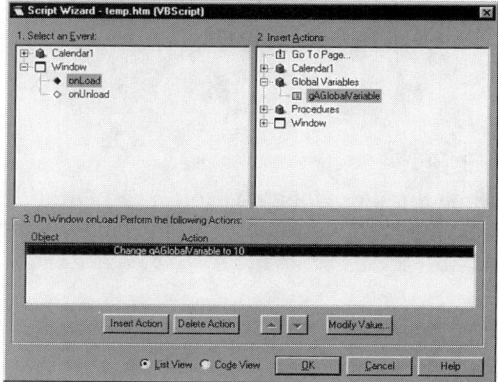

Fig. 31.21   The List View editor.

The List View displays each of the statements from the script for the event you're handling. The List View provides the following several command buttons for editing the script:

- Insert Action

- Delete Action

- Move Action Up

- Move Action Down

- Modify Value

Say that you wanted to select the next day on the Calendar control before setting gAGlobalVariable to 10. Select the NextDay action and then press the Insert Action button. When you've pressed the Insert Action button, a new command will appear above the command setting gAGlobalVariable (see Figure 31.22).

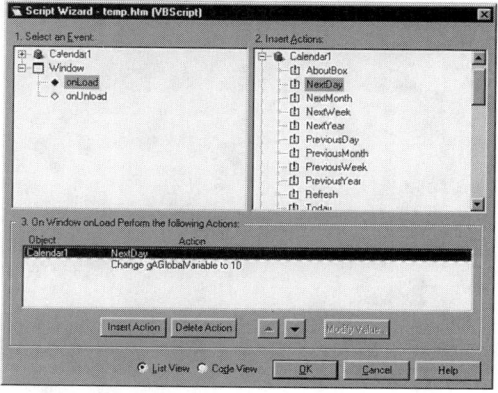

Fig. 31.22   Inserting an action.

Perhaps the actions you've entered are in the wrong order in the List View. To change the order of actions, use the Up and Down arrow buttons. Figure 31.23 shows the List View after pressing the Up arrow key. Of course, pressing the Delete button would remove the action just added to the script.

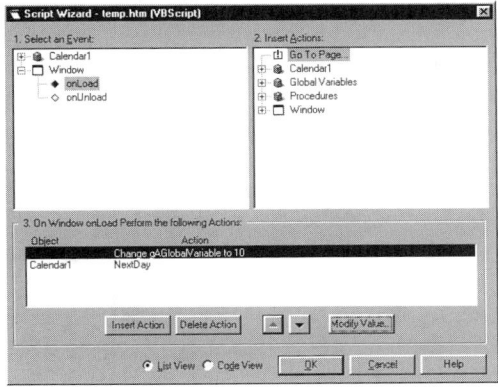

Fig. 31.23 Moving an action up.

Obviously, pressing the down arrow would return the script to the order shown in Figure 31.22.

Editing Scripts in the Code View
The List View is good for making simple scripts quickly and easily. However, many times the application will require more sophisticated programming. The Code View provides developers with a rudimentary editor for including VBScripts that you hand code. To take a look at the Code View, select the Code View radio button. Next press the right mouse and select New Procedure from the menu as shown in Figure 31.24.

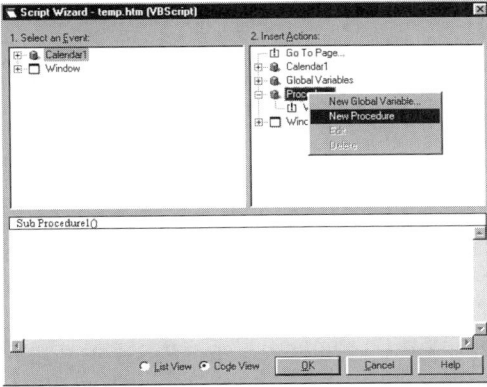

Fig. 31.24 Getting started with the Code View.

VI

ActiveX

Typically, you will change the name of the procedure to a useful name and then code the logic for the procedure. Figure 31.25 shows a coded procedure.

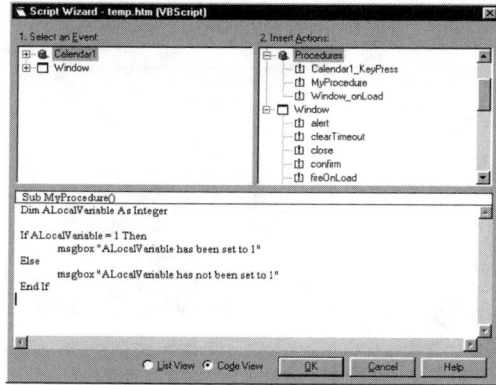

Fig. 31.25   A coded procedure in Code View.

Notice that MyProcedure is now included under the procedure item in the Action window. If you're familiar with Visual Basic or VBScript, you'll notice that MyProcedure has no End Sub. This is because the ActiveX Control Pad inserts the End Sub for you.

If you switch back to the List View or if you open a procedure developed in the Code View in the List View, the ActiveX Control Pad will only show a message as shown in Figure 31.26.

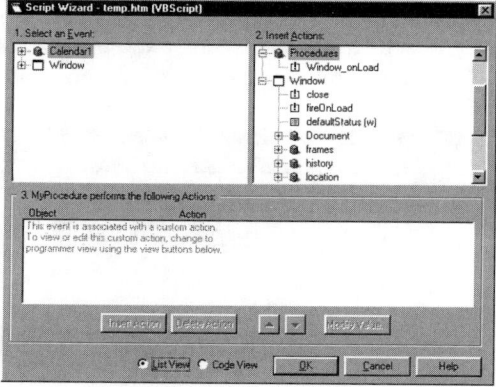

Fig. 31.26   Code View procedures in the List View.

When you close the Script Wizard, the ActiveX Control Pad adds the VBScript to your HTML document. Depending on the procedures you've created, you may have several VBScript tag pairs within the HTML document. Listing 31.1 shows the HTML document you've been playing with throughout this chapter.

Listing 31.1   VBScripts Inserted by the ActiveX Control Pad

```
<HTML>
<HEAD>
    <SCRIPT LANGUAGE="VBScript">
<!--
dim gAGlobalVariable

-->
    </SCRIPT>
    <SCRIPT LANGUAGE="VBScript">
<!--
Sub MyProcedure()
  Dim ALocalVariable As Integer

  If ALocalVariable = 1 Then
              msgbox "ALocalVariable has been set to 1"
  Else
              msgbox "ALocalVariable has not been set to 1"
  End If

end sub
Sub Window_onLoad()
call Calendar1.NextDay()
gAGlobalVariable = 10
end sub
-->
    </SCRIPT>
<TITLE>New Page</TITLE>
</HEAD>
<BODY>
    <SCRIPT LANGUAGE="VBScript">
<!--
Sub Calendar1_KeyPress(ByVal KeyAscii)
call MyProcedure()
end sub
-->
    </SCRIPT>
    <OBJECT ID="Calendar1" WIDTH=372 HEIGHT=279
     CLASSID="CLSID:8E27C92B-1264-101C-8A2F-040224009C02">
        <PARAM NAME="_Version" VALUE="458752">
        <PARAM NAME="_ExtentX" VALUE="9843">
        <PARAM NAME="_ExtentY" VALUE="7382">
        <PARAM NAME="_StockProps" VALUE="1">
        <PARAM NAME="BackColor" VALUE="12632256">
        <PARAM NAME="Year" VALUE="1996">
        <PARAM NAME="Month" VALUE="6">
        <PARAM NAME="Day" VALUE="30">
    </OBJECT>
</BODY>
</HTML>
```

This listing was copied directly from the ActiveX Control Pad, so you can see that the formatting of the code leaves a little to be desired. Notice how the procedures MyProcedure and Window_OnLoad are not even separated by a blank line. Most programmers prefer that procedures be separated by white space and easily readable. However,

VI

ActiveX

since the Script Wizard makes building and editing scripts easier and more graphical, this is a minor complaint.

Inserting an HTML Layout

An HTML layout can be inserted in a Web page quite easily. HTML layouts are excellent for elements that will be repeated in numerous Web pages on your Web site. You can simply build the HTML layout once and then include it in any appropriate Web page. To include an HTML layout, take the following steps:

1. Start the ActiveX Control Pad, if it's not already running.

2. Start a new HTML document by adding an H1 heading with some text like My HTML Layout. Also, add a <BR> tag to make a break between the heading and the HTML layout. When you're finished, the screen should resemble Figure 31.27.

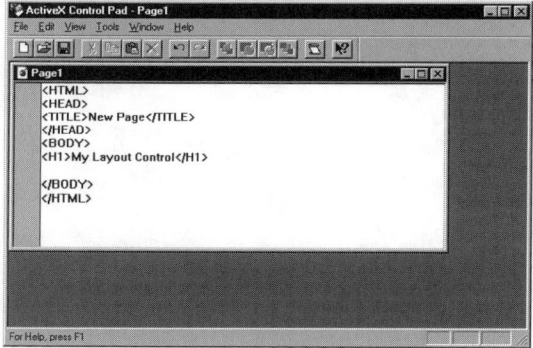

Fig. 31.27   Adding the H1 tag and heading text.

3. Insert the HTML layout that you created in the previous section. To do this, select Edit, Insert HTML Layout from the main menu. Then select the HTML layout you just created and press Open When You've Finished—your screen will look something like Figure 31.28.

   Notice that the gray margin bar now shows an HTML Layout button. Pressing this button launches the Layout Editor as described previously.

4. Save your HTML page to a file.

Now that you've completed the HTML document, you can test your work using Microsoft Internet Explorer 3.0. These next steps take you through testing out your HTML document:

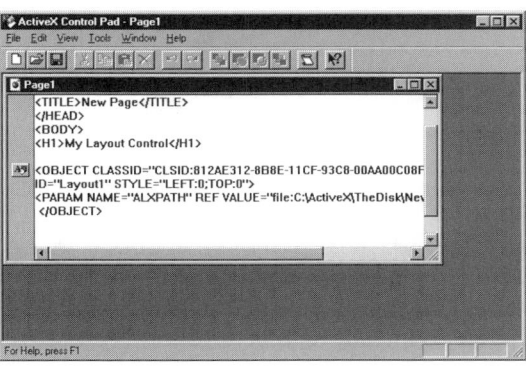

Fig. 31.28   Adding an HTML layout.

1. Start Microsoft Internet Explorer 3.0.

2. Open your HTML document by choosing File, Open or by typing the fully qualified path to the document.

3. If you've done everything correctly, the HTML document will look something like Figure 31.29.

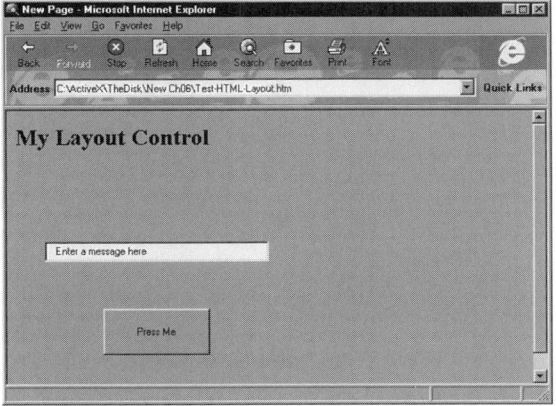

Fig. 31.29   HTML layout in Microsoft Internet Explorer 3.0.

4. Now enter some text in the text box. Notice when you type that the color of the text changes to the color selected previously.

5. Next, press the cmdPressMe button. You get the alert box shown in Figure 31.30.

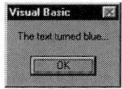

Fig. 31.30 Pressing the cmdPressMe button.

Inserting an Object

An HTML layout is itself an object, so inserting other objects in a Web page is quite easy. HTML layouts are excellent for elements that will be repeated in numerous Web pages on your Web site. You can simply build the HTML layout once and then include it in any appropriate Web page. To include an object, follow these steps:

1. Start the ActiveX Control Pad, if it's not already running.

2. Select File, New HTML and start a new HTML file.

3. Now add an H1 heading with some text like My Calendar. Also, add a <BR> tag to make a break between the heading and the HTML layout.

4. Next you'll add an ActiveX object. Select Edit, Insert ActiveX Control from the menu bar. Select the Calendar control from the list. When you're finished, the screen should resemble Figure 31.31.

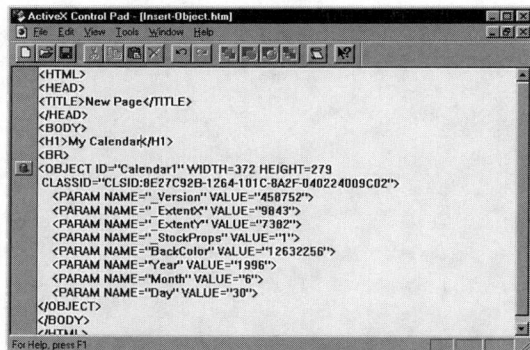

Fig. 31.31 Adding an object to a Web page.

5. Save your HTML page to a file.

Now that you've completed the HTML document, you can test your work using Microsoft Internet Explorer 3.0. To do so, follow these steps:

1. Start Microsoft Internet Explorer 3.0.

2. Open your HTML document by choosing File, Open or by typing the fully qualified path to the document.

3. If you've done everything correctly, the HTML document will look something like Figure 31.32.

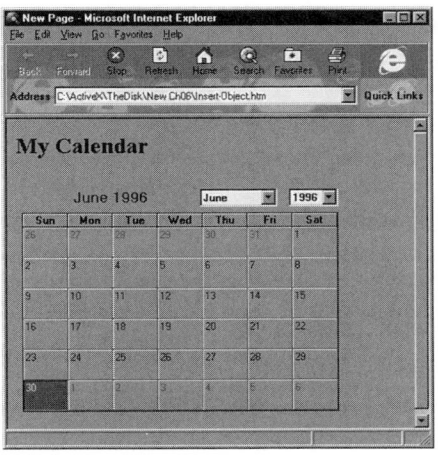

Fig. 31.32   Testing the page.

Customizing the ActiveX Control Pad Development Environment

The ActiveX Control Pad provides some limited ability to customize the development environment. You can customize the behavior of the following:

- HTML Layout Editor

- Script Wizard

The HTML Layout Editor provides a grid of dots that make it easy to align controls within the layout. The grid has the following configuration options:

- Vertical grid line spacing

- Horizontal grid line spacing

- Grid on/off

- Snap-to-grid

Figure 31.33 shows the dialog box for configuring these items. To obtain this dialog box, select Tools, Options, HTML Layout Options.

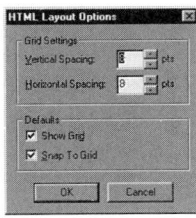

Fig. 31.33   HTML Layout editor configuration.

VI

ActiveX

The Script Wizard also allows limited customization of the Script Wizard environment. You can set the following options by selecting Tools, Options, Script Wizard from the toolbar:

- Default script view

- Script view font

- Default script language

Figure 31.34 shows the dialog box for configuring these items.

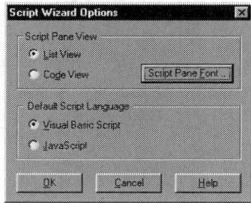

Fig. 31.34   Script Wizard configuration.

Index

Symbols

G

Check out Que® Books on the World Wide Web
http://www.mcp.com/que

As the biggest software release in computer history, Windows 95 continues to redefine the computer industry. Click here for the latest info on our Windows 95 books

Make computing quick and easy with these products designed exclusively for new and casual users

Examine the latest releases in word processing, spreadsheets, operating systems, and suites

Desktop Applications & Operating Systems

que® new users

what's new?

Que's Publishing Areas

Windows 95

Internet And New Technologies

The Internet, The World Wide Web, CompuServe®, America Online®, Prodigy® —it's a world of ever-changing information. Don't get left behind!

Find out about new additions to our site, new bestsellers and hot topics

Calendar of Events

DEVELOPER AND EXPERT USERS

ZD ZIFF-DAVIS PRESS

Que's Top 10 Titles

Macintosh & Desktop Publishing

In-depth information on high-end topics: find the best reference books for databases, programming, networking, and client/server technologies

A recent addition to Que, Ziff-Davis Press publishes the highly-successful *How It Works* and *How to Use* series of books, as well as *PC Learning Labs Teaches* and *PC Magazine* series of book/disk packages

Stay on the cutting edge of Macintosh® technologies and visual communications

Find out which titles are making headlines

With 6 separate publishing groups, Que develops products for many specific market segments and areas of computer technology. Explore our Web Site and you'll find information on best-selling titles, newly published titles, upcoming products, authors, and much more.

- Stay informed on the latest industry trends and products available
- Visit our online bookstore for the latest information and editions
- Download software from Que's library of the best shareware and freeware

que®

Complete and Return this Card
for a *FREE* Computer Book Catalog

Thank you for purchasing this book! You have purchased a superior computer book written expressly for your needs. To continue to provide the kind of up-to-date, pertinent coverage you've come to expect from us, we need to hear from you. Please take a minute to complete and return this self-addressed, postage-paid form. In return, we'll send you a free catalog of all our computer books on topics ranging from word processing to programming and the internet.

☐   Mrs. ☐   Ms. ☐   Dr. ☐

Name (first) ☐☐☐☐☐☐☐☐☐☐☐   (M.I.) ☐   (last) ☐☐☐☐☐☐☐☐☐☐☐☐☐☐☐☐☐

Address ☐☐☐☐☐☐☐☐☐☐☐☐☐☐☐☐☐☐☐☐☐☐☐☐☐☐☐☐☐☐☐☐☐
☐☐☐☐☐☐☐☐☐☐☐☐☐☐☐☐☐☐☐☐☐☐☐☐☐☐☐☐☐☐☐☐☐

City ☐☐☐☐☐☐☐☐☐☐☐☐☐☐☐   State ☐☐   Zip ☐☐☐☐☐ ☐☐☐☐

Phone ☐☐☐ ☐☐☐ ☐☐☐☐   Fax ☐☐☐ ☐☐☐ ☐☐☐☐

Company Name ☐☐☐☐☐☐☐☐☐☐☐☐☐☐☐☐☐☐☐☐☐☐☐☐☐☐☐☐☐☐

E-mail address ☐☐☐☐☐☐☐☐☐☐☐☐☐☐☐☐☐☐☐☐☐☐☐☐☐☐☐☐☐☐☐

Please check at least (3) influencing factors for purchasing this book.

Front or back cover information on book ☐
Special approach to the content ☐
Completeness of content ☐
Author's reputation ☐
Publisher's reputation ☐
Book cover design or layout ☐
Index or table of contents of book ☐
Price of book ☐
Special effects, graphics, illustrations ☐
Other (Please specify): _____ ☐

How did you first learn about this book?

Saw in Macmillan Computer Publishing catalog ☐
Recommended by store personnel ☐
Saw the book on bookshelf at store ☐
Recommended by a friend ☐
Received advertisement in the mail ☐
Saw an advertisement in: _____ ☐
Read book review in: _____ ☐
Other (Please specify): _____ ☐

How many computer books have you purchased in the last six months?

This book only ☐   3 to 5 books ☐
books ☐   More than 5 ☐

4. Where did you purchase this book?

Bookstore ☐
Computer Store ☐
Consumer Electronics Store ☐
Department Store ☐
Office Club ☐
Warehouse Club ☐
Mail Order ☐
Direct from Publisher ☐
Internet site ☐
Other (Please specify): _____ ☐

5. How long have you been using a computer?

☐ Less than 6 months   ☐ 6 months to a year
☐ 1 to 3 years   ☐ More than 3 years

6. What is your level of experience with personal computers and with the subject of this book?

	With PCs	With subject of book
New	☐	☐
Casual	☐	☐
Accomplished	☐	☐
Expert	☐	☐

Source Code ISBN: 0-7897-1028-5

7. Which of the following best describes your job title?

Administrative Assistant .... ☐
Coordinator .... ☐
Manager/Supervisor .... ☐
Director .... ☐
Vice President .... ☐
President/CEO/COO .... ☐
Lawyer/Doctor/Medical Professional .... ☐
Teacher/Educator/Trainer .... ☐
Engineer/Technician .... ☐
Consultant .... ☐
Not employed/Student/Retired .... ☐
Other (Please specify): _____ ☐

8. Which of the following best describes the area of the company your job title falls under?

Accounting .... ☐
Engineering .... ☐
Manufacturing .... ☐
Operations .... ☐
Marketing .... ☐
Sales .... ☐
Other (Please specify): _____ ☐

9. What is your age?

Under 20 ....
21-29 ....
30-39 ....
40-49 ....
50-59 ....
60-over ....

10. Are you:

Male ....
Female ....

11. Which computer publications do you read regularly? (Please list)

_____
_____
_____
_____
_____
_____
_____
_____
_____
_____

Comments: _____
_____
_____

Fold here and scotch-tape to ma